Dracul

Of the Father

The Untold Story of
Vlad Dracul

Vlad II Dracul
(illustration by Octavian Ion Penda)

A.K. Brackob

Dracul

Of the Father

The Untold Story of
Vlad Dracul

GAUDIUM

Gaudium Publishing

Las Vegas ◊ Oxford ◊ Palm Beach

Published in the United States of America by
Histria Books, a division of Histria LLC
7181 N. Hualapai Way, Ste. 130-86
Las Vegas, NV 89166 USA
HistriaBooks.com

Gaudium Publishing is an imprint of Histria Books. Titles published under the imprints of Histria Books are distributed worldwide.

Library of Congress Control Number: 202194791

ISBN 978-1-59211-027-8 (hardcover)

Contents

Contents

Introduction

"to compile a history, or to write any book whatsoever, is a more difficult task than men imagine. There is a need of vast judgement, and a ripe understanding.... history is in a manner a sacred thing, so far as it contains truth."

— Miguel de Cervantes Saavedra, *Don Quixote*[1]

Stories of Dracula have fascinated people around the world for generations. Both the fictional vampire created by the Irish author Bram Stoker at the end of the nineteenth century and the fifteenth century Prince called Vlad the Impaler, the man regarded as the historical Dracula, have become part of universal culture. Yet few realize that the Wallachian ruler dubbed Țepeș, who became infamous throughout Europe owing to a series of German pamphlets portraying him as a bloodthirsty tyrant, subsequently transformed in literature and film into a bloodsucking vampire, is not the original Dracula. Instead, that distinction belongs to his father, a Prince known as Vlad Dracul.

The elder Vlad, who gained the sobriquet Dracul or Dracula when Sigismund of Luxemburg, the Holy Roman Emperor, initiated him into the Order of the Dragon in February 1431, was among the most important political personalities of his day. He stands alongside his father, Mircea the Old, as one of the greatest rulers of Wallachia, the principality located between the Carpathian Mountains and the Danube River in Southeastern Europe that united with neighboring Moldavia in 1859 to form modern Romania. He far surpassed his more famous namesake in those qualities that define a great ruler. The renowned Romanian historian Nicolae Iorga characterized his leadership

---

[1]Miguel de Cervantes Saavedra, *Don Quixote*, Wordsworth Classics, 1993, p. 394.

abilities, writing that "He demonstrated energy and cleverness. He did not choose his friends except according to the needs of each moment."[2] Vlad Dracul struggled to protect the independence of his land, under the most difficult circumstances, against the threats posed by his powerful neighbors, the Ottoman Empire and the Kingdom of Hungary. In so doing, he in no small way contributed to the survival of his principality at a time when Turkish expansion in the Balkans expunged countries such as Bulgaria and Serbia from the map of Europe.

Vlad Dracul lived during tumultuous times, fraught with danger. The specter of the Black Death cast its shadow over Europe while at the same time a new chapter in the age-old struggle between East and West played itself out. The once-mighty Byzantine Empire, now in its death throes, desperately clung to life, while the Ottoman Turks advanced into Europe, posing the most serious challenge that Christendom had yet faced. But even when confronted with the Islamic threat, Christians could not unite. Religious strife, which within a century would lead to the outbreak of the Protestant Reformation, was another form of pestilence plaguing the continent, contributing to the incessant conflicts among the Christian states of Europe. George Sphrantzes, a Byzantine court official who served the last three Emperors of the Eastern Roman Empire, echoed the despair felt by many who lived during those troubled times, noting in his Memoirs: "I have written this about myself and about some of the events during the time of my unfortunate life. It was better for me if I had never been born, or if I had died as a child."[3] Under these circumstances, the survival of Wallachia, a country situated along the frontier between Christianity and Islam, demanded a shrewd and wise ruler at the helm. Vlad Dracul rose to meet the challenges of this troubled epoch and, in so doing, he became a representative figure of the early Renaissance, the type of prince later depicted by Niccolò Machiavelli in his classic treatise.

The story of the original Dracula is a tale filled with intrigue and suspense, honor and betrayal, war and peace. Vlad played an important role in the major events of his time. He fought the Turks when circumstances demanded, but he carefully avoided a potentially disastrous confrontation with the Sultan. When

---

[2]Nicolae Iorga, *Scrisori de boieri, scrisori de Domni*, Valenii-de-Munte, 1932, p. 158.

[3]Georgios Sphrantzes, *Memorii*, Bucharest, 1966, p. 2.

compelled to take up arms, he generally emerged victorious, but it was as a statesman, rather than as a military commander, that he truly excelled, winning valuable concessions from his more powerful neighbors. Time and again he demonstrated his exceptional leadership abilities. Walerand de Wavrin, a crusader from Burgundy who came to know him well, described Vlad as a ruler "renowned for his valor and wisdom," and "one who was very loved by his people."[4] Vlad Dracul left an important legacy. Subsequent Princes would adopt his policy of balancing the influence of one powerful neighbor off against another to preserve the independence of his country. He established a dynasty that ruled Wallachia well into the sixteenth century. Three of his sons — Vlad the Impaler, Radu the Handsome, and Vlad the Monk — eventually succeeded him on the throne; his sons and grandsons ruled Wallachia for forty-nine of the sixty-two years following his death.

Although Vlad ranks among the greatest Princes to have ruled Wallachia, he has received little attention from historians. Up to now, the only serious monograph devoted to the life and times of Vlad Dracul was a long article published by the Romanian historian Ilie Minea in the journal Cercetări istorice in 1928. Even though eminent scholars such as Francisc Pall and P.P. Panaitescu have subsequently made important contributions that elucidate certain aspects of his reign, for too long Vlad Dracul has not received the attention that he rightly merits, and, as a result, he has been denied his just place in history. Several books have been devoted to the study of his famous son, Vlad the Impaler, but any search for the historical Dracula must begin with the story of his father. It is a little known tale, but one that deserves to be told.

***

This book is the product of many years of research and writing. I am indebted to everyone who helped make it possible for me to tell the story of the original Dracula, but above all to my wife Dana, without whose hard work, dedication, loyalty, and moral support it could not have been realized. I would also like to express my gratitude to the "A.D. Xenopol" Institute of History of

---

[4]N. Iorga, "Cronica lui Wavrin şi Românii" in *Buletinul Comisiei istorice a României*, vol. VI, Bucharest, 1927, pp. 81, 104.

the Romanian Academy, especially Academician Alexandru Zub and Dr. Dumitru Ivănescu, as well as Mrs. Carmen Voroneanu, librarian of the Institute, for their cooperation in the realization of this project and for facilitating access to the materials needed for my research. Finally, I would also like to thank Marcel Popa, Director of Editura Enciclopedică in Bucharest, and Dr. Sorin Pârvu of the "Al.I. Cuza" University of Iaşi for their unwavering support.

Dracul

Of the Father

The Untold Story of Vlad Dracul

"The Draculas were... a great and noble race."

— Bram Stoker, *Dracula*

Preceding page:
Badge of the Order of the Dragon

Chapter I

The Name of the Father

"He must, indeed, have been that Voivode Dracula who won his name against the Turk..."

— Bram Stoker, *Dracula[1]*

E arly in the year 1431, Holy Roman Emperor Sigismund of Luxemburg held court in the German city of Nuremberg to preside over the Imperial Diet. The Emperor faced a complex series of problems. It was a period of great turmoil throughout Europe. In the West, the Hundred Years' War raged on between France and England; a nineteen-year-old peasant girl named Joan had breathed new life into the French army through her valor, but she had fallen captive in May of the previous year and in a few short months the English would burn the Maid of Orleans at the stake in Rouen on charges of witchcraft and heresy, giving rise to one of the great legends of this age. Conflicts among the city-states of Italy persisted and, although the Council of Constance had recently settled the Great Schism, disension continued to plague the Catholic Church. The execution of religious reformer Jan Huss as a heretic at the opening of the Council in 1415 only served of fuel the reform movement he had inspired in Bohemia and it began to spread to neighboring lands in Central Europe; since 1419 a bloody war had

---

[1] Bram Stoker, *Dracula*, Wordsworth Classics, 1993, p. 200.

waged on between his followers, called Hussites, and the armies of the
Emperor. In Southeastern Europe the situation was critical. In the seventy-five
years since the Ottoman Empire had established a foothold on the continent,
the forces of Islam had imposed their rule over much of the Balkans. The
important Greek port city of Salonika had just fallen into the Sultan's hands
and the Turks threatened the very existence of the Byzantine Empire, having
repeatedly laid siege to Constantinople during the preceding decades.

As King of Hungary, Bohemia, Croatia, Dalmatia, etc., as well as Holy
Roman Emperor, Sigismund governed a vast territory stretching from the
borders of France in the west to the frontier with the Ottoman Empire in the
southeast, making him the most powerful ruler in Christian Europe at that time.
One of his principal concerns was to defend Christendom against the Turkish
onslaught. As he dealt with affairs of state in the imperial city of Nuremberg,
which four decades later the astonomer Johannes Müller would acclaim as "the
middle point of Europe,"[2] he took measures intended to strengthen his defenses
along the border with the Islamic Empire. On a cold day at the beginning of
February of that year, 1431, a young man named Vlad, probably then in his
early thirties, the son of a former ruler of the small Principality of Wallachia
located in this strategically important region where Christianity and Islam
battled for supremacy, stood before the Emperor in the city's cathedral poised
to receive his parental inheritance. Sigismund wanted a reliable man on the
throne of this land over which he claimed suzerainty, as "King of Cumania,"
and he believed that young Vlad, who had grown up at his court, fit the bill.

All of Nuremberg, and many important personalities from throughout the
Empire who had gathered in the city to attend the Imperial Diet, turned out for
the occasion. Among those present were Nicholas von Redwitz, Ban of Severin
and leader of the Teutonic Knights whom Sigismund had recently called upon
to defend the border with the Turks, Burgrave Frederick of Zollern, an ancestor
of the Hohenzollern family, which one day would provide the Kings of
Romania, the country created by the union of the Principalities of Wallachia
and Moldavia in 1859, and John Hunyadi, a young Transylvanian nobleman in
the service of the Emperor, who later became the principal leader of the
struggle against the Turks. Along with his formal investment as Prince of

---

[2]Quo. John Hale, *The Civilization of Europe in the Renaissance*, New York, 1994, p. 3.

Wallachia and Duke of Amlaş and Făgăraş, areas in southern Transylvania granted to Wallachian rulers by the Kings of Hungary in the fourteenth century as their vassals, the Emperor also awarded Vlad with the Order of the Dragon. Sigismund had founded this society, called the *Drachenordens* in German or the *Societatis draconistorum* in Latin, on December 13, 1408. Modelled on the Order of St. George established by the Angevin King of Hungary, Charles Robert, in 1318, he created this predominantly Hungarian crusading order as a brotherhood to propagate the Catholic faith and to defend it against all enemies, be they heretics, schismatics, or infidels, as well as to protect the King and his family against all foes, foreign and domestic. By 1431, it had become the most powerful political organization in Hungary. Its foreign membership had grown to include King Vladislav Jagiełło of Poland, King Alphonse V of Aragon and Naples, King Henry V of England, Grand Duke Vitold of Lithuania, and Serbian Despot Stephen Lazarević, among others. Now Vlad, a descendent of the ruling family of Wallachia, was poised to become the newest member of this elite society.

Arrayed in the formal costume of the Order, scarlet garments, signifying sacrifice, draped by a green mantle, representing the power of the dragon, Vlad knelt before the Emperor who placed upon his neck the gold insignia that he henceforth wore as a sign of his membership in this exclusive brotherhood. It consisted of a collar made of two separate gold chains, joined together at intervals by a double-barred cross. Attached to it was the emblem of the Society, a winged dragon coiled up in a circle with its tail wound around its neck and a cross fixed on its back stretching from neck to tail. Above was another cross, symbolizing the triumph of salvation, with a Latin inscription that read, lengthwise, "Oh, how merciful is God," and on its width, "Piety and Justice."[3] Vlad then swore an oath of vassalage to Sigismund, whom he referred to in a document issued shortly afterward as "our rightful lord."[4] Then the Emperor presented him with a royal scepter made of silver, a sign of his authority as Prince of Wallachia, and the flag of St. Ladislas of Hungary,

---

[3]Ilie Minea, "Vlad Dracul şi vremea sa," in *CI*, IV:1 (1928), pp. 99-100; and Emil Vîrtosu, "Din sigiliografia Moldovei şi a Ţării Româneşti," pp. 331-558 în *DIR, Intro*, vol. II, Bucharest, 1956, p. 365.

[4]Doc. 179 in *DRH, D*, pp. 280-281.

symbolic of the fight against the
infidels. The ceremony now completed,
Sigismund's biographer Eberhard
Windecke, an eyewitness to this event,
recounts that Vlad was led throughout
the city in a grand parade, accompanied
by fifes and trumpets, to his residence
in the Emperor's palace.[5]

Despite his investiture in
Nuremberg in the early days of
February 1431, Vlad's path to assuming
his father's throne in Târgoviște, the
capital of Principality at that time,
would still be a long one. More than five
years passed before he effectively became Prince of Wallachia. But
unbeknownst to all present at this solemn occasion, they had participated in an
event of lasting significance; when Sigismund of Luxemburg placed the
insignia of the Order of the Dragon around Vlad's neck at the cathedral in
Nuremberg that day, it marked the birth of another great medieval legend. Had
this otherwise minor episode in history not taken place there would be no
Dracula today. Neither the historical prince, nor the fictional vampire of the
same name, would be known throughout the world. What's in a name? Our
answer to the Shakespearean query must be the Dracula legend itself, which
during the past century has developed into an industry in its own right.

To understand how this event gave birth to this name of enduring historical
and literary importance, it is first necessary to look at the evolution of names
in general, and that of Dracula in particular. During the Middle Ages, people
in Europe generally used only a first name. There was no need for what we call
a family name as the vast majority of the population lived in isolated
communities and few during their lifetime traveled further than their
neighboring villages. In addition, Wallachia was a predominantly Orthodox
land where people generally baptized their children with only one name, unlike

Insignia of the Order of the Dragon

---

[5]Minea, "Vlad Dracul și vremea sa," pp. 98-99; and Ilie Minea, *Principatele române și politica occidentală a împăratului Sigismund*, Bucharest, 1919, pp. 204-205.

Catholic countries where they often received two names, the second being the equivalent of what we call today a middle name. During Vlad's time a second name was occasionally added to indicate a father, a place of origin, or some other distinguishing characteristic, but usually only when necessary to distinguish between two people with the same first name. For example, a diploma issued by Vlad on August 13, 1437, lists jupan Nanul and jupan Nan Pascal, as well as jupan Stanciul, the brother of Mircea, and jupan Stanciul Honoi, among the members of the Royal Council witnessing the document. The others present are recorded only by their first names.[6] In later centuries, this descriptive designation evolved into what we now call a last name or a family name. The practice began to take hold among the upper classes already in the sixteenth century, but peasants in Wallachia and elsewhere continued to use only a first name well into the nineteenth century.[7] As a result, the ruling dynasty of Wallachia had no family name. It was later dubbed Basarab, after the name of the ruler considered to be the founder of the principality. But it is incorrect to refer to Vlad as Vlad Basarab. He never used this name, nor did any of his contemporaries refer to him in this manner. Only in the following centuries did certain princes adopt this name, seeking to enhance their legitimacy by making dubious ancestral claims.

To complicate matters further, there existed no custom of numbering princes of the same name[8] as practiced in many Western countries. Modern historians have added this convention to distinguish more easily between the different princes bearing the same name. Using this system, the subject of our book is Vlad II, while his son is Vlad III. Instead, the fashion in Wallachia was to add a descriptive epithet to the Prince's name, such as 'the Old', 'the Handsome,' 'the Monk,' 'the Great', and many others, not always flattering, such as 'the Stupid' or 'Empty-headed,' 'the Bad,' or even 'the Impaler.' Because of his reception into the Order of the Dragon, and the insignia he wore bearing the image of the dragon, which, as we shall see, he also applied to his coat of arms, his great seal, and his coins, his contemporaries gave Vlad the sobriquet Dracul or Dracula, a Slavonic-Romanian name with several

---

[6]Doc. 86 in *DRH, B*, vol. I, pp. 150-151.

[7]N.A. Constantinescu, *Dictionar onomastic romînesc*, Bucharest, 1963, p. XXIII.

[8]P.P. Panaitescu, *Mircea cel Bătrân*, Bucharest, 1994, pp. 40-41.

meanings, but in this case with the sense of 'the Dragon.' While the Order of the Dragon faded out of existence in the years following Sigismund's death in December 1437, the name Dracula in its many variants remained forever attached to Vlad and his sons, especially his famous namesake.

Dracul is derived from the Greek word for dragon, drakon. The law code elaborated by the Athenian ruler Drako in the seventh century B.C. embodied it with a sense of stern justice, from which the term draconian derived, but the word for dragon is also related to *drakos* meaning 'eye,' as the mythological creature was traditionally associated with the idea of watching over or protecting something. The classical myth of the Hesperides, in which the dragon Ladon aided the three sisters charged by Hera with watching over the golden apples that she had received as a wedding gift when she married Zeus, exemplifies this, as does the story of Cadmus, who is said to have founded Thebes and introduced the alphabet to Greece after slaying the dragon that guarded the fountain of Dince. In old English literature, we can point to the tale of the dragon protecting the treasure hoard in the epic poem Beowulf. Fables of beautiful princesses locked away in castles guarded by fire-breathing dragons also originate from this concept of the dragon as protector.

The dragon was also a warrior symbol. British war chieftains bore the title Pendragon, as evinced in the Arthurian legends where King Arthur's father is Uther Pendragon; pen being Welsh for 'head' or 'chief' and dragon with the sense of warrior. The native inhabitants of ancient Dacia, which included the territory of Wallachia, bore a war standard consisting of a dragon in the form of a wolf's head attached to the body of a serpent as they unsuccessfully struggled to drive the invading Roman legions led by the Emperor Trajan from their land; this war standard is depicted on Trajan's Column in Rome which commemorates his victory over the Dacians. In ancient times, the dragon was also a symbol of fecundity and prosperity. With these images in mind, it is easy to see why Sigismund chose the dragon as the emblem of his crusading order, which sought to propagate and to defend the Catholic faith.

By the fifth century A.D., with the spread of Christianity, the dragon symbol took on an additional meaning; it came to represent the devil or demonic power generally. In Judaic-Christian belief, this concept dates back to the story of Adam and Eve in the Garden of Eden recounted in the book of

Genesis in the Old Testament where evil is represented by a serpent, "more cunning than any beast of the field" (3:1). The New Testament book of Revelation explicitly makes this association: "And war broke out in heaven: Michael and his angels fought with the dragon; and the dragon and his angels fought, but they did not prevail, nor was a place found for them in heaven any longer. So the great dragon was cast out, that serpent of old, called the Devil and Satan, who deceives the whole world; he was cast to the earth, and his angels were cast out with him" (12:7-9). The legend of St. George slaying the dragon, an allegory of the triumph of Christianity over evil, is another example of this. This added connotation proved of great importance in the development of the Dracula myth. It forged the link between Dracula and the forces of evil in the evolution of the modern myth.

Although the image of the dragon as warrior-protector existed side by side with that of it as a symbol of Satanic power, the first sense dominated during this period. Even in the mid-sixteenth century, when the true origin of the name Dracula was long forgotten, Anton Verancsics, Archbishop of Strigonia and Vice-Regent of Hungary, recorded that the name had come to be applied to the inhabitants of Wallachia generally. "It is believed that this name was given to them by the Turks," Verancsics wrote, "because some of their princes [of that name] governed their country skillfully, while outside of it they behaved bravely and honorably, worthy of praise thanks to their virtues. The glory of their forefathers passed down to them and their name spread to the entire people, and the Turks began to call them *draguli* after their brave Prince Dragula."[9]

Even if it is clear that the name Dracula originated with Vlad's initiation into the Order of the Dragon, already in the fifteenth century it became shrouded in mystery because of the dichotomy of the images it evoked. The dual sense of the name was used by some contemporaries for political and literary effect. In 1459, the pretender Dan, who challenged Vlad the Impaler's hold on the throne of Wallachia with the support of King Mathias Corvinus of Hungary, wrote to the leaders of the Transylvanian city of Braşov, located near the border, in response to their complaints about "the things done by Dracula,

---

[9]*Călători străini despre ţările române*, vol. I, ed. Maria Holban, Bucharest, 1968, p. 399.

our enemy, of how he has been disloyal to our lord, the King, and has gone over to the Turks." Then, employing a play on words, Dan quipped, "He has done this thing truly taught by the Devil [Dracula in the original]."[10] Later, in 1486, the anonymous author of the Slavic manuscript *The Story of the Voivode Dracula* wrote, "in Wallachia there was a Christian voivode of the Greek faith called Dracula in the Wallachian language, but in ours, the Devil, so evil was he."[11] As a result, many have insisted that the name Dracula was given to Vlad the Impaler because of his diabolical cruelty; by extension, they also imagine his father as a bloody tyrant to have earned the nickname "the Devil." After all, the fifteenth century Byzantine chronicler Dukas records that the elder Vlad "Dragulios was called thus because he evil and cunning in his way; therefore the name Dragulios is also translated as evil and cunning."[12] This idea was reinforced in later centuries when this became the principal meaning of the name. For example, when the Ottoman Porte appointed the Greek nobleman Kirita Drako as Prince of Moldavia in November 1675, he quickly changed his name to Antonie Ruset for the reason that it would be inappropriate for the people to refer to their Prince as "the Devil." Yet, in Greek, the name still preserved the noble sense of dragon.

But the Greek name also embodied the image of a stern ruler, and many of the German, but especially the Slavonic stories about Vlad the Impaler emphasize his draconian sense of justice. For example, one of the Slavonic tales claims: "So much did he hate evil in his country that if someone committed a crime, stole or robbed or lied or committed an injustice, none of them remained alive. Be he a great noble or a priest or a monk or an ordinary man, even if he was very wealthy, he could not escape death. And so feared was he that there was in a place of his a spring and a well; to this well and spring came many travellers from different places and many people went to drink from the well and the spring because the water was cold and fresh. At that well, in an uninhabited spot, he placed a large and splendid cup of gold.

---

[10]Doc. LXXIX in Ioan Bogdan, *Documentele privitoare la relatiile Tării Românești cu Brașovul și Țara Ungurească în sec. XV și XVI*, Bucharest, 1905, pp. 101-102.

[11] *Cronicile slavo-romîne din sec. XV-XVI*, ed. P.P. Panaitescu, Bucharest, 1959, p. 200.

[12] Ducas, *Istoria turco-bizantină*, Bucharest, 1958, p. 252 (XXIX, 8), emphasis added.

And whoever wanted to drink water, and drank from that cup, he put it back in its place, and all the while it remained there no one dared to take that cup."[13] These stories portray him as a medieval Drako, whose law code, as the orator Demades said of that of the Athenian ruler, was "written in blood." The nineteenth century Romanian poet Mihai Eminescu, in his "Satire III," called upon Vlad the Impaler to return and to take out his wrath on a corrupt and immoral society.[14] The name Dracula, inherited from his father, certainly contributed to this image.

Given the extensive propaganda concerning Vlad the Impaler's excessive cruelty spread throughout the continent during the fifteenth and sixteenth centuries by a series of German pamphlets, early best-sellers in the European publishing world, it is easy to see how later generations came to understand that he received this name due to the abhorrent crimes of which he was accused. Decades before Bram Stoker created the vampire Dracula, the Romanian historian and political figure Mihail Kogălniceanu referred to Vlad the Impaler as "the greatest monster of nature and horror of humanity." The year before Stoker published his novel, Ioan Bogdan, author of the first monograph on Vlad the Impaler, considered him to be "the sad product of some barbaric times and of an inherited pathological nature."[15] Another contributing factor to this negative portrayal of the historical Dracula was that for a long time little was known about his father. The historian Ilie Minea published the first and only serious monograph on Vlad Dracul's reign up to now in 1928.

But the derivation of the name Dracula from the Order of the Dragon was not limited to the case of Prince Vlad and his famous son. In the sixteenth century, the Hapsburg King of Hungary, Ferdinand I, brother of the Holy Roman Emperor Charles V, granted lands and renewed the title of nobility and coat of arms of a Transylvanian nobleman called Ladislas Drakulia of

---

[13] P.P. Panaitescu, ed., *Cronicele slavo-române*, Bucharest, 1959, pp. 201-202.

[14]"Satire III" in Mihai Eminescu, *Poems and Prose of Mihai Eminescu*, ed. A.K. Brackob, Palm Beach: Center for Romanian Studies, 2019.

[15]Quo. Ioan Bogdan, *Vlad Țepeș și narațiunile germane și rusești asupra lui*, Bucharest, 1896, p. X.

Semtesth.[16] Although some have argued that this family were descendants of Vlad the Impaler,[17] the evidence to support this assertion is unconvincing. This coincidence of name is most likely explained by positing that an ancestor of this aristocratic family also received the Order of the Dragon from Sigismund of Luxemburg and that the family name emanated from this honor. A decree issued by Prince Alexander Mircea, who ruled Wallachia from 1568 to 1577, confirming ownership of certain estates to the Monastery of Govora after they had been adjudged before the royal council mentions the Drăculeşti family who had disputed the monks' claim.[18] As the Order of the Dragon was a mainly Hungarian brotherhood, the boyars referred to in this document are certainly descendants of Vlad Dracul, the only known member of this elite society from Wallachia; he had granted lands that belonged to that monastery to some of his relatives and followers when the cloister was ruined during the revolt led by the boyar Albul the Great in 1438.[19]

As a reaction against the Devil image conjured up by the name Dracula, some have sought a completely different origin for the name. In his inaugural discourse prepared for his induction into the Romanian Academy in 1909, Augustin Bunea, a Greek-Catholic priest and scholar from Blaj in Transylvania, wrote that Vlad "is incorrectly named by writers 'Dracul' because he was not bad, but one of the best and hardest working Romanian princes. His name at baptism had to be 'Dragul' [Dear One].... From Dragul the Romanians created, according to the sense of their language, the name Draculus or Dracul."[20] A more recent study by Aurel Rădutiu refined Bunea's theory, arguing that Dracul was a taboo word in Romanian society and that the original name must indeed have been Dragul which German sources, substituting *k* for *g* according to linguistic practice, transformed into Drakula.

---

[16]Doc. 34 in *Documente privitoare la istoria Ardealului, Moldovei şi Tării Românesti*, vol. I, ed. Andrei Veress, Bucharest, 1929, pp. 33-34.

[17]see Pavel Binder, "Une famille noble roumaine de Transylvanie: les Drakula de Sintesti," pp. 301-314 in *RRH*, XXVII:4 (1988).

[18]Doc. 339 in *DIR, XVI, B*, vol. III, Bucharest, 1952, pp. 293-294.

[19]Doc. 3 in *DIR, XVI, B*, vol. III, pp. 3-5.

[20]Augustin Bunea, "Stăpânii Ţerii Oltului," in *Academia Română. Discursuri de recepţiune*, XXXIV, Bucharest, 1910, p. 26.

He asserts that the name had nothing to do with the Order of the Dragon, but was instead a shortened form of the name Dragomir.[21] This hypothesis, however, cannot be sustained for several reasons. Both Slavonic and German sources from the time use the *k* form; there existed no set rules of orthography during this period and the alteration of *k* and *g* in different sources is explained by the synonymous variants *dracon* and *dragon*. Princes in fifteenth century Wallachia did not use an additional name, apart from that of John, uniformly adopted by all anointed rulers of the Principality, for reasons that we will discuss later on, and, as we have already pointed out, the ruling dynasty did not have an established family name. Our protagonist's baptismal name was Vlad, not Dragomir. In addition, it must be remembered that among the upper classes in Wallachia during this time, the dominant language was Slavonic, or more accurately Middle Bulgarian. The primary meaning of the Slavonic word *drakula* was dragon, from the Greek *drako*. The alternative sense of devil or demon, with its associated taboos, became dominant only in the following centuries, especially as Romanian began to replace Slavonic as the principal language among the upper classes. Thus, there can be no doubt that the name Dracula resulted from the exceptional event of Vlad's reception into the Order of the Dragon. As we have seen, it was common practice to characterize princes using a descriptive epithet often derived from a distinguishing trait or characteristic. Vlad's use of the dragon symbol on his coat of arms, his great seal, and his coins reflects both the importance and the unique nature of this event and made it inevitable that this sobriquet would attach itself to him.

The negative implications of the label Dracula did not disturb everyone. The dual sense of the name intrigued Irish author Bram Stoker who came across it while doing research for his vampire novel in an account by the English traveller William Wilkerson who had visited Wallachia and Moldavia in the early nineteenth century. "Dracula in the Wallachian language means Devil," Wilkerson wrote in 1820. "Wallachians were accustomed to give it as a surname to any person who rendered himself conspicuous by courage, cruel actions, or cunning."[22] Stoker chose it as the name for his anti-hero, based on

---

[21] Aurel Răduțiu, "Despre numele 'Drakula'," pp. 25-37 in *AII, Cluj*, XXXV (1996).

[22] William Wilkerson, *Account of the Principalities of Wallachia and Moldavia*, London, 1820.

Vlad the Impaler, who he describes, through the voice of Professor Van Helsing, as "no common man; for in that time, and for centuries after, he was spoken of as the cleverest and the most cunning, as well as the bravest of the sons of the 'land beyond the forest.'"[23] Thus, the vampire legend became forever linked to the name Dracula.

Having established the origin of the name, we must now consider the distinction between its forms, *Dracul* and *Dracula*. In the first monograph on the life of Vlad the Impaler, published in 1896, Ioan Bogdan explained the two forms of the name by simply stating, "*Draculea* was certainly the popular form, while *Dracul* was the literary form of the name."[24] Later historians and philologists differentiated between the two variants, establishing that *Dracul* refers to Vlad the father and *Dracula/ea* to his son Vlad the Impaler. The philologist Grigore Nandris explained that "The ending -a/-e in Dracula/Draculea is the Slavonic genitive suffix of the -o- stems. Its meaning is 'the son of.'"[25] But this explanation is too neat for a period when grammatical rules were by no means fixed, but in a state of constant fluctuation. Slavonic documents usually employ the word *sin*, meaning "son of" to express a filial relationship. Thus, in his internal documents Vlad the Impaler referred to himself as "son of the old Voivode Vlad"[26] or "son of the great Voivode Vlad."[27] The genitive suffix -a/-e is not restricted to meaning "son of," but rather it implies "of" in the general sense. This makes it more difficult to establish a distinction between the two forms. As the renowned historian Nicolae Iorga once pointed out, "Between Dracul and Draculea there is not always a difference, just as with Negrul and Negrea, Lupul and Lupea, thus we also have Dracea."[28] The elder Vlad is sometimes called Dracul and

---

[23]Stoker, *Dracula*, p. 200.

[24]Bogdan, *Vlad Țepeș*, p. 61, emphasis added.

[25]Grigore Nandris, "A Philological Analysis of Dracula and Romanian Place-Names and Masculine Personal Names in -a/-ea," in *Dracula. Essays on the Life and Times of Vlad Țepeș*, ed. Kurt W. Treptow, New York, 1991, p. 231; also Constantinescu, *Dicționar onomastic*, p. XXIX.

[26]Doc. 115 in *DRH, B*, vol. I, pp. 198-200.

[27]Docs. 117, 118 and 120 in DRH, *B*, vol. I, pp. 201-206.

[28]N. Iorga, *Scrisori de boieri, Scrisori de Domni*, Vălenii-de-Munte, 1932, p. 143.

other times Dracula. The same is true of Vlad the Impaler. The name is first mentioned in a letter of the Wallachian boyar Albu to the burghers of Braşov in the 1430s where he refers to Vlad the father as Drakulia.[29] Andreas de Palatio, a participant in the Varna Crusade, in a letter dated May 6, 1445, also uses Dracula, and the fifteenth century Polish chronicler Jan Długosz calls him by the same name.[30] A letter of King Ladislas II of Hungary dated November 1, 1495, and sent to another of Vlad's sons, Vlad the Monk, addresses him in its salutation as "son of the late Voivode Draculea."[31] Meanwhile, the Royal Governor of Hungary, John Hunyadi, writing to the officials of Braşov on February 6 and March 30, 1452, specifies that the younger Vlad is the son of "Voivode Drakul."[32] Dan, the pretender to Vlad the Impaler's throne mentioned earlier, refers to his rival using Dracula in letters written in Slavonic, and Dracul in those composed in Latin,[33] while Hunyadi's son Ladislas, in an appeal to the leaders of Braşov, dated December 17, 1456, to support Dan against Vlad, calls the latter, "the disloyal Voivode Drakul."[34] From these examples we can see that contemporaries make no distinction between Dracul and Dracula; both variants are used interchangeably in the fifteenth century. Modern usage whereby the elder Vlad is called Dracul and the younger Vlad, Dracula, is merely an artificial convention to make it easier to distinguish between the two princes sharing the same name. If we accept the explanation that the -a/-ea ending represents a genitive suffix, it follows that Vlad the father was referred to as Dracula with the sense "of the Dragon," or more specifically the Order of the Dragon, while he was also called Dracul, or simply "the Dragon," but with exactly the same meaning. Likewise, both forms

---

[29]Doc. CCX in Bogdan, *Documente privitoare...*, pp. 250-251; also doc. 211 in *DRH, D*, p. 310.

[30]Francisc Pall, "De nouveau sur l'action de Ianco de Hunedoara (Hunyadi) en Valachie pendant l'année 1447," in *RRH*, XV:3 (1976), p. 458, nt. 68.

[31]Bogdan, *Vlad Ţepeş*, p. 50.

[32]Docs. 308 and 309 in *DRH, D*, pp. 423-426.

[33]Docs. LXXIX, LXXX, CCLXVIII, and CCLXIX in Bogdan, *Documente privitoare...*, pp. 101-104 and 324-327.

[34]Doc. 341 in *DRH, D*, pp. 461-462.

of the name were applied to the younger Vlad, but with the sole meaning of "the son of the Dragon."

Having established the origin and meaning of the epithet, it is also interesting to mention something about his baptismal name. Vlad is a name of Slavic origin. It is derived from the Slavonic verb meaning "to rule,"[35] making it a name truly fit for a prince. Variants on the name include Vladimir, Vladislav, Ladislas, and Vlaicu or Layko. It appears that Vlad Dracul was christened after his great uncle, Vladislav I, who ruled Wallachia from 1364 to 1376. The popularity of this name among Wallachia's ruling family is attested to by the fact that during the fourteenth and fifteenth centuries no less than four rulers went by the name Vlad, while two were called Vladislav, not to mention other royal offspring so christened who did not attain the throne.

What's in a name? Dragon or Devil? Brave warrior, wise leader, cruel tyrant, or deranged monster? All of these elements combine to make up the Dracula legend. As we have demonstrated, Dracula was both the name of the father and of the son. Thus, we can affirm that the elder Vlad was the original Dracula. Therefore, any search for the origins of the Dracula legend must begin on that winter day in 1431 when a little-known pretender to the throne of a far off Principality beyond the Carpathians stood before the Holy Roman Emperor in Nuremberg, the German city that unwittingly became the birthplace of the legend, and received from him the Order of the Dragon. Here, the story of the life and times of Vlad Dracul, the original Dracula, begins.

---

[35]Constantinescu, *Dicționar onomastic*, pp. 408-409.

Chapter II

Dracula's Realm

*"Wallachia... appears to be named such, not after Flaccus, the Roman commander who ruled Moesia or Dacia, sent there by Trajan with thirty thousand people, brought and colonized there to work the land and to ensure provisions for the Roman army which had constant battles with the Scythians and the Sarmatians, but from the word **walch**, which in the German language means Italian."*

— Baranyai Decsi Czimor János, sixteenth century Hungarian writer[1]

A lthough it came to be called Wallachia, the realm over which the man dubbed Dracul ruled knew several names. The ancients called it Dacia, and fifteenth century Byzantine writers such as Laonic Chalkokondyles and Kritoboulos of Imbros continued to refer to the land north of the Danube with this designation. Since the Cuman invasions of the twelfth century it also became known as Cumania. When Hungarian monarchs imposed their suzerainty over the land south of the Carpathians in 1233, they added "King of Cumania" to their list of titles;[2] Hungarian sovereigns maintained this title as late as the reign of Sigismund of Luxemburg[3] who

---

[1] Holban, ed., *Călători străini*, vol. III, p. 214.

[2] Doc. XCIX in Hurmuzaki, *Documente*, vol. I, p. 127.

[3] Doc. 2214 in *Urkundenbuch*, vol. IV, pp, 549-551.

formally invested Vlad as Prince in 1431. But, already in the fourteenth century, after the Cumans had been largely assimilated, this name was no longer in common usage.

Documents issued by the Hungarian chancellery call it the Transalpine land or Transalpinia. Just as Transylvania means "the land beyond the forest," Transalpinia means "the land across the mountains." Both of these designations reflect the perspective of the Hungarian conquerors who expanded east from the Pannonian plain to impose their rule over these territories. The Wallachian chancellery also employed this name in Latin language documents. In letters written in Latin and addressed to the burghers of Brașov and to John Hunyadi, Vlad calls himself "Voivode of the Transalpine land" or "Transalpine Voivode"[4] and in a Latin language decree he issued in 1431, allowing the Franciscan monks to proselytize in Wallachia, he refers to his country as "the Transalpine land," and to himself as "Prince of Transalpine Wallachia."[5]

In Slavic and Greek language documents issued by the Prince's chancellery, the country is called Ungrovalachia, meaning Hungarian Wallachia. For example, in his diploma for the monasteries of Tismana and Vodita, dated August 2, 1439, he calls himself "John Vlad, Voivode and Prince, by the grace of God and by the will of God, lord and ruler of all of the land of Ungrovalachia."[6] This designation reflects a Greek or Balkan perspective. From the eleventh century, the name Valachia referred to the mountainous region of Thessaly inhabited by a population of Latin origin, heavily engaged in pastoral activities. Thus, the term Ungrovalachia was applied to the land between the Carpathians and the Danube to distinguish it from the territory in northern Greece called Valachia.[7]

Fifteenth and sixteenth century Moldavian chronicles employ yet another name for the neighboring Principality, calling it Muntenia or the Mountainous Land. For example, the German-Moldavian chronicle, written near the end of

---

[4]Docs. 226, 228 and 275 in *DRH, D*, pp. 325-328 and 383-384.

[5]Doc. 179 in *DRH, D*, pp. 280-281.

[6]Doc. 89 in *DRH, B*, vol. I, pp. 154-156.

[7]Constantin C. Giurescu, "O nouă sinteză a trecutului nostru," in *RIR*, II (1932), p. 15.

the reign of Stephen the Great (1457-1504), tells how the most famous of Moldavia's rulers placed Vlad's son, Vlad the Monk, "as Prince in Muntenia, whose son [Radu the Great] is still alive today and is Prince in Muntenia."[8] This curious appelation again reflects a view from without. Although Wallachia is mountainous along its northern border, this rugged terrain does not characterize the Principality. The origin of the name is unknown, but it likely reflects the fact that the state had its origins in its mountainous region around Câmpulung, or possibly because of the shared border between the two Principalities along the Carpathians. But this name is never found in Wallachian documents from Vlad's time.

The Turks called the country Iflak, a name they also applied to Vlad's father Mircea. Ottoman chroniclers refer to Vlad as "Diraku ibn Iflak," meaning "Dracula, the son of Iflak." The Polish chancellery called the country Basarabia, after the Prince who consolidated the independence of the land south of the Carpathians by his resounding victory over King Charles Robert of Hungary at the battle of Posada in 1330. In his treaty with Poland in 1396, recognizing the suzerainty of Vladislav I over his Principality, Vlad I calls himself "Voivode of Basarabia."[9] while Vlad's father Mircea called himself "great Prince of the land of Basarabia" when he renewed his previous alliance with the Polish monarch in 1403.[10]

Papal documents from Vlad's time designate the country between the Danube and the Carpathians as Valachie or Wallachia, meaning land of the Vlachs, a term applied to Latin-speaking peoples in the Balkans. Over time, this name also assumed the broader meaning of shepherd, the predominant occupation of this population. The appelation of Vlach is derived from the German name for the Celts, Welsh. As the Celts who settled in Gaul became Romanized, they began to use it to refer to all Latin or Latinized peoples. The Slavs borrowed this term from the Germans under the forms Vlach, Valach, and Vlas. The Poles, for example, use Wolosey to designate a Wallachian or a Romanian, and Wlachi an Italian. In 1923, Mussolini's foreign ministry sent a

---

[8]Panaitescu, ed., *Cronicile slavo-romîne*, p. 34. See also Olgierd Gorka, "Cronica epocei lui Stefan cel Mare (1457-1499)," in *RIR*, IV, V.

[9]Doc. CCCXVI in Hurmuzaki, *Documente*, vol. I, part. 2, pp. 374-375.

[10]Doc. DCLII in Hurmuzaki, *Documente*, vol. I, part. 2, p. 824.

diplomatic note to the Polish Government, officially requesting that they cease to refer to their country as Wlochy and henceforth call it Italy. The Magyars, in turn, borrowed the name from the Slavs, calling Italians, Olaszi, and Wallachians or Romanians, Olah; the name of the famous sixteenth century Hungarian humanist Nicholas Olahus reflects his family origin. The Greeks also borrowed this term from the Slavs;[11] Vlachs are first mentioned in eleventh and twelfth century Byzantine chronicles, such as that of Anna Comnena, and the fifteenth century narratives of Byzantine writers George Sphrantzes and Michael Dukas refer to the land between the Danube and the Carpathians as Wallachia. Although Vlad calls his Principality Ungrovalachia in his official title, he still refers to his country simply as Wallachia or the Wallachian land in many of his documents.

That Dracula's Realm became known as Wallachia is in itself a curious development. In most cases, the name of a country is derived from that of its conquerors, even if the indigenous population assimilated them over time. For example, the Bulgars, a Turkic people from the east, who came to rule over the Slavic population south of the Danube in the seventh century A.D., were Slavicized over the course of several centuries, but the land they conquered became known as Bulgaria, and its inhabitants Bulgarians. In a similar manner, the land between the Carpathians and the Danube became known as Cumania, but by the fourteenth century this name had fallen into disuse. The reason this name was replaced by one reflecting the majority indigenous population, however, can be explained. Unlike the case of Bulgaria, the Cumans never formed a unified state in the area. They mixed with the Slavic ruling class, adopting their language and culture, but remained organized in voivodates and tribes.[12] This process of assimilation was well-advanced when Thocomer and Basarab united the land between the Danube and the Carpathians. As a result, the newly-formed Principality wedged between the Bulgarian Empire and the Kingdom of Hungary, both with pretensions of suzerainty over the land, came to be called after its most distinguishing characteristic, its majority Vlach population.

---

[11]Panaitescu, *Interpretări românești*, p. 97.

[12]Panaitescu, *Interpretări românești*, p. 96.

Located in Southeastern Europe, Dracula's Realm encompassed an area of approximately 47,000 square miles, situated between the Carpathian Mountains and the Danube River. During Vlad's reign, its neighbors included the Kingdom of Hungary, the Principality of Moldavia and the Ottoman Empire. The country's natural frontiers afforded it some protection from an enemy attack. The Danube, one of Europe's mightiest rivers, could only be safely traversed at certain points where the river narrowed and the currents slowed. The fifteenth century Ottoman writer Kivami pointed out the hazards posed by attempting to cross the Danube, claiming that "Each year it takes the lives of ten thousand Turks, without swords or knives, and without shedding blood."[13] Even where conditions were propitious, an enemy army found itself in great danger when it attempted to cross the river. It could take days for an army laden with supplies to effect a crossing, and with its forces divided it lay vulnerable to attack. For this reason control over the fortresses protecting the principal crossing points was of vital importance. The main crossing points into Wallachia during Vlad's time along the Danube were: Calafat, across from the fortress of Vidin; Turnu, across from the powerful fortress of Nicopolis, where a cylindrical tower fort, originally built during Roman times, protected the landing on the Wallachian side; Giurgiu, across from Ruse, where Mircea the Old built a stone fortress on the island nearest the shore to defend this frequently-traversed route; across from Silistra, on the Bulgarian side of the river, a fortress once held by Vlad's father; at Floci, near the point where the Ialomița emptied into the Danube; and at Brăila, Wallachia's principal port and gateway to the Orient. Crossing points of lesser importance included: where the Jiu River emptied into the Danube across from Rahova; at Zimnicea; across from Svistov; and across from the fortress at Tutrakan on the Bulgarian shore.

The mountains, likewise, offered a limited number of passages into the country. From the west, Wallachia could be entered via the Cerna River Valley, via Mehadia, and then along the Danube to Severin, which during Vlad's reign was in Hungarian hands. Murad II used this route to invade Transylvania from Wallachia in the summer of 1438. The Olt River Valley was the principal route leading from Sibiu, frequented merchants travelling to and from the Saxon city; Vlad entered the country here in the fall of 1436 to

---

[13]Mihail Gublogu, ed., *Crestomație turcă*, Bucharest, 1978, p. 178.

claim the throne. The main road leading into Wallachia from Braşov crossed the Carpathians at the Bran Pass, by way of Rucăr. This was the principal trade route linking Transylvania to the Wallachian port of Brăila. Less-travelled routes included the Argeş Valley, protected by the fortress of Poenari, where Basarab laid his ambush for Hungarian King Charles Robert in 1330, the Prahova Valley, Teleajen, the Buzău River valley, and the Jiu River Valley. The border with Moldavia, to the east of the Carpathians, which ran along the Milcov and Siret Rivers, presented no major geographical obstacles, thereby facilitating contacts between the neighboring Principalities.

By the end of his father's reign, the Ottomans held small territories north of the Danube, in Wallachia proper, around the fortresses of Turnu and Giurgiu, but, in September 1445, Vlad succeeded in reconquering the latter, which he held throughout the remainder of his reign. When Vlad assumed the throne in the fall of 1436, his country extended as far east as the Danubian port city of Brăila, but in 1439 he managed to recover territory in the Danube Delta once held by his father, including the key fortress of Kilia, from Moldavia, thus regaining for Wallachia an outlet to the Black Sea. In a decree dated September 8, 1439, he first entitles himself, "Voivode John Vlad, by the grace of God and though the will of God, ruler and Prince of all the land of Ungrovalachia to the great sea..."[14] This territory remained under his control until the winter of 1445-1446.

Wallachia was a land of geographic diversity, abundant in natural resources. Michael Bocignoli, a Ragusan who visited the Principality at the beginning of the sixteenth century, provides the following description of the country: "It extends in length from west to east for twelve days' journey, and in width, from south to north, for a journey of a little over three days. In this uninterrupted plain, the land is fertile, good for planting, except for the places where it is cut by swamps and forests."[15] Wallachia in the time of Vlad Dracul was heavily forested, making for a landscape quite different from that which we see today. Since ancient times, the thick forests, like the mountains to the

---

[14]Doc. 108 in Hajdeu, *Archiva istorica*, vol. I, part 1, pp. 84-85, emphasis added.

[15]Holban, ed., *Călători străini*, vol. I, pp. 175-176. A descendant of one of the leading families of the maritime republic on the Adriatic Sea, Michael Bocignoli visited Wallachia prior to 1512. His account was published in 1524.

north, provided a place of refuge for the indigenous populations in face of the numerous invaders who conquered or overran the country. The Romanian proverb, "The forest is the brother of the Romanian," reflects this time-honored reality. The district of Vlaşca, or the Vlach land, earned its name because it was a forest refuge where the native population withdrew to avoid subjugation. The adjacent district called Teleorman, which in Cuman means 'the crazy forest,' is another such area,[16] its name reflecting the difficulty the conquerors faced in penetrating the region; another example is the Great Forest, in the Ilfov district, where the future capital of Bucharest developed. Numerous rivers also cross the country, flowing down from the mountains and emptying into the Danube. The most important waterways running through the interior of Wallachia were the Motru, Jiul, Olt, Vedea, Teleorman, Argeş, Dâmboviţa, Ialomiţa, and Buzău rivers. Numerous lakes and ponds also dotted the landscape. The rivers played a key role in the development of the Principality. They sustained a thriving fishing industry and, in addition to navigation, they formed natural overland communication and transportation routes, cutting through the dense forests, in the absence of road construction.[17]

Wallachia was organized into administrative units called *sudstvo* in Vlad's time,[18] but later *judete*. A royal official known as a *sudeţ* administered each of these districts or counties. Most of them represented tribes or former voivodates,[19] united when Thocomer and Basarab established the Principality. Around 1581, a Genoese traveller, Franco Sivari, noted that "Wallachia is divided into sixteen large counties."[20] In Vlad's time, there were no fewer than seventeen districts, because the Ottomans had annexed Brăila in 1544 and transformed it into a Turkish raya, but there may have existed several more as over time the trend was toward consolidation. A tradition places the organization of *sudstvo* in Wallachia during Vlad's reign, in 1442, but they existed long before; we know that during the time of his father, Mircea the Old, Wallachia had well-defined districts. Most of their names are derived from

---

[16]Giurescu, "O nouă sinteză a trecutului nostru," in *RIR*, I (1931), p. 363.

[17]Panaitescu, *Interpretări româneşti*, pp. 133-134.

[18]Doc. 89 in *DRH, B*, vol. I, pp. 154-156.

[19]Panaitescu, *Interpretări româneşti*, p. 98.

[20]Holban, ed., *Călători străini*, vol. III, p. 14.

geographical features, especially river valleys around which they were centered. The only *sudstvo* mentioned in extant documents from Vlad's reign is Jaleş. Although we lack precise information, other *sudstvo* possibly in existence during his time included Vâlcea, Upper Jiul, Motru, Balta, Prahova, Ilfov, Brăila, Pāureţ, Gilort, Saac (also called Săcueni), Muscel, Buzău, Vlaşca, Romanţi, Lower Jiul, Ialomiţa, Teleorman, Argeş, Râmnic, Olt, and Dâmboviţa.

In addition to ruling over Wallachia proper, Vlad also held the title of Hertzog or Duke of Amlaş and Fãgãraş in southern Transylvania. The Hungarian Crown had granted these Duchies, with predominantly Wallachian populations, to the princes of the Transalpine land as perpetual estates. The larger of the two, Fãgãraş, also known as the Olt land, became a possession of Wallachian princes during the reign of Vlad's great-uncle, Vladislav I, who acquired the Duchy, located between the Saxon cities of Sibiu and Braşov, from King Louis the Great of Hungary. Vladislav first used the title "Duke of Fãgãraş" in a decree dated November 25, 1369."[21] In a subsequent document, dated July 16, 1372, he calls the Duchy his "new estate."[22] Amlaş, located west of Sibiu, became a domain of the princes of the Transalpine land during the reign of Vlad's uncle, Dan I, who obtained it during the civil war that plagued Hungary following the death of Louis the Great. The Duchies formed an integral part of the Principality; the same laws and customs applied there as did south of the Carpathians. Vlad effectively ruled over Amlaş and Fãgãraş since his coronation at Nuremberg in February 1431; they never came under the control of his brother and rival Alexander Aldea. There are five extant diplomas issued by Vlad confirming holdings in Fãgãraş to various boyars, more than for any other Prince, an indication of the important role played by the Transylvanian Duchies as a base from which to launch his bid for the Wallachian throne.

It is difficult to determine the population of Wallachia during Vlad's reign. In a society based on oral tradition, written records were sparse. No censuses were recorded and they did not register births and deaths or baptisms and marriages. Population estimates have ranged from as few as 266,000 to as

---

[21]Doc. 3 in *DRH, B*, vol. I, pp. 12-13.

[22]Doc. 5 in *DRH, B*, vol. I, pp. 14-17.

many as 750,000.[23] A journal entry by Cicco Simonetta, Chancellor to the Duke of Milan, dated May 10, 1476, helps to shed some light on this problem. Simonetta noted the visit to the Milanese court of the Italian doctor Francesco Fontana, an emissary of King Matthias Corvinus of Hungary. As part of his mission, Fontana presented a list of revenues for the Kingdom of Hungary, prepared by the Royal Chancellery in December 1475, which, fortuitously, Simonetta transcribed in his journal. Among other things, it reveals that, "From Wallachia, when the King is crowned, he receives a horse from each household; a horse from the nobles must have a value of 25 ducats, while one from ordinary people 15 ducats. And when the King takes a wife, each household gives him an oxen; and there are 40,000 households. In the time of King Ladislas, he received 60,000 oxen. Of this, he no longer takes anything, but they are all obligated to participate in the defense of the country."[24] This journal entry provides us with the oldest known statistical source for the population of Wallachia.

The decline in the number of households in the Principality, from 60,000 during the reign of Vladislav I or Ladislas Posthumous, that is to say during the time of Vlad Dracul, to 40,000 in 1475, is due both to wars with the Turks, especially Mehmed II's campaign against Vlad the Impaler in the summer of 1462, and the loss of the two Transylvanian Duchies, which Matthias Corvinus had removed from under the control of the Princes of the Transalpine land, even though they continued to bear the title, "Duke of Amlaş and Făgăraş." But despite this precious indication, the average size of a household in fifteenth century Wallachia is unknown, making it difficult to provide an accurate estimate of the population in Vlad's time. We know that during the eighteenth and nineteenth centuries the size of an average household was 4.5 persons. Fiscal policies, such as those described in the document recorded by Cicco Simonetta, which levied taxes per hearth or household, made extended families larger and more commonplace in the Middle Ages; as a result, the size of an average household in the fifteenth century may have been double, giving a

---

[23]Louis Roman, "Populatia Tării Românesti în secolele XIV-XV," in *RdI*, 39:7 (1986), pp. 669, 678.

[24]See Annex in Serban Papacostea, "Populatie şi fiscalitate în Tara Românescă în secolul al XV-lea," in *RdI*, 33:9 (1980), pp. 1785-1786.

total population of around 540,000 during Vlad's reign. Other evidence supports this assessment of Wallachia's population during the first half of the fifteenth century. As a general rule, barely one per cent of the population formed a country's military forces.[25] From the account of the Burgundian crusader Walerand de Wavrin, who visited Wallachia in 1445, we know that approximately six thousand men comprised Vlad's entire army.[26] Thus, five to six hundred thousand is a reasonable estimate of the population of Wallachia during the time of Vlad Dracul.

The vast majority of this population lived in rural communities, called *selo* (pl. *sela*) in diplomas emitted by Vlad's chancellery. The fifteenth century Byzantine chronicler Laonic Chalkokondyles noted that "they live in villages and are inclined to a pastoral life."[27] Likewise, Archbishop John of Sultanieh, who visited Wallachia during the reign of Vlad's father Mircea as an emissary of Tamerlane, observed that "They do not have large cities, but many villages and animals."[28] Research has identified approximately 2,100 villages in Wallachia up to the beginning of the seventeenth century,[29] but, as the documentary evidence has lacunae, their actual number was probably somewhat higher; of these, 2,045 are still in existence. Most of these settlements formed along river valleys. Population density was highest west of

---

[25]Hale, *The Civilization of Europe in the Renaissance*, p. 129. P.P. Panaitescu calculated the population of Wallachia during the time of Vlad the Impaler as 400,000 to 500,000. To obtain this figure, he used exaggerated contemporary estimates of the size of Vlad's army, placing it at up to 40,000 men, and he considered that ten percent of the population comprised the military, see Panaitescu, *Mircea cel Bătrân*, pp. 60-61. Although his resulting estimate of the size of the population during the first half of the fifteenth century is reasonably accurate, the means he used to calculate it are erroneous.

[26]Iorga, "Cronica lui Wavrin," p. 126.

[27]Chalcocondil, *Expuneri istorice*, p. 63 (II, 77).

[28]Holban, ed., *Călători străini*, vol. I, p. 39.

[29]Lia Lehr, "Factori determinanți în evoluția demografică a Țării Românești," in *SMIM*, VII, p. 163. Ion Donat, "Așezările omenești din Țara Românească în secolele XV-XVI," in *Studii*, IX:6 (1956), p. 77, identifies 3,220 villages and cities from extant documents from the period 1325-1625, but his figure includes numerous toponyms subsequently eliminated by Lehr.

the Olt River, the area known as Oltenia.[30] The size of villages in Wallachia varied. Five to ten households formed smaller villages, while larger ones had upwards of fifty; approximately twenty households comprised an average village during this period.

A small, but important segment of the population lived in urban centers. Franco Sivari noted the existence of "twenty-one large market towns" when he visited the Principality at the end of the sixteenth century.31 Slightly fewer cities existed during Vlad's time. Urban centers began to develop in Wallachia during the thirteenth century, when, as a consequence of the Crusades, which reopened contacts between East and West, trade with the Orient began to flourish. Unlike villages, cities were royal estates, each with its own charter granted by the prince. Most cities developed as markets along trade routes, and the revenues generated by transit taxes and duties on commercial transactions represented the most important source of monetary income for the royal treasury.[32] Many market towns arose in areas bordering on the hills and the plains, as places where the different products produced in each of these economic regions could be exchanged; the variety of goods available for trade allowed them to prosper. Cities that developed in areas that lacked this economic diversity usually formed along important trade routes.[33] Most towns grew up around clusters of villages and, despite their primitive fortifications, they became places of refuge as well as commerce for the surrounding rural population. Around these markets, various crafts and trades also began to develop as the urban population increased. In Wallachia, however, a significant portion of city dwellers continued to engage in agricultural production, cultivating nearby fields, and when they required highly-skilled craftsmen, the Wallachian elite frequently appealed to the Saxon cities of Transylvania.

Foreign immigrants played a key role in the development of the earliest cities in Wallachia, especially Saxons and Hungarians coming from Transylvania. Their organization and institutions reflect these influences. The

---

[30]Dinu C. Giurescu, *Ţara Românească în secolele XIV şi XV*, Bucharest, 1973, p. 32.

[31]Holban, ed., *Călători străini*, vol. III, p. 14.

[32]Panaitescu, *Interpretări româneşti*, p. 207.

[33]G.M. Petrescu-Sava, *Târguri şi orase între Buzău, Târgovişte şi Bucureşti*, Bucharest, 1937, pp. 87-89.

word for city, *oraş*, is derived from the Hungarian term, *varush*. The Slavic term for town or market, *târg*, was also frequently employed to designate an urban center. Towns were organized along the model of German cities, with citizens annually electing a mayor, called a *sudet*, and an assembly of twelve councilmen, called *pârgari* from the German word for citizen, *burgher*, via the Hungarian *polgar*, who governed the city. We know that in Câmpulung these elections took place on the third day of Easter in the town square in front of the church.[34] In addition to these elected officials, the prince appointed a royal official, called a *pârcălab*, responsible for overseeing the administration. In cities with royal courts, the prince also appointed a *vornic*.[35] Unlike the Saxon cities of Transylvania, stone walls did not protect any of the cities in Wallachia; trenches and wooden palisades served to defend the urban centers south of the Carpathians.

Located along the route crossing the Carpathians from Braşov, via Bran and Rucăr, Câmpulung, also called Longo Campo, was Wallachia's first capital and its oldest city. Saxon settlers coming south from Transylvania founded the city at the beginning of the thirteenth century when the Teutonic Knights took possession of the Bârsa land and began to extend their control across the mountains into what was then known as Cumania. They built a wooden fort here in 1211, which they replaced with a stone citadel in 1217. Câmpulung continued to grow even after King Andrew II of Hungary expelled the Teutonic Knights from the region in 1225. It is first attested to by the gravestone of one of the town's officials, Count Lawrence, buried there in 1300, around the time the Principality came into being. Even though the capital moved to Argeş during the reign of Basarab I, Câmpulung remained a royal residence, and Basarab's wife, Princess Margaret, helped to found a Catholic monastery here. The town was organized along the lines of Saxon cities in

---

[34]Constantin C. Giurescu, *Târguri sau orase şi cetăţi moldovene*, Bucharest, 1967, p. 125.

[35]V. Costăchel, P.P. Panaitescu, and A. Cazacu, *Viaţa feudală în Ţara Românească şi Moldova*, Bucharest, 1957, pp. 426-427.

Transylvania.[36] The oldest known charter for a Wallachian city is one granted to Câmpulung by Mircea the Old or his son Michael, mentioned in later diplomas.[37] It enjoyed the greatest autonomy of all the cities in the Transalpine land.

With the development of the Principality, Argeş (today Curtea de Argeş) flourished, and Basarab made it his capital, beginning construction here of a princely church and a royal court, which his son and successor, Nicholas Alexander, would complete. The new capital became a military target in 1330 when King Charles Robert led his army against Basarab in an ill-fated attempt to restore Hungarian suzerainty over the Transalpine land. By the early fifteenth century, Târgovişte began to replace Argeş as the capital. In his account of his travels through the area, Johann Schiltberger, a German squire who fell prisoner to the Turks at the battle of Nicopolis in 1396, wrote: "I was also in Wallachia, in its two capitals, which are called Argeş and Târgovişte."38 By the time of Vlad's reign, Argeş functioned as a secondary capital. Although he issued almost all of his exant diplomas from Târgovişte, on August 2, 1439, he issued a deed confirming the holdings and privileges of the monasteries of Tismana and Vodiţa from the royal court at Argeş;[39] on September 8 of that year, he also issued a decree granting trade privileges to merchants from Poland and Moldavia, specifying that it was "granted at Argeş and written at Târgovişte."[40] Argeş remained the seat of the Orthodox Metropolitanate in Wallachia throughout the fifteenth century. Vlad erected a Metropolitan Church in Argeş on the site of the present-day Monastery of

---

[36]Ştefan Olteanu, "Cercetări cu privire la geneza oraşelor medievale din Ţara Românească," in *Studii*, XVI:4 (1963), pp. 1276-1277; and "Câmpulung" in Predescu, ed., *Enciclopedia cugetara*, p. 160.

[37]Virgil Drăghiceanu, "Curtea Domnească din Argeş," in *BCMI*, X-XVI (1917-1923), p. 23. Diplomas issued by Prince Radu Mihnea in 1615 and Prince Leon in 1633 mention a privilege granted to Câmpulung by Michael in 1392, but, either it was issued later, during Michael's reign, or if the date is correct, it was granted by Mircea the Old. By the seventeenth century, when these diplomas were drafted, there was a great deal of confusion over the chronology of medieval princes.

[38]Holban, ed., *Călători străini*, vol. I, p. 30.

[39]Doc. 89 in *DRH, B*, vol. I, pp. 154-156.

[40]Doc. 108 in Hajdeu, *Archiva istorică*, vol. I, part 1, pp. 84-85.

Argeş, built by Neagoe Basarab at the beginning of the sixteenth century; the family crest of the Draculas emblazoned on the bell tower is all that remains of this construction.

Founded by Saxon settlers in the fourteenth century, Târgovişte developed from a village to a market town to become the capital of Wallachia in the first half of the fifteenth century. Situated between a hill region and a plain along the Ialomiţa River, where inhabitants from these areas met to exchange goods. It is first mentioned as a customs point in Mircea the Old's undated decree, circa 1403, granting trade privileges to merchants from Poland and Lithuania,[41] and again in a similar decree for merchants from Braşov on August 6, 1413.[42] Located along a major trade route linking Transylvania and the Danube, its name in Slavonic literally means market town — the city prospered and became a royal residence during the reign of Vlad's father Mircea the Old. Owing to its Saxon origins, Târgovişte was also the most important center of Catholicism in the Principality. The city's crest showed the Virgin Mary in prayer, probably denoting the significance of St. Mary's Catholic Church, built there in the fourteenth century.[43] In addition, the Monastery of St. Francis was the headquarters of the Friars Minor in Wallachia, whose Order enjoyed Vlad's patronage. An Italian visitor to Wallachia during the first half of the sixteenth century, Francesco della Valle, describes Târgovişte as "a not very large city located on a plain and surrounded by thick oak trees."[44] It owed its rise to prominence to its favorable geographic location, with forests, rivers, streams, and swamps protecting it from attack. The Ragusan writer Felix Petancic (c.1445- c.1520), in a treatise describing invasion routes used by the Turks, prepared for Hungarian King Vladislav II, describes Târgovişte as "the capital of Wallachia, the principal residence of the princes, made inaccessible not by walls or girded by fortifications, but by ditches, fences, and barricades, strengthened on the outside only by sharp stakes, and it is located between swamps which surround it, along with dense

---

[41]Doc. 1 in Hajdeu, *Archiva istorica*, vol. I, part. 1, pp. 3-4.

[42]Doc. 120 in *DRH, D*, pp. 197-198.

[43]Emil Vîrtosu, "Din sigilografia Moldovei şi a Ţării Româneşti," in *DIR, Introducere*, vol. II, pp. 493-494.

[44]Holban, ed., *Călători străini*, vol. I, p. 322.

forests and ponds, so that almost the entire surrounding region is impassable."45

The royal court at Târgovişte was erected on a high terrace along the right bank of the Ialomiţa River, on the eastern edge of the town's market. It first became a royal residence during the time of Mircea the Old, when Vlad's eldest brother, Michael, made it his seat when he began to share power with his father during the final years of his reign, referring to it in a diploma for the monasteries of Cozia and Codmeana as "My Majesty's city, Târgovişte."46 The main structure of the court during Vlad's time was the official residence, a one-story building, 29x35 meters, with a formal reception hall, 6x12 meters, where the royal council met and the prince received foreign dignitaries and other visitors. This building also incorporated the living quarters for the prince and his family and housed administrative offices, including the royal chancellery. A network of cellars ran beneath the main floor. Near the residence was the royal chapel, also constructed during the time of Mircea the Old. Next to the church stood the Chindie Tower, so-called because from here the authorities announced the end of daily activities in the city at the approach of sunset, a time of day called *chindie*. The imposing tower, which dominated the city's skyline, dates from the mid-fifteenth century and was quite possibly raised by Vlad as part of his efforts to protect the autonomy of his Principality. This cylindrical structure, nine meters in diameter, rises up from a pyramidal base, twenty-seven meters high. It served as an important observation point from which to protect the court and to survey the surrounding area. High stone walls surrounded the entire complex.[47] From here, Vlad conducted most of his affairs of state.

The Principality's most important economic center during Vlad's time was Brăila, the port city located along the Danube River on Wallachia's eastern frontier. It was a key point linking trade routes between East and West. Chalkokondyles calls it "the city of the Dacians in which they do more

---

[45]Holban, ed., *Călători străini*, vol. I, p. 444.

[46]Doc. 39 in *DRH, B*, vol. I, pp. 82-84.

[47]For a detailed description of the royal court at Târgovişte see, N. Constantinescu and Cristian Moisescu, *Curtea domnească din Tîrgovişte*, Bucharest, 1969.

commerce than in all the other cities of the country combined."[48] It developed from a small fishing village in the fourth century A.D., to a growing market town by the end of the twelfth or beginning of the thirteenth century.[49] It is first mentioned in a Spanish geography from 1350 as Drinago. Vlad's great-uncle, Vladislav I, granted privileges to merchants from Braşov and the Bârsa land to transport their goods along the route to Braylan "on their way to foreign lands."[50] Schiltberger recalls visiting "a city that is called Brăila, which is located on the Danube, and which is a port for boats and ships with which merchants bring goods from the land of the infidels."[51] Some indication of the scale of commerce passing through Wallachia's principal port is found in an Ottoman report from April 15, 1520, which records that "ships from the Black Sea, coming from Trebizond, Caffa, Sinope, Samsun, Istanbul, and other regions of the Ottoman Empire, go up the Danube to Brăila... Sometimes seventy to eighty ships arrive at Brăila from the Black Sea loaded with goods. These are sold, and grains are loaded in their place and they start back."[52]

The Burgundian crusader Walerand de Wavrin made this important commercial center his base when he came to Wallachia in the summer of 1445, attempting to rekindle crusading efforts in the aftermath of the Varna debacle. Brăila prospered not only from foreign trade, but also because of its flourishing fishing industry. Merchants from Transylvania came here to purchase fish, as demonstrated by Vlad's decree from 1437 granting trade privileges to merchants from Braşov and the Bârsa land.[53] Stephen the Great's privilege for traders from Lemburg, dated July 3, 1460, shows that Polish merchants regularly crossed Moldavia to purchase fish in Brăila and Kilia.[54] Vlad appears to have made frequent visits to the port city along the Danube; he is known to

---

[48]Chalcocondil, *Expuneri istorice*, p. 285 (IX, 505).

[49]Constantin C. Giurescu, *Istoricul oraşului Brăila*, Bucharest, 1966, pp. 35-35.

[50]Doc. 46 in *DRH, D*, pp. 86-88.

[51]Holban, ed., *Călători străini*, vol. I, p. 30.

[52]Quo. Giurescu, *Istoricul oraşului Brăila*, pp. 48-49.

[53]Doc. 243 and Addenda A in *DRH, D*, pp. 340-341 and 463-464.

[54]Doc. 21 and B. Petriceicu-Hajdeu, ed., *Archiva istorică a România*, vol. II, Bucharest, 1865, pp. 171-176.

have had a young mistress from Brăila named Kaltsunina, with whom he had an illegitimate son christened Mircea.[55]

Several other cities existed in Wallachia at the beginning of Vlad's reign. Slatina, a market town on the Olt River, is first mentioned as a customs point for merchants from Transylvania en route to Bulgaria in Vladislav I's decree of January 20, 1368.[56] Pitești, on the Argeș River, a day's journey down river from the former capital, first appears in Mircea the Old's initial endowment for the Monastery of Cozia on May 20, 1388. This same document also mentions Râmnicu Vâlcea,[57] simply called Râmnicu, from the Slavonic word *rabnic* or *rabna*, meaning lake or pond, a city founded by Saxon and Hungarian settlers on the upper Olt River. Five kilometers southwest of Râmnicu Vâlcea was Ocnele Mari, a small market town that prospered because of the nearby salt mines from which it derived its name; it first appears in an undated decree from later in Mircea's reign.[58] Târgșor, also called Novo Foro or New Market, near present-day Ploiești, is first mentioned as a customs point in Mircea's privilege for merchants from Brașov dated August 6, 1413.[59] It was the site of Vlad's final battle and his son Vlad the Impaler raised a church here[60] to commemorate his father's memory. Calafat first appears in a diploma issued by Dan II for the Monastery of Tismana on August 5, 1424, in which he mentions that his father, Dan I, granted customs revenues from this small market town located across the Danube from Vidin to the Monastery.[61] Târgu Jiu, located on the river of the same name, existed during Mircea's time, when its *sudeț* or mayor is mentioned in a royal decree,[62] but the city first appears in a diploma that confirms mills built by monks from Tismana in that city to the cloister originally established by Nicodim, issued by Dan II on March 20,

---

[55]Doc. CCXXIX in Bogdan, *Documente privitoare*, pp. 282-285.

[56]Doc. 46 in *DRH, D*, pp. 86-88.

[57]Doc. 9 in *DRH, B*, vol. I, pp. 25-28.

[58]Doc. 27 in *DRH, B*, vol. I, pp. 62-63.

[59]Doc. 120 in *DRH, D*, pp. 197-198.

[60]Constantin C. Giurescu, "O biserică a lui Vlad Țepeș la Târgșor," in *BCMI*, vol. XVII (1924), pp. 74-75.

[61]Doc. 53 in *DRH, B*, vol. I, pp. 104-107.

[62]Doc. 32 in *DRH, B*, vol. I, pp. 70-71.

1429, or April 9, 1430.[63] A circular sent by this same prince to customs officials throughout Wallachia at the beginning of 1431, to inform them of the privileges he recently granted to merchants from Braşov, lists additional cities:[64] Buzău, located along the river of the same name in the eastern half of the Principality; Floci, a city near the point where the Ialomiţa River empties into the Danube, in the vicinity of the present-day village of Piua Petrii, no longer exists, but in the fifteenth century it had an important fishing industry and was a prosperous commercial center, especially for the wool trade from which its name, Floci, derived; and Gherghiţa, along the Prahova River, the site of a royal retreat where the princes of Wallachia went to hunt and to fish in the nearby forests and ponds.[65] All of these towns and cities existed long before we find them first mentioned in extant documents.

On September 8, 1439, Vlad issued a decree granting trade privileges to merchants from Poland and Moldavia, specifying that "they will pay a customs tax of two Hungarian florins per wagon at Râmnicu... after which they will be free to go on in peace to the Turkish land..."[66] This has been mistakenly understood to refer to Râmnicu Vâlcea, but, in fact, it is the earliest mention in existing documents of the city of Râmnicu Sărat, located in eastern Wallachia along the river of the same name. It would have made no sense for traders from Poland and Moldavia, passing through Wallachia on their way to trade in Ottoman lands, to go out of their way to Râmnicu Vâlcea. The small town of Râmnicu Sărat was the gateway to Wallachia for travelers coming from Moldavia, as Paul of Aleppo, a seventeenth century visitor to the Principality who followed this route, mentions in his account of his journey.[67] Moldavian Prince Stephen the Great invaded Wallachia via this route and defeated Basarab the Young in a battle near Râmnicu Sărat on July 4, 1481, after which

---

[63]Doc. 64 in *DRH, B*, vol. I, pp. 124-125. This diploma is dated from Argeş on Palm Sunday which falls on the dates specified in 1429 and 1430. These years are established by comparing the list of members of the prince's royal council with other documents from Dan II's reign.

[64]Doc. 69 in *DRH, B*, vol. I, pp. 130-131.

[65]Petrescu-Sava, *Târguri şi oraşe*, p. 17.

[66]Doc. 108 in Hajdeu, *Archiva istorică*, vol. I, part. 1, pp. 84-85.

[67]Doc. 310 in Hajdeu, *Archiva istorică*, vol. I, part. 2, p. 87.

he installed Vlad's son, Vlad the Monk, on the throne.[68] Boyars from this city also sent a harshly-worded reply to the Moldavian prince, categorically refusing his request that they recognize Vlad's illegitimate son Mircea as prince in March 1481.[69]

Vlad also worked to recover cities that Wallachia had lost prior to his reign. In the summer of 1439, he seized Kilia, the strategic fortress and port city near the mouth of the Danube, also known as Lykostomo or "the mouth of the wolf," from Stephen II of Moldavia. His father had conquered Kilia from the Genoese in 1403-1404, but it fell into Moldavian hands in 1426 when Alexander the Good occupied it during the wars between Dan II and Vlad's brother Radu II. But Vlad again lost his outlet to the Black Sea to the neighboring Principality during the winter of 1445-1446. In the fall of 1445, he also recovered Giurgiu from the Turks; it is first mentioned in a document from 1403 in which Mircea the Old renews his alliance with King Vladislav I of Poland,[70] and again in a diploma dated May 11, 1409,[71] as a *grad*, a term used in Slavonic documents of the time with the sole meaning of fortress,72 but when Vlad's father renewed his treaty with Vladislav I on May 17, 1411, he calls Giurgiu, "our city."73 Its location at one of the principal crossing points along the Danube led to its development as a market town and a customs point.

Although they are only first attested to in documents subsequent to his reign, other towns also existed during Vlad's time. The most important of these were Bucharest and Craiova, both of which became important urban centers by the end of the fifteenth century. Bucharest, located along the Dâmbovita River, now the capital city of Romania, is first mentioned as a fortress in a diploma issued by Vlad's son, Vlad the Impaler, on September 20, 1459.[74] It

---

[68]Panaitescu, ed., *Cronicele slavo-române*, p. 34.

[69]Doc. CCXXIX in Bogdan, *Documente privitoare*, pp. 282-285.

[70]Doc. DCLII in Hurmuzaki, *Documente*, vol. II, part. 1, pp. 824-825.

[71]Doc. 35 in *DRH, B*, vol. I, pp. 75-77.

[72]N.A. Constantinescu, "Cetatea Giurgiu: originile şi trecutul ei," in *AARMSI*, series II, vol. XXXVIII (1915-1916), p. 496.

[73]Doc. 115 in *DRH, D*, pp. 186-187.

[74]Doc. 118 in *DRH, B*, vol. I, pp. 203-204.

then became the preferred residence of his brother Radu, who succeeded him in 1462, but it did not officially become the capital of Wallachia until 1659. Tradition dates the origins of Craiova, or "the King's city," to the thirteenth century; some attribute its founding to the Bulgarian Tsar John Asen, while others consider that it was the residence of Cuman rulers.[75] It is first mentioned in a diploma issued by Prince Basarab the Old on June 1, 1475, which lists a boyar called Jupan Neagoe from Craiova as a member of the royal council.[76] On January 31, 1496, Vlad's grandson, Radu the Great, issued the first diploma known to have been written at Craiova.[77] Another small market town was Tismana. It had a *ban* responsible for governing the region, first mentioned in a diploma granted by Vlad's son Radu for the nearby monastery on July 10, 1464;[78] the town prospered during the fifteenth century thanks to the important copper mines in the surrounding area, especially the one opened by Chiop Hanosh at Bratilova at the end of the fourteenth century. Mircea had granted royal revenues from this mine to the Monastery of Tismana,[79] a gift renewed by Vlad in his diploma for this cloister dated August 2, 1439.[80]

Wallachia, officially known as Ungrovalachia or the Transalpine land, was a prosperous country during Vlad's reign, with a population of well over half a million people. It was divided into numerous administrative districts and had as many as twenty cities and market towns. It was a land of geographic diversity, with mountains and plains, numerous rivers, lakes, and forests, and an abundance of natural resources. Its favorable position along international trade routes had generated abundant wealth that had led to the creation of the Principality between the Danube and the Carpathians, but its unfortunate location on the crossroads between East and West, on the frontier between Christianity and Islam, made it a battleground over which the neighboring superpowers sought to exert their control. This was Dracula's Realm.

---

[75]"Craiova" in Predescu, ed., *Enciclopedia cugetară*, p. 231.

[76]Doc. 148 in *DRH, B*, vol. I, pp. 243-246.

[77]Doc. 264 in *DRH, B*, vol. I, pp. 427-428.

[78]Doc. 124 in *DRH, B*, vol. I, pp. 209-213.

[79]Doc. 14 in *DRH, B*, vol. I, pp. 33-36.

[80]Doc. 89 in *DRH, B*, vol. I, pp. 154-156.

Chapter III

The Land of Draculas

"It was the ground fought over for centuries by the Wallachian, the Saxon, and the Turk. Why, there is hardly a foot of soil in all this region that has not been enriched by the blood of men, patriots or invaders."

— Bram Stoker, *Dracula*[1]

T he land over which Vlad Dracul ruled had a long and complex history. Since Antiquity it was a crossroads between East and West, Romans and barbarians, Orthodoxy and Catholicism, Christianity and Islam. Already in the fifth century B.C., Herodotus described this division between two distinct cultures by comparing the story of how the Greeks carried off the Asian princess Medea with that of Paris' abduction of Helen. According to the father of history, the Greeks were the aggressors in the legendary Trojan War: "Abducting young women, in their opinion, is not, indeed, a lawful act; but it is stupid after the event to make a fuss about it. The only sensible thing is to take no notice; for it is obvious that no young woman allows herself to be abducted if she does not wish to be. The Asiatics, according to the Persians, took the seizure of the women lightly enough, but not so the Greeks: The Greeks, merely on account of a girl from Sparta, raised a big army, invaded

---

[1]Stoker, *Dracula*, p. 20.

Asia and destroyed the Empire of Priam. From that root sprang their belief in the perpetual enmity of the Grecian world towards them — Asia with its various foreign-speaking peoples belonging to the Persians, Europe and the Greek states being, in their opinion, quite separate and distinct from them."[2] To understand the life and times of Vlad Dracul requires some perspective on the tangled past of this region, for, as the seventeenth century Moldavian chronicler Miron Costin once wrote, "Any story must begin from the beginning."[3]

In ancient times, the Balkans, including the land north of Danube that later became Wallachia, was called Thrace. Herodotus provides the earliest historical information we have of this area. "The population of Thrace," he observed, "is greater than that of any country in the world except India. If the Thracians could be united under a single ruler in a homogenous whole, they would be the most powerful nation on earth, and no one could cope with them..."[4] But the Thracians were divided into numerous tribes often at war with each another. The Getae or Dacians, often called Geto-Dacians, were the Thracian people generally regarded as the remote ancestors of the Romanians who inhabited Wallachia. They fought the Persian invaders led by Darius I in 514 B.C. Later, in 339 B.C., Meda, a daughter of the Getic King Cothelas, became the sixth wife of Philip II of Macedon, the father of Alexander the Great.[5] In the first century B.C. the Dacian King Burebista united most of the tribes north of the Danube and posed a serious enough threat to Roman interests in the area that Julius Caesar considered an expedition against him prior to his assassination on the ides of March in 44 B.C. But the danger to Rome ceased with the assassination of Burebista later that same year which led to the break-up of his Kingdom. Only in the second half of the first century A.D. did another Dacian ruler, Decebal, reestablish a Kingdom powerful enough to challenge Roman authority. After Decebal humiliated the legions of

---

[2]Herodotus, *The Histories*, trans. Aubrey de Sélincourt, Baltimore, 1968, p. 14.

[3]*Cronice atingătoare la istoria romînilor*, ed. Ioan Bogdan, Bucharest, 1895, p. 179.

[4]Herodotus, *The Histories*, pp. 311-312.

[5]Kurt W. Treptow, "Macedonia and the Geto-Scythian Conflict during the Final Thracian Campaign of Philip II, 342-339 B.C.," pp. 74-86 in *Macedonian Studies*, XI:1-2 (1994).

Emperor Domitian in A.D. 89, another Roman Emperor, Trajan, decided to take decisive action against the Dacians. After two long campaigns, in 101-102 and again in 105-106, he destroyed Decebal's Kingdom and Dacia became the final province added to the Roman Empire.

Roman rule in Dacia lasted less than two hundred years, but it proved a key factor in the formation of the Romanian population that came to inhabit Wallachia. The historian Eutropius tells how "Trajan, after conquering Dacia, brought here from all over the Roman Empire great numbers of people to plow the land and to inhabit the towns."[6] These settlers mixed with the native Thracian population, just as they had done earlier in the provinces south of the Danube. Over time, Latin became the predominate language among these people of diverse races. Despite the flawed history, it is interesting to note how people in Vlad Dracul's time grasped their past. Vlad's contemporaries included the Italian humanist Enea Silvio Piccolomini. One of the most influential scholars of his day, the future Pope Pius II recorded that the Getae "were defeated and subjugated by Roman forces. Then a colony of Romans was brought there to keep the Dacians under control led by one named Flaccus for whom Flacchia was named. After a long time the name changed, as is bound to happen, and it was called Valachia, and instead of Flacci the inhabitants were called Vlachs. This people even now has a Roman tongue, although greatly changed and barely understandable to someone from Italy."[7]

Although the Emperor Aurelian abandoned the province of Dacia between 271 and 275, Roman influence north of the Danube persisted. Bridgeheads on the left bank of the Danube, with a corresponding buffer zone of some 20 to 30 kilometers to defend against barbarian invaders, remained in Roman hands for a long time after.[8] The Emperor Constantine the Great enhanced these fortifications and reestablished Roman control over much of Wallachia in 328.[9] Cities and military outposts along the Danube also served as important

---

[6]Quo. *A History of Romania*, ed. Kurt W. Treptow, Iași, 1997, p. 36.

[7]Holban, *Călători străini*, vol. I, p. 472.

[8]D. Tudor, "Stăpânirea romană în sudul Daciei, de la Aurelian la Constantin cel Mare," in *RIR*, X (1940), pp. 223-224.

[9]D. Tudor, "Constantin cel Mare și recucerirea Daciei Traiană," in *RIR*, XI-XII (1941-1942), pp. 140-141, 144.

points of commercial and cultural exchange. Consequently, Roman influence north of the Danube continued through the reign of the Byzantine Emperor Justinian (527-565). Thus, for nearly half a millennium Roman culture made its mark upon Wallachia and the mixing of populations gave birth to a new people speaking a Latin tongue. "Romanian is a word derived over time from Roman," wrote Miron Costin in 1684, "and today, if you want to ask someone if they know Moldavian, you say to them: 'do you know Romanian?'... They have never used another name among themselves. Foreigners have named them in different ways."[10]

Still, in the mid-sixth century it is too early to speak of the existence of a Romanian people. Both during the period of Roman influence in Dacia and after various barbarian peoples overran the area, each contributing to a greater or lesser degree to the formation of this people. The most significant newcomers to the region were the Slavic tribes who came from the steppe and infiltrated the lands on both sides of the Danube during the fifth and sixth centuries. The Slavic element played a key role in the ethnogenesis of the Romanians; as the historian Ioan Bogdan categorically stated, before the Slavic invasions there can be no mention of a Romanian people.[11] Although the Slavs arrived in significant numbers, they did not absorb the Latinized population inhabiting Wallachia. The native people took refuge in the dense forests which covered much of the land at that time.[12] Nevertheless, Slavic influence was undeniable as they settled and imposed their rule throughout the region. The mingling of the Slavs with the Latinized population resulted in the evolution of the Romanian people who, in the time of Vlad Dracul, were called Vlachs or Wallachians.

In the seventh century, the Bulgars, a nomadic Turkic people from the east, swept south across the Danube and imposed their rule over the Slavs living there. They defeated the Byzantines and forced Emperor Constantine IV to recognize the Bulgarian state in 681. The Bulgars cooperated with the native Slavic aristocracy and over time the much larger Slavic population assimilated

[10]Bogdan, ed., *Cronice atingătoare*, p. 187.

[11]Constantin Giurescu, "O nouă sinteză a trecutului nostru," in *RIR*, I (1931), p. 349.

[12]S. Mehedinți, "Coordonate etnografice. Civilizația și cultură," in *ARMSI*, series III, XI (1931), p. 144.

them, forming the people known as the Bulgarians. Under Khan Krum (802-814) Bulgarian rule extended north of the Danube and strengthened Slavic influence in that area, installing a Slavic ruling class in former Dacia.

Up to the ninth century, Latin was the language of the Church in Wallachia. Christianity had slowly spread to Dacia beginning in the second and third centuries A.D. It gained a firm hold in the region after Constantine the Great declared it an official religion of the Roman Empire and a bishopric was established at Tomis on the Black Sea coast. Linguistic evidence supports this thesis. The basic religious vocabulary in Romanian is of Latin origin: church — *biserică* (Latin *basilica*), cross — *cruce* (Latin *crux-cis*), priest — *preot* (Latin *presbiterum*), God — *Dumnezeu* (Latin *dom(i)ne deus*), Easter — *Paşti* (Latin *pascha, -ae*), Christmas — *Crăciun* (Latin *creatio, - onis*), and angel — *înger* (Latin *angelus*), to give just a few examples. But the lack of a solid state structure north of the Danube left the Church loosely organized. This began to change in 864 when the Bulgarian King Boris converted to Christianity and adopted the name Michael. Although Rome and Constantinople struggled for supremacy over the Bulgarian Church for the next half century, the Greek Church gained the upper hand. Toward the end of Boris's reign, disciples of the Byzantine scholars Cyril and Methodius came to Bulgaria from Moravia; among them was Kliment of Ohrid (840-916) who played a key role in spreading Christianity throughout the Balkans. These missionaries introduced the Cyrillic alphabet and in 888 the Bulgarian Church officially adopted the Slavic rite. As the Bulgarian Empire at this time included the territory of former Dacia, the Church north of the Danube also began to use the Slavic liturgy and continued to do so until the seventeenth century.[13] Under Boris's son Simeon (893-927), the first Bulgarian ruler to adopt the title of Tsar, the Empire reached its peak and Slavic language and culture became entrenched in former Dacia. This period of Bulgarian rule was of vital importance for the formation of the future Principality of Wallachia. "All of the seeds of state and church life from which, beginning in the thirteenth century, arose our political institutions in the Middle Ages," observed the Romanian historian Ioan Bogdan at the end of the nineteenth century, "have their origins in the period

---

[13]Dimitrie Onciul, *Originile principatelor române*, Bucharest, 1899, pp. 136-140; and Alexandru Ştefulescu, *Mînăstirea Tismana*, Bucharest, 1903, pp. 10-11.

of Bulgarian influence: political and social organization in cnezates and voivodates, church hierarchy, the development of a nobility, or boyars, the Bulgarian language in the royal chancellery, in the church, in secular literature, and in private correspondence."[14]

In 1018, the Byzantine Emperor Basil II destroyed the First Bulgarian Empire, earning the epithet 'the Bulgar slayer.' For almost two centuries Byzantine rule again extended to the Danube. Remnants of the Bulgarian Empire north of the Danube broke up into autonomous fiefdoms called cnezates and voivodates. But the fall of Bulgaria did nothing to diminish Slavic cultural influence in the area; Basil II promptly issued a decree recognizing the autonomy of the Bulgarian Church, headed by an Archbishop with his seat at Ohrid, the last capital of the Empire. The Church north of the Danube was under the jurisdiction of the Bishop of Vidin, subject to Ohrid.[15] Despite attempts at rebellion, such as that led by Delean and Alusian, descendants of the last Tsars, in 1040, the Bulgarians did not succeed in restoring their Empire until the end of the twelfth century.

The power vacuum created by the collapse of the First Bulgarian Empire made it possible for other peoples to extend their influence over the territory of former Dacia. The first of these were the Hungarians, or Magyars, a Finno-Ugric people, who came to Europe from the Ural steppes and settled in the Pannonian plain at the end of the ninth century. Having converted to Catholicism under King Stephen I in the year 1000, they expanded their rule eastward over the territory that became known as Transylvania or "the land beyond the forest." They encountered resistance from several Bulgarian-Wallachian voivodates and cnezates, but by the end of the twelfth century Hungarian rule had reached the Carpathians. To consolidate their authority in Transylvania and to defend the borders of the Kingdom in the east and southeast, the Hungarian Kings brought settlers into the province and granted them special privileges. The first to arrive were the Szecklers, a Turkic people related to the Hungarians. They settled in the area along the eastern Carpathians and had an autonomous local administration overseen by a Count appointed directly by the King. Perhaps the most important immigrants to

---

[14] Ioan Bogdan, *Romînii şi Bulgarii*, Bucharest, 1895, p. 22.

[15] Onciul, *Originile principatelor române*, pp. 141, 143.

reach Transylvania in the late twelfth century were the Germans, generally referred to as Saxons, although they came from throughout the German lands and not exclusively from Saxony. Each group of Saxon settlers was led by a *gräve* and the villages and towns they founded were often named after their leader, as in the case of the principal Saxon center, Sibiu, called Hermannstadt. The Saxons established fortified cities and brought urban life to Transylvania, developing trades and commerce. The Saxon territories had an autonomous administration, directly dependent on the King. This status is reflected in the German name for Braşov, Kronstadt, literally 'the King's city.' Saxon privileges were secured in a general charter granted to them by King Andrew II in 1224. One of its provisions ensured the freedom of the people to elect their own magistrates, abolishing the hereditary rights claimed by many of the *gräves*.[16] The most important German cities near the border with the future Principality of Wallachia were Braşov and Sibiu.

The eleventh and twelfth centuries witnessed the arrival of new migratory peoples from the east who left their mark on the region. These peoples moved in relatively small bands numbering upwards of 15,000 fighting men; with their women, children, and slaves accompanying them the total reached 70,000.[17] Although the Byzantines regained control over the Balkans in the eleventh century with the fall of Bulgaria, on the other side of the Empire the Seljuk Turks crossed the Taurus Mountains in Anatolia and defeated a Byzantine army at Manzikert in 1071. This marked a watershed in the history of Asia Minor that had serious repercussions for Southeastern Europe later on. From the eleventh to the thirteenth centuries Turkish tribes continued to move into the area and replaced Greek with Islamic culture.[18] Another Turkic people, the Pechenegs, came to the Carpatho-Danubian region from the Ural steppes at the beginning of the eleventh century; in 1048, the warlord Kegen led 20,000 Pechenegs across the Danube at Silistria to enter the service of the Byzantine

[16] *History of Transylvania*, ed. Béla Köpeczi, Budapest, 1994, pp. 178-181.

[17] R. Rosetti, "Care au fost adevăratele efective ale unor armate din trecut," in *AARMSI*, series III, XXV (1942-1943), p. 729.

[18] L.S. Stavrianos, *The Balkans since 1453*, New York, 1958, p. 34.

Emperor.[19] During the latter half of this century a related Turkic people called
the Cumans also arrived. They defeated and assimilated the Pechenegs and
over the next two hundred years played a major role throughout this entire
region of Europe.

The Cumans occupied a vast area on both sides of the Danube. Unlike most
Turkic peoples, they converted to Christianity in large numbers soon after their
arrival, allowing them to mingle more easily with the existing population in
the region. They settled in significant numbers between the Carpathians and
the Danube so that the territory of the future Principality of Wallachia east of
the Olt River was called Cumania during the twelfth and thirteenth centuries.
Before their arrival in the Danube basin, they had come into close contact with
the Russians and absorbed Slavic cultural influences. They cooperated and
mixed with the local nobility in Southeastern Europe. In Bulgaria, the Cumans
helped to reestablish the Empire and provided the names for two of its
dynasties, the Asens and the Terters. They also played an important role in
Hungary, providing first a Queen and then a King during the second half of the
thirteenth century and their language became written in the *Codex Cumanicus*
printed by Geza Kún.[20] Descendants of the Cumans, called the Gagauz, are
found today in the Republic of Moldavia, southeast Ukraine, and the Dobrudja
region of Romania and Bulgaria.

The closing decades of the twelfth century saw the rebirth of the Bulgarian
Empire. In 1185, two brothers, Theodore and Asen, united the Bulgarian,
Vlach, and Cuman populations south of the Danube in rebellion against the
Byzantine Empire. Unsuccessful at first, the brothers fled north of the Danube
to garner support among the Cuman tribes ruling there. Asen is a name of
Cuman origin, but the Byzantine historian Niketas Choniates, who took part in
the campaign against the rebels, serving as secretary to the Emperor, refers to
the brothers as Vlachs: "The Vlachs hesitated at the beginning and refused to
join the revolt to which Peter and Asen tried to incite them, being uncertain of
the success of the enterprise. To free their compatriots of this fear, those of the

---

[19]N. Bănescu, "Cele mai vechi ştiri bizantine asupra românilor dela Dunărea-de-Jos,"
in *AIIN*, Cluj, I (1921-1922), p. 143.

[20]N. Iorga, "Imperiul Cumanilor şi domnia lui Băsărabă," in *ARMSI*, series III, VIII
(1927-1928), pp. 97-103.

same blood with them built a house of prayer under the name of St. Dimitrie the Martyr in which they gathered many of them of both sexes... behaving exactly as do those possessed by demons, they taught these self-intoxicated ones to say that God had decided to free the Bulgarian and Vlach peoples..." Choniates goes on to tell of a Byzantine priest taken prisoner by the rebels who "pleaded with Asen in his own language to set him free, for he knew the language of the Vlachs."[21] Stirred by nationalist sentiments of modern times, Romanian and Bulgarian historians have engaged in a long polemic over the ethnic origin of the two brothers. Trying to make claims of ethnic affiliation based on medieval sources is hazardous at best; the term Vlach also meant shepherd and many of these had been Slavicized. As John V.A. Fine, Jr., the preeminent American scholar on the history of the medieval Balkans, points out, "There is no evidence of any 'national' conflict or rivalry between these two people at this time. Thus the modern academic controversy, being over an issue of little relevance to the Middle Ages, is probably best dropped."[22] With the aid of the Cumans from north of the Danube the rebellion succeeded. Theodore donned purple boots, a traditional symbol of the authority of the Emperor, and adopted the name Peter, after a Bulgarian Tsar of the mid-tenth century who had been canonized by the Church, marking the foundation of the Second Bulgarian Empire with its capital at Trnovo.

But the loss of Bulgaria was only the beginning of the problems confronting Byzantium. Racked by internal strife, the Empire faced its greatest peril to date when the army of the Fourth Crusade, having initially been raised to free Jerusalem from the Saracens, sacked Constantinople in 1204 and established a Latin Empire. The Greeks regained possession of the imperial city half a century later, but the Byzantine Empire never recaptured its former glory. This left Bulgaria with a claim to be the rightful heir to the imperial tradition in Southeastern Europe; during the reigns of Kaloyan (1197-1207) and John Asen (1218-1241) the reborn Bulgarian Empire expanded its borders in the Balkans and extended its rule over Cumania north of the Danube. Meanwhile, the Kingdom of Hungary had reached the Carpathians and after the death of Tsar

---

[21]Quo. N. Bănescu, "O problemă de istorie medievală: crearea şi caracterul statului Asăneştilor (1185)," in *AARMSI*, series III, XXV (1942-1943), pp. 570, 575.

[22]John V.A. Fine, Jr., *The Late Medieval Balkans*, Ann Arbor, 1994, p. 13.

Kaloyan in 1207 it began to make inroads across the mountains and to challenge Bulgarian suzerainty in the area.

To defend southern Transylvania against the neighboring Cumans, King Andrew II of Hungary called in the Teutonic Knights in 1211, granting them the Bârsa land.[23] One of the three great military crusading orders of the Middle Ages, the Teutonic Knights had been established only a few years earlier, in 1198. With the fall of Jerusalem in 1187 and the debacle of the Fourth Crusade, these defenders of the faith had to look outside the Holy Land for other areas to propagate Catholicism. Thus, they came to the Bârsa land. German colonists accompanying the Knights founded the city of Braşov around 1215. During this same period Dietrich, a leader of the Knights, established the fortress of Bran, originally known as Dietrichstein, to defend one of the principal mountain passes leading to Cumania. To attract them to the area, the King had granted the Teutonic Knights a series of privileges: they had an autonomous administration, the liberty to setup markets, and the right to build wooden fortresses such as the one at Bran. Acting on the authority of the Pope, the Knights soon expanded the scope of their mission; they began to erect stone fortresses and they crossed the mountains into Cumania. They raised these castles at strategic points on both sides of the Carpathians, usually atop high rocky peaks, sometimes on the ruins of old Roman or Dacian forts. They constructed one such fortress, called Cetatea Neamţului or the Fortress of the German, at the junction of the Dâmboviţa and Dâmbovicioară rivers between Rucăr and Bran.[24] Their penetration south must be placed in connection with Papal efforts to convert the Cumans to Catholicism; to achieve this, the Pontiff established a Bishopric of the Cumans at Milcov as early as 1217. Not only did the Cumans, under a leader named Bortz, resist the Germanic invaders,[25] the Knights's usurpation of royal prerogatives also brought them into conflict with the Hungarian King. The Pope insisted that these new territories were subject exclusively to his jurisdiction and that the Knights acted solely on

---

[23]Doc. XLI in Eudoxia de Hurmuzaki and Nic. Densuşianu, eds., *Documente privitoare la istoria românilor*, vol. I, Bucharest, 1887, pp. 56-58.

[24]I. Puşcariu, "Cetatea Neamţului de la Podul Dâmboviţei în Muscel," in *AARMSI*, series II, XXX (1907- 1908), p. 12.

[25]Doc. 7 in *DRH, D*, pp. 15-17.

behalf of the Holy See.[26] Naturally, Andrew II disagreed. Unable to allow this challenge to royal authority to go unanswered, the King personally led an army against the Teutonic Knights at the beginning of 1225 and drove them from the area. Honorius III protested. He demanded that Andrew return the lands seized from the Knights which "we established through apostolic privilege not to be subjected to anyone other than the Roman Pontiff," including "a fortress which they built across the Carpathian Mountains with difficulty and at great expense,"[27] referring to Cetatea Neamţului. The Hungarian King refused the Pope, but realizing the need for reliable settlers to develop and to defend this underpopulated border region,[28] Andrew II retained the German colonists who had originally accompanied the Knights to southern Transylvania and whose privileges he had confirmed the previous year.

Following the expulsion of the Teutonic Knights, the struggle between Hungary and Bulgaria for control over Cumania continued. A war between the two powers around 1230 left Hungary in control of lands around Vidin and part of the region between the Olt and Danube rivers; as a consequence, in 1233 the Hungarian King created the Banate of Severin and assumed the additional titles of King of Bulgaria and Cumania.[29] Still, much of Cumania remained under Bulgarian control throughout the reign of Tsar John Asen. The Tartar-Persian chronicle of Rashid, written in 1303, refers to Cumania in 1241 as the land of the Bulgarians.[30] The conflict between Hungary and Bulgaria also assumed a religious character. Although the Bulgarian Church had submitted to Rome under Tsar Kaloyan after the crusaders took Constantinople in 1204, the union of Orthodoxy and Catholicism was nominal at best and soon forgotten. As Hungary and Bulgaria each strove to impose their rule over Cumania, the Catholic and Orthodox Churches, represented by the two competing powers, battled for the hearts and minds of its inhabitants. On November 14, 1234, the Pope advised Bela, the son and co-regent of Andrew II of Hungary, of the urgent need to bring the Vlachs living there under the

---

[26]Doc. LX in Hurmuzaki, *Documente*, vol. I, p. 82.

[27]Doc. 5 in *DRH, D*, pp. 10-14.

[28]Doc. LVIII in Hurmuzaki, *Documente*, vol. I, pp. 80-81.

[29]Docs. XCVIII and XCIX in Hurmuzaki, *Documente*, vol. I, pp. 126-127.

[30]Onciul, *Originile principatelor române*, p. 35.

authority of the Archbishop of Cumania. "As I have learned, in the Diocese of the Cumans there are some people called Vlachs, who, although they call themselves Christians, embrace different rites and customs in a single faith and commit acts that are contrary to that name," wrote Gregory IX. "Thus, ignoring the Roman Church, they receive religious rites not from our venerable brother, the Archbishop of the Cumans... but from some pseudo-bishops who practice the Greek rite, while others, Hungarians as well as Germans, together with other righteous believers from the Kingdom of Hungary, cross over to them to live there and, forming a single people with the aforementioned Vlachs, also ignore him and receive the aforesaid rites to the great indignation of righteous believers and to the great harm of the Christian faith."[31] By 1238, the Pope had abandoned hopes of convincing the Bulgarian Church to return to the union with Rome; he excommunicated Tsar John Asen and called upon the Hungarian King to organize a crusade against the schismatics and to seize Bulgaria.[32] But chaos soon struck the entire region as a new threat loomed on the horizon.

The Tatars, a Mongol people from the east, swept into Europe in 1241. The attack did not come as a complete surprise for these nomadic warriors had already imposed their rule over the Cumans living to the east of Hungary in 1239, leading many to seek refuge in Hungary and Bulgaria. A Hungarian prelate wrote to the Bishop of Paris amidst the attack, telling him that two Tatar spies had been captured and brought before Bela IV where "They declared that their objective is the subjgation of the entire world" and that their ruler is called *Zingiton* (Ghenghis Khan, meaning the King of Kings).[33] The Tatars defeated the Hungarian army and devastated the entire region as far west as Buda and the Dalmatian coast. Although their armies penetrated into Scandinavia and Germany and threatened to overrun the entire continent, the effect of their attack was blunted when news of the death of the Great Khan Ogödoi reached them in the spring of 1242, bringing an abrupt halt to their offensive. In the aftermath, Bulgaria and Cumania were left to pay annual tribute to the loosely-organized Tatar state known as the Golden Horde.

---

[31]Doc. 9 in *DRH, D*, pp. 20-21.

[32]Doc. CXXVI in Hurmuzaki, *Documente*, vol. I, pp. 168-169.

[33]Doc. CLIX in Hurmuzaki, *Documente*, vol. I, pp. 206-207.

Amidst these events, Tsar John Asen died in 1241 leaving the throne to his seven-year-old son Kaloman. The impact of the Tatar invasion and the lack of a strong ruler in Bulgaria opened the door for Hungary to extend its control over Cumania. To defend this area, King Bela IV called on another of the great medieval crusading orders, the Knights of St. John of Jerusalem, also known as the Knights Hospitallers; after reaching an agreement with Rembald, the Grand Preceptor of the Order, the King issued a diploma entrusting them with the banate of Severin and granting them extensive privileges. With certain specified exceptions, Bela ceded to the Knights all revenues due the royal treasury from Cumania for the next twenty-five years. This document also provides some information, albeit sparse, about the political organization of Cumania. Cnezates ruled by John and Farcas, located west of the Olt River, were placed under the authority of the Hospitallers. Another Cnezate in the same region ruled by the Voivode Litovoy was left to the Wallachians, but the King granted the Knights half of the revenues it owed to the Crown; the same exemption applied to the land of Seneslav, Voivode of the Wallachians, located east of the Olt.[34] Despite the presence of the Hospitallers, the struggle for control of Cumania intensified. The Knights of St. John have settled "in a highly endangered area on the border with the Cumans and the Bulgarians, "wrote Bela IV to the Pope in 1254, "from where they hope to propagate the Catholic faith among them, with the favor of the Apostolic Seat, all along the Danube to the sea...." But the King warned the Pontiff that Hungary and Europe faced the threat of a new invasion from the East: "The Tatars have made tributary the areas bordering the Kingdom to the east, that is Russia, Cumania, the Brodnici lands [Moldavia], and Bulgaria." That same year, the Franciscan missionary Wilhelm de Rubruquis, an emissary to the Great Tatar Khanate at Qara Qorum, reported that "from the mouth of the Don toward the west, up to the Danube, everything is under their control. And even beyond the Danube toward Constantinople, Wallachia, which is the land of Asen, and lesser Bulgaria all the way to Salonika, everyone pays them tribute."[35] Lacking sufficient manpower and resources to fulfill their mission, the Hospitallers withdrew from the region in 1260.

---

[34]Doc. 1 în *DRH, B*, vol. I, pp. 3-11.

[35]Doc. CCI in Hurmuzaki, *Documente*, vol. I, pp. 265-275.

While Hungary controlled a large portion of the future Principality of Wallachia during the second half of the thirteenth century, its hold on the area weakened with the decline of the Arpad dynasty. Already in 1257, internal pressures forced Bela IV to divide his Kingdom with his son Stephen. Stephen V married a Cuman princess named Elizabeth, and when Bela IV died in 1270 he remained the sole ruler of Hungary, but he died only two years later leaving his underage son Ladislas as his heir. The country fell under the control of a regency council and two rival factions of nobles struggled for supremacy. In these chaotic conditions, nobles in the border areas of the Kingdom seized the opportunity to throw off Hungarian suzerainty.

One of those who revolted against Hungarian rule was the Voivode Litovoy mentioned in the diploma for the Knights of St. John of 1247. With the departure of the Hospitallers from the area, Litovoy expanded his control over the Severin region and when the opportunity arose, sometime around 1273 or 1274, he began to assert his independence. Information about this insurrection comes from a diploma of Ladislas IV dated January 8, 1285, in which he praises the Magistrate George for his services to the Crown, including the suppression of Litovoy's revolt. "When we began our reign, when we were in our childhood, after the death of our beloved father," the King wrote, "Voivode Litovoy, together with his brothers, in their treachery, took under his control part of our Kingdom, located across Carpathians, and despite our appeals he refused to pay us the revenues due to us from those parts. I sent against him the aforementioned Magistrate George who... killed him, while he captured his brother, named Barbath and brought him to us. For his ransom, we extracted a large sum of money and thus, thanks to the services of Magistrate George, the tribute owed to us from those parts was restored."[36] This document also hints at the increasing wealth of the region south of the Carpathians, an important factor driving the move toward independence.

Despite the suppression of Litovoy's revolt, the situation in Hungary and Cumania continued to deteriorate. In 1278 Pope Nicholas III sent Philip, the Bishop of Firminy, as papal legate to Hungary and Cumania in an attempt to

---

[36]Doc. 13 în *DRH, D*, pp. 30-34; see also Doc. CCCLXXXIX in Hurmuzaki, *Documente*, vol. I, pp. 483- 484.

quiet the unrest and rebellion brewing in those parts.[37] Seeking to overcome the factional strife dividing his country, Ladislas IV sought help from his mother's relatives, the Cumans, to restore order in the Kingdom. To the dismay of Popes Honorius IV (1285-1287) and Nicholas IV (1288-1292), he had the Queen imprisoned and took a Cuman woman as his concubine and lived among them, adopting their ways;[38] thus, he came to be known as Ladislas the Cuman. But the King's efforts to reimpose royal authority antagonized the nobility even further and led to his assassination in 1290. His successor, Andrew III (1290-1301), a brother of Bela IV, fared no better. With his death in 1301 the Arpad dynasty came to an end; a state of anarchy prevailed in Hungary with a dozen large landowning families each asserting their independence.

With Hungary in disarray and Bulgaria weakened by internal strife, conditions were favorable at the end of the thirteenth century for the emergence of a new political organization in the area between the Carpathians and the Danube. Burgeoning trade between East and West in the aftermath of the Crusades feuled by the rise of an urban society in Western Europe and a corresponding demand for luxury goods brought steadily increasing wealth to this region located along the principal trade routes with the Orient. In 1304, Pope Benedict XI referred to Cumania as a rich and well-populated land with several bishops and many priests of the Greek rite.[39] The political fragmentation that characterized Europe during the Middle Ages resulted from the lack of economic ties between different regions. This all changed as trade began to flourish, cities developed, and the population increased; the need to secure expanding trade routes and the attraction of the wealth they generated sparked the formation of new, more centralized political structures. In the loosely knit lands known as Cumania, these factors, together with the turmoil in Hungary, led to the founding of the Principality of Wallachia.

While the details surrounding the origin of the Principality are obscure, the conditions in Hungary that favored its establishment are better-known. Seven years of anarchy and civil war followed the death of Andrew III in 1301, as

---

[37]Doc. CCCXXXV in Hurmuzaki, *Documente*, vol. I, pp. 414-416.

[38]Docs. CCCLXXVI and CCCLXXXV in Hurmuzaki, *Documente*, vol. I, pp. 467, 478-479.

[39]Doc. CCCCXLVIII in Hurmuzaki, *Documente*, vol. I, pp. 563-565.

various pretenders to the crown of St. Stephen pressed their claims, each supported by different factions among the nobility. One of the most important players in the ensuing struggle for the throne was Ladislas Apor, the Voivode of Transylvania. He ruled the province as a virtually independent fiefdom. Descendants of the Arpads through a female line, Charles Robert of the French Anjou family and Venceslav, a son of the King of Bohemia, both vied for the crown; the latter withdrew in 1305, ceding his claim to Otto of Bavaria who was then anointed and crowned as King of Hungary. But before Otto could consolidate his position, his rival, Charles Robert, gained a precious ally with the election of a French Pope, Clement V, in 1305. Many considered the new Pope, formerly the Archbishop of Bordeaux, as a pawn of Philip IV, the King of France, who intended to use him to expand French influence in Europe. One of the steps taken in this direction by Philip and Clement was the destruction of the Templar Knights and the confiscation of their wealth. The Pope excommunicated Otto as Charles Robert advanced into Hungary. Faced with this challenge, Otto fled east to Transylvania in 1307, hoping to gather support from the German population there, as well as from Ladislas Apor. But Ladislas also harbored royal aspirations; he promptly arrested Otto and imprisoned him in the fortress of Deva after confiscating the crown of St. Stephen and the royal insignia. Shortly thereafter, Otto was placed in the custody of a Wallachian voivode, possibly Stephen Maelat at Făgăraş where a castle had recently been constructed,[40] or across the mountains where Thocomer ruled. The unfortunate claimant was subsequently freed and returned to Bavaria where he continued to use the royal title until his death in 1312. Meanwhile, although Charles Robert had been crowned King of Hungary in 1308, two more years passed before Ladislas Apor recognized the authority of the new monarch and turned over to him the crown of St. Stephen, the symbol of royal legitimacy.[41] But troubles in Hungary persisted and for the next two decades the Angevin King struggled to restore order in his Kingdom.

The founding of the Principality of Wallachia is shrouded in myth; it is thought to have taken place between 1290 and 1310. Seventeenth century

---

[40] Adolf Armbruster, "Românii în cronica lui Ottokar de Stiria," in *Studii*, 25:3 (1972), p. 475; Gheorghe Brancovici, *Cronica românească*, Bucharest, 1987, p. 52.

[41] Doc. CCCCLI in Hurmuzaki, *Documente*, vol. I, p. 572.

chronicles record that Radu Negru, or Black Radu, crossed the mountains from Făgăraş in Transylvania, arriving first at Câmpulung, and then at Argeş: "he made the capital there, building the royal court and a church which is still there today. And he began to make order in the country, establishing counties, judges, boyars, and other things useful to the throne and the country, expanding it to the Danube and the Siret."[42]

But how much of this legend of a voivode coming down from Transylvania to found Wallachia, known in Romanian historiography as the *descălăcatul*, is true? The traditional name given to the founder of the Principality is simply Negru Vodă, literally the Black Voivode. Seventeenth century chroniclers added the name Radu because their sparse information about the early princes led them to equate the Black Voivode with Radu, Vlad Dracul's grandfather, who ruled Wallachia in the second half of the fourteenth century.[43] Although the tradition is clearly much older, the first written mention we have of the Black Voivode as the founder of Wallachia comes from a diploma issued by Prince Alexander Mircea for the Monastery of Tismana on January 8, 1569.[44] Unfortunately, it provides no help in identifying him. Some historians say that the legend of a *descălăcatul* in Wallachia has no basis in historical fact, but rather is a myth derived from the story of the founding of the sister Principality of Moldavia.[45] Others have drawn parallels between the story of the Black Voivode and the legend of William Tell and the founding of the Swiss Confederation.[46] Still others have conjectured the existence of another Prince named Radu at the end of the thirteenth century or identified the Black Voivode with different fourteenth century Wallachian Princes.

Most legends have some basis in historical fact; the story of the Black Voivode is no exception. The conditions in Hungary that precipitated Litovoy's failed revolt in northern Oltenia steadily worsened in the years

---

[42]Radu Popescu, *Istoriile Domnilor Ţării Româneşti*, Bucharest, 1963, p. 5.

[43]Onciul, *Originile principatelor române*, p. 31.

[44]Doc. 351 in, *DIR, XVI, B*, vol. III, pp. 303-304.

[45]Pavel Chihaia, *De la Negru Vodă la Neagoe Basarab*, Bucharest, 1976, p. 12.

[46]Gheorghe I. Brătianu, *Tradiţia istorică despre întemeierea statelor româneşti*, Bucharest, 1980, p. 97.

following the assassination of Ladislas the Cuman. This favored efforts to establish a unified state in Cumania. We know that from 1291 to 1324 there was no Hungarian governor, called a *Ban*, of Severin, indicating that the newly-founded Principality of Wallachia had likely incorporated this territory.[47] In addition, a diploma of Prince Matthew Basarab, dated April 12, 1636, mentions that he saw a diploma issued by the Black Voivode for the monastery of Câmpulung in 1291-1292.[48] Thus, it is plausible that the tradition concerning the founding of Wallachia by the Black Voivode around 1290 is true. But who was the Black Voivode and where did he come from?

Most historians have rejected the legend that the Black Voivode crossed the mountains from Făgăraş and unified Wallachia. The political situation in Transylvania at the time did not allow for such a scenario; also, Făgăraş did not become tied to Wallachia until the reign of Vladislav I (1364-1376). This element is clearly borrowed from the story of the founding of Moldavia by the Voivode Dragoş from Maramureş. This has led historians such as Gheorghe I. Brătianu to conclude that "the historical reality is another; the rise of a native power which, fighting at times with the Tatars and at times with the Hungarians, founded Wallachia."[49] While this explanation for the founding of the Principality does not conform with the historical information we possess, the legend of a *descălăcatul* cannot be rejected outright. First of all, virtually all sources refer to the establishment of Wallachia as a fairly sudden event, and indicate that the Black Voivode came from somewhere outside the Principality. For example, Vasile Buhăescul, a seventeenth century chronicler, records that in 1290 the Black Voivode "came down and founded Wallachia and died on the throne, ruling for twenty-four years."[50] A gradual unification of the country from within the native ruling class would have been a long, drawn-out process, as demonstrated countless times throughout European history. The available evidence does not indicate that such a process occurred in Wallachia. The hypothesis that a conqueror came from outside the country

---

[47]*Istoria românilor*, vol. III, Bucharest, 2001, p. 573.

[48]Ioan C. Filitti, "Despre Negru Vodă," in *ARMSI*, series III, IV, (1925) p. 36.

[49]Brătianu, *Trădiţia istorică*, p. 88.

[50]Vasile Buhăescul, "Istoria Ţării Româneşti şi Moldovei," in *RIAF*, XIV (1913), p. 156.

to impose his rule over it is more tenable than supposing that one of the existing voivodes suddenly gained sufficient power to force the others to submit to his authority. The Hungarians certainly used every possible means to prevent one of their vassals in this strategically important border region from accumulating enough power to challenge royal authority, especially after the suppression of Litovoy's rebellion. Thus, the legend of a *descălăcatul* appears to have a basis in historical reality. But if the Black Voivode did not come from Transylvania, where did he come from?

Our first clue to discovering the identity of the Black Voivode comes from his name itself — Negru Vodă. As we have seen in the case of the name Dracula, such epithets were given to remark distinguishing characteristics. Names such as Negru (Black) or Albu (White) generally remarked facial characteristics.[51] This interpretation is confirmed by Miron Costin who wrote that the first Prince of Wallachia "was named Negrul Vodă, that is 'the one whose face is black.'"[52] Our next clue comes from the name of the first documented ruler of Wallachia — Basarab. Basarab, or Băsărabă in its original form, is a name of Cuman origin; literally it means "the good father."[53] The earliest mention of his reign is found in a diploma issued by Charles Robert on July 26, 1324;[54] another act from 1329 tells us that Basarab ruled Wallachia as early as 1320-1321,[55] but we cannot precisely date the beginning of his reign. From another royal diploma, dated November 26, 1332, we learn that Basarab is the son of Thocomer,[56] or Tugomir, a name of Turkic/Slavic origin. A diploma issued by Prince Gavril Movilă on November 13, 1618, refers to Basarab's son and successor, Nicholas Alexander, as the *grandson* of the Black Voivode.[57] With these facts in mind, the most plausible explanation for the legend of the Black Voivode is that he was a Cuman-Tatar Prince who came

---

[51]Constantinescu, *Dicţionar onomastic*, p. LI.

[52]Bogdan, *Cronice atingătoare*, p. 193.

[53]Constantinescu, *Dicţionar onomastic*, p. 192.

[54]Doc. 15 in *DRH, D*, pp. 36-37.

[55]Doc. 18 in *DRH, D*, p. 41.

[56]Doc. 25 in *DRH, D*, pp. 49-52.

[57]Doc. 8 in *DIR*, XIII, XIV, XV, B, p. 12.

from lands in the east and imposed his rule over Wallachia.[58] Papal documents from the period that decry "incursions by Cumans, Tatars, schismatics, and hostile pagans" that had nearly ruined Hungary[59] support this conclusion. The Cuman-Slavic aristocracy that governed the land certainly facilitated the conquest. Another indication of the association of the Wallachian dynasty with the Tatars is found in a letter sent from Avignon by Pope John XXII to Charles Robert on August 5, 1331. In it, the Pontiff mentions the King's campaign in Wallachia the previous year as one "against the *Tatars*, enemies of the Catholic faith."[60] The dark skin of the Cuman-Tatar conqueror accounts for his epithet, the Black Voivode. According to legend, the Black Voivode died around 1314-1315 and was buried at Argeş, confirming the chronicler's assertion that he ruled for twenty-four years. Thus, we can identify the Black Voivode with Thocomer, the father of Basarab.

This hypothesis is further supported by the fact that throughout his reign of over thirty-five years Basarab maintained strong ties to the Tatar clans in the east and close relations with Bulgaria, another Tatar ally. The Wallachian dynasty appears to have come from the region of southern Moldavia, between the Prut and Dniester rivers, today in southwestern Ukraine; at the beginning of the fourteenth century, Abulfeda, an Arab scholar, referred to this territory as "the land of the Bulgarians and Turks."[61] The area came to be known as Basarabia as it was the land of origin of the Prince who gained fame throughout Europe following his remarkable victory over the King of Hungary in 1330.

When he inherited the throne around 1315, Basarab faced many challenges as he sought to consolidate the independence of the Principality founded by his father. Hungary gradually recovered from the anarchy of the previous decades as Charles Robert of Anjou worked vigorously to restore the authority of the monarchy. The new King secured his lands through a system of alliances with neighboring states, allowing him to concentrate on domestic matters; in 1320, he married Elizabeth, the sister of King Casimir of Poland, laying the

---

[58]Andrei Veres, "Originea stemelor tările române," in *RIR*, I (1931), p. 230.

[59]Docs. CCCCXLIV and CCCCXLV in Hurmuzaki, *Documente*, vol. I, pp. 557-560.

[60]Doc. 21 in *DRH, D*, pp. 44-45, emphasis added.

[61]Quo. Brătianu, *Tradiţia istorică*, p. 44.

basis for the future union of the two kingdoms under his son Louis. Charles Robert met the daunting task of bringing order to his troubled Kingdom with skill and tenacity, making him, as the distinguished Hungarian historian Pal Engel observed, "one of the most successful rulers of the Middle Ages."[62] After the death of Ladislas Apor in 1316, Charles Robert gained effective control over much of Transylvania, but only quelled a rebellion in the province, led by the sons of the late Voivode, in 1324 with the help of Cuman forces.[63] The Hungarian King also had to deal with the recently established Principality of Wallachia to the south over which he claimed suzerainty. The dispute between the two countries centered around the Banat of Severin which Wallachia had incorporated during the period of civil strife in Hungary. A series of border wars broke out in the area around Severin and Mehadia.[64] Consistent with his policy of trying to maintain peaceful relations with neighboring states so that he could deal more effectively with domestic problems, Charles Robert appealed to diplomatic means to resolve the dispute with his neighbor across the Carpathians. He sent Count Martin of Szalacs on several missions to negotiate with Basarab[65] and by 1324 good relations prevailed between the two countries. Wallachia maintained its autonomy and Basarab continued to hold Severin, but he accepted the suzerainty of the King and agreed to pay an annual tribute, known as the *censul*, to the Hungarian Crown.

But this state of affairs did not last long as tensions began to build. In a written statement dated June 18, 1325, the secretary of the Hungarian royal chancellery, Ladislas, a man "learned in medicine and science," declared that one Paulo, son of Iwanko of Ugol, came before him to testify that Stephen, a son of the Cuman Count Parabuh, had slandered Charles Robert and praised the Wallachian ruler, "*disloyal* to the holy Crown,... saying that the power of our lord, the King, could in no way stand against or compare with the power of Basarab."[66] The situation seems to have improved somewhat by 1327 when

[62]*A History of Hungary*, ed. Peter F. Sugar, Bloomington, 1994, p. 37.

[63]Kopeczi, ed., *History of Transylvania*, p. 205.

[64]Doc. 18 in *DRH, D*, p. 41.

[65]Doc. 15 in *DRH, D*, pp. 36-37.

[66]Doc. 16 in *DRH, D*, pp. 37-38, emphasis added.

Pope John XXII wrote to Basarab from Avignon praising his loyal service to the Catholic Church and asking him to receive Dominican inquisitors in the lands under his rule, "located in the Kingdom of Hungary."[67] But this letter also implies that Basarab harbored enemies of Hungary and the Church, especially Templar Knights from Germany and Poland who took refuge in significant numbers in Wallachia and Bulgaria during this period. By 1329, relations between the two neighbors had again taken a turn for the worse as Basarab gave shelter to the sons of Ladislas Apor, who had continued to oppose Charles Robert's authority in Transylvania.[68] The threat of an armed conflict between Hungary and Wallachia now loomed on the horizon.

Throughout his reign, Basarab maintained close ties with the Golden Horde. Like neighboring Bulgaria, Wallachia at this time formed part of the system of tributary states established by the Tatars in the aftermath of their invasion of Europe in the mid-thirteenth century. Basarab retained the lands ruled over by his family between the Prut and Dniester rivers. To strengthen ties with this area, the Wallachian Prince colonized settlers from the relatively densely populated region of Oltenia in the nearly deserted territory between the Siret and Prut rivers, to create a bridge between Wallachia and Basarabia. This region later became part of southern Moldavia, but as we learn from a letter to the King of Poland dated September 1, 1435, outlining the division of Moldavia between Princes Ilias and Stephen, long after the reign of Basarab it was still known as *Olteni*.[69] Accounts of the expedition to this area led by the Emir of Aîdîn, Umur Bey, in 1339-1341, confirm that Basarab ruled these areas. These Turks came here to defend Byzantine interests, including Kilia, against the Genoese; the Danube port is referred to as being "on the border of

---

[67]Doc. 17 in *DRH, D*, pp. 39-40.

[68]Ştefan Pascu, "Contribuţiuni documentare la istoria românilor în sec. XIII şi XIV," in *AIIN, Cluj*, X (1945), p. 166.

[69]Constantin C. Giurescu, "Oltenii şi Basarabia: colonizări muntene în sudul Moldovei în veacurile XIV şi XV," pp. 130-139 in *RIR*, X (1940); Doc 192 in Mihai Costachescu, *Documentele moldoveneşti înainte de Ştefan cel Mare*, vol. II, Iaşi, 1932, pp. 681-684. Petre Diaconu, "Kilia et l'expedition d'Umur Beg," in *RESEE*, XXI:1 (1983), p. 29 argues that the Emir's expedition reached Anchialos in Bulgaria and not Kilia on the Danube.

Wallachia."[70] The fact that the Tatars played an extremely important role in the history of this region of Europe well into the mid-fourteenth century is often overlooked; although a loosely organized confederation, the Golden Horde ruled over the land east of the Carpathians that became the Principality of Moldavia and claimed suzerainty over Wallachia and Bulgaria. In words remmiscent of Herodotus's description of the Thracians, the Byzantine chronicler Laonic Chalkokondyles affirmed that the Tatars 'would be the largest, most powerful, and strongest, as is no other people in the world, if they would not be scattered throughout many parts of the world in Asia and Europe... If united, and they would decide to live in the same country and to remain obedient to a single Emperor, no one in the entire world would be able to resist them so as not to be subjugated."[71]

Following the common practice of the day, both Basarab and his father Thocomer used marriage alliances to consolidate their political position. Tradition has preserved the name of Basarab's wife, Margaret or Marghita, and the fact that she was Catholic; although we have no information to indicate her origins, the marriage clearly had political undertones. Given the extent of French influence in fourteenth century Wallachia, which cannot be explained solely by ties to Angevin Hungary, one may speculate that Margaret came from France. For Basarab, religion was a matter of political expediency. As with many noble families of Cuman origin in the area where the Bishopric of Milcov had aggressively propagated the Latin rite, Basarab most likely had a Catholic upbringing. But at a time when the independence of Wallachia was defined in terms its relationship to Hungary, the principal Catholic power in the region, Basarab forged ties with certain heretical sects and with the Orthodox Church. We have already seen that he accorded refuge to Templar Knights persecuted in the West and considered by Rome during this period as the most dangerous heretical group in Europe. Because of his deviation from the Catholic Church, Charles Robert referred to Basarab in 1332 as a

---

[70]Quo, *Istoria românilor*, vol. III, p. 572; see also Mustafa A. Mehmet, "Aspecte din istoria Dobrogei sub dominația otomană în veacurile XIV-XVII," in *Studii*, 18:5 (1965), p. 1100.

[71]Laonic Chalcocondil, *Expuneri istorice*, Bucharest, 1958, p. 94.

"schismatic,"[72] a term applied to those of the Greek rite or other Christian sects split off from the Church of Rome; only five years before the Pope himself had called Basarab "a devout Catholic Prince."[73] From his marriage to Margaret, Basarab had several sons, but the only one we know by name is his eldest son and successor, Alexander, also called Nicholas Alexander. We also know of at least one daughter, Theodora, who married Alexander, the nephew and heir of Bulgarian Tsar Michael Shishman.

The marriage of Theodora to Alexander of Bulgaria consolidated the already close ties between the two neighboring states. When Bulgaria went to war against Byzantium in 1323-1324, Wallachia proved a staunch ally. The Byzantine chronicler Ioannes Kantakuzenus recorded that Basarab's troops participated alongside those of Michael Shishman against the Emperor in 1324.[74] Six years later, Basarab, along with Tatar forces, again came to the aid of Bulgaria, taking part in the disastrous battle at Velbuzd on July 28, 1330, in which the Serbs inflicted a massive defeat on the Bulgarians and their allies. Serbian chronicles say that Basarab took part personally in the battle and, reflecting the close ties between the Wallachian Prince and the Golden Horde, they refer to his troops as Wallachian-Tartars.[75] Tsar Michael Shishman was killed in the fighting after falling from his horse, leaving Basarab's son-in-law Alexander as the new ruler of Bulgaria. On the other side, the future Serbian Tsar Stephen Dušan distinguished himself commanding a cavalry unit in this battle.[76]

When news of the defeat at Velbuzd reached Hungary, many felt that Basarab was now vulnerable and that the time had come to take military action against the rebellious Prince and to bring the territory across the Carpathians back under the control of the Crown of St. Stephen. The Hungarian attack on Wallachia in 1330 was an extension of the power struggle ongoing in Tran-

---

[72]Doc. 25 in *DRH, D*, pp. 49-52.

[73]Doc. 17 in *DRH, D*, pp. 39-40.

[74]Maria Holban, "Despre raporturile lui Basarab cu Ungaria Angevină" in *Studii*, 20:1 (1967), p. 12.

[75]N. Iorga, *Studii și documente*. vol. III, Bucharest, 1901, p. 11.

[76]Fine, *Late Medieval Balkans*, pp. 271-272.

sylvania since the death of Ladislas Apor in 1316. The architects of the campaign were Transylvanian Voivode Toma de Szécsény and Count Dionysius, castellan of the fortress of Mehadia; their declared objectives were the recovery of Severin, which Basarab continued to hold, and the removal of the troublesome Prince who harbored the sons of Ladislas Apor, archrivals of Toma and Dionysius and opponents of Angevin power in Transylvania. Swayed by the arguments of these nobles and their supporters in favor of military action, the *Chronicon pictum Vindobonense*, which provides the most extensive account of the campaign, tells us that Charles Robert gathered a large army and set out against Basarab in September 1330, "even though the Voivode had always faithfully paid the tribute owed to His Majesty, the King."[77]

The royal army set out from Temesvar (Timişoara) and headed southeast, crossing the mountains into the Severin district. The invaders met little or no resistance and promptly occupied the strategic Danubian fortress; the King placed it under the command of Dionysius. Basarab now faced a difficult situation. Not only had the defeat at Velbuzd weakened his military capacity, but it deprived him of assistance from his Bulgarian allies. Given these circumstances, the Wallachian Prince resorted to diplomacy in an attempt to end the conflict with the Hungarian King. According to the *Chronicon pictum Vindobonense*, which provides the most extensive account of the campaign, "Basarab sent emissaries worthy of great honor to the King to say to him: 'Because you, my lord and King, have troubled to gather an army. I will pay for your trouble with 7000 silver marks and I will peacefully turn over to you Severin and all that belongs to it, which at present you hold by force, and in addition to this I will faithfully pay each year the tribute that I owe to your Crown and I will send at least one of my sons to serve at your court with my money and at my expense."[78] The peace terms proposed by Basarab were extraordinarily generous, reflecting both the gravity of his situation and the wealth of his Principality. The offer to pay 7000 silver marks in war reparations is in itself remarkable. This was the equivalent of 1,680,000 dinars or 1,447

---

[77]G. Popa-Lisseanu, ed., *Fontes Historiae Daco-Romanorum, Fasciculus XI: Chronicon pictum Vindobonense*, Bucharest, 1937, p. 109.

[78]Popa-Lisseanu, ed., *Fontes Historiae Daco-Romanorum*, XI, p. 109.

kilograms of 800% silver or 74 kilograms of fine gold; to give some idea of what this sum represented, it should be noted that in the late fourteenth century the Moldavian Prince Petru Muşat loaned the King of Poland the much lower sum of 3000 silver rubles and received the province of Pocuţia as collateral, while it took decades for the King to repay only part of the principal.[79] Basarab's offer sparked a debate in the royal camp. A Czech nobleman, Count Donch, advised Charles Robert to accept the terms: "Lord, this Basarab speaks to you with great humility and honors you; for this, reply to him in your letter with the favor of royal benevolence, full of love and compassion..." Surprisingly, however, the pro-war Transylvanian faction won out. The King refused the Wallachian Prince's proposal and told his emissaries: "Tell Basarab this: 'he is the shepherd of my sheep and I will remove him from his hiding places by his beard'."[80] The Hungarian objective remained the removal of Basarab from the Wallachian throne.

Having decided to continue the war, the Hungarian army advanced slowly eastward in the direction of Argeş, the capital of Wallachia. Basarab wisely refused to meet the Hungarians in open battle; he harassed the invaders[81] and employed scorched-earth tactics to slow their advance and bought precious time as he awaited the arrival of troops from his Tatar allies. His tactics had the desired effect: Although they had not engaged in battle, the situation of the Hungarian army became critical by late October as the weather grew colder and they lacked sufficient food and water. By the time he reached Argeş, Charles Robert had a change of heart. Negotiations between the two sides resumed and the King now agreed to Basarab's terms on the condition that he provide logistical support to ensure the safe and quick return of the royal army to Transylvania.

Basarab feigned peace but prepared for war as Tatar reinforcements had now arrived. The route taken by the royal army in its retreat to Transylvania

---

[79]Dinu C. Giurescu, "Relaţiile economice ale Ţării Româneşti cu ţările peninsulei balcanice," in *Romano-slavica*, XI (1965), p. 168; Radu Manolescu, *Comerţul Ţării româneşti şi Moldovei cu Braşovul*, Bucharest, 1965, p. 19; and Ilie Minea, "Războiul lui Basarab cel Mare cu regele Carol Robert," in *CI*, V-VII (1929-1931), p. 338.

[80]Popa-Lisseanu, ed., *Fontes Historiae Daco-Romanorum*, XI, pp. 109-110.

[81]Doc. 35 in *DRH, D*, pp. 65-66.

and the location of the subsequent battle of Posada are disputed by historians. The most likely route seems to have been along the Argeş river valley as contemporary sources say that the Hungarian army was lost and not on a main road, making it highly unlikely they had followed one of the frequently-travelled routes along the Olt river valley or the Câmpulung-Rucăr-Bran-Braşov road; from the capital of Argeş, this would be the most direct route back to Transylvania. In effect, Basarab proffered the Hungarians a shortcut home, but he had a surprise in store for them along the way. When the royal army entered a narrow pass, probably in the vicinity of the fortress of Poenari, the Wallachians, supported by Tatar troops and possibly some Templar Knights, sprang a carefully-prepared ambush on the King's army.[82] The attack came to be known as the battle of Posada, a term used to refer to a fortified passage or crossing and not the name of a locality. The *Chronicon pictum Vindobonense* describes the ensuing battle: "The innumerable masses of Wallachians, from high upon the cliffs, running from every part, showered down arrows upon the Hungarian army in the valley below, along a road that should not even be called a road, but more properly a narrow path, where, unable to maneuver, the best horses and soldiers fell in battle because, as a result of the steep cliffs... they could not attack the Wallachians on either side of the road, nor could they advance, nor did they have where to run, being trapped there; the King's soldiers were caught like fish out of water."[83] The King himself narrowly escaped death, having changed clothes with Desiderius, the son of Count Dionysius, who was subsequently killed in the fighting.[84] The battle began on Friday, November 9, and lasted until Monday, November 12. The King later described it as a "hostile attack launched with brutality in some narrow and heavily forested places, surrounded by powerful fortifications."[85] Charles Robert managed to flee incognito, with a portion of his army, but the Hungarians suffered heavy losses; the dead included royal Vice-Chancellor Andrew Albensis.[86] In addition to those killed, the Wallachians and their Tatar

---

[82]Doc. 37 in *DRH, D*, pp. 67-69.

[83]Popa-Lisseanu, ed., *Fontes Historiae Daco-Romanorum*, XI, p. 110.

[84]Ilie Minea, *Informaţiile româneşti ale cronicii lui Ian Długosz*, Iaşi, 1926, p. 13.

[85]Doc. 29 in *DRH, D*, p. 57.

[86]Doc. CCCCXCVII in Hurmuzaki, *Documente*, vol. I, pp. 622-623.

Depiction of the Battle of Posada from
the *Chronicon pictum Vindobonense*

allies took many prisoners, horses, and large quantities of plunder. The King's royal seal also disappeared amidst the chaos. The battle of Posada marked the most devastating defeat of a Hungarian army since the Tatar invasion of the previous century. News of Basarab's victory spread throughout Europe.[87] Around the same time, the Tatars launched an attack on Transylvania from the east.[88] The battle of Posada secured the independence of the newly established Principality; throughout the remainder of his reign, Charles Robert never again took up arms against his neighbor to the south.

Basarab remained a strong ally of the Tatars until the end of his reign and in so doing preserved the independence of Wallachia. In 1343, after the death of Charles Robert, Basarab sent Alexander, his son and heir to the throne, with a Wallachian army to join the Tatars in an unsuccessful attack on Transylvania.[89] But despite political tensions, ties to the powerful neighboring Kingdom continued. Angevin Hungary had a significant influence on political, social, cultural, and economic life in Wallachia. Charles Robert introduced Western feudal customs and a new style of government to Hungary based on Western feudal principles. Naturally, these also spread across the Carpathians. For example, French dress-style became fashionable among the elite and the nobility adopted heraldic symbols like those their Hungarian counterparts; the Wallachian coat of arms displayed on coins minted during the fourteenth and fifteenth centuries borrowed elements from the seal of Angevin Hungary.[90] Hungarian influence was especially strong in urban centers such as Câmpulung, Argeş, Râmnicu Vâlcea, and Târgovişte where Hungarians formed a significant part of the population. The young Wallachian state adopted many aspects of Hungarian public administration; terms such as *oraş* (city), *ban* (governor), *hotar* (border), and *pârcălab* (castellan), among others,

---

[87]Emil C. Lăzărescu, "Despre lupta din 1330 a lui Basarab Voevod cu Carol Robert," in *RI*, XXI: 7-9 (1935), p. 246.

[88]Gheorghe Brancovici, *Cronica Românească*, p. 55.

[89]E. Lăzărescu, "In legătură cu relaţiile lui Nicolae Alexandru-Voevod cu Ungurii," in *RI*, XXXII (1946), pp. 130-132.

[90]Brătianu, *Tradiţia istorică*, p. 93.

were borrowed from the Hungarian language, along with many toponyms of Hungarian origin.[91]

Nor did Basarab cut ties completely with the Catholic Church. A letter from Pope Clement VI to Louis the Great of Hungary dated October 17, 1345, tells of the conversion of Basarab's son Alexander to Catholicism, along with other commoners and nobles from Wallachia and Transylvania.[92] This political gesture should be viewed in connection with the changing political situation within the Golden Horde. After the death of Khan Uzbek in 1342, Tatar policy became increasingly anti-Christian[93] and their hold on the areas bordering Hungary tenuous. The Pope hoped to strengthen the Catholic cause even further. On June 2, 1348, Clement VI addressed an invitation to the Franciscan monks in Hungary to send some of their brothers to *Cumania* to strengthen the faith of those recently converted and to convert others.[94] Of course, none of this would have been possible without Basarab's consent.

Basarab, Vlad Dracul's great-great grandfather and the man who secured the independence of Wallachia, died at the end of 1351 or the beginning of 1352. His son Alexander, who upon his conversion to Catholicism took the additional name Nicholas, succeeded him as prince. By previously making Alexander his associate ruler, Basarab had assured a smooth transition of power, eliminating disputes over succession, something very important for the security of the Principality given the dangers surrounding it.

Nicholas Alexander assumed the throne during a new period of upheaval. Around the time of Basarab's death, Hungary launched an offensive against the Tatars driving them from the region east of the Carpathians that came to be called Moldavia. Voivode Dragoş, from the Maramureş region north of Transylvania, ruled the newly-conquered territory on the King's behalf. Although Tatar attacks persisted throughout the fourteenth and fifteenth

---

[91]Giurescu, "O nouă sinteză," in *RIR*, I (1931), p. 352.

[92]Doc. 32 in *DRH, D*, pp. 60-61.

[93]Gheorghe I. Brătianu, "Originile stemelor Moldovii şi Ţării Româneşti" in *RIR*, I (1931), p. 59.

[94]Doc. VIII in Eudoxia Hurmuzaki, ed., *Documente privitoare la istoria românilor*, vol. I, part. 2, Bucharest, 1890, pp. 7-8.

centuries, this effectively removed them from the political equation in the Carpatho-Danubian region.

South of the Danube, Bulgaria was also in decline. In the early part of the century, under Tsar Svetoslav (1300-1322), the Bulgarian Empire extended its rule along the Black Sea coast. But soon after, the Genoese expanded their influence in the Pontic area, challenging both Bulgarian and Byzantine interests. The devastating defeat at Velbuzd in 1330 was a severe blow to the Bulgarian Empire. In its aftermath, a revolt broke out in the eastern part of the Empire led by a Bulgarian boyar of Cuman origin named Balika; the Byzantines and the large Greek population living in the coastal cities supported the rebellion. The new state, with a Greek administration, had its capital at Kaverna. In 1346, Balika intervened in the Byzantine civil war on the side of the Paleologus family, sending 1000 troops, under the command of his brothers, Dobrotitsa and Theodore, to aid the regent, Empress Anne of Savoy. Dobrotitsa distinguished himself in the service of the Byzantines and married the daughter of the most powerful member of the regency council, Alexis Apokoukus. When his brother Balika died in 1354, Dobrotitsa became ruler of the land along the Black Sea coast stretching from Varna north to the mouth of the Danube, that came to be called Dobrudja after him. Because of his ties to the Imperial family, he also received the title of Despot.

Relations between Bulgaria and Wallachia cooled in the early 1350s when Tsar John Alexander divorced Nicholas Alexander's sister Theodora to marry his mistress of the same name, a Jewess converted to Christianity. All these factors forced Alexander to reconsider Wallachia's foreign policy. He now sought an accommodation with Charles Robert's son and successor Louis the Great. The King sent Demetrius, the Bishop of Oradea, on a series of diplomatic missions to Wallachia and, as a result of his efforts, by the end of 1354, Alexander had acknowledged Hungarian suzerainty.[95]

Alexander's ties to the Catholic Church facilitated the renewal of political relations with Hungary. Basarab had originally arranged a marriage for Alexander with an Orthodox princess from Bosnia. A son, Vladislav, also called Vlaicu, resulted from this union. Later, before his conversion to

---

[95]Doc. XXVIII in Hurmuzaki, *Documente*, vol. I, part. 2, pp. 37-38.

Catholicism in 1345, Alexander married a Catholic princess named Clara. We have no additional information about her background, but she may have been an Italian, possibly from Venice. Alexander's second marriage resulted in the birth of several children: two sons, Radu and Voislav, and three daughters, Ana, Elizabeth, and Anca. Like his father, Alexander arranged marriages for his children to achieve political aims. Ana married her cousin Stratimir, son of Tsar John Alexander of Bulgaria; Elizabeth married the Hungarian Duke of Oppeln, a relative of Louis the Great's wife Elizabeth, and, finally, in 1360, a Ragusan emissary, Nicole Luccari, negotiated the marriage of Anca to Uros, the son and successor of Serbian Tsar Stephen Dushan.[96]

Nicholas Alexander remained in good relations with Hungary through 1359. A diploma issued by Louis the Great on August 29 of that year grants estates in Transylvania to some Wallachian boyars who had fled to Hungary "when the Transalpine Voivode Alexander Basarab did not want to recognize us as his rightful lord... they remained faithful to Our Majesty."[97] This document reflects the division within Wallachia after Basarab's death and Alexander's reluctance to submit to Hungarian suzerainty. The defeat of the Tatars in Moldavia in 1353 appears to have been the decisive factor in forcing his change of policy. When Louis the Great toured Transylvania in 1359, Alexander, as his vassal, came before the King to pay homage; in a solemn ceremony, most likely held at Alba-Iulia in December of that year, the Wallachian Prince presented gifts to his sovereign and prostrated himself before the monarch, acknowledging his suzerainty.[98]

Although Alexander paid formal homage to the King, he had never fully reconciled himself to the idea of accepting Hungarian overlordship. Political necessity had dictated his decision. Even as he openly acknowledged the King as his suzerain, Alexander sought ways to protect his autonomy and looked for opportunities to assert his independence once more. His ties to the Catholic Church had served him well, allowing him greater flexibility in his foreign

---

[96]Virgiliu Drăghiceanu, "Curtea domnească din Argeș," in *BCMI*, X-XVI (1917-1923), p. 17; and Pavel Chihaia, *Din cetățile de scaun ale Țării Românești*, Bucharest, 1974, pp. 181, 311.

[97]Doc. 40 in *DRH, D*, pp. 73-75.

[98]Lăzărescu, "Relațiile lui Nicolae Alexandru cu Ungurii," pp. 133-134, 139.

policy, but as a vassal of Hungary they had the opposite effect. To counter this, the Prince sought to formalize ties with the Greek Orthodox Church which represented the vast majority of his subjects. Supported by Metropolitan Ianchint of Vicina, Nicholas Alexander sent repeated requests to Patriarch Calixtus to establish a Metropolitanate in Wallachia. After difficult negotiations, in May of 1359 the Patriarch agreed to appoint Ianchint, at the Prince's request, as "the true hierarch of all Wallachia" on the condition that Alexander and his heirs agree that the Wallachian Church will remain under the jurisdiction of the Patriarch and that, at Ianchint's death, they will only accept a hierarch sent by the Ecumenical Synod.[99] Alexander further strengthened his ties to the Orthodox world by providing financial support to the monastic center at Mount Athos, especially the Cutlumuz Monastery.[100] Thus, while Alexander paid homage to Louis the Great in Transylvania, at home Ianchint was setting up the new Metropolitanate in Argeş with the precise scope of countering Hungarian influence.

Soon after he returned from his audience with Louis the Great, Alexander's opportunity to reassert his independence presented itself. A new event took place to alter the balance of power in the region. Toward the end of 1359, a Romanian voivode from Maramureş, Bogdan of Cuhea, led a revolt against Hungarian rule. He crossed the mountains into Moldavia, drove out the successors of Dragoş and proclaimed the independence of the Principality. With the Hungarians out of Moldavia, Alexander seized the opportunity to break the bonds of vassalage and to stop paying annual tribute to the Angevin King. Wallachia maintained its independence from Hungary throughout the rest of his reign. Louis the Great later complained that Alexander "forgot all of the benefits he received from us and, as an ingrate, while he still enjoyed this earthly life, he did not hesitate to renege with bold daring the bond by which he was bound before us, as well as the letters of agreement concluded between us."[101] Nicholas Alexander, Vlad Dracul's great grandfather, died on November 16, 1364; his eldest son, Vladislav, succeeded him on the throne.

---

[99]Docs. 9 and 10 in *DIR, XIII, XIV, XV, B*, pp. 13-16.

[100]"Primul Testament al lui Hariton" in *Fontes Historiae Daco-Romanae*, vol. IV, Bucharest, 1982, pp. 285-293.

[101]Doc. 42 in *DRH, D*, pp. 78-80.

By the end of Alexander's reign, the Ottoman Turks, a new force to which the fate of Wallachia and the entire region would be tied for the next five hundred years, had established a foothold in Southeastern Europe. Osman Bey (1284-1326) laid the basis of the future Ottoman state in Anatolia, but his son and successor, Orhan (1326-1359), established the foundations of an Empire, doubling its size. The Turks became involved in European affairs, intervening in the Byzantine civil wars on the side of John VI Cantecuzenus; Orhan married the Emperor's daughter Theodora and sent troops to relieve Salonika, then under siege by the Serbian Tsar Stephen Dušan. By 1354, the Ottomans gained a permanent base in Europe when, in the aftermath of a devastating earthquake, they occupied Gallipoli, the principal crossing point between Asia and Europe. Having gained this foothold on the continent, the Turks took advantage of the chaotic situation in the Balkans to expand further into Europe. The Turkish advance in Southeastern Europe at this time was nothing more than a series of random conquests where and when the opportunity presented itself. Ottoman expansion in both Asia and Europe continued under Orhan's son Murad I (1360-1389). He took Adrianople in 1362 and made it his capital, thereby brazenly declaring Ottoman intentions to impose Muslim rule over Christian Europe.

Several things favored Ottoman expansion in Europe at this time. The Black Death had reached Constantinople in 1347 aboard Genoese ships arriving from the Black Sea port of Caffa; it spread throughout the continent during the following decades decimating up to one-third of the population. Europe had also entered a period of social and economic crisis that sparked major peasant uprisings in France (1358), England (1381), and Transylvania (1437). The British historian Rodney Hilton explains that "society was paralysed by the increasing costs of the social and political superstructure — costs which were not being paid for by any increase in society's productive resources."[102] Southeastern Europe was a collection of small states frequently in conflict with one another making them easy prey for the powerful, centralized Ottoman Empire. All of Europe was divided. The long, intermittent struggle between France and England known as the Hundred Years' War kept the states of Western Europe from focusing their attention elsewhere, and the

---

[102] Rodney Hilton, *Class Conflict and the Crisis of Feudalism*, London, 1985, pp. 241-242.

Catholic Church, theoretically a unifying factor, was itself divided into opposing camps by the Great Schism. In addition, the Catholic and Orthodox Churches had never reconciled. These factors and a host of others prevented any unified Christian opposition to the Islamic invaders.

On the other side of the coin, the Ottmans possessed significant advantages. Driven by a zealous religious ideology, founded on the idea of *jihad*, and having a highly centralized administration, the Turks did not have to deal with the types of problems that divided Europe. The Sultan apportioned the lands of his Empire employing what is known as the *Timariote* system, creating a non-hereditary aristocracy with no limits on their military service; all lands were held at the Sultan's discretion and could be passed on from father to son only with his express consent. This was diametrically opposed to the Feudal system in Europe where nobles jealously guarded their power and privileges, ruling over semi-autonomous fiefdoms. Equally important was the organization of the Janissary corps at the beginning of the reign of Murad I; this provided the Sultan with a professional standing army, the likes of which Europe had not seen since Roman times. The ranks of the Janissaries were filled by means of the *devshirme*, essentially a tax on male Christian children. These children, aged eight to eighteen, were carefully selected from Christian families having more than one son and living in territories under Ottoman rule; the recruits were then assigned to estates in Anatolia, converted to Islam, and trained as warriors. Fiercely loyal, the Janissaries became the Sultan's personal bodyguard and his elite fighting force. Finally, driven by an Islamic concept of world domination, with the Sultan as both the political and spiritual leader, the Ottomans confronted Christian Europe from a position of unity and strength that Europeans could not match.

Louis the Great was determined to bring Wallachia back under Hungarian suzerainty, and the death of Nicholas Alexander seemed to afford him the perfect opportunity. From his capital at Visegrad, Louis issued an order on January 5, 1365, to mobilize the royal army for a campaign against Wallachia, declaring that Alexander's son "Vladislav, following the bad habits of his father..., refused to recognize us in any way as his rightful lord."[103] But the Hungarian army that gathered at Temesvar that spring ultimately had another

---

[103]Doc. 42 in *DRH, D*, pp. 78-80.

destination. Abandoning the offensive against Wallachia, probably because he received intelligence that Vladislav was well-prepared to meet the attack, the King redirected his forces south against Vidin, then ruled by Vladislav's cousin and brother-in-law, Stratimir.

Around 1360 Tsar John Alexander had divided his Empire between his two sons, Stratimir and Šišman. Stratimir ruled over the western part with his capital at Vidin, while his half-brother Šišman, John Alexander's son by his second marriage, ruled over the eastern part from Trnovo. The division of the country amounted to a death sentence for Bulgaria. Vidin was a major commercial center in the region, especially for trade with Ragusa and the Dalmatian coast, and a strategically important fortress on the Danube; from here Louis hoped to extend Hungarian influence and to spread Catholicism south of the Danube. The Hungarians took the city by storm on May 30, 1365, and captured Stratimir and his wife, Vladislav's half-sister Ana. The Bulgarian Tsar and Tsarina were exiled to Humnic in Croatia where they remained in custody for the next four years. With Vidin now under Hungarian rule, Vladislav decided to acknowledge Louis the Great's suzerainty, entitling himself "Ladislas, by the grace of God *and his Majesty the King*, Transalpine Voivode and Ban of Severin."[104]

With the Hungarians advancing in the Balkans and the Ottoman threat omnipresent, Byzantine Emperor John V Paleologus made the unprecedented decision to travel to Hungary to seek assistance from Catholic Europe to drive back the Muslim invaders. Never before had a Byzantine monarch left the Empire except at the head of a conquering army. But the Turks were not the only peril Byzantium faced. Pope Urban V wrote to John V in early 1366 advising him to return to union with the Roman Church, menacingly reminding the Emperor that Constantinople was threatened on one side by the King of Hungary and on the other by the King of Cyprus, aided by many Latins.[105] Meanwhile, Šišman attacked Black Sea ports held by Dobrotitsa and the Byzantines. On the surface, negotiations in Buda between John V and Louis the Great proceeded well. In July, Urban V again wrote to the Emperor, this time to congratulate him on his intention to unite with the Church of Rome, together

---

[104]Doc 46 in *DRH, D*, pp. 86-87, emphasis added.

[105]Doc: LXXX in Hurmuzaki, *Documente*, vol. I, part. 2, pp. 111-112.

with his entire people.[106] But, at the same time, the Pope wrote to Louis the Great, warning him not to place too much faith in the promises of the Greeks, and to offer them help against the Turks only after the Emperor and his sons return to union with the Church of Rome.[107] When negotiations concluded, John V made his way overland via Temesvar, Sebeş, Mehadia, and Severin to Vidin, on the Danube, where he embarked on a ship for the voyage home. The route was feasible only because of Vladislav's alliance with Hungary. But along the way, probably around Nicopolis or at Varna on the Black Sea coast, the Bulgarians under Shishman captured the Emperor and held him prisoner.

The Emperor was fortunate in that his cousin, Amadeus of Savoy, had come to Constantinople on a crusading expedition. The man known as the Green Count, after the color of his armor, recovered Gallipoli from the Turks in May 1366. When news of John V's capture reached Constantinople, Amadeus advanced up the Black Sea coast, took back Messembria from the Bulgarians, and laid siege to Varna, demanding that Šišman release the Emperor. The Green Count appealed to the Emperor's ally Dobrotitsa, whose capital was then at Kaliakra, for assistance.[108] By the end of 1366, their combined actions led to the safe return of John V. To strengthen ties between Byzantium and Dobrotitsa around this time, John V's son Michael Paleologus married one of Dobrotitsa's daughters. Desperate for aid from the West, John V stayed true to his word and travelled to Rome where he personally converted to Catholicism before the Pope on October 18, 1369. But his efforts were in vain. Despite papal appeals, no significant aid from the West was forthcoming and the union of the two Churches could not be realized. "As Michael VII had so tragically demonstrated nearly a hundred years before," John Julius Norwich, the acclaimed historian of the Byzantine Empire, keenly observed, "union could not be unilaterally imposed from above; the Emperor had no control over the souls of his subjects."[109] Ultimately, John V had no choice but to renew his

---

[106]Doc. LXXXVII in Hurmuzaki, *Documente*, vol. I, part. 2, pp. 127-129.

[107]Doc. LXXXIII, in Hurmuzaki, *Documente*, vol. I, part. 2, p. 119.

[108]N. Iorga, "Veneţia în Marea Neagră, I. Dobrotici," in *AARMSI*, series II, XXXVI (1913-1914), pp. 1046-1047; and Francisc Pall, "Encore une fois sur le voyage diplomatique de Jean V Paléologue en 1365/66," in *RESEE*, IX:3 (1971), p. 539.

[109]John Julius Norwich, *Byzantium: The Decline and Fall*, New York, 1996, p. 332.

peace treaty with Murad I, placing him in the humiliating position of being the Sultan's vassal.

Meanwhile, to rebuild his Empire, the Bulgarian Tsar Shishman allied with the Sultan and, with Ottoman military assistance, he attacked Hungary in 1367, laying siege to Vidin. In these circumstances, Vladislav proved an indispensable ally for Louis the Great. He supplied the city with desperately needed victuals[110] and helped the King fend off the Bulgarian-Turkish attack. Then, on January 20, 1368, at the request of the Hungarian court, Vladislav confirmed his peace treaty with Louis the Great and granted trade privileges to the Transylvanian city of Braşov.[111] But despite these manifestations of peace, storm clouds loomed on the horizon. Vladislav never intended to remain a vassal of the King of Hungary and he patiently awaited the opportunity to reassert Wallachia's independence.

Vladislav's most reliable ally throughout this period was Dobrotitsa. The two neighboring lands seem to have forged an alliance already during Nicholas Alexander's reign through the marriage of his son Radu to Dobrotitsa's daughter Kalinikia, probably arranged by Metropolitan Ianchint who had strong ties to Dobrotitsa's lands. In 1367, while Vladislav fought the Bulgarians and Turks beneath the walls of Vidin, Dobrotitsa launched an offensive against John Šišman's Empire from the east, seizing the Danubian port city of Silistra where he made his son Terter local ruler.[112] Throughout this period, Dobrotitsa engaged in a long war with Genoa as the Italians sought to monopolize trade along the Black Sea coast. In the course of this war, which did not formally end until 1387, after the Despot's death, Genoa managed to seize control of the strategic Danubian port city of Kilia.

An opportunity soon presented itself for Vladislav to throw off the Hungarian yoke. The burden of Hungarian rule and the aggressive Catholic proselytizing of the Franciscan missionaries caused increasing unrest among the largely Orthodox population in Vidin and the surrounding territory. By late

---

[110]Doc. 50 in *DRH, D*, pp. 90-91.

[111]Doc. 46 in *DRH, D*, pp. 86-87.

[112]Ernest Oberlander-Tarnoveanu, "Quelques remarques sur les émissions monétaires médiévales de la Dobroudja méridionale" in *RRH*, XXVII: 1-2 (1988), p. 113.

summer of 1368, a full-scale rebellion had broken out and threatened to spread to the Banat region of Hungary. Although Hungarian officials at Vidin blamed Šišman for inciting the revolt and asked "Vladislav, the Transalpine Voivode, to send, if not more, at least three or four of his flags,"[113] the King clearly viewed the Wallachian Prince as the source of his troubles in the region. In September of that year, Louis again mobilized his army for war against Vladislav.[114] The Hungarians launched a two-pronged attack in October 1368. The King led a force against Severin in the west, while the Voivode of Transylvania invaded from the north, via the Bran pass, in an attempt to reach Argeş. A contemporary Hungarian chronicler, Johannes de Küküllew, records that Vladislav "stood guard along the Danube with a large army, on the border with Bulgaria, to impede the crossing of the King's army. Meanwhile, Voivode Nicholas forced the crossing of the Ialomiţa River [most likely the Dâmboviţa River] where the Wallachians had built trenches and fortifications and encountered a large army of the Voivode Vlaicu, led by Count Dragomir, the Castellan of Dâmboviţa. He defeated them in a fiérce battle in which many fell and the commander himself [Dragomir] fled. But after that, he [Nicholas] advanced too far and entered the bogs with reeds and narrow passages; then the Wallachians, striking from the forests and mountains, attacked him, and he, the Voivode, with many other brave men and leading nobles... met death here. And when the Hungarian soldiers separated from the army of the Voivode retreated and tried to escape, the Wallachians surrounded them... in a swampy, desolated area and killed many of them, so that few were able to escape.... The body of Voivode Nicholas could only be recovered from the clutches of the Wallachians after a bloody battle..."[115]

But by late November, Louis's army received reinforcements, with the arrival of troops led by Nicholas Garai, and managed to force the crossing of the Danube "against the attacks of the soldiers and archers of Laicu, Voivode of the Wallachians, who fired arrows like a rainstorm." Küküllew adds that the Hungarians "forced the enemy to flee and they dispersed like smoke. Then the

---

[113]Doc. 53 in *DRH*, *D*, pp. 93-95.

[114]Doc. 51 and 52 in *DRH*, *D*, pp. 91-93.

[115]Quo. Victor Motogna, "La războaiele lui Vlaciu-Vodă cu Ungurii," in *RI*, IX: 1-3 (1923), p. 18.

army entered the Severin land and occupied it."[116] As winter was upon them, the Hungarians withdrew after consolidating and garrisoning the fortress of Severin. The King's success was ephemeral. With help from Dobrotitsa, and reinforced by Dragomir's victorious troops, Vladislav quickly regained Severin and traversed the Danube. Coming to the aid of the rebellious local population, the Wallachians occupied Vidin on February 12, 1369. By now anti-Hungarian and anti-Catholic sentiment had reached a boiling point. The arrival of Vlaicu's men sparked the outbreak of a massacre which claimed the lives of the Franciscan missionaries in that city. But the Wallachian Prince's offensive did not end here. Vladislav also attacked Hungarian positions in southern Transylvania, burning the Monastery of St. Nicholas at Talmesch, along the Olt River, twenty kilometers south-southeast of Sibiu.[117]

Louis the Great could not allow this defeat to go unanswered. By April, he had gathered a new army and set out against Vladislav. The impending conflict forced both sides to negotiate. By mid-summer they reached a peace agreement; Louis agreed to restore Vladislav's brother-in-law Stratimir to the throne in Vidin. On August 29, 1369, the King wrote to Peter, the Ban of Bulgaria: "We have freed the Tsar of Vidin on the guarantee of Voivode Vlaicu and of Dobrotitsa and we have promised to return his country to him, on the condition that he give us his two daughters as hostages."[118] Stratimir also had to promise to prevent further violence against Catholics in his lands. To ensure this, at the encouragement of her mother, Nicholas Alexander's widow, the Catholic Princess Clara, Tsarina Ana, Stratimir's wife, converted to Catholicism.[119] Finally, as Vidin was an important commercial center for trade between Transylvania and Ragusa on the Adriatic coast, Stratimir granted trade privileges to merchants from Braşov.[120]

---

[116]Quo. Alexandru A. Vasilescu, "Cetatea Dâmboviţa" in *BCMI*, XXXVIII (1945), p. 32.

[117]Doc. CXIII in Hurmuzaki, *Documente*, vol. I, part 2, p. 149.

[118]Doc. 54 in *DRH, D*, pp. 95-96.

[119]Doc. CXXII Hurmuzaki, *Documente*, vol. I, part. 2, p. 158.

[120]Doc. I in Gr.G. Tocilescu, ed. *534 documente istorice slavo-române*, Bucharest, 1931, p. 3: and P. Dragulev, "Scrisoarea Ţarului Strasimir dela Vidin către negustorii Braşoveni," in *RIR*, IX (1939), p. 295.

Vladislav emerged as the clear victor in this confrontation. Not only did he succeed in returning Stratimir to the throne and in forcing Louis to accept his rule over Severin, as part of the peace settlement the King also granted Vladislav and his successors the Duchy of Făgăraş in southern Transylvania. With the acquisition of this predominantly Romanian populated territory, the Wallachian Prince now added "Duke of Făgăraş," to his title,[121] which he referred to in a diploma from 1372, granting the market of Scherkkengen (today Sercaia) and several villages in this region to his relative Ladislas of Dobka, in recognition of his services against the Bulgarians and the Turks, as his "*nove plantacions.*"[122] In return, Vladislav again recognized the suzerainty of the Crown of St. Stephen and agreed to protect Catholicism. On November 25, 1369, he issued a decree ordering all Catholics in his Principality to accept a new bishop sent as the representative of the Bishop of Transylvania to whom the Catholic Church in Wallachia was subordinate.[123] But despite the urging of his step-mother Clara, a devout Catholic, Vladislav did not respond favorably to Pope Urban V's appeal to him in April 1370 to return to union with the Church of Rome so that he may become an "Athlete of Christ" in recognition of his military victories.[124] It should be noted that Vladislav's refusal came only six months after the Byzantine Emperor himself had submitted to Rome.

Like his father before him, Vladislav, while protecting Catholicism, shrewdly took steps to strengthen Orthodoxy in his country as a counterbalance to Hungarian political interests which were inextricably linked to Catholic propaganda. He supported the Orthodox monastic center at Mount Athos, rebuilding the Cutmuluz Monastery.[125] On this occasion he met the monastery's abbot, Hariton, who subsequently became the Metropolitan of Wallachia. Vladislav also made gifts to the Lavra Monastery on Mount Athos, including an inscribed icon donated by him and his wife Ana.[126] More

---

[121]Doc. 3 in *DRH, B*, vol. I, pp. 12-13.

[122]Doc. 5 in *DRH, B*, vol. I, pp. 14-17.

[123]Doc. 3 in *DRH, B*, vol. I, pp. 12-13.

[124]Doc. CXXIII in Hurmuzaki, *Documente*, vol. I, part 2, p. 159.

[125]Doc. 11 in *DIR, XIII, XIV, XV, B*, pp. 16-19.

[126]N. Iorga, "Muntele Athos în legatură cu ţerile noastre," in *AARMSI*, series II, XXXVI (1913-1914), pp. 459-460.

importantly, he strengthened the Church by seeking the approval of the Patriarch to establish a second Metropolitanate in Wallachia, strategically located at Severin to counter Hungarian-Catholic proselytizing in this area. The Ecumenical Synod approved the plan in October 1370, appointing Daniil Kritopoulas, who took the monastic name Antim, as Metropolitan in Severin because "with the passage of time, as the population of the country happens to be larger, almost innumerable, a single hierarch is not enough for such a large people..."[127] This new Metropolitanate remained subordinate to Argeș,[128] but henceforth, until Wallachia lost the Severin land in the early fifteenth century, the Principality had two metropolitans, one at Severin and the other at Argeș.

The most important step that Vladislav took to strengthen Orthodoxy, however, was to establish monasteries in his country. These served as religious, cultural, and educational centers, and also played an important role in political and economic life. The introduction of monasticism to Wallachia was the work of a monk named Nicodim, the most important cultural and religious figure in the Principality during the fourteenth and fifteenth centuries.

Born of a Greek father and Serbian mother, Nicodim took his monastic vows at Mount Athos. He spent several years in Serbia, helping to organize the Church there. Then, around 1369, when the conflict between Orthodoxy and Catholicism in the borderlands between Wallachia, Bulgaria, and Serbia was at its height, he led a group of Serbian monks to Wallachia where they received Vladislav's support and protection. By 1372, Nicodim and his followers had raised the Monastery of Vodita in the Severin land, receiving generous financial contributions and material donations from the Wallachian Prince. These included villages exempted from all royal works and taxes. In addition, Vladislav recognized the autonomy of the monastery, declaring that after Nicodim's death neither the Prince, nor the Metropolitan, nor anyone else could appoint the new abbot, and that the monks would be free to choose their

---

[127]Doc. 15 in *DIR, XIII, XIV, XV, B*, p. 22.

[128]Doc. V in Eudoxia de Hurmuzaki and N. Iorga, eds., *Documente privitoare la istoria românilor*, vol. XIV, part 1, Bucharest, 1915, pp. 6-7.

own leader in the manner that Nicodim established.[129] This "rule of Nicodim" came to govern all monasteries in Wallachia.

Vodita was a modest construction along the banks of Danube with a small church dedicated to St. Anthony. But Nicodim, hearing God's call, determined to found a larger monastery at a less vulnerable location in the interior of the country. While travelling in the heavily-forested, mountainous areas of northern Oltenia, he met a child who led him to a place in the cavernous mountains. According to legend, Nicodim entered a small cave, located above a larger one through which a stream flowed, to mediate and to pray. There he encountered a large snake that hissed and opened its mouth to bite the monk. Nicodim calmly made the sign of the cross using a lead crucifix he wore around his neck. The snake fled and fell from the cave and died instantly, leaving its imprint on the stone above the lower cave. Nicodim then descended and blessed the site where he raised the monastery called Tismana.[130] The legend of the founding of Tismana has all the elements of an allegory for the victory of Christianity over the forces of evil, represented by the serpent, an image that contributed to the development of the Dracula myth. During Vladislav's reign a small wooden church was raised on the site. Under his successors, Radu and Dan, a stone monastery was constructed. Tismana became the most important religious center in Wallachia during the fourteenth and early fifteenth centuries. Nicodim remained here as abbot until his death at the end of 1406. His followers spread the monastic tradition to the neighboring lands of Transylvania and Moldavia. Nicodim also served as a political advisor to Wallachian princes. As a theologian, he corresponded with Evtimiy, the Bulgarian Patriarch at Trnovo, the leading spiritual figure in the Slavic Orthodox world, on various moral and religious issues. He also compiled and illustrated a Slavonic translation of the Holy Scriptures which remains one of the cultural and artistic treasures of Wallachia dating from this period.

Vladislav's efforts to maintain his autonomy were carefully planned. The situation in the Balkans changed when Šišman, once an ally of the Turks,

---

[129]Doc. 6 in *DRH, B*, vol. I, pp. 17-19.

[130]Stefulescu, *Mănăstirea Tismana*, pp. 51-54.

Nineteenth century depiction of the Monastery of Tismana

began to support the Serbs against the Ottomans. Hoping to drive the Muslims from Europe, Serbian leaders organized an offensive against the Turks in 1371. On September 26, the two sides met in battle at Cernomen on the Marica River. It resulted in a major victory for the Sultan that opened the way for further Ottoman expansion in the Balkans. This directly threatened Šišman's Empire. Following the principle that the enemy of my enemy is my friend, by late 1372, Vladislav found himself in an alliance with the Sultan against both Hungary and Šišman's Bulgaria. By the summer of 1374 he had seized the important Danubian city of Nicopolis from the Bulgarians[131] and appears to have extended his control over Rucăr in the Carpathians. In response, Louis the Great had placed an embargo on salt imports from Wallachia at the beginning of 1373.[132] Meanwhile, Pope Greogory XI forbade the sale of arms to the Turks and Wallachians because they used these weapons against Christians.[133] Vladislav failed to hold Nicopolis, but the conflict with Catholic Hungary

---

[131]Doc. 63 in *DRH, D*, pp. 107-108.

[132]Doc. 61 in *DRH, D*, p. 106.

[133]Doc. CLII in Hurmuzaki, *Documente*, vol. I, part 2, p. 207.

continued throughout the remainder of his reign. Louis took measures to strengthen his border defenses; he built a powerful stone fortress at Bran[134] on the site of the wooden fort that the Teutonic Knights had constructed at the beginning the thirteenth century. In the early sixteenth century, the humanist Nicholas Olahus, a Transylvanian native, described Bran as "indescribably strong, like a bolt and gate for Transylvania, located in a steep place from where you enter into Wallachia."[135] To defend the fortress, also called Terciu by the Hungarians and the Saxons, Louis brought in English archers,[136] the most renowned bowmen in Europe at that time.

Vladislav died around 1376, shortly after his teenaged half-brother Voislav, both apparently victims of the plague. Although the sparsity of crowded urban centers lessened the impact of the Black Death in Wallachia in comparison with many other parts of Europe,[137] it still wreaked havoc on the Principality. "Fear of the plague" was among the reasons given to the Patriarch by the elderly Metropolitan Ianchint for his not making the journey to Constantinople to attend the Holy Synod.[138] In his last will and testament, written in July 1378, Hariton, the former Abbot of the Cutlumuz Monastery who had become Metropolitan of Wallachia, declares that he is deathly ill "and tried in the most powerful manner by *the plague which is now rampant.*"[139] Vladislav had no sons and so his half-brother Radu succeeded him on the throne. Numismatic evidence indicates that Vladislav had earlier made Radu his associate ruler,[140] thus ensuring a smooth transfer of power.

Radu, dubbed Negru by seventeenth century chroniclers who mistook him for the founder of the Principality, was Vlad Dracul's grandfather. Writing

---

[134]Doc. 67 in *DRH, D*, pp. 110-112.

[135]Holban, *Călători străini*, vol. I, p. 492.

[136]N. Iorga, *Istoria armatei româneşti*, vol. I, Vălenii-de-Munte, 1910, p. 91.

[137]Lia Lehr, "Factori determinanţi în evoluţia demografică a Ţării Româneşti," in *Studii şi materiale de istorie medie*, vol. VII, Bucharest, 1974, p. 189.

[138]Doc. VI in Hurmuzaki, *Documente*, vol. XIV, part 1, pp. 7-8.

[139]Doc. 21 in *DIR, XIII, XIV, XV, B*, pp. 28-32, emphasis added.

[140]Octavian Iliescu, "Domni asociaţi în ţările române în secolele al XIV-lea şi al XV-lea" in *Studii şi cercetări de istorie medie*, II: 1 (1951), pp. 41-43.

during Vlad's reign, Eberhard Windecke, Sigismund of Luxemburg's biographer, called him Pankraz the Wise, Pankraz being a corrupt form of Ban Radu,[141] an indication of the esteem he had earned as ruler of Wallachia. Radu is a name of Slavic origin, meaning 'happy'. Its variants include Radoslav or Radomir.[142] Like Vlad, it was a popular name among the Wallachian elite; there were four rulers named Radu during the fourteenth and fifteenth centuries. Radu had two wives. The first, Ana, probably a Serbian princess, bore him a son named Dan. Although Nicolae Iorga has suggested that she was a Byzantine princess,[143] and others a daughter of Oltenian boyars,[144] Radu's second wife and Vlad Dracul's grandmother, Kalinikia, was most likely a daughter of Dobrotitsa.[145] She bore him Mircea and other sons.

Unfortunately, relatively little information has survived about Radu's reign. We know that he fought to maintain Wallachia's independence against Hungary. A contemporary Italian chronicle, *Cronaca Carrarese*, written by Galeazzo and Bartolomeo Gatari, tells of a great battle in the summer of 1377 between Louis, the King of Hungary, and Radano, the infidel Prince of Bulgaria, a confusion because of the Slavic aristocracy that ruled Wallachia. Radu received Ottman military assistance in his battle with the Hungarians, while the Venetians, perhaps because of his mother's family ties, supplied him with arms despite the Pope's interdiction of their sale four years earlier. Although Louis claimed victory in his foreign correspondence[146] and possibly regained Severin, in late October he decried heavy losses suffered "in our recent expedition against the Transalpine Wallachians."[147] To attract the support of his Saxon subjects in southern Transylvania for a new campaign against Wallachia, the King wrote to the officials of Brașov on November 19, promising them that "if the Transalpine land will fall into our hands," he would

[141]Constantin Giurescu, *Istoria românilor*, vol. I, Bucharest, 1942, p. 421.

[142]Constantinescu, *Dicționar onomastic*, pp. 355-357.

[143]N. Iorga, *Chestiunea Dunării*, Vălenii-de-Munte, 1913, p. 154.

[144]P.P. Panaitescu, *Mircea cel Bătrân*, Bucharest, 1944, p. 46-48.

[145]Sergiu Iosipescu, *Balica, Dobrotița, Ioancu*, Bucharest, 1985, p. 125.

[146]G.I. Brătianu, "L'expédition de Louis I-er de Hongrie contre le prince de Valachie Radu I-er Basarab en 1377," in *RHSEE*, II: 4-6 (1925), pp. 76-77; 80-82.

[147]Doc. CXCVII in Hurmuzaki, *Documente*, vol. I, part 2 pp. 248-249.

lower customs taxes.[148] Yet, despite repeated efforts throughout the remainder of his reign, Louis the Great failed to subjugate the "Land across the Mountains."

Despite the ongoing struggle with Hungary, Radu did not adopt a policy hostile to the Catholic Church. Instead, he appears to have tried to distance the Catholic Church in Wallachia from Hungarian domination by establishing a Bishopric at Argeş, directly dependent on Rome rather than on the Bishop of Transylvania. This again may reflect Clara's influence. On July 15, 1379, Pope Urban VI granted the Franciscans permission to establish monasteries in Serbia and Wallachia.[149] A new Catholic church, dedicated to St. Nicholas, was built in the capital of Argeş, and, in 1381, Urban VI appointed Nicholas Anthony as bishop for the Wallachian diocese. Perhaps because of his sagacious religious policy, Radu was subsequently dubbed "the Wise."

Near the end of Radu's reign, a new period of political crisis engulfed Hungary. Building on the successes of his father, Charles Robert, Louis the Great had strengthened Hungary and become one of Europe's most powerful monarchs. When his maternal uncle Casimir of Poland died without an heir in 1370, Louis assumed the added title of King of Poland. The joining of the two Kingdoms under the same ruler created a superpower in Eastern Europe with the potential to dominate half of the continent. But the union was a fragile one and in peril from the moment of its inception for Louis had not yet produced an heir. His second wife, Elizabeth of Bosnia, bore him three daughters, but no son. The King attempted to overcome this problem betrothing his oldest daughter, Catherine, to Louis, the Duke of Orleans and brother of French King Charles V, but his plan failed when Catherine died shortly thereafter. Next, he arranged for the engagement of his infant daughter Mary to Sigismund of Luxemburg, son of Holy Roman Emperor Charles IV. Theoretically, this made Sigismund heir to the thrones of Hungary and Poland, but the marriage had not yet taken place when Louis died in 1382. This sparked a major political crisis. The Polish nobility refused to accept Mary and Sigismund as their sovereigns and Sigismund's attempts to assert his claim by force failed. After a long series of conflicts and negotiations, a compromise was finally reached; the nobles

---

[148]Doc. CLXXXIX in Hurmuzaki, *Documente*, vol. I, part 2, pp. 242-243.

[149]Doc. CCVII in Hurmuzaki, *Documente*, vol. I, part. 2, pp. 268-268.

agreed to recognize Louis's youngest daughter, Hedwiga, as Queen of Poland. She was crowned in October 1384. Next, the critical question of marriage was debated, for whoever married Hedwiga would become the next King of Poland. The man chosen was Jagieŀło, the pagan Grand Duke of Lithuania, on the condition that he convert to Catholicism. He did so and then married Hedwiga on February 18, 1386. Adopting the Christian name Vladislav, he was crowned King on March 4 of that year. The union of Poland and Lithuania created a new power in Eastern Europe, one that would rival Hungary in the following decades.

The situation in Hungary was no less turbulent, reminiscent of the period following the death of Andrew III at the beginning of the century. Although Mary was crowned Queen after the death of Louis the Great, the opposition of Queen Mother Elizabeth to her pending marriage prevented Sigismund from being crowned King. Elizabeth planned to rule as regent, with the help of the powerful Palatine Nicholas Garai. Sigismund attempted to force the issue in 1385, arriving in Hungary to claim his bride and his throne, but he was driven out by the regents. Meanwhile, a new pretender appeared on the scene in the form of Charles of Durazzo, the King of Naples and a distant relative of Louis I. Educated in Buda, Charles enjoyed the support of part of the nobility. He landed in Dalmatia in the fall of 1385 and made his way to the Hungarian capital where he was crowned as Charles II on December 31, 1385. Elizabeth, appalled at the audacity of the Neapolitan King, immediately began plotting against him. On February 24, 1386, less than two months after his reign began, agents of the Queen Mother assassinated Charles. The late King's supporters could not let this deed go unpunished. In reply, they killed Nicholas Garai and took Elizabeth and Mary captive. The Queen Mother was strangled to death some months later. With civil war rampant, Sigismund returned to Hungary in the fall of 1386 to free his captive fiancée and to press his claim to the throne once more. This time he had the support of a powerful faction of nobles who, tired of the ongoing domestic strife, saw him as a means to restore order in the Kingdom. Mary was freed and on March 31, 1387, nineteen-year-old Sigismund of Luxemburg, the man who later placed Vlad Dracul on the throne of Wallachia, became King of Hungary.

Amidst the turmoil engulfing neighboring Hungary, Vlad Dracul's grandfather, Radu I, died around 1383. His eldest son Dan succeeded him on the throne. Little is known about Dan's reign. A Bulgarian ballad tells of "Dan Voivode Ban, who rules over many lands... over fortresses, monasteries, and mountains, over the wide plain, over the numerous villages."[150] Another ballad speaks of Dan as living in a village called Satul din Vale (the Village in the Valley) and drinking wine with the villagers.[151] The little information available to us indicates that Dan took advantage of the disarray in Hungary; he appears to have regained Severin and continued his attack north against the fortress of Mehadia, where a diploma issued by Sigismund in 1390 recalls "the time when Voivode Dan invaded with his powerful army... the said places of our fortress of Mehadia."[152] As a result of this conflict with Hungary, Dan seems to have gained the small Duchy of Amlaş, near Sibiu. Queen Maria had granted this estate to the Bishop of Transylvania on June 1, 1383,[153] but the upheaval in Hungary and the need to secure peace along the southern border of the Kingdom forced the transfer of this territory to the ruler of the Transalpine land on the same terms as Făgăraş, which Wallachian Princes had ruled since the time of Vladislav I. Dan also completed the building of the Monastery of Tismana. The only surviving document from his reign grants and confirms villages and other privilege to this monastery. Dan recounts that "at the beginning of the reign granted to me by God, I found in the land of My Majesty, at the place called Tismana, a monastery, not in all of its parts yet finished, which the holy departed most venerable Voivode Radu, the father of My Majesty, raised from its foundation, but he did not finish it due to the shortness of his life. For this reason, My Majesty willed that, as his successor on the throne, to be his successor also in this and to continue the charity of my father and for my own soul to finish building this church dedicated to the Holy Mother of God, the Virgin Mary..."[154] This document is also significant as it

---

[150]Quo. Ion Donat, "Aşezările omeneşti din Ţara Românească," in *Studii*, IX:6 (1956), p. 81.

[151]N. Şerbănescu and N. Stoicescu, *Mircea cel Mare (1386-1418)*, Bucharest, 1987, p. 43.

[152]Doc. 76 in *DRH, D*, pp. 123-125.

[153]Doc.CCXIX in Hurmuzaki, *Documente*, vol. I, part 2, p. 278.

[154]Doc. 7 in *DRH, B*, vol. pp. 19-22.

is the first written evidence we have of the presence of Gypsy slaves in Wallachia.

Dan had at least three sons, Vlad, John, and Dan, but they all were apparently still quite young at the time of his death. To ensure a smooth succession, numismatic evidence indicates that Dan had made his half-brother Mircea associate ruler. This proved to be a wise precaution as Dan's reign was cut short when he died in battle against the Bulgarian Tsar John Šišman on September 23, 1386. His successor, Mircea, Vlad Dracul's father, would become the most celebrated prince in Wallachia's medieval history.

Chapter IV

The Father's Father

"A wise man ought always to follow the paths beaten by great men, and to imitate those who have been supreme, so that if his ability does not equal theirs, at least it will savour of it."

— Niccolò Machiavelli, *The Prince*[1]

Mircea the Old assumed the throne of Wallachia in the fall of 1386, during a time of tumultuous political change in the region. Hungary and Poland emerged from the chaos following the death of Louis the Great as separate, but powerful states competing to extend their influence in the Black Sea region to control the important East-West trade routes. Meanwhile, the Ottoman advance in the Balkans continued and the forces of Islam would soon reach the Danube. The small Principality between the Carpathians and the Danube struggled to preserve its autonomy amidst the pressure exerted upon it by these three regional superpowers. Fortunately, in Mircea the Old, whom the Turkish chronicler Leunclavius dubbed "the bravest and most able of Christian Princes,"[2] Wallachia had a leader capable of

---

[1]Machiavelli, *The Prince*, p. 41 (VI).

[2]Johannes Leunclavius, *Historia Musulmana Turcorum de monumentis ipsorum exscripta*, Frankfurt, 1591, f. 418.

confronting these new challenges. He set the example that his son Vlad would strive to emulate.

Mircea was the son of Radu the Wise and his second wife Kalinikia, the daughter of Despot Dobrotitsa. Some sources hint at a conflict between him and his older half-brother Dan, but they confuse later events. The two brothers worked closely together, just as their father Radu had done with his elder half-brother Vladislav, and Dan had named Mircea his associate ruler; this ensured a smooth transition of power when he fell in battle against the Bulgarian Tsar Šišman. The name Mircea is said to be a diminutive form of Dimitrie.[3] It is derived from *mir*, the Slavonic word for peace,[4] but, with danger all around, Mircea's reign was far from peaceful. Still, he rose to meet every challenge and he ruled Wallachia with astuteness and dexterity for over thirty years, leaving such a strong imprint on the history of the Principality that, even long after his death, his successors looked back upon his reign as a point of reference.

Some historians claim that Mircea received the epithet 'the Old' to distinguish him from a later Prince, Mircea the Shepherd, who ruled Wallachia in the mid-sixteenth century.[5] But the name is first found in a diploma issued by Neagoe Basarab on June 28, 1519, long before the reign of Mircea the Shepherd (1545-1554; 1558-1559), which refers back to "the days of Voivode Mircea the Old."[6] It is more plausible that the epithet attached itself to his name as a sign of the respect and esteem with which later generations regarded him. It was common, for example, to refer to village elders as "old and wise men," as a sign of deference. Mircea, having given shape to the political and administrative institutions of his country, had such a strong impact on the history of his land that his descendants looked back upon him as a wise elder, thus explaining the sobriquet 'the Old.'

Since the time of Nicholas Alexander, a common cause joined Wallachia to its neighbor Moldavia — the struggle against Hungarian domination. When

---

[3] Şt. Nicolaescu, "Domnia lui Alexandru Vodă," in *RIAF*, XVI (1915-1922), p. 225.

[4] Constantinescu, *Dicţionar onomastic*, pp. 322-323.

[5] Vîrtosu, *Titulatura domnilor şi asocierea la domnie*, p. 123.

[6] Doc. 147 in *DIR, XVI, B*, vol. I, p. 146.

Mircea took the throne, Peter I (c. 1375-1392), a descendant of Bogdan I who had proclaimed the independence of the Principality in 1359, ruled Moldavia. Through his mother, Margaret or Muşata, Peter had ties to the ruling family of Lithuania.[7] When Lithuanian Grand Duke Jagiełło became King of Poland these ties transformed into relations of vassalage as Moldavia accepted the suzerainty of the Polish Crown on May 6, 1387,[8] to counter the threat posed by Hungary. This bond was strengthened the following year when Vladislav Jagiełło solicited a loan of 4,000 silver rubles from the Moldavian Prince, offering the region of Pocuţia, to the north of Moldavia, as collateral. Peter responded by sending 3,000 silver rubles, the equivalent of 360,000 gold galbens, to the King,[9] money desperately needed by the Polish monarch to consolidate his hold or the throne and to fend off the attacks of Sigismund who had not yet renounced his claim to the Polish Crown. Both Moldavia and Wallachia allied with the Bosnian ruler Tvrtko (1353-1391) to oppose Sigismund's plans to bring their lands back under Hungarian control. To concentrate his military efforts in this direction, Sigismund concluded an armistice with Vladislav on August 2, 1388.[10] But the new Hungarian King had spread his military resources too thinly and Poland could not be expected to sit idly by and watch Hungary extend its domination east of the Carpathians, thereby threatening the prosperous trade route linking the Polish commercial center of Lemburg (today, Lvov in Ukraine) with the Black Sea port of Akkerman (today, Belgrad-Dnestrovskiy in Ukraine). This forced Sigismund to postpone plans for an offensive in the region. But Hungary continued to represent a serious danger to the independence of Wallachia. Mircea needed help to counter the threat posed by his more powerful neighbor; in the summer of 1389, with the mediation of his ally Peter I, the Wallachian Prince opened negotiations with Poland. On January 20, 1390, Mircea concluded a treaty of mutual assistance with King Vladislav against "the hostile attacks of

---

[7]C. Ciohandru, *Alexandru cel Bun*, Iaşi, 1984, p. 41.

[8]Docs. 162 and 163 in Costăchescu, ed., *Documentele moldoveneşti*, vol. II, pp. 599-603.

[9]Doc. 164 in, Costăchescu, ed., *Documentele moldoveneşti*, vol. II, pp. 603-606.

[10]Doc. CCXLVIII in Hurmuzaki, *Documente*, vol. I, part. 2, p. 309.

Sigismund, the King of Hungary, and those of his vassals or any of his subjects."[11]

But the Hungarian threat was not the only problem Mircea faced when he ascended the throne of Wallachia. Up to now, the Principality had limited dealings with the Turks, and the Wallachians had often found themselves allied with the Ottomans against Hungary or Šišman's Bulgaria. Relations between Wallachia and the Ottomans began to change, however, as the Sultan's armies encroached upon the Danube and imperiled the lands of Wallachia's long-time ally Dobrotitsa. Around the time when Mircea became Prince, Dobrotitsa died. His son Terter, also called Ivanko, succeeded him as Despot of the lands along the Black Sea coast reaching inland to the Danube and the border with Šišman's Bulgaria. More than two decades of war with Genoa had reached an end by the time of Dobrotitsa's death; Ivanko concluded the formal peace treaty ending the conflict with the Genoese on May 27, 1387. The agreement restored peaceful relations and regulated commerce between the two sides, stipulating customs taxes and according the Genoese the right to maintain a consul, a trading house, and a Catholic church in Dobrudja.[12] During this time, with Murad I engaged in campaigns in Anatolia, a league of Serbian and Bosnian rulers, led by the Serbian King Lazar, launched an offensive against the Ottomans in the Balkans, winning a series of battles and skirmishes against them. Neither Ivanko nor Shishman took part in these attacks, but, as vassals of the Sultan, they were obligated to lend aid to the Turks under these circumstances. But the Turkish chronicler Mehmed Neshri tell us that "These two scoundrels, revolting against the Sultan, did not come to the army."[13] Thus, in 1388, Murad I sent his Grand Vizier, Ali Cenderli, with a powerful army to punish his recalcitrant subjects. The Turks overran Bulgaria and Dobrudja. Šišman fled to his fortress at Nicopolis on the Danube where he eventually surrendered and again swore allegiance to the Sultan who then restored his lands to him. Ivanko was less fortunate. He perished in the fighting, while Ali Pasha occupied parts of Dobrudja.

---

[11]Doc. CCLVIII and CCLXII in Hurmuzaki, *Documente*, vol. I, part. 2, pp. 315-316 and 322.

[12]Doc. 24 in *DIR, XIII, XIV, XV, B*, pp. 34-40.

[13]*Cronici turcești*, vol. I, p. 110.

Mircea presumably sent troops to Ivanko's aid, but the death of Dobrotitsa's son now placed the Wallachian Prince in direct conflict with the Turks. Ivanko had no children. This left his nephew, Mircea, the eldest son of Ivanko's sister Kalinikia, as heir to the Despotate along the Black Sea coast. The energetic young Prince moved quickly to extend his control over the lands between the Danube and the Black Sea, seizing Silistra and other areas occupied by Ottoman forces during Ali Cenderli's campaign. By 1389, Mircea had added "Despot of the lands of Dobrotitsa and Lord of Silistria" to his title.[14] Although he now ruled over this area, Dobrudja maintained a separate political and administrative structure and Greek remained the official language in the province.[15] Mircea attempted to consolidate his hold over this newly-acquired territory by granting some estates there to boyars from Wallachia; a Greek-language document dated March 28, 1412, tells of a village near Kaliakra owned by Mircea's logofăt, Baldovin.[16]

The Turks did not stand in his way when Mircea pressed his claim as the rightful heir to the lands of Dobrotitsa. The Ottomans, at this time, were busy in Serbia. In the summer of 1389, Sultan Murad I led his troops against Lazar and his allies. The two armies met in battle at Kosovo Polje on June 15 of that year. Although some have claimed that Mircea sent a contingent to aid Lazar against the Turks, there is no convincing evidence to support this assertion; it results from the desire of nationalist Romanian historians to connect Wallachia's greatest Prince with this famous battle. It is inconceivable that Mircea, in hostile relations with both Bulgaria and Hungary at this time, would have sent military aid to Lazar, an ally of both Šišman and Sigismund. Besides, with the acquisition of Dobrudja he had already stretched his resources to their limit; nor could he ignore the need to protect his own frontiers against his hostile neighbors. The battle of Kosovo marked the death knell of medieval Serbia, which less than half a century before, under Tsar Stephen Dušan, had been poised to dominate the Balkans and threatened to conquer Constantinople itself. The Turks routed the Serbian armies. Lazar was captured and then

---

[14]Doc. CCLXII in Hurmuzaki, *Documente*, vol. I, part. 2, p. 322.

[15]Oberländer-Târnoveanu, "Quelques remarques," p. 121.

[16]Doc. 36 in *DRH,B*, vol. I, pp. 77-78; Constantin C. Giurescu, "În legătură cu Mircea cel Bătrân," in *RIR*, XV (1945), pp. 414, 431.

executed on the Sultan's order. Murad I was then himself killed when Lazar's son-in-law, Miloš Obravič, infiltrated the Ottoman camp and plunged a dagger into his chest. But this did nothing to change the outcome of the conflict. Murad's son Bayezid quickly seized control and, to prevent any dispute over his succession, he ordered that his brother Yakub be strangled to death immediately. Despite the decimation of its armies at Kosovo, Serbia lived on as a vassal of the Sultan until its final absorption into the Ottoman Empire in 1459.

The new Sultan hastened the pace of Ottoman expansion in the Balkans, as well as in Anatolia; Bayezid became known as *Yildirim*, the Thunderbolt, because of his rapid actions and movements. With an Ottoman attack on Wallachia now imminent, Mircea faced an increasingly perilous situation. Surrounded by enemies, he traveled to Lemburg where he renewed his alliance with King Vladislav in July 1391.[17] But Mircea stood alone against the Sultan because Poland at this time had no direct interest in halting the Ottoman advance so long as it seriously inconvenienced Vladislav's principal enemy, the King of Hungary. The inevitable occurred later that year when an Ottoman force under Firuz Bey made the first Turkish incursion "into Wallachia which," the Ottoman chronicler Kemalpashazade admits, "at that time was not yet subjected,"[18] while Bayezid campaigned in *Rumelia*, as the Ottomans called the European portion of their Empire. According to the Turkish chronicler Idris Bitlisi, Firuz Bey returned from Wallachia with "great plunder and many sturdy sons and beautiful daughters that he captured as slaves, choosing the fifth part for the Sultan."[19] Mircea could not afford an extended conflict with Turks. With Bayezid's armies threatening the Principality, another Turkish chronicler, Mehmed Pasha, records that "Mircea, the Voivode of Wallachia, submitted and obliged himself to pay tribute."[20] His treaty with the Sultan came to be known as the "Capitulations" or *Ahidname*; Mircea agreed to pay annual tribute in the sum of 3,000 galbens, but maintained the

[17]Doc. CCLXXV in Hurmuzaki, *Documente*, vol. I, part. 2, pp. 334-335.

[18]Quo. Aurel Decei, *Relaţii româno-orientale*, Bucharest, 1978, p. 153, nt. 1.

[19]*Cronici turceşti*, vol. I, p. 156.

[20]*Cronici turceşti*, vol. I, p. 290.

independence of his Principality.[21] Although for many years historians considered the Capitulations to be an eighteenth century forgery, their authenticity is now widely accepted.[22]

Despite the Capitulations agreement, Mircea remained wary of the Ottoman threat. In search of potential allies, he fostered diplomatic contacts with various Anatolian rulers along the Black Sea coast opposed to the Sultan. The danger to Wallachia increased dramatically in the summer of 1393 when the Ottomans conquered Šišman's Bulgaria and transformed it into a Turkish pashalik; the Bulgarian Tsar was killed and Patriarch Evtimiy, who had led a desperate resistance against the Muslim invaders at Trnovo during the three month siege of the city, was exiled. The Turks may also have taken Silistra from Wallachia at this time. With the Ottoman Empire now at Wallachia's borders, the Principality began to suffer periodic raids from irregular troops known as *Akingi* or *Agazi*. The fifteenth century Italian writer Giovanni Maria Angiolello, a confidant of Mehmed the Conqueror, explained that these troops "are not paid, except by the booty they may gain in guerilla warfare. These men do not encamp with the rest of the army, but go traversing, pillaging, and wasting the country of the enemy on every side, and yet keep up a great and excellent discipline among themselves, both in the division of the plunder and in the execution of all their enterprises."[23] Mircea acted quickly in face of these attacks. Realizing the futility of trying to fend off these incursions, he decided instead to take the offensive against these Islamic terrorists.

With Bayezid engaged in Anatolia, Mircea received intelligence from the Emir of Sinope that a favorable moment had arrived for him to make his move against the *Akingi*. He carefully planned the assault, determined to prove to the Thunderbolt that he too could strike with lightning speed. Mircea boldly selected Karnobat, one of the main *Akingi* bases deep in the Balkans, as his target. In the fall of 1393, the Wallachian Prince crossed the Danube, probably

---

[21]Doc. 1 in Dimitrie A. Sturdza and C. Colescu-Vartic, eds., *Acte şi documente relative la istoria renascerei României, vol. I (1391-1841)*, Bucharest, 1900, pp. 1-2.

[22]Mustafa Ali Mehmed, *Istoria turcilor*, Bucharest, 1976, p. 128; Ştefan Ştefănescu, *Tara Românească de la Basarab I "Întemeietorul" până la Mihai Viteazul*, Bucharest, 1970, p. 117.

[23]Quo. Decei, *Relaţii româno-orientale*, p. 152.

at Giurgiu, and headed south. On horseback, the journey to Karnobat took approximately 36 hours, travelled in four stages.[24] This daring attack, striking near the heart of the Empire, took the Turks completely by surprise; according to Bitlisi, the Wallachians "devastated Karnobat and many among the Muslims became martyrs."[25] Mircea returned to Wallachia with great plunder and many slaves,[26] having, for the moment, seriously diminished the capacity of the *Akingi* to cause harm to his Principality.

Bayezid could not let such audacity go unanswered. He left Anatolia, which the Ottomans called *Rum*, and hastily returned to Rumelia, determined to make order in the European portion of his Empire. In the winter of 1393-1394, the Sultan set up court at Serres and summoned all of his Christian vassals in the Balkans there to settle various disputes. Among those in attendance were the Byzantine Emperor Manuel II, the Emperor's brother Theodore, despot of Morea, and Serbian ruler Stephen Lazarević; the Prince of Wallachia was notably absent. An open conflict with the Ottomans was now inevitable. This forced Mircea to reconsider his foreign policy. The alliance with Poland would be of no use to him in the face of a Turkish attack; nor could he any longer depend on Moldavia, also an important factor in his relations with Poland, for support following the death of Peter I in 1392. Up to now Mircea's foreign policy, like that of his predecessors, had been dictated by the notion that Hungary represented the greatest threat to Wallachia's independence. This all changed when the Ottoman Empire became Wallachia's new neighbor to the south; the Turkish peril now drew Wallachia and Hungary together in a common cause and relations between Mircea and Sigismund gradually began to improve. At the end of May 1394, Sigismund sent the Hungarian nobleman Gregory Bethlen to Wallachia as his emissary; the Transylvanian Voivode Frank de Szécsény, from whom Bethlen was ordered to receive instructions before his departure, facilitated the negotiations with Mircea.[27]

---

[24]Decei, *Relaţii româno-orientale*, p. 155.

[25]*Cronici turceşti*, vol. I, p. 156.

[26]*Cronici turceşti*, vol. I, p. 113.

[27]Doc. 80 in *DRH, D*, p. 129.

While more urgent matters in Anatolia forced Bayezid to return there in the spring of 1394, delaying his attack on Wallachia, negotiations between Mircea and Sigismund dragged on. They had not yet reached a formal agreement in the fall of 1394 when the Sultan crossed back over to Europe to lead his armies against the recalcitrant Voivode of *Iflak*, the Ottoman name for Wallachia. Bayezid's attack would culminate in one of the most famous battles in the history of the Principality. In late September, Ottoman forces crossed the Danube at Nicopolis and occupied the Wallachian fortress of Turnu, called Little Nicopolis, on the opposite bank. From here, the Sultan proceeded in the direction of Târgovişte; Mircea harassed the Ottomans as they advanced, but retreated before their superior force as he could not risk a pitched battle. An eighteenth century chronicle of the Catholic Monastery of St. Francis in Târgovişte records that Bayezid set fire to the city and the monastery.[28] From here the invaders set out in the direction of the capital, Argeş. Meanwhile, according to the Byzantine chronicler Laonic Chalkokondyles, "Mircea gathered the army of his country, but did not plan to descend upon him [Bayezid] to give battle; instead, with great care, he placed the women and children in the mountains near Braşov for shelter. After that he followed with his army close to Bayezid through the oak forests of the country which are numerous and cover all parts of the land making it difficult for an enemy to move and not easy to conquer."[29] As the Ottomans marched though Wallachia, both Sigismund and the Transylvanian Voivode Frank de Szécsény closely monitored the situation from locations near the border in southeastern Hungary and southern Transylvania.[30] Hungary had provided Wallachia with some material assistance, but, as they had not yet concluded a treaty, the King's intention was not to lend Mircea military support, but to ensure that the Ottomans did not cross the border into Transylvania. Mircea stood alone against the might of the Ottoman Empire.

---

[28]B.P. Hajdeu, *Archiva istorică a României*, vol. I, part. 2, Bucharest, 1865, p. 47.

[29]Laonic Chalcocondil, *Expuneri istorice*, trans. Vasile Grecu, Bucharest, 1958, p. 64 (II, 79).

[30]Viorica Pervain, "Din relaţiile Ţării Româneşti cu Ungaria la sfârşitul veacului al XIV-lea" in *AIIA, Cluj*, XVIII (1975), p. 96.

The Sultan's forces held the advantage in terms of numbers, equipment, discipline, and experience. But the Wallachians too had some things going for them; as they were defending their homeland, they knew the terrain intimately and possessed the element of surprise. The wily Prince used these things to his full advantage. As the Turks neared Argeş, they entered a swampy, heavily-wooded area which prevented the deployment of their forces in a manner that would allow them to exploit their numerical superiority. Mircea seized this opportunity to strike back at the Empire. Here, on October 10, 1394, the battle of Rovine was fought. According to Turkish sources, the battle took place near the Argeş River; *Rovine* does not refer to a specific location, but is a Slavonic term meaning ditch or swamp. The Ottoman chronicler Orudj bin Adil described the ensuing conflict: "Mircea, the Infidel, bringing his army with him, came against Sultan Bayezid and, upon meeting one another, a great battle took place, so that on the side of the Muslims, as well as on the side of the Infidels, many were slaughtered."[31] The fierceness of the fighting at Rovine was remembered for centuries after. Writing near the end of the seventeenth century, the chronicler George Brankovici recalled, "never was there such a terrible battle as that one; the blood of the soldiers spilled until it reached the fetlocks of the horses."[32] The result was a hard won victory for Mircea. The Sultan, having suffered heavy losses, and with winter drawing near, retreated back across the Danube.

Mircea had defended his Principality brilliantly, but victory came at a heavy cost. With his military forces depleted and resources running low, the conclusion of an alliance with neighboring Hungary was now imperative; all the more so because his victory at the battle of Rovine was ephemeral at best and he knew that the spring thaw would bring with it the return of Turkish armies determined to pillage the land and to drive him from the throne. Under these circumstances, negotiations between Wallachia and Hungary resumed with renewed intensity. Sigismund ultimately hoped to form a broad anti-Ottoman alliance and to lead a crusade to drive the Turks from Europe and to extend Hungarian hegemony over all of Southeastern Europe. Part of his plan was to negate Polish influence in the region. The immediacy of the Ottoman

---

[31]*Cronici turceşti*, vol. I, p. 48.

[32]Gheorghe Brancovici, *Cronica românească*, p. 61.

threat had drawn Wallachia closer to Hungary, but Moldavia remained firmly in the Polish camp. At the end of 1394, Stephen I succeeded to the throne as the representative of the pro-Polish faction in the country; on January 6, 1395, the new Prince swore allegiance to Vladislav I, promising to stand with him against their mutual enemies, including the King of Hungary and Mircea, referred to in this treaty as "the voivode of Basarabia."[33] While Stephen renewed his Principality's ties of vassalage to the Polish Crown, Sigismund was in the Szeckler lands in Transylvania, preparing to cross the mountains to invade Moldavia. Toward the end of January, Sigismund won a victory over the Moldavians at the battle of Hindau, today Ghindoani, south of the fortress of Neamț. On February 3, the Hungarian army encamped before this fortress,[34] the principal stronghold protecting Moldavia's border with Transylvania, constructed during the reign of Peter I. Failing to take the citadel, the King could not capitalize on his previous victory, and with pressing matters awaiting him in Transylvania, Sigismund left Moldavia, arriving in Brașov by February 14.[35]

Sigismund's failure to bring Moldavia under his control did not represent a major setback to his plans for a campaign against the Turks because the participation of that Principality was not a strategical necessity. Wallachia, on the other hand, represented an essential element in any scheme for a new crusade. The lengthy negotiations of the previous year between Hungary and Wallachia finally paid off as both sides now realized the urgent need to conclude an agreement. With Sigismund across the border in Brașov, Mircea set out from his capital at Argeș, passing through Câmpulung, Rucăr, and Bran, to meet him. On March 7, 1395, the King and the Prince concluded a treaty formalizing the alliance between Hungary and Wallachia. Negotiations had been difficult partly because Mircea refused to accept the inclusion of any clause in the agreement that could be construed as a recognition of Hungarian suzerainty. The result was a narrowly-focused treaty in which both sides agreed to provide mutual assistance "against those terrible, cunning sons of

---

[33]Doc. 167 in Costăchescu, ed., *Documentele moldovenești*, vol. II, pp. 611-615.

[34]Docs. 81 and 82 in *DRH, D*, pp. 130-131.

[35]Ilie Minea, *Cetatea Neamțului*, Iași, 1943, p. 7; Giurescu, "O nouă sinteză a trecutului nostru," in *RIR*, II (1932), p. 18.

evil, enemies of the name of Christ, and unforgiven enemies of ours, the Turks."[36] Interestingly, Mircea noted that the document was "sealed with our small seal for lack of the larger one." Seals were the principal means of authenticating documents during this time and the Prince's large seal would normally be applied to any act of such importance; for this reason, Mircea made special mention of the fact that he had to use his small seal. In all likelihood, Mircea's large seal was lost during the battle of Rovine the previous fall and had not yet been replaced. On this occassion commercial privileges between Wallachia and Braşov were also renewed.[37]

Mircea counted on his alliance with Hungary to provide him with much needed military support as Turkish forces now massed along his southern frontier. Sigismund held true to their agreement and made immediate plans to send an advance force of some 400 men under the command of Stephen de Losoncz, the former Ban of Macva, to Wallachia. On April 6, the King ordered Gregory Bethlen, who had handled the negotiations with Wallachia during the previous year, to join this expeditionary force as his personal representative.[38] Sigismund, meanwhile, remained in Transylvania to gather a larger army with which he intended to come to Mircea's aid. A contemporary French chronicle tells us that Stephen de Losoncz had specific instructions from the King "to find out the manner in which they [the Turks] could be attacked and to return with reliable information."[39]

The Ottomans, however, had no intention of sitting idly by while Sigismund made his preparations to enter Wallachia. They had maintained a bridgehead at Turnu since the previous fall and used this base to gather an army with orders from the Sultan to invade the Principality, oust Mircea, and to place in his stead Vlad, the eldest son of Mircea's brother Dan. Vlad Dan apparently went into self-imposed exile sometime after his father's death in search of outside assistance to help him press his claim to the throne; Mircea's proclamation of his young son Michael as associate ruler several years earlier

---

[36]Doc. 87 in *DRH, D*, pp. 138-142.

[37]Docs. 88 and 89 in *DRH, D*, pp. 142-143.

[38]Doc. 93 in *DRH, D*, pp. 149-150.

[39]Quo. Giurescu, "În legătură cu Mircea cel Bătrân," p. 426.

may have determined him to do this. As tensions mounted between Mircea and the Turks, the pretender received a warm welcome at the Ottoman Porte. He probably accompanied the Sultan to Wallachia during the campaign of the previous fall for Bayezid certainly had no intention of transforming the Principality into a pashalik and needed a legitimate candidate with a strong base of support among the native population to place on the throne. The fifteenth century Hungarian chronicler Johannes de Thurocz provides indications that Vlad Dan worked from Turnu during the winter of 1394-1395 to gather support among dissatisfied factions within the country.[40] Given the long history of animosity between Wallachia and Hungary, and the aggressive Catholic proselytizing of the latter, there were certainly many amongst the predominantly Orthodox population of the Principality who disapproved of Mircea's alliance with Sigismund. The Sultan was too preoccupied elsewhere to participate personally in this new Ottoman campaign. On April 16, 1395, he captured Salonika. Bayezid then proceeded to Athens and on to Brusa, the capital of the Asian portion of his Empire, as he prepared for a new seige of Constantinople.[41] Nevertheless, a significant Turkish force gathered at Turnu, including contingents led by the Sultan's Serbian vassals, Stephen Lazarević, Marko Kraljević, and Constantine Dragošević, the father-in-law of Byzantine Emperor Manuel II. This army penetrated into the interior of the country in early May. They likely advanced along the Olt River valley which afforded them both maximum opportunity for plunder and ease of movement north toward the important city of Râmnicu and the capital of Argeş as it was a well-populated and frequently-travelled route. Mircea now prepared to confront this new Ottoman invasion.

Reinforced by the troops led by Stephen de Losoncz, the Wallachian Prince hurried south determined to halt the Turkish advance. The two forces met in battle on May 17, 1395. This second battle of Rovine, so-called because it also took place in marshlands, albeit at a different location than that of the previous year, was another fierce encounter. Thurocz describes how the King sent Stephen de Losoncz to Mircea's aid, "but, being overwhelmed by the numbers of the enemy, he was killed in a bloody battle with heavy losses on both sides,

---

[40]Pervain, "Din relaţiile Ţării Româneşti cu Ungaria," p. 98.

[41]Tahsin Gemil, *Românii şi otomanii*, Bucharest, 1991, p. 81.

losing the battle and at the same time his life. After the death of their commander, his soldiers fled, leaving the enemy great booty and many prisoners.[42] The Ottoman forces also suffered heavy losses before finally winning the day; Serbian commanders Marko Kraljević and Constantine Dragošević died in the fighting.[43] Mircea now fled northward to await help from Sigismund, while Vlad Dan and the Ottomans advanced toward the capital of Argeş.

According to a contemporary Bulgarian chronicle, after his defeat at the second battle of Rovine, Mircea "fled to the Hungarians."[44] In reality, although he abandoned Argeş to the invaders, Mircea continued to hold Câmpulung where he awaited help from Sigismund. Difficulties raising an army had delayed the King's departure for Wallachia;[45] in late June, he was in the vicinity of Braşov making final preparations for his campaign against the Turks. From here he advanced into Wallachia via the Bran pass. On July 6, the Royal army encamped around Câmpulung[46] where Sigismund and Mircea conferred to plan their counter-offensive against Vlad Dan and the Ottoman invaders supporting him. The combined Wallachian-Hungarian army now possessed numerical superiority; the recent battle and the likely withdrawal of some contingents from the country for use elsewhere had reduced the Ottoman force. Sigismund and Mircea appear to have retaken Argeş and Râmnicu and proceeded down the Olt valley with little opposition. Their objective was the fortress of Turnu, on the Danube, which Vlad Dan and his Turkish allies had used as a base for their latest incursion into the country; possession of this citadel had allowed for the uncontested crossing of men and material from Nicopolis, the recently acquired Ottoman stronghold on the opposite bank. When they besieged the fortress intense fighting began. "Three times the banner of the King fell to the ground and three times it was raised again," relates the French chronicle of St. Denis, "as the King continuously

---

[42]Quo. Panaitescu, *Mircea cel Bătrân*. p. 254.

[43]George Sp. Radojicic, "La chronologie de la bataille de Rovine: in *RHSEE*, V:4-6 (1928), pp. 136-137.

[44]Quo. Panaitescu, *Mircea cel Bătrân*, p. 242.

[45]Doc. 105 in *DRH, D*, pp. 171-174.

[46]Doc. 94 in *DRH, D*, pp. 150-151.

encouraged his men to fight for Christ."[47] In the face of these repeated assaults, the citadel fell to the royal army. Sigismund wrote that, "attacking them with strength, we took the fortress with the help of Christ.... After that, we left faithful castle guards in that fortress."[48] Mircea had regained the strategic points previously lost, but Vlad Dan remained at large in Oltenia where he had found a base of support among the native population opposed to Mircea's pro-Hungarian policy.

Unfortunately for Mircea, Sigismund could not remain in Wallachia to follow-up on his victory. Soon after he captured Turnu, the King received news that his pregnant Queen had died after a fall from a horse had provoked a miscarriage. The death of Maria was a serious blow to the young King. Not only had he lost a beloved wife and a potential heir, but he now feared for his throne as the legitimacy of his claim to the Crown of St. Stephen was based on his marriage to the daughter of Louis the Great. On the northern border of his Kingdom, the Poles prepared to attack. Vladislav also claimed the Hungarian throne through his marriage to Louis's youngest daughter, Hedwiga, but fortunately for Sigismund, Johannes de Kanisa, the capable Archbishop of Strigoniu, fended off the invaders without necessitating the presence of the King in this region. But there remained a very real danger that certain factions among the Hungarian nobility might use the occassion of Maria's death and Sigismund's absence from the country to organize a revolt to undermine the King's authority. As a result, the two armies now went in separate directions. Sigismund headed northwest on his way back to Hungary, while Mircea returned to Argeş hoping to consolidate his hold on the Principality. By August 25, the King had reached Severin[49] and prepared to cross the mountains. With the enemy force divided, Vlad Dan seized the opportunity to strike back as the royal army trekked through the mountain passes leading from the Severin land to the Banat in Hungary. In a diploma dated June 6, 1397, Sigismund recalled the ensuing attack: "we climbed the peaks of the mountains to a place called Posada [not to be confused with the site of the battle of the same name in 1330] in the ordinary language, through some narrow paths surrounded by large

---

[47]Quo. Panaitescu, *Mircea cel Bătrân*, p. 257.

[48]Doc. 99 in *DRH, D*, pp. 154-158.

[49]Doc. 95 in *DRH, D*, pp. 151-152.

bushes where numerous Wallachians laid in ambush, and they attacked us violently from the dark and thick forests, hurling spears and firing poison arrows."[50] Sigismund escaped back to Hungary, but with his victorious campaign suddenly transformed into a bitter defeat.

Having vanquished the Hungarians, and with domestic affairs now preoccupying Sigismund, Vlad Dan gained the upper hand in his struggle with his uncle for the throne of Wallachia. The arrival of Ottoman reinforcements in September further strengthened his position.[51] The country was now split, with Vlad controlling the western portion of the Principality and Mircea the eastern part. At this point, the Patriarch of Constantinople tried to mediate the conflict. He directed his emissary, the Metropolitan of Mytilene, on the Aegean island of Lesbos: "You have been chosen to go to *the parts of Wallachia* to do all that you have been instructed verbally by our humbleness and that which is contained in the letters to *the Princes* there."[52] These efforts came too late. In early October, Stephen I of Moldavia intervened in Wallachia to help Vlad Dan. They forced Mircea to flee across the mountains to Transylvania where he continued to rule the duchies of Amlaş and Făgăraş. Vlad I was now Prince of Wallachia.[53] But the fighting did not end here. As Ottoman reinforcements continued to arrive, Vlad Dan and his Turkish allies launched an offensive against Transylvania, reaching Braşov and Temesvar.[54] This expedition had the character of a raid intended to finish off Mircea, as well as to pillage and to cause destruction in the Hungarian lands. On December 10, 1395, Paul de Armaninis, the Ambassador of Mantua to Hungary, reported from Buda that Sigismund had to cancel a scheduled meeting with his brother, King Venceslas IV of Bohemia, because of these attacks.[55]

[50]Doc. 99 in *DRH, D*, pp. 154-158.

[51]Ilie Minea, *Informaţiile româneşti ale cronicii lui Ian Długosz*, p. 15.

[52]"Acta Patriarchatus Constantinopolitani," doc. 50, in *Fontes Historiae Daco-Romanae*, vol. IV, p. 250, emphasis added.

[53]Octavian Iliescu, "Vlad Ier, voivode de Valachie" in *RRH*, XXVII:1-2 (1988), p. 79.

[54]Ştefan Pascu, "Contribuţiuni documentare la istoria românilor în sec. XIII şi XIV," in *AIIN, Cluj*, X (1945), p. 218.

[55]Gemil, *Românii şi otomanii*, p. 81.

The loss of Wallachia represented a major setback to Sigismund's plans for an anti-Ottoman crusade. In a diploma dated December 8, 1397, the King decried the events two years earlier when "our enemy, Voivode Vlad, who was at that time placed and raised to the leadership of our Transalpine land by the aforesaid Turks, was there with a large army of Turks and Wallachians."[56] Despite this impediment, Sigismund continued with his efforts to organize the long-delayed crusade intended to drive the Turkish infidels from Europe. Having lost Wallachia by arms, the King now tried to win it back to the Hungarian cause though diplomatic means. The negotiations that followed also served as a cover for intelligence-gathering operations. On March 21, 1396, Maternus, the Bishop of Transylvania, wrote to the officials of Sibiu: "The possessor of this letter, Johannes Tatar, a man in the service of the royal court, was sent by our lord, the King, with certain important messages to the Voivode Vlad.... we ask you to send to Vlad, together with the aforementioned Johannes Tatar, a capable and worthy man, knowledgeable in the Wallachian language, and order this emissary of yours to spy, quietly and secretly, and to gather news of the Turks and other information."[57] Efforts to draw Vlad I into an anti-Ottoman coalition failed. Encouraged by his ally, Stephen I of Moldavia, Vlad Dan instead opened negotiations with Poland. On May 28, 1396, as "Voivode of Basarabia and Count of Severin," having "recently" attained the throne, he swore allegiance to Polish King Vladislav I and his wife Queen Hedwiga, explicitly recognizing them as the rightful sovereigns of Hungary.[58]

Although Wallachia remained outside the Hungarian camp, the crusade that Sigismund had long dreamed of leading finally began to take shape. Bayezid's renewed siege of Constantinople hastened its realization. With the imperial capital in dire straits, the Byzantine chronicler Dukas recalls how "Emperor Manuel, not knowing what to do and not having help from anywhere, wrote to the Pope, to the King of France, and to the King of Hungary announcing the blockade and the desperate situation facing Constantinople and that if they would not come quickly to help and to provide assistance he will surrender the

---

[56]Doc. 101 in *DRH, D*, pp. 160-169.

[57]Doc. 97 in *DRH, D*, pp. 153-154.

[58]Doc. CCCXVI in Hurmuzaki, *Documente*, vol. I, part. 2, pp. 374-375.

city into the hands of the enemies of Christianity."[59] Sigismund heeded the
Emperor's call for help and by February 1396 he had concluded a treaty with
Manuel II. Preparations for war now began in earnest. The Great Schism
divided the Catholic Church at this time, but the Hungarian King managed to
convince the rival Popes, Boniface IX in Rome and Benedict XIII in Avignon,
to set aside their differences for the moment and each sent out calls for a
crusade against the Turkish infidels. Through letters and emissaries,
Sigismund personally appealed to Christian rulers throughout Western Europe
to join in the crusade; he wrote to the French King Charles IV, telling him how
the Sultan boasted that he would go to Rome and feed his horses oats on the
altar of St. Peter's Basilica. The German monk Johann Trittheim tells us that
in this way the King "gathered in a short time a large army against the Turks."[60]

The call to arms did not go unheeded as nobles throughout Europe began
to rally to the Christian cause. The most enthusiastic response came from
Burgundy where John of Nevers, the son of Duke Philip the Fair, gathered a
large contingent of knights and set out for Buda in late April. France also
answered the appeal from the heir of the Angevin kings of Hungary. Among
the French nobles who headed east that summer to take up arms against the
Turks were Count Philip de Artois, Admiral Jean de Vienne, Marshal Jean le
Maingre, called Boucicaut, and Lord de Coucy. In the midst of the Hundred
Years' War, France and England set aside their differences momentarily as the
Duke of Lancester joined the crusaders with a contingent of English knights.
German knights, led by Count Palatine Ruppert and John of Zollern, the
Burgrave of Nuremberg, also came to take part in Sigismund's grand venture.
Brimming with confidence, the crusaders did not fully grasp the gravity of the
task at hand. The atmosphere was almost festive; a contemporary French
chronicle recounts that Boucicaut joined the crusade, "first because he desired
above all to fight the Turks, then for the excellent food to which he had been
treated on earlier occassions by the King of Hungary."[61] As these crusaders
rendezvoused at the Hungarian capital, the Turkish noose tightened around

---

[59]Ducas, *Istoria turco-bizantină*, Bucharest, 1958, p. 78 (XIII, 8).

[60]Quo. Serban Papacostea, "Mircea la Nicopol (1396): O mărturie ignorată," in *RdI*,
39:7 (1986), p. 697.

[61]Quo. Panaitescu, *Mircea cel Bătrân*, p. 262.

Constantinople. The Byzantines received some much-needed relief when Venice, in anticipation of the upcoming crusade, sent galleys to the beleaguered imperial capital.[62] All the pieces were finally falling into place.

A substantial force of crusaders from all over Europe had gathered at Buda. It is said that Sigismund, "looking over the large number of his soldiers, remarked that with such a great army he could not only defeat the Turks, but if the sky were to fall they could hold it up with their lances."[63] Manuel II later recounted that "a vast army gathered at Nicopolis, comprised of Hungarians, Frenchmen, and Burgundians, at which all of the barbarians trembled merely upon hearing their names."[64] But to have a clear idea of the size of this force it must be remembered that European armies during this period were small in comparison with later centuries[65] and that medieval sources notoriously exaggerated figures for literary effect. In reality, Sigismund had a total of around 10,000 troops, even though contemporary accounts give estimates a high as 200,000.[66] This army set out for Temesvar where Mircea, the exiled Prince of Wallachia joined them with a force of approximately 1,000 men. Because of his experience and knowledge of the terrain, the King assigned Mircea to lead the advance guard; the Byzantine chronicler Chalkokondyles recorded that Sigismund "had with him the Dacians [Wallachians], a brave people, to show them the way and to open the road for the army."[67] From Temesvar, the crusaders proceeded to Orşova, where they crossed the Danube around August 13, 1396.

Among those who made this crossing was Johann Schiltberger, a fifteen-year-old squire from Bavaria in the service of a knight called Reichartinger. The Ottomans captured the youth at the battle of Nicopolis and he spent the

---

[62]Appendix LV in N. Iorga, "Veneţia în Marea Neagră, II" in *AARMSI*, series II, XXXVI (1913-1914), p. 1117.

[63]Brancovici, *Cronica românească*, p. 60.

[64]"Manueles Paleologus" in *Fontes Historiae Daco-Romanae*, vol. IV, p. 336.

[65]Hale, *Civilization of the Renaissance in Europe*, p. 78. Before 1500, 12,000 to 30,000 men comprised a large army.

[66]R. Rosetti, "Care au fost adevăratele efective ale unor armate din trecut," in *AARMSI*, series III, XXV (1942-1943), pp. 734, 740-741.

[67]Chalcocondil, *Expuneri istorice*, p. 59 (II, 69).

next thirty years of his life travelling throughout Asia as a slave of the Turks
and the Mongols. When he finally returned home, he entered the service of
Duke Albert III of Bavaria and wrote a journal of his travels, providing us with,
among other things, a first-hand account of the Nicopolis campaign. He
recounted how the army of crusaders, "crossed the Danube into Bulgaria and
headed toward a city called Vidin, which is the capital of Bulgaria. Then the
Prince of the country and of the city [Stratimir] voluntarily pledged his allegiance to the King. Then the King garrisoned the city with 300 men, cavalry
and good infantry." Vidin and the surrounding territory controlled by Stratimir
was all that remained of the once mighty Second Bulgarian Empire since the
fall of Trnovo in 1393. The last Bulgarian Tsar, Mircea's uncle through his
marriage to Ana, the sister of Mircea's father Radu, made a desperate gamble
by opening the gates of the city to the crusaders, hoping that they would help
him to restore the former glory of his Empire or at least ensure its survival.
From Vidin, the crusaders marched along the Danube to Rahova. "In that place
there were many Turks who did not want to surrender the city," recalled
Schiltberger. "Then the citizens rose up and drove out the Turks by force and
submitted to the King; many of the Turks were killed, while others were taken
prisoner. The King also garrisoned this city with 300 of his men."[68] Up to now,
the crusaders had encountered little serious resistance. The initial objective of
the campaign, as Sigismund had told Byzantine emissary Emanuil
Philanthropeno earlier that summer, was to reach the port city of Varna on the
Black Sea coast.[69] Continuing their march to the sea, the crusaders advanced
along the right bank of the Danube in the direction of Nicopolis.

Once he reached Nicopolis, Sigismund expected the arrival of additional
troops. The new Transylvanian Voivode, Stibor de Stiboricz, a Pole from
Slovakia, led an army into Wallachia, intending to neutralize Vlad Dan so that
he would be unable to assist the Turks south of the Danube and then to join the
King's forces at Nicopolis. Vlad I, supported by Ottoman soldiers, tried to
block Stibor's advance. A difficult battle ensued with heavy losses on both
sides. The fighting degenerated to the point where Stibor and Vlad Dan
engaged in single combat. The Wallachian Prince was severely wounded in

---

[68]*Călători străini*, vol I, pp. 28-29.
[69]Iorga, "Veneția în Marea Neagră, II," p. 1089.

this encounter and forced to flee with his troops.[70] The Transylvanian Voivode's victory opened the way for an unimpeded march to Nicopolis and removed Vlad I as a potential threat to the Christian army advancing along the Danube.

By mid-September, the crusaders led by Sigismund had reached Nicopolis where Stibor's force joined them. Built on a rocky plateau overlooking the Danube, the Roman Emperor Trajan is credited with founding Nicopolis whose Greek name means "City of Victory." The name proved ominous to the Christian force now camped before its walls. From this highly defensible position, the Turkish garrison prepared to offer stiff resistance. As a result, the fortress could not easily be taken by assault and the crusaders prepared for a prolonged seige. For over two weeks they tried to take the city by various means, including mining the large round tower protecting the stronghold, but to no avail. Finally, they prepared to set it ablaze.[71]

Meanwhile, the Sultan made plans of his own. Although it meant raising the seige of Constantinople, Bayezid, true to his sobriquet 'the Thunderbolt,' prepared to move quickly north to relieve Nicopolis. Orudj bin Adil wrote that when he received news of the advance of the crusaders led by the King of Hungary, "Sultan Bayezid set out with ten thousand volunteers and met the infidels near Nicopolis."[72] Another Turkish chronicler adds that the Sultan first went to Trnovo where he made preparations for his counter-offensive.[73] From here, he proceeded north to the Danube. A decisive battle between Muslim and Christian forces was now imminent.

According to Schiltberger, when he received news of the impending arrival of the troops led by the Sultan, "King Sigismund blocked their path a mile from the city with his army." The crusaders abandoned plans to set fire to the fortress as they prepared for battle. The long-awaited moment when they would confront the enemy of Christendom was now at hand. At this point, Schiltberger relates that "the Prince of Wallachia, called Mircea, came and

---

[70]Doc. 101 in *DRH, D*, pp. 160-169.

[71]N. Iorga, ed., "Cronica lui Wavrin şi românii," in *BCIR*, IV (1927), p. 139.

[72]Mihail Guboglu, ed., *Crestomaţie turcă*, Bucharest, 1978, p. 217.

[73]*Cronici turceşti*, vol. I, p. 113.

asked the King for permission to make a reconnaissance of the enemy." In typical medieval fashion, he provides exaggerated numbers. Schiltberger claims that Mircea reconnoitered the Ottoman force with 1000 of his men; realistically, he probably engaged about 100 troops from his total force of 1000 in this type of operation. After completing his mission, Schiltberger says that Mircea reported to Sigismund "that the enemy had 20 flags with him, and that under each flag there were over 10,000 men."[74] The numbers are completely out of proportion with what we know of medieval armies. A *flag* was the equivalent of a modern regiment. It usually numbered around 500 men, but not more than 1000. Any more than that could not be held together under a single banner in this midst of battle. Thus, if we accept that Mircea's reconnaissance revealed 20 flags in the Turkish camp, it confirms Orudj bin Adil's estimate of 10,000 Ottoman troops under Bayezid's command, rather than the 200,000 claimed by Schiltberger.

The stage was set for a decisive confrontation between two forces of approximately equal strength, although the Ottomans may have enjoyed a slight numerical superiority. In the Christian camp, a council of war was now held. Schiltberger recalled that "the King wanted to prepare the battle order. Then the Prince of Wallachia asked that he be permitted to lead the first attack, which the King heartily approved. But the Duke of Burgundy [John of Nevers], hearing this, protested against this honor going to another, saying that he had come from afar with a great army... which had cost him a great deal."[75] Now the effects of the lack of a unified command and an overconfidence bordering on arrogance made themselves apparent in the Christian camp. Chalkokondyles confirms that "the Celts [French], being proud and uncalculated, as usual, wanted the victory to be theirs alone, so, heavily armed, they attacked first, as if they could destroy the barbarians in one blow."[76] The crusaders made a serious blunder in not using troops experienced in combat with the Turks in the front lines. The King was conscious of this and wanted Mircea to lead the attack, but he lacked the authority to impose his decision. According to Trittheim, "Sigismund believed that one who knew the ways and

---

[74]*Călători străini*, vol. I, p. 29.

[75]*Călători străini*, vol. I, p. 29.

[76]Chalcocondil, *Expuneri istorice*, p. 62 (II, 75, 76).

customs of the enemy and who had fought with them before should be appointed to lead the assault."[77] The King was not alone in his desire to use experienced troops; a young Wallachian boyar who fell prisoner in the battle later recalled that Lord de Coucy "made it a habit to keep Wallachian noblemen, who knew the ways of the lands occupied by the Turks, near him as armed companions."[78] But pride and arrogance won out over sound strategy and tactics. The fateful battle occurred on September 25, 1396. With the Ottomans occupying the high ground, John of Nevers led his heavy cavalry in a charge against the disciplined troops forming the Ottoman center; the lack of coordination and discipline among the patchwork army of crusaders proved fatal. "The Celts [French] were defeated," Chalkokondyles relates, "and they began to flee in panic and without any order. They fell over their own army while the Turks pursued them.... Seeking to cross the Danube in haste, much of the army perished in the river."[79]

The battle of Nicopolis once again confirmed that the days when heavily-clad knights in shining armor would rule the battlefields of Europe were over. In his study of the battle, the Turkish historian Aziz Suryal Atiya concluded, "The victory was won by the party that possessed an unflinching unity of purpose, a strict and even ruthless discipline, prudent tactics, and wise leadership."[80] Nicopolis firmly established Ottoman military superiority. It would take two centuries for Europeans to bridge the gap. Bemoaning the battle of Mohacs that transpired on August 29, 1526, and sounded the death knell of medieval Hungary, Bishop Paulo Giovio wrote to the Holy Roman Emperor Charles V, explaining, "The Turks are better soldiers than ours for three reasons: first, because of discipline, which is rare among us; second, because they throw themselves into battle with fervent conviction, into the mouth of death, for they believe that each one has written on his forehead how and when

---

[77]Quo. Papacostea, "Mircea la Nicopol," p. 697.

[78]Iorga, ed., "Cronica lui Wavrin," p. 139.

[79]Chalcocondil, *Expuneri istorice*, p. 62 (II, 76).

[80]Quo. Rosetti, "Care au fost adevăratele efective," p. 735.

he will die; and third, because the Turks live without bread and without wine, and usually rice and water are enough for them."[81]

The Christian force at Nicopolis was decimated. Many were killed and others were taken captive, including John of Nevers, who bore a large share of the responsibility for the debacle, and Marshal Boucicaut. Trittheim recorded that "King Sigismund made it to the sea with difficulty and went by ship to Constantinople, escaping death. Palatine Ruppert returned to Heidelburg dressed as a poor beggar."[82] Many of those taken captive, such as the young squire Johann Schiltberger, were sold into slavery. Important noblemen, such as Marshal Boucicaut and John Nevers, were ransomed for large sums of money. John of Nevers went on to become Duke of Burgundy (1404-1419); his son and successor, Philip the Good (1419-1467), would become one of the most illustrious rulers of fifteenth century Europe. Sigismund fled Nicopolis aboard ships that the Venetians had sent to the Danube to provide logistical support for the crusaders as the Ottomans forced Schiltberger and other prisoners to taunt the King from the banks overlooking the river. The architect of the failed crusade made his way to the Byzantine capital, where he consulted with Emperor Manuel II, and from there to Ragusa on the Adriatic coast; Sigismund did not return Hungary until three months after the disaster.

Immediately following his great victory, Bayezid moved west with characteristic agility, cutting off the crusaders's escape routes through Bulgaria and Serbia. At the same time, he took Vidin and transformed the last remnants of the medieval Bulgarian state into a Turkish pashalik. Stratimir had gambled and lost when he threw in his lot with the crusaders; the last Bulgarian Tsar was captured and sent to Brusa as a prisoner where he lived out the rest of his days. Five hundred years would pass before Bulgaria would rise from the ashes and reappear on the map of Europe. Wallachia remained the only escape route open to most survivors who had avoided capture. Mircea and

---

[81]Quo. P.P. Panaitescu, *Interpretări româneşti*, Bucharest, 1947, p. 150.

[82]Quo. Papacostea, "Mircea la Nicopol," p. 698.

Stibor were among those who made their way north to Transylvania, but the appearance of Vlad Dan and his troops hindered their flight.[83]

Wounds Stibor suffered in the fighting at Nicopolis made his journey back to Transylvania all the more difficult, but he recovered quickly and was determined to seize the initiative, fearing an imminent Ottoman attack on Hungary.[84] The Transylvanian Voivode could not tolerate an ally of the Sultan on the throne of Wallachia; he intended that the Principality to the south remain a buffer between Hungary and the Ottoman Empire. Taking advantage of the fact that the main Ottoman force had withdrawn south for the winter, Stibor again gathered an army, which included Mircea and his troops, and reentered Wallachia through the Bran Pass in late November 1396. Their objective was to oust Vlad I and to restore Mircea to the throne. This attack, coming so late in the year and on the heels of the disastrous defeat at Nicopolis, caught Vlad Dan unprepared. Stibor and Mircea marched through Rucăr and Câmpulung virtually unimpeded. Unable to mount a counterattack, Vlad I fled before the invaders and took refuge in the fortress of Dâmbovita, south of Câmpulung. A diploma issued by Sigismund a year later, in which he recounts Stibor's valiant deeds, recalls how the Transylvanian Voivode laid seige to the citadel until "the Voivode Vlad was forced from the aforesaid fortress.... and coming out from there with his wife, his children, and with his entire entourage, he abandoned the fortress of Dâmbovita into our hands."[85] Vlad I and his family were taken prisoner and brought to Hungary. By the end of 1396, Mircea once again ruled Wallachia.

Following Vlad Dan's capture, Mircea worked to consolidate his hold on the Principality. Potential rivals still remained at large. A Ragusan accounting ledger records that 60 perpers were given to "John, son of the late voivode Dan, arrived in Ragusa on July 28, 1397."[86] John likely escaped Wallachia and fled to the Dalmatian coast following the defeat of his brother Vlad I. The

---

[83]Iorga, *Istoria armatei românești*, vol. I, p. 93; docs. 99 and 101, in *DRH,D*, pp. 154-158, 160-169.

[84]Pascu, "Contribuțiuni documentare," p. 219.

[85]Doc. 101 in *DRH, D*, pp. 160-169.

[86]Quo. P.P. Panaitescu, "Relațiile Țării Românești și ale Moldovei cu Raguza," in *Studii*, 2:4 (1949), p. 110.

youngest of Dan's sons, his namesake, remained in the service of his uncle Mircea. The newly restored Prince also had to fend off Ottoman raids in 1397 and prepared for a rumored invasion in 1398, but the Turks made no concentrated effort north of the Danube at this time because Bayezid focused his attention on Anatolia. The Sultan conquered Karaman in 1398 and by 1399 most of Asia Minor, with the notable exception of Trapezunt in the east, had fallen under Ottoman domination. Mircea's position was further strengthened when Sigismund and Vladislav I signed a peace treaty in July 1397 in which the Poles renounced their claim to the Crown of St. Stephen and recognized Hungarian suzerainty over Wallachia.[87] Ties to Hungary were reinforced when the King granted Mircea a royal estate in Transylvania, near Koloszvar (Cluj), which included the fortress of Huedin (Bologa),[88] as insurance in the event that he was forced to flee Wallachia in the face of another Turkish attack.

By 1399, Europe was again in Bayezid's center of attention and Mircea feared a new invasion. On March 23, 1399, Sigismund wrote to Count Johannes de Paszto, a former court official, ordering him to gather troops to aid Mircea in the event of an attack: "Yesterday, I received a letter from.... Prince Mircea, Transalpine Voivode, written near Little Nicopolis [Turnu], telling that Bayezid himself, the Lord of the Turks, is at the city of Adrianople with a very large army, on this side of the sea, from where in five days he could easily arrive at the Danube." The King emphasized the need for swift action, declaring that "we must have no doubt and we must greatly fear that the Wallachians, finding themselves without our assistance, will not remain faithful and steadfast, but will submit in a short time to the Turkish yoke. If this would happen, and God forbid that if should, you know very well in what danger and peril our country would find itself."[89] But, although Ottoman raids continued, Wallachia did not confront a major invasion at this time as the Sultan directed his resources toward tightening the noose around Constantinople.

[87]Panaitescu, *Mircea cel Bătrân*, p. 274.

[88]Iosif Pataki, "Ceva despre relaţiile Ţării Româneşti cu Ungaria," in *SMIM*, II, Bucharest, 1957, p. 423.

[89]Doc. 105 in *DRH, D*, pp. 171-174.

The atmosphere in the Byzantine capital was now one of despair. Only outside help could save the remnants of the once-mighty Eastern Roman Empire. From Rome, Pope Boniface IX issued a call for a new crusade, but after the debacle at Nicopolis little interest could be roused for another such grand endeavor. Manuel II sent emissaries throughout Europe to plead for assistance to save his beleagured Empire from falling into the hands of the Turks. In September 1399, a modicum of help arrived from France after Charles VI sent a fleet of six vessels to Constantinople under the command of Marshal Boucicaut, eager for revenge against the Turks after his capture at Nicopolis. The French broke through the Ottoman blockade, but the small force of some twelve hundred men could not save Constantinople from the Turks. Boucicaut told Manuel that he must personally travel to the West to seek help, as only in this way could he raise sufficient resources to save his Empire from Bayezid's armies. Realizing that armed resistance was the only option left open to him, the Emperor left his capital, accompanied by Boucicaut, on December 10, 1399; Manuel spent the next three years travelling in Italy, France, and England, working against time to try to garner the men, materiel, and financial resources that alone could prevent the fall of Constantinople into Ottoman hands.

While Manuel II travelled throughout Europe striving to save his Empire from the Turks, north of the Danube Mircea worked vigorously to strengthen his own position as the Ottoman threat seemed omnipresent. The Wallachian Prince had not been on good terms with neighboring Moldavia since Stephen I had supported Vlad Dan against him in 1395-1396. Following Stephen's death in 1399, the Poles intervened in the Principality to assure the succession of a candidate amenable to them so that Moldavia would remain in the Polish sphere of influence; their choice fell upon Iuga, a son of Roman I. But Poland faced a political crisis following the unexpected death of Queen Hedwiga on July 17, 1399. Mircea now saw an opportunity to secure his northeastern border. In the spring of 1400 he intervened in Moldavia on behalf of another son of his former ally Roman I, Alexander. Moldavian chronicles record that "on April 23 Voivode Alexander took the throne of Moldavia, while Voivode

Iuga was taken prisoner by Voivode Mircea."[90] In an effort to ensure good relations in the future, the two princes concluded a treaty fixing the border between their principalities.[91] Mircea's bold initiative in intervening in Moldavia to place Alexander on the throne paid off as peaceful relations between the two neighboring states persisted throughout the remainder of his reign.

With Constantinople surrounded, in the fall of 1400 Bayezid sent a large force to plunder Wallachia and Hungary. They attacked Oltenia and the Banat where they met only token resistance, but as Turkish troops prepared to cross the Danube to return to Ottoman territory with their plunder and numerous captives destined to be sold into slavery, Mircea launched a surprise counterattack and nearly annihilated the invaders.[92] Despite this victory, the Ottoman threat to Wallachia loomed ever larger as the alliance with Hungary proved ineffectual. Sigismund's hold on the Crown of St. Stephen had always been tenuous, but the death of Maria and the disaster at Nicopolis had made the situation even worse. The King tried to purchase the loyalty of leading nobles by giving away numerous royal holdings to his supporters; of 230 castles and estates in the Crown's possession at the end of Louis the Great's reign, Sigismund retained only 47 of these by 1407.[93] Nevertheless, a revolt broke out in Hungary in the spring of 1401 and the King was taken prisoner. A council of barons ruled the country for over half a year until Sigismund was restored to the throne after agreeing to marry Barbara Cillei, the daughter of one of the most powerful Hungarian landowners, Hermann Cillei. Following his liberation, the King still faced revolts in Bosnia, Dalmatia, and Transylvania. Then, in 1403, Ladislas of Naples, the son of Charles of Durazzo who had briefly held the throne of Hungary in 1385, landed on the Dalmatian

---

[90]Panaitescu, ed., *Cronicile slavo-romîne*, p. 6; Mihail Kogălniceanu, *Cronicile României*, vol. I, Bucharest, 1872, p. 136.

[91]Doc. CXLVI, Ioan Bogdan, *Documentele lui Ştefan cel Mare*, vol. II, Bucharest, 1913, pp. 330-336; Doc. 22 in Ion Ionaşcu et al., eds. *Relaţiile internationale ale României*, Bucharest, 1971, pp. 129-132.

[92]N. Iorga, *Acte şi fragmente*, vol. III, Bucharest, 1897, pp. 4-5.

[93]János Bak, "The Late Medieval Period" in Peter F. Sugar, ed. *A History of Hungary*, Bloomington, 1994, p. 55.

coast with the full support of Pope Boniface IX, "to occupy the throne of Hungary and to set right the miserable state of affairs there."[94] By the end of that year, Sigismund had fended off this challenge and pardoned those who had opposed him, finally restoring order in his Kingdom.

The crisis in Hungary had left Mircea without his most important ally against the Turks. As a result, he apparently resumed ties of vassalage to the Ottoman Empire in 1401. Bayezid also had a vested interest in peace along the European borders of his Empire at this time; a new threat from the Orient had arisen to menace the Sultan's Anatolian frontier. Tamerlane (1336-1405), a descendant of the great Ghenghis Khan, had rebuilt the Mongol Empire to include most of Central Asia after he seized the throne at Samarkand in 1369. By the end of the century he had defeated the Golden Horde and threatened Ottoman holdings in Asia Minor. The Mongol advance north of the Black Sea drove Tatar tribes west. Some fled to Moldavia where they fell into slavery. Other tribes came to Wallachia where Mircea allowed them to settle or to pass through the country on their way to Adrianople where they planned to join forces with Bayezid to fight the Mongols.[95] That Mircea facilitated the crossing of Tatar troops destined to supplement the Sultan's army is a reflection of the peaceful relations between Wallachia and the Ottoman Empire at this time. These renewed ties of vassalage are also attested to in a memoir written by the Dominican monk John, the Archbishop of Sultanich in Anatolia, whom Tamerlane had sent to Paris to negotiate an alliance against the Ottomans: "next to the Great Sea, or Pontica, is Wallachia, a large country. It has its own prince, and although the Turk has captured many of them and has made them pay tribute, nevertheless, he has not imposed his rule on this country as he has on the others."[96]

The year 1402 found Manuel II in Paris. He had spent the past two and a half years treating with the leaders of Catholic Europe trying to obtain help to breath new life into his dying Empire, but he had little to show for his efforts. Time was of the essence as the Ottoman noose tightened around the Byzantine

---

[94]Doc. CCCXLVII in Hurmuzaki, ed., *Documente*, vol. I, part. 2, pp. 421-423.

[95]Mustafa A. Mehmet, "Aspecte din istoria Dobrogei sub dominaţia otomană," in *Studii*, 18:5 (1965), pp. 1102-1103.

[96]*Călători străini*, vol. I, p. 39.

capital and it increasingly seemed as if the Emperor would never again see his homeland. Constantinople stood on the brink of capitulation. But just when things looked their bleakest, the relief that Manuel had desperately sought arrived like manna from heaven. On July 28, 1402, the armies of Tamerlane and Bayezid met in battle on the Chubuk plain near Ankara. Some have claimed that Mircea, as a vassal of the Sultan, participated in person alongside Bayezid's forces at the battle of Ankara, but it has been demonstrated that the evidence to support this claim is derived from a translation of an Ottoman chronicle that confuses the Wallachian Prince with Serbian ruler Stephen Lazarević,[97] known to have fought bravely alongside the Sultan against Tamerlane. Although there is no compelling evidence that Mircea personally took part in the battle, Orudj bin Adil recorded that when Bayezid set out to confront Tamerlane, "he brought with him numerous soldiers, among them *Akingi* and *Cerahori* [mercenaries], as well as soldiers from Wallachia. He gathered the army of Laz and the Serbian one, also taking along Laz-oglu [Stephen Lazarević]."[98] This well-informed Ottoman chronicler, who was born around the time of these events, clearly distinguishes between the Wallachian and Serbian troops in the Sultan's army, thus providing convincing evidence that Mircea at least sent a contingent to fight alongside the Ottomans at Ankara. In any event, the battle resulted in an overwhelming victory for Tamerlane. Bayezid himself fell captive and in one swift blow the Mongol ruler brought the mighty Ottoman Empire to its knees. Chalkokondyles could only explain the shocking Turkish defeat by saying that "Bayezid, having achieved unmeasured power, was humbled by God so that he would not continue with thoughts of such great power."[99] The blockade of Constantinople dissipated almost immediately. Tamerlane's victory postponed the fall of Byzantium to the Turks for another half a century. Bayezid committed suicide in captivity in March of the following year and a civil war broke out among his sons, each of whom sought to impose his rule over remnants of the Empire. Manuel II, having received the welcome news of the Ottoman defeat while in Paris, made

---

[97]Aurel Decei, "A participat Mircea cel Bătrân la lupta de la Ankara?" in *RIR*, VII (1937), p. 355.

[98]*Cronici turceşti*, vol. I, p. 49.

[99]Chalcocondil, *Expuneri istorice*, p. 79 (II, 109).

his way back to the imperial capital, where he arrived in June 1403, still hopeful that a concerted Christian military effort could be organized to finish off the Turks.

The outcome of the battle of Ankara abruptly terminated Mircea's dependence on the Ottomans. He saw an opportunity to recoup some of his losses of the previous decade, but with the unstable political situation in the region, Wallachia still needed a reliable ally. With Hungary in disarray, Poland represented the most viable alternative. The death of Hedwiga in 1399 had destabilized Poland, but the situation had greatly improved by 1401 when Vladislav I concluded an alliance with his cousin Vitold, Grand Duke of Lithuania. Alexander the Good, Mircea's protégé in Moldavia, had renewed that Principality's ties of vassalage to the Polish Crown on March 12, 1402,[100] and he now facilitated a reconciliation between Mircea and Vladislav. They revived their previous alliance and, in 1403, Mircea granted trade privileges in Wallachia to merchants from Lemburg and throughout Poland and Lithuania.[101]

The Wallachian Prince now moved to take advantage of the situation in the Danube basin where the troubles in Hungary and the Ottoman Empire had created a power vacuum. When war broke out between Genoa and Venice in 1403, Mircea sided with the Venetians who had previously aided his father Radu in his war with Louis the Great. Since their long war with Dobrotitsa, the Genoese had controlled Kilia (Lykostomo), the strategically important fortress and port city located on the northern branch of the Danube River near the outlet to the Black Sea.[102] Mircea now seized Kilia from the Genoese. Meanwhile, at the beginning of 1404, the Venetians destroyed the Genoese fleet at Mondon, thus assuring that Kilia remained in Wallachian hands. Mircea also appears to have recovered Turnu around this time and worked to secure the left bank of the Danube, constructing a stone fortress at Giurgiu.

---

[100]Doc. 171 in Costăchescu, *Documentele moldovenești*, vol. II, pp. 621-622.

[101]Doc. DCLII in Hurmuzaki, *Documente*, vol. I, part. 2, pp. 824-825; and Doc. 1 in Hajdeu, *Archiva istorică*, vol. I, part. 1, Bucharest, 1865, pp. 3-4; see also Doc. 7 in Ionașcu, et al. eds, *Relațiile internaționale*, pp. 94-95.

[102]Nicolae Iorga, *Studii istorice asupra Chiliei și Cetății Albe*, Bucharest, 1899, pp. 60, 274.

Now that the Ottoman threat had diminished with the defeat and capture of Bayezid at Ankara, little interest could be roused in the West for a campaign that Manuel II hoped would deliver a coup de grâce to the forces of Islam. Nor did Tamerlane express any interest in finishing off the Ottomans. The Mongol Emperor returned several Anatolian states such as Karaman and Sinope to their former rulers, but he left the Ottomans many of their possessions in western Anatolia over which he claimed suzerainty; of Bayezid's sons, Isa was appointed Emir of Brusa, while Mehmed continued to govern Manisa, just as he had done under his father. Another of Bayezid's sons, Suleiman, escaped after the battle of Ankara and made his way to Adrianople where, with the help of Grand Vezir Ali Cenderli, he proclaimed himself Sultan and effectively ruled the European portion of the Empire. To consolidate his position, Suleiman came to an agreement with the Byzantines; prior to Ankara, the Emperor had been a vassal of the Sultan, now Suleiman accepted Manuel II as his sovereign. The peace was sealed by the newly-proclaimed Sultan's marriage to the Emperor's daughter. In addition, Suleiman released Byzantine prisoners and restored Thessalonika, certain Aegean Islands, and Black Sea ports up to Varna to the Greeks. For his part, Manuel II, realizing that he could not expect significant aid from the West, embraced this arrangement which offered the Empire a new lease on life.

Although now an ally of Byzantium, Suleiman's relations with other Christian states in Southeastern Europe, most notably Wallachia, deteriorated. Disputes along the Danube, raids by the *Akingi*, and Mircea's desire to recover lost territories such as Dobrudja, led to renewed conflicts. Because of the escalating Ottoman peril, Mircea again drew closer to Hungary where Sigismund now had firm control of the situation; in the spring of 1404, the King wrote to Philip, the Duke of Burgundy, telling him, among other things, that the Voivode of Wallachia had reported new victories against the Turks.[103] To strengthen ties between Hungary and Wallachia, the King placed the fortress of Bran under Mircea's authority;[104] Sigismund probably did this to compensate for the fact that help from Hungary had been slow to arrive in

---

[103]Doc. CCCLIII in Hurmuzaki, *Documente*, vol. I, part. 2, p. 429.

[104]Ioan Moşoiu, *Branul şi Cetatea Branului*, Bucharest, 1930, p. 14; Panaitescu, *Mircea cel Bătrân*, pp. 194-194.

Wallachia on previous occassions. Persistant difficulties in financing the defense of the Kingdom's southern border also compelled the King to entrust Mircea with the maintenance of this strategic point. Today, the picturesque Bran Castle is one of Romania's most frequented tourist attractions, where visitors from all over the world are invariably deceived into believing that it is Dracula's castle. In reality, although Mircea controlled the fortress throughout the remainder of his reign, neither his son, Vlad Dracul, nor grandson, Vlad the Impaler, ever had possession of Bran Castle, which had reverted to Hungarian control by the time they ruled Wallachia.

A common interest in opposing Ottoman expansion drew Wallachia and Hungary ever closer. In the fall of 1406, Mircea visited the venerable Abbot Nicodim at Tismana where he granted a diploma confirming the monks's fishing and pasturing privileges. Interestingly, the Prince mentions that he issued the document "as My Majesty was going to Severin to meet with the King, then I arrived at the monastery in the month of November, on the 23nd day, together with all the abbots of the monasteries and all My Majesty's boyars."[105] In frail health, Nicodim was not among those who accompanied Mircea to Severin to meet Sigismund. He died a month later at the monastery he had founded. Undoubtedly, plans for a new campaign against the Turks dominated the agenda of the conference at Severin. Sigismund took several initiatives around this time to prepare for war with the Ottomans. As a defensive measure, he ordered the Saxon cities in Transylvania to build new fortifications or to improve existing ones. The King also drew Bayezid's most dependable Christian ally, Serbian despot Stephen Lazarević, who, along with the Byzantines, had made peace with Suleiman, into the anti-Ottoman alliance. Finally, he appointed one of his most reliable and trustworthy lieutenants, Filippo Scolari, as count of Temes, making him responsible for the defense of Hungary's frontier with the Ottomans.

Born in Italy in 1369, Filippo Scolari, better-known as Pippo de Ozora or Pippo Spano, came from a poor noble family of Florentine merchants. He studied in Germany and then travelled to Hungary as an assistant to the Italian merchant Lucca della Pecchia who procured luxury goods for the Bishop of Strigoniu, the highest ranking Catholic Church official in the Kingdom. As

---

[105]Doc. 32 in *DRH, B*, vol. I, pp. 70-71.

Florence held a virtual monopoly over commerce in Hungary during this time, it is no surprise that young Pippo remained there to handle the Bishop's accounting matters. At Strigoniu, in 1395, he met the King. Impressed by the young Italian, Sigismund took Pippo to his court where he experienced a meteoric rise. In 1398, he married Barbara de Ozora, the daughter of a leading Hungarian nobleman, and began calling himself Pippo de Ozora. Fiercly loyal to his benefactor, Pippo helped to free the King from prison and later saved Sigismund's life during the rebellions of 1401-1403. In recognition of his services, in 1404 the King named him Count of Temes and in 1408 Ban (in Hungarian, *ispan*) of Severin, from which his sobriquet, Spano, is derived. He went on to accumulate numerous other titles and he became a member of the regency council that governed Hungary during Sigismund's absence. He promoted Italian culture in Hungary. The Italian painter Masolino (1383-c. 1447) figured among those who spent time at his court. He also introduced Italian architectural designs in the churches and fortresses he built. A highly intelligent man with a talent for foreign languages, Pippo Spano was also a capable military leader; in 1407-1408 he distinguished himself in the campaign against the Turks in Bosnia.[106]

Sometime after his meeting with Sigismund at Severin, probably in coordination with the Hungarian offensive in Bosnia, Mircea launched an attack on Ottoman positions along the left bank of the Danube, recapturing the stronghold of Silistra and most of Dobrudja north of Varna. Suleiman's position had become vulnerable after the death in 1407 of his gifted Grand Vezir Ali Cenderli, the power behind the throne and the man responsible for preventing a deblace and holding the European portion of the Empire together following the disaster at Ankara. A Greek inscription from 1408 found in the city recalls how Mircea "liberated Silistra from the Turks."[107] The Wallachian

---

[106]Ioan Haţegan, "Banatul şi începuturile luptei antiotomane," in *RdI*, 31:6 (1978), pp. 1027-1031; Adolf Ambruster, "Un aliat italian al domnilor români: Pippo Spano," in *MI*, XI:2 (1977), p. 43.

[107]Quo. *Istoria Românilor*, vol. IV, p. 187; Anca Ghiată, "Aspecte ale organizării politice in Dobrogea," in *RdI*, 34:10 (1981), p. 1888; and Andrei Pippidi, "Sue une inscription grecque de Silistra," in *RESEE*, XXIV (1986), pp. 323-332 who argues that Mircea recovered Silistra in 1403 and that it remained under Wallachian rule until 1419.

Prince hoped to recover the lands of Dorbotitsa which he considered his rightful inheritance; the capture of Silistra was a step in this direction. It soon became apparent that significant help from Hungary to achieve these objectives was not forthcoming. Affairs in the West preoccupied Sigismund. In addition, Hungary once again began to press its claim to Severin, long a source of dispute between the two neighboring countries. As a result, Mircea abandoned his alliance with Sigismund. The break occurred at some point during 1408. In December of that year, Sigismund established a new crusading society, the Order of Dragon. The 24 founding members included Pippo de Ozora and Serbian despot Stephen Lazarević, both key figures in the struggle against the Ottomans. Mircea is notably absent from the list. The only plausible explanation for this is that the King of Hungary and the Prince of Wallachia were no longer in good relations at this time. Had things stood differently, Mircea may have become the original Dracula. Another indication of this change is that earlier, in 1408, the King regarded Kilia, which Mircea controlled, as a reliable base against the Turks; after the break, Sigismund began making plans to conquer the strategic Danubian port.[108] But the King was increasingly drawn away from affairs in Southeastern Europe following his election as Holy Roman Emperor in 1410.

The alliance with Hungary having failed, Mircea sought security by renewing ties with its rival, Poland. Through his aunt, the Bulgarian Tsarina Ana, wife of Stratimir of Vidin, Mircea was a distant relative of the Polish King via the latter's marriage to his first wife, Hedwiga.[109] In an undated letter to Vladislav I, Mircea refers to him as his "parent" (in Slavonic, *roditel*), a term of respect used to reflect virtually any degree of kinship, and added, "I am yours, and my children, as many as there are, are your children and grandchildren as they are mine."[110] In 1409, the Wallachian Prince renewed trade privileges for merchants from Lemberg and throughout Poland and Lithuania.[111] On February 6, 1410, Vladislav Jagiełło validated his previous

---

[108] Florin Constantiniu and Serban Papacostea, "Tratatul de la Lublău (15 marie 1412)" in *Studii*, XVII:5 (1964), p. 1138.

[109] Pavel Chihaia, *Din cetățile de scaun ale Țării Românești*, Bucharest, 1974, p. 182.

[110] Doc. DCLIII in Hurmuzaki, *Documente*, vol. I, part. 2, p. 825.

[111] Annex II in Panaitescu, *Mircea cel Bătrân*, p. 353.

treaty with Mircea.[112] They concluded a new agreement on May 17, 1411, while Mircea inspected his recently-constructed fortress at Giurgiu and closely monitored the situation south of the Danube, where his protégé Musa had recently seized power, pledging mutual assistance against "the raids and hostile attacks of the King of Hungary, his vassals, or any of his subjects."[113] The new theater of war between Hungary and Poland was in the north where, beginning in 1409, the Teutonic Knights, aided by Sigismund, fought against Vladislav I and his Lithuanian allies. The decisive battle in this conflict took place at Tannenberg (Grünwald) on July 15, 1410, where the Poles won a great victory; they decimated the Knights's cavalry and the Grand Master himself laid dead on the battlefield before Sigismund's troops could arrive to help their allies. As a result of this victory, Lithuania, fearing that Poland had now grown too strong, began to assert its independence. With their alliances in disarray, Poland and Hungary reached a stalemate and returned to the negotiating table.

With Hungary and Poland at war in the north, Mircea faced the Ottoman threat alone. Suleiman continued his policy of hostility toward Wallachia and sanctioned frequent raids by the *Akingi* against the Principality. Unable to obtain help from European states, Mircea renewed his contacts with rulers along the Black Sea coast of Anatolia, especially those of Karaman and Sinope, who had a common interest in opposing Ottoman aggression. With the civil war between Bayezid's sons now in full swing, the wily Prince sought to turn the situation to his advantage.

When Mircea began his diplomatic offensive, the Ottoman Empire was split in two; Mehmed, who had defeated his brother Isa, ruled in Rum and Suleiman in Rumelia. Another of Bayezid's sons, Musa, had been captured with his father at the battle of Ankara. Tamerlane freed Musa when Bayezid committed suicide and allowed him to take his father's body to Brusa for proper burial. Musa allied with his brother Mehmed for a time, but later fled to Karaman where he awaited an opportunity to stake his own claim. Meanwhile, Suleiman, claiming to be the one true Sultan, attacked Mehmed and the two struggled for control of Asia Minor.

---

[112]Annex III in Panaitescu, *Mircea cel Bătrân*, p. 354.

[113]Doc. 115 in *DRH, D*, pp. 186-187.

According to the Ottoman chronicler Mehmed Neshri, Mircea "very much
weakened by the *Akingi* in Rumelia," sent emissaries to Karaman in 1409 and
began negotiations with Musa, offering to support him against Suleiman.[114]
Ottoman sources maintain that the initiative belonged to Mircea. Another
chronicler, Kodja Husein, cites a fanciful letter the Wallachian Prince
purportedly sent to Musa at Karaman: "Upon your fortunate arrival, I will hand
over to you all my wealth, and I have a daughter, as beautiful as the moon, and
she will be your slave, and we will serve you with all we have in my country,
with wealth and with people."[115] Byzantine chroniclers, on the other hand,
claim that Musa initiated the contact. Dukas writes that the Ottoman prince
crossed the Black Sea to Wallachia and "Meeting there with the Voivode
Mircea, he told him who he was and from where and why he came,"[116] while
Chalkokondyles adds that "Musa came to Wallachia by sea from Sinope. He
negotiated with Mircea, offering him land and revenues in exchange for
help."[117] If Musa came seeking Mircea's assistance, then it is likely that he was
still acting in concert with his brother Mehmed at this time, for the latter had
much to gain by attacking Suleiman in Europe so as to force his withdrawal
from Anatolia. But, although Mehmed stood to benefit as well, the most
probable explanation remains that Mircea encouraged Musa's ambition and
enticed him to come to Wallachia. The Prince had used his diplomatic ties with
the emirs along the Anatolian coast in the past to coordinate anti-Ottoman
strategy. Also, the marriage of Musa to one of Mircea's daughters, recorded
by Ottoman chroniclers, is confirmed in a letter from 1411 sent by the Patriarch
of Constantinople, Eftemie II, to a Russian prince.[118] Finally, with Hungary
and Poland at war, Mircea needed help against Suleiman; what better way to
obtain it than to find an ally in the Turkish camp.

Having accepted Mircea's proposal, Musa left Karaman and "returned to
Isfendiar [Sinope]," Neshri continues, "and from there, taking a ship, he
crossed to Wallachia. The Bey of Wallachia, being very pleased, received him

[114]*Cronici turceşti*, vol. I, p. 114.

[115]*Cronici turceşti*, vol. I, p. 443.

[116]Ducas, *Istoria turco-bizantină*, Bucharest, 1958, p. 122 (XIX, 1).

[117]Chalcocondil, *Expuneri istorice*, p. 114 (IV, 171).

[118]N. Şerbănescu and N. Stoicescu, *Mircea cel Mare*, Bucharest, 1987, p. 30.

with respect and honor and feasted him and gave him many gifts. After this, giving him his daughter, he made him a prince in his land.[119] While negotiations to bring Musa to Wallachia were underway, the Byzantines, Suleiman's staunch allies, got wind of Mircea's plans and conspired against the Wallachian Prince. Chalkokondyles attests to the hostile relations between Mircea and the Greeks at this time, revealing that "here in Byzantium, they received a son of Mircea and they promised him that they would bring him to the throne with the help of their friend Suleiman."[120] The son referred to here is probably one of the several illegitimate children spawned by Mircea whom Chalkokondyles tells us "had relations often with his mistresses."[121] In any event, Mircea foiled the plot to oust him by seizing the initiative. As preparations for the offensive against Suleiman progressed, the Prince intensified his diplomatic efforts to gain support for his plans to intervene in the Ottoman civil war, sending emissaries to Venice in May 1410;[122] Mircea had been on good terms with the Republic of St. Mark since their collaboration in the war against Genoa in 1403-1404. Meanwhile, Serbian Despot Stephen Lazarević also pledged military assistance.

"Mircea gladly received Musa," Chalkokondyles continues, "and provided for his needs and gave him an army, including Wallachians led by Dan [Mircea's nephew]."[123] These preparations did not go unnoticed. Dukas relates that "The western pashas, who defended the areas along the Danube, found out about Musa's arrival in Wallachia and wrote to Suleiman about what happened and told him that if he would not quickly cross over to the Thracian parts, Musa will take the West as his inheritance."[124] When everything was ready, Musa and Dan traversed the Danube at Mircea's stronghold of Silistra, where there were no Ottoman forces to hinder their crossing, and invaded Rumelia in early summer of 1410. They encountered only token resistance as they advanced south to Adrianople and joined with Stephen Lazarević; Musa then entered the

---

[119]*Cronici turceşti*, vol. I, p. 114.

[120]Chalcocondil, *Expuneri istorice*, p. 114 (IV, 171).

[121]Chalcocondil, *Expuneri istorice*, p. 64 (II, 78).

[122]Panaitescu, *Mircea cel Bătrân*, p. 317.

[123]Chalcocondil, *Expuneri istorice*, p. 114 (IV, 171).

[124]Ducas, *Istoria turco-bizantină*, p. 122 (XIX, I).

Ottoman capital where he proclaimed himself Sultan. Meanwhile, Suleiman, heeding the advice of his lieutenants, gathered his army and crossed the Straits back into Europe to confront Musa's challenge. The two armies met in battle at Cosmedion, in the Golden Horn, on June 15, 1410. Suleiman defeated Musa and his allies and drove them back to Adrianople where he won another victory over his brother on July 11 and recaptured the capital. Musa and Dan now fled to Wallachia to regroup and to consult with Mircea.

In the months that followed, Musa courted the beys and pashas of Rumelia from his base in Wallachia, determined to win them over to his cause before launching a new attack. He found a receptive audience. The loss of Ali Cenderli had taken its toll. Chalkokondyles explains that "Suleiman became apathetic and was only interested in partying, so the state of affairs became unstable. Thus, his highest officials became disappointed in him.... And the Greeks sent emissaries to him and they advised him not to neglect everything and to party all the time as his throne is in danger and not at all secure in the face of his brother. But he did not pay attention to any of this."[125] Having secured important allies in Suleiman's camp, Musa, with Mircea's support and with Dan and a contingent of Wallachian troops at his side, launched a second invasion of Rumelia in February 1411. Once again, Adrianople was the objective. Musa took the capital with relative ease on February 11 after many of Suleiman's officials abandoned him and went over to his brother. Suleiman fled toward Constantinople to seek help from his Byzantine allies, but he was captured and killed en route. The ruler of the small Principality north of the Danube had successfully placed his candidate on the throne of one of the most powerful empires of his day. Mircea's bold foreign policy initiative had born fruit.

Mircea remained Musa's closest ally throughout the Ottoman prince's brief reign. The Wallachian Prince used his close relations with Venice to mediate a treaty of alliance between the new Sultan and the Republic of St. Mark. A Venetian chronicle records that "This Musa got along better [than other sultans] with the Christians and with the Venetians who regularly came to his

---

[125]Chalcocondil, *Expuneri istorice*, p. 115 (IV, 174).

lands."[126] In recognition of his support, the new Sultan turned over several cities on the left bank of the Danube to the Wallachian Prince.[127]

But victory for Mircea meant defeat for Byzantium. Manuel II lost his closest ally with the death of Suleiman and the crafty Emperor now sought ways to strike back; he opened negotiations with Mehmed who continued to rule the Asian part of Bayezid's former Empire from Brusa. Musa, meanwhile, hoping to deal Byzantium a decisive blow, now laid seige to Constantinople. A decade had passed since Ottoman troops had surrounded the walls of the imperial capital and nearly forced its capitulation, but in the ensuing years the Byzantines had strenghtened their defenses and the city could easily withstand an assault by a Turkish force far less powerful than in the days of Bayezid. Mircea continued to back Musa and Wallachian troops led by his nephew Dan participated in this seige of Constantinople. Under the walls of Byzantium, Dan's own princely ambitions awakened. Dukas records that Mircea's nephew, "found himself with Murad in the expedition against Constantinople and, as one who was prepared for any act of war, he himself accompanied the Turks in reconnaissance and he secretly went about the city." Hoping to obtain Byzantine support, Dan deserted and, "making himself known to the Emperor, he took part in the Byzantine attacks and demonstrated great courage against the Turks."[128] The Byzantine chronicler apparently confuses Murad II's seige of Constantinople, which began in June 1422, with that of Musa in 1411. But in the summer of 1422 Dan arrived in Hungary from where, with Sigismund's help, he prepared to take the Wallachian throne from Radu Praznaglava who enjoyed Ottoman support. In addition, all the evidence we possess ties Dan to Musa, not to Murad. The would-be Prince remained in Byzantium, which was hostile to Mircea, hoping for an opportunity to press his claim to his father's throne. But the removal of his enemy Musa remained the Emperor's immediate concern. After a debacled attempt to raise up Suleiman's young son Orhan against Musa that ended with Salonika also coming under seige, Manuel II reached an understanding with Mehmed. Aided by the Byzantines, Mehmed crossed the straits into Europe in the summer of 1412 and attacked Musa at

---

[126]Quo. Panaitescu, *Mircea cel Bătrân*, p. 317.

[127]Iorga, *Chestiunea Dunării*, p. 161.

[128]Ducas, *Istoria turco-bizantină*, p. 252 (XXIX, 7).

Adrianople. But the Anatolian ruler met with defeat and hastily retreated to his stronghold in Asia Minor.

Despite this reprieve and Mircea's unwavering support, Musa's hold on Rumelia began to weaken. Relations with Serbia deteriorated when the new Sultan refused to honor promises to Stephen Lazarević to turn over lands in Macedonia. But Musa's domestic policy proved even more damaging. Influenced by the radical Sheik Bedreddin Mahmud, one of the most brilliant intellectual figures of his day, the new Sultan alienated many of the Ottoman elites who had helped him overthrow his brother Suleiman. Musa named Bedreddin *Kadiasker*, a military judge and the highest ranking official in the Ottoman judiciary. The Sheik preached an ideology of social equality and religious tolerance which, together with Musa, he sought to put into practice. This did not sit well with Ottoman aristrocrats who frowned upon Musa's good relations with Christian states such as Wallachia and Venice and rebelled against the new Sultan's practice of confiscating the wealth of large landholders and promoting ordinary men to high positions. These policies created widespread unrest among the Ottoman elites; Chalkokondyles affirms that they "were unhappy with the authoritarian rule of Musa and crossed over to Mehmed."[129] Capitalizing on his situation, Mehmed launched a new invasion of Europe in the summer of 1413. The two brothers met in battle at Çamurlu, not far from Sofia, on July 5. Musa fought bravely, but was vastly outnumbered and Mehmed emerged victorious. Musa fled toward the Danube, hoping to reach Wallachia where, with Mircea's help, he could rebuild his forces, but he was captured, taken to Mehmed, and then strangled.[130] For the first time since the days of Bayezid the Thunderbolt, both the Asian and European parts of the Ottoman Empire were united under a single ruler. The Ottoman civil war had effectively come to an end.

Mircea now faced a precarious situation. Although Musa was captured before he could reach Wallachia, some of the officials loyal to him managed to cross the Danube to safety. Orudj bin Adil records that "Musa had a subject

[129]Chalcocondil, *Expuneri istorice*, pp. 117-118 (IV, 178-179).

[130]Chalcocondil, *Expuneri istorice*, p. 120 (IV, 183).

called Azep who, fleeing, went to Wallachia."[131] Another of those who escaped was Sheik Bedreddin. Having aided and abetted Mehmed's enemies, Mircea realized the need to prepare for renewed Ottoman attacks on his Principality. Already in the summer of 1412, when Mehmed first challenged Musa, the Wallachian Prince had sent emissaries to Hungary to participate at the Congress of Buda to discuss the renewal of his alliance with Sigismund. On this occasion, plans for a new anti-Ottoman campaign were discussed, which included the restoration of Bulgaria, but Mircea had no interest in joining such an effort so long as Musa retained his hold on Rumelia. The events that followed the defeat of the Teutonic Knights at Tannenberg compelled the Wallachian Prince, who as late as May 1411 had renewed his alliance with Vladislav I against the Hungarian King, to seek an accommodation with Sigismund. Negotiations between Poland and Hungary resulted in the Treaty of Lublau, signed on March 15, 1412. This treaty ended the conflict between the rival Kingdoms and established the basis for their future cooperation. A significant clause in the treaty refers to Moldavia. Hungary recognized the preeminence of Polish interests in Moldavia, first established in 1387 when Petru Muşat accepted the suzerainty of the Polish King, but obligated the Principality east of the Carpathians to contribute military support to the anti-Ottoman struggle led by the King of Hungary. In the event of non-compliance, the two regional superpowers secretly agreed to divide Moldavia between them. The agreement does not mention Wallachia as it was an Ottoman ally at this time, but the treaty does stipulate Hungary's claim to Kilia, then in Mircea's possession.[132] Kilia interested Sigismund not only strategically, as a base of operations against the Ottomans, but also economically, because of its importance as an outlet for German merchants from Transylvania to participate in the prosperous eastern trade and to challenge the commercial monopoly in the Orient held by the Venetians with whom Sigismund fought for control of

---

[131]*Cronici turceşti*, vol. I, p. 51.

[132]Doc. CCCCI in Hurmuzaki, ed., *Documente*, vol. I, part 2, pp. 483-487. See also Constantinescu and Papacostea, "Tratatul de la Lublău"; and P.P. Panaitescu, "Legăturile Moldo-Polone în secolul XV şi problema Chiliei," in *Romanoslavica*, III (1958), p. 99.

the Dalmatian coast.[133] In any event, after Musa's defeat Mircea hastened to come to terms with Hungary. The two countries renewed their former agreements and, on August 6, 1413, the Wallachian Prince confirmed trade privileges for merchants from Braşov.[134]

When he resumed the alliance with Hungary, Mircea agreed to send one of his sons as a hostage to Sigismund's court. This was a common practice at the time to ensure the loyalty of a vassal to his suzerain. The term hostage is somewhat misleading; the so-called hostage lived and worked at his sovereign's court and enjoyed all of the honors and privileges due to someone of his rank and stature. The Wallachian Prince chose to send his son Vlad, perhaps not yet in his early teens, to the court of the Hungarian King. A diploma issued by Sigismund on March 19, 1430, makes reference to "Layko [Vlad], son of the late, renowned, and great Mircea, Voivode of our Transalpine land, raised at our court."[135] Although it is possible that young Vlad was sent to the Hungarian court as early as 1404-1408 when Mircea enjoyed good relations with Sigismund, 1413 is a more probable date as the King likely required some guarantee from Mircea after the breakdown of their previous agreement. Vlad presumably adapted easily to his new environment as his mother, Mara, came from a powerful Hungarian landowning family. The experience of growing up at Sigismund's cosmopolitan court certainly benefitted young Vlad and prepared him for his future role as Prince of Wallachia; he had the opportunity to learn foreign languages, participate in Western feudal society, and observe political dealings at the court of one of Christian Europe's most powerful rulers.

As Mircea braced himself for the Sultan's wrath, Mehmed worked to consolidate his hold over the newly-won European portion of his Empire. He rewarded the Byzantines and the Serbs who had helped him to defeat Musa. The new Sultan restored all of the lands and privileges that Suleiman had accorded to the Byzantines and, like his brother, Mehmed also accepted the Emperor as his nominal suzerain. According to Dukas, the Sultan sent

---

[133]Şerban Papacostea, "Kilia et la politique orientale de Sigismund de Luxembourg," in *RRH*, XV:3 (1976), pp. 421-436.

[134]Doc. 120 in *DRH, D*, pp. 197-198.

[135]Doc. 172 in *DRH, D*, pp. 273-274.

emissaries to Manuel II, instructing them to "Go and say to my father, the Emperor of the Romans, that, with the help of God and the collaboration of the Emperor, my father, I have taken my parental inheritance. From now on I am and I will be obedient to him as a son to a father, for I am not ungrateful and I will not appear in the eyes of anyone as an ingrate...".[136] Meanwhile, Mehmed did not forget that Mircea supported Musa against him and determined to punish the Wallachian Prince. Chalkokondyles notes that the Sultan "sent an army against Dacia [Wallachia] and plundered this country. And the Prince of Dacia, sending emissaries to him, concluded a peace treaty on the condition that he bring the tribute that he owed to Emperor Mehmed."[137] The Byzantine chronicler refers here to raids by the *Akingi* which forced Wallachia to resume paying tribute to the Ottomans for the first time since the days of Bayezid the Thunderbolt. Mircea also gave up control of the Ottoman cities on the right bank of the Danube that Musa had granted to him earlier.

While diplomatic maneuvering and the resumption of tribute payments managed to buy Mircea a reprieve from Ottoman assaults, the Prince did not abandon his king-making ambitions. Suleiman's son Orhan, who the Byzantines had originally raised against Musa, fled toward Wallachia after Mehmed's victory, hoping to find support there for his imperial ambitions, but before he could reach the Danube he was captured and brought before his uncle who had him blinded and then sent him to Brusa. Having settled affairs in the Balkans, Mehmed set out against his enemies in Asia Minor, intent on recovering territories lost after the battle of Ankara. Faced with renewed Ottoman aggression, the Emirates on the Anatolian Black Sea coast intensified their long-standing diplomatic contacts with Wallachia and other Christian countries, hoping to find a way to fragment Ottoman power once again. Before long, a new pretender to the Ottoman throne surfaced, claiming to be Mustafa, another son of Bayezid, presumed to have perished at the battle of Ankara.

While Ottoman and Byzantine chronicles, favorable to Mehmed, portray Mustafa as an imposter, it cannot be ruled out that he was truly Bayezid's son. In any event, he managed to present himself as a legitimate contender for the throne. The Anatolian Emirs supported him as an alternative to Mehmed, while

---

[136]Ducas, *Istoria turco-bizantină*, p. 132 (XX, 1).

[137]Chalcocondil, *Expuneri istorice*, p. 120 (IV, 183).

many of those who had backed Musa rallied to him; most important among these was Sheik Bedreddin who seems to be the one who convinced Mustafa to stake his claim. Mehmed Neshri records that Bedreddin boasted: "he is my disciple and he revolts for me."[138] Since the days of Musa, Bedreddin stood at the forefront of a revolutionary religious and social movement. Educated at such important centers of learning as Konya, Cairo, and Mecca, Bedreddin Mahmud was one of the leading scholars of his time, writing numerous books on philosophy, theology, and Islamic law. He preached a form of pantheism and promoted religious tolerance, seeking to break down the barriers between Islam, Christianity, and Judaism; he also advocated the redistribution of wealth and notions of collective property. There can be no doubt that Bedreddin awakened Mustafa's ambitions and that his movement provided the base of power from which the pretender launched his challenge to Mehmed.

By the beginning of 1415, diplomatic efforts to organize support for Mustafa's bid for the throne were in full swing. On January 20, the Venetian Senate received two emissaries from Mustafa, one Turk and one Greek, asking for help against Mehmed. But the Venetians, reluctant to become directly involved in the conflict so as not to jeopardize their commercial interests in the Levant, recommended that Mustafa first obtain the support of their ally Mircea in Wallachia and promised some assistance should he succeed.[139] The Emirs of Anatolia, especially the rulers of Karaman and Sinope, facilitated contacts between Mustafa and Mircea in the spring of 1415, but here again, observes the Ottoman chronicler Idris Bitlisi, Bedreddin played a key role, "as earlier, through his ties to Musa Celebi, he was friends with the Prince of Wallachia."[140] As a result, Mustafa followed in Musa's footsteps; he left Karaman for Sinope and from there traveled by boat to Wallachia. His arrival in the capital of Argeş is recorded in a diploma granted by Mircea confirming ownership of the villages of Beala and Preslop to a boyar named Vlad and his

---

[138]*Cronici turceşti*, vol. I, p. 117.

[139]Iorga, *Acte şi fragmente*, vol. III, pp. 6-7.

[140]*Cronici turceşti*, vol. I, p. 162.

relatives, issued "in the month of June, on the 10th day, in the year 6923 [1415] and indiction 8, at the time when Mustafa Celebi arrived."[141]

Mircea had once more committed himself to the role of king-maker. Chalkokondyles recounts how "Mustafa crossed into Dacia [Wallachia] and, remaining there for a long time with 300 men, he made contact with the leading Turks, negotiating separately with each of them."[142] Mircea placed Wallachian troops at Mustafa's disposal and the pretender soon began leading raids south of the Danube. A report from Ragusa, dated August 18, tells that Mustafa, within two months after his arrival in Wallachia, launched attacks on Bulgaria and had won over two Danubian beys to his cause.[143] But despite some successes, most notably winning over Tineit, the Bey of Nicopolis, to his cause, Mustafa failed to gather the kind of support among the Ottoman elites that Musa had amassed against Suleiman. Chalkokondyles explains that "he did not achieve anything as Mehmed, among other things, was a decent man and he knew how to treat well the leading Turks, being of a gentle nature; and he declared outright that Mustafa is not the true child of Bayezid."[144] Another reason that the Ottoman aristocracy in Rumelia did not flock to Mustafa was their wariness of his association with Bedreddin and the radical reforms advocated by the Ottoman cleric.

Although Mustafa garnered limited support among the Ottoman elites, his ties to the popular Bedreddin won him the loyalty of many lower class Muslims. The threat became so serious that Mehmed abandoned his campaign against Karaman in the early summer of 1416 and prepared to return to Rumelia to quell the unrest; Mehmed now readied for a full-scale attack and ordered the Ottoman fleet to the Danube to prevent Mustafa from crossing. At this point, Venice intervened on behalf of Mircea's protégé. On May 29, 1416, the Venetian fleet commanded by Pietro Loredano entered the Dardanelles and decimated the Turkish fleet at Gallipoli, sinking 27 of their ships; the result of the battle ensured the naval supremacy of the Republic of St. Mark for decades

---

[141]Doc. 38 in *DRH, B*, vol. I, pp. 80-82.

[142]Chalcocondil, *Expuneri istorice*, p. 130 (IV, 203).

[143]Aurel Decei, *Istoria imperiului otoman*, Bucharest, 1978, pp. 78-79; Gemil, *Românii și otomanii*, p. 97.

[144]Chalcocondil, *Expuneri istorice*, p. 130 (IV, 203).

to come.[145] Although it benefitted the plans of Mircea and Mustafa, Venetian involvement was motivated above all by the desire to protect its trade monopolies. They displayed little confidence in the Ottoman pretender's eventual success and by July the Republic had concluded a new peace treaty with Mehmed.

As Mustafa prepared to cross the Danube, Sheik Bedreddin, the true architect of the revolt against Mehmed, joined his disciple in Wallachia. Bedreddin arrived in the Principality after the suppression of a failed revolt in Aydîn intended to keep Mehmed pinned down in Anatolia while Mustafa launched his attack in Rumelia. They now laid plans for a two-pronged offensive in Europe; Mustafa was to lead his forces south to Thessaly, while Bedreddin stirred up unrest in Dobrudja and Bulgaria, with the intention of leading his followers south to join with Mustafa. The Ottoman chronicler Solakzade Mehmed Hemdemi confirms that Bedreddin "had an agreement with Börüklüge [Mustafa]."[146] With preparations now complete, and the Danube crossing secure from interference as a result of the Venetian victory at Gallipoli, Mustafa launched his invasion accompanied by troops provided by Mircea. By now Mehmed had reached Adrianople where, Dukas informs us, "he found out that Mustafa, with Tineit [the bey of Nicopolis], had crossed the Danube, having Wallachians with them and not a small army of Turks and that they were heading for Thessaly."[147] Things did not go well for the pretender. Mehmed inflicted a decisive defeat on the invaders and Mustafa and Tineit fled to Salonika where they sought refuge among Mehmed's Byzantine allies. The Sultan laid seige to the city, demanding that the rebels be turned over to him. This provoked the most serious crisis in Ottoman-Byzantine relations since Mehmed had accepted Manuel II as his suzerain and both sides eagerly sought to avoid a conflict. Dukas purports that the Emperor wrote to the Sultan saying, "I, as you well know, have promised you to be like a father to you and you like a son to me.... I will honor my oaths, but you do not want to honor them.... As for the refugees, there can be no talk and my ears cannot hear of turning them over to you; for this would no longer be the doing of an Emperor, but that of a

---

[145]Decei, *Istoria imperiului otoman*, p. 77.

[146]*Cronici turceşti*, vol. II, ed. Mihail Guboglu, Bucharest, 1974, p. 133.

[147]Ducas, *Istoria turco-bizantină*, p. 154 (XXII, 3).

tyrant... But because I am committed to being as a father to you, I swear to you by God... that the refugee Mustafa and his companion Tineit will be kept under guard for as long as you rule and as long as you live on this earth."[148] Mehmed took the Emperor at his word and averted a crisis.

Although he had eliminated Mustafa as a potential threat, the Sultan's problems in the Balkans persisted. While his disciple was trapped at Salonika, Bedreddin, with Mircea's assistance, had set out from Silistra and, preaching his gospel of social equality, incited the first peasant uprising in Ottoman history. Holding to the plan established with Mustafa, he gathered a ragtag force of some 3,000 men in Dobrudja and Bulgaria and proceeded to march on the Ottoman capital. But these rebels proved no match for veteran Turkish troops. Before reaching Adrianople, Bedreddin was defeated and captured; the Ottoman cleric was then taken before Mehmed at Serres who ordered him hanged on December 16, 1416.[149] Having crushed the rebellion, the Sultan now made plans to deal with Wallachia, where Mircea had been a thorn in his side since the days of Musa.

While the alliance with Hungary had secured Wallachia's northern frontier and allowed Mircea to direct his attention south of the Danube, he received little help from the King in his efforts to overthrow Mehmed I. The Sultan remained on peaceful terms with Serbia, another Hungarian ally, and had taken no aggressive action against the Kingdom. More importantly, Sigismund, having assumed the added role of Holy Roman Emperor, had to set right affairs in Europe before turning his resources against the Turks. Nor were the Byzantines any longer clamoring for aid against the Ottomans thanks to the good relations prevalent between Manuel and Mehmed. Sigismund had by no means abandoned his dream of leading a great crusade against the Turks, but he set it aside for the moment to direct his attention toward healing the divisions within Christian Europe. With this goal in mind, in November 1414, the Holy Roman Emperor announced the convocation of a Church Council at Constance in Switzerland.

---

[148]Ducas, *Istoria turco-bizantină*, pp. 156, 158 (XXII, 5).

[149] Gemil, *Românii și otomanii*, p. 98.

Addressing the Council on July 13, 1415, Sigismund outlined a program intended to bring peace and unity to Europe: to resolve disputes within the Church, such as the movement led by the reformer Jan Huss in Bohemia; to settle the Great Schism; to end the long war between England and France; and, finally, to achieve the union of the Orthodox and Catholic Churches. The participants at the Congress included a delegation from Wallachia, as well as the neighboring Principality of Moldavia. A memoir by Ulrich von Richenthal, a participant at the Council, mentions that a boyar named Dragomir or Tugomir represented Mircea at Constance.[150] This may be Dragomir from Shegarcea, listed among the witnesses in the Prince's diploma dated June 10, 1415, mentioned earlier in connection with Mustafa's arrival in Argeş.[151] Ulrich also noted the presence of delegates from several Wallachian cities with Catholic communities who had accompanied Dragomir: Argeş (Ergx), Câmpulung (Langnaw), Turnu (Zürm), Târgovişte (Newmarckt), and others whose names cannot be identified with certainty.[152] Although the Wallachians played a minor role at the Church Council, their presence there reflected the Holy Roman Emperor's awareness of Wallachia's importance for realizing the objectives he presented before the representatives of Christendom gathered at Constance.

One of the first items on the Council's agenda was to address the crisis in Bohemia, provoked by the growing reform movement led by Jan Huss (1369-1415). A precursor of the Protestant movement launched by Martin Luther a century later, Huss preached against the corruption and abuses of the clergy and advocated a return to Christianity's more humble origins. His movement also embraced social and political aspirations, awakening Czech patriotism in protest against German control of the Church in Bohemia. Huss had been inspired by the Lollard movement in England, led by the Oxford scholar John Wycliffe (c.1320-1384), which had played an important role in the great peasant uprising in England in 1381. Wycliffe condemned the doctrine of transubstantiation and opposed monasticism and the privileges of the

---

[150]Constantin I. Karadja, "Delegaţii din ţara noastră la conciliul din Constanţa (în Baden) în anul 1415," in *ARMSI*, series III, VII (1927), p. 63.

[151]Doc. 38 in *DRH, B*, vol. I, pp. 80-82.

[152]Annex in Karadja, "Delegaţii din ţara noastră la conciliul din Constanţa," p. 82.

priesthood and the Church hierarchy, arguing that individuals had direct access to God; as a result, he favored the translation of the Bible into the vernacular. The Czech reformer developed these ideas to the great consternation of the religious and secular leaders of Europe. With the memory of the violent popular uprising in England still vivid, the hierarchs of Christendom resolved to put a quick end to the stirrings in Bohemia. Huss accepted an invitation to discuss his views on Church reform before the Council after having received a personal guarantee of safe conduct from Sigismund, but the overture was merely a ruse. After his arrival at Constance, Church officials seized Huss, placed him on trial for heresy, and condemned him to burn at the stake. They naively believed that his execution would stifle the threat he represented to the political and religious establishment.

The next task before the Council was to restore unity within the Catholic Church by ending the Great Schism. With rival popes in Rome and Avignon since 1378, the Council of Pisa had tried to resolve the dispute in 1409 by electing a new pontiff, but in the end the rift only deepened as the appearance of a third Pope further divided Catholic Europe. On this issue the efforts of the Council of Constance proved more fortuitous. The delegates representing the rival factions set aside their differences and, with the election of Martin V as Pope in 1417, the Great Schism came to an end.

The drive for Christian unity also entailed efforts to heal the schism between the Catholic and Orthodox Churches that had divided Christianity since the Pope and the Patriarch had excommunicated one another in the eleventh century. The Council of Pisa had taken a step in this direction when it elected a Greek Pope, Alexander V, on June 5, 1409. On Christmas day of that year, Byzantine Emperor Manuel II had written to the new Pope, expressing his conviction that a union of the two Churches might now be possible.[153] Such hopes quickly vanished with the death of Alexander in May of the following year and the election of the depraved John XXIII as his successor. By the time the Council of Constance took up the question of reuniting the Catholic and Orthodox Churches, Manuel II enjoyed excellent relations with Sultan Mehmed I and Church unity, an idea abhorred in the Orthodox world since the sack of Constantinople in 1204, did not rank high on the

---

[153]Minea, *Principatele române şi politica orientală a împăratului Sigismund*, p. 144.

Emperor's agenda. But Manuel was a shrewd ruler and the vicissitudes of politics had taught him always to keep his options open. While he hesitated to commit to the union of the Churches, the Emperor proposed that Catholic wives be found for his sons John and Theodore as a first step in this direction. While the Greeks skirted the issue, the Catholics, as demonstrated by the condemnation of Huss at the outset of the Council, showed no interest in compromise or reform, thereby impeding any sincere effort at restoring unity between the two Churches. Richenthal places the blame for the failure to make headway on this question at Constance squarely on the shoulders of the Roman Church: "If the Catholic Church would have reformed then," he wrote in his memoir, "the Orthodox Church would have united with her and the schism between East and West would have thus come to an end."[154]

Despite these setbacks, the Council of Constance did take a symbolic step toward the union of the Eastern and Western Churches. The highest-ranking Orthodox prelate to make the journey to Switzerland was the Metropolitan of Kiev, Gregory Ţamblac, who had been sent to the Council by his sovereign, Grand Duke Vitold of Lithuania, an active proponent of Church unity. Tamblac was a Bulgarian cleric, born and educated at Trnovo where he studied under the venerate Patriarch Evtimiy. After the fall of Bulgaria in 1393, he went to Serbia and then to Constantinople where entered the service of the Patriarch. When Constantinople formally recognized the Church in Moldavia at the beginning of Alexander the Good's reign, Ţamblac was sent to the Principality to oversee its organization. He remained in Moldavia for several years at the Monastery of Neamţ, the most important religious center in the Principality during this period, and gained a reputation as an important theologian. At some point he entered into a dispute with his superiors at Constantinople. He then went to Lithuania where Vitold had him invested as Metropolitan of Kiev.[155] Tamblac arrived at Constance on February 17, 1418, as the Council neared its close. Backed by the Grand Duke of Lithuania and the King of Poland, he formally submitted the Orthodox Church in the lands ruled by Vitold and Vladislav to the Church of Rome in a solemn ceremony in

---

[154]Quo. Karadja, "Delegaţii din ţara noastră la conciliul din Constanţa," p. 77.

[155]P.P. Panaitescu, *Alexandru cel Bun*, Bucharest, 1933, pp. 16, 18.

the presence of Sigismund of Luxemburg on February 25.[156] Nevertheless, this union was symbolic and fleeting. The Council registered no significant progress in bridging the gulf between Orthodoxy and Catholicism.

Although the Council had ended the Great Schism, it could not heal the divisions within Catholic Europe. Sigismund, despite travelling to London and Paris, failed to mediate an end to the conflict between England and France, and the Hundred Years' War dragged on until 1453, the year Constantinople finally fell to the Turks. Nor did the burning of Huss end the dissension in Bohemia. The Hussite movement was driven underground for a time, but in 1419 it erupted into a full-scale revolt against imperial and papal authority that would preoccupy the Emperor until the end of his reign. Sigismund had intended for the Council of Constance to remedy the ills plaguing Christianity in hopes that he could then organize a great crusade to banish the Turkish infidels from Europe and eventually from the Holy Land as well. In this regard, the Council proved an utter failure. For Wallachia it meant that no grand coalition would materialize to remove the imminent danger posed by the Ottoman presence along the Danube.

The failure of Mircea's plans to oust Mehmed now left Wallachia exposed to the Sultan's fury. With the Council of Constance and efforts to mediate the conflict between England and France preoccupying Sigismund, no significant Hungarian assistance could be expected to help defend against the inevitable attack. In addition, Mircea's most important Anatolian allies had also submitted to Sultan. Once again, Wallachia stood alone against the might of the Ottoman Empire. Mehmed, meanwhile, having executed the rebel leader Bedreddin and having reached an agreement with Manuel II to neutralize Mustafa, now prepared to lead his armies, which included contingents from Karaman and Sinope, north against Wallachia at the beginning of 1417.

Mehmed did not set out on a campaign of conquest against the Principality north of the Danube, but rather on a punitive expedition. Dukas specifies that the Sultan intended to punish Mircea for his support of Mustafa and that he

---

[156]Constantin I. Karadja, "Portretul și stema lui Grigorie Țamblac," in *AARMSI*, series III, XXVI (1943- 1944), p. 145.

"plundered and burned and caused great damage."[157] The Ottomans had no strategic or military interest in conquering Wallachia at this time. The objectives of the campaign were to recover Dobrudja and to secure the Danube border against further attacks, to punish Mircea for his aiding Mehmed's opponents, and to force Wallachia once again to recognize Ottoman suzerainty and to resume the payment of annual tribute to the Porte. To achieve these goals, the Sultan's army seized Dobrudja and dispersed along the Danube, attacking strategically important fortresses held by the Wallachians. One by one, the Danubian citadels of Isaccea, Ieni-Sale, Silistra, and Turnu fell into Turkish hands. Dobrudja remained under Ottoman rule for the next 460 years. Meanwhile, according to an anonymous Ottoman chronicle, "Sultan Mehmed stopped on the banks of the Danube, besieged the fortress of Giurgiu, and sent the *Akingi* into Wallachia. They gathered much plunder,"[158] and, the Turkish chronicler Sa'adeddin adds, "captured strong boys and beautiful young girls."[159] Mircea could do little to oppose the numerically superior Ottoman forces attacking from several directions. He retreated before the invaders so as the keep his army intact, taking refuge in the mountains.

His position now untenable, another Ottoman chronicler, Kodja Husein, records that Mircea "sent a letter of submission and apology, together with tribute for three years. He also sent along the renowned emir Minnet-bey, who was a man of Musa Celebi."[160] Minnet-bey is probably the official Orudj bin Adil refers to as Azep, a name simply meaning military leader. While it is possible that Mircea sent Minnet-bey as an emissary to negotiate on his behalf, it is more likely that Mehmed demanded that he hand over Musa's adjutant to eliminate another potential threat. By sending tribute for three years, Mircea compensated the Sultan for the period since 1414 when he had last paid tribute. In so doing, Ashik-Pasha-Zade writes that the Wallachian Prince "completely

---

[157]Ducas, *Istoria turco-bizantină*, pp. 160 (XXII, 6).

[158]Quo. N. Iorga, "Cronicele turceşti ca izvor pentru istoria românilor," in *ARMSI*, series III, IX (1928-29), p. 5.

[159]*Cronici turceşti*, vol. I, p. 307.

[160]*Cronici turceşti*, vol. I, p. 445.

submitted and sent his sons to serve at the Porte."[161] The sons Mircea handed over to the Sultan as hostages to guarantee his future good conduct were presumably Radu and Alexander. Having achieved the objectives of his campaign, Mehmed now adopted the added title of *Gazi*, meaning warrior for Islam; prior to setting out against Wallachia, the Sultan had not led his armies against a Christian state, a prerequisite to earn this designation.[162] Mircea, having failed in the role of king-maker and lacking outside help to continue the anti-Ottoman struggle, now had to accept the inevitable and to resume his status as a vassal of the Sultan. In so doing, he protected the Principality from unauthorized Turkish raids and brought peace to his land.

During Mircea's long reign, the organizational structure and administrative apparatus of the Principality reached maturity. Like his predecessors, he also paid great attention to the Church, the backbone of the state. He confirmed the possessions and privileges of existing monasteries such as Tismana, Vodița, Codmeana, and Snagov, and added to these. Tismana, founded by Nicodim during the reigns of Vladislav and Radu, remained the most important monastery in Wallachia. Mircea's generous donations to Nicodim's monastery included several villages, with exemptions from royal taxes and works, mills, including that "which My Majesty's mother, Princess Kalinikia, requested to the monastery at Bistrița, which previously belonged to the Archimandrite Basea," and revenues due to the royal treasury from the newly-established copper mines at nearby Bratilova leased to Chiop Hanosh.[163] Monasteries built during Mircea's reign included Cozia, Bradeț, Vishina, Dealul, Glavcioc, Strugalea, Govora, Bolintin, and Săracinești. Of the monasteries raised by Mircea, Cozia was far and away the most important. In his first diploma for the newly-established monastery, dated May 20, 1388, the Prince declared that "My Majesty decided to raise from its foundation a monastery in the name of the Holy Trinity... at the place called Călimănești on the Olt, which was previously the village of My Majesty's boyar Nan Uboda, who with love and

---

[161]*Cronici turcești*, vol. I, p. 85; Mehmed Neshri also records that Mircea sent his sons to serve at the Porte, *ibid*, p. 116.

[162]Nagy Pienaru, "Relațiile lui Mircea cel Mare (1386-1418) cu Mehmed I Celebi (1413-1421)," in *RdI*, 39:8 (1986), p. 784.

[163]Doc. 14 in *DRH, B*, vol. I, pp. 33-36.

Mural painting depicting Mircea the Old and his son Michael
from the Monastery of Cozia

with zeal, respecting the wishes of My Majesty, donated it to the afore-mentioned monastery." He provided it with several villages, exempted from royal taxes and works, mills, fisheries, annual endowments of food and clothing from the royal reserves, 300 *salase* of Gypsies (meaning approximately 2000 slaves),[164] revenues generated from customs taxes collected at Genune,[165] and exemptions from all customs taxes applicable to the monk's trading activities throughout the country.[166] In May 1413, the Prince commissioned Master Hanosh at Bratilova to forge a bell for the monastery inscribed "in the days of the Great Voivode John Mircea and Voivode Michael."[167] Mircea made Cozia the most important monastery in the land after Tismana. By the mid-fifteenth century, Cozia had surpassed Tismana as the most important monastic center in the land and, after the fall of Constantinople, the abbot of the monastery founded by Mircea on the banks of the Olt became the successor of the Metropolitan of Wallachia.[168]

Following the example of his grandfather and his uncle, Mircea also supported the principal center of Orthodox monasticism at Mount Athos, especially Cutlumuz, which he referred to as "our monastery."[169] Continuing the religious policy of his father Radu, Mircea also fostered the Catholic Church in Wallachia, keeping it independent of the Church in Hungary and directly dependent on the Holy See. Rome continued to appoint Italians to head the diocese in the Principality. As we have seen, the Prince sent a sizeable delegation to participate at the most important Church Council of the epoch at Constance. Mircea also rebuilt the Catholic monastery at Târgoviște that had been destroyed during Bayezid's invasion of Wallachia in 1394, and his

---

[164]Docs. 9, 10, 17, 20, 25, 26, 27, and 28 in *DRH, B,* vol. I, pp. 25-30; 42-45, 47-49, 58-65. A *salasa* was a Gypsy household comprised of a family or an extended family.

[165]Doc. 37 in *DRH, B,* vol. I, pp. 78-80.

[166]Doc. 30 in *DRH, B,* vol. I, pp. 66-67.

[167]Minea, *Principatele române și politica orientală a împăratului Sigismund,* p. 110.

[168]Kurt W. Treptow, *Vlad III Dracula,* Iași, 2000, pp. 90-91.

[169]Iorga, "Muntele Athos în legătură cu țerile noastre," pp. 464-465.

Catholic wife Mara is credited with having helped to raise the Church of St. Mary in the same city.[170]

Limited information has survived about Mircea's family. An undated diploma for the Monastery of Snagov confirms the donation of a village in the Buzau River valley by Mircea's brother *Jupan* Staico;[171] the title *jupan,* implying that he was a high-ranking boyar is derived from the Slavonic word *zupan,* used to designate a leader of village communities. Later documents mention another brother, Stan, who served in the Royal Council under Mircea's sons Radu, Alexander, and Vlad Dracul.

Mircea's wife, Mara, came from the powerful Toma family in Hungary, with extensive holdings in the southwestern part of the Kingdom around Lake Balaton. Mara was a relative of Ladislas de Losoncz, who served as Voivode of Transylvania from 1376 to 1391.[172] Radu the Wise conceivably arranged for the marriage of his younger son to a relative of the influential Transylvanian Voivode during a lull in the conflict with Hungary or as part of a peace accord. On February 2, 1400, Sigismund wrote to Mircea's wife, the Princess of Wallachia, ordering her to rectify abuses committed by the administrators of her estates in the county of Zala against residents of the market town of Kesztel.[173]

At least four sons resulted from Mircea's marriage to Mara — Michael, Radu, Alexander, and Vlad — all of whom ascended to the throne at different times following the death of their father. Mircea had designated his eldest son, Michael, as associate ruler as early as 1391, when he was still a child, bestowing upon him the title of Voivode.[174] He did this to keep the throne within his bloodline and to ensure a smooth transition of power upon his death. As he reached adulthood, Michael took on increasing responsibilities, having his own royal residence at Târgoviște which became the second capital of the

---

[170]Cristian Moisescu, *Tîrgoviște: Monumente istorice și de artă,* Bucharest, 1979, p. 90.

[171]Doc. 34 in *DRH, B,* vol. I, pp. 73-74.

[172]Iosif Pataki, "Ceva despre relațiile Țării Românești cu Ungaria," pp. 427-428.

[173]Annex I in Panaitescu, *Mircea cel Bătrân,* pp. 351-352.

[174]Doc. 15 in *DRH, B,* vol. I, pp. 36-39.

Principality. Many have considered the other sons, Radu, Alexander, and Vlad, as illegitimate because Mircea only mentions Michael in his diplomas and Chalkokondyles asserts that he had several illegitimate children, but this assumption is incorrect. Although they are not mentioned in chancellery documents, there was no established formula at this time for listing all legitimate male offspring in official acts. Michael is mentioned because of his role as associate ruler, not because he is Mircea's only legitimate son. In his letter to King Vladislav of Poland cited earlier, Mircea refers to "my children, as many as there are,"[175] certainly implying the existence of several legitimate male offspring. There is a mistaken belief that both legitimate and illegitimate male children had an equal claim to the throne during this period, but, as we shall see later on, this was not the case at the beginning of the fifteenth century. Furthermore, if Radu, Alexander, and Vlad had been illegitimate, it would have negated their value as hostages. Thus, along with their older brother, Radu, Alexander, and Vlad were legitimate offspring of Mircea and his Catholic Hungarian wife Mara. In addition to these four sons, we also know of two daughters; one, as we have seen, married the Ottoman Sultan Musa, while the other, Anna, married one of the leading nobles of Serbian Despot Stephen Lazarević.[176]

Mircea died on January 31, 1418. The funeral procession carrying the earthly remains of Wallachia's most distinguished ruler since Basarab left the capital of Argeş and made its way to Râmnicu and then up the Olt River valley to the Monastery of Cozia, which he had founded and where he was laid to rest on February 4. Michael succeeded his father as Prince, but the smooth transition of power that Mircea had envisioned proved ephemeral. With the Ottomans and the Hungarians both intent on maintaining Wallachia in their respective spheres of influence, Mircea's successors readily found outside help to press their individual claims to the throne. The lack of primogeniture meant that, from a legal standpoint, each had an equal claim to his father's inheritance, and the neighboring powers did not hesitate to exploit this in their own interest. The stage was now set for a long period of intermittent civil war of which Vlad Dracul would eventually become one of the main protagonists.

---

[175]Doc. DCLIII in Hurmuzaki, *Documente*, vol. I, part. 2, p. 825.

[176]Şerbănescu and Stoicescu, *Mircea cel Mare*, p. 30.

Chapter V

Interregnum

"to appeal to foreigners for assistance... is an excellent prelude to slavery."

— Niccolò Machiavelli, *The Discourses*[1]

Shortly after the death of Mircea the Old, his widow Mara set out for her native Hungary. Although we have no precise information about the scope of her journey, there is enough evidence for us to conjecture that, apart from dealing with affairs on her family estates near Lake Balaton, the dowager Princess frequented the royal court at Buda on a diplomatic mission on behalf of her son Michael for whom closer ties to Hungary were now of vital importance. During her stay in the Hungarian capital, she undoubtedly also spent time with her younger son Vlad, now entering adulthood, a hostage at Sigismund's court for the past several years. Among other things, mother and son probably spoke of Mircea's death and the current state of affairs in the Principality. Mara's return to Wallachia is noted by a scribe in a diploma Michael granted to the monasteries of Cozia and Codmeana on June 22, 1418, confirming all of the donations and privileges previously

---

[1]Niccolò Machiavelli, *The Discourses*, New York, 1986, p. 478.

accorded to them by his father and grandfather, written "at Târgoviște, at the time when Your Majesty's mother, the Princess, came from the Hungarians."[2]

Thanks to Mircea's careful preparations, Michael, who, as associate ruler, had become increasingly involved in affairs of state during the preceding years, assumed the throne upon his father's death without opposition. At the time of his coronation, Mircea's eldest son was in his early thirties. The document mentioned above also tell us that he had two sons, Radu and Michael. We have no information about his wife, but there can be no doubt that the marriage of Mircea's designated heir served political purposes and that his spouse likely came from one of the leading noble families of Hungary or Poland. But despite Mircea's efforts, in anticipation of the day when his son would rule alone, and the veneer of a smooth transition of power, the dissension within the country that Mircea had driven underground after he had regained the throne from Vlad I at the end of 1396 began to resurface. Although he had been destined to rule since birth, Michael lacked his father's political savvy and had to look for outside help to maintain his authority.

The main reason for Mara's visit to Hungary was to secure support for her son from the authorities in Buda. Pro and anti-Hungarian factions had divided the Wallachian nobility, and Oltenia, where Vlad Dan had found a strong base of support two decades earlier, was the focal point of anti-Hungarian sentiment in the country. As tensions mounted after Mircea's death, Michael decided to send his mother, the dowager Princess, to her native Hungary to seek assistance. One of those keenly aware of the danger facing the new Wallachian Prince was Pippo de Ozora, the Count of Temeș, whose lands bordered Oltenia. On June 20, 1418, as Mircea's widow made her way back to Wallachia, Pippo informed Palatine Nicholas Garai, who oversaw the affairs of the Kingdom in Sigismund's absence, that "we have received news that Michael, Voivode of the Transalpine land, faces unrest among the barons and inhabitants of his land and that if this situation continues he is in danger of losing the throne."[3]

---

[2]Doc. 42 in *DRH, B*, vol. I, pp. 86-88.

[3]Quo. B. Iványi, "München levéltárai magyar szempanthól." in *Levéltáry Közlemények*, vol. XII, Budapest, 1934, p. 67.

These internal threats increasingly drove Michael into the Hungarian camp and he became reliant on his larger neighbor to maintain his position. This further widened the divisions within the country and also upset the delicate balance that Mircea had achieved among the powerful neighboring states. His need to draw closer to Hungary led Michael to abandon the peace agreement that his father had concluded with Mehmed I in 1417 and to cease paying tribute to the Sultan. This had inevitable repercussions. It once again exposed the Principality to the Ottoman peril and made its ruler dependent upon Hungarian support to resist the domestic and foreign dangers threatening his hold on the throne.

This dependence on Hungary also left the new Wallachian Prince extremely vulnerable to pressure from the neighboring Kingdom which claimed suzerainty over "the Transalpine land." The fortresses of Bran, which Sigismund had earlier ceded to Mircea, had long represented a major sticking point in relations with Transylvania, especially with the city of Braşov. Merchants from Braşov and the surrounding Bârsa land had been displeased ever since the King had turned over this key citadel to the Wallachian Prince and repeatedly complained to the royal court of abuses committed by officials stationed there by Mircea and Michael. The instability in Wallachia following Mircea's death renewed pressure to return Bran to Hungary. Michael tried to redress the complaints of the Transylvanian merchants by ordering his castellans at the fortress of Dâmbovita and customs officials at Rucăr and Bran, called Terciu in documents of the time, "to stay out of the way of these Braşovians, do not loot them, but take from them only the proper customs tax; even more, be lenient with them.... so that they do not complain anymore to My Majesty's parent [referring here to Sigismund], as they have up to now..."[4] But despite the Prince's efforts, pressure intensified and on June 7, 1419, Sigismund ordered Michael de Nades, Count of the Szecklers, to take possession of the fortress and, "when you take control of the castellans of our aforesaid fortress of Terciu, do not let them ask the aforementioned citizens and guests [merchants from Braşov and the Bârsa land] to pay any customs taxes on their things and their goods for sale or on any other goods of theirs." The King motivated his decision by saying that Mircea and Michael had

---

[4]Doc. 40 in *DRH, B*, vol. I, p. 85.

"deprived them in various ways of their ancient liberties."[5] Sigismund was not, however, unsympathetic to Michael's plight. To ease opposition to the Prince and his pro-Hungarian policy, on September 29, 1419, the King issued an edict of religious toleration for "all those in the land of Ungrovalachia... that their monasteries and all their churches and monks and priests and all the people who live in the country may live according to their faith, but serve us righteously."[6] Interestingly, the document mentions that Agathon, Nicodim's successor as abbot of the Monastery of Tismana, appeared before the Holy Roman Emperor to solicit this decree. The archimandrate of Wallachia's most important monastery, located in Oltenia, the hotbed of anti-Hungarian and anti-Catholic sentiment in the country, would have been a logical choice as an intermediary between Michael and the factions opposing him. Given that Sigismund was a fervent Catholic, determined to crush heresy and to restore unity to Christendom, the magnanimity of this unparalleled gesture can only be explained by his concern over the tense political situation in the Principality. That the King issued such a document, carefully drafted in Slavonic rather than Latin, the official language of the Hungarian chancellery, is indicative of Michael's position as his vassal, a status Mircea had painstakingly avoided, but which his son, out of necessity, assumed, possibly as consequence of Mara's visit to Hungary.

Michael, having thrown in his lot with Hungary and having reneged on his obligations to the Sultan, now faced renewed conflict with the Ottomans. Contemporary Venetian chronicles record a series of battles between the Hungarians and the Turks: "It is heard from the Danube that the Turks fought the Hungarians under Pippo of Florence. The Turks were first defeated... But they returned and defeated the Hungarians..."[7] The Ottoman armies brought with them their own candidate to replace Michael as Prince, his brother Radu, who had remained as a hostage at the Porte since Mircea had made peace with Mehmed I early in 1417. As the rules of succession in Wallachia recognized no concept of primogeniture, even though he was not Mircea's first-born son, Radu had a legitimate claim to the throne and, therefore, he was able to attract

---

[5]Doc. 127 in *DRH, D*, pp. 208-209.

[6]Doc. 128 in *DRH, D*, p. 210.

[7]Quo. N. Iorga, *Studii și documente*, vol. III, Bucharest, 1901, p. IX.

support among dissatisfied elements within the country. But, for the moment, Michael, bolstered by Sigismund's trusted lieutenant Pippo de Ozora, maintained his hold on the throne and the Turks retreated south of the Danube for the winter.

Historians have long held that Mircea's nephew Dan, and not his son Radu, accompanied the Ottoman armies to Wallachia against Michael. This errant conclusion is based on a confused passage in Dukas and a misreading of a fragment from the chronicle of Johannes Thurocz mentioning a war between Mircea and Dan. Scholars interpreted this as a struggle between Michael and Dan II, but a prominent figure mentioned in this account is Stephen de Losoncz, ban of Macva, who died fighting alongside Mircea against Vlad I in 1395.[8] This misinterpretation arose because the chronicler refers to Vlad as Dan, after his father, a practice not uncommon in medieval sources. In addition, there is no documentary evidence to support the conclusion that Dan followed Michael on the throne; the first extant acts emitted by the Wallachian chancellery following Michael's reign are those of Radu II.

The Turks, with Radu at the fore, returned to Wallachia in the spring of 1420. A contemporary Byzantine annal notes "great devastation and plunder committed by the Turks in Wallachia."[9] By summer they had driven Michael from the throne and occupied the Principality, forcing him to take refuge across the border in Transylvania. On July 27, Vladislav I of Poland wrote to Sigismund informing him that the Turks "entered Wallachia full of fury and went throughout the land killing and plundering and subjugated it completely; with grave threats they extracted an oath of allegiance from its inhabitants, took tribute and many gifts, and left it under the threat of their garrisons."[10] The battles continued as Ottoman contingents raided Transylvania and southern Moldavia. By August, Ottoman troops had captured the fortress of Severin from the Hungarians and marched into the Banat. Michael and his

---

[8]Octavian Iliescu, "Emisiuni monetare ale Ţării Româneşti din secolele al XIV-lea şi al XV-lea," in *Studii şi cercetări de numismatică*, vol. II, Bucharest, 1958, p. 320; Viorica Pervian, "Lupta anti-otomană a ţărilor române în anii 1419-1420," in *AAIA, Cluj*, XIX (1976), p. 73.

[9]Quo. Academia Română, *Istoria Românilor*, vol. IV, p. 305.

[10]Quo. Pervian, "Lupta anti-otomană a ţărilor române în anii 1419-1420," p. 71.

Hungarian allies counterattacked. At some point, Mircea's son died in the fighting and, according to Leunclavius, the Turks took his sons Radu and Michael prisoner;[11] they apparently died in captivity for they were never heard from again. Radu II now ruled Wallachia. The fall of the Principality south of the Carpathians into the Ottoman sphere of influence altered Sigismund's plans to open a trade route to the Black Sea along the Danube; on August 25, 1420, the King wrote to the Teutonic Knights that he had abandoned this project because Kilia had fallen to the Turks.[12]

Border wars between the Hungarians and the Ottomans continued throughout the fall of 1420; on October 24 Turkish troops devastated Orăstie across the mountains in Transylvania.[13] While the winter months brought the struggle to a halt, in the spring of 1421 fighting resumed as a large Ottoman force led by Mehmed's son and heir Murad invaded Transylvania through the Bran Pass in early April, burning and looting Brașov and the Bârsa land.[14] During this attack, Radu II presumably recovered the fortress at Bran that Sigismund had withdrawn from Michael two years earlier for in a document issued later that year we find the citadel again in Wallachian hands.[15] The Turkish onslaught caused such great devastation that, on September 5, the King granted Brașov and the surrounding villages of Honigberg (Harman), Petersberg (Petresti), Brenndorf (Bod), Heldsdorf (Halchiu), Weidenbach (Ghimbav), and Wolkendorf (Vulcan) a one year tax exemption, which he extended to ten years on June 4, 1422, after the full extent of the damages became apparent, ordering them to use these revenues to rebuild and to strengthen their fortifications.[16]

As evidenced by the King's letter announcing that Kilia had fallen into Ottoman hands, Hungarian political circles saw Radu II as merely a puppet-

---

[11]N. Iorga, *Istoria Românilor*, vol. IV, Bucharest, 1937, p. 11.

[12]Pervian, "Lupta anti-otomană a țărilor române în anii 1419-1420," p. 74.

[13]Doc. LXVI in Andrei Veress, "Vechi istorici unguri și sași despre istoria românilor," in *ARMSL*, series III, IV (1929), p. 333.

[14]Ibid.; Doc. CCCCXXV in Hurmuzaki, *Documente*, vol. I, part. 2, p. 515.

[15]Doc. 134 in *DRH, D*, pp. 218-220.

[16]Docs. XII-XIV in Hurmuzaki, *Documente*, vol. XV, part 1, Bucharest, 1911, pp. 11-12.

ruler for the Sultan. Sigismund disparagingly dubbed him *Prazna Glava*, a Slavonic expression meaning 'empty-headed' or 'stupid'. But the new Wallachian Prince enjoyed a solid base of support among the native population and proved a more capable ruler than enemy propaganda suggests. In a diploma issued on April 6, 1427, at Câmpulung, when the King had accompanied his armies into Wallachia to drive out Radu, Sigismund himself admitted that "A great number of the inhabitants of our Transalpine land, called Vlachs... sided with Radu Praznaglava and the Turks and turned away, like lost souls, from the path of the true faith."[17]

Although the Hungarian Court refused to recognize the new Prince officially, the Saxons of Braşov and the Bârsa land negotiated with Radu to end the fighting between the neighboring states. Having suffered the wrath of a combined Ottoman-Wallachian invasion the month before, the Saxons came before the Wallachian Prince to purchase peace. In the treaty concluded on May 17, 1421, Radu writes, "My Majesty promises from this day, when the Braşovians *gave us their wealth so as to be peace between us* and to be one country with the country of My Majesty, to live in peace and good understanding with all of Braşov and all of the Bârsa land, and My Majesty promises that their enemies will be the enemies of My Majesty, while the enemies of My Majesty will be the enemies of the Braşovians and of all of the Bârsa land..." As a condition of peace, the Prince ordered the Saxons not to harbor any of his political opponents, most of whom had fled to Hungary: "And do not keep bad people among you," he wrote, "whom My Majesty does not love. They are not to live among you."[18]

To consolidate his hold on the Principality, Radu sent emissaries to King Vladislav of Poland. Conflict between Poland and Hungary had erupted again in 1420 when Sigismund had favored the Teutonic Knights in their renewed clashes with the Poles;[19] Vladislav had countered by aiding the Hussite rebels in Bohemia against him. Vlad I had undertaken a similar diplomatic initiative in 1396, attempting to protect Wallachia from Hungarian aggression by

---

[17]Doc. 157 in *DRH, D*, pp. 251-252.

[18]Doc. 133 in *DRH, D*, pp. 217-218, emphasis added.

[19]Veniamin Ciobanu, *Ţările române şi Polonia*, Bucharest, 1985, pp. 34, 36.

aligning the Poles and the Ottomans against them. Radu's father Mircea had also used alliance with Poland as a counterpoise to Hungary. Now firmly installed on the throne, on June 1, 1421, the new Prince granted a diploma confirming possession of ponds along the Danube from Sapatul to the mouth of the Ialomița River with all their revenues "to the Monastery of Cozia, the burial place of my father, in his eternal memory." This same document shows him as ruler of Wallachia, including the Banate of Severin, as well as Duke of Amlaș and Făgăraș and ruler of the Danube Delta to the Black Sea, implying his possession of Kilia.[20] A second diploma issued shortly thereafter confirmed all of the gifts and privileges with which Mircea had endowed Cozia and its associate monastery Codmeana.[21]

Only days after Radu II concluded his peace treaty with Brașov, an event occurred that upset the delicate political situation in Southeastern Europe. Sultan Mehmed I had spent the spring of 1421 in Rumelia directing military operations against Hungary. When he prepared to cross the straits to Anatolia in early May, Emperor Manuel II personally escorted him and dined with the Sultan as an affirmation of the good relations that continued to exist between the Byzantines and the Ottomans. But soon after, Mehmed died unexpectedly during a hunt when he suffered an attack of epilepsy and fell from his horse. His eighteen-year-old son Murad now assumed the throne, proclaiming himself Sultan. Radu, having worked closely with Murad during the invasion of Transylvania that spring, continued to enjoy Ottoman support.

Despite the transfer of power taking place in the Ottoman Empire, relations between Radu and Transylvania remained peaceful throughout the remainder of 1421. In the fall, two emissaries from Brașov, Revel Hanash and Cîrstea from Râsnov, came to Târgoviște to request that the Prince renew the trade privileges that Mircea had accorded them in 1413. Radu granted their petition on November 21.[22] Around this time, he also sent word to his brother Alexander who had accompanied him from the Porte and now governed the region around Rucăr on his behalf, to enforce the provisions of the trade

---

[20]Doc. 48 in *DRH, B*, vol. I, pp. 95-98.

[21]Doc. 49 in *DRH, B*, vol. I, pp. 98-100.

[22]Doc. 134 in *DRH, D*, pp. 218-220.

agreement. This document, in which Radu addresses his brother as *"Tsar Alexander,"*[23] a title use in Slavonic to refer to sons of princes,[24] is the first mention in historical sources of the future Prince Alexander Aldea.

The personal relationship forged by Mehmed I and Manuel II had maintained peace between their respective Empires for nearly a decade. Now, with the passing of Murad and with Manuel aged and in ill-health, relations between the Turks and Byzantines underwent a dramatic change which also had repercussions for Wallachia. A growing pro-war faction in Constantinople led by the Emperor's son and designated successor, John VIII, and Demetrius Cantacuzenus disapproved of Manuel's policy of rapprochement with the Ottomans. They favored opposing Murad's succession by setting loose the pretender Mustafa, held in custody by the Byzantines in accordance with the agreement concluded between Manuel and Mehmed in the fall of 1416. After a heated debate in the imperial council, the Byzantine chronicler George Sphrantzes, a confidant of Manuel II, records that the aged Emperor yielded to his son, telling him, "Do as you please! For I, my son, am old and sick and near death, while the throne and its concerns I have given over to your care, so do as you please."[25] The Mustafa affair proved as disastrous for the Byzantines as it had been for Mircea five years earlier. Although the Ottoman pretender managed to assert his control over Rumelia for a short time, he reneged on promises made to his Byzantine sponsors to return the port of Gallipoli to the Greeks. In any event, Murad soon inflicted a crushing defeat on Mustafa's forces, captured the pretender, and ordered his immediate execution. Bent on vengeance, Murad now directed his fury against the Byzantines. On June 8, 1422, Ottoman forces began to encircle the imperial capital. For the first time in a decade Turkish armies pitched their tents beneath the walls of Constantinople. The Emperor had foreseen the results of John VIII's confrontational policy. Sphrantzes relates that Manuel told him privately, "I fear that his plans and efforts may bring about the sudden collapse of this house. For I foresaw his thoughts with Mustafa and how he believed that he

---

[23]Doc. 135 in *DRH, D*, p. 220, emphasis added.

[24]Onciul, *Originile principatelor române*, p. 202.

[25]Georgios Sphrantzes, *Memorii, 1401-1477*, Bucharest, 1966, p. 12 (VIII, 3).

would succeed and I have seen the results of his successes and the danger in which he has placed us."[26]

Shortly after the seige of Constantinople began, a Byzantine delegation led by Demetrius Paleologus, another of Manuel's sons, set out for Hungary.[27] This trip had a twofold purpose: to seek Hungarian cooperation against the Turks and to prepare the way for an official visit by John VIII to Buda to negotiate a formal alliance with Sigismund. This delegation also included Mircea's nephew Dan who had taken refuge in Constantinople when Musa beseiged the city in 1412. Manuel, in an effort to extract the Empire from the perilous situation created by his son's ill-advised initiative in setting up Mustafa against Murad, hoped, with Hungarian support, to place Dan on the throne of Wallachia and thereby distract the Sultan's attention from the seige of the imperial capital. It appears that Radu's exiled political opponents had already contacted Dan and proffered him their support in his bid to claim his father's inheritance. Dukas writes that "Dan paid homage to the Emperor and asked his permission to leave straight for home. The Emperor, according him all honors, placed him on one of the largest ships and sent him via the Black Sea to Akkerman. The boyars from Wallachia he found there proclaimed him Prince."[28] Demetrius and Dan made the journey to Hungary by way of Akkerman, then overland through Moldavia, because Radu held Kilia, making the shorter route via the Danube and through Wallachia impracticable.

While the Byzantines awaited outside help, Murad II, lacking the patience necessary for a prolonged seige, ordered a general assault on the city on August 22. But the walls of Constantinople proved impregnable. The wily old Emperor, meanwhile, engaged in further secret diplomatic manuevering to relieve the pressure on the Empire. Manuel conspired with the rulers of Karaman and Sinope to raise up Mehmed's younger son, also named Mustafa, against his brother. The failure to take the city by storm and the appearance of this new threat in Anatolia forced Murad to abandon the seige of Constantinople on September 6. Once again, the Fates had intervened to save

---

[26]Sphrantzes, *Memorii*, p. 60 (XXIII. 8).

[27]Sphrantzes, *Memorii*, p. 16 (XII, 2).

[28]Ducas, *Istoria turco-bizantină*, p. 252 (XXIX, 7).

the imperial city. But Manuel had played his last hand. On October 1, a delegation from Anatolia brought the young Prince Mustafa to Byzantium to pay homage to the Emperor and to coordinate strategy. Sphrantzes tells us that when they came before Manuel "they marvelled at the very sight of him and said in amazement that he resembled their law-giver Mohammed, for as his enemy Bayezid had once said of him, even someone who does not know the Emperor at all at the very sight of him would say, 'he must be the Emperor.'" Late in the afternoon of that same day Manuel suffered a stroke that left him half-paralyzed.[29] The survival of the Empire now depended on his son John VIII.

Although Murad quickly stifled the threat posed by Mustafa in Anatolia and had his younger brother strangled, in what had become the tradition of the Osmanli house, trouble appeared in Europe where the Hungarians, taking advantage of the situation in the Ottoman Empire, sent Dan against Radu. The Byzantine-Hungarian scheme to strike back at the Ottomans by supporting the son of Dan I succeeded. In September 1422, Dan II, backed by Hungarian troops, forced Radu and his Turkish allies to flee south of the Danube and seized the throne of Wallachia; in the five years that had elapsed since the death of Mircea the Old, Wallachian rulers had become completely dependent upon the neighboring great powers for their rank.

When Dan won the support of the Hungarian Crown in his bid to claim his father's throne, Mircea's son Vlad, still serving at Sigismund's court, became disenchanted. Vlad almost certainly felt that the King's choice of a candidate to place on the throne of Wallachia should have fallen on him and not on his cousin Dan. After all, he had been educated at the Hungarian court and had spent years in the King's service. In addition, he certainly felt that the throne should be kept within his father's bloodline. But Sigismund decided that Vlad's youth and inexperience represented a handicap for a ruler in the troubled Principality and chose instead the more mature Dan with his proven military skills. Undoubtedly, Dan's having received the blessing of the Byzantine Emperor also weighed heavily in his decision. Young and ambitious, Vlad refused to let the King's verdict deter him. Given the tense relations prevailing between Hungary and Poland, Vlad saw an opportunity to seek backing elsewhere to make his own bid for the throne. Mircea may have

---

[29]Sphrantzes, *Memorii*, p. 14 (XI, 2).

arranged for the betrothal of his youngest son to a member of the Polish royal family, so Vlad naturally turned to Vladislav I for support when he decided to press his claim to his father's inheritance. Sigismund later recalled how "Layko, son of the late, renowned, and great Mircea, Voivode of our Transalpine land... following bad advice, secretly fled from our court and from our country and, wanting to head toward other lands, he arrived with all his companions in our region of Scepusiensium, near the border with Poland." The King went on to say that a force led by Court Martin of Ujvar pursued Vlad, "blocking the way of the aforementioned fugitive in some narrow passes in those mountains and surrounded him and all of his voivodes and those who followed them, and, although he fought bravely and defended himself with the best war materiels available, they captured him and brought him back and turned him over to Our Majesty."[30] As this document indicates, the young prince had already gained a following and, although his ambitions had been foiled for the moment, Vlad had clearly announced his intention to stake his claim to his father's inheritance.

As a vassal of the Hungarian King, Dan II, like Michael before him, had to prepare to face renewed Ottoman assaults on the Principality. Sigismund had engineered Radu's overthrow and the Turks could not let this provocation go unanswered. In December 1422, Radu, having obtained reinforcements from the Sultan, launched a counterattack, hoping to catch his rival unprepared in the midst of winter, but Dan had readied himself for his assault and Hungarian troops under the command of Pippo de Ozora were on hand to help him drive back his enemies. They pursued the invaders back across the Danube, raided the area around Silistria,[31] and, according to an anonymous Turkish chronicle, "caused much harm in Rumelia."[32] This led to further Ottoman reprisals. Radu and the Turks tried again at the beginning of 1423, but Pippo and Dan inflicted

---

[30]Doc. 172 in *DRH, D*, pp. 273-274.

[31]Docs. VII and VIII in Hurmuzaki, *Documente*, vol. VIII, p. 3.

[32]N. Iorga, "Cronicele turceşti ca izvor pentru istoria românilor," in *ARMSI*, series III, vol. IX (1928-1929), p. 6. Ottoman chronicles mistakenly refer to all Wallachian rulers during the period after Mircea's death as Dracul, but the date Hegira 826 (15 December 1422 to 4 December 1423) makes it clear that the chronicle refers to an attack by Dan.

a resounding defeat on their enemies on February 26.[33] Ottoman raids led by Mehmed Bey, whom Murad had assigned to maintain pressure on Wallachia, continued throughout the year. Neshri tells us that "making incursions, they saturated themselves with plunder."[34] By the fall, the situation had grown so serious that Sigismund was forced to withdraw troops engaged against the Hussites in Bohemia to send them to the Danube to fight the Turks. On October 25, Ragusan officials congratulated the King on the recent victories of his armies in Wallachia and Bulgaria.[35] Despite persistent Ottoman efforts to reinstall Radu, Dan, with strong Hungarian military support, most notably that of the acclaimed Italian warrior Pippo de Ozora, maintained his hold on the throne.

Dan is a name with symbolic meaning for a ruler, being derived from Hebrew, meaning 'judge' or 'lord'.[36] One of his first acts as Prince was to renew the trade privileges received by the merchants of Braşov "from the ancestors of My Majesty for customs taxes in the markets of My Majesty's country and along the road from Braşov to Brăila."[37] This document also reveals that Wallachia continued to hold the fortress at Bran that Radu had seized back from Hungary in 1421. The King probably left the border stronghold in Wallachian hands as a gesture to help Dan win domestic support; the withdrawal of the citadel from Michael had certainly undermined his position at a critical time. But still, the new Prince owed his rank to Hungarian military assistance. Dan's situation improved when Hungary and Poland again patched up their differences and signed a new treaty at Kesmark on March 30, 1423, renewing the agreement concluded at Lublau ten years earlier, thus allowing Sigismund to direct more of his overstretched resources to defending the Kingdom's southern border. As a result, the potential to form a new coalition against the Ottomans began to materialize.

---

[33] Quo. Alexandru A. Vasilescu, *Urmaşii lui Mircea cel Bătrân*; Bucharest, 1915, p. 24, nt. 4.

[34] *Cronici turceşti*, vol. I, p. 118.

[35] Vasilescu, Urmaşii lui Mircea cel Bătrân, p. 24.

[36] Constantinescu, *Dicţionar onomastic*, p. 39.

[37] Doc. 136 in *DRH, D*, pp. 221-222.

One of the most ardent proponents of such a coalition was Byzantine co-Emperor John VIII. Following Manuel's stroke and paralysis, John effectively ruled the Empire and actively pursued a policy hostile to the Ottomans. This caused his father some consternation. Manuel confided to his personal secretary George Sphratzes: "My son is the Emperor, which is as it should be, and he may have been a great Emperor, but not for these times. He has a grand vision and thinks on a large scale in a way that was necessary in the great days of our ancestors, but today, as the events unfolding before our eyes demonstrate, our state does not need an Emperor, but a good caretaker."[38]

Like his father had done a quarter of a century earlier when Bayezid's armies placed a stranglehold on the imperial capital, John VIII set out for the West in November 1423, hoping to convince the rulers of Catholic Europe to organize a crusade against the Turks to relieve the beleagured Eastern Empire. He made his voyage by ship to Venice and then overland to Milan and Mantua, but had little to show for his efforts. He only obtained vague promises of support from the Italian city-states in the event that an anti-Ottoman coalition could be organized; as the realization of any such expedition demanded that the Holy Roman Emperor take the lead, John continued on to Buda where he arrived in early June 1424. The Byzantine ruler spent eight weeks in the Hungarian capital, during which he participated alongside Sigismund in the procession marking Corpus Christi Day on June 22. Their discussions, however, bore little fruit as the Hungarian King, in consultation with the Pope, conditioned direct assistance to Byzantium on the reunification of the Catholic and Orthodox Churches.

One of the people John VIII met during his sojourn at the Hungarian court was a young prince from Wallachia named Vlad. Mircea's son apparently made a positive impression on the visiting dignitary. The restless youth, whose ambitions had been frustrated by Sigismund's support of Dan II, now asked the King's permission to join the Byzantine Emperor's suite and to depart with him from Buda. Sigismund granted his request. Hence, Vlad accompanied John VIII on his journey back to the imperial city where he remained for the next several years. Dukas records Vlad's presence in Byzantium where "he stayed at the palace of Emperor John, dressed in military uniform, and each

---

[38]Sphrantzes, *Memorii*, pp. 58, 60 (XXIII, 7).

day held council with young men adroit in war and rebellion, for at that time there were a good number of Wallachians in Constantinople."[39]

Before leaving Hungary, John dispatched a courier to the Byzantine capital with a coded message for his father, informing him of his pending return. Sphrantzes relates that this messenger, "upon his arrival, asked to see the Emperor because he had something urgent to tell him..." As Manuel convalesced in bed, the Emperor's personal secretary received the courier in his stead: "Then, taking me aside, he handed me the coded letter and revealed to me from where and when he had set out on his journey. And, as soon as I deciphered it, I went and read it to him [the Emperor].... And when I read him the paper, that he is in good health and that he is setting out for the lands around Wallachia and that ships should come to the locality called Kilia to pick him up and bring him home, he [the Emperor] was filled with great joy."[40] John made his way to Kilia via Transylvania and Moldavia, carefully avoiding Wallachia and the route along the lower Danube. Recalling the fate suffered by his grandfather John V on his return from Hungary in 1366, when he was taken prisoner after embarking on a ship at Vidin for his voyage home, the Emperor carefully selected his itinerary. John had good reason to be concerned for his safety. The Ottomans controlled the key fortresses along the lower Danube and Turkish troops had invaded Wallachia only months before. A diploma issued by Sigismund on July 10, 1424, while John VIII was still in Buda, mentions that Nicholas Csáki, the Voivode of Transylvania, had recently "sent a large number of his fighting men to our Transalpine land, to help our faithful servant, the great Dan, Voivode of our Transalpine land, against the attacks of the barbarous Turks who then conspired to enter our aforesaid land."[41] By travelling through Transylvania and Moldavia on his way to the Wallachian port of Kilia, located at the mouth of the Danube, John VIII avoided the Ottoman peril. As Moldavia remained a vassal of the Polish King, the Treaty of Kesmark signed the previous year, reestablishing peaceful relations between Hungary and Poland, made this route a secure one for the Byzantine Emperor's journey home. Moldavian tradition records that Prince

---

[39]Ducas, *Istoria turco-bizantină*, p. 250 (XXIX, 6).

[40]Sphrantzes, *Memorii*, pp. 16, 18 (XIII, 2-3).

[41]Doc. 140 in *DRH, D*, pp. 225-227.

Alexander the Good, his wife Marina, and Metropolitan Joseph greeted John VIII upon his arrival in the Principality and escorted the imperial entourage to the port city of Galați from where they continued their journey by boat along the northern branch of the Danube to Kilia. The Monastery of Neamț houses an icon the Byzantine Emperor is said to have offered as a gift to the Metropolitan on the occassion of his passing through Moldavia.[42]

John VIII's visit to Hungary did nothing to revive the crusading spirit in the West that had steadily waned since the fiasco at Nicopolis. The troubles in Bohemia preoccupied Sigismund and, in the fall, with the help of Stephen Lazarević, he opened negotiations with the Turks. On November 25, the King wrote to Lithuanian Grand Duke Vitold, telling him that he did not attend the Diet at Vienna because he was engaged in discussions with emissaries from Sultan Murad.[43] These contacts resulted in a short-lived peace agreement that allowed Dan some time to consolidate his position in Wallachia.

During this brief respite, Dan obtained permission from Sigismund to establish a mint in Wallachia. On November 10, 1424, the Wallachian Prince informed the burghers of Brașov that "Because My Lord, the King, has granted me the throne and received me as his righteous and faithful servant, he has also granted me a mint, so that it will be in My Majesty's country as it is in his country, thus to strike coins also in My Majesty's country." Dan went on to revise the customs taxes to be paid in Wallachia by merchants from Brașov, in accordance with the privileges he had previously granted them, to reflect the lower value of his new coins. The Prince's attempts to compel Transylvanian merchants to use his coins in their transactions in Wallachia caused them to protest to the King. On April 4, 1425, Sigismund admonished his vassal for his attempts to oblige commercial agents from Brașov and the Bârsa land to utilize "your coins, which in the Wallachian tongue are called ducats," in their transactions because "the receipt of these coins by them could bring them,

---

[42]Panaitescu, *Alexandru cel Bun*, pp. 28-29; Ilie Minea, *Despre Dimitrie Cantemir*, Iași, 1976, p. 89 nt.; Alexandru Elian, "Moldova și Bizanțul în secolul al XV-lea" in *Cultura moldovenească în timpul lui Ștefan cel Mare*, ed. M. Berzu, Bucharest, 1964, p. 123, nt. 2.

[43]Viorica Pervian, "Lupta antiotomană la Dunărea de Jos în anii 1422-1427" in *AIIA, Cluj*, XXVI (1983-1984), p. 98.

without a doubt, heavy losses." He then ordered Dan "not to force or to constrain in any way the citizens of our aforementioned city and district to receive your coins." The King then sternly warned his vassal, "Do not do otherwise with regard to these matters if you want to continue to enjoy our generosity."[44] As Dan depended on Hungarian military support to maintain his hold on power, he had no choice but to renounce his attempts to impose a monetary monopoly over Wallachian trade. Nevertheless, he had made his first endeavor to return to the policy of autonomy that Mircea had so successfully pursued.

The revised trade privileges Dan issued for Braşov in November 1424 continue to show Bran as a Wallachian possession. But shortly thereafter, perhaps as a rebuke to the Prince for his monetary policy, Sigismund once again removed the citadel protecting the mountain pass connecting Braşov with the Principality to the south from Wallachian hands. The Transylvanians now reciprocated for what they had viewed as abuses by Wallachian authorities and imposed new taxes on merchants from the neighboring land. This led Dan to complain to the burghers of Braşov about the measures instituted by the castellans at Bran against his merchants. In an undated letter, he wrote from Argeş that "the castellans at the fortress of Terciu plunder My Majesty's people and they have set heavy customs taxes and persecute the *poor men* and do them harm although they are without guilt."[45] In documents from the time, "poor men" denotes merchants, as they are not part of the landowning aristocracy. The situation deteriorated and, as the leaders of Braşov had no authority over the royal officials stationed at Bran, the matter came before Sigismund. On February 3, 1426, the King commanded the castellans and customs agents assigned to the castle in the Carpathians to cease imposing "unjust assessments and taxes on the possessions and goods" of the merchants passing through there, "especially those from our Transalpine land."[46]

---

[44]Doc. 146 in *DRH, D*, pp. 234-236.

[45]Doc. XVI in Bogdan, *Documente privitoare*, p. 31, emphasis added. Bogdan dates this letter 1427-1431, but it seems more likely to have been written prior to Sigismund's order to the officials at Bran to cease these practices.

[46]Doc. 148 in *DRH, D*, pp. 236-238.

Amidst these continuing trade disputes, at the beginning of summer in 1425 the peace concluded between the Hungarians and the Turks the previous fall came undone. Radu II, backed by Ottoman troops, once again crossed the Danube in an effort to retake the throne. The boyars opposed to Hungarian domination had consistently supported Radu, but now he also received covert help from Alexander the Good of Moldavia, who had his sights set on the Wallachian port of Kilia. Dan appealed to the King for assistance. On September 3, Sigismund wrote to the Ragusans, telling them that he sent "an army under the command of the renowned Captain Pippo de Ozora, Count of Temes, against the Turks, and another, under the command of the celebrated captain Nicholas Csáki, the Voivode of Transylvania, likewise against the Turks, the enemies of Christ, to help the illustrious Transalpine Voivode Dan."[47] Their arrival tipped the balance in Dan's favor. On October 20, Ragusan officials reported to the King: "We have learned from reliable sources that Your Majesty's army sent against the Turks who attacked the domain of Voivode Dan fought with great courage in such a way that few Turks were able to escape."[48] A combined force under Dan and Pippo de Ozora, accompanied by Fruschin, son of the late Tsar John Shishman, crossed the Danube and attacked Ottoman positions around Vidin in an attempt to revive the defunct Bulgarian Empire. Faced with this threat, the Sultan launched a counterattack and by late November the Ottomans had defeated Pippo and driven back the invaders, but the onset of winter brought the fighting to a standstill. Dan continued to rule Wallachia, but more than ever his position depended upon Hungarian military might.

Radu stayed close to the Danube during the winter months, working to win the support of boyars concerned about the increasing Hungarian domination of their country. With Ottoman troops at his disposal, Radu devised a plan to overthrow Dan. He intended to incite a revolt among the nobility to coincide with a new invasion of the Principality; he also counted on assistance from Alexander the Good, with whom he had concluded a secret alliance, to attack Dan in the northeast. But before their plot could be brought to fruition, Dan's spies uncovered certain details of the plan and learned of the clandestine

---

[47]Quo. Vasilescu, *Urmașii lui Mircea cel Bătrân*, p. 27, nt. 4.

[48]Quo. Vasilescu, *Urmașii lui Mircea cel Bătrân*, p. 27, nt. 5.

involvement of Alexander of Moldavia in the scheme. Dan immediately complained to Sigismund who, in turn, protested to Vladislav of Poland about the actions of his vassal in direct violation of their treaty. The Polish King then sent an emissary to Moldavia to investigate the charges and to order Alexander to contribute troops to fight alongside the Poles and Hungarians against the Turks. The Moldavian Prince apologized for his imprudence and promised to comply with the orders of his suzerain.[49]

With a Turkish invasion imminent, Dan renewed his allegiance to Sigismund,[50] and the King prepared to send military assistance to Wallachia. Invoking the terms of the Treaty of Lublau, renewed at Kesmark in 1423, the Hungarian King also called on Poland and Lithuania to contribute troops for a joint campaign against the Ottomans; these forces were to gather at the Wallachian port city of Brăila on the Danube by June 24, 1426; in early May, at Vladislav's insistence, Alexander issued a writ of safe-conduct for Polish and Lithuanian troops to pass through Moldavia.[51] But Radu and the Turks struck before the promised assistance could reach Dan. On May 30, the two cousins met in battle. Radu, "accompanied by many Turks and disloyal Wallachians," devastated Dan's army in this confrontation and Sigismund's ally barely escaped with his life. Radu now occupied a large portion of Wallachia, but a Hungarian force under the command of Stephen Pohernok arrived to sustain Dan. They launched a counterattack and after "a hard-fought battle... they obtained a glorious and triumphant victory" over Radu and the Turks.[52] The war, however, had only just begun.

When news of Dan's initial defeat by Radu and the Turks reached Sigismund, he wrote to Cardinal Henric de Beaufort, papal legate in Bohemia, explaining that he failed to attend the Diet at Nuremberg because of illness and that he now intended to go personally to Wallachia to aid Dan against the Turks.[53] In conformity with their previous agreement, 5000 troops from

---

[49]Vasilescu, *Urmaşii lui Mircea cel Bătrân*, p. 28.

[50]Doc. CCCCXLV in Hurmuzaki, *Documente*, vol. I, part. 2, p. 534.

[51]Doc. 178 in Costăchescu, *Documentele moldoveneşti*, vol. II, pp. 642-644.

[52]Doc. 219 in *DRH, D*, pp. 316-318.

[53]N. Iorga, *Acte şi fragmente*, vol. III, Bucharest, 1897, pp. 80-81.

Poland, Lithuania, and Moldavia, under the command of Jan Kobilenski, assembled at Brăila on June 24 to unite with Hungarian forces in a joint effort against the Ottomans.[54] But despite his stated intentions, Sigismund failed to show up. The ongoing conflict with the Hussites in Bohemia continued to preoccupy the King. In mid-July, he wrote to Vladislav, asking the Polish King to order his forces to remain in Brăila, because he was sending two of his nobles to receive them and "to take them to Voivode Dan."[55] But two months passed, and still no one arrived. The costs of maintaining this army that seemingly had nowhere to go mounted. Finally, Vladislav's patience with his Hungarian counterpart wore out and he ordered the frustrated would-be crusaders to return home to their respective countries at the end of August.

Soon after they departed, Sigismund reversed himself, and on September 4 he once more announced his intention to lead an expedition to Wallachia, but Vladislav wisely refused to commit his troops for a second time. Despite his professed intention, the Hungarian King again postponed his departure for Wallachia. Still hoping to avenge the humiliating defeat at Nicopolis thirty years earlier and to lead a new Christian coalition against the Turks, Sigismund continued negotiations with his long-time enemy, Venice, but an agreement with the Republic of St. Mark proved elusive. In the interim, Pippo de Ozora had arrived to aid Dan against Radu. The fiercest fighting occurred in Oltenia where anti-Hungarian sentiment was strongest. By October, Dan and Pippo had driven Radu and the Turks from Wallachia and, once again accompanied by Fruschin, they attacked Ottoman positions across the Danube. In recognition of his services against the Turks in this campaign, Sigismund granted the Bulgarian prince possession of the castle at Lipova the following year.[56] Although they won a series of minor victories, they could not sustain an offensive and soon returned to consolidate their victory in Wallachia.

---

[54]Ilie Minea, *Informaţiile româneşti ale cronicii lui Ian Długosz*, Iaşi, 1926, p. 17.

[55]Quo. Vasilescu, *Urmaşii lui Mircea cel Bătrân*, p. 30, nt. 1.

[56]Doc. CCCCXLVI in Hurmuzaki, *Documente*, vol. I, part. 2, pp. 534-535. This document is incorrectly dated in 1426. Lipova was held by Pippo de Ozora until his death at the end of 1426, so it could not have been granted to Fruschin until after that date. Given that the diploma was issued at Marienburg (Feldioara) the likely date is April or May 1427 when Sigismund is known to have been in that locality.

The realization that Dan's hold on the throne was tenuous at best hastened their return. Unable to trust many of his own boyars and faced with an imminent counterattack by Radu and the Turks, he depended more heavily than ever on Hungarian military aid to maintain his position. In early November, Dan sent his Logofăt, Coico, to Lipova, where he met with Sigismund, Pippo, and other Hungarian officials, to discuss "the ways and means by which we can sustain Voivode Dan on his throne." The King wrote that on the advice of Pippo and his nobles "we have decided that, for the safety and personal security of Voivode Dan, we must maintain at all times one thousand men alongside Voivode Dan, that is 100 cavalry and 900 infantry." Furthermore, he ordered that the cost of this personal bodyguard be paid for from the Hungarian treasury.[57] But before this decision could be implemented, Radu, supported by Ottoman troops, launched his attack, this time forcing Dan to flee across the mountains to Transylvania. Once more a son of Mircea ruled the Transalpine land.

Amidst turmoil in Wallachia, Alexander the Good occupied the Danubian port city of Kilia and its surrounding territory. The Prince had long had his eye on this stronghold and seized the opportunity to extend Moldavian control to the mouth of the Danube. Ostensibly, his annexation of the strategically important Wallachian fortress could be justified as a move to prevent its fall into Ottoman hands, but the Moldavian ruler had no intention of relinquishing control of the port, even after Dan and his Hungarian allies had driven the Turks out of Wallachia. As a result, Kilia remained a point of contention between the two neighboring principalities until it finally fell to the Ottomans in 1484.

In late December 1426, Sigismund arrived in Braşov where he began to gather an army to reinstall Dan as Prince of Wallachia. Hungarian preparations for a counteroffensive suffered a setback on December 27 when Pippo de Ozora, the Italian warrior who had ably coordinated the defense of the southern border of the Kingdom against the Ottomans for the past two decades, died suddenly at the age of fifty-seven. But additional help arrived from an unexpected source. Driven by the crusading spirit of yore, long since waned in most of Christendom, the adventurous Prince Don Pedro, second son of King

---

[57]Doc. 151 in *DRH, D*, pp. 242-245.

Alphonse of Portugal, journeyed across the breadth of Europe, accompanied by four hundred knights, determined to join in the struggle against the Turkish infidels.[58] His presence in the army preparing to cross the Carpathians at the beginning of 1427 to drive the Ottomans from Wallachia is mentioned by Stephen de Rozgony, the Count of Gyor, in a letter dated January 25, who refers to him as "the illustrious Prince, the King of Portugal." The Count writes that Pedro and Dan, accompanied by Hungarian and Szeckler forces, "set out yesterday for the Transalpine land to capture and hold the Voivode Radu, if they can, and, if the waters of the Danube will be frozen, to continue on to devastate the Turkish land, burning and plundering it as possible, and to advance to the shores of the sea."[59] The task before them was difficult. The army "suffered from severe hunger, extreme cold, and other scarcities, and endured very many losses."[60] After an arduous campaign, "Voivode Dan, thanks to the collaboration and leadership of the illustrious Lord Pedro...," recalls Sigismund in a diploma granted on July 2 of that year, "was restored to his throne."[61] A Venetian report, dated April 3, indicates that, by late March, Dan and his allies had occupied Wallachia, causing great consternation at the Porte, where "all say with one voice that it [the Ottoman army] is preparing to go to the Danube to oppose the forces of the Hungarians and the Wallachians who are now set out on this route and want to cross into Greece."[62] Sigismund himself crossed the mountains to Câmpulung in early April,[63] from where he coordinated the activities of his victorious armies as they completed the recovery of Wallachia by capturing the strategic Danubian forts of Turnu and Giurgiu.

With the Turks now driven out of the Principality south of the Carpathians, the King returned to Transylvania. Dan's position, however, remained insecure. Sigismund had complained on April 6, while he was still at

---

[58]N. Iorga, "Un prinț portughez cruciat în Țara Românească a secolului al XV-lea" in *ARMSI*, series II, XXXVIII (1915-1916), pp. 333-337.

[59]Doc. 153 in *DRH, D*, pp. 247-249.

[60]Doc. 162 in *DRH, D*, pp. 258-261.

[61]Doc. 161 in *DRH, D*, pp. 257-258.

[62]Quo. Iorga, "Un prinț portughez," pp. 335-336.

[63]Docs. 155-157 in *DRH, D*, pp. 250-252.

Câmpulung, that "A large number of the inhabitants of our Transalpine land, called Wallachians, took the side of Radu Praznaglava and the Turks."[64] Realizing that he remained in danger of losing Wallachia, the King began planning a new expedition against the Ottomans. As soon as he arrived at Marienburg (Feldioara) on April 8, Sigismund dispatched a letter to a German prince, declaring that "we have decided that this summer we will set out again to fight the Turks, and we hope, with the help of God, to reconquer the Danube, and in this way to do a great service to Christendom."[65] But the Ottomans struck first. In May, the Turkish army that Venetian intelligence had reported in early April was preparing to go to the Danube, attacked Wallachia, trying to reinstall Radu as Prince, as well as Hungarian positions along the Danube north of Vidin. This forced Sigismund to hasten his plans. On June 1, the King ordered the delay of a trial at Monyoros (Maierush) because the litigants "will set out together with their lord in our royal army which, with the help of God, we will soon raise in our Transalpine land against the barbarian Turks."[66] But things did not proceed as quickly as Sigismund might have hoped. The Hungarian King encountered persistent problems in raising an army, especially for military actions outside the borders of his Kingdom, because the nobles resisted feudal levies. Various attempts at military reform throughout Sigismund's reign had done little to improve this situation. Finally, on July 9, Lorand Lepes, the Vice-Voivode of Transylvania, also delayed judgement of a case pending before him, "owing to the setting out of our army, now raised, for the Transalpine land against the Turks,"[67] and indeed, around July 12, Sigismund led his troops through the Bran pass into Wallachia.

The King intended to secure Wallachia for Dan while marching across the Principality to the area around Severin where a sizeable Ottoman force led by Sultan Murad threatened Christian positions along the Danube. On July 27, the Hungarian army reached the Cerna River, some fifty kilometers west of Râmnicu Vâlcea. By this time, news had reached Sigismund of the death of his staunch ally, Serbian Despot Stephen Lazarević. Lazarević's death on July 19

---

[64]Doc. 157 in *DRH, D*, pp. 251-252.

[65]Quo. Pervian, "Lupta antiotomană la Dunărea de jos în anii 1422-1427," p. 112.

[66]Doc. 159 in *DRH, D*, pp. 255-256.

[67]Doc. 163 in *DRH, D*, p. 261.

shifted the focus of the fighting between the Ottomans and the Hungarians to Serbia. Already, in May 1426, the Despot had made provisions to cede the Macva region, including the key Danubian fortresses of Golubac and Belgrade, to the Hungarian King when he died. Sigismund now hurried to defend his interests in Serbia against the Turks who also coveted these important citadels. In mid-August, the royal army left Wallachia and arrived at Orşova where it crossed the Danube into Serbia. Hungarian troops garrisoned Golubac and then Belgrade, where the King arrived on September 17. Don Pedro of Portugal appears to have accompanied Sigismund throughout this campaign. Early in 1428, the Portugese prince and his men left Belgrade and made their way home via Venice and Florence where they enjoyed formal receptions. Later, as Duke of Coimbra, the Pope would praise Pedro for his crusading efforts in North Africa.[68]

Following a winter respite, war resumed in Serbia in the spring of 1428. The new Despot, Lazarević's nephew and adopted son George Branković, faced fierce Ottoman assaults as the Sultan hoped to capitalize on dissension in the Principality following Lazarević's death to extend his control over as much Serbian territory as possible. Sigismund held the powerful fortress at Belgrade with little difficulty, but elsewhere intense fighting broke out. The fortress at Golubac became the focal point of the conflict. Although Dan had to retain the bulk of his forces at home to protect against a new attack by Radu, he did send Wallachian contingents to help Sigismund defend Gobulac. Royal secretary Caspar Slik wrote to the Mayor of Frankfurt in Germany, informing him that "The Turks arrived at the Danube with all their army and their might and are encamped near the fortress of Golubac, but they have not yet managed to take it, their attack being repulsed. But at the present moment the Despot is working to achieve a peace treaty for a period of three years between our Lord and the Turks, but negotiations have not yet been finalized.... If anyone tells you that we have lost a great number of men do not believe him because we have not lost more than two hundred men, and those who were killed were poor peasants from Wallachia under the command of Lord Zawisch."[69] But, despite Slik's optimism, fighting resumed and on June 3 the fortress fell to the

---

[68]Iorga, "Un prinţ portughez," pp. 336-337.

[69]Doc. CCCCLXI in Hurmuzaki, *Documente*, vol. I, part 2, pp. 551-552.

Ottomans. Meanwhile, Radu II, supported by Turkish troops, once again attempted to seize the throne of Wallachia. Heavy fighting ensued, but Dan, with help from Stephen Rozgony, who had succeeded Pippo de Ozora as Count of Temes, defeated the invaders; they could not, however, prevent the Ottomans from regaining possession of Giurgiu and Turnu which the Wallachian Prince had recovered the previous year. This time Radu himself died in the fighting. His brother Alexander appears to have fled to Moldavia. The information coming out of Wallachia that summer, however, was confused. On August 25, Grand Duke Vitold of Lithuania wrote that he had received news that, after the battle at Golubac, "the Turks had crossed the Danube into Wallachia, which also belongs to the King of the Romans,... and that the Governor of that territory, who is called Dan, has been captured or killed."[70] In reality, Dan had finally eliminated his long-time rival for the throne. The peace negotiations mentioned by the King's secretary dragged on until February 1429 when Sigismund at last concluded a three-year peace treaty with Murad II, recognizing the status quo in Wallachia and Serbia, both of which paid tribute to the Sultan, but remained vassals of the Hungarian King.

In January 1429, even before the formal treaty with the Ottomans had been sealed, Sigismund met his allies Vladislav and Vitold at Luck to settle disputes that had arisen since their previous meeting at Kesmark. The Hungarian King's main purpose was to obtain, by hook or by crook, the port of Kilia at the mouth of the Danube. He saw this as the means by which Hungary could compete with its archrival Venice for control of the prosperous trade between the Orient and Central Europe. Despite attempts to come to terms with the Republic of St. Mark over the previous years their ongoing dispute over the Dalmatian coast proved an obstacle too great to be overcome. Sigismund went so far as to complain to Pope Martin V that he had been forced to make peace with the Turks "because of the tyranny of the Venetians."[71] But when Vladislav's vassal Alexander of Moldavia had seized Kilia and the surrounding territory at the end of 1426, he had thrown a wrench into Sigismund's plans. The persistent conflicts with the Turks during the previous two years had forced him to leave

---

[70]Quo. Vasilescu, *Urmașii lui Mircea cel Bătrân*, p. 34, nt. 12.

[71]Quo. Vasilescu, *Urmașii lui Mircea cel Bătrân*, p. 39.

this problem on the back burner, despite Dan's complaints to his suzerain about the abusive action of the Moldavian Prince. The armistice with the Sultan now afforded Sigismund the opportunity to realize his objective.

As Kilia now lay in Moldavian hands, the Hungarian King used the occassion of the summit at Luck to try to convince his counterparts to invoke the clause in the Treaty of Lublau calling for the partitioning of Moldavia between Hungary and Poland in the event that the Principality refused to contribute to the anti-Ottoman struggle. This would have placed Kilia under Hungarian rule. Sigismund reproached Alexander for his secret dealings with Radu and the Turks and remarked that because of his machinations Moldavia had not suffered an Ottoman attack since 1421. Vladislav, however, stood by his Moldavian vassal and refused to agree to such a measure. The Polish King countered Sigismund's arguments, pointing out that when he called upon Alexander to supply troops and to facilitate the passage through Moldavia of Polish and Lithuanian forces to join the campaign against the Ottomans planned for the summer of 1426, the Prince complied without hesitation. Vladislav subtly reminded the Hungarian King that the campaign did not take place because of the failure of his own troops to arrive at the appointed place on time.

Having failed to convince his allies to proceed with the partitioning of Moldavia, Sigismund now demanded that the fortress and its surrounding territory be restored to Wallachia. This would return Kilia to the Hungarian sphere of influence, in accordance with the existing agreements between Hungary and Poland. But Vladislav hesitated to acquiesce in this as well. After prolonged discussions, they decided to establish a commission to study the issue. As Vladislav claimed suzerainty over Moldavia and Sigismund over Wallachia, they agreed to submit the matter to the arbitration of Vitold, who would decide the status of Kilia, based on the evidence submitted by the special commission, at a conference at Troky on April 23. Poland, however, also had a vested interest in trade with the Orient. Vladislav did not want the strategic Danubian port to fall into Hungarian hands and so he worked clandestinely to undermine the arbitration process. Sigismund's renowned penchant for delay aided the Polish King's machinations. Hungarian delegates failed to arrive at Troky on time and discussions over the fate of Kilia broke down, much to the dissatisfaction of Dan who now decided to employ other means to recover his lost territory.

Dan came to realize that Sigismund never intended for Kilia to return to Wallachian control. For several years, the King had planned to bring his long-time allies, the Teutonic Knights, to the Danube and to entrust them with defending the border with the Ottomans. The fact that similar schemes under Andrew II and Bela IV in the thirteenth century had failed miserably did not deter Sigismund. On July 2, 1426, he wrote to Lorand Lepes, the Vice-Voivode of Transylvania, telling him of his intentions and ordering him to reach an agreement with the nobles, the Saxons, and the Catholic bishops as to how this plan could be carried out without violating the rights of any of the privileged groups in the province.[72] Three years later, Sigismund put his scheme into action. The list of over twenty fortresses the King intended to cede to the Knights included Mehadia, Orşova, the Saan Island, and two claimed by Wallachia — Kilia, on its eastern frontier, and Severin, on its western border.

Frustrated at the failure of diplomacy to resolve the dispute over Kilia, Dan decided to take matters into his own hands. In May 1429, Dan invaded southern Moldavian and attacked the fortress. Although he failed to take the citadel, he plundered the surrounding area. This led Alexander to complain to Vitold who intervened on his behalf with the King of Hungary to try to oblige Dan to return the cattle and goods seized in the attack. Sigismund replied that he had been too preoccupied with affairs in Bohemia to intervene in the dispute between Wallachia and Moldavia. The King had not authorized Dan's attack on Moldavia. The Wallachian Prince's bold initiative came as a surprise to Sigismund, forcing him to set aside other matters and to attempt to revive diplomatic efforts to resolve the dispute over Kilia.

The Hungarian King now sent two emissaries, accompanied by two Wallachian delegates, to Vitold to present their case for the restoration of Kilia and its surrounding territory to Wallachia. Dan's representatives brought with them "a description of the borders and the places which the Voivode of Moldavia had occupied."[73] In response to these renewed pressures for the restitution of Kilia to Wallachia, Alexander the Good ordered that obstacles be placed in the Danube where the northern branch empties into the sea. This cut-off shipping on the Danube, isolating the Wallachian port of Brăila to the

---

[72]Doc. CCCCLI in Hurmuzaki, *Documente*, vol. I, part 2, pp. 539-540.

[73]Quo. Vasilescu, *Urmaşii lui Mircea cel Bătrân*, p. 39, nt. 1.

detriment of Wallachian as well as Transylvanian merchants. On August 30, Sigismund wrote to Vitold complaining of the actions of the Moldavian Prince, telling him that the obstructions Alexander had placed in the river had recently prevented twelve ships from passing through those waters; some of these ships were sunk, while others were forced to turn back.[74] By this time, however, the Hungarian King could no longer find support among his allies over the matter of Kilia. Alexander removed the obstacles from the Danube and the strategic fortress remained in his possession.

This outcome did not please Dan. Relations between Wallachia and Hungary grew increasingly tense. Not only did Sigismund's lack of firm support for the return of Kilia disappoint the Prince, but his suzerain's plan to bring the Teutonic Order into the region further alienated Dan as he lost Severin to the Knights, whose leader, Nicholas von Redwitz, obtained the title of Ban of Severin from the King in 1430.[75] Dan now broke with Sigismund and turned to his long-time enemy, the Sultan, to whom he had begun paying tribute in accordance with the treaty signed in February 1429, for support. With Turkish assistance, Dan launched a new assault on Kilia in the spring or summer of 1430. He again failed to take the citadel, but the combined Wallachian-Ottoman force divided into four groups and burned and plundered southern Moldavia causing Alexander to protest to both Sigismund and Vladislav.[76] The Wallachian Prince also began to offer refuge to the King's enemies. In a diploma dated December 6, 1433, and issued at Basel in Switzerland where a new Church Council had recently convened, Sigismund recalls that he had confiscated lands from a Transylvanian nobleman, Lado de Byzere, and his sons, who had "fled to Wallachia, subjected then as now to the barbaric Turks... and to the late Dan, Voivode of the Transalpine land, who then, in defiance of Our Majesty, was, of his own free will, on the side of the aforesaid Turks, where the aforesaid Lado, fighting as an unbeliever with all his might against Our Majesty and against our loyal subjects until the end of his life, together with his aforementioned sons, ended his earthly life as a

---

[74]Vasilescu, *Urmașii lui Mircea cel Bătrân*, p. 39, nt. 2.

[75]Doc. CCCCLXXI in Hurmuzaki, *Documente*, p. 564.

[76]Nicolae Iorga *Studii asupra Chiliei și Cetății-Albe*, Bucharest, 1899, p. 88. Iorga incorrectly places these events in 1429.

traitor."[77] Dan's new anti-Hungarian foreign policy certainly won him domestic support, but it also cost him the backing of several key boyars, the most important of which was his Vornic, Albu, who went into exile in Moldavia where Alexander the Good began to draw closer to Sigismund.

The death of Vitold in a riding accident on October 27, 1430, upset the delicate ties uniting Hungary, Poland, and Lithuania in common cause. The new Grand Duke, Swidrigaillo, backed by Sigismund, began to assert Lithuania's independence from Poland. This led to a series of military confrontations in which Moldavia sided with Hungary and Lithuania against the Poles. With Dan an ally of the Sultan, and Alexander an ally of Hungary, and the dispute over Kilia still unresolved, tensions between the two neighboring principalities now reached a breaking point. Domestic opposition no longer threatened Dan's hold on the throne, but the dangers posed by his hostile neighbors to the north loomed large. Still he remained confident that he could maintain his position and establish his own family dynasty so that his sons Danciul and Basarab[78] could succeed him on the throne. To improve his situation in these perilous times, Dan made a goodwill gesture to the Saxons of Transylvania on January 30, 1431, according favorable trade privileges to merchants from Braşov and the Bârsa land,[79] albeit under false pretenses.[80] But as his cousin Radu had learned, such a move in itself could not resolve his differences with the Hungarian King.

Throughout this period, Mircea's son Vlad remained at Constantinople waiting for an opportunity to press his claim to his father's throne. He was now a young man in his prime. It is likely that, Vlad, having maintained his contacts with Poland where he had attempted to flee to seek support for a bid for the Wallachian throne in 1422, took a Polish wife, perhaps a relative of Vladislav I, during his sojourn at the imperial palace. Mircea may have arranged for this marriage around the time he renewed his alliance with the Polish King in 1411. She bore him his first son around 1428 or 1429 whom he christened Mircea

---

[77]Doc. 209 in *DRH, D*, pp. 307-309.

[78]Docs. 59-61 in *DRH, B*, vol. I, pp. 115-118.

[79]Doc. XVII in Bogdan, *Documente privitoare*, pp. 32-38.

[80]Alexandru A. Vasilescu, "Privilegiul comercial latinesc al lui Mircea cel Bătrân din 25 august 1413, acordat Braşovenilor, este fals," in *RIR*, XIII (1943), pp. 78-96.

after his father. When news reached the Byzantine capital that his cousin Dan no longer enjoyed Sigismund's backing, Vlad realized that the moment he had long awaited had finally arrived. According to Dukas, he gathered his followers who had joined him in exile in Constantinople and "went to the border of Wallachia and there gathered many more; they assembled day by day and formed a powerful army."[81] The Byzantine historian's reference to "the border of Wallachia" certainly refers to Transylvania where Vlad probably arrived in the fall of 1430. Presumably, he travelled by sea to Moldavia and then overland to Transylvania. His strong ties to Schässburg (Sighisoara in Romanian; Segesvár in Hungarian) suggest that he settled in this Saxon city upon his arrival there. Around 1431, his wife gave birth to his second son, his namesake, the future Vlad the Impaler. The exact date and place of birth of the historical Dracula are unknown, but there is a strong possibility that he was born in Transylvania, perhaps even in Schässburg. In any event, having found here additional support among Wallachian boyars who had taken refuge in Hungary following Dan's break with Sigismund, Vlad now prepared to go before the man at whose court he had been raised to ask that he be installed on his father's throne. Early in 1431, the son of Mircea the Old set out for Nuremberg where Sigismund, as Holy Roman Emperor, presided over the Imperial Diet. But Vlad's long journey home had only just begun.

---

[81]Ducas, *Istoria turco-bizantină*, pp. 250, 252 (XXIX, 6).

Chapter VI

The Great Pretender

"Noble patricians, patrons of my right,
Defend the justice of my cause with arms;
And, countrymen, my loving followers,
Plead my successive title with your swords."

— Shakespeare, *Titus Andronicus*[1]

When he arrived in Schässburg in 1430, Vlad acquired a house on the main square of the fortified city, opposite the imposing Gothic-style Catholic church, known as the Monastery Church, that had been raised the previous year; both of these buildings still stand today in the historic center of one of the finest surviving examples of a medieval German town, earning it the nickname "the Pearl of Transylvania." Built on a hilltop overlooking the Târnava River valley on a site inhabited since antiquity, Schässburg in the time of Vlad Dracul was a burgeoning urban center. First attested to in the thirteenth century at the time of the great influx of Saxon settlers to Transylvania, it differed from other German cities in the region, such as Brașov, Sibiu, and, to a lesser extent, Bistrița, which, because of their location along key passes near the borders of the Kingdom, controlled

---

[1]Act I, scene 1.

important international trade routes. Instead, crafts flourished in Schässburg and the city became organized around a network of guilds which dominated its economic and political life. Some of these associations, such as those of the furriers, the butchers, the tailors, the tanners, the goldsmiths, the locksmiths, the blacksmiths, the coopers, the rope-makers, the weavers, the shoemakers, and the barbers are recalled in the names of the extant towers that once defended the burg against attacks by the Turks, Tatars, and other enemies.

From Schässburg, the pretender to the throne of Wallachia, accompanied by his supporters and attendants, set out on a journey of a thousand kilometers to the imperial city of Nuremberg in Germany shortly after Christmas of that year. The route that Vlad and his entourage likely followed took them through Kolosvár (Cluj), Nagyvárad (Oradea), the Hungarian capital of Buda, which he now revisited after an absence of over six years, Pressburg (also called Pojony, today's Bratislava), and Vienna before they finally reached their destination. Given that an average day's journey during this period covered some forty kilometers,[2] and the certainty of formal receptions in Buda and Vienna, and perhaps at other places along the way, the delegation had to travel for at least a month to reach the city at the heart of the Holy Roman Empire. Sigismund arrived at Nuremberg, where the Imperial Diet was set to begin its deliberations, prior to Vlad, making the trip of slightly over two hundred kilometers from Constance, where he was in mid-January,[3] in approximately a week. The two men now met for the first time since Vlad's departure for Constantinople in the summer of 1424. The moment Mircea's son had long awaited, when he could finally lay claim to his father's throne, had seemingly arrived.

Sigismund had decided to crown Vlad as the new Prince of Wallachia before either party set out for Nuremberg. Considering the time needed to travel great distances and the expense involved, it is inconceivable that Vlad would have made this long voyage merely to plead his case before the Emperor. Also, bearing in mind that information could only be gathered as fast as those bringing it could ride, it is hardly possible that Sigismund would take a decision of this nature on the spur of the moment without first obtaining

---

[2]Hale, *Civilization of the Renaissance in Europe*, p. 147.

[3]Doc. 2105 in *Urkundenbuch*, vol. IV, pp. 424-425.

reliable information from his intelligence sources about the situation in Wallachia, something that required sufficient time to gather. His biographer, Eberhard Windecke, writes that Vlad sent emissaries beforehand to inform the Emperor of Dan's death and the desire of the boyars of the country to place him on the throne.[4] Windecke's account is clearly erroneous. Dan was alive and well at that time, ruling from Târgoviște as an ally of the Sultan. Sigismund could not have believed that Dan had died and therefore decided to appoint Vlad to fill the void. Instead, he sought to replace Dan because he had allied himself with the Ottomans, and Wallachia could no longer be counted upon as a vassal state of Hungary. The true motive that brought Vlad to Nuremberg was that the Emperor desired to place a reliable man on the throne of the Transalpine land. Windecke's allusion to Dan's death is erroneous or merely a literary device to express the idea that the Prince had turned away from Hungary. Certainly, Dan's new pro-Ottoman stance, which, Sigismund later recalled, he had adopted "in contempt of Our Majesty... of his own free will,"[5] and the fact that he harbored declared enemies of the Hungarian King, provided the Emperor, who still included "King of Cumania"[6] among his numerous titles, with all the motivation he needed to implement measures to replace his recalcitrant vassal.

A sizeable entourage accompanied Vlad to Nuremberg, including boyars who had joined him in exile in Constantinople and many pro-Hungarian nobles who had deserted Dan at the beginning of 1430 and who now supported Vlad in his bid for the throne. Although we have no specific information about the boyars in his suite, in a document issued at Nuremberg immediately after his investiture, the newly-crowned Prince mentions a "Marschal." Romanian scholars have translated this as *Vornic*,[7] the equivalent of Court Marschal or Palatine. This interpretation has led some to equate this official with Voico,[8] a powerful boyar known to have joined Vlad in Transylvania and the first to hold

---

[4]Constantin M. Kogălniceanu, "Cercetări critice cu privire la istoria românilor," in *RIAF*, XII:1 (1911), p. 45.

[5]Doc. 209 in *DRH, D*, pp. 307-309.

[6]Doc. 2214 in *Urkundenbuch*, vol. IV, pp. 549-551.

[7]Doc. 179 in *DRH, D*, pp. 280-281.

[8]Bogdan, *Documente privitoare*, p. 249.

Fifteenth century depiction of Nuremberg from the *Nuremberg Chronicle*

the position of *Vornic* in Vlad's royal council. But this hypothesis is mistaken. Voico still served in Dan II's royal council at this time and is listed among the witnesses to the trade privileges that Prince granted to Braşov on January 30, 1431.[9] Had he abandoned Dan the following day, he still could not have been present at Nuremberg in time for Vlad's coronation. If not Voico, then who was the "Marschal" referred to by Vlad? Our most important clues lie in the document itself, a Latin-language privilege granting Franciscan monks the right to propagate Catholicism in Wallachia. In it, Vlad writes that he gave the document "to be noted with our name by our Marschal, a copy of which, in the common language of the Transalpine land [meaning Slavonic], we have sent for greater surety." The attributes of the "Marschal" implied in this text included the composition, translation, authentication, and dispatching of official acts. These are all functions of the dignitary known as the *Logofăt* or Chancellor. Thus, the Marschal referred to in this decree is, in fact, Vlad's *Logofăt*, Stephen, one of his most trusted associates. Although we have no information about Stephen prior to this time, he was probably among those boyars known to have kept company with Vlad at the court of the Byzantine

[9]Doc. 175 in *DRH, D*, pp. 276-278.

Emperor. There are additional reasons to believe that Stephen is the official mentioned in this document. In addition to his responsibilities as head of the royal chancellery, the *Logofăt* also oversaw Church-related matters, thereby making his direct involvement with a decree of this nature a necessity. We also know that on other occasions Vlad sent Stephen as an emissary on his behalf to Sigismund;[10] he almost certainly played a key role in the negotiations that preceded Vlad's enthronement at Nuremberg.

Presumably, Vlad's investiture took place at the cathedral at Nuremberg; ceremonies of this nature were invariably religious affairs. The date was most likely February 8, which fell on a Thursday in the year 1431. A visitor to Wallachia in the seventeenth century, Paul of Aleppo, son and secretary to Patriarch Macarius of Antioch, present at the coronation of Prince Constantine Şerban (1654-1658), records that the inauguration ceremonies for Princes of this land customarily took place on Thursday.[11] Assuming that this tradition predates the time of Vlad Dracul, it confirms the proposed date; even though the event took place outside of the Principality, it was imperative that the customs of the land be meticulously respected to uphold the legitimacy of Vlad's claim. Acting on the authority of the Emperor, who presided over the solemnity, the Archbishop anointed Vlad, who shortly after proclaimed himself, "by the grace of God, Prince of Transalpine Wallachia and Duke of Amlaş and Făgăraş," and declared Sigismund, in his capacity as "Holy Roman Emperor and King of Hungary, Bohemia, Dalmatia, Croatia, etc." as "our natural Lord," thereby formally recognizing him as his sovereign. Now consecrated as ruler by divine right, in accordance with another custom of his ancestors, Vlad adopted the surname John, an appelation of religious significance that all Wallachian Princes had assumed since the time of Basarab. Finally, Sigismund presented him with a silver scepter, a symbol of Vlad's authority as Prince of Wallachia. According to Windecke, a group of boyars brought this scepter from the Principality for the Emperor to confer upon the new ruler in accordance with "the law of the country and custom of the land."[12] Although some have rejected this account because Dan still ruled

---

[10]Doc. 249 in *DRH, D*, pp. 345-346.

[11]B.P. Hajdeu, *Archiva istorică*, vol. I, part. 2, Bucharest, 1865, p. 104.

[12]Panaitescu, *Mircea cel Bătrân*, p. 195.

Wallachia and insisted that Sigismund provided a new scepter for Vlad's coronation, Windecke's version cannot be discounted. One of the boyars who deserted Dan may have stolen the scepter, called a *buzdugan*, and taken it to Transylvania and from there to Nuremberg; there are several other documented cases of theft from the royal court and treasury by refugee boyars in the fifteenth century.[13]

Now officially invested as Prince of Wallachia, the Emperor next bestowed the Order of the Dragon upon Vlad. The significance of this moment, as we discussed in the first chapter, was that as result of this honor he became known as *Dracul* or *Dracula*. Sigismund had established the *Societatis draconistorum* on December 13, 1408. The oath sworn by those inducted into the superior class of the Order, reserved for foreign rulers of which Vlad now became a member, promised brotherhood, friendship, mutual assistance, and alliance with the Hungarian King and his allies. In addition, members committed themselves to destroy and to persecute enemies of the faith, to serve, to propagate, and to defend Catholicism with zeal, and to fight with all their might against pagans, and especially the Turks.[14] This implied that Vlad, although ruler of a predominantly Orthodox land, had to embrace Catholicism. This was not difficult for him to do given that his mother, Mara, who had passed away sometime around 1427,[15] was a Hungarian Catholic and that he had spent the formative years of his youth at Sigismund's court in Buda where he was raised in the Catholic tradition. Vlad, like his father, also had a Catholic wife. Apart from their military and religious obligations, members of the Society pledged to help one another personally, as well as to assist widows and orphaned children of dead members of the Order; they also had to take part at the funerals of fellow members or, if this was not possible, to pay to have thirty masses said for his soul and to wear mourning clothes for a day. The insignia of the Order, which the Emperor placed around Vlad's neck on this occasion, was to be worn at all times. The official costume — scarlet garments with a green silk

---

[13]For examples, see docs. XXVII and CXXVII in Bogdan, *Documente privitoare*, pp. 47-48 and 157-159.

[14]Vîrtosu, "Din sigiliografia Moldovei și a Țării Românești," in *DIR, Intro*, vol. II, p. 364.

[15]Panaitescu, *Mircea cel Bătrân*, p. 50.

cloak — was worn for ceremonial events such as Vlad's reception into the Order. On Fridays, members had to wear a black costume or to pay for five masses to be said,[16] probably to commemorate Christ's crucifixion on a Friday. Membership in this elite Society created a personal bond between Vlad and his sovereign. In addition to awarding him membership in the Order of the Dragon, Sigismund also presented his vassal with the flag of St. Ladislas of Hungary, another symbol of the struggle against the infidels.

A grand parade followed the ceremony in which Vlad was led from the cathedral to his residence at the imperial palace amidst throngs of spectators who had gathered to witness the event. Here, at Sigismund's court, he issued his decree for the Franciscan monks. Indubitably, this act was linked to his reception into the Order of the Dragon and served as proof of his devotion to the Catholic faith. In it, he recounts that the Emperor had "decided to send some pious monks, brothers of the Order of the Friars Minor, to the Transalpine land, which is lacking any spiritual consolation from the Holy Roman Church,... who will work to spread and to preserve the true faith in the aforesaid Transalpine land." In his newly-acquired capacity as Prince, Vlad ordered "any and all inhabitants of the Transalpine land, monks and servants of any rank, condition, or status under our jurisdiction... not to attempt to disturb, to interfere with, or to cause them harm in any way."[17] To obtain his parental inheritance, Vlad had thrown in his lot with the Catholic, pro-Hungarian camp, but his decree lacked any force. Although he had been formally proclaimed Prince of Wallachia, he had yet to assume the throne, and the road to Târgoviște would be longer and more arduous than Vlad or anyone present in Nuremberg during those heady days in early February of 1431 could have anticipated.

Unfortunately for Vlad, the political situation in the region at this time was in a state of flux. Even before news of his coronation reached the area, events were set in motion that would impede his chances of ever reaching Târgoviște. Alexander the Good now seized the initiative in his ongoing dispute with Dan over control of Kilia. The Wallachian Prince had twice invaded Moldavia during the previous two years, the last time accompanied by Turkish troops.

---

[16]Minea, "Vlad Dracul și vremea sa," p. 100.

[17]Doc. 179 in *DRH, D*, pp. 280-281.

Fearing that Dan, with Ottoman support, might yet succeed in recovering the port city at the mouth of the Danube, the Moldavian Prince decided to strike first and readied his troops to invade Wallachia. Convinced of the need to intervene in the neighboring Principality and to place on the throne a Prince resigned to accept Moldavian control over Kilia,[18] Alexander the Good turned to another of Mircea's sons, like himself named Alexander, but also known as Aldea, who had sought refuge in the Principality east of the Carpathians after Dan had defeated his brother Radu. When relations between Wallachia and Moldavia deteriorated, Alexander Aldea found support there to make his own bid for his father's throne.

Accompanied by Wallachian supporters, the most important of whom was Albu, formerly one of Dan II's leading boyars, but who had also served on the royal council during the final years of Mircea's reign, Alexander Aldea led Moldavian forces into Wallachia in the spring of 1431. The move caught Dan by surprise and forced him to flee across the Danube to his Ottoman allies. Alexander II now ruled from Târgoviște, ending for the moment the conflict between Moldavia and Wallachia over Kilia.

The third of Mircea's sons to assume the throne, Alexander Aldea has been a subject of academic controversy. Several scholars, most notably Nicolae Iorga, have claimed that he was not Mircea's son at all, but rather a boyar named Aldea who took the name Alexander to honor his patron, Alexander the Good of Moldavia.[19] But for a boyar from outside the ruling dynasty to have pretended to the throne, he first would have needed to accrue substantial power. There is, however, no evidence of a boyar by this name having served in the royal council during the preceding decade. In fact, the only Aldea to appear in Wallachian documents up to this time was a boyar who served in the royal council during the early years of Mircea's reign and who, in 1398, together with his wife Bisa, donated the village of Chireashov to the Cutlumuz Monastery at Mount Athos in commemoration "first of our lord, Voivode John Mircea, then of our parents and of myself and my wife because it is our

---

[18]Veniamin Ciobanu, *Țările române și Polonia*, Bucharest, 1985, pp. 44-45.

[19]N. Iorga, *Istoria românilor*, vol. IV, p. 31; also Panaitescu, *Alexandru cel Bun*, p. 52; and C. Cihodaru, *Alexandru cel Bun*, Iași, 1984, p. 269.

monastery."[20] But this Aldea could not be the boyar suggested by Iorga as he was certainly an elderly man at that time and there is no trace of him in documents after 1400. Alexander II generally refers to himself by his Christian name in his letters and diplomas. He styles himself "John Alexander, Voivode and Prince, son of Voivode Mircea,"[21] claims uncontested by his contemporaries. These considerations, together with Radu II's decree in which he addresses his brother as "Tsar Alexander,"[22] invalidate Iorga's hypothesis.

Alexander was a fashionable name throughout the region during this epoch owing to the legendary status of the son of Philip II of Macedon. One of the most popular books of the period was a Slavonic translation of *Alexandria*, a Greek novel about the life of Alexander the Great.[23] But Alexander II was undoubtedly christened after his great-grandfather, Nicholas Alexander. The name, of Greek origin, means "one who protects people."[24] The other name by which he came to be known, Aldea, is an epithet that appears most frequently in letters of Vlad Dracul, who mentions his elder brother exclusively by this name. Aldea was a diminutive form of Alexander.[25] It is a name of Germanic origin, a variant of Aldo, a saint in the Catholic calendar, derived from *Ald*, meaning "old" or "vigorous" in medieval German.[26] There is only one extant letter in which Alexander calls himself Aldea, a hasty dispatch to Hungarian officials written at Buzău, most likely in 1434. It contains numerous errors and awkward formulations. For example, the greeting employs an unusual formula not found in any other document of the period: "From the Wallachian Voivode and Prince, son of Mircea, from Voivode *Alde*..."[27] This clumsy formulation

---

[20]Doc. 19 in *DRH, B*, vol. I, pp. 46-47.

[21]Doc. 199 in *DRH, D*, p. 297.

[22]Doc. 135 in *DRH, D*, p. 220.

[23]V. Costăchel, P.P. Panaitescu, and A. Cazacu, *Viața feudală în Țara Romînească și Moldova*, Bucharest, 1957, p. 531.

[24]Constantinescu, *Dicționar onomastic*, p. 7.

[25]Kogălniceanu, "Cercetări critice," p. 44; and Șt. Nicolaescu, "Domnia lui Alexandru Vodă Aldea," in *RIAF*, XVI (1915-1922), p. 238.

[26]Constantinescu, *Dicționar onomastic*, p. 180.

[27]Doc. 192 in *DRH, D*, pp. 291-292. See note 72 in this chapter for comments on the dating of this document.

and the use of the diminutive form of the Prince's name, not to mention numerous other errors and omissions, indicate that it was not penned by a professional scribe. The only plausible explanation is that the Prince, far from the royal court at Târgoviște, did not have a chancellery official on hand to draft this urgent message. Despite an age difference of perhaps ten years and the fact that they had not seen each other for some twenty years and now vied for their father's throne, it is only natural that Vlad referred to his sibling using the diminutive form of his name, all the more so because to use his proper name, the meaning and significance of which Vlad, with his ties to the Greek world, was all too aware, would also acknowledge his legitimacy.

Alexandru Aldea
Prince of Wallachia, 1431-1436
By Octavian Ion Penda

Alexander II's first order of business as Prince was to consolidate his position and to prepare for the inevitable Ottoman counterattack. In this task, he was greatly aided by Albul, formerly one of the most important members of Dan II's royal council. As Vornic under Dan II, he had already gained extensive power and had strong ties to Transylvania where the Prince sent him in April 1428 to settle a border dispute involving the Duchy of Amlaș.[28] Disgruntled over Dan's pro-Ottoman policy, he fled to Moldavia at the beginning of 1430. A son of a boyar called Tocsaba, another name of Cuman origin, Albul again assumed the office of Vornic under Aldea, making him the most important dignitary in the Principality after the Prince himself. But Albul played a role unprecedented for a court official in Wallachia up to this time. He virtually became co-ruler

---

[28]Doc. 164 in *DRH, D*, pp. 262-263.

of the country. In the letter to Hungarian officials mentioned above, Alexander informs them of a forthcoming attack by Ottoman forces on Transylvania and writes, "if this army will come against Transylvania, I will also be with it; but if I will not come with it, I will send Albul with it."[29] Vlad Dracul consistently refers to the two together, as if they jointly rule Wallachia; for example, he accuses officials of Braşov of "bringing copper to Aldea and to Albul," against the orders of Sigismund.[30] Because of the unparalleled authority held by this boyar during the reign of Alexander Aldea, he would be remembered as Albul the Great. Taking into account the unique position Albul held and the fact that Alexander appears to have been in frail health at various times throughout his reign, it is plausible that Albul fled to Moldavia with the intention of engineering the rise of Alexander to the throne.

In addition to Albul, other Wallachian boyars threw in their lot with Alexander. Some of these, such as Stanciul, had served his brother Radu and presumably had accompanied him into exile in Moldavia. Others, like Iarciul, had followed the same course as Albul and had abandoned Dan at the beginning of 1430, ending up in Moldavia where they offered their allegiance to the new pretender. A final category included boyars who had remained loyal to Dan II up to the time he was forced to flee south of the Danube; these included Nan Pascal, Cazan, and, for a short time, Voico. In a royal decree probably issued in the summer of 1431, the Prince commands villagers in Boruşi, on the estates of Voico in the county of Vâlcea, who had risen up against the boyar, previously one of the key members of Dan's royal council, "to be obedient... to the one who has done me great service... to Jupan Voico, because you are his ancient and rightful estate... obey him and honor him."[31] By November 1431, when we have the first extant list of members of Alexander's royal council, Voico's name is conspicuously absent, indicating that by this date he had taken refuge in Transylvania where we know he joined Vlad's entourage. Voico apparently fled in haste, for, with winter rapidly

---

[29]Doc. 192 in *DRH, D*, pp. 291-292.

[30]Doc. 185 in *DRH, D*, pp. 285-286.

[31]Doc. 70 in *DRH, B*, vol. I, pp. 131-132. George D. Florescu, *Divanele domneşti din Ţara Românească*, Bucharest, 1943, p. 91, identifies this village with Boroşteni, near Vulcan in the county of Vâlcea.

approaching, he wrote to the burghers of Braşov: "My brothers, you know well that I was your friend during the time of my lord, Voivode Dan, and that I was your brother and that I will continue to be. But you know well in what kind situation I find myself. For this reason I ask of you, if God will so instruct you, to provide me with a long fur coat, and if God will help my lord, Voivode Vlad, for one of these we will pay you for two or three."[32]

By now aware of Sigismund's intention to place his younger brother on the throne and the steps the Emperor had already taken in this direction, Alexander moved quickly to try to convince the Hungarian King to accept the fait accompli and to confirm him as ruler of Wallachia. To do this he enlisted the help of Peterman, a wealthy merchant from Câmpulung and a close friend of Albul,[33] a man held in high regard by Sigismund who had granted him estates in Transylvania.[34] The new Prince also called upon the officials of Braşov for help, requesting that "in the moment in which My Majesty's boyar Peterman arrives there, give him a good man to accompany him to Oradea,"[35] where they presumably met with Sigismund's representatives. Peterman's mission, almost certainly at Albul's initiative, succeeded. Hungarian officials now countermanded plans to install Vlad, who by this time had returned to Transylvania from Nuremberg, on the throne of Wallachia.

The fact that his older brother had managed to seize the throne before him certainly came as a great disappointment to Vlad. But although Sigismund accepted Alexander as the new ruler of Wallachia, Vlad maintained his title and privileges. As compensation for abandoning plans to place him on the throne of the Transalpine land, the Emperor installed Vlad as ruler of the duchies of Amlaş and Făgăraş in southern Transylvania, holdings generally reserved for the Prince of Wallachia. These territories never came under Alexander II's jurisdiction. Unlike his predecessors since the days of his father Mircea, Aldea titles himself solely as ruler "over all of the land of

---

[32]Doc. 178 in *DRH, D*, p. 280.

[33]Albul is listed as the primary witness to Peterman's last will and testament drafted in 1425 in which he bequeaths his wealth to the Monastery of Cozia, see Doc. 57 in *DRH, B*, vol. I, pp. 112-113.

[34]Doc. 256 in *DRH, D*, pp. 356-357.

[35]Doc. 203 in *DRH, D*, p. 299.

Ungrovalachia" in his internal documents. During his long reign, Sigismund had learned many times that circumstances could change rapidly and it suited him to keep Vlad ready should the need arise to intervene south of the Carpathians. Unlike the numerous other pretenders throughout the fifteenth century, Vlad had been crowned by the Holy Roman Emperor himself and effectively held dominion over lands traditionally reserved for rulers of the Principality. But for now, the would-be Prince remained the Great Pretender to the throne of Wallachia.

Alexander Aldea owed his success in obtaining recognition from the Hungarian Crown in large measure to dramatic changes taking place on the political scene in Eastern Europe at this time. The delicate alliance between Hungary, Poland, and Lithuania, first established at Lublau in 1412, and then repaired at Kesmark in 1423 and Luck in 1429, broke down following the death of Grand Duke Vitold in a riding accident on October 27, 1430. Tensions between Hungary and Poland resurfaced. Encouraged by Sigismund, the new Grand Duke, Swidrigaillo, sought to assert Lithuanian independence. On June 9, 1431, he concluded an alliance with the Teutonic Knights against Poland. Meanwhile, Alexander the Good, up to now a loyal vassal of Vladislav, also joined this new anti-Polish league. Relations between Moldavia and Poland had deteriorated; Alexander, disappointed by the King's hesitant support on the issue of Kilia and faced with Turkish attacks, now sought to draw closer to Hungary, the leading force in the anti-Ottoman struggle. Vladislav, in turn, accused Alexander of spreading heresy after he refused to arrest a former Franciscan monk Jacob, one of the leading exponents of Hussitism in Moldavia, in April.[36] Aldea benefitted from these changing political currents. To win Moldavia over to the Hungarian camp, Sigismund confirmed Alexander II as Prince of Wallachia and accepted the status quo with regard to Kilia.

The anticipated Ottoman counterattack intended to restore Dan came in the summer of 1431. Around mid-June, Aldea wrote to the officials of Brașov and the Bârsa land informing them that "four great lords — Feriz Beg, Azbuga, Caracea Beg, and Balaban Beg — are ready with their armies at Silistra on the Danube and another army awaits at Turnu, while Sultan Murad is three days away from me; therefore, my brothers, together with you I can resist them, but

---

[36]Minea, "Vlad Dracul și vremea sa," p. 105.

without you I cannot, so gather your forces and stay ready so that at the moment when you receive word from My Majesty in that same moment come to my aid."[37] Meanwhile, Alexander the Good also sent forces to aid his protégé in Wallachia. In early July, royal officials in Transylvania had received intelligence that these troops had gathered at Putna, in the Vrancea region of southern Moldavia, and that the Great Vornic intended "to lead these troops into the Transalpine land." Despite the recent shifts in alliance, they remained wary of Moldavian intentions, fearing a possible attack on Transylvania, and awaited the arrival of an emissary from Alexander the Good.[38] The situation soon became clear when Aldea wrote to Braşov that "on the orders of my lord, the King, four flags of Moldavians have arrived." This meant approximately 2000 troops. The Prince went on to ask them "to help me with bows, arrows, arms, and anything you can."[39] When the moment arrived, Aldea dispatched an urgent message to Braşov: "be aware that the Turks have invaded at the Danube at all the crossings... hurry as quickly as you can, day and night, to come to my aid."[40] These efforts bore fruit. A Ragusan report dated September 6 tells of the defeat of the Turks who had invaded Wallachia that summer.[41] Dan, who had accompanied these Ottoman forces, apparently died in the fighting.[42] For the moment, Alexander II had secured his position.

Vlad's prospects of attaining the throne improved at the beginning of the following year as the political landscape continued to change. The unexpected

---

[37]Doc. 191 in *DRH, D*, pp. 290-291. The editors propose May 1432 as the date of this letter as suggested originally by Ioan Bogdan (Doc. XIX in *Documente privitoare*, pp. 40-41), but it is better seen as reflecting events in the summer of 1431, a date also accepted by Ilie Minea ("Vlad Dracul şi vremea sa," pp. 103-104).

[38]Doc. 181 in *DRH, D*, pp. 282-283.

[39]Doc. 195 in *DRH, D*, pp. 293-294. Also dated May 1432 by the editors of this collection, but more likely it is from 1431 for the reasons stated above.

[40]Doc. 193 in *DRH, D*, pp. 292-293.

[41]Vasilescu. Urmaşii lui Mircea cel Bătrân, p. 44.

[42]According to a Serbian chronicle, "in the year 6940 [September 1431-August 1432], on June 1, Voivode Dan died fighting bravely against the Turks" (Quo, Vasilescu, *Urmaşii lui Mircea cel Bătrân*, p. 47). The correct date must be 6939, placing Dan's death on June 1, 1431, but he was killed fighting alongside the Turks and not against them.

death of Aldea's patron, Alexander the Good, on January 1, 1432, meant that the Wallachian Prince could no longer depend on Moldavian support because of the uncertain political situation in the neighboring Principality. Nor could he rely upon Hungary for military assistance against the Turks. Sigismund had set out for Italy for his long-delayed coronation as Emperor by the Pope and events in the West continued to take precedence over the struggle against the Ottomans. Alexander II had additional reasons to feel insecure in his alliance with the Hungarians; Vlad ruled the duchies of Amlaş and Făgăraş, traditionally reserved for rulers of the Transalpine land, and continued to use the title Prince of Wallachia with the Emperor's tacit consent. Weighing these factors and realizing the imminent danger of renewed Ottoman attacks on Wallachia, Aldea felt constrained to come to terms with the Sultan. Sometime after January 15, 1432, when he granted the village of Goleşti near Argeş to the Monastery of Cozia in "eternal memory of My Majesty's father,"[43] Alexander set out for Adrianople where he submitted to Murad II. As Aldea had no sons, he left twenty sons of leading Wallachian boyars as hostages; in a subsequent letter to Hungarian authorities, the Prince explained his actions: "I did what I did and I went to him out of fear. All of this I did from fear, as they took my country and began to threaten me and I sent the children of boyars there."[44] Their presence at the Porte is confirmed by Bertrandon de la Brocquière, an emissary of Philip the Good, the Duke of Burgundy, who noted that he saw "twenty gentlemen from Wallachia who were hostages for the aforesaid country" at Adrianople in the summer of 1433.[45]

One of Aldea's obligations as a vassal of the Porte was to accompany the Ottoman army with Wallachian contingents when called upon by the Sultan. As the three-year peace agreement concluded between the Hungarians and the Ottomans in 1429 expired, Murad II prepared to launch a new attack on Transylvania. The Wallachian Prince readied his troops and joined the Ottoman offensive; he did so partly out of obligation, but he almost certainly saw it also as an opportunity to eliminate his rival. By mid-April, Ragusan

---

[43]Doc. 73 in *DRH, B*, vol. I, p. 135.

[44]Doc. 192 in *DRH, D*, pp. 291-292.

[45]Quo. Kogălniceanu, "Cercetări critice," p. 47; and Minea, "Vlad Dracul şi vremea sa," p. 106.

sources already knew of the upcoming attack on Transylvania. Ottoman forces, led by Ali Bey, the Beylerbey of Rumelia, crossed the Danube at Nicopolis in early June and proceeded north to Târgoviște. Almost simultaneously, another Ottoman army struck western Transylvania around the Iron Gates. On June 10, officials of Brașov conveyed to Hungarian authorities that their spies reported that the Turks "have gathered a large armed force in the Transalpine land," and that on Wednesday, June 11, they would encamp at Finta,[46] some thirty kilometers southwest of Târgoviște. From here a detachment of *Akingi* set out against Moldavia, but Alexander the Good's son and successor Iliaș stood ready and annihilated the attackers.[47] Aldea accompanied the principal invasion force led by Ali Bey that crossed into Transylvania via the Bran pass. This combined Wallachian and Turkish force attacked Brașov on June 24, the feast day of John the Baptist;[48] town councillors fell captive and the invaders plundered the Bârsa land and adjacent Szeckler territories for three days. After taking many captives and much plunder, Ottoman troops withdrew south, and the Beylerbey returned to Adrianople where he arrived on July 22.[49] The invasion of 1432 marked the most devastating attack on Transylvania since 1421.

The disastrous events of the summer of 1432 revived Vlad's hopes of seizing the throne with which he had already been invested. Sigismund's grand experiment of entrusting the defense of the southern border of the Kingdom to the Teutonic Knights had proved a failure. On March 7, 1432, even before the Ottoman assaults had begun, the Knights assigned to protect the region had written from Severin to their Grand Master complaining of insufficient revenues and a lack of manpower to strengthen the fortresses in their possession. When Ottoman forces attacked the area around the Iron Gates that summer, they captured three of the citadels the Knights had been assigned to defend and took much plunder and many captives destined to be sold into

---

[46]Doc. 196 in *DRH, D*, pp. 294-295. The editors have incorrectly dated the document June 20.

[47]Gemil, *Românii și otomanii*, p. 111, nt. 274; Iorga, *Studii și documente*, vol. III, p. X.

[48]Andrei Veress, "Vechi istorici unguri și sași," in *ARMSL*, series III, vol. IV (1929), p. 334.

[49]Iorga, *Studii și documente*, vol. III, p. X; Kogălniceanu, "Cercetări critice," p. 49.

slavery.[50] The King now charged Vlad with coordinating the defense of southern Transylvania. The Prince later admonished the burghers of Braşov: "You know very well that our lord, the Kaiser, has assigned me to defend these borders, and that without my approval you are not to make peace with Wallachia."[51]

As the defense of this region necessitated adequate finances, Sigismund, whom Vlad, with his German upbringing, referred to as *Kesar* or Kaiser, granted the Great Pretender to the Wallachian throne the right to establish and to operate a royal mint. Vlad then wrote to the burghers of Braşov: "You know well that it is the order of our lord, the Kaiser, that I set up a mint. Therefore, hand over to my men iron and everything else that is necessary for a mint so that we may begin our work."[52] Vlad established his new mint in Schässburg, most likely in the house that also served as his residence.

Turkish raids in Transylvania continued throughout the summer of 1432. On August 10, an Ottoman contingent attacked Sibiu. News of the devastation reached Sigismund in Italy. On December 14, he wrote from Siena to Michael Jakch, Count of the Szecklers, requesting details about the extent of the damages suffered by the Saxon lands in southern Transylvania.[53] In the aftermath of the Ottoman attacks, the King took action to reorganize defenses in the region. Difficulties in financing had long hindered efforts to protect the area from Turkish incursions. Although the King had granted the Teutonic Knights revenues from royal mints in Sibiu and Braşov, the Hospitallers

---

[50]Minea, "Vlad Dracul şi vremea sa," p. 117.

[51]Doc. 173 in *DRH, D*, pp. 274-275. For considerations on the dating of this document see note 98 in this chapter.

[52]Doc. 232 in *DRH, D*, pp. 329-330. The editors of this collection date this undated document from the period 1437-1443, but Vlad uses the term *Kesar* in his letters to refer exclusively to Sigismund, who died on December 9, 1437, and not his successors as King of Hungary, Albrecht or Vladislav, neither of whom held the title of Holy Roman Emperor. Furthermore, the letter refers to the *Krastoshi*, a reference to the Teutonic Knights who left the area after 1435. Thus, the letter must be dated 1431-1435 and the context makes it most likely around the time we have suggested here.

[53]Doc. XXIII in Hurmuzaki, *Documente*, vol. XV, part. 1, pp. 16-17.

complained that these did not provide significant income.[54] In a revealing letter
sent by Sigismund from Siena in Italy on February 24, 1433, to the Saxons in
Kolosvár and Bistriţa, the King writes that the German cities in southern
Transylvania, "for their more effective defense... against attacks made by the
Turks, have regularly sent, at the cost of a remarkable sum of money, some
spies to our Transalpine land and sometimes to Turkey... and when they, acting
on reliable information from those spies and from other people, realize that the
aforementioned Turks will enter those parts with hostile intentions, they
regularly place in the mountains, at great expense, a large number of men to
defend the mountain passes in those parts which stretch... from the Făgăraş
land to the Haţeg district, so that the Turks cannot get through; thus, during
this past year, in the time of the invasion of the above-mentioned Turks, they
maintained two thousand men in the aforementioned mountains."[55] Sigismund
went on to order that Kolosvár and Bistriţa, cities located further from the fray,
contribute their share to these defense expenditures. Apart from small
garrisons stationed in various strongholds, defense of the border region
depended on timely and accurate information so that an army could be
mustered when necessary to meet a potential threat. Standing armies were too
costly to maintain and the day of the professional soldier had not yet dawned;
the bulk of the military consisted of feudal levies commanded by nobles. In
this type of system, intelligence gathering operations, such as that described
by Sigismund, played a key role.

The fact that Făgăraş, ruled by Vlad, had been cut off from Wallachia and
was now incorporated into the defensive system of southern Transylvania
provoked a great deal of unrest among the local population. Increased taxation
to cover defense outlays certainly ranked high among the causes of their
discontent. A monk at the Monastery of Kertz, located in the Duchy, echoed
the turmoil in southern Transylvania at this time in a transcription of the works
of St. Augustine in which he noted, "this book was finished in the year of our
Lord 1433 at the time of the uprising of the Wallachians in Făgăraş."[56] This
revolt appears to have coincided with plans for a new Wallachian-Ottoman

---

[54]Minea, "Vlad Dracul şi vremea sa," p. 122, nt. 1.

[55]Doc. 205 in *DRH, D*, pp. 300-303.

[56]Ştefan Pascu, *Bobîlna*, Bucharest, 1957, p. 82.

attack on Transylvania. On May 16, Michael Jakch, Count of the Szecklers, wrote to the officials of Braşov, warning them to take measures to protect against an invasion and "not to be somehow duped by those deceitful Wallachians," promising that "we will come to your aid with all our men."[57] But an attack did not materialize that summer. Vlad managed to bring the situation in Făgăraş under control, and the Duchy continued to serve as the base from which he hoped to launch an attack on Wallachia to seize the throne from his brother. But, as affairs in the West, where a new Church Council had opened at Basel in 1431, preoccupied Sigismund, the time to launch an offensive had not yet arrived and Vlad continued to play the role of Prince-in-waiting.

The situation in neighboring Moldavia had changed dramatically since the death of Aldea's protector, Alexander the Good. Like Mircea in Wallachia, Alexander had tried to secure a smooth transition of power by making his eldest son, Iliaş, associate ruler as early as 1414.[58] Born on July 20, 1409, Iliaş was the son of Alexander and his first wife Neaksha, or Anna, a great-granddaughter of Bogdan I, who had established the independence of the Principality in 1359. Alexander had arranged for the marriage of his designated heir to Maria, a sister of the Polish Queen Sophia, in October 1425. But Alexander had several sons and, as happened in Wallachia after the death of Mircea, disputes broke out among them as each aspired to the throne. Iliaş's most important rival was his half-brother Stephen, also called Stetco, born in 1411, the eldest son of Alexander and his long-time mistress Stanca.[59] An ambitious woman, Stanca had insisted that Alexander recognize Stephen as a legitimate heir, a necessary prerequisite for an illegitimate offspring to have a realistic opportunity of one day wearing the crown. After Alexander's death,

---

[57]Doc. 208 in *DRH, D*, pp. 306-307.

[58]*DRH, A*, vol. I, p. 28.

[59]Panaitescu, ed., *Cronicele slavo-romîne*, p. 6. The Anonymous Moldavian Chronicle erroneously dates Iliaş's wedding to Maria on October 23, but the correct date is undoubtedly October 21, which fell on a Sunday in that year, the day in which marriage ceremonies were commonly performed. This conclusion is supported by the fact that the chronicle specifies that the princess arrived on Saturday and that the wedding took place the following day. See L. Simanschi, "Precizări cronologice privind istoria Moldovei" in *AIIA, Iaşi*, VII (1970), p. 76.

Stanca began to encourage her son's ambitions and soon prompted him to challenge Iliaş.

Aldea's relations with Moldavia had also changed following his protector's death. His facilitating the Ottoman attack on Moldavia in the summer of 1432, when Turkish troops had used Wallachia as a staging ground for their raid on the neighboring Principality, had certainly created tensions between the two neighboring Principalities. Family connections, however, led to the breakdown in relations between Wallachia and Moldavia. While a refugee at the court of Alexander the Good, Aldea appears to have married one of Stanca's daughters, making him the brother-in-law of Iliaş's rival, Stephen.[60] As the conflict between the two half-brothers intensified, Stephen fled to Wallachia in May 1433. The seventeenth century Moldavian chronicler Grigore Ureche records that "Voivode Iliaş wanted to kill his brother Voivode Stephen, and Voivode Stephen fled to Muntenia."[61] Meanwhile, Iliaş, who harbored enmity toward Stanca and blamed her for inciting rebellion, ordered the drowning of Stephen's mother.[62] He also reorientated Moldavia's foreign policy, accepting the suzerainty of Polish King Vladislav I, his brother-in-law, in June 1433.[63]

As a result of these events, by the fall of that year Aldea began making peace overtures to Hungary. Having accompanied the Ottoman forces that had burned and pillaged Transylvania the year before, his task was not an easy one. All the more so because he had to proceed cautiously so as not to provoke the ire of the Sultan. In addition, Vlad stood poised across the mountains ready to move against his brother as soon as he received Sigismund's approval to launch an invasion. We know that, at the end of 1433, Sigismund still considered Wallachia as belonging to the Ottoman camp. In the diploma cited in the previous chapter condemning the Transylvanian nobleman Lado de Byzere for treason, issued at Basel in Switzerland on December 6, 1433, the recently-crowned Holy Roman Emperor asserts that his traitorous subject "withdrew to Wallachia" during the time of Dan II, "subjected then, *as it also*

---

[60]Minea, *Vlad Dracul şi vremea sa*, p. 134.

[61]Kogălniceanu, ed., *Cronicele României*, vol. I, p. 141.

[62]*Istoria românilor*, vol. IV, pp. 318-319.

[63]Doc. CCCCLXXXII in Hurmuzaki, *Documente*, vol. I, part. 2, pp. 580-581.

is now, to the barbaric Turks,"[64] a clear indication that relations between Hungary and Wallachia had not yet improved since the events of the summer of 1432.

But before intensifying efforts to improve relations with Hungary, Aldea first sought to secure his border with Moldavia. He provided military assistance to his brother-in-law Stephen who now prepared to avenge his mother's assassination and to attempt to usurp the throne from his half-brother. The Polish chronicler Jan Długosz records how Stephen returned to Moldavia in the fall of 1433 and seized the throne with help from the Turks and Wallachians,[65] forcing Iliaş to flee to his relatives in Poland. Grigore Ureche explains that "Voivode Stephen had fled to Muntenia for fear of his brother; there he received help and an army, and returning to the country, he came against his brother, Voivode Iliaş, to drive him from the country to the place called Laloni where they fought, and Stephen was victorious over Iliaş, and Stephen assumed the throne of the country."[66] Civil war ensued, as Iliaş regrouped and returned with a force of his own only to suffer another defeat at the hands of Stephen at Dărmaneşti on February 1, 1434. Iliaş again sought help from his brother-in-law, King Vladislav, but the Polish Diet intervened, hoping to bring stability to the vassal state, and ordered that he be held at Sieradz.[67] Aldea's brother-in-law now ruled Moldavia.

Having acquired an ally in Moldavia, Alexander II now turned his attention to Hungary, hoping to forestall Vlad from launching an attack against him. Albul almost certainly played a key role in this diplomatic maneuvering to neutralize Vlad, and his efforts paid off. To convince the Hungarians of their goodwill, Aldea and Albul ransomed Transylvanian citizens taken captive during the recent Ottoman attacks on the province. In an undated letter to the burghers of Braşov, Aldea writes, "I am working for you, so that you will have peace, and your captives, as many as I have been able, I have ransomed. And as many captives as there are at Nicopolis, I have sent word to Nicopolis not

---

[64]Doc. 209 in *DRH, D*, pp. 307-309, emphasis added.

[65]Minea, *Informaţiile româneşti*, p. 23.

[66]Kogălniceanu, ed., *Cronicele României*, vol. I, p. 142.

[67]Minea, Principatele române şi politica orientală a împăratului Sigismund, p. 238.

to send them on until you are able to ransom them."[68] In another letter, this one to the burghers of Sibiu, the Prince claims to have obtained freedom for "three thousand prisoners"[69] from the Sultan. Although wary of Aldea's professed loyalty, Sigismund preferred peaceful relations with Wallachia as the conflict in Bohemia continued to preoccupy the King. The time for Vlad to throw down the gauntlet had not yet arrived.

The alliance between Wallachia and Moldavia further complicated matters for Vlad. Despite the thaw in relations between Hungary and the Transalpine land, a cold war persisted between the Great Pretender, ruling over the southern Transylvanian duchies, and the Prince south of the Carpathians, aided by his powerful Vornic Albul. Vlad had tried to open negotiations with Moldavia, but Stephen refused to recognize his legitimacy and, contrary to accepted practice, he seized the emissary Vlad had sent to the court at Suceava. In a letter to the officials of Braşov, Vlad complained that "the Moldavians took him captive, bound him, and turned him over to Aldea and to Albul, and they also confiscated all of the goods that I had in Moldavia. Now, wanting to ransom my servant from Aldea and from Albul, they are asking more than a thousand gold florins for him."[70] Clearly, the Moldavian Prince took Vlad's ambassador prisoner and turned him over to Aldea to demonstrate that he only recognized his brother-in-law as the legitimate sovereign of Wallachia, with jurisdiction over all Wallachian subjects. In response to these hostile acts, Vlad took retaliatory measures against the Moldavians, apparently with Sigismund's tacit

---

[68]Doc. 225 in *DRH, D*, pp. 324-325.

[69]Doc. 197 in *DRH, D*, pp. 295-296.

[70]Doc. 187 in *DRH, D*, pp. 287-288. The editors date this letter November 1431-1432 after Bogdan (Doc. XXXVII in Bogdan, *Documente privitoare*, pp. 59-61), but the spring of 1434 is a more likely date because Vlad also complains in this letter that "my servant Vlad has come to me and told me that you have thrown him out and have not allowed him to carry out the task which I have assigned him." In addition, Aldea's ally Stephen ruled Moldavia at this time, having recently driven out his brother Iliaş with whom Vlad enjoyed good relations, but who was hostile to Aldea. This scenario would also explain the goods in Moldavia that Vlad accuses the authorities there of having confiscated. Bogdan's dating of these documents is generally faulty because he erroneously believed Aldea's reign ended in 1433 and that Vlad ruled Wallachia for a brief time in 1432.

approval. In another letter, he wrote to the Saxons of Braşov, "You know well what kind of friends the Moldavians are to me. For this reason, I have been permitted to have my servants go throughout the land of my lord, the Kaiser, and wherever they find Moldavians to arrest them and to take from them whatever they are carrying with them, and to bring them to me." But the Saxons, interested in peaceful relations with the two neighboring Principalities, necessary for the trade on which their prosperity depended to flourish, refused to cooperate. "I understand, however, that you follow my servants," Vlad sternly reproached them, "and do not allow them to take hold of those people disloyal to my lord, the Kaiser, and to me."[71]

Soon after he managed to restore peaceful relations with Hungary, Aldea again found himself in a delicate situation as the Ottomans planned a new assault on Transylvania for the summer of 1434. Aldea had informed Hungarian officials of Turkish intentions and travelled to Moldavia where he met with his ally, Stephen, in the spring of that year. When he returned to Wallachia and arrived in Buzău, Alexander II received further details concerning the upcoming attack and sent a hastily-written dispatch to the Palatine, Nicholas Garai, and to Stephen Rozgonyi, the Count of Temes. Aldea informed them that, "I asked for help from Moldavia, and the Moldavian Prince has the same feelings for the King that I have." The Prince wrote that, "you should know that the Turks will come with their army to Transylvania and that I will accompany them or, if I do not come with them, I will send Albul along with them." He also provided detailed intelligence concerning the Ottoman force preparing to invade. The Prince now declared himself ready to break with the Sultan and to throw off the Turkish yoke if the Hungarians would provide the necessary military support: "when your army will meet them, at that moment I will withdraw from their army. Many times the Turks have betrayed me, and now I wish to do the same to them, so as for there not to remain a trace of them!" Aldea further proposed that the Ottoman pretender Daud Celebi, be sent with an army to lead a counteroffensive: "send Sultan Celebi, as quickly as possible, with an army, and I will also give him half of

---

[71]Doc. 190 in *DRH, D*, pp. 289-290. The editors date this letter 1432-1433 after Bogdan (Doc. XL in Bogdan, *Documente privitoare*, pp. 63-64), but, for the same reasons outlined in the previous note, I maintain that the spring of 1434 is a more likely date.

my army, and we will strike at the Lord of Rumelia himself and at Lord Hamza as soon as Celebi will arrive."[72] Alexander II's ambitious plan recalled the days when his father Mircea played the role of king-maker in Ottoman politics. But Wallachia no longer could sustain such ambitions, and although peaceful relations prevailed between Hungary and the Transalpine land, officials such as Michael Jakch warned against being "tricked by those villaneous Wallachians."[73]

Prior to his trip to Moldavia, Alexander II had travelled to Adrianople to pay homage to Murad II. During this visit, he probably first learned of Ottoman plans for a new raid on Transylvania. The events of 1432 still fresh in their minds, Aldea's meeting with the Sultan provoked concern among Transylvanian leaders. Vlad hoped to turn this situation to his advantage and to launch an invasion south of the Carpathians. In a letter to the burghers of Brașov, Vlad wrote, "you know well that Aldea went to the Turks not for your benefit, but to bring harm upon you, to bring the Turkish army to plunder you, as they have plundered you before. Therefore, I ask you as my brothers, prepare for me one hundred firearms, with all they require, and bows and arrows and shields, as many as you can, and give me men to help me, as many as you can spare, for I want to go, if God will help me, and drive him out of the country."[74] Vlad was not alone in doubting Aldea's intentions. In a harsh letter addressed to "all the citizens of Sibiu, both great and small," the Wallachian Prince accuses them of "fabricating lies, that I have abandoned the King and gone over to the Turks.... whoever lies, may dogs fuck his wife and his mother. If I have gone to the Turks, I have done it out of necessity, to bring peace to my land, what is left of it, and for all of you, and I freed three

---

[72]Doc. 192 in *DRH, D*, pp. 291-292. The editors date this letter May-June 1432 after Bogdan (Doc. XXX in Bogdan, *Documente privitoare*, pp. 49-53), while Iorga, *Scrisori de Domni*, proposes 1435, but the context of the letter makes 1434 the more likely date.

[73]Doc. 208 in *DRH, D*, pp. 306-307.

[74]Doc. 198 in *DRH, D*, pp. 296-297. The editors date this letter October 1432-March 1433 after Bogdan (Doc. XXXIX in Bogdan, *Documente privitoare*, pp. 62-63), but for the reasons stated in previous notes 1434 is the most probable date.

thousands slaves, yet you say that I want to plunder the country of my lord, the King, with the Turks."[75]

Although no detailed information about the Ottoman raid on Transylvania that summer had survived, Serbian chronicles mention that by mid-May Turkish forces were in Wallachia[76] from where they launched their attack. The invasion coincided with another uprising in Făgăraş, as the heavy duties imposed to finance the defense of southern Transylvania provoked further civil strife. On June 2, Michael Jakch ordered the officials of Braşov to take severe action against the rebellious Wallachians who had taken refuge in the mountains, and to kill the rebels and to take captive their women and children.[77] Conflict between noble and peasant was acute throughout Transylvania at this time, as both the landowners and the Church, in desperate need of revenues, sought to extract heavier duties from their serfs. In response, the peasants attempted to invoke their ancient right to move from one estate to another to seek more favorable conditions. The aristrocracy then tried to impede their movement and bind them to the land. In an attempt to keep the situation from spinning out of control, on August 28, 1434, the Voivode of Transylvania ordered certain nobles not to impede their serfs from moving from one estate to another after they have paid the *terragiis*, a special tax required for a serf to leave his estate, and other debts.[78] Vlad, with help from Braşov and Michael Jakch, managed to bring the situation in Făgăraş under control, but Transylvania remained a tinderbox ready to explode.

The Turkish raid in the summer of 1434 concentrated on Braşov and the Bârsa land. An assessment of the damages inflicted by the Ottoman invaders records destruction to the city's walls and towers, and the devastation of St. Peter's Church and Monastery.[79] The burning and pillaging by Turkish forces

---

[75]Doc. 197 in *DRH, D*, pp. 295-296. The editors date this letter July 1432 after Bogdan (Doc. XXIII in Bogdan, *Documente privitoare*, pp. 43-44), but for reasons previously stated, 1434 is a more likely date.

[76]Iorga, *Studii şi documente*, vol III, p. XV.

[77]Doc. 2197 in *Urkundenbuch*, vol. IV, p. 523.

[78]Doc. CCCCLXXXIX in Hurmuzaki, *Documente*, vol. I, part. 2, p. 588.

[79]Doc. XXIX in Hurmuzaki, *Documente*, vol. XV, part. 1, pp. 20-21. This report compiled by officials of Braşov is dated October 16, 1434.

in this region was extensive. Because of the devastation, Sigismund, while at Pressburg on April 7, 1435, exempted Brașov from payment of a special tax imposed at the Council of Basel.[80] Three days later, the Holy Roman Emperor decreed that wood from the royal forest reserves be provided to residents of the Bârsa land to help them rebuild their homes burned by the Turks the year before.[81]

Aldea's grandiose scheme to turn the tables on the Turks never materialized, albeit through no fault of his own. The Hungarians did not set loose the Ottoman pretender Daud Celebi, nor did they prove capable of mobilizing a force strong enough to launch a counterattack against the Islamic invaders. Under these circumstances, Alexander II could not openly betray the Sultan. In the absence of Sigismund, the defense of the Kingdom's southern border lacked cohesion and Transylvanian officials proved incapable of mounting anything more than a passive resistance against Turkish attacks. There appears to have been little cooperation amongst these responsible for protecting the frontier: Michael Jakch, the Count of the Szecklers, responsible for the southeastern border of the Voivodate, the Wallachian pretender Vlad, charged with protecting the southern border between Brașov and Sibiu, Transylvanian Voivode Ladislas Csáki, absent from the province for most of his tenure, Vice-Voivode Lorand Lepes, who governed in his absence but lacked the necessary authority to formulate a coherent defensive strategy, the Count of Severin, Nicholas von Redwitz, leader of the Teutonic Knights manning the fortresses in the southwestern region along the Danube, who had proved completely ineffective in combatting the Turks and would soon abandon the region as the Knights of St. John had done before them, and, finally, Pippo de Ozora's successor as Count of Temes, Stephen Rozgonyi, an experienced warrior, but lacking the leadership qualities that had made Pippo an outstanding military commander, capable of undertaking independent military enterprises against the Turks in Sigismund's absence. The King's declared intentions of returning to the Kingdom after an absence of nearly five years seemed to be the remedy sought by all parties. On October 7, 1434, Vlad wrote to the burghers of Brașov from Merghindeal, in the Duchy of Făgăraș:

---

[80]Doc. XXX in Hurmuzaki, *Documente*, vol. XV, part. 1, p. 21.

[81]Doc. XXXI in Hurmuzaki, *Documente*, vol. XV, part. 1, p. 21.

"I send you news that a man came to me from my lord, the Kaiser, on Wednesday, October 6, and he brought good news for me and for you also, news which Janosh the Brave will tell you."[82] The good news mentioned by Vlad was likely the King's intention to return to Hungary to resume command of the struggle against the Turks. Vlad hoped that this meant that he would finally be able to attain his father's throne that had eluded him for so long. With this scope in mind, he sent his trusted lieutenant, Logofăt Stephen, to meet the Emperor at Pressburg at the end of December 1434. Michael Jakch was also present at the imperial court at this time.[83] But despite his best laid plans, Sigismund delayed his long- awaited return to eastern Hungary until 1436 as the conflict in Bohemia continued to take precedence.

Despite his involvement in the Ottoman attack, Aldea managed to maintain good relations with Hungary. He had secretly provided Hungarian officials with accurate information about Ottoman plans, troop strength, and movements, and his intention to revolt against the Turks could not be realized through no fault of his own. The intelligence he provided certainly helped limit damages suffered during the recent invasion. For the moment, he served Hungarian interests better by feigning allegiance to the Sultan than by turning against the Turks on his own, without Hungarian military support to back him up, which could only result in his removal and replacement by a Prince more pliant to Ottoman interests. As a result, Vlad had to bide his time in southern Transylvania, watching and waiting from his base in Schässburg and ruling over the duchies of Amlaş and Făgăraş.

Meanwhile, the instability that had marked Moldavian politics since the death of Alexander the Good grew more acute. Following the death of Polish King Vladislav I on May 31, 1434, Iliaş, with the help of his sister-in-law

---

[82]Doc. 213 in *DRH, D*, pp. 311-312. As with all of Vlad's letters in Slavonic, the original document does not indicate the year, but, as October 6 fell on a Wednesday only in 1434 during this period, we can precisely date when it was written.

[83]Doc. 249 in *DRH, D*, pp. 345-346. The editors incorrectly date this document December 29, 1437. Sigismund died on December 9 of that year and the term Kaiser used in this letter could only refer to him and not to Albrecht or Vladislav, his immediate successors, who bore only the title of King. The correct year is 1434 when Sigismund is known to have spent the winter months in Pressburg.

Queen Sophia, who now ruled Poland as regent for her young son Vladislav III, managed to escape confinement and began to gather troops for a new invasion of Moldavia to recover the throne he had lost to his brother Stephen. Iliaş made his move in the summer of 1435. He chose a fortuitous moment, for Aldea had taken severely ill and rumors of his death began to circulate. On July 29, 1435, Michael Jakch wrote from Bistriţa to the officials of Braşov who had "made known to us that Aldea, the Transalpine Voivode, has closed his eyes forever..."[84] News of Aldea's death, however, was premature. The Prince had recovered by October 15 when he issued a diploma for the Monastery of Cozia, confirming to it the village of Cărareni,[85] but the severity of his illness and the potential for instability in the Principality in the event of his passing meant that Stephen could not rely on military assistance from Wallachia as he had previously done. The armies of the two brothers met in battle at Podraga, in northern Moldavia, on August 4, 1435. This time Iliaş triumphed, winning an important, albeit not decisive victory over Stephen. At this point, Polish officials intervened to restore peace to the troubled Principality as the conflict between the two siblings posed a serious threat to their economic interests in the region, especially the important trade route linking Lemburg and Akkerman. The sixteenth century Polish chronicler Joachim Bielski records: "At that time the King [Vladislav III], through emissaries, made peace between Iliaş and Stephen..."[86] As a result of the agreement, Stephen recognized Iliaş as Prince and, in return, was made associate ruler and given territories in southern Moldavia. Iliaş wrote to the King of Poland from Suceava on September 1, 1435, officially informing Vladislav III, to whom he paid homage in separate acts in both Latin and Slavonic that same day,[87] that "we have given to our beloved brother, Voivode Stephen, from our inheritance, the following district, the city of Kilia with the customs and the surrounding territory that belong to that city, and the city of Vaslui and the surrounding

---

[84]Doc. 218 in *DRH, D*, pp. 315-316.

[85]Doc. 76 in *DRH, B*, vol. I, p. 138.

[86]G.I. Năstase, "Istoria moldovenească din Kronika polska a lui Bielski" in *CI*, I (1925), p. 118.

[87]Docs. 193 and 194 in Costăchescu, ed., *Documentele moldoveneşti*, vol. II, pp. 684-688.

territory belonging to that city, and the district of Tutova and the market of Bârlad with all its surrounding territory, and the mills of Covurlui and the city of Tecuci with all its surrounding territory, and Oltenii."[88] For the moment, Polish authorities had managed to bring the situation in Moldavia under control.

The powerful Vornic Albul had managed to maintain political stability in Wallachia during Aldea's bout with death in the summer of 1435. The ties to Hungary that he had forged as one of Dan II's leading boyars continued to serve him well in this task. While Vlad worked to gather support to invade Wallachia to oust his brother, Albul worked to improve relations with Hungary, and especially with the Saxon city of Braşov, among Wallachia's most important trade partners. One of purposes of Logofăt Stephen's mission to Pressburg, where he joined Peter Urosh, an emissary from Braşov, and representatives from Sibiu at the end of December 1434, was to discuss relations with Wallachia together with the Emperor, Michael Jakch, and other royal officials. From a letter Vlad addressed to the burghers of Braşov in early 1435, we learn that they imposed certain trade restrictions which Braşov failed to respect: "you are not abiding by what you discussed with me, but you are bringing copper to Aldea and to Albul. For this reason, my boyar [Stephen] and your man Peter went to the Span [Michael Jakch] and they will tell you that the Span said that all copper should go to the royal mints, as is the command of our lord, the Kaiser."[89] Vlad sent his emissaries Jonash, Stanislav, and Nanesh to Braşov to ensure that all supplies of copper be sold to the royal mint that he had established in Schässburg, and threatened all smugglers with the death penalty. In addition, Vlad's letter reveals that ties with Moldavia were also on the agenda at Pressburg. Tense relations had existed since Prince Stephen had seized Vlad's property in that Principality and handed over one of his emissaries to Wallachian authorities. To prevent such a thing from

---

[88]Doc. 192 in Costăchescu, ed., *Documentele moldoveneşti*, vol. II, pp. 681-684.

[89]Doc. 185 in *DRH, D,* pp. 285-286. The editors place this document in November-December 1431 after Bogdan (Doc. XXXV in Bogdan, *Documente privitoare*, pp. 57-58), a date that must be rejected for reasons discussed in previous notes. As we know that Stephen and Peter Urosh were in Pressburg in late December 1434, the context of Vlad's letter makes early 1435 the most plausible date.

happening again, Vlad ordered the Saxon burghers: "And as many people as are found there from Moldavia, do not let any of them slip though your hands for our lord, the Kaiser, and the Span, by their orders, have commanded that they be held until our emissaries return from Moldavia. Let it not be otherwise." The emissaries likely discussed the return of the confiscated goods and compensation for the man taken hostage as a prelude to reestablishing normal relations.

It appears that a decision had been made at Pressburg that winter to resume normal relations with Wallachia and Moldavia, at least until such a time as Sigismund's plans for a new crusade against the Turks could be brought to fruition. After his emissaries returned from Moldavia, in the spring of 1435, Vlad addressed another letter to the burghers of Braşov, this time authorizing them to trade with both Wallachia and Moldavia: "It is my will that you make peace with whomever you desire and trade and feed yourselves, with Moldavians or with Wallachians, only do not bring there old money or copper. And when I will want to break peace with them, I will inform you a week before about this so that you will not suffer losses."[90] As a result, on May 26, 1435, Stephen renewed the trade privileges for the merchants of Braşov that they had originally received from his father Alexander the Good.[91] Given Vlad's hostile relations with Stephen of Moldavia, we cannot, however, exclude the possibility that he aided Iliaş against his brother when he returned to the country in the summer of 1435. Vlad's strong ties to Poland, especially to the family of Vladislav I, with whom Iliaş was related by marriage, support such a conjecture.

Ottoman troops entered Wallachia during the summer of 1435, during Alexander II's severe illness, to ensure that, if should Aldea die, the Hungarians would not enter the country and impose their candidate, Vlad, on the throne, as well as to launch a new attack in the area around Severin and southwestern Transylvania. According to Windecke, Wallachian forces took

---

[90]Doc. 183 in *DRH, D*, pp. 284-285. The editors date this letter November-December 1431 after Bogdan (Doc. XLIV in Bogdan, *Documente privitoare*, pp. 67-68), an untenable date for reasons stated earlier. The context places this letter in the spring or early summer of 1435.

[91]Docs. 189 in Costăchescu, ed., *Documentele moldoveneşti*, vol. II, pp. 676-677.

part in this new Turkish assault that marked the death knell of the Teutonic Knights in the region.[92] By October 10, Nicholas von Redwitz, the leader of the Hospitallers in the region, had relinquished the title of Ban of Severin. Early the following year, Sigismund named Hungarian nobleman Franco de Talloucz to fill the vacant post.[93]

Although Aldea cheated death in the summer of 1435, he never fully recovered his health. This created further instability in the Principality, as many of the leading boyars began to think of possible successors, who, apart from Vlad, included Dan II's sons Danciul and Basarab. Certainly some also resented Albul's powerful position. As a result, several boyars took refuge in Transylvania where they joined Vlad. This had been a persistent problem throughout Aldea's reign, amplified by the fact that Vlad was no ordinary pretender; not only had the Holy Roman Emperor invested him as Prince of Wallachia, but he effectively governed the two duchies in southern Transylvania, traditionally the purview of the ruler of the Transalpine land. Whenever Aldea enjoyed amicable relations with Hungary he tried to compel the burghers of Braşov to remove his enemies from their midst. In an undated letter from around the time of Voico's defection in 1431, the Prince writes, "I had hoped to receive help and much good from you. But you do not listen to me, and where there is a thief or a robber, he takes refuge with you and you feed my enemies who consume my parental inheritance and the treasury of Wallachia. Therefore, either turn over to me my enemy and wealth, or do not complain against me for I will send to the King to complain about you."[94]

---

[92]Vasilescu, *Urmaşii lui Mircea cel Bătrân*, p. 50. Sigismund's biographer mistakenly identifies Vlad as the Wallachian Prince who contributed to the defeat of the Teutonic Knights.

[93]Minea, "Vlad Dracul şi vremea sa," p. 137.

[94]Doc. 222 in *DRH, D*, pp. 321-322. The editors date this document 1436, but it should be dated 1431, around the time when Voico fled to Transylvania to join Vlad. I opt for this earlier date because Aldea says "You know well that my lord, the King, does not support me as he supported Voivode Dan, but he accepted me as his adopted son." The reference to Dan and Aldea's apparent close relations with Sigismund appear logical only in the period prior to when he made peace with the Sultan in 1432. After the events of 1432, Sigismund understandably never placed the same faith in Alexander as an ally.

Alexander II also attempted to win over some of his opponents. In another undated letter from around the same time to the burghers of Braşov, he writes, "among you there is My Majesty's boyar, Jupan Antonie. Consequently, I have sworn to him, on my faith and the soul of My Majesty to come without any fear to My Majesty. Therefore, send him away with honor from among you, to come without fear to My Majesty, in accordance with the command of My Majesty."[95] If, as Ioan Bogdan supposes, the boyar Antonie mentioned in this letter can be identified with Anton, whom we later find serving as Vlad's *Camaraş* or Chamberlain,[96] Aldea's efforts clearly failed.

By 1436, Vlad's star was on the rise. Sigismund returned to the region for the first time since he had concluded the peace agreement with the Sultan in 1429, determined at long-last to organize a new crusade against the Ottomans. Aware of Aldea's fragile health and leery of his past dealings with the Turks, the Emperor preferred a reliable man on the throne of Wallachia — a member of the Order of the Dragon. In April 1436, Sigismund spent the Easter holiday at Seghedin where he sought to put order in affairs in the eastern part of his Kingdom.[97] Vlad journeyed there to meet with the Emperor for the first time since his coronation at Nuremberg in 1431. The prospect of renewed hostilities between Wallachia and Hungary did not sit well with the Saxons of Braşov who sought to protect their prosperous trade relations with the Principality south of the Carpathians. Before leaving for Seghedin, Vlad wrote a reproachful letter to the burghers of Braşov: "You yourselves know what a great task the Kaiser has placed upon me, to defend this border, and that you are not to make peace with Wallachia without my permission. Yet My Majesty, bowing to your wishes, has permitted you to feed yourselves and to have peace,

---

[95]Doc. 204 in *DRH, D*, p. 300. The editors date this letter in 1433 after Bogdan (Doc. XXVI in Bogdan, *Documente privitoare*, p. 47), but hostile relations between Wallachia and Hungary at that time preclude this date. It most likely dates from 1431.

[96]Doc. 204 in *DRH, D*, p. 300. The editors date this letter from 1433, based on Bogdan (Doc. XXVI in Bogdan, *Documente privitoare*, p. 47), who dates this letter 1431-1433, but it is most likely from 1431 for if Antonie is Anton, as Bogdan proposes, he is later found as one of Vlad's trusted officials, making it improbable that he would receive such a proposal from Aldea. In addition, Aldea's strained relations with Braşov in the period 1432-1433 prelude his making such a request then.

[97]Docs. 2255, 2256, and 2258 in *Urkundenbuch*, vol. IV, pp. 597-601.

as is fitting among people, but as for the mountains and the passes, you are under no obligation to anyone to defend them. Yet you do not think well of me and my servants, who each day shed their blood for you and for everyone. But because you have heard that My Majesty will go to my lord, the Kaiser, you have instructed your evil men to pillage My Majesty's servants and you have taken their horses and everything that belongs to them. You shall regret this, for My Majesty will not permit my servants to suffer these losses, and for one, I will take from you two or more. And what My Majesty's servant Voloder tells you, believe him, for they are my words."[98]

Vlad's meeting with Sigismund in the spring of 1436 emanated from the Emperor's intention to launch a new crusade against the Ottomans. The Peace of Arras had brought a temporary halt to the Hundred Years' War, making possible the participation of English and French troops in such an enterprise. The Emperor had finally managed to bring the situation in Bohemia under control, and the Diet of 1435 had reorganized the Hungarian army in an attempt to make it a more effective fighting force. Sigismund again actively began to promote the union of the two Churches and proposed moving the Council of Basel to Buda in this scope.[99] The Emperor had even come to an understanding with his long-time nemesis Venice, after concluding an armistice with the Republic of St. Mark in 1433 and a peace treaty in 1435, to support such an endeavor. In addition to his Christian allies, Sigismund had also engaged in

---

[98]Doc. 173 in *DRH, D*, pp. 274-275. The editors date this document December 1430-January 1431 after Bogdan (Doc. XXXII in Bogdan, *Documente privitoare*, pp. 54-55), but this is based on the false assumption that Vlad's only meeting with Sigismund took place at the time of his coronation in Nuremberg in February 1431. This letter cannot be placed prior to Vlad's investiture as Prince, for the letter opens "John Vlad, Voivode and Prince. My Majesty writes to all the burghers of Braşov and wishes you good health." Likewise, it closes with "John Vlad, Voivode by the grace of God, Prince." Vlad could not have used the surname John or the title of Prince prior to his coronation. Furthermore, there is no evidence to indicate that Vlad was assigned to protect the southern border of Transylvania at such an early date, all the more so because the Teutonic Knights had just come to the area for this exact purpose. The only plausible date for this letter is the spring of 1436 when Sigismund is in eastern Hungary and plans are underway to organize a new anti-Ottoman crusade.

[99]Minea, *Principatele române şi politica orientală a împăratului Sigismund*, p. 244.

extensive diplomatic efforts to secure the participation of the Sultan's enemies in Anatolia in an offensive against the Ottoman Empire. By forcing the Turks to fight a war on two fronts, he hoped diminish their military strength and make them more vulnerable to attack. Through the mediation of the King of Cyprus, he had reached an agreement to this effect with Ibrahim Bey, the ruler of Karaman, and he hoped that Shah Ruh, Tamerlane's son and successor, would also join the coalition.[100] Part of the Emperor's grand strategy included placing Vlad on the throne of Wallachia where he needed a reliable ally.

The situation in Moldavia deteriorated further in the spring of 1436, thereby ruling out the participation of that Principality in any Christian coalition against the Ottomans. Despite the peace settlement that Polish diplomats had negotiated between Ilias and Stephen the previous summer, fighting resumed between the two siblings as Stephen was not content with his inferior rank. The armies of the rival brothers met in battle at Piperești, near the Prut River, on Thursday, March 8.[101] The result was a victory, albeit not a decisive one, for Stephen. The country now became a dual monarchy, with Ilias ruling the northern part from Suceava, and Stephen the south from Vaslui;[102] both brothers now bore the title of Prince, and each maintained a separate court and royal council.

Upon his return from his meeting with Sigismund, Vlad began to implement measures to prepare for an eventual invasion of Wallachia. He instructed the officials of Brașov: "do not allow anyone to cross the mountains into Wallachia, neither for commerce, nor as an emissary, nor for any reason whatsoever. Whoever wishes to go there must first ask permission from Jonash the Brave, and whoever Jonash will allow shall be free to go..." In the same letter, Vlad again rebukes the burghers of Brașov for not respecting their agreements with him: "you promised before me that you will return the house of Hanesh the bow-maker to him, but, after I left, you took it from him again. It grieves me deeply that you have not kept the promise that you made in my

---

[100]Gemil, *Românii și otomanii*, p. 112.

[101]Panaitescu, ed., *Cronicele slavo-romîne*, p. 6.

[102]Simanschi, "Precizări cronologice," pp. 77-78; and Ștefan Gorovei, *Mușatinii*, Bucharest, 1976, p. 51.

presence."[103] Hanesh probably supplied arms to Vlad, and the Saxons may have taken this action against him as a goodwill gesture to Aldea.

The last extant diploma from the reign of Alexander II is dated June 25, 1436, from Târgoviște. In it, he confirms to the Monastery of Cozia all of its previous endowments, including villages, customs revenues, fisheries, mills, and gypsy slaves, "to sustain the godly monks in eternal memory of the holy departed Prince of Ungrovalachia, My Majesty's father." The boyars serving in the royal council at that time, listed as witnesses to this document, include Albul, Radu of Sahac, Stanciul the brother of Mircea, Vâlcsan of Florea, Radu of Borcea, Nan Pascal, Tatul Sârbul, Iarciul, *Spătar* Stancea, *Vistier* Stanciul, *Stolnic* Vlaicu, *Păharnic* Barbul, and *Logofăt* Cazan.[104] Most of these nobles had served Aldea faithfully since the beginning of his reign. But with the Prince's health failing him and the threat of an invasion looming from the north, an alarming number of boyars began to abandon Aldea. Certainly, Vlad enticed some of them to defect as he intensified preparations for an attack. The Great Pretender embraced the maxim that Machiavelli later expounded in *The Prince*: "although one may be very strong in armed forces, yet in entering a province one has always need of the goodwill of the natives."[105] Beset by illness, Aldea tried in vain to stem the tide of refuges fleeing to Transylvania. In late July or early August, he wrote to the officials of Brașov, demanding that they extradite rebel boyars who had recently fled to the Saxon city: "First, the Spătar Stan came among you. I sent you word to turn him over to me, but you did not listen to my words. Then Todor fled, stealing horses that belong to Wallachia. Again I sent word for you to turn him over to me, but still you did not listen to me. I have struggled for you, so that you may have peace, and your captives, as many as I have been able to, I have ransomed.... There among you are Stanciul, Tatul, Vasile, and Ulan, and they also took horses from my court. If you cherish your peace, send them to me bound. If you do not send them to

---

[103]Doc. 189 in *DRH, D*, pp. 288-289. The editors date this document November-December 1431 after Bogdan (Doc. XXXVIII in Bogdan, *Documente privitoare*, pp. 61-62), but I contend that 1436 is the more likely date.

[104]Doc. 77 in *DRH, B*, vol. I, pp. 138-140.

[105]Niccolò Machiavelli, *The Prince*, p. 16.

me, you will not have peace with me."[106] We know that these boyars had only recently fled from Wallachia for three of them were serving on Alexander II's royal council as late as June 25: the *Spătar* Stan or Stancea, Tatul Sârbul, and Stanciul, either the brother of Mircea or the *Visiter*. There can be no doubt that these are the boyars referred to in Aldea's letter as they were the only high-ranking officials in a position to take horses from the Prince's court.

Aldea's threats did not produce the desired results. As Vlad prepared for war, he sternly warned the burghers of Brașov, "do not make peace with the Wallachians; if you make peace, be forewarned that I will break that peace. In addition to this, I ask you: I have some wagons there that I have asked you to build for me. Hurry with these and make an effort for me and bring them to Cohalm, and men from Cohalm will bring them to me. Their cost will be paid by my *Cămăraş*, Anton."[107] The newly-constructed wagons that Vlad asked the Saxons burghers to finish quickly and to deliver to him were undoubtedly part of his preparations for the forthcoming campaign south of the Carpathians.

As preparations continued, Vlad sent his representatives to Brașov to discuss plans for the upcoming offensive. On July 16, 1436, the Great Pretender was in Făgăraş, the seat of the Duchy he had ruled for the past five years, from where he wrote to officials of the Saxon city: "I have learned of all that has been said and organized and agreed upon with you by our boyars, Spătar Dumitru, Logofăt Stephen, Kayka Hausporopulos, and Magistrate Johannes, your fellow citizen, concerning our affairs, as well as with us on your part, and that they meet with our approval.... For this reason, as long as

---

[106]Doc. 225 in *DRH, D*, pp. 324-325. The editors date this letter July-December 1436, but it is unlikely to have been sent later than August of that year.

[107]Doc. 184 in *DRH, D*, p. 285. The editors date this letter November-December 1431 after Bogdan (Doc. XXXIII in Bogdan, *Documente privitoare*, p. 56), but, as I have pointed out earlier, his chronology is faulty. This document must be dated in the summer of 1436 when Vlad is preparing to invade Wallachia. Another indication supporting 1436 as the likely date is that in the same letter Vlad writes: "My Majesty makes known to you that Sibiu has relinquished the old ducats; therefore, you should no longer use them either, for if I find that someone is using the old ducats I will punish him." We know that in 1436 Hungarian ducats were appreciated by increasing their silver content in an effort to stop the decline of the currency's value, and that this contributed to the peasant uprising that broke out in the province the following year.

Contemporary painting believed to be Vlad Dracul

we live on this earth, we will forever preserve them in our memory, in an undying spirit of brotherhood and friendship.... And we ask you as dear friends to do the things that you have promised and bring them to conclusion by your actions." He signed the letter, "Your friend Vlad, son of the belated Prince Mircea, Voivode of Transalpine land."[108] Although the letter is vague and convoluted, according to the style of the time, recommending an emissary, in this case Magistrate Johannes, to provide details verbally, clearly the two sides

[108]Doc. 226 in *DRH, D*, pp. 325-326.

had reached an agreement concerning aspects of the planned campaign and regulating relations between the parties once Vlad assumed the throne. Vlad's *Spătar*, Dumitru, mentioned in this document, is likely the same Jupan Dumitru that Aldea had sent to Braşov in 1431 to complain about their harboring refugee boyars.[109] At some point, Dumitru defected to join Vlad and he assumed the role of *Spătar*, or Sword-Bearer, making him commander of the pretender's military forces. The presence of Vlad's *Spătar* alongside his trusted lieutenant Stephen at the negotiations with the Saxon leaders indicates that military preparations for the upcoming attack were on the agenda of the meeting at Braşov. This letter, mentioning both a *spătar* and a *logofăt*, supports the contention that Vlad maintained a full-fledged royal council during the years he spent in Transylvania as a pretender to the throne of Wallachia. Never before had a claimant to the princely title been so well-prepared to assume power.

By late August, Aldea's health had again taken a turn for the worse. Vlad now wrote to the officials of Braşov, telling them that "people have come to me from Wallachia and told me that Aldea is dead. If he has not yet died, he is gravely ill and will die soon. Therefore, I ask you as my brothers and good friends to lend me your aid and to accompany me. I will leave you at the foot of the mountains while I go against them with my men. If it becomes necessary, I will return to you, but if God will help me, as I hope He will, for there is no one to stand against me, you will come to me when I have succeeded. And the Schässburgens will also go with me."[110] In response to these developments, the Bishop of Transylvania, George Lepes, his brother, Vice-Voivode Lorand Lepes, and Michael Jakch, the Count of the Szecklers, met at Bod, fifteen kilometers north of Braşov, from where they drafted a letter on August 31 to officials of the Saxon city and the Bârsa land ordering them to send delegates there for a meeting on Sunday, September 2, to discuss "the immediate raising of troops from among you to be sent to help Prince Vlad, Voivode of the Tran-

---

[109]Doc. 222 in *DRH, D*, pp. 321-322. See note 94 in this chapter for argument on dating.

[110]Doc. 182 in *DRH, D*, pp. 283-284. The editors date this letter November-December 1431 after Bogdan (Doc. XXXIV in Bogdan, *Documente privitoare*, p. 57), but for reasons discussed earlier this dating is erroneous. The likely date is late August 1436, when Vlad is readying his forces to cross into Wallachia.

salpine land." They went on to mention that this was to be done in accordance with a letter to Transylvanian authorities from Sigismund providing instructions to this effect,[111] probably issued after his meeting with Vlad in the spring of that year.

By September 5, Vlad was on the move, writing to the officials of Braşov from his camp at Roya, recommending to them his emissary Johannes Hanesh who was charged with informing them of the latest developments.[112] This may be the same Hanesh the bow-maker referred to in an earlier letter by Vlad. The location of his camp, Roya, has not been positively identified. Nicolae Iorga has proposed Boitsa, near Turnu Rosu, south of Sibiu, as the probable site.[113] Another possible location is the village of Boia in the Upper Jiu region of Wallachia, near Jupâneşti in the present-day county of Gorj. Mention of this village is first found in a diploma issued by Prince Peter the Young on June 4, 1561,[114] but the document makes it clear that it existed long before that time. If Boia is, in fact, Roya, it would mean that Vlad had crossed into Wallachia around the beginning of September and that Hanesh was sent to inform them of the progress of the campaign. Either of these two possible locations for Vlad's camp on September 5 allows us to deduce that his invasion route ran through the Olt River valley, rather than the oft-travelled Bran Pass. This also took him to Mircea the Old's burial place at the Monastery of Cozia. Perhaps it was here, standing before his father's tomb for the first time and casting his eyes upon his votive portrait that today still adorns the inner sanctum of the church, that Vlad truly felt he had finally laid claim to his father's legacy.

Although we have no information about the campaign itself, we know that Vlad's endeavor was successful. Presumably, he initially chose to concentrate his attack in the western part of the country where the strongest resistance to a Prince favored by Hungary could be aniticipated. Apparently, this time the rumors of Aldea's death proved correct. As he had anticipated in his previous letter to Braşov, Vlad met little resistance. By late September 1436, more than

---

[111]Doc. 227 in *DRH, D*, pp. 326-327.

[112]Doc. 228 in *DRH, D*, pp. 327-328.

[113]Iorga, *Istoria românilor*, vol. IV, p. 56; and Doc. 2271 in *Urkundenbuch*, vol. IV, p. 616.

[114]Doc. 181 in *DIR, B, XVI*, vol. III, p. 150.

Small seal of Vlad II Dracul

five and a half years after his investiture at Nuremberg, Vlad finally assumed his father's throne. The long wait had ended. No longer the Great Pretender, he now rightfully bore the title, "John Vlad, Voivode and Prince of all of the land of Ungrovalachia and of the parts across the mountains, Duke of Amlaş and Făgăraş."[115]

---

[115]Doc. 82 in *DRH, B,* vol. I, pp. 145-146.

Chapter VII

Between the Cross
and the Crescent

"the Turks are as many as the sands of the sea, and no one can stand against them."

— former Vornic Neagu to the burghers of Braşov, 1480[1]

V lad's seizure of the throne in the fall of 1436 caught the Turks by surprise. Although Sigismund had not yet completed preparations to launch his crusade against the Ottomans, Aldea's passing created the opportunity to implement the first phase of the plan — the installation of Vlad as Prince of Wallachia. Fortuitously, when Vlad crossed the Carpathians through the Olt River valley, the Sultan was engaged in a campaign against Karaman where the ruler of the eastern Anatolian Emirate, Ibrahim Bey, had taken up arms against Murad II in compliance with the agreement he had

---

[1]Doc. CCXXIV in Bogdan, *Documente privitoare*, pp. 272-277. Undated letter, which Bogdan correctly dates March-April 1480 after its contents. Neagu served as Vornic under Vlad Dracul's son Radu the Handsome and as an adviser to Basarab the Young, also known as the Little Impaler, at the time this letter was written.

reached with emissaries of the Holy Roman Emperor.[2] Sigismund's notorious procrastination, however, had resulted in the failure to synchronize attacks in the east and the west. In response to the events north of the Danube, the Beylerbey of Rumelia hastily organized a raid in mid-October to punish the rebellious Principality whose new ruler refused to pay tribute to the Sultan.

News of the Ottoman attack on Wallachia had reached Constantinople by November 17, 1436, when Johannes of Ragusa, a delegate sent by Catholic officials gathered at Basel to the Byzantine capital the previous year to facilitate negotiations for the union of the two Churches, reported to the Council that, "a few weeks ago, the Turks made an expedition to Wallachia which had revolted. Many captives were taken and sold into slavery or tortured. Prior to this, they had lived in peace with the Turks by paying tribute."[3] Despite these losses, Vlad maintained his hold on the throne and repelled the invaders. The failure of Ottoman attacks on Wallachia that continued into the winter months is recalled by the chronicler Orudj bin Adil, a contemporary of these events, who records that Turkish troops led by Shah Melek, "crossing at Vidin, made an incursion into Wallachia. He was unlucky, however, as it was a very harsh winter, and because of the cold many men suffered frostbite to their hands and feet."[4] Vlad's victory over the Turks marked the first significant blow that Christian forces had dealt to the Ottomans since Alexander Aldea, backed by Moldavian forces, had ousted Dan II in the spring of 1431. News of the young Wallachian Prince's triumph spread throughout Europe. The Burgundian emissary Bertrandon de la Broquière recorded that on March 16, 1439, during discussions at the Council of Florence concerning plans for a crusade to drive the Turks from Europe, Byzantine Emperor John VIII's Chamberlain, John Torzellois, remarked the necessity of obtaining the cooperation of the Prince of Wallachia, "who can provide more than 15,000 cavalry, among the strongest, most capable, and renowned soldiers in all the world."[5]

---

[2]Gemil, *Românii și otomanii*, p. 112.

[3]Doc. XVII in Iorga, *Notes et Extraits*, vol. IV, pp. 25-30.

[4]*Cronici turcești*, vol. I, p. 52.

[5]Quo. Minea, "Vlad Dracul și vremea sa," pp. 86, 192. See also Bertrandon de la Broquière, *La voyage d'Outremer*, Paris, 1892, pp. 263-265.

Having successfully repelled the Ottoman attacks on the Principality, Vlad now began the task of consolidating his hold on power. Although extant documents from his reign are scarce, from the surviving evidence we can extrapolate that Vlad pursued a policy of reconciliation intended to unite the opposing factions among the nobility. He realized that only in this way could Wallachia overcome the internal strife that neighboring foreign powers had exploited to interfere in domestic politics. The fact that he had entered the country virtually unopposed allowed the new Prince to adopt such a generous attitude toward his former opponents. Of the thirteen boyars listed as serving on Aldea's royal council on June 25, 1436, the date of the last known diploma issued by his chancellery, there is evidence to suggest that as many as twelve either received positions at Vlad's court or the renewal of privileges granting tax and labor exemptions on their lands. Although we cannot always exclude the possibility that a particular document refers to a different boyar with the same name, as these nobles generally appear in diplomas and letters with only one name and there are sometimes spelling modifications from one document to the next, in most cases it is clearly the same person. We have already seen that several of Aldea's boyars — including his Spătar Stancea, Tatul Sârbu, and Stanciul — had fled to Transylvania during the final months of his reign, where they presumably joined Vlad. Tatul Sârbu, Stanciul, the brother of Mircea, and Stanciul Hanoi (either Aldea's Vistier Stanciul or his Spătar Stan) served on Vlad's royal council as early as January 20, 1437,[6] the date of the earliest extant diploma issued after he assumed the throne. Radu Borcea and Nan Pascal appear on Vlad's council by July 18 of that year,[7] and on August 1 Vâlcsan of Florea is listed among its members.[8] By August 2, 1439, Vlad had appointed Iarciul to the council. In documents from 1445, we find that Aldea's Logofăt Cazan had succeeded Stephen as head of Vlad's chancellery,[9] making

---

[6]Doc. 80 in *DRH, B*, vol. I, pp. 142-144.

[7]Doc. 81 in *DRH, B*, vol. I, pp. 144-145.

[8]Doc. 83 in *DRH, B*, vol. I, pp. 146-147.

[9]Doc. 98 and 99 in *DRH, B*, vol. I, pp. 172-175. From a diploma issued by Vladislav II on January 2, 1450, we discern that Cazan, who served both Aldea and Vlad as Logofăt, was the son of Radu of Sahac, providing further evidence of the latter's reconciliation with Vlad. See Doc. 101 in *DRH, B*, vol. I, pp. 176- 177.

it likely that up to that time he had served as the latter's deputy. Even Albul, Alexander II's right-hand man, and Radu of Sahac, the second most important member of his council, although they no longer served at court, both received the renewal of royal exemptions from taxes and labor for their holdings in a diploma dated August 13, 1437.[10] The same act extends identical privileges to Aldea's Stolnic Vlaicul, Vâlcsan of Florea, and Dragomir of Berendei, a boyar who served on the council in 1432.[11] Another document from August 1 of that year confirms similar privileges for a village belonging to Nan Pascal, Tatul Sârbul, and Stanciul.[12] Aldea's Paharnic Barbul is the only member of his royal council from 1436 who cannot be found in any of the surviving documents from Vlad's reign. Even the scribe Calcio who penned the diploma of June 25, 1436, continued to work in the chancellery when Vlad become Prince. All of this clearly indicates that Vlad made a concerted effort to reconcile with his former opponents.

In addition to making peace with his onetime adversaries, Vlad did not forget those who had stood by him during his years as a pretender. It is not surprising that a large portion of his surviving diplomas confirm lands and privileges to his supporters in the Duchy of Făgăraş, which had served as his base while awaiting his opportunity to occupy the throne. On January 20, 1437, Vlad confirmed possession of the villages of Voivodeni, Sasciorii-Loviştea, and part of Sâmbata-de-Sus to Roman, exempting them from royal taxes and works.[13] On July 18, Stan, the son of Tatul, Ursul, Radu, Stan, the son of Bara, and Godea received a diploma renewing similar privileges for the village of Mărgineni and its surroundings.[14] Later, in 1441, the Prince confirmed privileges for the holdings of Teodor and his two brothers in the Duchy.[15] On April 23 of that year he also renewed tax and labor exemptions for lands in both Făgăraş and Wallachia belonging to Stanciul Moenescul and his five sons,

---

[10]Doc. 86 in *DRH, B*, vol. I, pp. 150-151.

[11]Doc. 73 in *DRH, B*, vol. I, p. 135.

[12]Doc. 82 in *DRH, B*, vol. I, pp. 145-146.

[13]Doc. 80 in *DRH, B*, vol. I, pp. 142-144.

[14]Doc. 81 in *DRH, B*, vol. I, pp. 144-145.

[15]Doc. 92 in *DRH, B*, vol. I, pp. 159-160.

Moian, Stoica, Sin, Vlad, and Michael, and their children, granting them half of the village of Voila in the Duchy.

In accordance with the agreements that Logofăt Stephen and Spătar Dumitru had negotiated the previous July, Vlad renewed trade privileges for the merchants of Braşov on January 24, 1437.[16] These were essentially the same preferred customs duties that Mircea had granted them in 1413.[17] It specified taxes for a variety of imported and exported goods transported "on the route from Braşov to Brăila," with transit fees to be paid at Târgşor, Târgovişte, and Dâmboviţa. For goods imported from the Orient, brought by ship to the port at Brăila, a standard three percent duty applied. For reasons that remain obscure, Vlad issued a second, identical privilege for Braşov on April 8, 1437.[18] Both documents specify that the burgher Mehel and Andreiash, the Judeţ of Râşnov, had come to Târgovişte on behalf of the burghers of Braşov to conclude this agreement. Probably the latter act was issued as a copy of the original accord which had somehow been lost, only to turn up centuries later in a Russian archive.[19]

Although Vlad worked hard to consolidate his hold on the throne, unfortunately for him his security depended not only on his own efforts, but also on Hungarian military support. Despite his recent victory, the Turkish threat loomed large. Although they had failed to subdue Vlad, Ottoman forces led by Ali Bey set out on a punitive expedition against Hungary early in 1437 and "with the army of Rumelia, he crossed the Danube," where, according to the Ottoman chronicler Müneggimbasi, he "devastated and pillaged the environs of Temesvar for about forty days, and then returned to the imperial seat with great plunder."[20] In light of these recent developments, Sigismund wrote from Prague to Transylvanian Vice-Voivode Peter Cseh on February 7,

---

[16]Addenda A in *DRH, D*, vol. I, pp. 463-464.

[17]Doc. 120 in *DRH, D*, vol. I, pp. 197-198.

[18]Doc. 243 in *DRH, D*, vol. I, pp. 340-341. Interestingly, both the privilege of January 24 and that of April 8 contain the same error in dating, giving indiction 24. The correct indiction for the year 6945 (September 1436-August 1437) is 15.

[19]Ştefan T. Esanu, "Un document necunoscut de la Vlad al II-lea Dracul, in *Magazin Istoric* (August, 1970), pp. 77-78.

[20]*Cronici turceşti*, vol. II, p. 243.

1437, telling him to prepare to defend against further Turkish attacks on the province, and informing him that in a short time he intended to lead a large army against the Ottomans.[21] But even though the installation of Vlad on the throne of the Transalpine land had been seen as a prelude to this new crusade against the Turkish infidels, Sigismund's plans for concerted action against the Ottomans soon ground to a halt. Murad II had managed to crush the rebellion in Anatolia led by Ibrahim Bey, but he maintained him on the throne of Karaman as a vassal so as not to provoke an attack by Shah Ruh.[22] This ended hopes of forcing the Sultan to fight a war on two fronts. Trying to coordinate joint action among the Christian states of Europe continued to prove a daunting task. In January 1437, Pope Eugenius IV wrote to the Papal Nuncio in Hungary, instructing him to preach for a crusade against the Turkish infidels.[23] Wary of an Ottoman attack, Henric de Thamasy, Jakch's associate as Count of the Szecklers, wrote from Bistrița to officials of Brașov on June 8, 1437, asking for news from Wallachia of Turkish movements and promising assistance should they attack.[24] But trouble brewing within the Kingdom assured that Hungarian military might would remain at home. In addition, the issue of Church Union remained an impediment to launching an offensive against the Ottomans.

Conflict within the Catholic Church hindered efforts toward union. Pope Martin V had summoned a General Church Council which opened at Basel in 1431. But the Pope died in February of that year and his successor, Eugenius IV, tried to move the assembly to Italy so that he could exercise greater influence over it. The new Pope sought to defend the idea of papal supremacy against those religious and secular leaders who argued that a General Church Council derived its authority directly from God and, therefore, was superior to the Pontiff, a dispute that had intensified after the Council of Constance. The delegates resisted the Pope's efforts to assert control over the Council, and the conflict continued for the next several years, despite Sigismund's efforts to mediate between the two sides, to the detriment of prospects for Church unity.

---

[21]Pascu, *Bobîlna*, p. 102.

[22]Gemil, *Românii și otomanii*, p. 112.

[23]Doc. DXXXIV in Hurmuzaki, *Documente*, vol. I, part. 2, pp. 633-635.

[24]Doc. 247 in *DRH, D*, pp. 343-344.

Eugenius gradually gained the upper hand and on, September 18, 1437, he issued a bull dissolving the Council of Basel. The Pope then summoned a new General Council, for the specific task of resolving the differences between the Catholic and Orthodox Churches, which opened at Ferrara in Italy on January 8, 1438. The ultimate objective of the Council was to unite Chistendom so that it could wage a holy war against the forces of Islam.

Byzantine Emperor John VIII remained one of the staunchest advocates of concerted military action against the Turks and he believed that only through the union of the Orthodox and Catholic Churches could he hope to realize such a plan. Prior to his death, Manuel II had warned his son against such a course of action. Sphrantzes recalls how "The late Emperor said to his son, Kir Emperor John, when they were alone with only myself present, speaking of a synod: 'My son, we know well and true that in the depths of the hearts of the pagans they greatly fear that we will come to an agreement and unite with the Latins. They consider that if this would happen the Christians in the West will come to our aid and cause them great harm. As a result, preoccupy yourself with the question of a synod, and always consider it, especially when you need to frighten the infidel; but never try to do anything for this to take place, for I do not believe that our people are disposed to find a means of unity and peace and understanding, but they want to return to as it was in olden times. But this being virtually impossible, I fear that it would make the schism even worse! And then we will have exposed ourselves in the eyes of the pagans.' The Emperor [John], however, as I observed, did not approve of his father's words and he rose up and left without saying anything."[25] John VIII did not heed his father's advise and, on November 27, 1437, the Emperor left Constantinople for Italy at the invitation of the Pope, determined to reunite Christendom as a means of obtaining Western military support against the Turks. Patriarch Joseph and numerous religious leaders from throughout the Orthodox world, including Damian, the Metropolitan of Moldavia, joined the Emperor in Ferrara.

Although there is no conclusive evidence of Wallachian participation, Vlad likely sent representatives to the Council, just as his father Mircea had done two decades earlier when Christian leaders had gathered at Constance. As ruler

---

[25] Sphrantzes, *Memorii*, p. 58 (XXIII, 5-6).

of a predominantly Orthodox land, Vlad, with his affinities to Catholicism, undoubtedly supported the union of the Churches with the political advantages it offered him. On October 22, 1438, a Florentine merchant named Anton de Piscia received 46 gold florins from the papal treasury as "reimbursement for an equal sum he paid to Wallachian delegates for their expenses for two months." Vatican records also show that on June 13, 1439, the Medici family received "364 gold florins representing an equal sum paid to...," among others, "the Wallachian ambassadors... for their expenses up to May 22."[26] Although scholars have assumed that this refers to payments made for Moldavian representatives for whose participation at the Council there exists irrefutable evidence, these same accounting records mention these delegates as deputies "of the Prince of Moldavia." Thus, Wallachian participation at the Council of Florence cannot be ruled out. Still, given the troubled relations between Vlad and the new Hungarian King Albert of Hapsburg, it is unlikely that the Wallachian Prince sent high level representatives.

Financial considerations and an outbreak of the plague caused the Council to move from Ferrara to Florence at the beginning of 1439. Discussions centered around questions of Church doctrine dividing Catholicism and Orthodoxy, and the pressing need to organize concerted military action to drive the Ottomans from Europe and also to recover territories lost to them in Anatolia. On December 2, 1438, Eugenius IV wrote to Sigismund's successor Albert, informing him that negotiations were underway with the Greeks to unite with the Church of Rome and that he was hopeful of positive results.[27]

As Manuel II had predicted, the Ottomans were not indifferent to the discussions underway in Italy. After John VIII left Constantinople aboard Venetian galleys, Sphrantzes informs us that the Sultan convened a council of war and proposed to lay siege to the city, "not so much for the purpose of taking it, but so as to force the Emperor to return from his journey." All of Murad II's advisors counselled him to do this except for his Grand Vizir, Halil Pasha. He told the Sultan, "'if you wage war on Constantinople, it will more likely be a motive for the Emperor, out of necessity, to say to the Latins, 'I

---

[26]Quo. C. Auner, "Moldova la saborul din Florența," in *Revista catolică*, IV (1915), p. 391.

[27]Doc. DXLIV in Hurmuzaki, *Documente*, vol. I, part. 2, pp. 643-644.

accept everything that you say!' And then all that we fear will be realized. Abandon this plan and wait to see what will happen. If they come to an agreement, you have a peace treaty with them bound by oath; then in the future you can act as you see fit. But if, as is more likely, they do not reach an agreement, then things will have worked out better for us and you can do as you please with even greater confidence.' And this advice convinced the Sultan to abandon his intentions."[28]

Eighteen months after the Council opened the two sides reached an agreement. In return for promises of military support, the Greeks conceded the major doctrinal questions under dispute. These included: the *filioque* in the Nicene Cneed whereby Catholic doctrine affirmed that the Holy Spirit proceeded from the Father *and the Son*, rather than solely from the Father as the Orthodox Church maintained; the existence of Purgatory; the use of unleavened bread in communion; and the supremacy of the Pope. In return, Catholic leaders agreed to organize a two-pronged attack against the Ottomans, on land and sea, planned for the spring of 1440. On this basis, Catholic and Orthodox leaders signed the act of union, known as the *Laetentur Coeli*, meaning 'let the heavens rejoice,' on July 5, 1439.

But the agreement between the Greeks and the Latins was feeble at best. No sooner had the ink dried on the accord than strong opposition, led by the Metropolitan of Epheseus, Mark Eugenicus, the only Orthodox leader present at Florence who defied both the Emperor and the Patriarch and refused to sign the agreement, arose throughout the Orthodox world. By February 1440, the Patriarchs of Jerusalem, Alexandria, and Antioch had all condemned the Union. As Ureche aptly put it, "instead of union, greater disunion resulted,"[29] just as Manuel II had feared and Halil Pasha had anticipated. Chalkokodyles explains that "when the Greeks arrived home, Pope Eugenius did not send them any help of significance. Immediately, the Greeks began to reconsider and were sorry that they had reconciled with the Pope."[30] According to Dukas, this led many to cry, "It is much better for the Turkish turban to rule from the

---

[28]Sphrantzes, *Memorii*, p. 60 (XXIII, 10).

[29]Kogălniceanu, *Cronicele României*, p. 139.

[30]Chalcocondil, *Expuneri istorice*, p. 180 (VI, 301).

center of the city than the Latin tiara."[31] Although the agreement reached at Florence officially remained in force until the fall of Constantinople, for neither the Emperor nor the Patriarch denounced it, and on December 12, 1453, Cardinal Isidore, former Metropolitan of Kiev, celebrated a mass at the Cathedral of St. Sophia to officially consecrate the Union, for all intents and purposes the Council was a failure.

Apart from the prolonged debate over the question of Church unification, civil strife that broke out in Transylvania in the summer of 1437 also hindered Sigismund's attempts to organize a crusade against the Turks. Rising tensions between landlords and peasants had plagued the eastern province of the Kingdom of Hungary for nearly a century. Throughout the fourteenth and fifteenth centuries, the burden on the peasantry steadily increased. In 1342, Charles Robert imposed a tax of 18 dinars per peasant household. Then, in 1351, Louis the Great issued a decree transforming the *dijma*, the royal tax appropriating one-tenth of peasant production, into the *nona*, that is "To gather from all our serfs, from the plowmen, and from those who have vineyards... the ninth part of all their grains and of all their wine..."[32] As these fiscal measures became increasingly oppressive and the nobility infringed on traditional peasant liberties, an uprising broke out in Transylvania in 1365-1366. The nobility crushed the revolt and obtained the right to judge and to sentence to death peasants found guilty of theft and other acts of disorder. The lower classes also directed their animosity against the Church which held vast estates. For example, in 1375 Ottho, Abbot of the Klus Monastery, reported to Transylvanian Vice-Voivode Ladislas that Wallachian and Hungarian peasants had risen up and burned numerous houses on the Monastery's estates.[33]

Beginning in the fourteenth century, throughout Europe the feudal system entered a period of crisis. While feudal structures varied from one region to the next, two main elements characterized the system. The first was that it was based on production on individual small holdings. The second and most

---

[31]Ducas, *Istoria turco-bizantină*, p. 328 (XXXVII, 10).

[32]Quo. Pascu, *Bobîlna*, p. 41.

[33]Doc. CLXXV in Hurmuzaki, *Documente*, vol. I, part. 2, pp. 225-226.

important element is described by British historian Rodney Hilton as "the exploitative relationship between landowners and subordinated peasants, in which the surplus beyond the subsistence of the latter, whether in direct labour or in rent in kind or in money, is transferred under coercive sanction to the former."[34] As climatic changes affected harvests and the population declined as a consequence of the Black Death, the nobility placed increasingly stringent demands on the peasants. The rise of trade, the development of urban centers, and the formation of larger state structures all put additional stresses on an already overburdened system. One of the principal means in which landowners responded to this crisis was to restrict peasant movement from one estate to another. This became one of the main causes of tension between nobles and peasants throughout this period. In an effort to ameliorate the situation, Sigismund had issued a decree on February 9, 1410, guaranteeing to all serfs the right of free movement from one estate to another after they paid the *terragiis* and any debts they may have accumulated.[35] But despite the King's edict, by 1437 the nobility had virtually brought peasant movement to a standstill.

The spread of the Hussite movement throughout Central Europe further accentuated peasant discontent. The burning at the stake of Czech religious reformer Jan Huss at the Council of Constance on January 6, 1415, had radicalized the movement which took on a pronounced anti-feudal character. The teachings of Oxford scholar John Wycliffe, which had contributed to the English peasant revolt in 1381, inspired Huss. His doctrine challenged the authority of the Roman Catholic Church, which he called "the Synagogue of Satan," and denied the role of the clergy as an intermediary between man and God. As Hussites believed that people could appeal directly to God, they did not recognize saints or the Virgin Mary or the authority of the Pope. They also declared that indulgences are fraudulent and denied the existence of purgatory. Likewise, they preached social equality, declaring that only those who work

[34]Rodney Hilton, "A Note on Feudalism," in Rodney Hilton, ed., *The Transition from Feudalism to Capitalism*, London, 1976, p. 30.

[35]Doc. CCCLXXXIX in Hurmuzaki, *Documente*, vol. I, part. 2, pp. 470-471.

could eat, and opposed capital punishment.[36] In 1426, Hussites in Transylvania held a synod to organize the struggle against the Catholic Church and feudal exploitation. But the persecution of the movement that Sigismund had vigorously prosecuted since 1419, when war with the Hussites, then led by Jan Zizka, had broken out, led many to seek refuge in other lands. Hussites from Transylvania and as far away as Bohemia found safe haven in Moldavia where Alexander the Good accorded them protection.

In a telling letter dated March 5, 1431, John de Ryza, the Catholic Bishop of Baia, Moldavia's former capital, complains to the Bishop of Krakow about Alexander the Good's increasing hostility toward the Catholic Church and his favorable attitude toward the Hussites: "We personally presented ourself before the Prince of the country, together with this Jacob [a Hussite leader] who, feeling that he enjoyed the protection of the Prince, rebuked us, at our question as to why he escaped from prison in Krakow and fled from the lands of Hungary, with the answer that if the Roman Church were not in error, and if all of the land of Hungary had not fallen into error, he would not have come to the land of Moldavia, and that in all of Hungary he did not find a single true and perfect priest, and that our lord, the Pope, is neither true, nor perfect because he maintains his court in great luxury and encourages the obscenity of whores.... We cannot hold our own against him [the Hussite leader Jacob] because we are so few and the Prince protects him against all of the true believers in Christ and it would be difficult for us to oppose the protection of the Prince. The Prince has granted him a residence in Bacău where he lives as a true heretic, having with him an apostate of the Order of the Friars Minor who gives communion in both forms as often as his followers desire, baptizes them, and hears their confessions, and the Prince of the country has given him and his disciples a written diploma that states that anyone who disturbs him or his Hussite disciples will pay to the Prince a fine of twenty Turkish gold ducats, and for this reason he has become so daring and is not afraid of anyone..." John de Ryza went on to ask the Bishop of Krakow to intervene with King Vladislav

---

[36]Holban, ed., *Călători străini*, vol. I, pp. 69-73. Papal inquisitor Jacob de Marchia, assigned to Transylvania in 1436-1437 to combat the spread of the heresy, compiled a list of 64 points representing Hussite beliefs.

to convince the Moldavian Prince to arrest or to expel the Hussites.[37] The Polish King addressed a letter to Alexander on May 6 of that year, calling on him to take action against the heretics, and warning him of the dangerous connection between Hussitism and peasant unrest,[38] but Vladislav's recalcitrant vassal continued to afford protection to the Hussites. As a result, Moldavia became a base for the spread of Hussite propaganda into Transylvania.

Trouble brewed in 'the land beyond the forest' where discontent among the lower classes intensified. Aware of the potential dangers, the Bishop of Transylvania, George Lepes, firmly believed the Hussitism stood at the root of the problem. Seeking a solution to alleviate the threat to the social order in the province, on May 8, 1436, he addressed an invitation to Franciscan monk Jacob de Marchia, Papal Inquisitor, to come to Transylvania to eradicate the perilous Hussite heresy that had spread there "from Moldavia and other parts... infecting many people, both men and women, from our flock."[39] But the Bishop failed to understand that Hussitism was a symptom and not the cause of the disease plaguing the province. Lepes himself provided the spark that would ignite rebellion. After decades of devaluation, a new Hungarian dinar was issued in 1436, appreciating its value by 1000%; he then decreed that all tithes owed to the Church, which the Bishop had not collected since 1433, be paid solely in the new currency.[40] This affected not only Catholic peasants, mainly Hungarians and Saxons, but also Orthodox Wallachian peasants who, because they lived on Roman Catholic lands, were obliged to pay the tithe to the Church.[41] Peasants began refusing to pay the inflated tax, and they beat and drove away those sent out by the Bishop to collect it. Lepes responded by excommunicating anyone who could not or would not pay the tax. This led peasants to address their grievances to secular authorities; they complained

---

[37]Holban, ed., *Călători străini*, vol. I. pp. 64-66.

[38]Mihail P. Dan, *Cehi, slovaci și români*, Sibiu, 1944, p. 97, nt. 50.

[39]Doc. DVIII in Hurmuzaki, *Documente*, vol. I, part. 2, pp. 604-605.

[40]Doc. DXX in Hurmuzaki, *Documente*, vol. I, part. 2, pp. 614-620; Octavian Iliescu, *Moneda în România*, Bucharest, 1970, p. 40; and János Bak, "The Late Medieval Period," in Peter F. Sugar, ed., *A History of Hungary*, Bloomington, 1994, p. 60.

[41]Béla Köpeczi, ed., *History of Transylvania*, Budapest, 1994, p. 224.

that their family members died without receiving the last rites, were given no funeral, and were denied burial in the church cemetery, and that "their sisters and daughters, against the customs and ritual which must be held in the Holy Roman Catholic Church, were married without the blessing of the Church."[42] As neither side backed down, rebellion was imminent.

Amidst this explosive situation, Jacob de Marchia arrived in Transylvania. An Italian monk of the Franciscan Order, Pope Eugenius IV had sent him to Bosnia in 1432, where he became Chief Vicar and Papal Inquisitor; he quickly earned a reputation as a stern defender of the faith. As the more radical Hussites had fled Bohemia after Sigismund restored order in the province and formally assumed the throne he had inherited from his brother, the heresy found fertile ground in eastern Hungary and Transylvania. Both George Lepes and Bishop John of Nagyvarad believed that Jacob de Marchia was the man for the job and Pope Eugenius agreed. On September 11, 1436, the Pope appointed him as Papal Inquisitor to Hungary, with instructions to eradicate the heresy.[43] This 'Torquemada of Transylvania' did not hesitate to employ torture and both corporal and capital punishment as the tools of his trade, making him a worthy predecessor to the infamous Spanish inquisitor.

Jacob managed to suppress the heresy in eastern Hungary with relative ease; on December 7, 1436, the Archbishop of Strigoniu, the Kingdom's chief prelate, wrote to Eugenius IV, praising the Inquisitor for having eradicated Hussitism in Hungary and for having converted many schismatics to the Catholic faith.[44] But the situation awaiting him in Transylvania was an altogether different matter. Bishop John of Nagyvarad reported to the Pope on December 1, 1436, that the Inquisitor had gone to Transylvania where the heretics had taken up arms against the Catholic clergy, killing several priests and destroying Church property. He added that, by condemning to death large numbers of heretics, Jacob managed to convince many to return to the true faith.[45] In his own account of his activity in Transylvania, the Inquisitor claims

---

[42]Doc. DXX in Hurmuzaki, *Documente*, vol. I, part 2, pp. 614-620.

[43]Doc. DVI in Hurmuzaki, *Documente*, vol. I, part 2, p. 603.

[44]Doc. DXIII in Hurmuzaki, *Documente*, vol. I, part 2, p. 608.

[45]Doc. DXI in Hurmuzaki, *Documente*, vol. I, part 2, p. 606.

that "of all of these heretics, I, Brother Jacob, with the help of the Holy Spirit, through my preaching, converted 25,000 people from among the priests and the laity."[46] But things were not as rosy as Church officials painted them. If anything, the harsh measures applied by the Inquisition further aggravated the situation; summary trials and burnings at the stake galvanized opposition to the Church and fueled the social unrest that had been brewing in the province. When the peasants rose in revolt, they forced Jacob de Marchia to abandon his mission in Transylvania.[47]

One of the first areas to which the flames of rebellion spread was the Duchy of Făgăraş, ruled by Vlad. There, Wallachian serfs living in three villages belonging to the Monastery of Kertz refused to pay the taxes demanded by the Church and took up arms. After a series of violent clashes, the authorities crushed the insurrection. Abbot Michael, a monk of the Cistercian Order, wrote to Sigismund describing the aftermath and "the rotting limbs of the schismatics, the enemy Wallachians, who had laid waste to the monastery with fire and committed theft of all kinds."[48] Violent unrest also manifested itself in the neighboring Saxon lands. At the end of April 1437, Vice-Voivode Lorand Lepes, Bishop George's brother, promised them assistance against "the evildoers and plunderers who have risen up and caused great harm."[49] Hungarian authorities desperately tried to keep a lid on the situation, but things were rapidly spiraling out of control.

The insurrection gained momentum as it spread to central Transylvania. There peasants and their allies, who included urban dwellers and even some representatives of the lesser nobility, gathered at Bobâlna, near Alperét, some fifty kilometers north of Kolosvar, where they established a fortified camp upon a hill some 695 meters high, commanding the surrounding plain. This makeshift stronghold resembled Taborite camps in Bohemia, indicating that some of the rebel leaders, who included Ladislas Biro, *Jude* Vincent and Ladislas Bana from Alperét, Antonio from Magyar Bogath, Magistrate

---

[46]Holban, ed., *Călători străini*, vol. I, p. 73.

[47]I. Makurec, "Husitismul în România," in *RI*, XIV:1-3 (1928), p. 42.

[48]Quo. Pascu, *Bobîlna*, p. 79.

[49]Doc. DXIX in Hurmuzaki, *Documente*, vol. I, part. 2, pp. 613-614.

Antonio and Gall from Kend, Magistrate Thomas from Zeek, John, son of Magistrate Jacob of Kolosvar, Ladislas, the son of Gall from Anthus, who is designated as "Captain and Warrior," and Magistrate Paul of Vajdaháza, "leader of the assembly of Hungarian and Wallachian inhabitants in these parts of Transylvania," had training in Hussite tactics and strategy. In contrast to the earlier violence in southern Transylvania, those who gathered at Bobâlna did so with peaceful intentions, proclaiming their loyalty to the King and hoping to reclaim what they considered to be their "ancient liberties" through negotiation. Upon hearing of the extent of the social unrest in the province, Ladislas Csáky hurried to Transylvania, which he had rarely visited during his tenure as Voivode. Under his leadership, the nobles established their camp at Kápolna, opposite Bobâlna. Around mid-June 1437, the peasants sent emissaries to the leaders of the aristocracy to present their grievances, but the nobles "refused their requests and took their emissaries captive. Then they were beheaded and cut to pieces on the orders of the great Ladislas Csáky, Voivode of Transylvania." The Voivode's refusal to engage in any discussion with the disgruntled peasants meant a declaration of war.

Ignoring the lessons learned after nearly two decades of conflict in Bohemia, Transylvanian authorities assumed that they could quickly crush the rebellion, as they had done in the past, through a decisive show of force. The most important officials in the Voivodate had gathered at Kápolna to lead their troops against the rebels at Bobâlna. Ladislas Csáky, "together with Lorand, his Vice-Voivode, and with the help of Henric de Thamasy and Michael Jakch, Counts of the Szecklers, went against them." Also present was Bishop George Lepes. "And once the battle began, many fell and were killed on both sides," according to the text of the official agreement ending the conflict. In reality, the fortified camp, defended with skill and determination by the rebels, proved impregnable to cavalry attack, and the aristocracy suffered a humiliating defeat. Voivode Ladislas Csáky numbered among those killed in the fighting. The nobles now prepared to accept a negotiated settlement.

An agreement between the two sides was drafted at Bobâlna on June 30 and finalized at the Convent of the Blessed Virgin Mary at the Monastery of Klus, outside Kolosvár, on July 6, 1437. In it, the rebels, calling themselves the "Universitias Hungarorum et Valachorum in his Partibus Transylvanie," professed their loyalty to the King, declaring that the sole purpose of their uprising was "to regain their liberties given to them in ancient times by the holy Kings, which now... are openly ignored or completely abolished." The accord reduced the tax burden which had steadily increased over the past century and limited the obligation to work on the landlord's estate to one day per year. The annual tax, known as the *censum*, was reduced to ten new dinars, to be paid on the feast day of King St. Stephen, August 20. The agreement also addressed the principal grievances that had provoked the uprising in terms favorable to the peasants. It guaranteed that "each and every person of free status, after they pay the rightful *terragiis* and any debts they have accumulated, shall be free to leave, unimpeded, to go wherever they wish." The peasants also obtained the right to make a will, so that "if someone does not have a wife, a legal heir, or a blood relative, they may leave their property and goods to whomever they chose by testament, and the lord of the estate may not alter that testament." To curb previous abuses, the text declared that only "The goods of those without a wife, children, or blood relatives, and who die without leaving a testament become the property of the lord of the estate." The agreement reduced the back taxes owned to the Bishopric of Transylvania to five new dinars. By far the most innovative aspect of the accord was the provision stating that "henceforth, every year before the feast of the Ascension, two wise elders worthy of trust from each village, estate, and city shall gather at the above-mentioned hill at Bobâlna, together with the aforementioned captains.... who will ask those elders if their lords respect their liberties or not and if any noble violates this agreement... he shall be considered an oath-breaker and the other nobles shall shun him and not come to his aid." Finally, the two sides agreed to send a joint delegation to Sigismund to obtain the decree of King St. Stephen, and to respect the text of that document should it modify the terms of their accord.[50]

The peace settlement was doomed from the start for the nobles had no intention of abiding by the terms of the agreement. It did, however, buy them time to regroup their forces. For this purpose, the nobles convoked an extraordinary Diet, without awaiting authorization from the King or the appointment of a new Voivode, also attended by Saxon and Szeckler leaders. This assembly opened at Torda on September 8, but peasant opposition forced

---

[50]Doc. DXX in Hurmuzaki, *Documente*, vol. I, part. 2, pp. 614-620.

them to abandon that town and to reconvene at their stronghold at Kápolna. Here, on September 16, they concluded an historic agreement that became known as the "Union of the Three Nations" and would serve as the constitutional foundation of the Principality during the following centuries. In effect, it regulated relations among the three privileged groups, each of which enjoyed a direct relationship to the King. It is important to remember that during this time the term "nation" did not carry with it ethnic connotations, nor did it include all the inhabitants of the land. Instead, it referred to specific categories of men defined by their privileged status rather than their ethnic origin. To avoid confusion with the modern sense of "nation," it is better to refer to these groups as "estates."

The compact signed at Kápolna on September 16 by the leaders of the nobility and the Saxon and Szeckler elites stated the intention of each of the parties to provide mutual assistance "to oppose all those who fight against this Kingdom, regardless of the nature of the enemy, and they have sworn to be bound together inseparably in the defense of this Kingdom.... and whenever there will occur a hostile attack or a disturbance of any kind against one of the aforesaid parties, that is against the nobles, the Saxons, or the Szecklers, and that party will call upon another of the parties to come to their aid, the party called upon obliges itself to set out the next day to assist the other..." The signatories also united behind the Church, taking an oath "to bring to an end completely and entirely any anterior causes of envy or hostility of any kind whatsoever between the venerable servant of Christ, lord and father George Lepes, Bishop of Transylvania, and the Church clergy, on the one hand, and the nobles, Saxon, and Szecklers, on the other, and none of the parties shall dare to do anything to rekindle these disputes."[51] The subsequent renewal of the accord left no doubt as to its original purpose: "To eradicate and to destroy the evil uprising of the accursed peasants, as well as to defend these parts against the attacks of the barbaric Turks."[52]

Having joined forces, the ruling classes of Transylvania now prepared to crush "the evil uprising of the accursed peasants." Tensions mounted as both sides readied themselves for renewed hostilities. The two camps once again

---

[51]Doc. DXXI in Hurmuzaki, *Documente*, vol. I, part. 2, pp. 621-622.

[52]Doc. XXXVIII in Hurmuzaki, *Documente*, vol. XV, part. 1, pp. 24-25.

met in armed conflict, on September 30, this time at Delloapáti, south of Bistritz; after a hard-fought battle, in which the nobles gained a slight advantage but could not subdue the rebels, negotiations resumed. The two sides finalized a new agreement on October 10, modifying the Bobâlna accord, which, like the previous one, was sealed at the Convent of St. Mary's Monastery near Kolosvár. The most important change involved raising the annual tax, known as the *censum*, which the Bobâlna settlement had fixed at not more than 10 dinars for each serf, by applying a graduated tax-rate according to the individual's wealth. For example, a peasant who owned a plow with eight oxen was required to pay 1 gold florin, the equivalent of 100 dinars, per annum, while a peasant with a plow drawn by four oxen was assessed at half a florin, or 50 dinars annually. The lowest tax rate, applied to those serfs with little or no property, was 12 dinars a year, meaning that even the poorest peasants now paid more than the maximum amount of 10 dinars agreed upon at Bobâlna three months earlier. In addition, the *censum* was now to be paid in two installments, the first of which was due on St. Martin's Day, November 11. Despite the increased fiscal burden, the provision limiting the obligation to work on the landlord's estate to one day per year remained unchanged. Likewise, the right of peasants to move from one estate to another after paying the *terragiis* and any accumulated debts remained inviolable. The agreement also affirmed the landlord's right of judgement over his serfs, but it stated that if the peasant felt that his landlord's judgement was unfair, he could appeal to another village or town, where both parties, the landlord as well as the serf, must accept whatever is decided there."[53]

As part of the Delloapáti Accord, the two sides again agreed to send delegates to the Emperor, who was then in Prague, not later than November 1, to seek his approval. Clearly, Sigismund was the last, best hope to ensure a peaceful settlement to the conflict in Transylvania, but problems elsewhere had for too long preoccupied the Hungarian King. The peasants had hoped that the King would put at their disposal the original decree of King St. Stephen, which popular tradition held specified the rights and obligations of serfs, but such a document almost certainly never existed. It is unknown if the proposed delegations ever reached Sigismund or what position he may have adopted

---

[53]Doc. DXXIII in Hurmuzaki, *Documente*, vol. I, part. 2, pp. 623-627.

regarding the negotiated settlements. After a reign of over fifty years as King of Hungary and twenty-seven as Holy Roman Emperor, Sigismund passed away on December 9, 1437.

Despite these previous agreements, the nobility never intended to abide by their terms. Their strategy was to weaken peasant resistance until they could regain the upper hand. The rebels were also keenly aware that, lacking direct intervention by the King in the conflict, the nobles would again attempt to quell the uprising by force, as they had tried to do at Delloapáti. This realization radicalized the movement that, despite strong Hussite influences, had continued to profess loyalty to King and Church, and that thus far had sought to improve conditions within the existing social system. Now a full-scale rebellion broke out. One of the reasons that this occurred was that lesser nobles and members of the urban middle class joined the rebels in increasing numbers. A member of the lower nobility, Antonio Magnus, one of the rebel leaders who had signed the Delloapáti Accord, emerged as one of the movement's principal leaders. Other leaders included Master John of Kolosvár, Michael the Wallachian from Vireog, a blacksmith from Ujfalace named Valentin, and Ladislas Ban from Alperét. A decree from 1438 declares the noblemen Michael and David from Zsuk in Transylvania as traitors for siding with the peasants during the rebellion of the previous year.[54] The rebels now abandoned their efforts to improve conditions and openly called for the abolition of serfdom and class privilege. The fifteenth century Hungarian chronicler Antonius Bonfinius records that "Antonio, in Transylvania, *devising new things and gathering a large number of armed peasants under the banner of abolishing serfdom*, abandoned his loyalty to the King.... Antonio, gathering his troops, devastated the nobility; many were killed, and villages and towns that opposed them were first pillaged and then burned and destroyed.... The peasant Martin dared to do similar things in the region called Nir, between the Someş rivers."[55] A contemporary Saxon register from Sibiu likewise notes that "In the year of our Lord 1437, a certain Hungarian, one Antonio Magnus, rose

---

[54]Doc. DXXXVII in Hurmuzaki, *Documente*, vol. I, part. 2, p. 637.

[55]Annex in Pascu, *Bobîlna*, p. 233, emphasis added.

up and gathered around him the rebellious masses and tried with them to subjugate all of Transylvania, especially the nobles."[56]

Rebels attacked Torda, Dés, and other towns in central Transylvania, and tried to spread the flames of rebellion to the Saxon and Szeckler lands in the south and east. In early December, Nagyenyed (Aiud) fell to the insurgents, but the nobles counterattacked and reclaimed the town on December 15. Still the rebels pressed on. Antonio Magnus led his forces against Kolosvár and captured the city around December 10. The insurgents now possessed a fortified stronghold in the heart of Transylvania from where they hoped to spread revolution. Upon entering Kolosvár, peasants stormed the prison and freed those held captive by the Ancien Regime in a gesture that foreshadows the storming of the Bastille at the outbreak of the French Revolution three and a half centuries later. As the rebels exacted their vengeance, they slaughtered many nobles and burned and pillaged St. Mary's Monastery outside the city. With the situation spiraling out of control, the newly-appointed Voivode, Desediu de Losoncz, a Transylvanian landlord with estates centered at Alperét, near Bobâlna, where the uprising had begun, assumed command of the nobles's forces and, with help from troops sent by the authorities in Buda, laid siege to Kolosvár. On January 9, 1438, Desediu de Losoncz, Lorand Lepes, and other noble leaders, along with Michael Jakch, Count of the Szecklers, invoked the Kápolna Accord and called upon the Saxons to come to their aid.[57] With Saxon help, during the second half of January the nobles took the city by storm, crushed the rebellion, and captured its leaders.

Having quelled the uprising, the nobles now took their vengeance upon rebel leaders, determined to make an example of them to demonstrate to the peasants what happens to those who dare to challenge the ruling estates. The above-mentioned Saxon register records that "The nobles killed this Antonio near the Monastery of Kolosvár and then cut him to pieces, while at the town of Torda they executed nine of his accomplices, whom they then impaled on a hill just outside Torda."[58] But the nobles did not limit themselves merely to

---

[56]Doc. DXXXVI in Hurmuzaki, *Documente*, vol. I, part. 2, pp. 636.

[57]Doc. DXXXV in Hurmuzaki, *Documente*, vol. I, part. 2, p. 636.

[58]Doc. DXXXVI in Hurmuzaki, *Documente*, vol. I, part. 2, p. 636.

reprisals against the leaders of the uprising. Bonfinius recalls that "a great number of peasants were punished: some had their eyes gouged out; others had their noses and ears cut off; some had their lips cut off; others received their punishment by having their hands cut off..."59 Thus, an entire generation bore the scars of rebellion as a reminder to their children and grandchildren of the price of insurrection. To consolidate their victory, representatives of the nobility and the Saxon and Szeckler elites met at Torda where, after condemning to death and impaling captured rebel leaders, they renewed the Kápolna Accord on February 2, 1438.60 Ultimately, the uprising was doomed to failure; the rebels could offer no viable alternative to the existing socio-political system. But tensions remained high as the burden of serfdom continued to weigh heavy on the peasants. By 1514, when a new rebellion would rock Transylvania, the obligation of the serfs to work on the landlord's estate, which the Bobâlna agreement had set at one day a year, had increased to one day per week.61

Apart from the incidents involving the villages held by the Kertz Monastery, which were considered as lands belonging to the Catholic Church and therefore required to pay the tithe demanded by Bishop Lepes in the new currency, Vlad's holdings in Transylvania, the Duchies of Amlaş and Făgăraş, remained for the most part unaffected by the peasant uprising. Peasants in these territories enjoyed relatively better conditions than their counterparts in other areas of Transylvania because the laws and customs of the Transalpine land, where the feudal regime was less stringent, applied there as well. Unlike serfs in Transylvania, who gave one-ninth of their production, the *nona*, to their masters, those in Wallachia owed their landlord the *dijma*, or one-tenth of their yield. Still, the extent of the rebellion gave Vlad cause for alarm. Clearly, he could no longer rely on help from Transylvania against the Turks, all the more so following the death of his protector, Sigismund, at the height of the uprising. As Sigismund left no male heir, his son-in-law, Albert of Hapsburg, who had married his daughter Elizabeth, succeeded him on the throne of Hungary. Albert and Elizabeth were crowned King and Queen on January 1, 1438. But

---

59Annex in Pascu, *Bobîlna*, p. 233.

60Doc. XXXVIII in Hurmuzaki, *Documente*, vol. XV, part. 1, pp. 24-25.

61*Istoria românilor*, vol. IV, p. 145.

the new King lacked Sigismund's authority and had to concern himself above all with consolidating his position. All of these factors forced Vlad to reconsider his foreign policy to protect himself against the Ottoman threat.

Finding himself without reliable military support to fend off a Turkish attack, Vlad decided to prevent such a calamity by making peace with the Sultan, just as his father Mircea had done under similar circumstances. The Byzantine chronicler Dukas tells us that "Dragoulios, the Voivode of Wallachia... crossed the straits and met with Sultan Murad at Brusa."[62] Vlad set out on this journey to Anatolia, which would take him away from his Principality for a minimum of six to eight weeks, sometime around February 1438.[63] Whether or not Albert knew of Vlad's intention to travel to the Porte to purchase peace from the Turks is unclear, but on Valentine's Day the new King addressed a letter to the officials of Brașov and the Bârsa land, informing them, "I have written to our faithful servant, the great Vlad, Voivode of our Transalpine land, telling him not to disturb you or to cause you any damages, but on the contrary to protect you from attacks, especially the attacks of the barbaric Turks."[64]

Upon his arrival in the Asian capital of the Ottoman Empire, Dukas writes that Vlad, "paying homage to him [the Sultan], submitted and promised that when Murad will need to cross into Hungary he will accord him passage, and that he will go before him as far as the borders of Germany and Russia. Murad was overjoyed by this promise, and he had him sit at his table and he drank together with him and he received him with all honors and many gifts for him and his suite, who were more than three hundred, and he embraced him and then he let him leave."[65] Vlad appears to have developed an excellent personal relationship with the Sultan, something that would serve him well later in his

---

[62]Ducas, *Istoria turco-bizantină*, p. 254 (XXIX, 10).

[63]Although many have argued that Vlad submitted to the Sultan at the beginning of his reign (see, for example, Virgil Ciocîltan, "La campagne ottomane de Transylvanie," in *RRH*, XV:3 (1976), pp. 439-440), for reasons outlined above, this certainly occurred after Sigismund's death, a conclusion also supported by Aurel Decei, *Istoria imperiului otoman*, Bucharest, 1998, p. 87.

[64]Doc. 251 in *DRH, D*, pp. 347-349.

[65]Ducas, *Istoria turco-bizantină*, p. 254 (XXIX, 10).

reign. In fact, many of Murad's adversaries held the Sultan in high regard. Dukas characterized Murad by saying that "he respected treaties that he concluded under oath to the letter, unchanged and undisturbed.... he received emissaries with pleasure, and he let emissaries leave in peace because he hated war and loved peace. For this reason, the Father of Peace rewarded the infidel with a good, peaceful death, and not one by the sword."[66] Although the tribute paid by Wallachia would steadily rise during the second part of the fifteenth

Sultan Murad II
By Octavian Ion Penda

century, the first half of the century was a period of relatively little inflation, making it likely that Vlad agreed to the same terms as those accepted by his father Mircea and that the amount to be paid annually to the Sultan remained 3000 galbens. Ottoman chronicles from this period are ambiguous and often confuse or combine different events, but the account of Idris Bitlisi indicates that Vlad "set out for the Porte *without being called*" and that he brought with him "tribute for *two years*, as well as many gifts."[67] This confirms our hypothesis that Vlad went to the Sultan of his own initiative during the second year of his reign. Vlad had made the long voyage to Brusa to secure his position, but his enemies at home used the occasion of his absence from the Principality to attempt a coup d'état.

Albul appears to have withdrawn from public life following Aldea's death. The former *Vornic* acknowledged Vlad as Prince and, in return, received a

---

[66]Ducas, *Istoria turco-bizantină*, p. 284 (XXXIII, 6).

[67]*Cronici turcești*, vol. I, p. 166, emphasis added.

diploma renewing exemptions from royal taxes and labors for his estates.[68] But Albul harbored secret ambitions. After Vlad set out for Anatolia, the man who had once wielded power in Wallachia nearly equal to that of the Prince now sought to claim the throne for himself. We learn of this revolt from a diploma issued by Prince Mircea the Shepherd on April 1, 1551, confirming possession of the villages of Glodul and Hința to the Monastery of Govora. In it, the Prince recounts that "these aforementioned villages belonged to the holy monastery from the beginning of our country Wallachia.... And then, in the days of Voivode Vlad the Impaler, there was a boyar who was called Albul the Great. He took the aforementioned villages by force and he plundered the holy monastery.... And after this, in the days of Voivode Vlad the Impaler, this boyar, Albul the Great, made himself Prince over the land of Voivode Vlad the Impaler, but Vlad set out with his army against him and captured him and killed him and all of his family. Then, Voivode Vlad saw that the holy monastery was deserted, so he gave those villages, Glodul and Hința, to some of his servants."[69]

Historians have long believed that this document refers to a revolt against Vlad the Impaler, just as the text seems to imply. It has been used as evidence of the younger Vlad's conflicts with the boyars, a favorite theme of Marxist historiography which strove to portray the Impaler as a proto-Communist hero, struggling to curb the abuses of the nobility.[70] There are several problems, however, with such an interpretation of this document. First of all, who was the Albul who rose up against Vlad the Impaler? The boyar Albul, son of

---

[68]Doc. 86 in *DRH, B*, vol. I, pp. 150-151.

[69]Doc. 3 in *DIR, XVI, B*, vol. III, pp. 3-5. Vlad's son Vlad the Monk and his grandson Radu the Great later restored the villages of Hința and Glodul to the Govora Monastery (see Docs. 210, 233, and 290 in *DRH, B*, vol. I, pp. 335-336, 373-374, and 471-474).

[70]See, for example, Barbu T. Câmpina, "Complotul boierilor și răscoala din Tara Românească" in *Studii și referate privind istoria Romîniei*, part. I, Bucharest, 1954; and Ștefan Andreescu, *Vlad Țepeș (Dracula)*, Bucharest, 1998, p. 90-91. American historians Radu Florescu and Raymond T. McNally also adopted this position in their works on Vlad the Impaler, see Radu R. Florescu and Raymond T. McNally, *Dracula: A Biography of Vlad the Impaler*, New York, 1973, p. 61. It is also present in more recent works such as the Romanian Academy's multi-volume synthesis, *Istoria românilor*, vol. IV, pp. 350-352.

Tocsaba, who served as Vornic under both Dan II and Alexander Aldea, vanishes without a trace from historical documents beginning in 1438. Although some contend that this same Albul tried to overthrow the younger Vlad,[71] it seems highly improbable that this boyar, who first appears as a member of the royal council under Mircea the Old, would suddenly reappear after an absence of twenty years to make a bid for the throne. If the document in question does not refer to this Albul, then who is the boyar in question? The only boyar named Albul referred to in documents from the time of Vlad the Impaler is the *Vistier* of the pretender Dan III who tried to overthrow the younger Vlad in 1460,[72] but his status as an official serving the son of Dan II rules him out as a usurper. This incongruity has led others to postulate the existence of yet another Albul, an older brother of Dan III's Vistier who, as a result, is called 'the Great,'[73] an appellation sometimes used to distinguish between two related persons of the same name. But there is no evidence to corroborate the existence of such a person. It is a case of creating facts to support a hypothesis. Therefore, we must conclude that the Albul specified in Mircea the Shepherd's diploma is Aldea's Vornic, the only boyar in the first half of the fifteenth century to wield sufficient power to earn the epithet 'the Great' and with enough might to dare to seize the throne for himself, even though he was not of royal descent.

But if Albul the Great tried to usurp the throne for himself, then clearly he rebelled against his and Aldea's arch-rival, Vlad Dracul, and not against Vlad the Impaler.[74] Still, to confirm this hypothesis, the question as to why the document quoted above makes reference to Vlad the Impaler must answered. In chapter I, we demonstrated that contemporaries used the names *Dracul* and

---

[71]Nicolae Stoicescu, *Dicţionar al marilor dregători*, Bucharest, 1971, p. 15; Rădutiu, "Despre numele Drakula," p. 30, nt. 4.

[72]Doc. CCLXIX in Bogdan, *Documente privitoare*, pp. 325-327.

[73]Andreescu, *Vlad Ţepeş (Dracula)*, pp. 90-91; and Pavel Chihaia, *Din cetăţile de scaun ale Ţării Româneşti*, Bucharest, 1974, p. 73. Andreescu posits that Albul Tocsaba was the father of Albul the Great and Dan III's Vistier, but we know that his eldest son was named Stancea and, like his father, held the position of Vornic during the reign of Vladislav II, see Stoicescu, *Dicţionar al marilor dregători*, p. 24.

[74]This idea is first suggested in Treptow, *Vlad III Dracula*, Iaşi, 2000, p. 81.

Dracula interchangeably to refer to both Vlads. As time passed, the distinction between father and son blurred even more. The lack of historical writing in fifteenth century Wallachia, incomplete records, and the fact that several Princes bore the same name contributed to this situation. Through his terror tactics in campaigns against both the Turks and the Saxons of Transylvania, the younger Vlad had earned the sobriquet, 'the Impaler,' but this did nothing to alleviate the confusion. By the time of Mircea the Shepherd (1545-1554; 1558-1559), who issued the diploma recounting Albu's revolt, Vlad the Impaler also referred to Vlad Dracul. Another document emitted by the chancellery of this same Prince confirms this supposition. In a diploma confirming ownership of the village of Izvoranii to the Monastery of Snagov dated June 26, 1558, Mircea the Shepherd declares that "My Majesty read the ancient diplomas of Voivode Vlad the Impaler, and of Voivode Vladislav the Old, and of Voivode Basarab the Old."[75] In typical fashion, the Princes mentioned are listed in chronological order; Vlad the Impaler refers to Vlad Dracul, Vladislav the Old to his successor Vladislav II, (1447-1456) and Basarab the Old most likely to Basarab the Young (1478-1481) or Neagoe Basarab (1512-1521). Furthermore, we still possess Vlad Dracul's original diploma referred to here by Mircea the Shepherd, confirming possessions, including the village of Izvoranii, to the Monastery of Snagov, dated June 30, 1441.[76] There are no extant diplomas issued by his son for this Monastery. Thus, there can be no doubt that Mircea the Shepherd uses the name Vlad the Impaler to refer to Vlad Dracul and that his diploma of April 1, 1551, recalls an uprising led by Albul the Great against him.

Yet this sixteenth century diploma is not the only evidence of the coup d'état engineered by Albul after Vlad left the country to make peace with the Sultan. In an undated letter to the burghers of Braşov, Albul makes it clear that he seized power following Vlad's departure: "I give you news of the Voivode, Dracula, whom you have placed here. Those among you to whom he is dear can kiss him goodbye, for you shall see him no more, for I place my trust in God that from where he has gone he shall not return. Yet for all the good I have done for you, you have shown no gratitude to me.... Whoever wishes may

[75]Doc. 100 in *DIR, XVI, B*, vol. III, pp. 85-86.
[76]Doc. 95 in *DRH, B*, vol. I, pp. 164-166.

bring iron and copper and any other goods; and whoever is owed a debt is free
to collect it. But you plunder the houses of those poor men who prepare to
come here via Prahova or Teleajen, each with what he can, and you intimidate
them so as not to come."[77] This letter clearly implies that Vlad had set out for
Brusa and that Albul did not expect him to return from there. The certainty
with which he makes this assertion leads one to speculate that perhaps the
former Vornic had used his contacts among Ottoman officials to try to ensure
the failure of Vlad's peace mission. This would mean that a conspiracy to seize
the throne from Vlad was afoot prior to his departure, but Albul underestimated
the Prince's diplomatic skill and did not anticipate that Vlad and Murad would
get along so well personally. The letter also proves that Albul had assumed the
prerogatives of the Prince, declaring free trade. A simple boyar, for Albul held
no title under Vlad and did not serve in his royal council, would not have
presumed to make such a declaration. A mention in Polish archives of an oath
of allegiance to the Polish King by a pretender John Albul, using the title
Palatine of Basarabia,[78] provides further evidence that Albul had seized power.
John was the surname assumed by all rulers of Wallachia, which the Poles
called Basarabia, since the founding of the Principality. The title Palatine was
the Latin equivalent of Vornic; as he was not of royal blood, Albul perhaps
hesitated to call himself Prince.

As the previously-mentioned letter indicates, the officials of Braşov
hesitated to show favor to Albul, perhaps fearing reprisals from Vlad should
he return, but also because they were uncomfortable about the legitimacy of
his claim to power. The usurper, however, realized that he needed to gain
Saxon support if he hoped to maintain his position. On April 2, Albul assured
the burghers of Braşov that "I have no hostile intentions toward you. You may
go about freely and you will have no problems, for we would like you to be

---

[77]Doc. 211 in *DRH, D*, p. 310. The editors date this document 1434-1435, but the
reference to the assistance provided by Braşov to place Voivode *Dracula* in Wallachia
makes it clear that this letter could only have been written after Vlad assumed the
throne in the fall of 1436. Albul also implies that Vlad had departed for the Porte,
making February-March 1438 the most probable date.

[78]Iorga, *Studii şi documente*, vol. III, p. XIV; and Iorga, *Studii istorice asupra Chiliei
şi Cetăţii-Albe*, p. 74.

our brothers as you were before."[79] But the officials of Braşov waited to see how the situation evolved. Still, Albul persisted. In another undated letter to the burghers of Braşov, the former Vornic wrote: "I am forever your brother in all that you need. Arrange things so that... one of your men is with me at all times, never absent from here, so that I can tell you what I know."[80]

Despite the initial success of his revolt, Albul failed to win the support of Vlad's principal boyars; even those who had served with him under Aldea were reluctant to join him, as indicated by the fact that no significant changes occurred in the composition of Vlad's royal council between 1437 and 1439. Those who had not accompanied their Prince to Brusa probably fled south of the Danube following Albul's coup d'état to await his return and to prepare for their counterattack. Although he could garner enough military support to forcibly take power, Albul encountered strong opposition, as evidenced by his devastation of the Monastery of Govora. Vlad had worked hard to secure a broad base of support and the results of his efforts became apparent during this time of crisis. Most leading boyars were disinclined to throw in their lot with a usurper from outside the ruling dynasty, a situation unprecedented in the history of the Principality up to that time.

As a result, upon his return from Anatolia, Vlad crossed the Danube with a significant force and easily crushed the rebellion. Albul was killed in the fighting, but some of his family and supporters escaped to Transylvania, the traditional place of refuge for disgruntled Wallachian boyars. Albul's son Stancea later become Vornic under Vladislav II. Another of Albul's men, Neagoe, had managed to flee across the Carpathians with 200,000 aspers, the equivalent of 4,000 gold florins, from the royal treasury. Having learned of this from his intelligence sources, Vlad wrote sternly to the burghers of Braşov: "A servant of Albul, one Neagoe, has fled there and taken with him money

---

[79]Doc. 201 in *DRH, D*, p. 298. The editors date this document 1433-1434, but the text of the letter, which specifies the day and month it was written, make it clear that Albul has assumed the prerogatives of ruler of Wallachia making April 2, 1438, the most likely date.

[80]Doc. 202 in *DRH, D*, p. 299. The editors date this document from 1433-1434 after Bogdan (Doc. CCIX in Bogdan, *Documente privitoare*, pp. 249-250), but the spring of 1438 when Albul briefly assumed power is a more likely date.

belonging to My Majesty, two hundred thousand aspers, and left them at Rijnov with Cârstea Madramen and Michael the Bulgarian. And so, I have sent My Majesty's Spătar, Dragota, for you to turn over that money to him so that he can bring it to My Majesty. Do not do otherwise, for if you will not give it to him be forewarned that I will make war."[81]

Throughout this period, we can detect a steady deterioration in relations between Wallachia and Braşov, first revealed in Albert's letter of February 14, 1438, to officials in Braşov and the Bârsa land, who had previously expressed their concern to the King that Vlad may undertake some hostile actions against them.[82] Despite the trade agreements concluded during the previous year, commercial relations remained a point of contention. These problems, however, seem to have arisen in part because of abuses committed by royal officials stationed at Bran Castle, rather than any measures taken by Saxon authorities. In a letter dated April 26, 1438, addressed to military and customs officials assigned to the fortress, Albert accuses them of imposing abusive customs taxes "on each Wallachian from the Transalpine land who came with their property and goods to our city and land, and because of this our citizens and merchants from Braşov and our Bârsa land, when they happen to go to the Transalpine land, bringing with them their property and goods so as to earn a living, are prevented from doing so in these parts and are pillaged in a similar manner through the payment of much higher duties...." Therefore, the King ordered his men "not to demand unfair or illegal customs taxes" from Wallachian merchants, so that merchants from Braşov and the Bârsa land, "in the future, will not be hindered in any way in the said Transalpine land."[83] The problem of refugee boyars also soured relations between the two neighbors. In another undated letter to the burghers of Braşov, Vlad admonishes them: "I have written you before and I am writing to you again now that whoever leaves this country without My Majesty's written permission, you are to stop them and to send word to My Majesty. If they are honest men, they can continue on with their property, but if they have stolen horses we shall punish them as evil

---

[81]Doc. 239 in *DRH, D*, p. 335. The Spătar mentioned here, Dragota, is another of Vlad's military commanders, an adjutant of the Great Spătar Dumitru.

[82]Doc. 251 in *DRH, D*, pp. 347-349.

[83]Doc. 252 in *DRH, D*, pp. 349-350.

men. You should know that they have depleted this country of horses. If you do not do this be aware that I will make war on you. Do not let it be otherwise."[84] Although the exact causes remain obscure, after Vlad crushed Albul's revolt, relations between Wallachia and the Saxons of Transylvania took a turn for the worse.

The death of Sigismund had created a new rift between Hungary and Poland. The conflict centered on control over Bohemia. Hussite leaders, who had spent the past two decades fighting the Hungarians, refused to accept Albert of Hapsburg as Sigismund's heir and instead offered the crown to Polish King Vladislav III. Vladislav proposed that his younger brother Casimir be made King of Bohemia, and Polish forces prepared to cross the border to press his claim and to drive out Albert who had been crowned in Prague on June 29, 1438. The Poles now sought to enlist Ottoman support against the Hungarians, and Vlad, with his strong ties to the Polish royal family, seems to have played a key role in these negotiations. Marginal notes added by an unidentified third party to a letter penned by Jodocus de Helpruna, sent from Vienna on September 11, 1438, to Johannes von Bachenstein, an official of the Council of Basel, describing recent events in Transylvania, point out that "the Prince of Wallachia is related by marriage to the King of Poland" and consider this as one of the reasons that the Ottomans attacked Transylvania that summer."[85] Hungarian nobles also accused the Poles of colluding with the Ottomans in a letter dated September 15.[86] If Vlad, as part of his mission to Brusa, helped to negotiate Polish-Ottoman cooperation against Hungary, it would explain Dukas's assertion that he promised the Sultan, of his own accord, safe passage through Wallachia and agreed to accompany Ottoman forces against Hungary.[87] The Poles could justify their alliance with the Ottomans in the same way that French King Francis I rationalized his cooperation with the Sultan against Charles V a century later: "I cannot deny that I very much want to see the Turk powerful and ready for war, not for his own sake, for he is an infidel

---

[84]Doc. 250 in *DRH, D*, p. 347.

[85]Quo. Virgil Ciocîltan, "Între sultan şi împărat: Vlad Dracul în 1438," in *RdI*, 29:11 (1976), p. 1777.

[86]Veniamin Ciobanu, *Ţările române şi Polonia*, Bucharest, 1985, p. 49.

[87]Ducas, *Istoria turco-bizantină*, p. 259 (XXIX, 10).

and the rest of us are Christians, but to erode the power of the Emperor and involve him in crippling expense."[88]

Murad II also had his own reasons for launching an attack against Hungary at this time. Sigismund's death and the recent peasant uprising in Transylvania made that province, which promised the invaders great plunder, particularly vulnerable; in addition, the Sultan wished to punish the Hungarians for their role in inciting the rebellion in Karaman. When he arrived in Adrianople and began to muster his army, Mehmed Neshri tell us that the Sultan sent word to his vassals, George Branković in Serbia and Vlad in Wallachia, instructing them to ready their troops to join him in an attack on Hungary. He records that "Dracula replied: 'I am ready to serve my Sultan. I accept to lead his horse by its reins.'"[89] In other words, Vlad, who knew the terrain as well as anyone, agreed to lead the vanguard for the attackers, perhaps another indication of his complicity in helping to organize the campaign. By the end of May, Murad had assembled his army at his European capital and prepared to march on Transylvania. Although contemporary sources estimate the size of the Ottoman army that went against Transylvania that summer at anywhere from 70,000 to 300,000 troops,[90] Murad's force likely numbered no more than 30,000 fighting men, apart from the 2,000 to 3,000 men each contributed by Vlad and George Branković.

Murad II set out with his army from Adrianople in early June and made his way north to the Danube. En route, Serbian troops commanded by despot George Branković joined him and served as the Sultan's advance guard until they reached Vidin where this combined force crossed the river into Wallachia. There, Vlad awaited the Sultan with his contingent. As he was the most familiar with the terrain that lay ahead, the Wallachian Prince replaced

---

[88]Quo. Hale, *Civilization of Europe in the Renaissance*, p. 40.

[89]*Cronici turcești*, vol. I, p. 120.

[90]The author known as "Captivus Septemcastrensis" speaks of 300,000 Turkish troops (N. Iorga, *Acte și fragmente*, vol. III, p. 8), while Johannes von Bachenstein estimates the Ottoman army at 100,000, including "15,000 armed women" (Quo. Ciocîltan, "Între Sultan și Împărat," p. 1773). Ottoman sources, such as Orudj bin Adil, give between 70,000-80,000 men (*Cronici turcești*, vol. I, p. 53), a more realistic figure if we assume it includes non-combattants accompanying the army.

Branković at the head of the army and guided them across the mountains into Transylvania. They proceeded north along the left bank of the Danube. An anonymous Ottoman chronicle informs us that Murad "passed by a fortress of the cursed Hungarian called Severin. He fired a few cannon volleys, but did make an effort to take it; he then traversed the narrow pass called the Iron Gates, after which, passing in front of the fortress of Orşova, he stopped at the banks of the Cerna River. From there he passed before the fortress of Mehadia and that of Karansebesh [Caransebeş]."[91] The Ottomans did not concern themselves with these fixed fortifications, but were satisfied with burning and pillaging everything that fell prey to them along the way. On August 7, 1440, King Vladislav of Hungary and Poland issued a new diploma confirming the holdings of the Macskási family in the Karansebesh district as their original deeds had been lost when their estates were devastated during the Turkish invasion two years earlier.[92] Murad had not embarked on a campaign of conquest. Had the Ottomans set out to do so, they could certainly have taken several of these citadels, but as they were located behind enemy lines, they lacked the means to hold them for an extended period, meaning that any assault on them would be a frivolous waste of time and resources. Besides, the Sultan knew that the small garrisons manning these fortresses represented no threat his powerful army. From the outset Murad had intended this campaign as a punitive expedition to pillage and to gather captives to be ransomed or sold into slavery. With Orthodox and Catholic leaders gathered in Italy to discuss Church union, the Sultan realized that an offensive at this time designed to conquer additional Christian territories could work against Ottoman interests by driving the two sides closer together. As we have seen, similar considerations led him to abandon the idea of a new siege of Constantinople after Emperor John VIII left to participate at the Council of Florence.

From Karansebesh, Vlad guided Turkish forces east to the Hatszeg land, following the route traversed by Emperor Trajan's Roman legions over thirteen hundred years earlier when they stormed the Dacian capital of Sarmizegetusa. But before reaching the vestiges of Decebal's once-proud city, they had to penetrate a narrow man-made pass called the Iron Gate, the portal

---

[91]Quo. Aurel Decei, *Relaţii româno-orientale*, Bucharest, 1978, p. 216.

[92]Doc. DLXX in Hurmuzaki, *Documente*, vol. I, part.2, pp. 671-673.

to Transylvania. Legend attributes its construction to Alexander the Great, but, although it dates from antiquity, the Macedonian ruler never set foot in these parts. Here Ladislas Kende, a Transylvanian-Wallachian noble, and his family, who had been charged by Sigismund with protecting this pass and its bridge, the principal route for salt mined at Vyzakna (Ocna Sibiului) to be transported to Hungary, offered token resistance. But the overwhelming Ottoman force could not be impeded. They devastated the Kende family estates in the Hatszeg land as they continued their advance. The following year, King Albert granted new royal diplomas to Ladislas Kende and his family, confirming their holdings and their concession to administer the bridge at the Iron Gate, as the original documents issued by Sigismund had been lost during the invasion.[93]

From Hatszeg, the Sultan's army, with Vlad at the fore, marched northeast, pillaging the environs of the Saxon city of Broos (Orăştie) before moving on to Mühlbach (Sebeş). We are fortunate to possess an eyewitness account of the events that transpired at Mühlbach, left to us by a Dominican monk, George of Hungary, writing under the pseudonym of Captivus Septemcastrensis,[94] meaning "Captive from the Seven Citadels" or Siebenburgen, the German name for Transylvania. Saxon colonists had settled Mühlbach around the beginning of the thirteenth century. An imposing church built in the fourteenth century dominated the town square and remains one of the most splendid examples of Gothic architecture in Transylvania. Mühlbach became an educational center for the surrounding area, boasting a school located in the city's Dominican convent; the town's priest Anthony, one of its leading citizens, had received his doctorate from the University of Vienna. George had come to Mühlbach from Ramosch (Romos), a village 25 kilometers southwest of the town, to study at the Dominican school, perhaps under this same Anthony, a widely respected scholar and cleric.

While working as a clerk at the Vatican four decades later, the Dominican monk wrote a book entitled, *Tractatus moribus, condicionibus et nequicia*

---

[93]Docs. DLIV and DLV in Hurmuzaki, *Documente*, vol. I, part.2, pp. 653-656.

[94]Francisc Pall, "Identificarea lui 'Captivus Septemcastrensis,'" in *RdI*, 27:1 (1974), p. 98. George's book on the Turks enjoyed great popularity in Europe during the late fifteenth and throughout the sixteenth century. No fewer than 11 Latin-language editions and 7 German language translations of work were published.

Turcorum (*Treatise on the Customs, Way of Life, and Wretchedness of the Turks*), first published in Rome in 1480, in which he recalled the Ottoman attack on Mühlbach, an event that had a decisive impact on the rest of his life. In it, George remembers, "At that time, I was a young man of fifteen or sixteen years old and I had left my place of birth during the preceding year to come to the fortified city, called Sebesh by the Hungarians and Mühlbach in German, to study. It was well-populated at that time, but not well-fortified, and when the Turks came and beseiged the town, the Prince of Wallachia [Vlad], who had come there with the Sultan,... spoke with the leading citizens at the walls of the city and advised them to make peace and to remain calm because they did not have the power to resist the Turks who were many and well-armed." After deliberations, town leaders, including Anthony, Herman Mewlmeuster, Martin Vlich, and Zacharia, surrendered Mühlbach to the Sultan, hoping in this way to avoid bloodshed and the destruction of the city. Without a doubt, they had known and worked with Vlad during his years as a pretender in Transylvania, and they trusted that he would do his best to protect them.

But soon after they yielded the city to the Turks, George tells us that the Sultan ordered his troops to begin to plunder and to take captives: "Then two brave and noble brothers among us rose up and said that they will fight against all the Turks because it is better to die a hundred times than to surrender themselves into the hands of the Turks with their women and children." Those who chose to resist barricaded themselves in the town's strongest tower. Among them was young George who recalled that "One of these brothers stayed next to me in the loft of the tower all throughout the night and all of us who were there expected that we would be killed and that none of us would come out of there alive. Near dawn of that terrifying night, the Sultan came there personally and ordered that all of the young men, women, and children be selected, and that they would be taken with him to Turkey to his imperial seat. Seeing this, the citizens went to the Prince of Wallachia and asked him to take care of their families in the land where they would be taken. I was still in the loft of the tower, where I had remained alone, now thinking that I would escape undetected. But all at once I began to smell smoke and heard a strange noise coming from all sides, and then I saw that they had set fire to the tower at its base. There was too much smoke and it became too hot, and I knew that the loft where I was hidden would not hold up against the approaching flames for very long, so I tried to climb down without making any noise, but I fell as a large and heavy piece of wood came down and struck me and nearly killed me, making a great noise. From that moment my misfortune began as I was captured and placed in chains and taken across the Danube to Adrianople, the capital of the Sultan."[95] The Ottomans devastated the city and took numerous captives before moving on. Joducus de Helpruna reported from Vienna to the Council of Basel that "Mühlbach is totally destroyed."[96]

Vlad seems to have played a similar role at nearby Kelling (Câlnic), convincing town leaders, including the cleric Lawrence, to surrender so as to avert a massacre at the hands of the Turks. Under the circumstances, the Wallachian Prince had given Saxon leaders at Mühlbach and Kelling sound advice. The fortifications protecting these towns had not been improved in recent decades and were wholly inadequate to withstand an Ottoman assault. As the days passed, the Turks grew increasingly confident. No Hungarian army had materialized to challenge them and Murad's intelligence sources reported that none was likely to appear any time soon.

There are several explanations for the failure of the Hungarians to mobilize a force to oppose the Turkish invaders. First of all, King Albert was engaged in Bohemia where Polish forces had crossed the border, at the invitation of Hussite leaders, in an attempt to claim the crown for Vladislav III's brother Casimir. Although he ultimately defeated the Poles, the conflict kept Albert in the Czech lands throughout the summer and fall of 1438. In addition, the peasant revolt that had been brutally repressed only months before had seriously damaged Transylvania's defensive capacity. Despite the Kápolna Accord, nobles, fearing for the security of their estates should they depart for military duty, refused to heed Voivode Desideu de Losoncz's call to arms. When Desideu tried to compel them to do so by confiscating lands from those

---

[95]Iorga, *Acte și fragmente*, vol. III, pp. 8-10 in the original Latin version. For a contemporary German translation, edited by the noted humanist Sebastian Franck, a friend of Protestant reformer Martin Luther who himself wrote a preface to one of the German editions of the book by 'Captivus Septemcastrensis,' see A. Decei, "Informațiile istorice ale lui 'Captivus Septemcastrensis," in *AIIN, Cluj*, VII (1936-1938), pp, 689-693.

[96]Quo. Ciocîltan, "Între sultan și împărat," p. 1771.

who refused, powerful nobles such as Ladislas and Stephen Báthory went over the Voivode's head and complained to Queen Elizabeth about his abusive actions. The Báthory brothers told the Queen that they were unable to obey the Voivode's order because serfs on their estate at Feyerd (Feiurdeni), north of Kolosvár, had risen up and destroyed their property and killed one of their overseers. On August 10, 1438, Elizabeth wrote to Desideu de Losoncz, ordering him to restore the confiscated lands to the Báthorys.[97] Because of the continued danger of peasant unrest, on May 22, Albert had granted permission to the brothers Gregory, Nicholas, and Anthony Bethlen, representatives of another of Transylvania's leading aristocratic families, to build a fortified castle at Bethlehem (Beclean).[98] An additional indication of the devastating impact of the peasant revolt on Transylvanian defenses is found in a letter dated September 14, 1439, in which the King complains to Bishop Lepes about the reluctance manifested by serfs on royal estates to take up arms against the Turkish invaders the year before.[99] The inability to coordinate military action against the Ottomans is also explained by the fact that, since the death of Pippo de Ozora, the region lacked a strong leader capable of taking the initiative; Desideu de Losoncz had been selected as Voivode from among the ranks of the Transylvanian nobles as a compromise solution during a period of crisis and, because of this, proved incapable of exerting his authority over them. As a result, the Saxon lands had to stand alone against the Turkish onslaught in the summer of 1438.

With Transylvania's defenses in disarray, the Turks could move about unimpeded. This situation permitted the Sultan to divide his force, sending out contingents to ravage and to plunder, as well as to forage for food and supplies, while he proceeded with the main body of his troops to Sibiu, the region's wealthiest and most important city. An anonymous Ottoman chronicle records how Murad "ordered all of his commanders to organize in groups and to go out on pillaging expeditions in all directions. Thus, he devastated the country of the enemy and took great plunder."[100] Fortifications provided the

---

[97]Doc. DXLI in Hurmuzaki, *Documente*, vol. I, part.2, pp. 641-642.

[98]Doc. DXLII in Hurmuzaki, *Documente*, vol. I, part.2, pp. 642-643.

[99]Doc. XLII in Hurmuzaki, *Documente*, vol. XV, part.1, pp. 26-27.

[100]Quo. Decei, Relaţii româno-orientale, p. 216.

Transylvanians with their only means of defense. Throughout his long reign, Sigismund had actively promoted the construction and improvement of walls, towers, and other fortifications to defend the cities of his realm, particularly those located in vulnerable border regions such as Transylvania. The efficacy of these manmade defenses was now put to its severest test to date. From Joducus de Helpruna's letter and its marginal notes, we learn that the walls of Weissenburg (Alba Iulia), the residence of the Voivode, failed to keep out the Akingi who devastated the city and plundered its Catholic Cathedral, the seat of Bishop Lepes.[101] Nearby Krako (Cricau) also suffered at the hands of the invaders; as a result of the destruction, on January 27, 1439, the Bishop exempted town officials from paying dues owed to the Episcopal Seat.[102] Other towns fared better. The well-built fortifications of Kokelburg (Cetatea de Baltă), Mediasch (Mediaș), and Schässburg (Sighişoara), defended with bravery and skill by their inhabitants, kept out the Turkish marauders who had to content themselves with pillaging their suburbs and the surrounding countryside. It is also possible that Ottoman troops spared Schässburg because of Vlad's connection with that city.

Meanwhile, the Sultan, attended by his vassals, Vlad and George Branković, laid seige to Sibiu. Here, the King's capable representative Anton Trautenberger, Prefect of the district, whom Sigismund had appointed to that post in 1432, directed the city's defense.[103] The wealthiest and most populous urban center in Transylvania at that time, Sibiu presented a tempting target for the Turkish invaders thirsting for plunder. But Hermannstadt, as the town was commonly referred to in those days, was an especially well-fortified city, and throughout his reign Murad had demonstrated that he lacked the patience to engage in a prolonged seige of the type necessary to force its capitulation. Machiavelli aptly describes the predicament facing a would-be aggressor intent on attacking a German city of this type: "they are fortified in such a way that every one thinks that taking them by assault would be tedious and difficult, seeing they have proper ditches and walls, they have sufficient artillery, and they always keep in public depots enough for one year's eating, drinking, and

---

[101]Quo. Ciocîltan, "Între sultan și împărat," pp. 1771-1772.

[102]Doc. 2327 in *Urkundenbuch*, V, pp. 20-21.

[103]Decei, *Relații româno-orientale*, p. 217.

firing. And beyond this, to keep the people quiet and without loss to the state, they always have the means of giving work to the community in those labours that are the life and strength of the city, and in the pursuit of which the people are supported; they also hold military exercises in repute, and moreover have many ordinances to uphold them."[104] The Ottomans could only hope to find a hidden weakness in the fortifications or to convince some of the defenders to betray their town.

While they attempted to take the city, Ottoman forces also plundered the surrounding countryside; they did, however, spare the nearby Duchy of Amlaş, as it belonged to Vlad. Despite the Sultan's efforts, Sibiu proved impregnable. A native of the city, the sixteenth century humanist Nicholas Olahus (1493-1568), a man who corresponded with Erasmus and rose to become archbishop of Strigoniu and later regent of Hungary, described his hometown as "a large and powerful city... it is very well fortified; apart from its walls, which are wide and solid, there are numerous towers and a moat with wide and deep waters which surround it all along the outside, except on the eastern side. Outside the walls, the city is surrounded on all sides by wide and deep ponds in three or four rows... because of this the enemy does not have access to the city walls anywhere except along the roads which lead from different regions to the city gates. And these are so strong, having stakes, bolts, and other improvements, that the city cannot be conquered except by starving it, or through the negligence of the citizens or dissension among them, such as often threatens strong cities."[105] Realizing its futility, Murad raised the seige after only eight days.[106]

By now the bulk of the Ottoman force had reassembled and it began to move east. This took it through Vlad's most important Transylvanian domain,

---

[104]Machiavelli, *The Prince*, p. 82 (X).

[105]Holban, ed., *Călători străini*, vol. I, p. 492. Olahus provides this description in his book *Hungaria* written in Latin around 1536-1537. Although it dates from a century after Murad's seige, the fortifications he describes were largely the same as those protecting the city in the summer of 1438.

[106]Gustav Gündisch, "Siebenbürgen in der Türkenabwehr, 1395-1526," in *RRH*, XIII:3 (1974), p. 426. An anonymous Ottoman chronicle relates that the Sultan remained at Sibiu "five to ten days," see Decei, *Relaţii româno-orientale*, p. 217.

the Duchy of Făgăraș, which, thanks to the Wallachian Prince's status as the Sultan's ally, escaped devastation by the Turks. Their next target was the lucrative Bârsa land, with its administrative center at Brașov, described by the celebrated German humanist Sebastian Münster as "the second city of the country [Transylvania] after Sibiu."[107] Murad had trespassed in these parts before, alongside Vlad's brother Radu in the spring of 1421. This time, he decided not to test the city's recently improved fortifications. Instead, Ottoman troops ravaged its suburbs and went about freely through the Bârsa land, burning and pillaging and taking numerous captives, so that Helpruna reported to Bachenstein on September 11 that the Turks had completely devastated the district.[108]

Murad's sojourn in Transylvania lasted over six weeks. Mehmed Neshri records that, "Entering the Hungarian vilayet, they overran it for forty-five days and laid waste to it. They took so much plunder that only Allah knows how much."[109] The main body of the Ottoman army had covered a distance of approximately 500 kilometers since it had crossed into Hungarian territory at Severin. Given the poor condition of the narrow roads, the numerous wagons, camels, and other pack animals loaded with tents and supplies, not to mention the plunder and captives taken along the way, the main force, whose column stretched for 30 to 40 kilometers, could not advance more than 15 to 20 kilometers per day. Thus, it could take two days for the entire force to assemble at a designated location. Through the use of signals and swift riders carrying messages, communications between the different parts of the army were maintained, while individual units on horseback could break off and strike quickly at much greater distance. As we know the Turks halted for eight days before Sibiu, we must conclude that estimates found in Ottoman sources,

---

[107]Holban, ed., *Călători străini*, vol. I, p. 508. Sebastian Münster (1459-1552) published his *Cosmographia* or *Beschreibung aller Länder* in Latin and German in 1544. His description of the world enjoyed widespread circulation throughout Europe during the sixteenth century, with translations appearing in French, English, and Italian.

[108]Ciocîltan, "Între sultan și împărat," p. 1771.

[109]*Cronici turcești*, vol. I, p. 120.

placing the duration of the campaign at 45 days to two months,[110] appear accurate. Although it has been argued, using Helpruna's letter, that the incursion lasted only 23 days, because he states that the Turks entered Hungarian territory on August 7,[111] it is more plausible that they withdrew around that date. Helpruna could not have received in Vienna the details of the campaign contained in his letter of September 11 had it terminated as recently as August 30. Nor could the Ottoman army have advanced at a pace of over 30 kilometers per day. The historian Francisc Pall has correctly observed that, "taking into account distance that had to be covered and the slowness of communications at that time, it would be impossible to admit that the expedition began, took place, and ended in the course of a single month, that is to say August."[112]

The Sultan's army exited Transylvania via the Bran Pass, ignoring the fortress here as the small garrison stationed there could do nothing to impede their crossing. The Ottoman chronicler Sa'adeddin tells us that "when they reached the land of Wallachia, Dracula gave them a great feast, as was proper, and offered many valuable gifts."[113] The banquet celebrating the Sultan's triumph almost certainly took place at the royal court at Târgovişte. Here Murad also rewarded Vlad for his services. Helpruna, in his letter, reported that Anthony and other leading citizens of Mühlbach had been killed, but the marginal notes correct this erroneous information, stating that "Anthony is not dead, but he is alive and was taken captive to Wallachia where, with 55 other leading citizens of Mühlbach and their families, they were given by the Turkish Sultan to the Wallachian Prince Fleyko [Vlad] who had guided the Turkish Emperor."[114] Father Lawrence and the leading citizens of Kelling had the same

---

[110]*Cronici turceşti*, vol. I, pp. 87, 120, 292, 310, 343, and 404; and *Cronici turceşti*, vol. II, p. 134. The shortest estimate for the duration of this campaign found in Ottoman sources is 40 days, and the longest 4 months, but most chronicles give 45 days or 2 months.

[111]Ciocîltan, "Între sultan şi împărat", pp. 1770-1771.

[112]Francisc Pall, "Ştiri noi despre expediţiile turceşti din Transilvania în 1438," in *AIIC*, I-II (1958-1959), p. 21.

[113]*Cronici turceşti*, vol. I, p. 310.

[114]Quo. Ciocîltan, "Între sultan şi împărat", p. 1773.

The Wallachian capital of Târgovişte from a sixteenth-century engraving

good fortune. Vlad had kept the promise he made to protect those Saxon leaders when he convinced them to surrender their towns to avoid bloodshed and almost certain death.

Even though he had failed to provide any military assistance against the Ottomans, King Albert did not look favorably upon those who had chosen to surrender their towns to the Sultan without a fight. After Vlad freed the captives that Murad had turned over to him, they sought the King's permission to return to their homes. Although he allowed most of them to repatriate, Albert refused to let those he considered responsible for the decision to surrender to do so. In a decree addressed to Transylvanian officials, dated January 31, 1439, he accused the cleric Anthony, Hermann Mewlmuester, Martin Vlich, and Zaharia of Mühlbach of treason because "they surrendered themselves, of their own free will, together with that city of ours, to the barbaric Murad, lord of the Turks, who at that time, as an enemy, together with his powerful Turkish army, entered our lands in Transylvania to plunder them." The King went on to say, "it has come to our attention... that some of the above-mentioned citizens, residents, and guests, at present under the domination of those Turks in the Transalpine land, about whom it is said that they are not guilty in connection with the aforementioned treason... desire to come and to return to our above-mentioned town and seat of Mühlbach and to their old homes to live." Albert then ordered Transylvanian authorities to allow those "who wish to return over the course of time from the above-mentioned Transalpine land and from Turkey back to our aforementioned town of Mühlbach, excepting the previously-mentioned traitors, the cleric Anthony, Hermann, Martin, and Zaharia, to return freely and unharmed, together with their children, families, property, and goods..."[115]

The vast majority of those taken captive by the Turks in Transylvania were not so fortunate as those whom the Sultan had given to Vlad as a reward for his loyal service. After leaving Târgoviște, the Ottomans headed south to Giurgiu where they crossed the Danube, laden with booty and with numerous captives in tow. Contemporary sources claim that the Turks took as many as 30,000 captives. Just as with troops figures provided by medieval sources, these numbers are highly exaggerated. The entire population of the region, pillaged by the Turks in the summer of 1438 did not exceed 500,000; under these circumstances, it is impossible to admit that in no more than two months the Sultan's forces rounded up well over 5% of the total population. Despite this, there is no doubt that the Ottomans took several thousand prisoners, perhaps as many as 10,000. Those who had the misfortune of falling captive to the Turks now embarked on what amounted to a forced death march of some twenty days to the Ottoman capital at Adrianople.

The horror faced by those abducted by the Turks is described in a letter from Bartholomew of Yano, Guardian of the Franciscan monks stationed at Constantinople, to Albert de Sorteano, a leading member of his Order in Italy, dated December 12, 1438. Bartholomew obtained his information from a monk who survived the march and had the good fortune to be ransomed shortly thereafter. Bartholomew describes how "the priests, the monks, and the young and old men, for as long as they could go on, were led in irons tied to the tails of horses, while the rest of the people, together with the women and children, were driven along like a herd of sheep with the help of dogs, without mercy or pity; those who fell behind because of exhaustion, thirst, and especially pain, were killed on the spot." Many died before reaching Adrianople. The dead bodies were tossed into carts. The Franciscan monk depicts the grotesque sight in the Ottoman capital following the Sultan's return from Transylvania: "a large number of corpses lie outside the houses, partly rotting, partly eaten by

---

[115]Doc. 257 in *DRH, D*, pp. 357-358.

dogs, so that it would seem unbelievable to someone if they did not see it with their own eyes. Sometimes the dead bodies are thrown in front of Latin merchants; if someone, not so much out of pity but because of the horrible smell, tries to bury them or to take them from there, he is absolutely forbidden from doing so unless he first pays to do this."[116]

Some of the survivors of the death march were ransomed, such as the monk who provided Bartholomew with the information he reported to Albert de Sorteano, but the majority were sold into slavery. The slave trade prospered throughout the Levant and the Black Sea region during this period. Interestingly, Italian merchants, especially the Genoese, were among the most active participants in this trade, purchasing their fellow Christians from the Turks and reselling them like cattle at slave markets, such as those at Akkerman, Caffa, and Tana, for prices ranging from four to ten florins each.[117] Slavery was widespread at this time throughout the Muslim world, as well as in Russia. While the Sultan generally claimed one-fifth of those taken, as well as a similar portion of all booty, selling their captives into bondage provided Ottoman soldiers with an important source of revenue, alongside the spoils they seized during their pillaging expeditions.

Bartholomew of Yano witnessed in disgust how "Turkish peasants and shepherds, armed with a bow or a sword, many bent with age and riding donkeys, return after a few days, each bringing with him through the middle of Constantinople three or four young men bound to the Venetian and Genoese merchants here. Sometimes they stop for everyone to see and swear at them and beat them. And no one dares to say anything against this."[118] Among those sold into bondage was young George, the student taken captive at Mühlbach after the Turks set fire to the tower where he had attempted to hide. In his memoir, he recounts how he spent the next twenty years in Anatolia, "in the most horrifying and difficult captivity, in constant fear and danger. Seven times I was sold and seven times I was purchased for money. All my masters were barbaric until I ended up with a clergyman of a church. After spending

---

[116]Quo. Pall, "Ştiri noi despre expediţiile turceşti," pp. 18-19.

[117]N. Iorga, "O mentiune neobservată a românilor la bizantini," in *RI*, XIX:4-6 (1933), p. 159.

[118]Quo. Pall, "Ştiri noi despre expediţiile turceşti," p. 20.

time there with him and accompanying him all the time, I came to know more about their religion than they did, so that people came from far away to listen to me and to see me." In 1458, the Muslim cleric, whom George recalled, "came to love me as his own child," gave him his freedom.[119] The former slave then went to the island of Khios, then under Genoese rule, where he joined a Dominican monastery. He later went to Rome, where he served as a papal secretary and drew on his experiences in captivity and the intimate knowledge he had acquired of the religion and customs of the Turks to write his book. George died in Rome on July 3, 1502, at around the age of eighty.[120] Most, however, were not as lucky as the Dominican monk who lived to tell the tale of his time in bondage; they spent the rest of their lives in servitude. Bartholomew of Yano claimed that the Turks had abducted ten to fifteen thousand Christians annually during the previous twenty to thirty years and that many, especially the young, abandoned their Christian faith and embraced Islam to improve their situation; he estimated that during the previous four decades tens of thousands of Christians had reneged their faith under such circumstances.[121]

Given the success of the Sultan's expedition in terms of the vast quantities of plunder and numerous captives taken, and the inability of Transylvanian authorities to organize any serious opposition, Murad ordered a second attack on the province in the fall of 1438. Fearing precisely such a move, on September 21 the newly appointed Count of the Szecklers, Emerik Bobek, ordered the burghers of Braşov to take measures to strengthen defenses at Bran to stave off another Ottoman incursion.[122] These efforts were in vain. In October a sizeable Turkish force, estimated by Bartholomew at 20,000 men, crossed the Danube and headed north. Vlad facilitated their passage through Wallachia, but, as the Sultan did not take part personally in this new incursion, he was under no obligation to accompany them across the border to Transylvania.

---

[119]Decei, "Informaţiile istorice," pp. 691-692.

[120]Pall, "Identificarea lui 'Captivus Septemcastensis'" pp. 99-100.

[121]Pall, "Ştiri noi despre expediţiile turceşti," p. 20.

[122]Doc. 2317 in *Urkundenbuch*, vol. V, pp. 13-14.

As Bobek had anticipated, the Turks entered the province via the Bran Pass. They passed by Braşov, making no attempt against the city's powerful fortifications, and raided the Szeckler lands that had escaped unscathed during Murad's campaign. Again they met no organized resistance and marauded freely about the unprotected villages and countryside, gathering large quantities of booty and many captives. The Guardian of the Franciscan Order at Constantinople reports the fanciful figure of 30,000 captives, but without a doubt they herded several thousand more prisoners back to Adrianople. Although he was unaware of the dealings between the Ottomans and the Poles that had precipitated the events he described in his letter from Constantinople, Bartholomew of Yano expressed his disgust over the complicity of Christian merchants in supplying iron, steel, and even weapons to the Muslims: "These days I saw forty mules loaded with steel, taken from this city to Adrianople. For this reason the Turks themselves laugh at the Christians, saying outright: 'you see, you fools, your blindness! You yourselves provide us with the arms with which we destroy you!'"[123]

Around this time, Vlad's Polish wife bore him a third son, whom he christened Radu after his grandfather, Radu the Wise. The future Prince, known as Radu the Handsome, is first mentioned in a diploma dated August 2, 1439, confirming the possessions and privileges of the monasteries of Tismana and Vodiţa "to remain unaltered and unchanged as long as My Majesty shall live, and as long as My Majesty's sons, Mircea, Vlad, and Radu shall live."[124] As the previous extant document to mention Vlad's sons, a deed confirming the village of Vlădeşti, near Argeş, with exemptions from royal taxes and works, to the boyar Bodin, dated August 23, 1437,[125] who had originally received this estate from Dan II as a reward for his military services against the Turks, makes reference only to Mircea and Vlad, we can conclude that Radu was born between these dates. It also appears that Vlad's wife died shortly thereafter, perhaps as a result of childbirth, a not uncommon occurrence during this period due to a lack of proper hygiene and inadequate medical care.

---

[123]Pall, "Ştiri noi despre expediţiile turceşti," pp. 22-23.

[124]Doc. 89 in *DRH, B*, vol. I, pp. 154-156.

[125]Doc. 87 in *DRH, B*, vol. I, pp. 151-153.

Like his father Mircea, Vlad realized the need to try to maintain a delicate balance between the two great powers bordering on his Principality. Soon after the second Ottoman incursion in Transylvania, the Wallachian Prince addressed letters, first to Queen Elizabeth and later to King Albert, trying to repair the damage his involvement in these events had done to his relations with neighboring Hungary. Unfortunately, the original documents have not survived, but we learn of their contents from the marginal notes subsequently added to Helpruna's letter to Bachenstein of September 11, 1438, by a well-informed, albeit anonymous, source. Vlad explained to the royal couple that he had been constrained to assist the Turks, "out of fear of death and the devastation of his country." He also asked the King "to assign him a fortified place in Hungary where he could take refuge in similar cases so that he would not be compelled to fight against the Hungarians."[126] His releasing of those prisoners taken by the Turks at Mühlbach and Kelling whom Murad had handed over to him upon reaching Wallachia was certainly part of his strategy make amends to the Hungarian monarch. But Albert did not respond to Vlad's overtures to reestablish friendly relations. As we have seen, the King accused those Saxon leaders whom the Wallachian Prince had persuaded to surrender their towns of treason and refused to allow them to repatriate. He also began to support a pretender to Vlad's throne. In a document Albert issued on October 9, 1439, he mentions "our faithful servant Basarab, son of the late Transalpline Voivode Dan," as commanding a cavalry unit in the royal army then engaged against the Turks in Serbia.[127]

Having had his attempts at reconciliation with Hungary rebuffed, Vlad now focused on improving relations with neighboring Moldavia and strengthening his ties to Poland. At the same time, he also sought to regain an outlet to the sea, vital to Wallachian trading interests. The Principality had come into existence and prospered because of its strategic location controlling important trade routes linking the Orient with Central Europe, but the loss of Kilia, seized

---

[126]Quo. Ciocîltan, "Între sultan și împărat," p. 1777.

[127]Victor Motogna, "Un document privitor la Laiota Basarab," in *RI*, X:1-3 (1924), p. 123. The editor of the document mistakenly concluded that it referred to Laiotă Basarab, also known as Basarab the Old, who ruled Wallachia intermittently between 1473 and 1477.

by Alexander the Good during the wars between Radu II and Dan II, had hindered Wallachian commerce flowing through the Danubian port city of Brăila. Now, Vlad sought to exploit similar circumstances in Moldavia, where tensions continued between the two brothers who jointly ruled that country, to recover this lost territory.

Close ties to the Polish royal family made Vlad and Iliaş natural allies, and the two had cooperated together in the past against Stephen, who had received support from Alexander Aldea. The marginal notes to Helpruna's letter insist that Vlad was related by marriage to Polish King Vladislav III, but also state that "the Prince of Wallachia or the Transalpine land, called Fleyko, is a kin of the two Princes of Moldavia."[128] We know that Iliaş's wife Maria was a sister of Queen Sophia of Poland, daughter of the Prince of Kiev, Andrew Olegmandovich. If, as we suspect, Vlad's first wife was another of Sophia's sisters, it would explain the kinship bond between Vlad and Iliaş suggested in these notes, although their author mistakenly assumes these ties also extended to the latter's brother Stephen.

Relations between the two rival siblings in Moldavia had remained tenuous after, at Polish insistence, they had agreed upon the division of the Principality in 1435. Neither brother saw this as a permanent settlement. Stephen certainly viewed it as a provocation when, around the end of 1438, Iliaş officially proclaimed his eleven year old son Roman as associate ruler and heir apparent.[129] By late spring of 1439, conflict again broke out between the two Moldavian Princes. Stephen took control of the key port city of Akkerman and improved its fortifications;[130] as it was the most important commercial center

---

[128]Quo. Ciocîltan, "Între sultan şi împărat," p. 1777. The Latin terms used to express kinship in this letter, "sororius" for kin, possibly cousin or brother in law, and "affinis" for related by marriage, are not precise and, therefore, open to differing interpretations.

[129]Doc. 11 in Costăchescu, *Documentele moldoveneşti*, vol. II, pp. 31-34. This document, dated March 12, 1439, is the first in which Roman is accorded the title Voivode, indicating his status as associate ruler. His investiture with this rank occurred after June 20, 1438, the date of the last known document in which he is mentioned without this title, see Doc. 7 in *ibid.*, pp. 23-26.

[130]An inscription found at Akkerman, dated November 10, 6948 (1439), attests to the fact that Stephen strengthened the fortress after he seized it from Iliaş, see Ioan Bogdan, "Inscripţiile dela Cetatea-Albă," in *AARMSI*, series II, vol. XXX (1907-1908), pp. 313-

in the Principality, its loss was a major blow to Iliaş, denying him an important source of revenues. As a result, Iliaş turned to Vlad for help. The two rulers forged an alliance formalized by the betrothal of Iliaş's daughter, perhaps named Maria, after her mother, but who later in life adopted the monastic name Eupraxia,[131] to the Wallachia Prince. As she was quite young at the time, around twelve or thirteen years old, it is uncertain when the marriage was consummated, but it was by no means unusual during this era for a girl to enter wedlock shortly after puberty. Maria bore Vlad at least two children, a daughter, named Alexandra,[132] and a son, also christened after his father, the future Prince Vlad the Monk.

Vlad now attacked southern Moldavia, where Stephen ruled, and seized Kilia at the mouth of the Danube, along with its surrounding territory, that had previously belonged to Wallachia. Kilia, the port city founded by the Byzantines in the twelfth century, was also known by its Greek name, Lykostomo, meaning "mouth of the wolf"; in his *Descriptio Moldaviae*, Prince Dimitrie Cantemir explains that it "received this name from Greek sailors because it seemed to throw out waves as from the throat of a wolf."[133] His

---

325. Bogdan dates this inscription November 10, 1440, but the Byzantine style new year fell on September 1, and given that the inscription is in Greek and that Stephen took the citadel in 1439, I apt for November 10, 1439, as the correct date. Ştefan Andreescu, "Une ville disputée," in *RRH*, XXIV:3 (1985), p. 224; and Vîrtosu, *Titulatura domnilor*, p. 168.

[131]The Polish chronicler Jan Długosz informs us of Vlad's marriage to a daughter of Iliaş, see Minea, *Informaţiile româneşti*, p. 37. Vlad the Monk recalls, "my mother, the nun Eupraxia" in diplomas providing endowments to the monasteries of Filoteiu and Cutlumuz on Mount Athos, see docs. 202 and 231 in *DRH, B*, vol I, pp. 323-326 and 370-371. Eupraxia was a frequently-used Greek monastic name, meaning 'happiness' or 'success,' see Constantinescu, *Dicţionar onomastic*, p. 54.

[132]His daughter is attested to in a diploma issued by Prince Radu Şerban on January 20, 1604, confirming the villages of Satul Mare and Vâlcana to a boyar called Vintila of Săteni. The document specifies that Vlad the Impaler had purchased these two villages as a dowry for his sister Alexandra (see Doc. 116 in *DIR, XVII, B*, vol I, pp. 106-108). If, as this document indicates, she attained marriageable age during Vlad the Impaler's principal reign (1456-1462), it means that she was born between 1440 and 1447.

[133]Dimitrie Cantemir, *Descriptio Moldaviae*, Bucharest, 1973. pp. 85-86. See also Iorga, *Studii istorice asupra Chiliei şi Cetăţii Albe*, p. 31

possession of this territory is first affirmed in a decree granting trade privileges to Polish and Moldavian merchants, dated September 8, 1439, in which he entitles himself "Voivode John Vlad, by the grace of God and through the will of God, ruler and Prince of all the land of Ungrowallachia *to the great sea*, and Duke of Amlaș and Făgăraș."[134] Soon after the fighting broke out in Moldavia, the Poles again intervened to protect their economic and political interests in the region. Although he had lost Kilia, Stephen had gained ground in his struggle with Iliaș. Since the 1435 settlement between the two brothers, the Polish King had only allowed Iliaș to pay homage to him as Prince of Moldavia, thereby recognizing his superior rank. With Stephen's acquisition of Akkerman, a port city vital to Poland's commercial interests in the Black Sea region, he could now claim equal status with his elder half-brother. As a result, in September 1439, both siblings paid homage separately to Vladislav III, each titling himself "Prince of the land of Moldavia."[135] At the same time, Vlad also consolidated his ties to Poland and Moldavia, granting commercial privileges to merchants from those two lands.[136] This was the first trade agreement concluded between Poland and Wallachia since the days of Mircea the Old. In it, he facilitates the passage of these merchants south of the Danube, reflecting the cooperation between the Poles and the Ottomans against Hungary, and Vlad's involvement in their alliance.

When the Council of Florence adjourned in the summer of 1439, preparations began in earnest to launch a two-pronged attack, by land and by sea, against the Turks in the spring of 1440, but Murad did not sit idly by awaiting the Christian offensive. The Sultan campaigned in Serbia, determined to strengthen Ottoman

---

[134]Doc. 108 in B.P. Hajdeu, *Archiva istorică*, vol. I, part. I, Bucharest, 1865, pp. 84-85, italics added. The Moldavian chronicle of Vasile Buhăescul states that only later, during the wars between Stephen the Great and Radu the Handsome, in the 1460s and 1470s, "the border between the two countries was fixed at the Milcov River," see Vasile Buhăescul, "Istoria Țerii Românești și a Moldovei," in *RIAF*, XIV (1913), p. 162.

[135]Docs. 206 and 207 in Costăchescu, *Documentele moldovenești*, vol. II, pp. 712-715. Writing from Suceava on September 8, Iliaș confirms to the King his submission as a loyal vassal after he recently returned from Lemburg, where he had personally paid homage to Vladislav III. Stephen's act of submission is dated September 25 from Bârlad.

[136]Doc. 108 in Hajdeu, *Archiva istorică*, vol. I, part. I, pp. 84-85.

defenses along the Danube. His principal target was the Serbian capital at Smederova, located at the junction where the Morava River flowed into the Danube, down river from Belgrade; George Branković had recently built a powerful fortress here, but fearing persistent Ottoman encroachments on Serbian territory, despite his participation alongside the Sultan in the campaign of 1438 in Transylvania and the marriage of his daughter Mara to Murad in 1435, he opened negotiations with Albert to turn it over to Hungary. But his desperate efforts to save the city from the Sultan failed. After a three month seige, Smenderova fell to the Turks in August 1439.

With Serbia on the verge of total collapse, and the Ottomans having flaunted the inability of the Hungarians to protect their southern border since Sigismund's death, the Hapsburg King took urgent measures to defend against Turkish incursions along the Danube. One of Albert's most important moves was to appoint John Hunyadi, along with his younger brother of the same name, as Bans of Severin, making them responsible for defending the region through which the Sultan's forces had marched unopposed the summer before.[137] Born in 1407, John Hunyadi had demonstrated his military prowess while serving in the army under both Sigismund and Albert; following his appointment as Ban of Severin, he experienced a meteoric rise, acquiring both titles and vast amounts of wealth in the process. Hunyadi soon became the leader of the anti-Ottoman struggle in southeastern Europe and the dominant figure of his epoch. As he governed the land adjacent to Wallachia in the name of the Hungarian King, Vlad would have to deal with John Hunyadi as both friend and foe for the remainder of his reign.

With the fall of Smederova to the Turks, Albert hurried to Serbia to try to recover the territories that had recently been lost. But the King encountered resistance from the nobles when he attempted to levy troops, a problem that had persistently plagued Sigismund as well, and, as a result, he could raise fewer than 20,000 men. As we have seen, his force included a contingent commended by Dan II's son Basarab, whom the Hapsburg ruler hoped to place on the throne of the

---

[137]Doc. DLVIII in Hurmuzaki, *Documente*, vol. I, part. 2, pp. 657-658. In this document, dated September 27, 1439, the King obligates himself to repay the Hunyadi brothers, Bans of Severin, for personal expenses incurred in defending the region against the Turks during the previous three months.

Transalpine land in Vlad's stead. An attempt to install the pretender in Wallachia was likely projected for the spring of 1440 as part of the plan to launch a crusade to drive the Turks from Europe agreed upon at Florence. In this way, the King hoped to assure the cooperation of Wallachia, which John VIII's Chamberlain considered essential to the success of the enterprise. But these designs were thrown into disarray when Albert died of dysentery, a common cause of death among soldiers, on October 27, 1439, while campaigning in Serbia. Queen Elizabeth was then pregnant, but, as she had not yet given birth to an heir to the throne, a succession struggle broke out in Hungary. This meant that efforts to organize a crusade had to be put on hold. Albert's death also had important consequences for Vlad; Polish King Vladislav III, with whom the Wallachian Prince enjoyed good relations, ultimately attained the crown of St. Stephen. An opportunity for reconciliation with Hungary now presented itself, and Vlad, like his father before him, sought to take advantage of any occasion to counterbalance the influence of one neighboring power against another to protect the autonomy of Wallachia.

Chapter VIII

The Sword of Damocles

"it is found in ordinary affairs that one never seeks to avoid one trouble without running into another; but prudence consists in knowing how to distinguish the character of troubles, and for choice to take the lesser evil."

—Niccolò Machiavelli, *The Prince*[1]

A lbert's untimely passing threw Hungary into a state of disarray. Those who favored a hereditary monarchy, especially large landowners such as Palatine Ladislas Garai and the Queen's relatives, the powerful Cillei family, rallied around Elizabeth who, on February 22, 1440, gave birth to an heir. With the backing of Albert's Habsburg relatives in neighboring Austria, and having employed Hussite mercenaries under the command of Jan Jiskra in Bohemia, the Queen Mother arranged for the coronation of her infant son, who became known as Ladislas Posthumous, with the crown of St. Stephen, the ancient symbol of the authority of Hungarian monarchs, on May 5. Meanwhile, those nobles who insisted upon the right of the Diet to elect the King, as well as those concerned with the immediacy of the Ottoman threat, proposed to offer the throne to sixteen year old Polish King

[1]Machiavelli, *The Prince*, p. 177 (XXI).

Vladislav Jagiełło. Known for his close ties to Poland, Vlad may have played a role in these events. The account left to us by the Burgundian crusader Walerand de Wavrin tells of a meeting that included Hunyadi and others concerned with the Ottoman threat, among them "many nobles from Wallachia, to consult and to see in what manner they could at least bring a halt to the plundering raids by the Turks in the future and likewise to decide what each in his place needed to do under the assumption that such attacks would continue.... They formed an embassy, which they sent to the Kingdom of Poland, to King Lancelot [Vladislav]."[2] The young King accepted their proposal and was crowned on July 17, but the existence of two claimants to the throne meant that civil war once again plagued Hungary.

As the architects of the plan to offer the Hungarian Crown to Vladislav had intended, it broke the alliance of convenience between the Poles and the Ottomans and altered the balance of power in the region. Upon receiving news of the union of Hungary and Poland under the same monarch, the Sultan lept into action. He led his army north to the Danube and, in July 1440, beseiged the powerful Hungarian-controlled fortress at Belgrade, the gateway to Central Europe. But throughout his reign, Murad had demonstrated an aversion to engage in prolonged sieges. He quickly surrounded the fortress on both land and water and made determined efforts to topple its walls and to take the citadel by storm, but the Croatian noblemen John Tallóczi, commander of the garrison at Belgrade, skillfully defended the stronghold and kept the Turks at bay. Soon emissaries from Vladislav arrived and appealed to Murad to raise the siege, reminding him of their previous cooperation. The Sultan, realizing that Belgrade could not be taken without subjecting it to a lengthy blockade, agreed to withdraw his forces and returned south with the bulk of his army. Nevertheless, conflicts along the Danube border persisted, some involving Vlad's forces as he continued to cooperate with the Ottomans; a diploma issued by Vladislav on August 9, shortly after his coronation as King of Hungary, rewards the two Hunyadi brothers, both named John, for their services as Bans of Severin in defending the Kingdom's frontier, "especially against the lairs of Dracul's men."[3] The younger John died soon after from wounds he had

---

[2]Iorga, "Cronica lui Wavrin," pp. 67-68.

[3]Doc. 259 in *DRH, D*, pp. 359-362.

received in earlier fighting. But despite these incidents, the ascension of Vladislav to the throne of Hungary created conditions for a thaw in relations between Wallachia and its powerful neighbor, thanks in large measure to Vlad's ties to the Polish royal family. As a result, by the time Murad raised the seige of Belgrade in the fall of 1440, the two neighboring countries resumed normal relations. It is also likely that around this time those Saxon leaders whom Albert had banished for surrendering their towns to the Turks in the summer of 1438 were finally allowed to return home. Although he repaired relations with Hungary, Vlad still continued to pay tribute to the Sultan, striving to maintain a delicate balance between the two superpowers on his borders.

The architect of the revival of the union between Poland and Hungary that had ceased to exist following the death of Louis the Great in 1382 was John Hunyadi. He lobbied for Vladislav's election as King of Hungary, hoping in this way to heal the rift between the two rival Catholic powers so that they could concentrate their forces to oppose the Ottoman threat. One of the most capable military commanders of his day, Hunyadi's talent and ambition propelled him to become the most powerful man in Hungary and the leader of Christendom in its struggle against the Turks. His father, Voicu, was a nobleman of Wallachian origin from the Hatszeg region in southern Transylvania, and his mother was a Catholic Hungarian noblewoman. Voicu had faithfully served Sigismund who, on October 18, 1409, shortly after John's birth, rewarded him with vast estates around Eisenmarkt (Hunedoara in Romanian; Hunyadvár or Vajdahunyad in Hungarian from which his surname, Hunyadi, derived). His extensive holdings included, apart from the town and its castle, thirty-five villages, a customs point, and salt, gold, and silver mines.[4] Voicu's domains were among the largest in the region, rivally those of nearby Deva. Sigismund also presented him with a coat of arms — a raven, with its wings slightly opened, carrying a ring in its beak. From this raven symbol emanated the family name Corvinus.

John Hunyadi began his career in the service of Sigismund's staunch ally Serbian Despot Stephen Lazarević. He went on to forge a close and lasting bond with the important Ujlaki family and worked for a time under the Bishop

---

[4] Annex 4 in Bogdan, *Românii în secolul al XV-lea*, pp. 228-229.

of Zagreb. Then, in 1430, he caught the attention of the Holy Roman Emperor. He became part of Sigismund's retinue and presumably went with him to Nuremberg where he witnessed Vlad's investiture as Prince of Wallachia in February 1431. Later that year, he accompanied his sovereign to Italy. He gained valuable military experience there assisting Sigismund's ally Filippo Maria Visconti, the Duke of Milan, against their common enemy, Venice. This afforded him the opportunity to observe the brilliant condotierre Francesco Sforza. He left Italy with the Emperor in January 1434 to attend the Church Council then assembled at Basel in Switzerland. Here he first met Cardinal Giuliano Cesarini, who presided over the assembly; the two later worked together to coordinate military efforts against the Ottomans. Hunyadi continued in Sigismund's service until the latter's death in December 1437. An important stage in his development as a military commander came in 1436-1437, when he fought in Bohemia where he had the opportunity to learn first-hand Hussite military tactics; he subsequently adapted their reliance on infantry and light artillery, as well as their practice of using wagons, not only for transport, but also to construct improvised fortifications, for use in his later campaigns against the Turks.[5]

By 1441, Vladislav, with Hunyadi's help, had gained the upper hand in the civil war, having defeated forces loyal to the Queen Mother at Bátászek. He now controlled most of the Kingdom, except for some areas along the border with Austria, where Duke Frederick had intervened on behalf of the infant Ladislas, and Bohemia and northern Hungary which Elizabeth's ally Jan Jiškra held firmly under his control. As a reward for their services, in March 1441, the new King appointed John Hunyadi and Nicholas Ujlaki as Voivodes of Transylvania. The former also assumed the title of Count of Temes, in addition to that of Ban of Severin, while the latter that of Ban of Macva. In so doing, Vladislav placed the defense of the Kingdom's southern border in the capable hands of John Hunyadi; for the first time since the death of Pippo de Ozora in December 1426 the region had the strong leadership it needed to confront the Ottoman threat. This also sparked hopes that the long delayed crusade to drive the Turks from Europe, agreed upon at Florence, would soon be underway.

---

[5]Camil Mureşanu, *John Hunyadi: Defender of Christendom*, Palm Beach: Center for Romanian Studies, 2019, pp. 54-58.

John Hunyadi, Governor of Transylvania

Wavrin records that shortly after Vladislav's coronation as King of Hungary, he summoned a council at which "barons from Poland and many great lords from Wallachia participated, to consult about the most suitable measures to take to resist the false and perverse plans of the Great Turk."[6]

But as long as the situation in Hungary remained unstable, such ambitions plans had to be set aside. After the battle at Bátászek, the dispute over the crown of St. Stephen reached a stalemate. This led Eugenius IV to intervene. In February 1442, the Pope sent Cardinal Giuliano Cesarini to Hungary to mediate a resolution to the conflict and to garner support for the organization of a crusade.[7] Cesarini's efforts bore fruit. The two sides reached an agreement on November 23, 1442; it recognized Vladislav as King and betrothed him to Elizabeth, while proclaiming the infant Ladislas his legitimate heir. But before the ink could dry on this settlement, Elizabeth unexpectedly passed away on December 19. The Vatican's efforts to bring peace to Hungary continued, but papal representatives could only achieve a two-year armistice between Vladislav and his opponents, Duke Frederick of Austria, acting as guardian for Ladislas Posthumous, and Jan Jiškra.

The civil strife in Hungary worked to Vlad's advantage. Vladislav's ascension to the Hungarian throne and Vlad's close ties to Poland reduced the threat posed by the pretender Basarab who had enjoyed Albert's support. The Wallachian Prince also benefitted from revenues generated by the royal mint in Schässburg that he had originally received from Sigismund. It appears that Albert revoked this privilege following the campaign of 1438, but we find the mint again functioning under the authority of the Wallachian Prince following Vladislav's coronation; a letter from Hunyadi and Ujlaki to the officials of Braşov, dated October 16, 1441, indicates that the new King granted the Transalpine Voivode the right to strike royal coins, "for the defense of the Kingdom of Hungary, to aid and to assist in that defense, which is our responsibility."[8] A shrewd politician, Vlad also used the crisis in Hungary to improve relations with the faction represented by the Queen Mother. In 1441,

---

[6]Iorga, "Cronica lui Warvin," p. 69.

[7]Doc. DLXXXI in Hurmuzaki, *Documente*, pp. 689-690.

[8]Doc. 266 in *DRH, D*, pp. 366-368.

Paul, the Catholic Bishop of Argeș, lent a substantial sum of money to Elizabeth to finance her military efforts.[9] He could only have done this with the tacit consent of the Wallachian Prince who actively intervened in Church affairs throughout his reign.

During the period of tense relations with Albert and the disarray in Hungary following his death, Vlad took measures to consolidate his position with regard to the religious institutions in his country. As the Church played a key role in almost every aspect of life in the Principality, no ruler could ignore its importance. Although Wallachia remained a predominantly Orthodox land, the Prince also had to accord special attention to the Catholic Church, as it represented an important segment of the urban population, and also because of its potential as an agent for the spread of Hungarian influence south of the Carpathians. For this reason, both Vlad's father Mircea and his grandfather Radu had worked to support a Catholic Church free from the control of Hungarian religious authorities. Vlad continued this policy. As we have, immediately after his coronation at Nuremberg in 1431, he granted a privilege to the Franciscan monks, allowing them to proselytize the Catholic faith in Wallachia. Because of his close relations with the Order of the Friars Minor, Vlad sought to name Michael, a Franciscan priest at their monastery at Târgoviște, to replace the Abbot of the Cistercian monastery at Kertz, in the Duchy of Făgăraș, with whom the Prince had had a series of disputes. As a result of his conflicts with the Transalpine Voivode,[10] the Cistercian Abbot, also named Michael, resigned on August 28, 1440, in favor of another member of his Order, Johannes de Bornequel.[11] Vlad, however, won the day and the Franciscan priest from Târgoviște became Abbot of the Monastery of Kertz,[12] thereby strengthening the Wallachian Prince's control over the Catholic Church in his lands.

---

[9]Doc. DLXXIII in Hurmuzaki, *Documente*, vol. I, part. 2, p. 677. Bishop Paul is listed among those guaranteeing the Queen's payment of 8500 gold florins to Henric Czeczko for his military services.

[10]Doc. 2342 in *Urkundenbuch*, vol. V, pp. 28-30.

[11]T.G. Bulat, "Un document al mănăstirii Cîrtișoara referitor la noi (1440)," in *RI*, XI:10-12 (1925), 287- 288; and Doc. 2387 in *Urkundenbuch*, vol. V, pp. 60-62.

[12]Doc. 90 in *DRH, B*, vol. I, p. 157.

Nor did Vlad neglect the Orthodox Church which, despite the Union of Florence, remained an important means of countering Hungarian influence in the Principality. The Prince appears to have financed the construction of a new church for the Metropolitanate at Argeş where a portion of the bell tower bearing his family crest can still be seen, although the church itself was demolished during the reign of Neagoe Basarab (1512-1521), who constructed the present-day church on its foundations.[13] As we have seen, the Monastery of Govora, near Râmnicu Vâlcea, had been completely destroyed during Albul's insurrection. Vlad had granted some of its holdings to loyal boyars, including some of his relatives,[14] who had opposed the usurper; the document from 1551 tells us that when "Voivode Vlad saw the holy monastery devastated, for this reason he gave these villages, Glodul and Hinta to some of his servants."[15] Among these were Voinea of Ocne and Cârstea.[16] Nevertheless, he did not ignore the needs of the Church. On September 16, 1440, he granted a site at Licura, not far from Govora, to the prelate Dorotei to

---

[13]Pavel Chihaia, *Din cetăţile de scaun ale Ţării Româneşti*, Bucharest, 1974, p. 60. Chihaia speculates that Vlad built the church at Argeş as a burial place and that it was dedicated on August 15, 1439, the feast of the Assumption at the Virgin Mary to whom it was dedicated, but there is no proof of any of this. He bases his assertion on the fact that there is an extant document placing Vlad at Argeş on August 2, 1439, and that he returned to Târgovişte shortly before September 9. But extant documents from Vlad's reign are too scarce to allow us to trace his movements with any certainty. As a royal court continued to function at Argeş, along with the Metropolitanate, Vlad certainly visited the city numerous times. Furthermore, although it is likely that Vlad built the church in question, it is possible that he merely improved on an existing construction. All we know for certain is that he raised the bell tower that bears his coat of arms. See also Doc. 318 in Hajdeu, *Archiva istorică*, vol. I, part. 2, p. 148. The "Life of Patriarch Nifon" recounts how the Metropolitan Church at Argeş was torn down by Neagoe Basarab and a new church erected on its foundations.

[14]We discern this from a decree issued by Prince Alexander Mircea (1568-1577) settling a dispute over lands between the Monastery and members of the Drăculeşti family, see Doc. 339 in *DIR, XVI, B*, vol. III, pp. 293-294.

[15]Doc. 3 in *DIR, XVI, B*, vol. III, pp. 3-5.

[16]We discern this from diplomas issued by Vlad the Monk and his grandson Radu the Great restoring these villages to the Monastery of Govora. See docs. 210, 233, and 290 in *DRH, B*, vol. I, pp. 335-336, 373- 374, and 471-474.

build a new monastery, at the same time endowing it with six vineyards.[17] Later, Vlad began to rebuild the devastated monastery at Govora, granting it a mill at Râmnicu Vâlcea and a vineyard at Copacel.[18] His sons Vlad the Impaler and Vlad the Monk continued this work, but it was his grandson Radu the Great who raised it to become one of the most important monasteries in Wallachia at the end of the fifteenth century.[19] Vlad also granted diplomas to the monasteries of Blăgoveștenia,[20] Tismana and Vodița,[21] Glavacioc,[22] Snagov,[23] and Codmeana,[24] as well as the hermitage at Sărăcinești.[25]

Although Vladislav's ascension to the throne improved Vlad's relations with Hungary, the meteoric rise of John Hunyadi who, along with Nicholas Ujlaki, now governed neighboring Transylvania, created new tensions between Hungarian authorities and the Wallachian Prince. A remarkable leader with a strong personality, in a relatively short time Hunyadi accumulated a vast fortune, along with political power, controlling large tracts

---

[17]Doc. 91 in *DRH, B*, vol. I, pp. 157-159. Later documents inform us that Licura subsequently came under the control at the Monastery of Cozia, see doc. 470 in *DIR, XVI, B*, vol. IV, pp. 479-480. The church raised by Dorotei at Licura survived to the beginning of the nineteenth century, see "Licura" in Predescu, *Enciclopedia cugetară*, p. 490.

[18]Doc. 268 in *DRH, B*, vol. I, pp. 433-437. Pavel Chihaia, "Deux armoires sculptées appartenent aux voivodes Vlad Dracul et Neagoe Basarab," in *Revue Romaine d'Histoire de l'Art*, I:1 (1964) claims Vlad founded the Govora Monastery (also Chihaia, *Din cetătile de scaun*, p. 60), but a diploma for the monastery issued by Radu the Great on March 22, 1497, mentions that it existed in the time of "our grandparents and great-grandparents," meaning that it dates as early as the reign of Mircea, doc. 273 in *DRH, B*, vol. I, pp. 443-446. In fact, it was originally a Catholic monastery, built during the time of Bulgarian Tsars Peter and Asan at the end of the twelfth century, see "Govora" in Predescu, *Enciclopedia cugetară*, p. 371.

[19]Radu Floresco, *Le monastère de Govora*, Bucharest, 1965.

[20]Doc. 88 in *DRH, B*, vol. I, p. 153.

[21]Doc. 89 in *DRH, B*, vol. I, pp. 154-156.

[22]Doc. 94 in *DRH, B*, vol. I, pp. 162-164.

[23]Doc. 95 in *DRH, B*, vol. I, pp. 164-166.

[24]Doc. 98 in *DRH, B*, vol. I, pp. 172-173.

[25]Doc. 79 in *DRH, B*, vol. I, p. 141.

of land throughout the Kingdom; his holdings included 25 castles, 30 towns and over 1000 villages, making him the largest landowner in Hungary, with domains far exceeding those of the King himself.[26] The young King, who in no small measure owed the crown of St. Stephen to Hunyadi, could not disregard the wishes of his powerful military commander. The Transylvanian Voivode's ties to the family of Dan II proved a sources of tension in his relations with Vlad. According to Nicholas Olahus, Hunyadi's sister Marina had married his grandfather Manzilla, a Wallachian boyar of Dan I's clan;[27] there may also have existed kinship bonds between Dan I and the Transylvanian Voivode's father, Voicu. In any event, Hunyadi favored the descendants of Mircea's brother Dan and, as a result, he took Dan II's son Basarab, whom Albert had supported as a pretender to the Wallachia throne, under his tutelage, although he did not yet go so far as to defy the King and set him up as a challenger to Vlad.

Around the beginning of 1441, Vlad decided to move the royal mint he operated in Schässburg to Braşov. City officials there sought the prestige and financial benefits associated with having a royal mint located in their town; Vlad, on the other hand, undoubtedly saw this as a means of strengthening relations with this key Saxon city just across his border, which also happened to be Wallachia's most important trade partner. Needless to say, the town fathers in Schässburg did not look favorably upon this decision. When Vlad sent his Cămăraş Anton there to effect the transfer, he encountered stubborn resistance. In an undated letter to the burghers of Braşov, Anton wrote: "I am your friend, and I want to honor you; it is better that this [mint] be located at you than in another place. Because of this, when the burghers of Sighişoara [Schässburg] realized that I wanted to move the mint to you, they came to me and they said to me: 'How can you move the mint to Braşov, to take this honor from us and to give it to the Braşovians? When the Voivode [Vlad] faced hard times, the Braşovians did not take him in, but we took him upon our heads, and now you go there? We would rather die than accept this disgrace...' I answered them, 'I will do what the Voivode has told me to do.' They replied, 'we will

---

[26]János Bak, "The Late Medieval Period," in Sugar, ed., *A History of Hungary*, p. 64; and Kopeczi, ed., *A History of Transylvania*, p. 227.

[27]Holban, *Călători străini*, vol. I, p. 487.

not let the iron be taken from the depository.' I told them, "you do not have the authority to stop anything." And then they said to me, "wait until Saturday, fifteen days from now, so that we can send a man to the Voivode.' I agreed to let them." Anton suggested that the burghers of Braşov also send an emissary to Vlad and asked them to keep him informed, "because I am striving to do my best for your benefit and will tell my lord how much help he will have from you, so that he may have a happy heart, and have only goodwill toward you, all for your honor."[28] Despite the efforts of the officials of Schässburg to preserve the mint in their town, Vlad stuck to the decision to move it to Braşov as its relocation to the powerful neighboring Saxon city brought with it important political advantages.

But as John Hunyadi began to assert control over Transylvania and to coordinate military action against the Ottomans, he viewed the Wallachian Prince's control over this source of revenue as an infringement on his own authority. Even before the Transylvanian Voivode took official action to change this situation, impediments to Vlad's minting activities began to appear. In their letter of October 16, 1441, Hunyadi and Ujlaki, then returning from a successful campaign against the Turks in Serbia, wrote, "we have heard that the renowned Vlad, the Transalpine Voivode, considers that it is becoming unfavorable and difficult to continue to strike royal coins among you, which he has been assigned to do by our illustrious lord, the King..." They went on to express their intention to assume control of monetary activities in the territories they governed: "it is fitting that in our lands and districts we should have the right and the legal authority to arrange for the continued minting of coins..." The Transylvanian Voivodes, however, ordered the officials of Braşov "not to permit any impediments until our arrival there..." They had apparently convinced the King to approve their plan and announced, "it is our intention to go without delay, setting aside other matters, to the above-mentioned Transalpine Voivode, where we are sent to discuss several issues

---

[28]Doc. 233 in *DRH, D*, pp. 330-331. The editors date this document 1437-1443, but it is unlikely to have been written during Albert's reign. It certainly dates prior to October 16, 1441, when we learn from Hunyadi and Ujlaki's letter to Braşov that Vlad's mint was functioning there, see Doc. 266 in *DRH, D*, pp. 366-368. 1437 remains a possibility, but I opt for late 1440 or early 1441 as a more likely date given the context.

Coins emitted by Vlad Dracul

by our lord, the King... thus, until that time, do not allow anyone to interfere with his striking coins."[29] Shortly thereafter, Vlad lost possession of his mint in Transylvania and no longer benefitted from the revenues it generated. He did, however, continue to strike coins in Wallachia bearing his distinctive dragon symbol. But the loss of the royal mint at Braşov only marked the beginning of the problems facing the Wallachian Prince.

Hunyadi's rise to power marked the revival of Hungarian military efforts against the Ottomans. In the summer of 1441, the last Serbian stronghold, Novo Brdo, fell to the Turks forcing Despot George Branković to take refuge in Hungary where he held vast estates. In the fall of that year, Hunyadi led a successful raid against the Ottomans in Serbia. Upon his return, Ishak Beg, commander of the Ottoman garrison at Smederovo, launched an attack against him, fully expecting to annihilate the invading force, but Hunyadi routed the Turks, forcing them to retreat hastily behind the walls of their fortress. It was a minor victory, but one important for Christian morale after having suffered

---

[29]Doc. 266 in *DRH, D*, pp. 366-368.

repeated defeats at the hands of the Ottomans. Both sides now prepared for renewed conflict as the young King received intelligence from Ragusan officials that Murad planned an attack on Hungary for the following spring.[30]

In February 1442, the Sultan sent Mezid Beg, governor of the Vidin district, with a force of 16,000 men to attack Transylvania. Vlad, respecting the terms of his agreements with the Porte, facilitated the passage of Ottoman troops through Wallachia, but, as Murad did not personally lead this expedition, the Wallachian Prince was not obliged to participate. The invaders seem to have entered Transylvania via the same route they used in the summer of 1438. Despite receiving intelligence foretelling of this attack well in advance, the Hungarians again had difficulty raising an army, and for a time it appeared that the Turks would once again march through the province unopposed; in his History of the Hungarian Kings, the seventeenth century Moldavian chronicler Miron Costin recalls that Mezid's army "did extensive damage, burning and plundering all of Transylvania." But, unlike his predecessors, John Hunyadi would not allow such an incursion to go unchallenged. Mezid Beg led his troops up the Mureş River Valley, in the direction of Weissenburg, where Hunyadi and Bishop George Lepes awaited the arrival of Ujlaki with reinforcements. But as help was slow to arrive, Hunyadi and Lepes hastily assembled an army and set out to confront the intruders. Mezid, however, had learned of their plans and they fell into a Turkish ambush. In the ensuing battle at Sântimbru, along the Mureş River, on March 18, the Ottomans inflicted a crushing defeat on the Hungarians; according to Costin, "Corvin [Hunyadi] alone did not fall into the hands of the Turks, but escaped by fleeing. The Bishop fell down from his horse as he jumped across a stream and there the Turks captured and killed him."[31]

Despite the death of Bishop Lepes and his forced retreat back to Weissenburg, the Transylvanian Voivode refused to be dismayed. Ujlaki arrived with reinforcements and Hunyadi, determined not to allow the invaders to escape with their booty and captives, wasted no time in launching another attack. His boldness on the heels of the defeat at Sântimbru took the Turks by

---

[30]Francisc Pall, "Le condizioni e gli echi internazionali della lotta antiottomana del 1442-1443," in *RESEE*, III:2 (1965), pp. 442-443.

[31]Miron Costin, *Opere*, Bucharest, 1958, p. 281.

surprise, but his reputation preceded him. Mezid ordered that should the Voivode, who could be easily identified by his distinctive armor, attack again, he was to be targeted by Ottoman troops. The Pasha knew that without their leader, the Hungarian army would flee the battlefield. The Transylvanian Voivode's spies learned of Mezid's order, so Hunyadi changed clothes and armor with one of his officers, Simion de Kamonya, who subsequently died in the fighting. As the Ottoman army, seemingly victorious and laden with plunder and captives, prepared to exit Transylvania via the Iron Gate, Hunyadi struck. The attack occurred at Voskopu, near the source of the Bistrița River. The Voivode carefully selected the time and place of the attack, using the terrain to compensate for the numerical inferiority of his force; with this victory of his illustrious ancestor in mind, Nicholas Olahus explains, "the passage is narrow and difficult, this is why the Turks who attacked Transylvania from here were often badly defeated by a small army."[32] The Fates also favored Hunyadi that day. The Ottoman commander, Mezid Beg, died instantly when he was struck by a cannon ball; his sons also fell in the battle. In a diploma recounting these events, Vladislav writes that "Mezid Beg, another Turkish Voivode, together with a powerful army of sixteen thousand armed men, penetrated into our above-mentioned Transylvanian parts to devastate them. Although an initial encounter took the previously-mentioned Voivode John by surprise, and he was wounded and forced to flee and some of his comrades-in-arms suffered losses, they still left there on the field many of the enemy who thus won a bloody victory, but, on the fifth day, in a new battle, the defeated overcame the victorious and won for God a glorious revenge. The villainous enemy mentioned above paid for the thievery that he had committed with a hasty death for both him and his sons."[33] The Turks scattered and fled, abandoning their booty and captives. Although he still lacked sufficient force to take the offensive, Hunyadi had won an important victory that sparked new life into the Christian cause.

Dan II's son Basarab was among those who took part in Hunyadi's successful counter-offensive. In reprisal for Vlad having withdrawn his mint from Schässburg, town leaders lent their support to his rival, and Basarab

---

[32]Holban, ed., *Călători străini*, vol. I, p. 488.

[33]Doc. 269 in *DRH, D*, pp. 372-373.

established his base outside their city. Hunyadi later repaid the burghers for supporting his protege by opening a new mint in their town,[34] which also helped generate additional revenues for his campaigns against the Turks. As news of the impending Ottoman invasion of Transylvania spread, the challenger for the Wallachian throne sought to use the opportunity to win political capital among the Saxons. On January 21, 1442, Basarab, entitling himself "Transalpine Voivode," wrote to the burghers of Braşov from his camp outside Schässburg, offering to come to their defense personally, "with five or six hundred men or more."[35] The Turkish attack, however, came via the Iron Gate rather than the Bran Pass, and he ultimately linked up with the Transylvanian Voivode's army to join in the fighting at Voskopu that resulted in the defeat of Mezid Beg. But despite Basarab's activities, the threat to Vlad's throne came from another direction.

News of Mezid Beg's demise caused great consternation at the Porte. In recent years the Ottomans had grown accustomed to plundering Transylvania at will and the shock of this defeat led the Sultan's advisors to seek an

---

[34]On June 6, 1443, as he prepared to set out on the Long Campaign, Hunyadi wrote to the burghers of Braşov informing them of his decision to open an additional mint in Schässburg and asking them to supply the materials needed for this purpose, see Hurmuzaki, *Documente*, vol. XV, part. 1, p. 28. On September 29, Hunyadi's Italian minter Cristofor gave officials at Braşov a receipt for the supplies he received from them for the new mint at Schässburg, see Hurmuzaki, *Documente*, vol. XV, part. 1, p. 29.

[35]Doc. CCLXXIV in Bogdan, *Documente privitoare*, pp. 330-331. Bogdan attributes this letter to Basarab Laiotă, also called Basarab the Old, and dates it 1460, following a suggestion by Nicolae Iorga. In Hurmuzaki, *Documente*, vol. XV, part. 1, p. 50 (doc. LXXXVIII), it is dated 1459. Both of these dates are incorrect because during that time Dan III, not Basarab Laiota, was the recognized pretender to the Wallachian throne. At the beginning of the twentieth century, when these document collections were published, little was known of Basarab II, and his role as a pretender in Transylvania during this time was overlooked by the editors of these compilations. The context of the letter make it clear that it should be attributed to Basarab II and dated in 1442, on the eve of Mezid Beg's invasion. Although his interpretation of events differs, Constantin Stoide independently reached the same conclusion about the dating of this document, see Constantin A. Stoide, "Basarab al II-lea (1442-1444) in *AIIA, Iaşi*, XVII (1980), p. 281.

explanation for this sudden turn of fortune. Suspicion fell upon the Wallachian Prince, whose ties to the Polish and now Hungarian King were well-known, and who may even have had a hand in Vladislav's accepting the Hungarian Crown. Vlad's enemies at the Porte included the Sultan's secretary, Phadulah, and Ishak Beg, commander of the Ottoman garrison at Smederova; the latter, according to Ashik-Pasha-Zade, warned Murad, "Do not believe that Dracula is your friend; he is treacherous."[36] After some discussion, the Sultan decided to call Vlad to Adrianople; Bartholomew of Yano wrote from Constantinople in February 1443 that, when news of Mezid Beg's defeat "reached the ear of the Turk, at first he was amazed; then he became very angry and sent for the Prince of Wallachia, who, although a Christian, is his subject and is called Diracule."[37] Walerand de Wavrin learned later from both Vlad and his son Mircea that the Sultan sent the Subashi commanding the fortress at Giurgiu, whom he describes as "a very subtle and elegant man," to the Wallachian Prince as his emissary: "He presented himself on behalf of the Great Turk, his master, bringing elaborate gifts and warm greetings and attestations of friendship, saying that the aforesaid Turk, his master, was very desirous to maintain ties of friendship and alliance with him, and that to achieve this the

---

[36]*Cronici turcești*, vol. I, p. 88. The same account is given by Mehmed Neshri, *ibid.*, p. 121. Dukas asserts that Vlad was accused of betraying the Sultan during the 1438 campaign in Transylvania, but his chronology and presentation of these events is muddled, see Ducas, *Istoria turco-bizantină*, p. 262 (XXX, 5). He does, however, provide an indication that the events he describes actually occurred later, after 1440, "in that time the King was a child," a reference to Ladislas Posthumous, *ibid.*, p. 258 (XXX, 2). The most reliable sources indicate that Murad was pleased with Vlad's services during the campaign of 1438. Had the Sultan harbored doubts about him at that time, he would not have rewarded him when they reached Wallachia and turned over important captives to him. Clearly, suspicion concerning Vlad arose when Vladislav became King of Hungary because the Wallachian Prince had previously played a role in facilitating contacts between the Poles and the Ottomans and the immediate cause for the measures taken against him was that officials at the Porte believed, as Bartholomew of Yano's letter tells us, "that he knew about the defeat caused by the Christians," see Annex 1 in Bogdan, *Românii in secolul al XV-lea*, p. 220.

[37]Annex 1 in Bogdan, *Românii în secolul al XV-lea*, pp. 216-222.

aforesaid Turk requested that, if possible, he consent to come to him to the city of Adrianople."

The invitation to the Porte sparked a heated debate at the court at Târgovişte. Wavrin continues, "The Prince of Wallachia, hearing the proposal made by the Great Turk through this Subashi, received him with great honor and gave him many valuable gifts. With regard to what the Subashi proposed, he consulted with the princes and nobles of his country to decide what would be best to do. The latter, however, firmly advised him not to go in person but to send an embassy...." This did not satisfy the Subashi, whose mission it was to entice the Wallachian Prince to the Ottoman capital. He worked hard to persuade Vlad who finally relented and accepted Murad's invitation, "setting aside the advice he received and the decision he had reached with the high princes and great nobles of his country."[38] Undoubtedly, Vlad would never have agreed to set out for Adrianople had he believed that he had done something to incur the Sultan's wrath.

When he reached Adrianople, nothing appeared out of the ordinary. Murad received Vlad at his camp on the outskirts of the city with all appropriate honors, "together with his barons, whom the latter had brought with him."[39] Perhaps the Sultan's advisors had not yet finished debating the question of Vlad's possible implication in Mezid Beg's defeat. Wavrin relates that, "The day after the arrival of the Prince of Wallachia, the Great Turk ordered a large banquet. And the Great Turk sat in a pavilion completely lined with dark red velvet, as if it were a reviewing stand, decorated and adorned with rich pillows covered in fine cloth, sewn with gold and silk threads, and as this pavilion was raised above the ground about ten feet, the one inside it could look out over all his captains and people. Outside this pavilion, on the ground, sat the Prince of Wallachia on some pillows and some carpets sewn with gold thread; he sat to the right of the Turk, while to his left were seated his Beylerbeys... and all of the other nobles were seated in a large semi-circle that stretched from his right hand to his left in such a way that the Great Turk could see everyone as they

---

[38]Iorga, "Cronica lui Wavrin," pp. 61-62.

[39]Annex 1 in Bogdan, *Românii în secolul al XV-lea*, pp. 216-222.

ate."[40] Undoubtedly, Vlad could sense tension in the atmosphere and, as the banquet progressed, he began to feel as if the Sword of Damocles dangled over his head.

When the banquet ended, Murad withdrew to his tent and sent for Vlad, who arrived accompanied by the Subashi of Giurgiu who had escorted him to Adrianople. We do not know what words the two exchanged, but clearly the Wallachian Prince's adversaries at the Porte had won the Sultan's ear; Dukas considers Vlad's demise the result of "pretexts invented by Phadulah."[41] Murad ordered Vlad's arrest and sent him to the fortress at Gallipoli where he was placed in irons and held prisoner. But the Sultan appears to have intended solely to punish Vlad. Wavrin tells us that he allowed "all those who had accompanied the Wallachian Prince as his attendants to leave; even more, the Turk provided them with an escort to accompany them to the border of their land." Nor did Murad back a pretender to the Wallachian throne. Instead, the country remained under the nominal authority of Vlad's eldest son and heir apparent Mircea, who had already been designated associate ruler, just as his father Mircea had done with his eldest son Michael, until his father's return. The Burgundian crusader says that at that time Mircea was a boy "of thirteen or fourteen years old, not yet competent to rule such a Principality, especially in time of war."[42] The Sultan, however, appears to have sent along an advisor and a bodyguard to assist him in this task.[43]

Rumors of Vlad's fate sent shockwaves throughout the region. Although imprisoned not far away in Gallipoli, his whereabouts were unknown and reports reached Constantinople that Murad had ordered his execution. The Guardian of the Franciscan Order in the Byzantine Capital believed, as late as February 1443, that, following the banquet, "he [Vlad] was taken prisoner and he [the Sultan] ordered his beheading."[44] When those who had accompanied

---

[40]Iorga, "Cronica lui Wavrin," p. 62.

[41]Ducas, *Istoria turco-bizantină*, p. 262 (XXX, 5).

[42]Iorga, "Cronica lui Wavrin," p. 63.

[43]Annex 1 in Bogdan, *Românii în secolul al XV-lea*, pp. 216-222. Bartholomew of Yano told of this in his letter from Constantinople, reporting that Murad "sent a Turkish captain to Wallachia to take the throne and to govern the country for his use."

[44]Annex 1 in Bogdan, *Românii în secolul al XV-lea*, pp. 216-222.

Vlad to Adrianople returned home with the news of what had transpired, Wavrin records that "a great sorrow spread over all the land of Wallachia."[45] But rather than seeking to oust Vlad permanently, Murad appears to have wanted to teach him a lesson to ensure his future good conduct. Dukas learned that "after he stayed for several days in the tower, he [the Sultan] asked him for his sons as hostages; he sent for them and they were brought and turned over, though they were still underage. Murad took them and sent them to the East, in Asia Minor, to a fortress called Nimpheon [Egrigöz], ordering that they be carefully guarded."[46] The two sons mentioned here are Vlad, around eleven years old at this time, and four year old Radu. As we have seen, the practice of providing hostages to an overlord as a show of good faith was widespread throughout Europe during this epoch. Leonardo Da Vinci commented on this phenomenon in his notebooks: "all communities obey and are led by their magnates, and those magnates ally themselves with and are constrained by their lord in two ways, either by blood relationship or by a tie of property; blood relationship when their sons, like hostages, are a surety and a pledge against any suspicion of their faith."[47] This aptly describes the situation Vlad faced as he handed over his two youngest sons to the Sultan.

When he decided to accept the Murad's invitation to Adrianople, Vlad sent two of the leading members of his royal council, Nanul and Logofăt Stephen, on a diplomatic mission to Hungary, presumably to inform authorities there what had transpired and the reasons for his decision. We know that they had

---

[45]Iorga, "Cronica lui Wavrin," p. 63. The age of majority for boys during this period was generally 14 to 15 years of age, although there are cases of Princes assuming the throne at an even younger age, such as Iliaş's son Alexăndrel who assumed the throne of Moldavia at the age of eleven, or Ladislas Posthumous who took the reigns of power at thirteen. For a discussion on this subject see Vîrtosu, *Titulatura domnilor*, pp. 223-225. Mircea, however, did not become Prince in his own right at this time, but rather ruled in his father's stead pending his return.

[46]Ducas, *Istoria turco-bizantină*, p. 262 (XXX, 5). Dukas's phrasing makes it clear that neither boy had yet reached puberty. The Ottoman chronicler Ashik-Pasha-Zade records that, "his two sons were imprisoned in the fortress of Egrigöz in the vilayet of Ghermian," see *Cronici turceşti*, vol. I, p. 88. Mehmed Neshri repeats this account, *ibid.*, p. 121.

[47]Leonardo Da Vinci, *The Notebooks of Leonardo Da Vinci*, Oxford, 1980, p. 284.

reached Sibiu by April 23, from a letter the two boyars sent to officials at Brașov. Two emissaries from that Saxon city, Bartholomew and Utuszh Gashpar, had come to Sibiu to ask Vlad's men if anyone from Brașov had come to the court at Târgoviște to meet with the Prince before their departure. Nanul and Stephen replied that, "while we were with our Prince, we did not see any emissary from you, nor did we hear of one."[48] The fact that the burghers sent emissaries to Sibiu to make their inquiry indicates that Vlad had departed Târgoviște for Adrianople sometime prior to this date.

Hunyadi did not look favorably upon Vlad's entertaining the Sultan's overtures and, when he received news of his fate at the hands of Murad, the Transylvanian Voivode used the opportunity to place his protégé Basarab on the Wallachian throne. In late May 1442, Dan II's son entered the country together with Hunyadi and a Transylvanian military force and drove out Mircea who fled south of the Danube, along with most of the members of Vlad's royal council. Possible exceptions include Vistier Șerban[49] and Tudor[50] who may have gone over to Basarab. Chalkokondyles recounts how "The Peons [Hungarians], led by Hunyadi invaded Dacia [Wallachia] and placed Dan [Basarab] there as Prince and ordered them [the Wallachians] to obey him. Their Prince, Dracula, was driven out and went to the Porte of the Emperor [Murad] and this Dan occupied the country, and those who sided with Prince Dracula were killed, wherever he found that one of them lived."[51] Logofăt Stephen, Paharnic Miclea, Tatul Sârbu, and Iarciul numbered among the possible victims of this bloodbath as they all suddenly disappear from the

---

[48]Doc. 267 in *DRH, D*, pp. 368-369.

[49]Stoide, "Basarab al II-lea," p. 291. His son Constantin is later found among the members of Basarab's brother Dan III's royal council on March 2, 1460, as he set out to challenge Vlad the Impaler for the throne, see Doc. CCLXIX in Bogdan, *Documente privitoare*, pp. 325-327.

[50]Tudor disappears from Vlad's royal council after 1441, but reappears under his successor Vladislav II, see Doc. 101 in *DRH, B*, vol. I, pp. 176-177 and subsequent documents emitted by this Prince.

[51]Chalcocondil, *Expuneri istorice*, p. 158 (V, 259). A Serbian chronicle also records Basarab's massacre of Vlad's supporters, although it mistakenly says that Mircea was beheaded, see N. Iorga, "L'élément roumain dans les annales serbes," in *RHSEE*, IV:7-9 (1927), p. 225.

documentary record around this time. Ottoman chronicler Sa'adeddin records that "the Hungarian King named in this province, in defiance of the Padishah, protector of the world, one of the descendants of the Princes of Wallachia."[52] In a diploma issued the following year, rewarding Hunyadi for his recent victories, King Vladislav recalls that after the defeat of Mezid Beg, the Transylvanian Voivode "moved to recover the Transalpine land, neighboring the above-mentioned Transylvanian parts, and it happened that, through his efforts and his strength, he defeated and ousted the hostile Voivode of those parts, and he named, on our behalf, as Prince and Voivode of those parts, the true heir to that throne, Basarab, son of the late Voivode Dan, and, in so doing, those parts came under the complete authority of this Crown."[53]

With Vlad out of the picture, events also began to unfold in neighboring Moldavia where fighting resumed between Ilias and Stephen. Deprived of his son-in-law's support, by September 1442, Ilias was driven out of the Principality and forced to take refuge in Poland. He tried to return the following year, but Stephen captured him and had him blinded, thereby eliminating him as a rival to the throne. Ilias lived out the remainder of his days in Poland. Stephen, however, had to come to terms with another of his half-brothers, Peter, who now became his associate ruler. As his long-time enemy Vlad no longer ruled in Wallachia, Stephen sought to secure his southern frontier by reaching an agreement with Basarab. Chalkokondyles tells of an alliance forged between the two Princes: "through an embassy sent to the Prince of Black Bogdania [Moldavia], he [Basarab] made peace and related himself by marriage to him [Stephen]."[54] As a result of these events, the Saxon chronicler Johann Filstich writes, "After John Corvinus defeated Mezid Pasha, Moldavia and the Transalpine land returned to obedience to the Kings of Hungary."[55]

When Murad learned that the Hungarians had entered Wallachia and installed a Prince of their choosing on the throne, he decided to take immediate

---

[52]*Cronici turceşti*, vol. I, p. 311

[53]Doc. 269 in *DRH, D*, pp. 372-373.

[54]Chalcocondil, *Expuneri istorice*, p. 158 (V, 260).

[55]Johann Filstich, *Tentamen Historiae Vallachicae*, Bucharest, 1979, p. 230.

action. Chalkokondyles recounts that the Sultan "prepared for war against the Dacians [Wallachians], to bring the son of Dracula to the throne."[56] As affairs in Anatolia detained Murad, he assigned the task to Shehabeddin, the Beyler-bey of Rumelia. Christian propaganda, militating for a new crusade against the Ottomans, painted their involvement in Wallachia at this time as an effort to transform the country into a Turkish pashalik. Bartholomew of Yano claimed that after Murad deposed Vlad, "he took all of the lands of the boyars and gave them to the Turks, where and how pleased; then he sent a Turkish captain to Wallachia to take the throne and to govern country on his behalf."[57] But despite these unsubstantiated claims, the purpose of the Sultan's intervention was to maintain Wallachia as buffer state. The Danube constituted the natural line of defense for the Ottoman Empire. Since ancient times, the principal communication artery in the Balkan Peninsula stretched from Adrianople through Philippopolis to Sofia and Niš, and on to Belgrade; this was the path Ottoman expansion followed on its way toward Central Europe.[58] The Roman Empire had withdrawn from Dacia because the Danube represented a more logical, defensible frontier. These same considerations also led the Sultans to consolidate the northern border of their Empire along this line.

Shehabeddin crossed the Danube in August with a large force, probably numbering between twenty to thirty thousand troops, although Christian sources give estimates ranging from eighty to one hundred and eighty thousand men. There is no mention of Mircea accompanying this army, but his presence cannot be ruled out, for the Turks surely intended to restore him as nominal ruler of Wallachia. When rumors of the pending Turkish attack had reached Basarab in mid-summer, he sent emissaries to the Sultan. According to Bartholomew of Yano, "they humbly asked for peace and promised to submit."[59] But Murad rejected these overtures. The new Prince now braced himself for an inevitable attack. Wavrin tells us that, "the Wallachians, finding out in time about their arrival, retreated to the mountains, abandoning all of the

---

[56]Chalcocondil, *Expuneri istorice*, p. 171 (VI, 282).

[57]Annex 1 in Bogdan, *Românii în secolul al XV-lea*, p. 220.

[58]P.P. Panaitescu, *Interpretări românești*, Bucharest, 1947, pp. 157-158; and Treptow, *Vlad III Dracula*, pp. 129-130.

[59]Annex 1 in Bogdan, *Românii în secolul al XV-lea*, pp. 216-222.

lowlands."[60] Basarab wisely chose not to engage the Ottomans until help could reach him from Transylvania; Idris Bitlisi writes how "that Prince, not being strong enough to confront the Islamic army, fortified himself in some rugged mountains and asked for help from the Hungarian King."[61] Having encountered no serious resistance, Shehabeddin grew overconfident. As a result, Bitlisi records that "he allowed his gazi soldiers to devastate and to gather plunder."[62] Dividing his force proved a tactical blunder that the Beylerbey of Rumelia would soon regret.

While a substantial portion of Shehabeddin's army was scattered about the country foraging and pillaging, John Hunyadi entered Wallachia with a sizeable force to join Basarab in a counterattack against the invaders. According to Sa'adeddin, Basarab "came down from inaccessible places, from high up in the mountains where he had taken refuge, and, uniting with the Hungarians, they all left to meet the Islamic army, and to take revenge."[63] Hunyadi's sudden appearance caught Shehabeddin, who, according to Ottoman sources, was already celebrating his victory, by surprise. Orudj bin Adil recounts that "while he [Shehabeddin] remained only with his Beys from the border areas and his janissaries, the cursed Hunyadi, coming with the Hungarian army, caught him unprepared, just as he had Mezid Beg. Placing in front of him his infidel foot soldiers, armed and dressed in mail, he [Hunyadi] positioned his cavalry at his rear. Then he attacked Shehabeddin Pasha unexpectedly with a vastly superior force."[64] The ensuing battle of Ialomiţa, so-named for the river along whose banks it was fought, occurred on Sunday, September 2.[65] It was a more hard-fought encounter than Ottoman chroniclers

---

[60]Iorga, "Cronica lui Wavrin," p. 65.

[61]*Cronici turceşti*, vol. I, p. 169. Bitlisi confuses the events surrounding Mezid Beg's assault on Transylvania and Shehabeddin's invasion of Wallachia, but this passage clearly refers to the latter.

[62]*Cronici turceşti*, vol. I, p. 170.

[63]*Cronici turceşti*, vol. I, p. 312. Sa'adeddin also confuses Shehabeddin's invasion with that of Mezid Beg, but the events described are those of August-September 1442.

[64]*Cronici turceşti*, vol. I, p. 54.

[65]Serbian chronicles differ on the date for the battle of Ialomiţa, placing it on September 2, 6 or 25 (see Iorga, *Studii şi documente*, vol. III, p. XVII and Iorga, "L'élément

suggest. In Vladislav's diploma of April 17, 1443, rewarding Hunyadi for his victories of the previous year, the King recalls that the Transylvanian Voivode, "courageously attacked them [the Ottomans] as they brutally plundered the aforementioned Transalpine land. When the two armies met, a fierce battle ensued with heavy losses on both sides. The battle lines collapsed and ferocious fighting continued until the evening when, finally, with the help of God, the battle ended, to our good fortune, and then the defeated were killed and the enemies were handed over as plunder to the prelates. Most of these were killed by being burned alive, rather than by the sword, while those who escaped by fleeing, most of them drowned."[66] This account reveals that Catholic priests accompanying the Hungarian army condemned the captured Islamic soldiers to death as heretics, for whom the prescribed punishment was burning at the stake.

Following this victory, the Wallachians donned Turkish clothing and prepared to confront the bands of marauding Turks that Shehabeddin had sent to pillage the land as they returned to the Ottoman camp on the banks of the Ialomița. Wavrin writes that these "infidels were loaded down with plunder and apart from this also brought with them large numbers of men and women that they had taken as slaves, along with a great number of cattle. These Turks, knowing nothing about the defeat of those at their camp, came in that direction well-disposed, singing songs of triumph and beating drums, as they believed they had conquered the entire country. But the Wallachians, who remained hidden in their camp, dressed in Turkish clothing, as I have said, soon transformed their joy into suffering."[67] Ialomița marked the most significant Christian victory over the Ottomans in recent years. Shehabeddin escaped, but his force was devastated and he was disgraced in the eyes of the Sultan.

---

roumain dans les annales serbes," p. 224), but several mention that it took place on a Sunday which in 1442 fell on September 2. This date is also confirmed by the letter of Bartholomew of Yano written only a few months after the battle (see Annex 1 in Bogdan, *Românii în secolul al XV-lea*, pp. 216-222), as well as a letter from the Venetian Senate to the Duke of Burgundy on February 2, 1443, see Pall, "Le condizioni e gli echi internazionali," p. 437.

[66]Doc. 269 in *DRH, D*, pp. 372-373.

[67]Iorga, "Cronica lui Wavrin," pp. 64-65.

Bartholomew of Yano reported from Constantinople that "all of the tents and pavilions of the defeated fell into the hands of the victors, together with approximately five thousand camels and numerous horses." Seeking to awaken interest in a crusade against the Turks, the Guardian of the Franciscan Order added that, "As a result of the victory, all the people of Wallachia, even the shepherds in the most isolated parts of the country, became rich; all of them now go about dressed in silk gowns and garments sewn with gold thread, that is in clothing and things taken from the defeated Turks, which these, in their arrogance, carry along with them everywhere."[68] The monk clearly intended his exaggerated picture of the outcome of the fighting in Wallachia to draw attention to the material benefits that could be obtained in battle against the Ottomans.

Having defeated the Beylerbey of Rumelia, Hunyadi now took the offensive. King Vladislav wrote that "first, he entered the Kingdom of Bulgaria, where he took the fortress of Vidin, together with the vast lands surrounding it, and then, later, together with the great Nicholas, his fellow Voivode, they struck in the lands of Ozora and Serbia."[69] In an attempt to inspire crusading efforts, Bartholomew of Yano greatly exaggerated their feats: "Because of these events, the Christians gathered enough courage so they mobilized and crossed [the Danube] until close to Adrianople, conquering many cities and fortified places, burning and destroying everything around."[70]

Hunyadi's victory at Ialomiţa echoed throughout Christendom and breathed new life into stalled efforts to launch a crusade to drive the Turks from Europe and to save Constantinople from doom. When news of the victory reached Venice, normally reticent to participate in military actions against the Ottomans that might threaten its commercial interests, Doge Francesco Foscari presided over a solemn procession in St. Mark's Square on November 4, 1442, to give thanks for what they hoped would mark the beginning of the end for the Ottoman Empire.[71] Hunyadi's military triumphs also inspired Pope

---

[68]Annex 1 in Bogdan, *Românii în secolul al XV-lea*, pp. 216-222.

[69]Doc. 269 in *DRH, D*, pp. 372-373.

[70]Annex 1 in Bogdan, *Românii în secolul al XV-lea*, pp. 216-222.

[71]George Lăzărescu and Nicolae Stoicescu, *Ţările române şi Italia până la 1600*, Bucharest, 1972, pp. 69-70.

Eugenius IV to renew efforts to organize the crusade previously agreed upon at Florence. On January 1, 1443, Eugenius issued a papal bull calling on Christian heads of state to provide financial and military assistance for a great crusade to drive the Turks from Europe.[72] A few days later, Eugenius sent Cardinal Cesarini, who had recently managed to negotiate a settlement to the internal conflicts plaguing Hungary since Albert's death, as Papal Legate to the Byzantine Empire, proclaiming that during the past year a small force of Hungarian, Polish, and Wallachian soldiers had defeated a great number of Turks and that, as a result, there is hope that Europe will soon be liberated from "the tyranny of the Turks."[73] Cesarini's task was to convince John VIII that serious efforts were now underway that necessitated his support. Understandably, the Byzantines remained skeptical.

The victory at Ialomiţa for the moment also secured Basarab's hold on the Wallachian throne. But the new Prince was fully aware that his country remained exposed to continued Ottoman attacks. As Christian leaders had not yet finalized a plan for concerted military action against the Turks, he renewed diplomatic contacts with the Sultan. Chalkokondyles recounts that, "as the governors of the Emperor [Murad II] who were located along the Danube, crossing secretly, did great damage to the country, he [Basarab] sent emissaries to the Emperor and, asking for peace, he succeeded in obtaining it, on the condition that each year he send three thousand bows and four thousand shields; and peace was made."[74] But like his father, Dan II, Basarab depended heavily on Hungarian assistance to maintain his position. Vlad was a popular ruler and enjoyed widespread support among the nobility, most of whom had remained loyal to him even as he languished in the tower at Gallipoli. Nor did Basarab's bloody reprisals against Vlad's supporters endear him to the people. Only two extant documents are known from Basarab II's brief reign — a diploma dated January 9, 1443, confirming the holdings of the Monastery of Cozia which curiously makes no mention of its founder, Mircea,[75] patriarch of the family with which his own battled for the throne, and another that same

---

[72]Minea, "Vlad Dracul şi vremea sa," p. 200.

[73]Doc. DLXXXI in Hurmuzaki, *Documente*, vol. I, part. 2, pp. 689-690.

[74]Chalcocondil, *Expuneri istorice*, p. 158 (V, 260).

[75]Doc. 96 in *DRH, B*, vol. I, pp. 167-168.

year confirming to the Cutlumuz Monastery at Mount Athos its holdings in Wallachia[76] — but neither lists the members of his royal council. Nevertheless, as we have seen, most of Vlad's leading boyars remained loyal to him. The extent of Basarab's dependence upon Hungary is reflected in a decree renewing trade privileges for merchants from Braşov and the Bârsa land issued by the Transylvanian Voivodes from Seghedin on March 2, 1443, based on the highly favorable terms they had obtained from Dan II with the complicity of his Logofăt Coico on January 30, 1431.[77] It also imposed the use of the Hungarian dinar on commercial transactions in the Principality. In a gesture that clearly infringed on the sovereignty of the Principality south of the Carpathians, and reflected Basarab's subservient status, Ujlaki and Hunyadi unilaterally established taxes to be paid by Saxon merchants at various customs points throughout Wallachia.[78]

Hunyadi had, in all probability, approved Basarab's efforts to obtain peace from the Sultan beforehand. Although he had not abandoned plans to take the offensive against the Ottomans, he realized the difficulties that needed to be overcome before he could do so. If the Turks could be diverted from attacking Wallachia for the moment, it would allow him time to make preparations for an offensive. The Transylvanian Voivode realized as well as anyone that organizing a successful crusade would not be any easy task. The internal divisions within Christendom had prevented Europe from joining together to halt the Ottoman advance. "Oh, Christian Princes, what have you been doing all this time?," decried Bartholomew of Yano in his letter of February 1443.

---

[76]Doc. 233 in Marta Andronescu, "Repertoriul documentelor Ţării Româneşti," in *BCIR*, XVI (1937- 1938), p. 73; and Doc. LXXXII in Hurmuzaki, *Documente*, vol. XIV, part. 1, p. 40.

[77]Doc. 175 in *DRH, D*, pp. 276-278. On this document, see Alexandru A. Vasilescu, "Privilegiu comercial latinesc al lui Mircea cel Bătrân" in *RIR*, XIII (1943), pp. 78-96, who convincingly demonstrates that the original act upon which Dan II's 1431 commercial privilege was based is a forgery and that officials from Braşov bribed Logofăt Coico to help them obtain these more favorable terms.

[78]Doc. 268 in *DRH, D*, pp. 369-371. For a critical analysis of this document see Francisc Pall, "Iancu de Hunedoara şi confirmarea privilegiului pentru negoţul Braşovenilor şi al Bîrsenilor în Ţara Românescă," pp. 63-84 in *AII Cluj*, IX (1966). The original document is also presented in an annex to this study, pp. 80-82.

"Why do you sleep? Why do you take up arms and fight one another — you who could, if only you would so choose, conquer and impose your faith on the entire world?"[79]

But stopping the Ottoman advance concerned not only Christians. When news of Hunyadi's military feats reached the Sultan's enemies in Asia Minor, they once again expressed their interest in coordinated action with the Europeans to fight the Ottomans. An anonymous Turkish chronicle tells of a court jester at Karaman who told his sovereign, "My Sultan, if you would attack from this side, and your brother John from the other, perhaps you could destroy the Osmanlis."[80] Both realized the advantages of forcing the Ottomans to fight simultaneously on two fronts. If they could prevent Murad from concentrating his military might against either, each would stand a better chance of defeating the Sultan's forces on their respective continents. According to Ashik-Pasha-Zade, the ruler of Karaman initiated diplomatic contacts to achieve this: "the emissary of Karamanoglu went to the Hungarian and said to him: 'You advance from there and I from here, so that Rumelia will be yours, and Anatolia mine. Likewise, let us take and give to Vîlk-oglu [George Branković] his vilayet."[81] But, as in the past, the slowness communications and transportation hindered coordinated military action. Nevertheless, John Hunyadi was determined to overcome these impediments and to take advantage of the opportunity to force the Ottomans to fight simultaneously on two continents.

Still, the arduous task of organizing a joint military action among the Catholic powers of Europe made it difficult to fix a timetable for the campaign. Hunyadi's successes of 1442 fueled optimism that a successful crusade could be organized to drive the Turks from Europe and relieve the beleaguered Byzantine capital, but the Vatican still faced the daunting task of first resolving the differences among the Christian states of Europe. Papal plans called for coordinated military campaigns on land and by sea. Hungarian and Polish troops led by King Vladislav would lead the attack by land to liberate the

---

[79]Annex 1 in Bogdan, *Românii în secolul al XV-lea*, pp. 216-222.

[80]N. Iorga, "Cronicele turceşti ca izvor pentru istoria românilor," in *ARMSI*, series III, vol. IX (1928-1929), p. 7.

[81]*Cronici turceşti*, vol. I, p. 89.

Balkans from the Turks, while a joint Christian fleet would block the straits to prevent the Ottomans from receiving reinforcements from Anatolia and to cut off an eventual retreat. One of the first to commit a fleet to this enterprise was Duke Philip the Good of Burgundy. Anxious to avenge the defeat of his father at Nicopolis, Philip had long harbored crusading ambitions. He sent one of his leading knights, Walerand de Wavrin, to command the Burgundian fleet. By the beginning of 1443, Venice, usually reluctant to participate in such an endeavor, had agreed to put ten galleys at the Pope's disposal. On May 8, Eugenius IV named his nephew, Francisco Condolmieri, the Cardinal of Venice, as Papal Legate and commander of the fleet.[82] But as the euphoria over the triumphs of the previous year began to dissipate, it became increasingly difficult to draw together the resources necessary from such an undertaking. In a sign of dampening enthusiasm for crusading efforts, Gaspar Schlick, the Chancellor of Bohemia, wrote around this time that the number of Turks killed at Ialomița was, in fact, 9,000, instead of the 30,000 initially reported, and he expressed doubts that Cesarini could gather a fleet.[83] Conflicts among the Italian city-states and difficulties in raising the funds necessary to finance the expedition also hindered his efforts. By the fall it was clear that the naval campaign had to be postponed. Eugenius IV wrote to Ragusa on December 17, blaming the Venetians, among others, for the delay.[84]

Despite these setbacks, Hunyadi pressed on with plans for a ground campaign, anxious to follow up on his victories of the previous year. On March 19, he wrote from Mediasch to the burghers of Brașov about his plans for an offensive against the Turks and asked them to supply arms and munitions.[85] He followed this up with another letter from the same city on June 23, requesting four hundred firearms and other supplies.[86] The immediate objective of the campaign he envisioned was the restoration of George Branković as ruler of Serbia, which had fallen to the Turks two years earlier. Both Serbia and Wallachia were important elements in Hungary's defensive

---

[82]Doc. DLXXXII in Hurmuzaki, *Documente*, vol. I, part. 2, pp. 691-693.

[83]Minea, "Vlad Dracul și vremea sa," p. 203.

[84]Pall, "Le condizioni e gli echi internazionali," pp. 451-452.

[85]Doc. XLIV in Hurmuzaki, *Documente*, vol. XV, part. 1, p. 28.

[86]Doc. XLVI in Hurmuzaki, *Documente*, vol. XV, part. 1, p. 29.

strategy, serving as buffer states between the Kingdom and the Ottoman Empire. The fall of Serbia to the Turks meant that the Islamic Empire now bordered Hungary itself. The force led by Hunyadi and the King south of the Danube included Wallachian troops[87] under Basarab who had fought the Turks at Hunyadi's side the previous year. In August 1443, Cardinal Cesarini had written to the Venetians that the forces engaged in the upcoming campaign against the Turks included "Voivode Barasida [Basarab] with twenty thousand cavalry."[88] In typical fashion, the numbers are highly exaggerated. Two thousands cavalry represents a more realistic estimate of the force Basarab could contribute. The Hungarians could not wait for the fleet. The Karamanlis had taken up arms against the Sultan as they had previously agreed and Hunyadi did not want to let the opportunity to force the Ottomans to fight simultaneously on distant fronts slip away. At the end of September, with Hunyadi, accompanied by Serbian Despot George Branković and the new Wallachian Voivode Basarab, leading the way, King Vladislav set out on what become known as the Long Campaign. Armistice negotiations with Jan Jiskra had delayed their departure, but the Hungarians hoped that this would work to their advantage as the Ottomans were not accustomed to mobilizing troops to fight major campaigns during the winter months.

The initial goal of the campaign was to liberate Serbia and to restore Branković, who had been in exile in Hungary since the fall of his country to the Turks in the summer of 1441, to his throne, but the crusaders also hoped to liberate the Balkans and to reach Constantinople. They crossed the Danube and took Smederovo from Vlad's nemesis Ishak Beg, whom Hunyadi had defeated two years before. This initial success bode well for the campaign. Hunyadi led his force of about 12,000 men south along the Morava River valley, while the

---

[87]Participation of Wallachian troops in this campaign is mentioned in the poem by the German minstrel Michel Beheim who wrote his account based on the testimony of one of the soldiers in the Christian army, Hans Magest, who later fell prisoner to the Turks at Varna, see Constantin I. Karadja, "Poema lui Michel Beheim despre cruciadele împotriva turcilor din anii 1443 şi 1444," in *BCIR*, XV (1936), p. 26 (v. 259).

[88]Iorga, *Acte şi Fragmente*, vol. III, p. 11. Iorga mistakenly interprets this to mean the Voivode of Basarabia, but the country was not referred to in this way in Italian sources. Barasida is clearly a distortion of Basarab, referring to the Prince of that name. The original text is "*Item Io vaivoda Barasida con chavali XXm.*"

King followed at a distance of two days march with another 18,000 to 20,000 troops. The Ottoman garrisons manning the fortresses en route abandoned their positions and retreated before the advancing Christian army. With Murad engaged against Karaman, the Ottomans found it difficult to muster an army to oppose them. Turkish forces in the region concentrated near Niš where they prepared to make a stand against Hunyadi.

On November 3, 1443, Christian and Ottoman troops clashed at Niš. Hunyadi encircled and easily routed the Turks, once more demonstrating his military genius. Despite the fact that he had not faced a regular Ottoman army, Niš was his most significant victory to date. News of the triumph spread throughout Europe: Venice, where the fleet was being readied, celebrated the victory on November 26; Eugenius IV presided over commemorations in Rome on January 10, 1444, while that same month Filippo Maria Visconti, the Duke of Milan, organized similar ceremonies to mark the occasion.[89] Christendom once again had reason to believe that Europe would soon be free of the Islamic intruders. But the repercussions of Hunyadi's victory at Niš did not end here. On November 8, Hunyadi addressed a letter to his fellow Voivode of Transylvania, Nicholas Ujlaki, describing his victory over the Turks. He pointed out that all along the way the Balkan peoples, "Bulgarians, Bosnians, Albanians, and Serbs," displayed their readiness to throw off the Ottoman yoke and greeted his army as liberators and provided them with provisions. He also called on Ujlaki to join him with additional troops,[90] but these were not forthcoming.

The victory at Niš provoked other problems that would plague the Ottomans for years to come. In Greece, Despot Constantine of Morea, the brother of John VIII, who became the last Byzantine Emperor, and who would breath his last breath in defense of Constantinople on that fateful Tuesday, May 29, 1453, launched a revolt against the Sultan, crossing the isthmus and invading central Greece, where he seized Ottoman strongholds. By 1445, he had taken most of Thessaly up to Mount Olympus, but the tide turned against

---

[89]Pall, "Le condizioni e gli echi internazionali," p. 461.

[90]Doc. DLXXX in Hurmuzaki, *Documente*, vol. I, part. 2, pp. 687-688.

him the following year and the Turks recovered the territories lost to the Greeks. They finally put down the rebellion in 1447.

A more significant revolt broke out in Albania led by George Castriota, better known as Scanderbeg. The son of Albanian nobleman John Castriota, George had spent time as a hostage at the Porte and subsequently converted to Islam, adopting the name Iskender or Alexander, from which his epithet Scanderbeg derived. He had gained important military experience serving in the Ottoman army and commanded a cavalry unit in the Turkish force that had gathered at Niš to oppose the Christian advance. Seeing an opportunity to recover his family lands that had fallen under Ottoman rule following the death of his father, Scanderbeg deserted the Turkish army at Niš as the battle began, along with a force of about three hundred Albanian cavalrymen loyal to him. He proceeded to his family's traditional stronghold at Croya where, with the help of a forged document, he convinced the Ottoman commander to turn over the fortress to him. He then announced his reconversion to Christianity, and took captive and then slaughtered the Turks that had garrisoned the town. Scanderbeg managed to unite most of the Albanian nobility and, for the next quarter-century, he led a fierce resistance against the Turks that continued even after his death in January 1468.

From Niš, Hunyadi pressed on toward Sofia. He encountered token resistance along the way and easily routed Turkish forces defending the city. The ease with which they had marched through Ottoman territory surprised even the Christians. On December 3, Hunyadi wrote to officials of Braşov and the Bârsa land of his victory at Sofia, optimistic that he could reach Adrianople in six to eight days.[91] But as soon as Murad had received news of the Christian offensive, he hurried back to Europe. The Christian failure to ready a fleet in time meant that the Ottomans could cross the straits unopposed and draw resources from Anatolia to deal with the crisis in Europe. To buy time until the Sultan arrived with reinforcements, Wavrin reports that the retreating Turks, as they "crossed through the mountains in flight, ordered the peasants who remained behind to block the roads and passes with as many trees as they could fell, making barricades of wood and stone, so that the Hungarians could only

---

[91]Doc. XLVIII in Hurmuzaki, *Documente*, vol. XV, part. 1, p. 29.

pass with great difficulty."[92] Harsh winter weather also hindered the Christian advance. A council of war held at Sofia, which included Hunyadi, King Vladislav, Branković, and Basarab, among others, decided to advance eastward through the Zlatica Pass on their way to Adrianople, rather than to follow the more southerly route through Philippopolis where they expected they would encounter heavier concentrations of Ottoman troops. Wavrin, who gathered his information from participants in the conflict, explained that "because the Turk had at his disposal a large number of people, especially compared to the King of Hungary, he kept to the open plain. At the same time, the King was advised to prefer narrow places, which were better suited to the small number of his soldiers. He did this. While the Turk, having faith in his great numbers, came to attack them there."[93]

By December 12, Hunyadi had reached the Zlatica Pass. The ensuing confrontation between Ottoman and Hungarian forces began with a fierce battle which, according to Polish chronicler Jan Długosz, lasted from morning to night, as the Christians attempted to force the pass.[94] They failed, and with their provisions running low and winter upon them, they were forced to withdraw shortly before Christmas. Conflicting reports circulated about what happened at Zlatica. Wavrin heard two such divergent accounts of the same events that he mistook them for separate campaigns. One told how the Christians repelled an Ottoman attack on their positions. This seems to have occurred when Hunyadi's advance unit arrived at the pass. The Ottomans hoped to defeat the smaller Hungarian force before the bulk of the Christian army could arrive, but the Transylvanian Voivode used the terrain to nullify the numerical superiority of the Turks and staunchly defended his position. "The Saracens," the Burgundian crusader relates, "were defeated, and the Great Turk [the Sultan] was forced to flee in disgrace.... it is said with certainty that on the day of battle more than forty thousand Turks died there and many more fell prisoner, while those who saved their lives could only do so by fleeing. Meanwhile, the Christians lost few men, but gained a great number of horses.... [Then] they held a council of war to decide if they should follow the

---

[92]Iorga, "Cronica lui Wavrin," pp. 77-80.

[93]Iorga, "Cronica lui Wavrin," p. 71.

[94]Minea, Informațiile românești, p. 32.

Turks or return to their country. And the council decided, after the victory they had achieved and the spoils they had won, to return to Hungary."[95] In fact, this initial Christian victory, on or around December 12, was far from decisive. Had he forced the Ottomans to flee, Hunyadi certainly would not have wasted the opportunity to press his advantage.

In reality, Chalkokondyles tells us that, after the failed Ottoman assault, the Sultan also held a council of war at which it was decided to hold the pass and to abstain from further attacks until the Hungarians began their inevitable retreat.[96] In a second account of the events at Zlatica, Wavrin tells how the crusaders struggled to cross the mountains, "but the trees, stones, and other impediments with which the Turks blocked the roads made it difficult for them to pass. It could be said that Lady Luck, who had up to then smiled upon the Christians, now turned her back on them. Then, suddenly, a bitter cold set in, accompanied by wind and sleet that completely transformed the mountains. Then, for three days a heavy snow fell...." Lacking provisions and with the men "not sufficiently well-clothed or covered to protect against the cold, many froze to death...." Faced with these harsh conditions, the Christian war council made the decision to retreat and "they organized infantry detachments to go before the army to clear the roads...." But before they managed to do this, "the Christians saw more than half of their men and over three-quarters of their horses perish. Those who managed to escape regarded it as truly a miracle of God."[97]

As the crusaders withdrew, the Ottomans began their counteroffensive, hoping to destroy the invaders. But Hunyadi, now bringing up the rear, remained vigilant. In a letter written en route, dated January 6, 1444, and addressed to officials of Braşov and the Bârsa land, the Transylvanian Voivode tells how he defeated a hasty Ottoman attack led by the Beylerbey of Rumelia, Kasam Pasha, who had replaced Shehabeddin after the defeat at Ialomiţa, near

[95]Iorga, "Cronica lui Wavrin," p. 71.

[96]Chalcocondil, *Expuneri istorice*, pp. 183-187 (VI, 307-314). The Byzantine chronicler incorrectly lists Vlad, "Drăculea, Prince of the Dacians," as fighting alongside Hunyadi during the Long Campaign, but as he errs in the chronology of events in Wallachia, he confuses him with Basarab.

[97]Iorga, "Cronica lui Wavrin," p. 80.

Melstica, on Christmas Eve. The Turks continued to harass the retreating Christian army. Another confrontation between Hunyadi and Beylerbey Kasam, near Kunovitsa, on January 2, 1444, had a similar outcome.[98] Here, Mahmud Celebi, brother of Grand Vizir Halil and brother-in-law of Sultan Murad, fell captive and was subsequently ransomed. Neither side was prepared to continue hostilities, and a tacit cease-fire entered into effect. As a result, George Branković regained control over much of Serbia. Meanwhile, Hunyadi and King Vladislav returned to Buda where they arrived in early February. Presumably, Basarab reached Wallachia at the head of his contingent around the same time; their return is mentioned in a poem by the German minstrel Michael Beheim, recounting this campaign.[99]

Despite their failure to penetrate the Zlatica Pass, Christian successes throughout the Long Campaign and the restoration of Branković as Despot of Serbia inspired hopes that with continued efforts the Turks could be forced out of Europe. Wavrin records what many at that time believed: "if they had crossed the mountains to Philippopolis and followed up their victory to the end, they would have reconquered, without a doubt, all of Greece. All the more so because Turkey tremored with fear upon hearing of the new Christian victories."[100] Branković had offered King Vladislav 40,000 florins to continue the campaign, but this could not be done without additional resources and coordinated action with the fleet, intended to prevent the Ottomans from drawing reinforcements from Anatolia. Certainly, many believed that the participation of the fleet would have made a decisive difference in the outcome of the campaign. It now remained to be seen if the Christians could muster the resources necessary for an all-out crusade, something they had proved incapable of doing since the disaster at Nicopolis in 1396.

Murad also faced a difficult situation. He had failed to conclude the war with Karaman because of the Hungarian attack, and he knew that, because of recent Christian successes, many in Europe now clamored for a crusade. The Sultan fully realized the dangers of having to fight major wars simultaneously

---

[98]Doc. XLIX in Hurmuzaki, *Documente*, vol. XV, part. 1, pp. 30-31. Hunyadi's letter of January 6, 1444, provides an important overview of the Long Campaign.

[99]Karadja, "Poema lui Michel Beheim," p. 26 (v. 259).

[100]Iorga, "Cronica lui Wavrin," p. 71.

on two continents. He also understood the mistake he had made by listening to those who had convinced him to arrest Vlad, who still languished in chains in the tower at Gallipoli. This had allowed the Hungarians to bring Wallachia completely under their control. When the Sultan gathered his advisors to decide what course of action to follow, Wavrin writes that Murad "admitted that the Hungarians and the Wallachian united together were a great power and that, as far as battle was concerned, gave serious cause for fear."[101] Under these circumstances, Vlad, whom many believed had been executed, now appeared as part of the solution to the Sultan's troubles in Europe. As the spring of 1444 approached, the pendulum began to swing back in favor of Vlad Dracul.

---

[101]Iorga, "Cronica lui Wavrin," p. 76.

Chapter IX

Vlad Dracul
and the Last Crusade

"I believe also that he will be successful who directs his actions according to the spirit of the times, and that he whose actions do not accord with the times will not be successful."

—Niccolò Machiavelli, *The Prince*[1]

V lad had suffered nearly two years of incarceration, but, manacled in irons in the dark, dreary confines of the tower at Gallipoli, it had seemed far longer. Walerand de Wavrin, who obtained his information directly from the Wallachian Prince, records that "he was held prisoner in horrible conditions for four years, where he endured great suffering and anguish, and from where he had lost all hope of escape, except by death." As he crossed the Dardanelles under guard, en route to the Sultan in Brusa, Vlad did not know what fate lay in store for him. Perhaps he anticipated that a public execution awaited him there, or possibly he sensed that the situation had

---

[1]Machiavelli, *The Prince*, p. 198-199 (XXV).

begun to change in his favor, but he could hardly have expected the warm reception that followed. "When he arrived," the Burgundian crusader continues, "he [Murad] told him that he wanted to live in peace and understanding with him, and that if he would take an oath and promise him that neither he, nor any of his subjects, would ever again declare war, that he [the Sultan] would also swear and promise in his turn to allow him to return freely and unharmed to his country, assuring him in writing that never in his life would he make war on him again. And even more, that if ever he [Vlad] will be forced to make war on anyone, he [Murad] would provide him assistance at his own expense...." Vlad did not hesitate to accept Murad's terms. Wavrin continues: "this proposal filled his heart with joy, and he did not hesitate to agree to what the Great Turk asked of him. Likewise, to reassure him, the Great Turk took on oath and ordered that letters be written specifying all that he had promised him."[2] His sons Vlad and Radu, up to then hostages at Egrigöz where, according to Dukas, Murad had ordered "that they be carefully guarded," were also restored to him. Then the Sultan allowed Vlad, whom Ottoman chronicles call *Dîraku ibn Iflak*, "to leave and to return to Wallachia, after each swore that from now on they will remain faithful to one another."[3]

Accompanied by his family and supporters, who had taken refuge south of the Danube when Basarab seized power and began his purge, as well as troops that the Sultan had placed at his disposal, Vlad returned to Wallachia in March 1444 to reclaim his throne.[4] Basarab, lacking popular support at home, found

---

[2]Iorga, "Cronica lui Wavrin," p. 76

[3]Ducas, *Istoria turco-bizantină*, p. 262 (XXX.5). Although, the Byzantine chronicler states in this passage that Vlad's younger sons remained hostages when he departed, he later confirms that following the Long Campaign the Sultan returned his sons to "Dragoulios and concluded a peace treaty bound by oath," p. 272 (XXXII.1).

[4]The date of Vlad's return has long been disputed. Most historians have argued that he regained the throne prior to the Long Campaign. For example, P.P. Panaitescu and Nicolae Stoicescu, "La participation des Roumains à la bataille de Varna (1444)" in *RRH*, IV:2 (1965), p. 224, who argue that the Sultan freed him as a consequence of Hunyadi's victory at the battle at Ialomiţa in September 1442; Camil Mureşanu, *John Hunyadi*, p. 90, who dates Vlad's return between March and October 1443; and Radu Constantinescu, "Quelques observations sur l'epoque de Vlad Tepeş (I); *RRH*, XVII:1

it difficult to raise a force to oppose him. He turned to his father-in-law, Vlad's long-time nemesis, Stephen II of Moldavia, who, Chalkokondyles tells us, "came to his aid in the war that he later had with Dracula,"[5] but it proved too little as the people rallied to their former Prince. In the ensuing conflict, Vlad easily routed his rival who perished in the fighting. His victory was so quick and decisive that Wavrin, in his account, merely states that he returned "to his country, where he was received with all the honors, esteem, and joy that he deserved as one who was very loved by his people."[6] The Burgundian crusader, however, glosses over the bloodshed that accompanied Vlad's return, as Basarab's relatives and supporters were either killed or fled the country. Among those descendants of Dan I who escaped Wallachia at this time was Manzilla of Argeș, the grandfather of the renowned sixteenth century humanist Nicholas Olahus, married to one of John Hunyadi's sisters.[7]

Another famous humanist, Enea Silvio Piccolomini, who served at the court of the Holy Roman Emperor, the Habsburg ruler Frederick III of Austria, at the time of these events, understood the factional strife in Wallachia as a struggle between Vlad's family and the progeny of Dan I. In his *Cosmographia*, the future Pope Pius II explains that, "Among the Wallachians in our time there were two factions, one of the Dans and the other of the Draguls, but as the latter were weaker than the Dans and were oppressed by them in many ways, they called on the Turks to aid them, and with the help of their forces they crushed the Dans, almost wiping them out."[8] This passage

---

(1978), pp. 29-30, who says Vlad retook the throne in February on March 1443. There has been a general desire among Romanian historians to connect Vlad with the Long Campaign, but some, most notably Constantin A. Stoide, "Basarab al II-lea (1442-1444), p. 299, have recognized that the evidence indicates this occurred after the Long Campaign. Nevertheless, Romanian historiography has still not reached a consensus. The Romanian Academy's recent synthesis, *Istoria Românilor*, vol. IV, states in the text that Vlad regained the throne in 1443 (p. 313), while in an annex it dates the end of Basarab's reign and the beginning of Vlad's second reign as around April 1444.

[5]Chalcocondil, *Expuneri istorice*, p. 158 (V, 260).

[6]Iorga, "Cronica lui Wavrin," p. 76.

[7]George Lăzărescu and Nicolae Stoicescu, *Țările române și Italia până la 1600*, Bucharest, 1972, p. 179.

[8]Holban, ed., *Călători străini*, vol. I, p. 472.

clearly refers to events in the spring of 1444. Piccolomini's observations influenced not only his contemporaries in their thinking about Wallachian affairs[9], but also many later historians who, beginning with A.D. Xenopol, tried to explain the ongoing struggles for the throne throughout the fifteenth and well into the sixteenth century in terms of an ongoing feud between the Drăculeşti and the Dăneşti families.[10] But, excepting the conflict between Michael and Radu II, and that between Alexander Aldea and Vlad Dracul, Ilie Minea has rightly pointed out that "One can only speak of a struggle between the Drăculeşti and the Dăneşti up to 1462, because from that time forward struggles took place between descendants of the same families."[11] Piccolomini's interpretation of affairs in the Principality as a Wallachian family feud, however, best describes events between 1442 and 1460, the period about which he wrote, and should not be extended beyond this time frame.

Vlad received a warm reception when he resumed the throne, but Wavrin tells us that "when his people learned of the contents of his treaty, as a result of which neither he nor they could any longer make war on the Great Turk as long as they lived, some rejoiced, while others became very sad. Those upset were among the youth who, as is true everywhere, exercise the use of arms of their own free will, while those who are older and more calm look only for rest and peace."[12] Clearly, a debate over whether to fight the Turks or to come to terms with them divided Wallachian society. The older generation, who had witnessed the devastation that decades of warfare had brought to the Principality, favored peace, resigning themselves to the futility of the conflict, a perspective best summed up in the words of the elderly boyar who later in the century wrote: "the Turks are as many as the sands of the sea, and no one can stand against them."[13] The youth, however, inspired by Hunyadi's recent

---

[9]See, for example, the account of Raffaelo Maffei (1451-1522), also known as Volterranus, who served as secretary to Pius II's successor Pope Paul II (1464-1471), in Holban, ed., *Călători străini*, vol. I, p. 478.

[10]See A.D. Xenopol, "Lupta între Drăculeşti şi Dăneşti," pp. 183-272 in *AARMSI*, series II, vol. XXX (1907-1908).

[11]Minea, *Principatele române şi politica orientală a împăratului Sigismund*, p. 151.

[12]Iorga, "Cronica lui Wavrin," p. 76.

[13]Doc. CCXXIV in Bogdan, *Documente privitoare*, pp. 272-277.

victories, eagerly sought the opportunity to demonstrate their military prowess, brimming with that confidence characteristic of the young of every generation, certain that they could change the world and alter the course of history. Although his own inclinations favored peace, Vlad had to work to create a consensus among his people because the dangerous geo-political situation of Wallachia, as a buffer state between the Kingdom of Hungary and the Ottoman Empire, demanded that he strive to maintain a balance of power between the two, both for his own sake and for that of his country.

Despite their successes during the Long Campaign, the Hungarians feared repercussions now that they had awakened the sleeping giant. Wavrin tells us that they took great pains "to find out the situation of the Great Turk, Murad Bey, and what he would do. Soon they received news that he had freed the Prince of Wallachia and that he had sent repeated calls to all those throughout his lands, asking for help and support from all the infidel lords, his neighbors, and informing them that he had made peace and union with the Prince of Wallachia and all of his Wallachian subjects, and that he intended to enter the land of Hungary at the end of August to avenge the injuries they had done to him and to extract reparations from the Hungarians for the losses that he had recently suffered."[14] As the Hungarians had maintained a firm grip on Wallachia during the reign of Basarab, the return of the independent-minded Vlad to the throne of the Transalpine land represented a blow to their interests, as well as an impediment to plans for launching a new crusade.

Because of its strategic location and military potential, Wallachia represented an important element in Christian planning for an offensive against the Ottomans. In 1443, with Basarab firmly in control of the Principality south of the Carpathians, Cardinal Cesarini, the architect of the forthcoming crusade, planned for the Christian army to march through Wallachia on its way to the sea coast, from where it would head south to join the fleet at Constantinople protecting the straits. In the fall of that year, Gaspar Schlick, the chancellor of Bohemia, wrote to Cesarini regarding this plan: "as for the route, which you wrote to me must go through Wallachia, I heartily approve, because mounted troops must avoid narrow passes through the mountains. The wide areas of the

---

[14]Iorga, "Cronica lui Wavrin," p. 77.

plains are preferable."[15] Such a strategy would also reduce the distance the crusaders needed to march through enemy territory. But Vlad's restoration upset these plans.

Basarab's demise took the Hungarians by surprise and left them without a ready alternative to Vlad. Given these circumstances and Vlad's strong base of support within the Principality, they sought instead to win him over to the anti-Ottoman cause. "But when they approached the Prince of Wallachia to ask for his help," Wavrin relates, "he excused himself, replying to the King and the Legate that he could do nothing in this regard, having in mind the solemn oath taken by the Great Turk to the effect that he would never again take up arms against him. And even more so, because only by taking these oaths had he escaped prison and the danger of death. After he received this response, the Cardinal of St. Angelo, the Legate of our Holy Father, the Pope, sent to him again, offering to free him from the oath and promises he made to the Turk, but nothing could be done to change his mind, and this made the Legate and the King of Hungary very unhappy."[16]

Despite the crusading fervor sparked by the successes of the Long Campaign and papal efforts to organize a fleet, Vlad's refusal to break his treaty with the Sultan dampened Hungarian enthusiasm for resuming the offensive. King Vladislav also harbored doubts that Pope Eugenius could pull together a fleet, and he knew that without adequate naval support a land campaign had little chance of success. Apart from this, Murad, acting on the counsel of his advisors, who were concerned about the troubles facing the Empire, and against his own better judgement, had proposed generous peace terms; the King feared that the Sultan might attack Hungary should he ignore his overtures. With these considerations in mind, the Hungarian Diet met in Buda in April 1444 to discuss what course of action to follow. Among those who lobbied for the continuation of hostilities was Serbian Despot George Branković. As the principal beneficiary of the campaign of 1443, he now dreamed of restoring Greater Serbia; on July 3, he rewarded Hunyadi with several estates in Hungary for his role in liberating a large portion of Serbia from

---

[15]Iorga, *Acte și fragmente*, vol. III, pp. 11-12.

[16]Iorga, "Cronica lui Wavrin," p. 78.

the Turks and restoring him to the throne.[17] In this manner, the Despot also hoped to purchase Hunyadi's continued support. Nevertheless, although preparations for a new crusade continued, they decided to send a delegation to Adrianople, led by Stoyka Gisdanich, to open peace negotiations with the Sultan.[18] The young King vacillated between those who clamored for continuing the war against the Turks and those who favored peace. Vladislav hoped that by negotiating with the Ottomans he could avoid a possible attack and obtain favorable terms to consolidate his recent victories in the event that, as had happened so often in the past, the resources needed to undertake a full-blown crusade did not materialize, but he also wanted to stay ready in case that they did.

The Hungarian embassy, headed by the King's emissary Stoyka Gisdanich, left Buda for Adrianople at the end of April. Upon reaching the Sultan's European capital, they found Murad amenable to the peace proposals put forward by the Hungarian King. One of the reason for this, Wavrin explains, was that "the Turks, by means of the Genoese, knew in detail everything that was being prepared in Venice in terms of an army, of which they were very much afraid."[19] Grand Vizir Halil Pasha and Serbian Despot George Branković, had lobbied to convince the Sultan to accept the Christian peace proposals, the latter indirectly through his daughter Mara, the wife of Murad II.[20] The two sides soon agreed to terms for a ten year peace agreement. Murad wrote to Vladislav on June 12, outlining the principal elements of the accord: "We inform Your Majesty that the beloved emissary Stoyka has told us, first of all, about Despot George, specifically that we must return his sons and his lands to him, while the said George shall be obligated to serve us in those

---

[17]Doc. DLXXXV in Hurmuzaki, *Documente*, vol. I, part. 2, pp. 696-698.

[18]Annex III.2 in Francisc Pall, "Ciriaco d'Ancona e la Crociata contro i Turchi," in *Académie Roumaine. Bulletin de la Section Historique*, XX (1938), pp. 62-63. Stoyka was a Serb who later became captain of the Hungarian garrison at Kilia when Hunyadi took possession of the port from Moldavia in 1448, see Francisc Pall, "Stăpânirea lui Iancu de Hunedoara asupra Chiliei şi problema ajutorării Bizantului," in *Studii*, 18:3 (1965), p. 629.

[19]Iorga, "Cronica lui Wavrin," p. 84.

[20]Mihail P. Guboglu, "Românii la bătălia de la Varna (10 nov. 1444) după izvoare turco-islamice şi europene," in *RA*, XLVII: 3 (1985), p. 270.

things he did previously. Out of brotherhood for Your Highness, I have agreed to this."

This same letter also reveals that through these negotiations the Hungarians also sought to make peace with Vlad. They reached an agreement whereby the Ottomans and the Hungarians would exercise joint sovereignty over Wallachia: "Likewise, he [Stoyka] told us, that with regard to Vlad, the Wallachian Voivode, he would like to reach a peace with him in this manner: that the said Voivode Vlad shall give me, first of all, the customary tribute, while in all our services to be obligated again as he was before, except that he shall no longer have to come personally to our court. We are satisfied with this out of love for Your Excellency, specifically that the Voivode Vlad shall pay tribute and that he shall continue to serve us in all of those things that he was previously bound to do and we are satisfied that he himself shall no longer have to come personally to our court, but that he shall send hostages, and that in the event that any of our people should take refuge in his lands that he shall send them back to us, and that we shall do the same if any of his subjects flee here."[21] The treaty recognized a joint Hungarian-Ottoman suzerainty over Wallachia, a status that would be renewed several years later when the Turks and the Hungarians once again met at the negotiating table. Given the geopolitical situation of Wallachia at this time, these terms were highly favorable to Vlad. Although the treaty obligated him to respect commitments to both superpowers, it limited the extent to which either could interfere in the country's domestic affairs. The final agreement likely resembled the terms of the armistice concluded a few years later between the Ottomans and the Hungarians, specified in Sultan Mehmed II's letter to John Hunyadi, then Governor of Hungary, dated November 20, 1451: "The Wallachian Voivode shall pay and give to My Majesty what is rightful in the form of tribute or other services. Likewise, he shall give what is rightful to the Kingdom of Hungary or to the Governor: obedience, submission, and obligations or other services.... [and] neither party shall appoint a Prince in the Transalpine land except for the one that shall be elected by that country."[22] As a result of the treaty, Vlad's two younger sons, Vlad and Radu, returned to the Porte as hostages.

---

[21]Doc. 273 in *DRH, D*, pp. 377-379.

[22]Doc. 305 in *DRH, D*, pp. 418-421.

Despite his uneasy relationship with Hunyadi, who had supported his rival Basarab, Vlad's ties to the King facilitated the rapprochement between Wallachia and Hungary. After the Ottomans and the Hungarians agreed to exercise joint suzerainty over Wallachia, Vlad confirmed the resumption of peaceful relations with the powerful neighboring Kingdom and restored trade privileges for merchants from Braşov and the Bârsa land on August 7, 1444. Vlad's acceptance of his status as a Hungarian vassal is reflected in the fact that, instead of renewing the privilege he had granted to Saxon merchants in 1437, he confirmed Hunyadi's decree of the previous year, which applied the tariffs set by Dan II in 1431, on the basis of the dubious Latin privilege of 1413 allegedly granted by Mircea. "Not long ago, the distinguished gentleman, Prince John Hunyadi, Voivode of Transylvania, confirmed the said letter of our father...," Vlad wrote to the burghers and elders of Braşov and the Bârsa land, "to preserve an everlasting peace between our two countries; for this reason, we, together with our barons and leading citizens who are in this Transalpine land, without any objections, wish to hold to and to maintain firmly that which is written in the letters of the aforesaid Princes, Mircea, Voivode of the Transalpine land, our father of happy memory, and John Hunyadi, Voivode of Transylvania."[23]

Since Vlad resumed the throne, tensions had run high between Wallachia and Transylvania. Hunyadi did not look favorably upon the man who had ousted his protégé and now ruled the Transalpine land, but Basarab's demise left him, for the moment, without a viable candidate to challenge Vlad. Apart from this, the international context demanded that the two set aside their differences and reach an accommodation. Despite the ensuing peace, disputes affecting commercial relations between the two neighboring states reveal that underlying political tensions persisted. In response to Hunyadi's demand that the Wallachians do nothing to impede Transylvanian merchants crossing the Carpathians from doing business in the Transalpine land, Vlad addressed a letter to Stoyka Harsean and all of the boyars in Oltenia, long the focal point of anti-Catholic and anti-Hungarian sentiment in the Principality, ordering them not to obstruct commerce in any way. "My Majesty commands that you do not harass those who come from the Hungarian land with goods," the Prince wrote to his nobles. "Furthermore, as for

---

[23]Doc. 275 in *DRH, D*, pp. 383-384.

their goods, you are not to let them return with so much as a strand of hair."[24] But problems continued as Hungarian officials stationed along the border, especially those at Bran, committed abuses against Wallachian merchants attempting to ply their trade in Transylvania.

In his decree of August 7, confirming privileges for traders from Braşov and the Bârsa land, Vlad complains that previous commercial agreements between the two neighboring lands "were ignored by certain customs officials and castellans of the fortress at Bran, and few wanted to preserve them."[25] The reestablishment of peaceful relations between Wallachia and Transylvania did not improve this situation. In a letter to John Hunyadi, Vlad decried persistent abuses by royal officials stationed at Bran, despite the fact that he had restored the Transylvanian Voivode's earlier decree: "Your Majesty should be aware that I have confirmed those few lines which you sent to My Majesty, saying that the poor men should have justice in accordance with the law established by previous Princes, and fulfilled Your Majesty's command, but you should know that Your Majesty's servants at Bran continue to abuse the poor men."[26] In a separate letter addressed to the burghers of Braşov around the same time, Vlad laments, "please understand me, for I have left my children to be butchered for the sake of Christian peace so that we, myself and my country, can belong to my Lord, the King. I have joined with you so that you will treat my subjects well and so that both yours and ours can feed themselves freely, both here and there. But now I see that my subjects cannot feed themselves freely because of those castellans at that fortress [Bran] who have robbed and plundered them in violation of the law..." He went on to warn them, "if you are my friends, tell those castellans to obey God and not to drive me away from my lord, the King, and the Holy Crown, as this is not my desire, but rather to

---

[24]Doc. 78 in *DRH, B*, vol. I, p. 141. This is an undated letter which, because of the context, I date 1444, but it could be dated at different times throughout his reigns, 1437-1442 and 1444-1447.

[25]Doc. 275 in *DRH, D*, pp. 383-384.

[26]Doc. 263 in *DRH, D*, pp. 363-364. The editors date this letter after March 7, 1441, when Hunyadi was appointed Voivode of Transylvania, but the contents of this letter refer to Hunyadi's act of March 2, 1443, establishing commercial privileges in Wallachia for Transylvanian merchants, and Vlad's subsequent act renewing these privileges. Thus the letter should be dated shortly after August 7, 1444.

have my subjects treated well by them, and for them to return to each what was taken, and for my subjects to have justice from them because I will not allow them to suffer these shameful losses." In this same act, Vlad demonstrated his commitment to peace with his Christian neighbors by renouncing the tariff on wax, one of Wallachia's principal exports, telling the burghers, "I have fulfilled your request and have permitted wax to be traded freely."[27] Despite difficulties in their commercial relations, Vlad had clearly drawn closer to Hungary on the eve of the Last Crusade.

But while the Hungarians and the Ottomans negotiated peace, the Vatican pressed forward with its efforts to raise a fleet and to organize a crusade. The successes of the Long Campaign breathed new life into these efforts that had repeatedly stalled since the Council of Florence. Raising a fleet was critical to plans for a new crusade. Walerand de Wavrin, one of the commanders of the naval expedition, explained the need "to send a naval force, galleys and other large ships, to guard the straits around Constantinople against a Turkish invasion. In other words, to impede the latter from crossing from Turkey and from Anatolia to Greece, for in this manner Greece will be easy to conquer."[28] While the Ottomans represented a formidable land power, the Christians, thanks to Venice's destruction of the Turkish fleet at Gallipoli in 1416, continued to dominate the sea, and they intended to exploit this advantage. Brimming with enthusiasm, Bartholomew of Yano, the Guardian of the Franciscan Order stationed at the Byzantine capital, claimed in his letter of February 1443 that as few as ten galleys would be sufficient to block the straits

---

[27]Doc. 253 in *DRH, D*, pp. 350-351. The editors date this document c. April 26, 1438, tying it to King Albert's letter of that date, ordering officials at Bran not to abuse Wallachian merchants, after Gustav Gündisch (Doc. 2311 in *Urkundenbuch*, vol. V, pp. 9-10). But 1444 is a more likely date as Vlad's reference to leaving his sons as hostages at the Porte, "to be butchered for Christian peace," clearly connects it with events in the summer of 1444, also a period of trade conflicts centered around Bran. Vlad's royal seal applied to this document, identical to the one attached to a letter from 1445, also supports this dating, as it differs from those used to authenticate documents during his first reign, which were presumably lost or destroyed.

[28]Iorga, "Cronica lui Wavrin," p. 72.

and to prevent the Turks from crossing.[29] But the task of raising a fleet capable of fulfilling this mission was by no means an easy one.

Many of the funds collected to finance the construction of a fleet had been embezzled or diverted to unrelated purposes. Meanwhile, the Christian powers insisted on dividing up the spoils even before the campaign got underway. Although the Byzantines held claim to the territories in question, the Catholic states did not bother to consult the Greeks as they redrew the map of Southeastern Europe. In return for their participation, the Venetians demanded both Gallipoli, the key to control over the Dardanelles, and Salonika, which it had lost to the Turks in 1430. Alphonse V of Naples claimed Athens and Patros, while the maritime republic of Ragusa located along the Adriatic coast sought Avlona and the fortress of Kanina.

Apart from Pope Eugenius, one of the principal backers of crusading efforts at this time was Philip the Good of Burgundy. Although anxious to avenge his father's defeat at Nicopolis, the ambitious Duke, who ruled over the most prosperous state in Europe, was even more interested in the prestige that the success of such as undertaking could bring. While nominally a vassal of the King of France, he had skillfully taken advantage of the Hundred Years' War between France and England and achieved de facto independence in 1435, when the Treaty of Arras freed him of the obligation to pay homage to his sovereign. He now hoped to transform his Duchy, with its capital at Dijon, into a Kingdom by playing a leading role in efforts to liberate Europe from the Turks. But Philip also had another motive for military involvement in the east. Burgundy, with its flourishing cities and textile industry, had important trading interests in the Orient threatened by the installation of Ottoman hegemony in the region. These reasons determined Philip join in the upcoming crusade. The Duke commissioned the Venetians, with whom he enjoyed close ties, to build the galleys he needed to take part in the naval campaign, and he appointed one of his closest advisors, Walerand de Wavrin, as commander of the Burgundian fleet.

By the spring of 1444, the Papacy had overcome the main obstacles to launching a naval expedition, and Eugenius IV was now confident that he

---

[29]Annex 1 in Bogdan, *Românii în secolul al XV-lea*, pp. 216-222.

could muster a sizeable fleet. On May 2, King Vladislav wrote to the Grand Master of the Teutonic Knights, informing him that the Pope had promised 38 galleys for the crusade: 12 from Venice, 10 from Aragon, 6 from Burgundy, 8 from Milan, and 2 from Rhodes.[30] As usual, the information coming out of Rome was overly optimistic. Enea Silvio Piccolomini provided a more accurate assessment of Christian naval capabilities; on May 27 he estimated that 25 triremes were then being equipped at Venice.[31] But the Hungarian King still harbored serious doubts that the Italian states could set aside their differences and launch a significant naval force; Wavrin tells us that in the summer of 1444, "the rumor circulated in Hungary that Our Holy Father could not come to an agreement with the Venetians."[32] Because of this, peace negotiations between Hungary and the Ottomans continued. But despite these reservations, by early July, a naval force, close to the size estimated by Piccolomini, prepared to set out for the straits. On July 4, eight papal galleys, commanded by Eugenius's nephew, Cardinal Francisco Condolmieri, left Venice. Three days later, eight Venetian galleys under Pietro Loredano, one of the Republic of St. Mark's most experienced naval officers,[33] and four Burgundian galleys commanded by Wavrin followed; a final Burgundian ship left port on July 8. Two Ragusan galleys joined this force en route.[34]

But as these men of war navigated through the waters of the Adriatic and Aegean seas on their way to seize control of the Bosphorus and the Dardanelles, the Sultan concluded peace treaties with the Christian states of Southeastern Europe. Murad reconfirmed his previous agreements with Vlad after accepting joint Ottoman-Hungarian suzerainty over Wallachia. Chalkokondyles writes that "The Dacians were to remain tributaries of the Sultan with what they had agreed to in the peace treaty that the Emperor had concluded with them earlier."[35] Murad also reached a separate accord with

[30]Minea, "Vlad Dracul și vremea sa,", p. 227.

[31]Pall, "Le condizioni e gli echi internazionali," p. 447.

[32]Iorga, "Cronica lui Wavrin," p. 84.

[33]Emil Diaconescu, "Politica orientală burgundă și turcii în sec. XIV și XV" in CI, I:1 (1925), p. 32.

[34]Minea, "Vlad Dracul și vremea sa,", p. 224, nt. 5.

[35]Chalcocondil, Expuneri istorice, p. 189 (VI, 317).

George Branković, restoring significant territory and important fortresses to the Serbian Despot, along with his blinded sons, Gregory and Stephen. This not only consolidated what he had won during the Long Campaign, but effectively restored much of Serbia, which only three years earlier the Ottomans had expunged from the map of Europe. Once a vocal proponent of continued military action against the Turks, Branković quickly became an advocate of peace. Soon after the Long Campaign, the Serbian Despot came to realize that, given present circumstances, he could win more at the negotiating table than on the battlefield; Branković accepted his status as a vassal of the Sultan and, in exchange, obtained remarkable concessions from the Porte. Mehmed Neshri explains his diplomatic success, claiming that "Vilk-oglu [Branković] gave numerous gifts to the Beys of Rumelia, and thereby, with the help of his florins, he persuaded the Sultan to make peace. The Sultan again accorded Vilk-oglu his lands and he took his two sons from the prison at Tokat and sent them back to their father."[36] While Neshri ignores Murad's own desire to settle matters in Europe, this passage attests to the diplomatic astuteness of the Serbian ruler. Undoubtedly, the Sultan's wife, Branković's daughter Mara, also helped to facilitate this accord. The Despot placed his seal on the agreement on August 15, and shortly thereafter he took possession of the promised lands and fortresses.

Negotiations between the Ottomans and the Hungarians had resulted in a ten-year peace accord between the two rival superpowers. Now, all that remained was for King Vladislav to ratify the agreement. Believing that he had secured peace in Europe, Murad crossed over to Anatolia on July 12 where he hoped to do the same by resolving the conflict with Karaman, which he did by concluding a treaty with Ibrahim Bey at the beginning of August. But up to the very moment that emissaries from the Sultan arrived at Seghedin in late July, Vladislav continued to play a duplicitous game of diplomacy. During the preceding weeks, the King had written to Scanderbeg in Albania and Stephen Tomash in Bosnia, encouraging them to take up arms against the Turks. Hunyadi wrote to Brașov as late as July 20, calling on the burghers to help him prepare for war.[37] But, having received no word from Rome, Vladislav, against

---

[36]*Cronici turcești*, vol. I, p. 123.

[37]Doc. 4 in Hurmuzaki, *Documente*, vol. XV, part 1, p. 31.

Das Ander Buch
Wie der Amurath ain Legation gen Hügern
sendet/begert fryd auff Zehen jar/vnd gibt das land
Mysiam den Christen wider.

Sixteenth century engraving of John Hunyadi receiving Ottoman emissaries at Seghedin

Hunyadi's advice, took a solemn oath and placed his seal on the peace treaty with the Ottomans in the presence of Murad's ambassadors at the end of the month.[38] Dukas specifies that Hunyadi did not swear to the treaty, but merely remarked, "I obey the King, I do not rule."[39]

After settling the conflicts threatening the security of his Empire in both Europe and Asia, Murad unexpectedly relinquished his throne in August 1444.

---

[38]Some Polish historians, most notably Oscar Halecki, have sought to vindicate Vladislav of charges of perjury by arguing that the King, although he initially signed the accord with Murad in June, had refused to ratify the treaty at Seghedin, see, for example Oscar Halecki, "La croisade de Varna" in *Bulletin of the International Committee of Historical Sciences* XI:4 (1939), pp. 485-495, but the evidence contradicts such assertions, see Francisc Pall, "Autour de la croisade de Varna: La question de la paix de Szeged et de sa rupture (1444); in *Académie Roumaine. Bulletin de la section historique*, XXII:2 (1941), pp. 144-158.

[39]Ducas, *Istoria turco-bizantină*, p. 272 (XXXII.1).

The motives behind the Sultan's abdication are complex. During the previous decades, the Ottoman Empire underwent a period of tumultuous change, marked by conflicts between the traditional Islamic aristocracy and a new emerging elite, comprised largely of Christian converts to Islam, that included the Jannissary corps and numerous slave servants who began to occupy key positions in the Ottoman administration.[40] As these domestic disputes became increasingly profound, Murad felt that he could no longer bear the pressures of his office, and the death of his eldest son, Aladdin, in the summer of 1444, intensified this sentiment. Having established peace on the frontiers of the Empire, the Sultan withdrew from public life, leaving the throne to his young son Mehmed, who nine years later would secure his place in history and earn the epithet 'the Conqueror' by breaching the once impenetrable walls of Constantinople, which henceforth became Istanbul, destroying the last remnant of Imperial Rome. But at this time, Mehmed was only a boy of twelve or thirteen, not yet prepared to rule an Empire.

Murad retreated to his palace at Manisa in Asia Minor, where he intended to live out the remainder of his days in tranquility, free from the burdens of state. But leaving an untried youth at the helm of the mighty Ottoman Empire made it a tempting target for many who had long suffered at the hands of the Turks. Mehmed Pasha records that, "When the Padishah left the throne to his son Mehmed, Karamanoglu sent an emissary to the Hungarian King and told him: 'The Padishah is old and has left his throne to an underaged son of his. Let us come to an understanding between us and advance and defeat the Turk.'"[41] Another Ottoman chronicler, Solakzade, reports that Ibrahim Bey wrote to Vladislav: "A taste for partying has filled the head of Osmanoglu, and he has left in his place as his successor a worthless brat who has not yet seen war and who has not yet ridden his horse through rocky places. And so, we must not let such an opportunity escape us and pass us by, for regret will do neither of us any good."[42]

---

[40]Gemil, *Romanii și otomanii*, pp. 117-119.

[41]*Cronici turcești*, vol. I, p. 293.

[42]*Cronici turcești*, vol. II, p. 136.

But the ruler of Karaman was not alone in calling on Vladislav to renounce peace with the Turks. Byzantine Emperor John VIII had learned of the peace negotiations between the Hungarians and the Ottomans from the Italian humanist Cyriaco Pizzicoli of Ancona, who was present in Adrianople during the talks,[43] and he wrote to the King on July 30 to express his dismay at the news, warning him not to trust the Sultan because he only negotiated out of fear.[44] But before the Emperor's letter or emissaries from Karaman could reach Vladislav, Giuliano Cesarini returned from Rome. The Pope had recalled him to Italy for consultations during the decisive phase of negotiations between the Hungarians and the Ottomans. When he reached Seghedin and learned that the King had just sealed a treaty with the Sultan, the Cardinal, who had worked diligently during the past two years to organize a crusade against the Turks, raged with anger. According to Wavrin, "Soon after the King of Hungary and the Great Turk exchanged oaths and made this peace agreement, the Cardinal of Saint Angelo returned from Rome and arrived in the Hungarian land. When he learned what had happened, he became very furious. He harshly criticized the King and all those who took part in his council, saying that under no circumstances could they conclude such a peace without the consent of Our Holy Father..." When he regained his composure, Cesarini told them: "Do you really believe that the Turk would have offered you peace and returned your fortresses to you if he were truly strong enough to attack you? Certainly not! On the contrary, Venetian and Genoese merchants have informed Our Holy Father that the Turk has sunk so low, and lost so many of his forces in battles up to now against you and others, in that he doesn't know where he can gather men, and that, now or never, the moment has arrived to reconquer Greece." "Apart from this," the Burgundian crusader continues, "he also told them that the army of Our Holy Father, that of the Duke of Burgundy, and that of the Venetians had at that very moment arrived at Constantinople to protect the straits."[45]

---

[43]Appendix III.1 in Pall, "Ciriaco d'Ancona e la Crociata contri i Turchi,' pp. 58-61 Cyriaco's letter to the Emperor is dated June 24, 1444, from Adrianople.

[44]Minea, "Vlad Dracul şi vremea sa," p. 232; and Minea "Informaţiile româneşti," p. 33.

[45]Iorga, "Cronica lui Wavrin," pp. 84-85.

His contemporaries regarded Giuliano Cesarini as one of the most capable members of the College of Cardinals. A highly educated man, Cesarini numbered Poggio Bracciolini and Enea Silvio Piccolomini, two of the leading humanists of the day, among his friends. The forty-six year old Cardinal was a skilled diplomat. He had played a role in peace negotiations between the French and the English, as well as in the campaigns against the Hussites in Bohemia; after presiding over the Council of Basel, he went on to become one of the architects of the Union of Florence.[46] Since his appointment as Papal Legate to Hungary in February 1442, Cesarini emerged as the driving force behind crusading efforts. He was not about to sit back and see all of his work squandered by the imprudent actions of the young King. Wavrin tells us that, "The Cardinal of Saint Angelo preached his message in Hungary with such passion that he convinced the King and his nobles to tear up the peace they had made with the Turks. As for their oaths and solemn promises, the Cardinal absolved them of these."[47] According to Długosz, Hunyadi joined Cesarini in urging the King to break the peace with the Sultan.[48] In any event, the Cardinal won the day and, on August 4, the King, joined by John Hunyadi and other leading nobles, swore a solemn oath before him, promising to muster their military forces and to cross the Danube at Orşova in September to liberate the lands of the Byzantine Empire from Turkish occupation.[49]

The Cardinal now had to act quickly lest news of the peace accord between the King and the Sultan reach the fleet protecting the straits and determine them to abandon their mission. To avoid such a scenario, Wavrin tells us that Cesarini "found three men who knew how to speak Turkish, dressed them in the Muslim fashion, and sent each by different routes to Constantinople, so that if one or two of them were captured the other would arrive with the message and annul the effects of the rumor. He entrusted each with a letter addressed to the Christian

---

[46]Pall, "Le condizioni e gli echi internazionali," p. 436.

[47]Iorga, "Cronica lui Wavrin," p. 85.

[48]Minea, *Informaţiile româneşti*, p. 33. Some less reliable sources claim that Hunyadi opposed breaking the treaty, but he had consistently advocated military action against the Turks and he certainly did not want to squander the opportunity presented by the arrival of the fleet at the straits.

[49]Doc. DLXXXIV in Hurmuzaki, *Documente*, vol. I, part 2, pp. 694-696.

forces comprising the fleet, in which he informed them that the King of Hungary is gathering a great force with which he will in a short time cross into Greece. Therefore, if by chance they hear it said that the King and the Turk have concluded a peace they should not believe this..."[50]

The Burgundians under Wavrin's command, who ventured into this part of the world for the first time, saw the crusade as a grand adventure. As they neared the straits, Wavrin sought information from his Venetian counterparts about the location of the ruins of ancient Troy. Inspired by the Homeric legends, he, together with his adjutants Pietre Vast and Gauvain Quieret, decided that if they spotted Turkish troops near the site where Agamemnon's thousand ships had long ago laid anchor to avenge the abduction of Helen of Troy, they too would follow in the footsteps of the legendary Greek heros of the *Iliad* and test their skill in battle against the Asian foe. Upon reaching the Dardanelles, they laid anchor. There, on the Anatolian shore, they observed the approach of Turkish infantry and calvary units. When he saw this, Wavrin "ordered the galleys brought near the shore so that his men could disembark. But at that very moment the sky grew dark and a fierce wind began to blow, so the patrons of the galleys and the sailers advised him not to approach the shore because if a great storm should break out, as signs indicated, the galleys would be smashed against the rocks and destroyed. Therefore, they lowered the galleys's small boats onto the sea and the men disembarked in groups and lined up on the shore."[51]

Wavrin, seconded by Quieret and Vast, commanded the troops that went ashore. These included a Venetian nobleman, Cristofle Cocq, a relative of Doge Francesco Foscari. Just before he set sail from Venice, Foscari had personally requested that Wavrin transport his relative to Constantinople aboard his galley. Cocq lept at the chance to fight the Turks and asked Wavrin to make him a knight and to allow him to join the expeditionary force, and the Burgundian commander consented. The ensuing skirmish between Christian and Ottoman troops marked the first military confrontation of the Last Crusade. The opposing forces numbered not more than a hundred men on each

---

[50]Iorga, "Cronica lui Wavrin," p. 86. Greece was frequently employed as a general term to refer to the lands south of the Danube during this period.

[51]Iorga, "Cronica lui Wavrin," p. 82.

side. Although the battle held no strategic significance, it once again revealed a fundamental problem that plagued crusading armies — a lack of military discipline. Soon after the fighting began, Wavrin tells us that the Christian lines broke when "An English archer, a nobleman, under the command of Pietre Vast, wanting to prove himself better than all the others, moved ahead of the other archers, abandoning his place in the lines. In turn, others, determined to demonstrate that they were just as brave as he was, began to hurry after him breaking the line that they had been ordered to hold. Meanwhile, the Turks, seeing their disorderly advance, pretended to flee, which caused all of the archers, together with their companions, to follow them. Then a Turkish Subashi on horseback, situated at the flank of the infantry, together with sixteen to twenty calvary, saw what was happening and moved to cut off the retreat of the Christian archers who pursued the Turkish infantry."[52] Despite this breakdown in discipline, Wavrin's men managed to drive off the Ottomans and to restore order. Both sides suffered several minor casualties, but only two Turks and two Venetian soldiers died in the fighting.

From here, Wavrin moved on to Gallipoli where he joined the Papal and Venetian fleets that had set out before him. Then, leaving the bulk of the Christian fleet at Gallipoli, Wavrin and Cardinal Condolmieri sailed on to Constantinople to meet with John VIII. After consultations with the Byzantine Emperor, it was decided that the Venetian and Papal fleets, along with the Burgundian galleys under Pietre Vast, would defend the Dardanelles at Gallipoli, as it was the principal crossing point for the Ottomans, while Wavrin, with the remainder of the Burgundian fleet and the two Ragusan galley would protect the Bosphorus.

Soon after the ships took up their positions, Turkish emissaries arrived under a white flag of truce at both the Bosphorus and the Dardanelles, requesting an audience with the Christian commanders. They presented copies of the peace treaty between the Sultan and the King of Hungary bearing the latter's seal. News of the accord threw the Christians into disarray. Both Wavrin and Cardinal Condolmieri withdrew to Constantinople to consult with the Emperor. They arrived in the Byzantine capital uncertain as to which course of action to follow, but the precautions taken by Cardinal Cesarini saved

---

[52]Iorga, "Cronica lui Wavrin," pp. 82-83.

the day. According to Wavrin, when he met Condolmieri at Constantinople, "he found him totally confounded by news of the peace treaty. But while they were together, one of the three messengers sent from Hungary arrived carrying the letters which the Cardinal of Saint Angelo had entrusted to him... warning that if they will hear any news concerning a peace agreement concluded between the King of Hungary and the Great Turk, not to believe this... He advised the Christians here to do everything in their power to guard the straits well so as not to allow the Turks to cross..." The Burgundian commander goes on to say that both he and the Cardinal "were very happy to hear this news because only a few hours before neither of them knew what advice to give to the other, whether to remain there or to return home."[53]

Meanwhile, Hunyadi and King Vladislav hurried to gather an army under the watchful eye of Cardinal Cesarini. They assembled a force comprised mainly of Hungarian, Saxon, and Polish troops, but given time constraints and the continued threat of hostilities with Frederick III of Austria, they had difficulty raising a sizeable army despite their earlier preparations. Vladislav also sought support from the Christian rulers of Southeastern Europe, but his efforts met with limited success. Having recovered much of his former territory, Serbian Despot George Branković categorically refused to break his treaty with the Sultan. The King once again sent emissaries to Vlad, who, Wavrin tells us, "limited himself to sending a certain number of Wallachians to accompany the King, but he candidly declared that he himself would not take up arms."[54] The troops promised by the Wallachian Prince were to join the Christian army en route. Bosnian ruler Stephen Tomash also contributed a handful of soldiers, but Scanderberg, who had seized his lands back from the Ottomans the previous fall, was in no position to venture away from Albania. All he could do to help was to keep Ottoman forces stationed in the region tied up so that they could not depart from there to oppose the crusaders. Likewise, Despot Constantine of the Morea created a diversion by attacking Turkish positions in Greece, occupying Athens and Thebes.[55] As a result, when King

---

[53]Iorga, "Cronica lui Wavrin," pp. 87-88.

[54]Iorga, "Cronica lui Wavrin," p. 85.

[55]Francisc Pall, "Un moment decisif de l'histoire du Sud-Est européen: La croisade de Varna (1444)," in *Balcania*, VII (1944), p. 115.

Vladislav, accompanied by Cardinal Cesarini and John Hunyadi, crossed the Danube at Orșova around September 22,[56] he had an army of no more than 12,000 men.[57]

---

[56]Dlugosz says the Christian army crossed the Danube on September 3 (see Minea, *Informațiile românești*, p. 33), but we know that the King did not arrive at Orșova until September 9. Most Romanian historians place the crossing around September 20 because of a diploma allegedly issued by Hunyadi at Orșova on that date for the monasteries of Vodița and Tismana, see doc. 97 in *DRH, B*, vol. I, pp. 168-171, and doc. 276 in *DRH, D*, pp. 384-387. This document, however, is of uncertain date, as the month is missing. In his history of the Tismana Monastery, Alexandru Stefulescu dates it October 20 (see Stefulescu, *Mînistirea Tismana*, pp. 162-168), but this is impossible as Hunyadi was then in Bulgaria en route to Varna; Ilie Minea opts for November 20, arguing that Hunyadi could only have granted such a diploma after the King's death, see Ilie Minea, *Din trecutul stăpânirii românești asupra Ardealului*, Bucharest, 1914, p. 25. But Alexandru Vasilescu has convincingly demonstrated that it is an eighteenth century forgery by Bishop Inochenție of Râmnicu as part of his efforts to defend the rights of the Orthodox Church during the Austrian occupation of Oltenia, see Al. A. Vasilescu, "Diplomele lui Sigismund I, regele Ungariei și Ioan Huniade, voevodul Transilvaniei, dela Mănăstirea Tismana, sunt false," pp. 1-115, in *RIR*, XIII. As Voivode of Transylvania, Hunyadi had no authority to issue such a diploma. In addition, the document refers to holdings that did not become possessions of the Monastery of Tismana until the following centuries and omits others that belonged to it in the fifteenth century. As result of the installation of Habsburg rule in Hungary and Transylvania, when the document was forged in the eighteenth century there was a resurgence of interest in Hunyadi because of the legitimacy that ties to the Corvinus family represented, see Veress, "Vechi istorici unguri și sași," p. 272, and doc. XXVI, pp. 298-300. We know, however, that the crossing took place only after September 22 when Vladislav addressed a letter to the Polish Diet from Orșova, justifying the upcoming campaign by accusing the Turks of not having complied with all the terms of the peace treaty, see Francisc Pall, "Autour de la Croisade de Varna: La question de la Paix de Szeged et de sa rupture (1444)," in *Bulletin de la Section Historique*, XXII:2 (1941), p. 154. The King also issued decrees from Orșova on September 21 and 22 concerning the rights of the citizens of Kolosvár, see Docs. 2507 and 2508 in *Urkundenbuch*, vol. V, pp. 146-148.

[57]Estimates of the size of the Christian army range from 8,000 to as many as 25,000 men. Wavrin provides the lower number (see Iorga, "Cronica lui Wavrin," p. 93), but the most accurate estimate is that of Andreas de Palatio from Parma, a participant in the campaign, who, in a letter dated May 16, 1445, gives a total at 16,000 Christian troops, including 4,000 Wallachian provided by Vlad who joined the King's army at

Having effected the crossing at Orşova, the army of crusaders slowly advanced along the right bank of the Danube. A caravan formed of hundreds of wagons laden with supplies, victuals, and nonessential luxury goods hindered their progress[58] so that they could cover no more than fifteen to twenty kilometers per day. This threatened the success of the campaign because it depended on the element of surprise, especially if the fleet failed to prevent the crossing of Ottoman troops from Anatolia. They also lost valuable time beseiging several fortresses of little or no strategic importance along the way. The Christian army's first encounter with the Turks came at Kladova, where they seized the fort from a small Ottoman garrison that offered little resistance. By September 26, the King encamped along the banks of the Timok River. Finding himself in urgent need of additional funds to pay his army, Vladislav ordered officials of Braşov and the Bârsa land to turn over to his representatives the royal tax, called the *censul*, normally due on St. Martin's Day (November 11.)[59] The following day, the crusaders reached Vidin. From here, they moved on to Nicopolis where they arrived in mid-October and made a half-hearted attempt to take the citadel while they awaited Vlad's arrival with reinforcements.

Vlad had reluctantly agreed to provide a Wallachian contigent to the King's army despite his misgivings about breaking his treaty with the Sultan. Perhaps Murad's abdication influenced his decision to do so. In any event, just before mid-October, he set out from Târgovişte and made his way to Nicopolis where he had previously agreed to meet the King, accompanied by his eldest son Mircea and approximately 4,000 troops that he had committed to the Christian enterprise. As he neared the Danube, Vlad's apprehension about the outcome of the Last Crusade steadily grew. The fifteenth century Italian humanist Filippo Buonaccorsi-Callimachus, who later served Casimir, Vladislav's

---

Nicopolis (see Minea, "Vlad Dracul şi vremea sa," p. 240). Therefore, Vladislav, crossed the Danube at Orşova with no more than 12,000 men.

[58]Minea, *Informaţiile româneşti*, p. 34; and Constantin I. Karadja, "Poema lui Michel Beheim despre cruciadele împotriva turcilor din anii 1443 şi 1444," in *BCIR*, XV (1936), p. 9. Długosz provides an inflated estimate claiming that over 2,000 wagons formed the caravan.

[59]Doc. 2509 in *Urkundenbuch*, vol. V, pp. 148-149.

brother and successor as King of Poland, describes the Wallachian Prince as "a highly superstitious man." Callimachus tells us that along the way to Nicopolis, the day before he reached the King, Vlad passed through a village called Sullonum where there lived a fortune teller renowned throughout the area. He decided to consult the seer, an elderly Bulgarian woman, bent with age. Vlad asked her about the prospects for the success of the crusade and she replied that the King would not emerge from battle victorious. The Prince certainly viewed this as a bad omen and it enhanced his sense of foreboding.[60]

When he reached the Christian camp before Nicopolis the following day and saw the small size of the King's army, Vlad's fear of pending disaster increased. He pleaded with Vladislav to turn back, remarking that the Sultan went hunting with more men than the King had at his disposal.[61] At this point, Polish chronicler Martin Bielski writes that Cardinal Cesarini intervened, telling the Wallachian Prince, "As soon as we reach the Hellespont we will find enough men who will join us against the Turks," to which Vlad replied with skepticism, "May God grant that things will be as this priest says."[62] Although the King, whom the Ottoman chronicler Müneggimbashi describes as "an arrogant youth,"[63] refused to heed his advice, Vlad considered the Cardinal and John Hunyadi as primarily responsible for the ill-advised decision to break the peace with the Sultan. Because of the latter's previous support of Basarab, bad blood existed between the Transylvanian Voivode and the Wallachian Prince. Chalkokondyles informs us that "John worked against him [Dracula] among the Hungarians around Emperor Vladislav," and that, after the crusaders crossed the Danube and moved along its banks, Hunyadi "robbed the [Wallachian] villages and spoke badly of him [Dracula] to the

---

[60]Minea, "Vlad Dracul şi vremea sa," p. 237. The village of Sullonum no longer exists and its precise location cannot be determined, but it must have been no more than thirty kilometers from Turnu for Vlad to have reached the King with his troops the following day.

[61]Minea, *Informaţiile româneşti*, p. 33; and Miron Costin, "Istorie de crăiia ungurească," in *Opere*, Bucharest, 1958, p. 285.

[62]Quo. P.P. Panaitescu and N. Stoicescu, "La participation des Roumains à la bataille de Varna (1444)," in *RRH*, IV:2 (1965) p. 225.

[63]*Cronici turceşti*, vol. II, p. 233.

Emperor of the Hungarians, saying that he is really on the side of the Turks and Murad, and that he would inform them of everything that was happening."[64] A heated argument erupted between the two during the consultations in the Christian camp before Nicopolis; Vlad is said to have drawn his sword against Hunyadi, but those present intervened to prevent them from duelling.[65] Vlad mistrusted Hunyadi and, despite Cesarini's assurances, he remained uneasy about the eventual outcome of the campaign. Still, determined to keep his commitment to the King, he provided him with the 4,000 troops he had promised, under the command of his sixteen year old son Mircea. Callimachus, however, reports that Vlad took his son aside and cautioned him not to risk his troops in battle if Christian success seemed doubtful.[66] According to Długosz, the Wallachian Prince also gave the King two fast horses and two loyal scouts with extensive knowledge of the terrain in the region and he told Vladislav to keep them by his side at all times as they will save him in case of danger.[67] Unfortunately, the young King later failed

---

[64]Chalcocondil, *Expuneri istorice*, p. 199 (VII, 333).

[65]Teodor Popa, *Iancu Corvin de Hunedoara*, Hunedoara 1928, p. 98.

[66]Minea, "Vlad Dracul şi vremea sa," p. 250, nt. 3.

[67]Minea, *Informaţiile româneşti*, p. 34; and G.I. Năstase, "Istoria moldovenească din Kronika polska a lui Bielski," in *CI*, I (1925), p. 119. The most reliable sources (Długosz, Callimachus, Bonfinius, and Andreas de Palatio) say that Vlad contributed 4,000 troops, although Beheim, whose figures are all highly exaggerated, gives the total of 7,000 (see Karadja, "Poema lui Michel Beheim," p. 28 [v. 327-329]) and Chalkokondyles absurd the figure of 10,000 horsemen (Chalcocondil, *Expuneri istorice*, p. 143 (V, 325). 4,000 is the maximum number of soldiers that Vlad could have contributed to such an enterprise and, if this total is correct, the Wallachian contingent comprised approximately 25% of the crusading force. In the past, there has been some confusion as to whether or not Vlad personally participated in the Varna campaign because of Chalkokondyles's assertion to this effect and the confused verses in Beheim's poem, but all other accounts clearly indicate that Vlad sent his son. Some have also mistakenly identified Vlad's son who took part in the crusade as Vlad the Impaler (see, for example, Minea, "Vlad Dracul şi vremea sa," p. 236), but this was due to a mistaken belief that Mircea had perished in battle against Basarab in 1442. There can be no doubt that Mircea commanded the Wallachian contingent. His brothers Vlad and Radu, both still too young to assume such a role, were hostages of the Porte

to heed Vlad's words of caution, but, as Miron Costin fatalistically remarked, "what is to be done, good advice cannot undo."[68] Vlad then returned to Târgoviște where he anxiously awaited news of the outcome of the campaign.

Although Hunyadi had accused Vlad of revealing Christian plans to the Turks, many suspected George Branković who had refused to participate in the campaign. In reality, the Ottomans had a myriad of other sources from which they could obtain information about the crusaders's strategy. However the news that the Hungarians had broken the peace treaty first reached the Porte, panic quickly set in among the Ottoman elite. The young Sultan showed little interest in the affairs of state and the Beys of Rumelia realized the urgent need for strong, experienced leadership. Seventeenth century Wallachian chronicler Radu Popescu writes that after the crusaders crossed the Danube, "When the Vizirs saw this, and that entertaining guests and drinking wine preoccupied Sultan Mehmed, they sent for his father, Sultan Murad, urging him to come quickly as they were losing their Empire."[69] A delegation from the Divan set out for Manisa and convinced Murad to come out of retirement.[70] The Sultan quickly gathered an army and, while Vlad tried in vain at Nicopolis to convince the King to turn back, Murad prepared to cross the straits.

Because the bulk of the Christian fleet had anchored at Gallipoli to prevent the Turks from crossing the Dardanelles, the Sultan, who had received this information from the Genoese, decided to cross the Bosphorus, where he arrived on October 16 with 3,000-4,000 men and some 500 camels laden with metal to construct cannons. Around the same time, another Turkish force, numbering several thousand men under the command of Grand Vizir Halil Pasha, occupied the European side of the strait. Thus, with the Ottomans controlling both sides of the Bosphorus, and the Christian fleet commanded by Walerand de Wavrin patrolling the water between them, determined to prevent

---

at this time as indicated in Beheim's poem, see Karadja, "Poema lui Michel Beheim," p. 41 (v. 745).

[68]Costin, "Istorie de crăiia ungurească," in *Opere*, p. 285.

[69]Radu Popescu, *Istoriile Domniilor Țării Românești*, Bucharest, 1963, p. 18.

[70]*Cronici turcești*, vol. I, p. 183.

the Sultan from passing over to the European side, the stage was now set for a test of strength.

Even before the Ottomans had taken up positions on both banks, Wavrin doubted that he had enough ships to impede their crossing. He consulted with the captain of the Ragusan galleys and "they reached the conclusion that if the Turk would come with a large force on the Turkish side of the strait, and his captain Halil Pasha on the other, with cannon and artillery at their disposal on both banks, it will be impossible to impede their crossing... For this reason, they sent Gauvain Quieret, Lord of Dreves, and John Bayart, treasurer of the army, to the Emperor of Constantinople to inform him that it will be impossible for them to prevent the crossing of the Turks if they will control both shores..." They asked John VIII to send out troops to secure the European coast, to which Wavrin promised to add all the men he could spare from his galleys, but the Emperor replied: "All that I have left is this fortress of Constantinople, where few people can still be found. I know my people well, and they are not strong and I cannot send them into battle... Therefore, do the best that you can on your own."[71] John did promise to contribute two galleys to the fleet when the Turks arrived, but, fearing the consequences of failure, the Emperor, despite his diplomatic efforts to encourage the crusaders, hesitated to become directly involved in fighting the Ottomans. Shortly after the fleet had arrived in the straits, he had sent his trusted advisor, George Sphrantzes, as an emissary both to the Christians and to the Sultan so as to protect Byzantine interests "according to which side would emerge victorious."[72]

Lacking the support of a land army and having only a few galleys at his disposal, Wavrin faced a hopeless situation as the Ottomans occupied both the European and Anatolian shores without opposition. In addition, severe weather made it increasingly difficult for the Christian fleet to hold its position. At this point, Wavrin tells us, "a Turk came from the shore, raising a small white flag attached to the tip of his lance, something which in their language and custom means an appeal for security so they can speak to someone. Lord Wavrin was advised to raise a similar one on his galley, which he did. Then the said Turk came and spoke to him in complete security on a small boat, saying these words: 'The King of Hungary and the Hungarians are perjurers; they have

---

[71]Iorga, "Cronica lui Wavrin," pp. 89-90.

[72]Sphrantzes, *Memorii*, pp. 66, 68 (XXXVI, 4).

broken the law. Murad Bey is going to battle against them.' Then, placing his right hand on the hilt of his sword, he said: 'And with this sword we will defeat them in battle.' And, after he said these words, he left."[73]

The Turks now prepared to effect the crossing. To do this they needed boats, and they depended on their allies, the Genoese, who had sided with the Ottomans to oppose the Venetians, their rivals for control of commerce in the Levant, to provide them. The Sultan handsomely compensated the merchants from Genoa for their assistance. Wavrin had been warned in advance that "the Genoese were committed to help the Turk in everything and with all their power, something that proved to be true... The said Genoese, at night, pretending to go out fishing, brought many large boats to the Turks on the other shore..." Wavrin's galleys tried to prevent the Genoese boats from crossing, "and they raised anchor and set out after them, cutting off their route. But as soon as the galleys neared the boats, they quickly retreated to the Turkish shore or to the Greek one." When the currents and the weather forced the galleys to return to anchor, the boats again began to cross. Thanks to the Genoese, the Sultan soon had all the boats he needed. Wavrin relates that, "A few Venetians, who pretended to be Genoese, also crossed into Turkey; and upon their return they brought news that they saw at the New Castle about thirty large boats, well-built, and provided with oars and with all that was necessary."[74]

The Burgundian commander provides the only eyewitness account of the crossing. He records that, as the Turks began their operation, "Around sunset it happened that a great storm broke out, a furious tempest that blew in from the Black Sea. Because of this, the galleys no longer had any power to maneuver using their oars to draw near the enemy. As a result of these circumstances, many Turks crossed during that night..." The small boats could traverse the 550 meters separating the two coasts despite the weather conditions, but "The severe storm and the harsh winds, as if the work of the Devil, was so strong that our galleys could barely maintain anchor. Seeing this, the Turks attributed their luck to the intervention of their gods. Not satisfied merely with this, they aimed their bombards and cannons on both banks and fired them at the same time, causing much damage to our galleys: some of

---

[73]Iorga, "Cronica lui Wavrin," p. 92.

[74]Iorga, "Cronica lui Wavrin," p. 88.

them were hit and ruptured, and a few men were killed and others wounded... The Turk then aimed a massive bombard against the galleys, capable of firing very heavy stones. It fired three shots in the direction of our ships, provoking great fear among those on board; but, with the help of God, it exploded after the third shot without hitting or causing damage to any Christian vessel. This is worth emphasizing, because if it would have made a direct hit on a galley, it would have sent it directly to the bottom of the sea... And so, the Turks managed to cross in two days and two nights, something that they could not have done in fifteen if the galleys could have maneuvered..."[75] Thus, the Christian fleet had completely failed in its mission to prevent Ottoman forces from crossing into Europe.

As the King's army, which now included Vlad's eldest son Mircea and up to 4,000 Wallachian troops, set out from Nicopolis, they had no idea that the Sultan was at that very moment crossing the Bosphorus with reinforcements from Anatolia, determined to stop the crusaders and to punish the Hungarians for breaking the peace treaty. Orudj bin Adil tells us that shortly after the Christians departed from Nicopolis, having failed to take the citadel, "Firuz Bey Oglu Mehmed Bey, Sanjakbey of Nicopolis, set out with his garrison and with *akingi* from the surrounding area and attacked the enemy army from behind. He defeated them, causing them to lose many unbelievers, and captured several infidels dressed in mail and armor and sent them to the Sultan..."[76] The Ottoman chronicler clearly exaggerates the success of this attack which did nothing to impede the crusaders's advance, but Mehmed Bey did capture several prisoners and he sent them to Adrianople where Murad had briefly stopped to prepare his army before setting out to confront the crusaders. Their interrogation undoubtedly yielded valuable information about the Christian army and its strategy.

Assuming that the fleet could fulfil its mission and prevent the arrival of Ottoman reinforcements from Anatolia, the crusaders intended to proceed east to the coast and then south to Adrianople and Constantinople to join with the naval force protecting the straits. If they succeeded in doing this, they felt certain that the remaining Turkish forces in the Balkans would be forced to

---

[75]Iorga, "Cronica lui Wavrin," pp. 91-92.

[76]*Cronici turceşti*, vol. I, pp. 55-56.

Sixteenth century engraving of the Christian army advancing toward Varna

surrender. Still confident that the Ottomans could not gather an army to oppose them, the crusaders meandered about on their march to the sea, beseiging several Ottoman fortresses along the way. They plundered Trnovo, the former capital of the Second Bulgarian Empire, and took Razgrad, where they set fire to twenty-eight Turkish boats on the Beli Lam River. As they neared the Black Sea, the King sent out contingents to capture various Ottoman strongholds in the region; these included Shumen, Provadiya, Kavarna, and Dobrotitsa's former capital of Kaliakra on the Black Sea coast, among others.

Another fortress taken by the crusaders was Petrus where, according to the poem of the German minstrel Michel Beheim, Mircea distinguished himself in battle. Beheim based his account of the Varna campaign on the testimony of Hans Magest, a Saxon soldier who served in the King's army and fell captive to the Turks at Varna. He spent the next sixteen years in captivity before he escaped and met the German minstrel, to whom he imparted his recollections of the campaign, at the court of Holy Roman Emperor Frederick III of Habsburg around 1460.[77] Beheim recounts that Mircea took charge of the assault on the stone fortress surrounded by a deep moat filled with rain water. The young Prince had ladders brought up and ordered his men to storm the walls, but this attempt to take the citadel failed; the Turks repelled the attack and killed thirty Christians in the process. Undeterred, the crusaders continued to batter the parapets with their artillery. Finally, they breached the walls and it became apparent to the Ottoman garrison that they could no longer withstand the Christian assault. Some of the Turks tried to escape via a secret underground tunnel, but Mircea had discovered this passage and waited at the exit with his men, killing all those who attempted to escape by this route. The citadel fell to the crusaders and they killed all fifty Ottoman troops that comprised the garrison.[78]

The assault on Petrus took place around the end of October. It was here that the King first received the news that the fleet had failed to prevent the Ottomans from crossing the straits. Vladislav now had to concentrate his forces to prepare for the inevitable showdown with the Sultan. Despite this disappointing news, the Christians remained confident; Murad had managed to cross with a relatively small force of no more than 3,000 men, and they expected that the fleet would proceed up the Black Sea coast with supplies and reinforcements to join the King's army. The crusaders, however, had lost

---

77Karadja, "Poema lui Michel Beheim," pp. 5-7; Iorga, *Studii și documente*, p. LXIX; and Minea, "Vlad Dracul și vremea sa," p. 205, nt. 1. Michel Beheim was born in Württemberg, Germany on September 27, 1416. He learned the lyric arts from the poet Konrad of Weinsberg. In 1448, he set out on his own, serving at the courts of Duke Albert III of Bavaria in Munich and Duke Albrecht III of Brandenburg. After 1454, he went to the court of King Ladislas Posthumous. Before the King's death on November 23, 1457, he left for Vienna to the court of Frederick III of Habsburg. He remained there for the next ten years, during which time he met Hans Magest, before returning to his native Germany where he died around 1479.

78Karadja, "Poema lui Michel Beheim," pp. 35-36 (V. 541-574). In his introduction to Beheim's poem, Karadja mistakenly asserts that Vlad the Impaler took part in the campaign (p. 12) because of the erroneous widely-held belief at the time that Basarab had killed Mircea in 1442. Beheim calls Mircea, *Trakle*, a form of Dracula, but it must be remembered that Vlad and all of his sons were referred to using different variants on this name in contemporary sources.

valuable time in taking fortresses of little strategic importance. In addition to the men he lost in these needless confrontations, the King also had to detach hundreds of troops from his small army to garrison the conquered citadels; this was a tactical blunder because the crusaders could only hold these fortresses if they succeeded in defeating the Ottomans in a major battle. The stage for just such a confrontation was set when the Christian army, led by King Vladislav, Cardinal Cesarini, and John Hunyadi, reached Varna on the Black Sea coast on November 9.

A thriving sea harbor since ancient times, the crusaders found Varna desolate. Wavrin writes that in the once-flourishing port city, "no human dwellings were seen, only some old walls."[79] As evening fell, they set up camp in a valley outside the town, which Długosz describes as one thousand steps in width, bordered by a mountain range on one side and a lake on the other.[80] Unbeknownst to the Christians, Sultan Murad, who had left Adrianople with his army at the beginning of the month, had also arrived at Varna. Wavrin tells us that, at dusk, the crusaders "saw large fires up in the mountains in several different places. The King then asked what these fires could mean; and several Greek Christians found near him answered him that it could be some peasants burning dried leaves and grass so that they would have fresh hayfields in the spring. But John Hunyadi, the Voivode of Hungary, told the King, 'Sire, if those are not the Turks come to do battle against you, then you should no longer believe anything I say.'"[81] That they could make such a confusion in the first place indicates the relatively small size of the enemy force. Mircea, with a contingent of Wallachian calvary, joined the Transylvanian Voivode as he set out on a reconnaissance mission that evening to confirm the arrival of the Ottomans.[82] Wavrin continues: "They went until they heard their distinctive drumbeats; this being sufficient, they returned to inform the

---

[79]Iorga, "Cronica lui Wavrin," p. 93.

[80]Minea, *Informațiile românești*, p. 34.

[81]Iorga, "Cronica lui Wavrin," p. 93.

[82]Karadja, "Poema lui Michel Beheim," pp. 37-38 (v. 627-630). Beheim recounts that the Wallachian Voivode led the reconnaissance, while Wavrin mentions only Hunyadi. In all likelihood, Mircea accompanied the Transylvanian Voivode.

Cardinal and the King that the fires in question were set by the Turks and that the next morning they will do battle."[83]

Although he remained at Constantinople, Wavrin obtained his information about the events at Varna from Christians who had fled the battle, as well as others who had fallen prisoner to the Turks and "were ransomed by the Genoese after they were brought to the fortress of Adrianople. The Genoese in question then brought them to Constantinople where the Christians, thus saved from slavery, told of the terrible happenings of that fateful day."[84] After Hunyadi and Mircea had verified the presence of the Sultan's army in the vicinity, the crusaders held a council of war to decide what action to take at daybreak. Vladislav, displaying youthful enthusiasm, wanted to launch an attack on the Ottoman camp, but Hunyadi and Cardinal Cesarini advised a more prudent course of action. The Burgundian crusader recounts that "the council decided that the King should wait there because Varna was located in a valley and the Turk could not come down from the mountains to engage the Christians in battle except through some narrow passages, especially a well-travelled road used by wagons in earlier times to bring goods to and from the port."[85] As he had done during previous encounters with the Turks, the practical-minded Hunyadi once again sought to use the terrain to his advantage. Meanwhile, Cardinal Cesarini occupied himself with spiritual matters, seeking to ensure the crusaders's success in the forthcoming battle with the Turkish infidels by invoking God's help as he said mass for the troops. Both sides now anxiously awaited daybreak.

Two armies of comparable strength faced each other outside Varna on the morning of Tuesday, November 10, 1444. The confrontation that took place that day would decide the fate of the Balkans for the next five hundred years. Christian accounts typically exaggerate the size of Ottoman armies either to explain defeat or to make a victory seem all the more heroic; Beheim, employing poetic license, gives the preposterous figure of 200,000 men.[86] In

---

[83]Iorga, "Cronica lui Wavrin," p. 93.

[84]Iorga, "Cronica lui Wavrin," p. 97.

[85]Iorga, "Cronica lui Wavrin," p. 94.

[86]Karadja, "Poema lui Michel Beheim," p. 47 (v. 934). To understand fully the absurdity of such a claim, one most keep in mind that if the fires the crusaders saw

reality, the Christian force, comprised of perhaps 15,000 troops, outnumbered the Turks. Murad had no more than 12,000 soldiers with him at Varna. The advantage, however, still lay with the Sultan who had an experienced, disciplined army at the center of which stood 5,000 janissaries.[87] This elite fighting force composed the bulk of Murad's army. Wavrin writes that, "The Turk personally commanded the main body of soldiers made up of the janissary infantry. These janissaries are Christian renegades and slaves, all archers, who wear white hats."[88]

Both armies divided into three corps. For the crusaders, Hunyadi, with approximately 3,000 men, held the left flank, bordering Lake Devna, and defended the main road coming down from the mountains. King Vladislav and Cardinal Cesarini held the center, while Hunyadi's brother-in-law Michael Szilagyi and two Polish nobles commanded the right flank. Mircea and his Wallachian contingent formed the reserve. Atop the mountains overlooking Varna, Karadja Bey commanded the advance guard, composed of approximately 3,000 Anatolian troops, mainly calvary. As we have seen, Murad held the center with his janissaries, while Rumelian forces, under Balta Ogli, a Bulgarian renegade who had led the Ottoman delegation at Seghedin when Vladislav ratified the peace treaty, brought up the rear.

Before dawn, Hunyadi ordered his troops to barricade the main road with large stones and trees. The battle began, according to Wavrin, when Karadja Bey led his men down the mountain and "packed the road leading down to the valley, approaching the barricades like a wave; all of the Saracens followed their commander in a great throng, each wanting to be first. John Hunyadi, the Voivode, stood guard at the base of the road, armed with a large lance, and knocked Karadja

---

burning up in the mountains on the evening of November 9 were merely those of the Sultan's advance guard, it would have taken more than a week, given road conditions and the difficulties of transportation, for the remainder of the Ottoman army to assemble at Varna. Turkish sources likewise exaggerate the size of Christian forces to emphasize the heroism of Islamic troops. Unfortunately, many modern historical works continue to give credence to the distorted figures often found in medieval sources.

[87]Minea, "Vlad Dracul şi vremea sa," p. 250. Andreas de Palatio, a participant in the battle, provides this figure in his letter written shortly after the failed campaign.

[88]Iorga, "Cronica lui Wavrin," p. 94.

Bey off his horse, along with all those in the front lines." The death of the Ottoman commander and their failure to break through the Christian lines, "came as such a hard blow to the Turks that they tried to turn and to flee.... Then the Voivode of Hungary, who had immediately observed the unfortunate situation of the Turks, sent some of his men along another pass, behind the mountain, where they began to kill the Turks who were all bunched together. Their lines completely collapsed, as those who had massed on the lower portion of the main road wanted to return, while those behind them wanted to advance, and they began to fight among themselves. Thanks to these circumstances, the Hungarians could kill them at will with great ease."[89]

As the Turks took flight, the Wallachian troops, until now held in reserve, came up and joined in the pursuit. Chalkokondyles writes that "the Dacians, in the confusion of the battle, when they saw that the Asians began to flee, they did not stop there, but headed directly for the encampment of the Sultan, and they plundered the goods and supplies of the Sultan and killed the camels,... After they finished doing this, and were loaded with plunder, they did not return to the battle and resume their positions in the lines, but they started to return to their camp."[90] Długosz likewise comments on the Wallachians's predilection for plunder and their lack of enthusiasm for fighting the Turks, saying that "the Wallachians put up little resistance.... and distinguished themselves by killing camels."[91] The dismal performance of the Wallachian contingent is not surprising. Reluctant to join the doomed crusade, Vlad had placed his sixteen year old son Mircea, a boy with little military experience, in command of the troops. In addition, the animosity between Hunyadi and Vlad certainly made cooperation between Wallachian and Transylvanian forces all the more difficult. But the most compelling explanation for the withdrawal of Wallachian troops from the Christian battle lines after Hunyadi's initial victory is found in Beheim's poem. The German minstrel asserts that when Murad found out about the presence of Wallachian troops in the Christian army, he

---

[89] Iorga, "Cronica lui Wavrin," pp. 94-95.

[90] Chalcocondil, *Expuneri istorice*, p. 197 (VII, 333).

[91] Minea, *Informaţiile româneşti*, p. 35. Andreas de Palatio also confirms that the Wallachians put up little resistance to the Turks, see Minea, "Vlad Dracul şi vremea sa," p. 249.

sent word to Mircea, ordering him to leave the battle or he would have his two brothers beheaded; as a result, the Wallachians retired, abandoning the Christians to their fate.[92]

Hunyadi's victory provoked panic among the Ottomans. When they saw the Hungarians driving back the Anatolian troops along the main road, Balta Ogli and his Rumelian contingent began to take flight, but Wavrin ominously notes that "The Great Turk, together with the main body of his army remained unmoved atop the mountain."[93] Murad acted quickly to rally his panic-stricken troops. The *Chronicle of the Slovenes* records that the Sultan, "brought before them a banner bearing an icon of Christ and above the banner he placed the peace treaty that the King had made with them; and he began to shout: 'Oh crucified one! Oh crucified one! Look upon your mass of infidels, who have not been incited by me. I have given them no reason to break their oath and to renounce the peace treaty that they made with me!' And with these words he turned the pagan army around and directed them again toward the King's camp."[94]

The crusaders brimmed with confidence following their success in this first battle. As they reformed their lines, Christian leaders consulted about what action to take next. Both the King and the Cardinal wanted to take the offensive and to attack the Sultan's position atop the mountain, but Hunyadi opposed this idea. An intense debate followed. According to Wavrin's account, the Transylvanian Voivode pleaded with the King, "Sire, you have won the battle today. Do not allow yourself to be tempted to place this result in the hands of fate by going to do battle with those archers atop the mountain, for they will kill your horses and will cause you to lose many men." But several Polish and

---

[92]Karadja, "Poema lui Michel Beheim," p. 41 (v. 734-746). Mircea is referred to here as *Trakle*. These verses confirm that Beheim is speaking of Mircea and not Vlad, as some, including Ilie Minea and Nicolae Iorga, have contended, for the poet makes it clear that the Sultan mentions his two *brothers* (*zwen bruder*), and not *sons*, see Minea, "Vlad Dracul și vremea sa," p. 236; and Iorga, *Studii și documente*, vol. III, pp. LXXI-LXXII.

[93]Iorga, "Cronica lui Wavrin," p. 95.

[94]Șt. Nicolaescu, "Letopisețul Țării-Rumânești," in *RIAF*, XI:1 (1910), pp. 111-112, nt. 1.

Hungarian nobles, some perhaps jealous that the glory of the victory in the opening confrontation belonged to Hunyadi, told the King: "Sire, the Voivode finished his battle well and the honor is his. This second battle must be ours." But the Transylvanian Voivode, the most experienced military commander present, intervened again to try to convince Vladislav and Cesarini not to take this foolhardy action. Gentlemen, do not lose what you have won. The Turk, who is atop the mountain, can do you no harm. If he will come here to fight, he will do this to your advantage. Remain here, in good order; tomorrow he must retreat or come to surrender to you. The greatest part of your men who fought are tired and, besides this, they have lost many lances and arrows. And night is approaching, the sun has set: because of this you will be at a great disadvantages to fight or to attack in the dead of night against those who will await you well-rested and in good order... In the name of God, do not put yourselves in a position to lose what has been won, for the strongest part of the entire enemy army is defeated." But most of those present at the council did not want to lose the momentum they had gained. Other Hungarian nobles argued against Hunyadi, saying, "That's fine, but precisely because the greatest part of the power of the Turks is defeated, we should attack what has remained of them to follow-up our victory, for this time our moment has arrived. Because if the Turk escapes us again, he will return against us, but if he will be killed or defeated, Greece will be reconquered with ease. Let us strike while the iron is hot."[95] This sentiment carried the day and the twenty year old King ordered his men to prepare to assault the Ottoman positions on the mountain.

An anonymous Ottoman chronicle describes the ensuing Christian attack as "a hard fought battle," with projectiles flying through the air "like a rain of death."[96] Vladislav, eager for glory, personally led the charge on the Ottoman center. Victory seemed within the crusaders's grasp; Wavrin learned from survivors of the battle that "the King and his Hungarians penetrated the enemy lines so deeply that the rumor began to circulate that the King had engaged the

---

[95]Iorga, "Cronica lui Wavrin," pp. 95-96.

[96]*Cronici turceşti*, vol. I, p. 183; and N. Iorga, "Cronicele turceşti ca izvor pentru istoria românilor," ARMSI, series III, IX (1928-1929), p. 7.

Great Turk in hand to hand combat."[97] But, just as Hunyadi had predicted, the janissaries, well-rested and confident, displayed the skill that had won them renown as an elite fighting force and did not fold under pressure. Chalkokondyles writes that they "maintained their positions and fought remarkably well. Then the horse of the Hungarian Emperor was wounded in the leg with an axe and fell. When he fell, those around him paid no attention, for they did not even see what had happened because of the chaos all around them."[98] Disaster struck as Vladislav fell to the ground; Mehmed Neshri tells us that a janissary named "Kodja-Hîzîr came down from his horse and cut off his head."[99] After the death of the King, the crusaders began to lose heart, but, according to the same anonymous Ottoman chronicle, Hunyadi rallied his men and "did not allow them to scatter. It is said that the cursed John, seeing that his army began to disperse, spoke thusly to the infidels [Christians]: 'We have come here for our faith, not for the King.' In this manner he regained control over the army and turned it around, attacking a few more times."[100] Wavrin relates that despite this setback, "the Hungarians and the Poles fought vigorously until it became completely dark so that you could not know to which of the two sides to attribute victory."[101] Ultimately, the Christian assault failed and, with their lines shattered, the crusaders fled the field of battle.

As the Wallachian contingent comprised up to one-fourth of the Christian ranks, their withdrawal from the battle may have influenced its outcome. Mircea and his men did not, however, abandon the crusaders in their moment of need. In the confusion of the retreat, they stepped in to lead the survivors to safety; Andreas de Palatio, one of those who made it back across the Danube, admitted that only those guided by the Wallachians managed to escape.[102] The retreat was chaotic. In the darkness of night, as the Christian lines collapsed, Wavrin tells us that "some, then others, began to flee, each believing that he was defeated, and they gathered, here a hundred, there two hundred, here

---

[97]Iorga, "Cronica lui Wavrin," p. 96.

[98]Chalcocondil, *Expuneri istorice*, p. 198 (VII, 336).

[99]*Cronici turceşti*, vol. I, p. 124.

[100]*Cronici turceşti*, vol. I, p. 183.

[101]Iorga, "Cronica lui Wavrin," pp. 96-97.

[102]Minea, "Vlad Dracul şi vremea sa," pp. 246-247.

thirty, there forty."[103] Chalkokondyles adds that they fled in disorder and during the retreat many brave men fell, no few among the Dacians [Wallachians]."[104] These small groups straggled north, reaching the Danube during the next two to five days. Mircea returned safely and reported to his father all that had happened. Cesarini survived the battle, but Wavrin eventually learned that "the Cardinal of St. Angelo, as he crossed the Danube, was robbed and drowned by Wallachians."[105] The Cardinal, who carried a substantial sum of gold and numerous luxury goods, proved a tempting target for brigands who took advantage of the chaotic situation to enrich themselves. He was not the only one to suffer such a fate. Chalkokondyles insists that while many Hungarians fell at Varna, "Many more, however, perished at the hands of the Dacians during the retreat."[106] Perhaps the animosity between the Wallachian Prince and the Transylvanian Voivode contributed to this. John Hunyadi himself escaped, reaching the Danube after two days and two nights where he crossed into Wallachia at Floci, together with the Archbishop of Lemberg.[107]

---

[103]Iorga, "Cronica lui Wavrin," p. 97.

[104]Chalcocondil, *Expuneri istorice*, p. 199 (VII, 337).

[105]Iorga, "Cronica lui Wavrin," p. 97. Długosz gives a similar account of Cesarini's fate, specifying that the Cardinal carried significant amounts of gold, see Minea, *Informațiile românești*, p. 36. Beheim claims that the Turks captured Cesarini and took him to Adrianople where he was skinned alive, see Karadja, "Poema lui Michel Beheim," pp. 46-47 (v. 914-919). The German minstrel clearly invented this tale for literary effect to emphasize the barbarism of the infidels. If the Turks had captured Cesarini, they would have likely ransomed a prisoner of his status for a large sum of money. In addition, we could expect to find his capture mentioned in Ottoman chronicles. Chalkokondyles, on the other hand, writes that "Cardinal Julian, an exceptional man in every respect, was killed by the Turks during the retreat, see Chalcocondil, *Expuneri istorice*, p. 199 (VII, 337). Wavrin and Długosz, however, are the most reliable sources concerning the fate of the Cardinal.

[106]Chalcocondil, *Expuneri istorice*, p. 200 (VII, 339). Despite the obvious exaggeration, the Byzantine chronicler evokes the chaos of the Christian retreat.

[107]Minea, *Informațiile românești*, p. 36; and Minea, "Vlad Dracul și vremea sa," p. 252. Długosz blames Hunyadi for the disastrous retreat.

Soon after Hunyadi entered Wallachia, Vlad ordered his arrest. Chalkokondyles writes that the Transylvanian Voivode "was captured by Dracula, the Prince of Dacians, who was his enemy... he captured him with thoughts of revenge and imprisoned him under guard."[108] A well-informed contemporary German source, *Gräffliche Zillische Cronnica*, also reports that after Hunyadi fled the battle of Varna, "he was arrested by Dracola Weywoda in Wallachia and held in the mountains."[109] The exact place of his incarceration is unknown, but given that we know he went directly to Braşov upon his release, the fortress of Dâmboviţa is a likely location.

Vlad had several reasons for taking this seemingly rash action. He had not forgotten their violent dispute before Nicopolis a month earlier, and now, with the loss of the King, with whom he had close ties, the Wallachian Prince looked with trepidation upon his future relations with Hungary where Hunyadi became ever more powerful. The Transylvanian Voivode had not only supported his rival Basarab, but, as we have seen, even after Vlad had concluded peace with Hungary in the summer of 1444, he continued to work against the Wallachian Prince. Vornic Radu Popescu's seventeenth century chronicle, *Histories of the Princes of Wallachia*, says that the Wallachian Prince arrested Hunyadi "because his army had done great damage to the country."[110] Other sources claim that Vlad blamed the Transylvanian Voivode for the disaster of the Last Crusade. The *Chronicle of the Slovenes* records how "Prince Dragul, Voivode of Wallachia, captured him and put him in prison because of the great harm that John had done to the Christian cause."[111] Although in the heat of the moment he felt justified in arresting Hunyadi, Vlad quickly realized that he had made an imprudent decision.

Some Romanian historians have refused to accept that Vlad arrested Hunyadi in the aftermath of the Varna debacle. Influenced by nationalist sentiments, they have rejected the existence of a conflict between these two personalities, both of whom they claim as national heroes, at such a critical

---

[108]Chalcocondil, *Expuneri istorice*, pp. 199-200 (VII, 337-338).

[109]Iorga, *Acte şi fragmente*, vol. III, p. 15, emphasis added.

[110]Popescu, *Istoriile Domnilor Ţării Româneşti*, p. 19.

[111]Nicolaescu, "Letopiseţul Ţării-Rumaneşti," p. 112, nt. 1.

Vlad Dracul arresting John Hunyadi after the Varna debacle

By Octavian Ion Penda

moment for the Christian cause. Even the most recent synthesis, *The History of the Romanians*, published by the Romanian Academy, overlooks the dispute between the two leaders at this time.[112] But the evidence that Vlad ordered Hunyadi's arrest as he returned from Varna is overwhelming. Hungarian, Polish, German, Italian, Byzantine, Slavonic, and Wallachian chronicles all make mention of this incident; it is impossible that such a diverse array of sources all fabricated the same story independent of one another.

Vlad did not, however, retain the Transylvanian Voivode for very long. Chalkokondyles relates that "The Hungarians, as they arrived home, found out that John had been captured; and they considered it a great and unbearable thing for a Hungarian of high rank to be held captive by Dracula. They sent word to him to free John; if he refused, they threatened to treat him as an enemy

---

[112]*Istoria românilor*, vol. IV, pp. 313, 345. The grand treatise compiled under the auspicies of the Romanian Academy claims that "Vlad Dracul facilitated the return home of John and the surviving troops," and that "The defeat at Varna did not, however, break-up the common anti-Ottoman front, especially the alliances with the Romanian lands." This thesis dates back to the early twentieth century and ignores overwhelming evidence to the contrary, see Augustin Bunea, "Stăpânii Ţerii Oltului," in *Academia Româna. Discursuri de recepţiune*, XXXIV, Bucharest, 1910, p. 29. Nicolae Iorga tried to argue that mentions of Hunyadi's arrest by Vlad are merely confusions with the incident following the battle of Kosovo in 1448 when Serbian Despot George Branković retained the then Governor of Hungary, see Iorga, *Studii şi documente*, vol. III, p. XXIV. Ilie Minea also refused to admit that Vlad retained Hunyadi, dating the previously-mentioned diploma for the monasteries of Vodiţa and Tismana November 20, 1444, from Orşova, making it impossible for the Transylvanian Voivode to have been delayed en route. Minea refuses to accept September as the month it was issued because the King was then present at Orşova and Hunyadi could not have infringed upon royal prerogatives by granting such a diploma, see Minea, *Din trecutul stăpânirii româneşti asupra Ardealului*, p. 25; and Minea, "Vlad Dracul şi vremea sa," pp. 252-253. As we have already seen, the diploma invoked by Minea does not indicate the month of its issue and Alexandru Vasilescu later convincingly demonstrated that it is a forgery, see Vasilescu, "Diplomele lui Sigismund I, regele Ungariei, şi Ioan Huniade, voevodul Transilvaniei, dela Manastirea Tismana, sunt false." Others, while admitting that Hunyadi was detained, insist that it happened by mistake and that Vlad, as soon as he became aware of this, freed him and accompanied him to Transylvania, see Panaitescu and Stoicescu, "La participation des roumains à la bataille de Varna," p. 230; and Mureşanu, *John Hunyadi*, p. 111.

and to attack him with all their army. When he [Vlad] received this news from the Hungarians, he became fearful of his situation, that the Hungarians... might plan a change and strike to remove him from the throne. Then he [Vlad] freed him [Hunyadi] and entertained him and then sent him to Transylvania via Braşov."[113] By November 25, the Transylvanian Voivode was in Braşov where he confirmed the privilege of merchants from the Saxon city to trade freely throughout Transylvania, originally granted to them by Sigismund of Luxemburg,[114] probably as a sign of gratitude to officials there for helping to secure his release. This means that Vlad released him no later than November 23, after holding him prisoner for approximately one week.

As Hunyadi returned safely to Hungary, few yet realized the full dimensions of the catastrophe at Varna that forever fixed its place in history as the Last Crusade. Confused and contradictory reports reached Constantinople where Wavrin and Cardinal Condolmieri waited with the Christian fleet; "some said that the King returned victorious to his country," the Burgundian crusader frustratingly noted, "while others said that he had his head cut off."[115] But soon the picture of an Ottoman victory emerged. The Byzantine Emperor had prepared for the possibility of such an outcome when he sent George Sphrantzes on his diplomatic mission to both sides on the eve of the crusade. Now John VIII, one of the leading proponents of the crusade, had to swallow his pride and dispatch emissaries to make peace with the Sultan and to congratulate him on his victory. Murad, believing that he had expunged the threat to the Empire, responded favorably to the Byzantine Emperor's overtures and, within a month of his victory at Varna, the Sultan once again retired from public life.

Eugenius IV was disheartened when he learned of the failure of the crusade. Hunyadi wrote to the Pope from Pest on May 11, 1445, informing him of the castrophe suffered by the Christian army at Varna, and blaming the failure of the crusade on the rulers of Wallachia, Bulgaria, Albania, and Constantinople, claiming that they did not provide the help that they had promised and, even

---

[113]Chalcocondil, *Expuneri istorice*, p. 199 (VII, 338).

[114]Doc. 2513 in *Urkundenbuch*, vol. V, p. 155.

[115]Iorga, "Cronica lui Wavrin," p. 97.

more, had acted treacherously.[116] It is no coincidence that Vlad is listed first among those incriminated by the Transylvanian Voivode. Yet, despite the debacle at Varna, neither Hunyadi, nor the Pope realized that it sounded the death knell for the age of the crusades that had begun in the eleventh century and marked the consolidation of Ottoman rule in the Balkans that would extend for over half a millennium. Within a decade, Constantinople would fall to the Turks. The crusade he had worked so tirelessly to organize having ended in distaster, Eugenius IV died in 1447 without having achieved his great dream of liberating Europe from the Turks during his pontificate. Although his successors continued to militate for joint Christian action to drive the Ottomans from Europe, the prerequisites necessary for such an undertaking had ceased to exist.

Everyone knew that, without Christian unity, attempts to drive the Turks from Europe were doomed to failure. Despite the efforts of such ardent proponents of crusading as Pope Pius II, increasing divisiveness plagued Europe. The rise of powerful rival states and continuing religious dissension, which within a century culminated in the Protestant Reformation, turned Christian Europe against itself. The crusading ideal could still inspire ambitious plans such as that for the creation of an anti-Ottoman League between France, Bohemia, and Venice in 1462, a sort of European Union of the fifteenth century. The eminent historian John Hale explains that, according to this initiative, "the other powers were to be invited to join. All must promise not to make war among themselves and to maintain a common security force as well as to contribute to a crusading army. Given its large scale, the project went further: there was to be a common law court to adjudicate members' quarrels, a general assembly of national representatives meeting regularly, and a servicing bureaucracy. It looked beyond a mechanism to push back the Turks to a permanent control of European divisiveness."[117] But such a proposals contravened the spirit of the times and could not overcome the problems facing this troubled age.

The death of Vladislav abruptly ended the union of the Hungarian and Polish Crowns, thereby weakening anti-Ottoman resistance as the two most powerful

---

[116]Doc. DXCV in Hurmuzaki, *Documente*, vol. I, part 2, pp. 715-717.

[117]Hale, *The Civilization of Europe in the Renaissance*, p. 133.

Christian states in Eastern Europe no longer presented a common front. In addition, both countries underwent a period of political turmoil in the aftermath of the Varna disaster. Because of disputes within the nobility, it took over two years before Vladislav's younger brother, Casimir, the Grand Duke of Lithuania, agreed to accept the Polish Crown. Casimir finally assumed the throne on June 25, 1447, thus restoring the union of Poland and Lithuania. Hungary also struggled with the question of succession. Many refused to believe that Vladislav had perished at Varna and some even deliberately tried to hide this fact for as long as possible because, in accordance with previous agreements between the opposing factions, Ladislas Posthumous was his designated heir. Hunyadi, who understood the need for a strong monarch to lead the struggle against the Ottomans, tried to offer the crown to Alphonso V of Naples and Aragon, to avoid the prospect of a child on the throne, the peril of which Shakespeare later deried in *Richard III*: "Woe to that land that's govern'd by a child!"[118] After prolonged negotiations, the rival groups reached a compromise; on June 5, 1446, the Diet at Pest recognized the boy Ladislas Posthumous as King, but unanimously chose Hunyadi as Governor of Hungary until he attained the age of majority. The Diet also confiscated the vast estates held by Serbian Despot George Branković in Hungary because he had refused to support the Christian coalition during the Varna Campaign. After a meteoric rise, John Hunyadi had succeeded in becoming the wealthiest and most powerful man in the Kingdom of Hungary.

But, as we have seen, in the immediate aftermath of the disaster at Varna, there was great confusion over Vladislav's fate. Many believed that both the King and the Cardinal survived the battle. The Ottomans, however, claimed that Vladislav had died in the fighting. Wavrin relates that they sent emissaries to the Venetian Captain Pietro Loredano, whose fleet stood at anchor before Gallipoli, and "they asked him to send someone to them, to the fortress of Gallipoli, so that they could show him the head of the King of Hungary. Loredano sent some of his men and the Turks showed them the head of a man with long blonde hair packed in a wooden crate filled with cotton. Upon their return, they told their Captain all that they had seen. But, on the other hand, most who had escaped slavery said that they had seen the King on several occassions and that he had black hair. Thus, things remained unclear and no

---

[118]Act II, Scene III.

one could imagine what had become of the King."[119] Ottoman sources claim that the King's head was preserved in a barrel of honey and sent to Brusa where it was washed in the Nilufer River and placed on a pike and carried through the city during celebrations to commemorate the victory at Varna.[120] Rumors that Vladislav did not perish at Varna persisted for several years. These gave birth to a legend according to which the young King, full of remorse for having committed perjury by breaking the solemn oath he had taken at Seghedin, for which God punished him by his cruel defeat at Varna, became a hermit and, guarding his anonymity, he followed the paths of pilgrims and finally ended up in Spain where he died some ten years later.[121]

By the time they had learned of the defeat of the crusaders at Varna, it was too late in the season for the Christian fleet protecting the straits to return home. Lord Wavrin and Cardinal Condolmieri decided to winter at Constantinople and Pera, intending to head back to their respective countries in the spring. But soon, Wavrin tells us, a rumor began to circulate in Constantinople that "some of the Greeks had saved him [Vladislav] and brought him to a powerful fortress where they kept him hidden. Some of the great nobles from Hungary accorded this rumor more credibility than any other, and they insistently and repeatedly asked Lord Wavrin to consent to enter the Black Sea in the spring and to voyage to all of the fortresses belonging to the Christians to see if the aforementioned King of Hungary could not somehow be found."[122] After consulting with Cardinal Condolmieri, Wavrin agreed to the Hungarians's request and began making plans to set out from Constantinople in the spring of 1445 in search of the lost King.

---

[119]Iorga, "Cronica lui Wavrin," pp. 97-98.

[120]Mihail P. Guboglu, "Românii în bătălia de la Varna (10 Nov. 1444) după izvoare turco-islamice şi europene," in *RA*, XLVII:3 (1985), p. 276.

[121]Pall, "Un moment decisif," p. 118.

[122]Iorga, "Cronica lui Wavrin," p. 99.

Chapter X

Seekers of the Lost King

*"I would like to make it clear to Your Excellency that we stand behind
our words, that we are devoted to the welfare of Christianity and that
we are pleased to have the opportunity now to work for this to the extent
that it is in our power to do so. But evil arises from this because we
Christians do not abandon our sinful ways and we quarrel amongst
ourselves."*

—Prince Basarab the Young to Toma, Burgermeister of Sibiu, 1481[1]

With the fate of King Vladislav uncertain, Walerand de Wavrin,
Captain General of the Burgundian fleet, decided not to return home
in the spring of 1445, but rather to go in search of the lost King. He
thought to voyage up the Black Sea Coast to the Danube and then to proceed
up river to Buda, hoping to obtain precise information about Vladislav's fate.
Wavrin's chronicle recalls that he "sent for the Hungarians who had been
ransomed and asked them if, together with all of his galleys, he could not
somehow navigate up the Danube all the way to Hungary. But they did not
know how to answer him. Then he summoned two sailors from Greece who

---

[1]Doc. 8 in Silviu Dragomir, *Documente nouă privitoare la relaţiile Ţării Româneşti cu
Sibiul în secolii XV şi XVI*, Bucharest, 1935, pp. 17-19.

had travelled the Danube on other occasions. Questioned in the presence of the Hungarians about the nature of the river in question and if he could reach Hungary via the Danube, they replied that he could not, but that he could very easily get to the fortress of Lykostomo [Kilia] or to Brilago [Brăila] and from there safely send someone overland to Hungary."[2]

Wavrin's discovery that he could not reach Hungary by ship reveals an important factor that influenced the historical development of Southeastern Europe. Until the end of the nineteenth century, the Iron Gates, with their dangerous rock formations lurking just below the water's surface, cut off the lower Danube from Central Europe. This impeded economic and cultural ties with Austria and Germany. Ships carrying goods from Vienna or Buda were unloaded at Belgrade; from there merchandise was transported overland to Sofia, Adrianople, and Constantinople. On the other hand, the Iron Gates helped to preserve the independence of the Principalities of Wallachia and Moldavia because the lower Danube did not prove useful to the Ottomans as they penetrated into Central Europe.[3] The river, which the ancient Greeks called the Istros, marked a logical and defensible border for Ottoman expansion in the Balkans. By garrisoning a series of fortresses along the course of the Danube they could effectively secure their hold over the region; these same considerations had long before led the Roman Empire to withdraw from its provinces in Dacia. In addition, the Danube also presented a significant natural obstacle in the way of Ottoman expansion. The fifteenth century Turkish chronicler Kivami illustrates this by recounting a debate at the Porte during Murad's reign: "The Danube itself is a water for *gazis*. Each year it takes the lives of ten thousand Turks, without swords or knives, and without shedding blood."[4]

Once he understood that he could not reach Hungary by ship, Wavrin relates that he "arrived at the decision, in agreement with the Hungarians and with his own knights and nobles, to enter the Black Sea and to investigate all

---

[2]Iorga, "Cronica lui Wavrin," p. 100.

[3]P.P. Panaitescu, *Interpretări românești*, Bucharest, 1947, p. 159.

[4]Mihail Gubloglu, ed., *Crestomație turcă*, Bucharest, 1978, p. 178, emphasis added. *Gazi* in this context means martyr for Islam. It is also used with the general sense of a warrior for Islam.

of the fortresses along the coast, going as far as the fortress of Lykostomo, which belonged to the Prince of Wallachia, to see if they could not obtain reliable information about the fate of the King of Hungary. At the same time, he would transport the Christian knights and nobles who had fallen prisoner at the battle of Varna home at his own expense. And if the King could not be found, and no reliable information about him could be obtained, as to whether he was dead or alive, then he would send Messieurs Pietre Vast and his secretary, Master Robert Lobain [to Hungary], together with certain letters addressed to the King, which would be given to him if he was found alive, as well as to the nobles of Hungary. The latter were invited to take up arms, as many of them as possible, and to return to Greece that same season and to unite with them [Wavrin and his men] as they have seven or eight galleys at their disposal with which they will proceed as far up the Danube as they can to effect a junction."[5] Having made this decision, the Seekers of the Lost King now began to prepare for the upcoming campaign as they awaited the arrival of spring to set out on their quest.

The sole source for details of the Danubian campaign of 1445 is Wavrin's account, which he related to his uncle Jehan de Wavrin, lord of Forestel, upon his return to Burgundy. The latter included it in his chronicle, *Anchiennes Chroniques d'Engleterre*. It also provides important information about the life of Vlad Dracul between 1442 and 1445. Walerand de Wavrin served as counsellor and Chamberlain to Duke Philip the Good of Burgundy; prior to assuming command of the Burgundian fleet sent to participate in the Varna Crusade, he distinguished himself at the siege of Calais, in 1436, an episode in the extended conflict between England and France that became known as the Hundred Years' War.

Apart from Wavrin, an anonymous fifteenth century Venetian chronicle mentions the campaign, based on a letter of the Bailiff of Constantinople reporting that the Papal Legate and the Captain of the Duke of Burgundy set out for the Danube to fight the Turks with seven galleys and a galliota and, they beseiged a fortress called Tusia.[6] The Italian humanist Giovanni Maria Angiolello likewise alludes to the events described by Wavrin in his *Historia*

---

[5]Iorga, "Cronica lui Wavrin," p. 100.

[6]Iorga, *Acte și fragmente*, vol. III, p. 11.

Turchesca.[7] The campaign of 1445 is also mentioned in a decree issued by the Transylvanian Vice-Voivodes George de Bala, Marcus de Herepe, and Stephen de Janusy on January 29, 1447,[8] as well as a conveyance granted by John Hunyadi as Governor of Hungary on October 12, 1447, for Nicholas Pogan and Emeric Zyndy, both of whom distinguished themselves during this campaign,[9] but neither document provides any detailed information.

After he reached his decision, "Lord Wavrin met with the Cardinal and explained to him in detail what he planned to do. As for the Cardinal, he had only words of praise for this initiative, declaring that if the Hungarians will gather a large force, and if he will be informed of this in time, that he will also come."[10] After he obtained Condolmieri's approval, Wavrin immediately began making preparations for the upcoming campaign: "he ordered the patrons, attendants, and sailors to prepare the galleys, and Jean Bayart, treasurer of the army, to purchase victuals and all of the things necessary to outfit the galleys for the voyage."[11] As Lent had already begun, they determined that the fleet would not be ready to depart until after the Easter holiday, which fell on March 28 that year. Wavrin spent Easter at Pera, near Constantinople, praying for the success of his mission. A day or two later, the fleet was ready as planned to set out in search of the lost King.

The Christians knew that they had nothing to fear from the Ottomans at sea, but they were cognizant of the fact that they could not match them on land. Wavrin realized that when the Turks saw the Burgundian galleys entering the Black Sea, they would remain on the alert all along the coast to see where they

---

[7]Donado Da Lezze, *Historia Turchesca*, Bucharest, 1909, p. 13. The editor of this edition, Ion Ursu, mistakenly attributed the chronicle to Donado Da Lezze. It provides only vague and confused information concerning the events of 1445.

[8]Doc. 2564 in *Urkundenbuch*, vol. V, pp. 185-186; and Doc. LVII in Hurmuzaki, *Documente*, vol. XV, part 1, p. 34. Hurmuzaki incorrectly dated this decree July 2, 1447, the Sunday after the feast of Saints Peter and Paul, but the correct date is January 29, "die dominica proxima past festum Sancti Pauli."

[9]*Urkundenbuch*, vol. V, pp. 210-211; and Doc. 284 in *DRH, D*, p. 394.

[10]Iorga, "Cronica lui Wavrin," p. 100.

[11]Iorga, "Cronica lui Wavrin," p. 101. The Burgundian fleet was leased from the Venetians and the owners of the galleys and their attendants accompanied them.

might disembark. Prior to the technological advances in the latter half of the fifteenth century that made possible Columbus's voyage across the Atlantic, medieval galleys generally navigated within sight of the shore, and their large crews meant that they required almost daily provisioning, especially for fresh water. Because of this, Wavrin points out that "the things those aboard the galleys needed to gather on land could not be obtained except by unexpectedly disembarking, without the knowledge of the Turks, seizing everything that they could get their hands on and then quickly returning aboard the galleys."[12] To deceive the Ottomans as to their intentions, the Burgundian commander decided to divide his fleet. He and Pietre Vast set out with two galleys up the Greek coast, while three other galleys, under Geoffrey de Thoisy and Regnault de Comfide, proceeded along the Asian shore in the direction of Trebizond. The two groups planned to meet halfway around the sea at Tana, a Venetian colony at the mouth of the Don River.

With the Hungarians who had been ransomed after falling prisoner to the Ottomans at Varna aboard his vessels, Wavrin advanced up the European coast of the Black Sea until he reached Messembria, a port city under Byzantine control, where he could safely take on provisions. The Greek commander of the fortress told him of a Hungarian noble who had escaped from the Turks and had taken refuge in the citadel two months before. He asked Wavrin to take this man aboard his galleys, explaining that he feared that if he continued to shelter him there it might provide the Ottomans with a pretext to besiege the town. This news provoked a great deal of excitement among those who had set out in search of the lost King, and for a moment it seemed that their mission would be capped with success. Wavrin tells us that, "When this news reached the ears of the other Hungarians aboard the galleys,... they imagined that it could be their King. But when they investigated more closely, they saw that it was not what they thought, but only an ordinary nobleman from their country whom they took with them."[13] Having taken on food and water, the Burgundian galleys left Messembria the following day.

Enjoying favorable winds, the galleys continued north until they reached Panguala (Mangalia), ancient Kallatis, founded in the sixth century B.C. by

---

[12]Iorga, "Cronica lui Wavrin," p. 102.

[13]Iorga, "Cronica lui Wavrin," pp. 102-103.

Greek colonists from Heraclea, a city-state located along the European coast of the Sea of Marmara. Wavrin recounts a story according to which the Amazon Queen Panthasilea founded the port city after Hercules and Theseus had passed through the realm of the legendary female warriors to fight Hippolyta and Menalipa. Herodotus claims that the Amazons came to this region after a war with the Greeks in which they were taken captive and transported by ship; they managed to kill their captors, but, as they did not know how to sail, they could not navigate their way back home and ran aground in Scythia. Here they mixed with the local population. "They have a marriage law," writes the father of history, "which forbids a girl to marry until she has killed an enemy in battle. Some of their women, unable to fulfill this condition, grow old and die in spinsterhood."[14] The interest Wavrin consistently displays in the legends and sites of antiquity reflects the spirit of the early Renaissance. The Burgundian crusader described Panguala as "very strange.... The port is protected by a large wall which extends into the waters of the sea, with a width of thirty to forty feet, enclosing the port and its entryway. In ancient times, no one could enter the realm of the Amazons, which today is called Scythia, by way of the sea, except by passing between the coast and that wall which extended for some twenty French leagues. But, at present, the said wall is ruined and collapsed in several places, and because of this, many ships, when they have the misfortune to be thrust there by storms and bad weather, strike against it and are destroyed. But despite this, from the surviving ruins one can get an idea of the ancient configuration of the place, when both the wall and the port were standing."[15]

The next day, the Burgundian galleys made their way to the mouth of the Danube, which Wavrin describes as "a wonderfully large river that empties into the Black Sea." He then continues: "They entered the mouth of the river and strove until they arrived at the fortress of Lykostomo, where they found the Wallachians." His account unequivocally proves that Kilia remained in Wallachian hands in 1445. Vlad had recovered the fortress near the mouth of the Danube, which his father had seized from the Genoese in 1403, but which the Moldavians had occupied during the reign of Dan II, in 1439 when he

---

[14]Herodotus, *The Histories*, pp. 277–279.
[15]Iorga, "Cronica lui Wavrin," p. 103.

intervened in the conflict between Moldavian Princes Stephen and Iliaș, after negotiating a marriage alliance with the latter. It is unknown if Kilia remained a Wallachian possession during the brief reign of Basarab II or if Vlad recovered it for a second time after he resumed the throne in 1444. But given the interest of Basarab's protector, John Hunyadi, in the Danubian port, and the fact that the Wallachian Prince had formed an alliance with Stephen of Moldavia by marrying one of his daughters, in all likelihood the fortress had not changed hands since Vlad first acquired it.

Upon their arrival at Kilia, the Burgundians sought information about Vladislav's fate, but the Wallachian officials stationed there could tell them nothing. As initially planned, Wavrin disembarked the freed Hungarian prisoners he had taken aboard his galleys, along with his embassy led by Pietre Vast, to send them overland to Hungary. The Burgundian commander undoubtedly chose to have them go to Hungary via Wallachia, instead of Moldavia, on the recommendation of Byzantine Emperor John VIII who enjoyed close relations with Vlad since the latter had spent several years at his court. Having learned nothing of the King's fate during their voyage up the Black Sea coast, Wavrin relates that the Hungarians "advised him to write a letter to John Hunyadi, the Voivode of Hungary, inviting him to put together a new army and to return to Greece, promising in turn that he would enter the Danube with six or seven galleys and proceed up river as far as possible to unite with him. Lord Wavrin entrusted it to Monsieur Pietre Vast, his secretary [Robert Lobain], and a nobleman called Jacques Faucourt. The Hungarians and the Wallachians calculated how much time it would take Monsieur Pietre Vast to complete this journey and they determined that over a month could pass before he returned. As a result, Lord Wavrin decided to reenter the Black Sea and to voyage along its coast from the point where they had left off to Caffa in the Thane [Azov] Sea and, after a month, to return and to go to city called Brilago [Brăila] to wait for the return of Monsieur Pietre Vast."[16] Having

---

[16]Iorga, "Cronica lui Wavrin," pp. 103-104. Wavrin uses Greece to refer to the lands south of the Danube. Nicolae Iorga identifies Pietre Vast as a Spanish Castillian or possibly Portuguese knight, (Vasq or Vasque), following the crusading tradition of Prince Pedro of Portugal who fought the Turks alongside Dan II and Sigismund, see Nicolae Iorga, "Les aventures 'Sarrazines' des Français de Bourgogne au XVᵉ siècle," in Constantin Marinescu, ed., *Melanges d'histoire générale*, Cluj, 1927, p. 17. There

agreed upon this plan, Pietre Vast took his leave from Wavrin and the Burgundian embassy set out from Kilia in the company of the Hungarians who were finally returning home after the debacle at Varna.

After raising anchor at Kilia, Wavrin continued his voyage in the Black Sea, hoping to encounter Ottoman vessels which he could engage in combat. The Burgundian galleys next stopped at Moncastro (Akkerman, today Belgorod-Dnestrovskiy in Ukraine), which Wavrin mistakenly identifies as a Genoese port. Although the Genoese held this fortress until the early fifteenth century and merchants from the seafaring Italian city-state continued to dominate trade in the port, at this time it was ruled by Stephen II of Moldavia who had recently improved its fortifications.[17] A bustling port, the Burgundian commander met here sailors from Trebizond and other Black Sea states. Still hoping to do battle with the Turks, Wavrin asked them if they had seen any Ottoman ships at sea, but they replied that the Sultan had forbidden Turkish naval vessels to leave port after he learned that the powerful Christian galleys had entered the Black Sea. Disappointed at this news, Wavrin went on to Caffa. Along the way, however, he had the good fortune to encounter three Ottoman ships laden with grain which he seized and took in tow to Caffa. At the key Genoese port city in the Black Sea, he met the three galleys commanded by Geoffrey de Thoisy and Regnault de Comfide. Wavrin's officers had underwent a series of adventures of their own since they began their voyage along the Asian coast; Thoisy had been taken prisoner in Georgia, but was later freed after the intervention of the Greek Emperor of Trebizond. Having reassembled his fleet, Wavrin now made his way back to the Danube with his two galleys to meet Pietre Vast at Brăila, while the three remaining ships made

---

is, however, no evidence to support this speculation. All we know for certain is that Pietre Vast was Wavrin's adjutant in the service of Duke Philip the Good of Burgundy.

[17]We know this from a Greek inscription attesting to the renovation of the citadel's fortifications carried out by Stephen after he took the city from his brother Iliaş, dated 10 November 6948, see Ioan Bogdan, "Inscripţiile dela Cetatea-Albă," pp. 313-325, who places it in 1440, but, as the inscription is in Greek and the Byzantine style new year fell on September 1, it can be dated November 10, 1439, even though the Moldavian chancellery, owing to Polish influence, used January 1 as the beginning of the new year.

their way back to Constantinople where they awaited further instructions from their commander.

The Burgundian fleet arrived at Wallachia's most important commercial port around the middle of May 1445. Johann Schiltberger, the young squire who had fallen prisoner to the Turks at Nicopolis in 1396 and escaped bondage thirty years later, describes Brăila as "a port for boats and ships with which merchants bring goods from the land of the infidels."[18] Three days after Wavrin laid anchor at Brăila, Pietre Vast, Robert Lobain, and Jacques Faucourt arrived there, accompanied by a Hungarian emissary. Vast reported to his commander that the Burgundian delegation had fortuitously reached Buda while the Diet was in session. The Burgundians were surprised to learn that, despite the presence of John Hunyadi in the Hungarian capital, they could obtain no certain information about the fate of King Vladislav. What they did not know was that the Transylvanian Voivode was party to an elaborate plan set afoot by Palatine Lawrence Héderváry, Dionsius Szécsi, the Archbishop of Strigoniu, and other members of the regency council. They conspired to feed doubts about the King's fate and to postpone declaring Vladislav dead so as to prolong their mandate to rule in his stead, thereby thwarting the ambitions of Frederick III to exert his right to rule the Kingdom as legal guardian of the legitimate heir Ladislas Posthumous, and buying time to negotiate a settlement to the succession dispute so as to avert another civil war. Just before the arrival of the Burgundian embassy in Buda, the Diet had decided that if Vladislav was confirmed dead, Ladislas Posthumous would be recognized as his successor on the condition that Frederick III renounce his tutorial rights and return the crown of St. Stephen.[19]

When Vast presented his credentials as emissary of the Captain General of Duke Philip of Burgundy, the Hungarians immediately brought him before the Diet where he handed over the letters addressed to the King and to John Hunyadi outlining Wavrin's proposal. After several days of intense discussions, the Hungarian leaders called back Pietre Vast to ask him what

---

[18]Holban, ed., *Călători străini*, vol. I, p. 30.

[19]Muresanu, *John Hunyadi*, pp. 113-117. Héderváry had gone so far as to forge a letter from John Hunyadi, dated November 20, 1444, from near Gallipoli, claiming the success of the campaign led by the young King.

assurances he could provide that Wavrin would meet them at the Danube with his galleys should they gather a land army. The Burgundian emissary replied: "I have his [Wavrin's] secretary [Robert Lobain] here with me and he has with him a blank paper signed by his commander upon which we can set forth all of the promises you require of him, on the condition, of course, that these are lawful and reasonable, and that you will give us assurances as to the number of soldiers that you can gather and set the time and place where we will meet one another." After Vast withdrew, a heated debate ensued, during which they interrogated several of the ransomed prisoners who had returned to Hungary with Burgundian help as to the veracity of Wavrin's proposal. With the succession crisis unresolved, this was no time for Hungary to commit its resources to a full-scale war with the Turks, all the more so because Murad's abdication and internal troubles within the Ottoman Empire offered them a respite by preventing the Turks from taking the offensive. Still, none of the factions struggling for power in Hungary at that time could refuse the crusaders outright and risk offending the Pope who sanctioned their mission. But the Burgundian proposal also presented opportunities. The faction opposed to Hunyadi, which included Ladislas Garai and others, saw it as a chance to send the powerful Transylvanian Voivode, who would be charged to lead any campaign against the Ottomans, away during this critical time, hoping to use his absence to gain the upper hand in the ongoing political struggle. Hunyadi and his supporters were well aware of this. To undermine this ploy, they sought to impose conditions on Hungarian participation that could delay the campaign or cause it to be aborted.

When they had reached an agreement as to how to respond to the Burgundian proposal, Hungarian officials again summoned Pietre Vast before them and presented their offer. They asked that Wavrin bring eight galleys up the Danube to Nicopolis, the sight of previous joint Burgundian-Hungarian military action against the Turks during the campaign of 1396, in mid-August, promising that they would join him there with 8,000 to 10,000 troops at that date. Apart from this, they insisted that Pietre Vast meet with the Prince of Wallachia on his way back and convince Vlad to participate with a large army, and that he go to Constantinople to bring back the Ottoman pretender Daud Celebi. Vast accepted these terms in Wavrin's name and set out for Brăila.

Because of his tense relations with Vlad, the Transylvanian Voivode, who knew of the Wallachian Prince's reluctance to join anti-Ottoman enterprises, deemed it unlikely that the Burgundians could persuade him to take part in a joint military undertaking. At the same time, there was nothing unusual about his requirement that the Wallachians also participate in the campaign because without them there was little chance of success for such an endeavor. Determined to fulfill his commitments, Pietre Vast stopped off at Târgoviște on his way back, where he had an audience with the Wallachian Prince. Unexpectedly, Vlad "promised him his full support, on the condition that the aforesaid Captain from Burgundy kindly remain with his galleys at Brăila until his people finish harvesting the grain from the fields. After that, he will gather as many soldiers as he can, so that, on the date and at the place established, he can be alongside those from Hungary. But before anything else, he wanted to speak with the Captain from Burgundy, but, as he was too far away, he promised to send his son [Mircea] to Brăila to enter into contact with the Captain, which he immediately did. Monsieur Pietre Vast then told the Prince of Wallachia that, as for himself, he was going to Constantinople, to the Emperor, [John VIII] to ask him for Soussy [Daud Celebi], a noble from Turkey, as well as five or six galleys, but that, upon his return, if he [Vlad] could be within five or six leagues of Brăila, and if he could send horses for the aforesaid Captain, he [Vast] would be able to bring him [Wavrin] and present him to him [Vlad]."[20]

The fact that Vlad readily agreed to take part in the anti-Ottoman campaign is not as surprising as it might seem at first. Since he had contributed to the Varna campaign, and especially after Murad's abdication, Vlad's relations with the Ottomans had taken a turn for the worse, and Turkish troops stationed along the Danube made frequent raids into Wallachia. These marauders inflicted substantial losses on the Principality. Vlad insisted that the Burgundian galleys remain at Brăila until the harvest was completed, not only to ensure that he could muster all available manpower, but also because he knew that their presence on the Danube would intimidate the Turks who would

---

[20]Iorga, "Cronica lui Wavrin," pp. 107-108. Vast asked Vlad if he could be within five or six leagues of Brăila, approximately fifteen to twenty miles, so that Wavrin could make the journey, meet with Vlad, and return to the port all in the same day.

not risk any provocative action. Thus, he assured his people of a peaceful harvest. Apart from this, Vlad jumped at the opportunity to induce the crusaders to direct their military resources against Ottoman positions along the Danube, thereby strengthening his own border defenses.

After his successful meeting with Vlad, Pietre Vast returned to Brăila and reported all of this to Wavrin who was very pleased at the success of his mission with everything that his emissary had agreed to in his name. The Burgundian commander now drafted a letter to Cardinal Condolmieri, informing him of all that Pietre Vast had accomplished in Hungary and Wallachia, and calling on him to keep his promise to join him on the Danube with as many galleys as he could bring. He also wrote to his lieutenant, Gauvain Quieret, who, because of illness, had remained behind at Pera with one of the Burgundian galleys, to join him. In addition, Wavrin instructed Vast to bring along a large bombard that he had left behind on one of the ships, as well as cannonballs and powder. Pietre Vast then boarded a small commercial ship that had brought goods from Constantinople to Brăila and now prepared for its return voyage.

Upon his arrival in the Byzantine capital, Wavrin's adjutant worked diligently to carry out his instructions. He convinced Cardinal Condolmieri to join the campaign with three of the papal galleys. Shortly after he reached Constantinople, Vast learned that Geoffrey de Thoisy and Gauvain Quieret had returned to Burgundy with one of the galleys, but, as three others remained in port at the Bosphorus and Wavrin already had two at Brăila, he could still provide the eight galleys that he had agreed upon with the Hungarians. Vast also convinced John VIII to allow Daud Celebi to join the crusaders, and he secured munitions in accordance with Wavrin's instructions. He then set out for Brăila with one of the galleys, eight to ten days ahead of the Cardinal and the other two Burgundian ships, arriving at the Wallachian port during the latter half of July.

While Pietre Vast made his way back from Constantinople, Vlad, as previously agreed, had set up camp in the vicinity of Brăila. When Vast arrived, Mircea, who had remained at the Wallachian port with Wavrin awaiting his return, sent word to his father to send horses so that he could bring the Burgundian commander to him. He did so immediately, and at the end of

July Vlad received Wavrin at his camp. The purpose of the meeting was to establish the details of the upcoming campaign; among those present were Mircea, Vast, and the Hungarian emissary who had accompanied him back from Buda. The Wallachian Prince thanked Wavrin for maintaining peace along the borders of his country during the harvest season as the Burgundian presence had made the Turks reluctant to conduct raids north of the Danube. He promised to provide sufficient grain and carts for transport to supply Wavrin's men. The two leaders then decided that after the remaining galleys arrived from the Byzantine capital, the Wallachians would accompany them on land as they proceeded up river to attack Silistra, which Wavrin learned "had previously been seized from the Wallachians and ruined so that none of its walls remained intact, but that it had since been rebuilt and repopulated. This was a crossing point that caused great damage to the land of the Wallachians." Apart from this, the Prince of Wallachia promised that, "to lead the galleys along the river, he would place at their disposal forty or fifty canoes, called *manocques*, built from a single piece of wood... long and narrow. Several Wallachians could fit in them; in some more, in others less."[21]

Although Vlad showed no reluctance to participate in anti-Ottoman military actions in 1445, in contrast to his attitude the previous year, he was not interested in all-out war with the Turks. The gratitude Vlad had expressed to Wavrin because his presence had allowed for a peaceful harvest indicates that raids by Ottoman garrisons stationed along the Danube had again become a serious problem for Wallachia. The Prince saw the presence of the crusaders on the Danube as an opportunity to recover important fortresses that had initially been lost to the Turks during the reign of his father Mircea, especially Silistra and Giurgiu. Vlad envisioned a limited scale enterprise, and he had no illusions about driving the Turks out of Europe. But the Prince also had personal motives for joining in the campaign; he hoped to exact revenge on certain Ottoman commanders who had wronged him in the past. Apart from this, Pope Eugenius had written to him in the spring to inquire about the fate of Cardinal Cesarini; at the same time, the Pontiff encouraged him to renew the struggle against the Turks.[22] By accomodating the Pope, Vlad hoped to

---

[21]Iorga, "Cronica lui Wavrin," p. 109. In Wavrin's account Triest denotes Silistra.

[22]Iorga, *Studii și documente*, vol. III, p. XXIV.

keep in check the animosity which Hunyadi, now the most powerful leader of Catholic Hungary, harbored against him.

With the details of the campaign settled, preparations began in earnest. Wavrin dispatched his faithful lieutenant Pietre Vast, who had already journeyed thousands of kilometers during the previous months to coordinate Christian efforts, back to Hungary to inform officials there that the promised galleys stood ready and that Vlad would accompany them on land with his army. Two days after Vast left for Buda, Cardinal Condolmieri laid anchor at Brăila with three papal galleys, aboard one of which was Bartholomew of Yano, Guardian of the Franciscan Order at Constantinople; Regnault de Comfide and Jacques de Thoisy also arrived with the two remaining Burgundian galleys. With the entire Christian fleet assembled, Wavrin greeted the Cardinal and informed him of all that he and Vlad had agreed upon.

As soon as news of the Cardinal's arrival with the remaining galleys reached Vlad, he dispatched Mircea, along with five or six of his leading nobles, to welcome the distinguished visitors and to provide for their needs. Among the boyars that accompanied the Prince's eldest son to Brăila was the head of the army, Spătar Dumitru, sent to coordinate joint action with the Christian fleet. Vlad himself returned to Târgoviște to deal with other matters before setting out on the campaign; on Saturday, August 7, he issued a diploma confirming lands, with exemptions from royal taxes and works, for Badea Ciutin and his sons.[23] Shortly after Mircea and Dumitru reached Brăila, a messenger arrived from Hungary with news that Hunyadi was still working to gather his army and that he would not reach Nicopolis until sometime around the feast of the birth of the Virgin Mary, which falls on September 8. Condolmieri, Wavrin, Mircea, and the other commanders present decided that, if time permitted, they would also attack other Ottoman positions along the Danube, in addition to Silistra, that lay on their way to Nicopolis; possible military objectives included Tutrakan, Giurgiu, and Ruse. The Seekers of the

---

[23]Doc. 99 in *DRH, B*, vol I, pp. 173-175. We learn of Dumitru's absence from the fact that he is replaced in the royal council on this date by his adjutant Spătar Neagoe. That Dumitru continued to held the office of Spătar in 1445 is confirmed by another document from that year confirming lands to the Monastery of Codmeana, see Doc. 98 in *DRH, B*, vol. I, pp. 172-173.

Lost King now prepared to resume their original role as crusaders. Wavrin and Cardinal Condolmieri then ordered their galleys to be cleaned, repaired, and provisioned for the upcoming campaign.

By mid-August, Vlad arrived at Brăila where his army had assembled. The commanders agreed that the Wallachians would proceed along the left bank of the Danube, keeping pace with the fleet, so as to supply the galleys and to provide help as needed. The eight ships comprising the Christian fleet left port on August 16. One of the Burgundian galleys flew the flag of Daud Celebi, a grandson of Sultan Murad I; in return for his cooperation, the Ottoman pretender made Pietre Vast promise that Wavrin would only turn over him and his entourage to the Hungarians, with whom he had collaborated in the past. While the Christians proceeded up the river to Silistra, the garrison there, which had learned of their plans through Turkish spies in Wallachia, prepared to meet them.

It took almost a week for the crusaders to cover the distance between Brăila and Silistra. Wavrin writes that "Throughout the journey, the Prince of Wallachia, who was accompanied on land by his entire army, frequently came to the river bank to speak with our Christian lords."[24] During these conversations, Vlad related to Wavrin many of the details about his life which the Burgundian commander subsequently recounted to his uncle who set them down in his chronicle. Wavrin's recollections also attest to the fact that Vlad was a highly cultured man, with a knowledge of several languages. When he recalls his discussions with different foreign leaders, such as John Hunyadi or Vlad's son Mircea, Wavrin specifies that these took place through an interpreter, but when he speaks of Vlad he mentions no need for an intermediary. Given that Vlad was raised at the court of Sigismund of Luxemburg, it is reasonable to assume that he learned Latin, German, and Hungarian there, in addition to Slavonic, the language of the Wallachian nobility in the fifteenth century. As he was regarded as a popular leader, he undoubtedly also spoke Romanian, the language of the majority of the population, especially among the lower classes of his country. During his years at the Byzantine capital, he acquired Greek as well, something that proved useful in forging a relationship with Murad II who also knew this language.

---

[24]Iorga, "Cronica lui Wavrin," p. 110.

Finally, although Vlad could have spoken to Wavrin in Latin, it is more likely that French also numbered among the languages spoken by the Wallachian Prince.

Two hours before they would have reached Silistra, Vlad told the Christian commanders aboard the galleys to lay anchor. As it was already late in the day, they made camp and held a war council where Wavrin, Condolmieri, Vlad, and the other commanders made plans for an assault on the city. The Wallachian Prince hoped to recover this key crossing point once traversed by Alexander the Great when he led his army against the Getae; since Roman times, when it was called Durostorum, Silistra had remained an important stronghold on the Danube. The Ottomans had seized the citadel, formerly held by Dobrotitsa, from Wallachia during Mehmed I's campaign against Mircea in 1416. As Cardinal Condolmieri, the Papal Legate, held overall command but had only three galleys, he insisted that Wavrin, who was chosen to lead the advance guard, fly the papal flag on his ship to balance the fleet politically, while one of the Wavrin's lieutenants, Regnault de Comfide, would fly the flag of the Duke of Burgundy. The attack on Silistra was set for sunrise of the following morning, and they decided that Wavrin would depart one hour ahead of the Cardinal.

Before sunrise, Wavrin's galleys stood at anchor before Silistra, with the Wallachians occupying the left bank of the river, all waiting the arrival of Condolmieri so they could begin the assault. As the Cardinal did not reach Silistra at the appointed hour, Vlad sent men to Wavrin to ask him if he knew the reason for the delay. As they spoke with the Burgundian commander, the Cardinal's galley came into view, but, to their amazement, Condolmieri had lowered his sails some three miles down river and lay idle. Wavrin became furious at this change of plan and angrily quipped to the Wallachians, "When you make a priest a chief of warriors, you can't expect much good to come of it."[25] He then sent a small boat to the Cardinal to inquire about the reason for the delay. By now it was nine o'clock in the morning, and with the temperature steadily rising, the summer heat began to make an attack on the fortress problematic. Thus far, the Ottoman garrison had not stirred, showing no sign of alarm at the crusaders's arrival. Wavrin became increasingly frustrated as

[25]Iorga, "Cronica lui Wavrin," p. 111.

the boat he had sent to the Cardinal did not return. Finally, Condolmieri raised his sails and the entire Christian fleet assembled before Silistra. Wavrin then went aboard the Cardinal's galley to find out what had happened. The Papal Legate informed him that the Wallachians with their canoes had entered a small river that feeds into the Danube and had captured a Turkish fisherman who, threatened with a painful death, revealed that "there are around thirty thousand knights hidden in the city of Triest [Silistra] and that all of the Subashis in the land of the Bulgarians are gathered there..." Under further interrogation by the Wallachians, the fisherman "also told them the names of all of the Subashis at that moment in the city."[26] Having learned this, the Cardinal concluded that he had to abandon plans to assault Silistra.

The Turks, who had readied for an attack on the city after receiving information about Christian plans from their spies in Wallachia, hoped that the crusaders would launch their assault before they learned of the overwhelming force they had assembled against them. When the Ottomans saw that no attack was forthcoming, they began to fire their artillery at the Christian fleet. While none of the galleys was hit, it did force them to move further up river, out of range of the Turkish guns. Next, the Ottomans attempted to entice the crusaders to attack. Around noon, they set fire to part of the city and put the women and children to begin screaming and feigned a retreat from the fortress, but to no avail, for Vlad and his men, who knew all of the Ottoman tricks, told Wavrin that "this is part of Turkish strategy to draw the Christians into an attack on the city."[27] Having failed to deceive the crusaders, the Ottomans next tried to intimidate them, bringing their entire force, armed in full battle gear, out to demonstrate along the river bank.

While Wavrin dined, Daud Celebi came aboard his galley to request an audience with him. The Ottomans pretender told him that he recognized the flags of several Subashis and that of the Ottoman garrison commander, and that if he could speak to them, he might convince them to come over to his side. Wavrin agreed to his proposal and went to see Cardinal Condolmieri who endorsed the plan. The Burgundian commander and his adjutant Regnault de Comfide hoisted white flags on their galleys and, with Daud Celebi aboard,

---

[26]Iorga, "Cronica lui Wavrin," p. 112.

[27]Iorga, "Cronica lui Wavrin," p. 112.

they slowly moved back down river. When Wavrin saw that the Turks had also raised a white flag of truce, he approached the shore. Daud then came out dressed in a gown of fine blue cloth, sewn with gold thread, and wearing a large turban on his head with a band of gold atop; he then stood up on a bench so that all the Turks on the shore could see him. Wavrin then lowered a small boat from the galley that went and brought back four Turks from the shore to meet with the Ottoman pretender. Daud sent a message to Ottoman commanders at Silistra, promising them favors if they would recognize him as their rightful ruler. Tensions ran high as both the Turks on the shore and the Christians aboard the galleys aimed their cannons at one another. The Ottoman leaders then sent back their reply, categorically refusing to recognize Daud Celebi, and affirming their loyalty to the Sultan, after which they began firing on the galleys. Wavrin and Comfide returned their fire as they moved their galleys back up river, out of range of the Turkish guns, but given the imprecision of the artillery of the day, neither side suffered any casualties.

After this, the Christian leaders consulted and, seeing that it was futile to remain before Silistra any longer, they decided to continue their course up river so they would arrive at Nicopolis on time to join with the Hungarians. Before they raised anchor, Daud Celebi, disheartened by the refusal of Ottoman commanders to recognize him, again came to Wavrin. The Ottoman pretender had become friendly with Vlad, who had extended to him an invitation to come ashore and to enjoy his hospitality during the voyage to Silistra. He now decided to accept the Wallachian Prince's proposal and asked Wavrin's permission to depart. The Burgundian commander, however, was a bit taken aback because Daud had previously made him swear a solemn oath that he would not turn him over to anyone but the Hungarians. During this epoch, such an oath was not to be taken lightly, even if the one who had insisted that it be made was now asking him to break it; to resolve the problem, Wavrin, Daud, and the Wallachian nobles who had come to escort him, all went before Cardinal Condolmieri who formally absolved the Burgundian commander of his oath. "Then," writes Wavrin, "without wasting any more time, he [Daud Celebi] and all the Turks went ashore to join the Prince of Wallachia."[28]

---

[28]Iorga, "Cronica lui Wavrin," p. 114.

Meanwhile, the galleys had run out of bread, and the oarsmen and mates were reduced to eating only boiled grain, so Wavrin set out the next morning with two galleys an hour or two ahead of the Cardinal to search for a suitable place where they could build large fires to bake bread. Vlad assigned Mircea to follow along with the canoes. Enjoying favorable winds, by late afternoon Wavrin arrived within a league of Tutrakan, where he found an appropriate site with sufficient wood where he could bake bread. Mircea reached the location where Wavrin had laid anchor around sunset because the canoes, powered only by oars, could not keep pace with the galleys using their sails. Soon after he disembarked, Vlad's son sent one of the leading Wallachian nobles, perhaps Spătar Dumitru, to the Burgundian commander with the following message: "The son of the Prince of Wallachia recommends himself to you and informs you that here you find yourself within two miles of the fortress of Turquant [Tutrakan]. Therefore, he requests that tomorrow morning you be ready to assault this fortress together with him, as he has five hundred Wallachians under his command."[29]

More than three hours had passed since they laid anchor, but Cardinal Condolmieri, who should have arrived before now with the remainder of the fleet, had not yet appeared. Wavrin became concerned and did not know how to respond to Mircea's invitation as he was reluctant to engage in any action without the Cardinal present. He consulted with his officers who all agreed that the remaining galleys would certainly arrive before morning. The Burgundian commander then sent his reply to Vlad's son: "I am hopeful that Monsignor Cardinal will also arrive, together with my other galleys, during the night so that tomorrow morning I will be ready. Send someone to inform me when you are prepared to cross, for it is my intention to go along and to attack that fortress with you."[30] Wavrin spent an anxious night, sleeping on deck with his men, awaiting Condolmieri's arrival, but at dawn there was still no sign of the Papal Legate.

At daybreak, on August 29, Mircea sent word to the Burgundian commander that he was ready to commence the attack. Although the remainder of the fleet had still not arrived, Wavrin did not hesitate to keep his promise;

---

[29]Iorga, "Cronica lui Wavrin," pp. 115-116.

[30]Iorga, "Cronica lui Wavrin," p. 116.

he immediately issued orders to sound the trumpets and raise the anchors and to follow the Wallachian canoes up river. As Mircea's men disembarked on the right bank of the Danube, the Turkish garrison, numbering around one hundred and fifty men, came out of the fortress and began to drive them back to the river before they could establish a bridgehead. Seeing this, Wavrin moved his galleys into position and began to fire his artillery to provide cover for Mircea and his troops. Once the Wallachians had secured a foothold, the Burgundian forces also came ashore. Wavrin divided his men into three corps: Dyeric de Vyane from Holland commanded the arbalesters, culvriniers, and artillerymen, while a knight from Henault, called the lord of Houes, led the infantrymen and galley hands, and the Burgundian captain himself commanded the rearguard. This forced the Turks to flee back inside the fortress and the Christians immediately began their assault. Enjoying numerical superiority, Wavrin tells us that both he and Mircea employed their troops so that "only half of their total effectives participated in the assault, while the other half went to rest aboard their ships or to tend to their wounds. Later, after they recovered, they returned to the assault, permitting the others to go to rest."[31]

The fortress at Tutrakan was of a simple square design with stone walls, typical of military architecture in the age before firearms became a decisive factor in warfare. It had been raised on the ruins of a fortress dating from Roman times, originally built during the reign of Emperor Diocletian. Small, square towers stood at three of its corners, while a large square tower built of massive stone masonry, over twenty feet high, which had recently been constructed to strengthen the citadel against attack in this new age of gunpowder, dominated the fourth corner. The Turks entered this tower by means of a wooden ladder; the upper part had a large wooden balcony, flanked by two wooden galleries from which the garrison could defend this bastion. An exterior courtyard ran outside the walls, protected by a trench and wooden palisades. The Christians easily took this exterior courtyard, but as they approached the walls, the Turks, especially those in the large tower, rained down heavy stones and other projectiles upon them. The Burgundian commander himself was slightly wounded in the attack when a stone thrown from

---

[31]Iorga, "Cronica lui Wavrin," p. 119.

the tower struck him on the upper arm and shoulder, but, in a foolhardy display of courage, he pressed on. Wavrin then ordered up his artillery, which included eight cannons, aimed them at the tower, and, together with his archers, arbalesters, and culvriniers, fired a barrage of projectiles, forcing the Turks to take cover inside the tower. The Wallachians and the Burgundians then stormed the fortress on all sides, taking everything except for the large tower, in which many of the Ottomans had taken refuge and now stubbornly defended.

The Christians could not take the large tower by assault because the Turks could still rain down rocks and stones from small windows and battlements upon anyone attempting to scale it. The Ottoman garrison hoped that it could hold out there until help from Silistra arrived. Wavrin next thought to mine the tower, but one of Mircea's men, who had participated in the construction of the bastion while a slave of the Turks, informed him that it was built of massive stone masonry, making this unfeasible. Meanwhile, the Subashi in charge of the garrison began to negotiate with the Wallachians, hoping to buy time for help to reach them, but the Christians quickly realized his ploy. Mircea and Wavrin then consulted and decided to set fire to the tower to try to force the Ottomans out.

They ordered their men to collect the wood from the palisades that had protected the exterior courtyard and to pile it up along the wall of the tower that faced into the wind so that the effect of the flames beating against the stone would intensify the heat inside. To set an example for their men, both Wavrin and Mircea began to carry wood. This inspired the others to work faster; in addition to wood from the palisades, they also brought straw, dried leaves and grass, and any other flammable materials they could find. The Turks inside the tower could do nothing because the culvriniers and artillerymen fired upon them whenever they tried to come out on the balcony, and their was no other position from which they could effectively defend that wall. After two hours of gathering wood, the pile reached nearly as high as the balcony. Then they lit it at the base and soon a massive bonfire was ablaze. The flames engulfed the balcony and reached the roof of the tower, itself made of large wooden shingles. Before long the heat inside the tower became unbearable and, with the roof collapsing above them, the Turks had no choice but to abandon their last bastion of defense, but they still had no intention of giving up without a fight. They opened the trap door in the floor and jumped down a passage with an opening at the base of the tower. The crusaders stood ready to meet them. Some of the Turks fought their way through the front lines, including the Subashi, dressed in a red caftan with a yellow collar that extended down upon his shoulders. The Ottoman garrison commander lunged at Wavrin with his sword drawn, but one of the Burgundian officers lept in front of his Captain with a battleaxe in hand and cut down the Subashi with a blow to the neck. All of the remaining Turks were then killed or captured. As the sun began to set on the horizon, the fortress at Tutrakan lay in Christian hands.

To the victors belong the spoils, but putting this into effect revealed some of the problems that consistently hindered Christian efforts to drive the Ottomans from Europe. The crusaders were as much soldiers of fortune as soldiers of Christ, and each sought to take captives who could later be sold or ransomed. Because prisoners represented an important source of revenue, the Christian soldiers began to fight amongst themselves, each trying to assert his claim to one of the captives. Wavrin tried to intervene to settle these disputes, but, unable to do so, he resolved the situation by ordering that all Turkish prisoners be killed. A massacre ensued, "Something which those who had been unable to take any prisoners, and had no hope of getting any, took great pleasure in doing; they killed them in the hands of those who had them."[32] But even this extreme measure did nothing to calm spirits. The crusaders began to fight over the belongings of the slaughtered Turks, tearing their caftans from their corpses, ripping them in two in the process, and quarreling over swords and sheaths, bows and arrows, and anything else of value. A frustrated Wavrin could do nothing. Finally, when there wasn't anything left to take, the situation seemingly resolved itself as each retired to his galley or canoe with what he had managed to seize.

By now, night had fallen, and with it a dense fog. The Burgundian commander had just boarded his ship when Mircea came to him to complain that those from the galleys had taken goods that rightfully belonged to his men. Wavrin replied that his own men made similar complaints against the Wallachians. The weary Captain, his wounded shoulder causing him discomfort, just wanted some peace and quiet to recover after this eventful day, but

---

[32]Iorga, "Cronica lui Wavrin," p. 120.

Mircea and the nobles accompanying him insisted on discussing these matters further, talking all the while Wavrin had his armor removed, leading him later to quip that "the Hungarians and the Wallachians are very talkative peoples." Exasperated, he finally told Mircea and his men, "Night has fallen. If the Turks were to come upon us now, they would capture us all, together with our galleys and artillery. Therefore, gather all of your men in your canoes. As for me, I am going to retire to my galley and tomorrow we can settle the disputes among our men."[33]

After he washed up and changed his clothes in his cabin, Wavrin, although he refused to treat his own wound, came out on deck with the surgeons and doctors under his command to check on the sick and wounded who numbered thirty or forty from his two galleys. Only one of his officers, Dyeric de Vyanne, had been wounded in the fighting when an arrow struck him in the leg. They had few provisions, apart from the bread they had baked the day before, water, and some wine that had soured during the long voyage. But despite the shortages, Wavrin had a feeling of satisfaction after his first victory over the Ottomans. He looked out from his galley and saw the tower off in the distance, still aflame, lighting up the night sky, its walls glowing red through the patches of fog; he later recalled how some of his men remarked to him that, "for a night of St. John, as that one was, they had never seen a more beautiful bonfire."[34]

Still, the Burgundian commander knew that he could let down his guard. He ordered the galleys anchored away from the shore, out of range of Ottoman bowmen, placed several sentries, and gave the command for his men to sleep dressed and with their weapons at hand. At dawn, the sentries sounded the alarm that the Turks had arrived. Wavrin saw from their banners that they had come from Silistra. He ordered his cannons aboard the galleys trained on them and they opened fire, forcing the Ottomans, who were too few to risk a confrontation with the crusaders, to retreat. Some of the Wallachians went ashore to give chase, but to no avail. In so doing, they discovered by chance important underground food deposits, desperately needed aboard the galleys whose provisions were nearly exhausted. Wavrin explains that, "In these

---

[33]Iorga, "Cronica lui Wavrin," p. 120.

[34]Iorga, "Cronica lui Wavrin," p. 121. It was August 29, the feast of the beheading of John the Baptist.

faraway lands, people dig deep holes in the ground in the form of a cistern where they stockpile grain, oats, and all sorts of produce, after which they cover them with large slabs of stone. On that morning, after a night during which a heavy dew had settled, it was easy to see that the earth above those cisterns was not wet like the ground all around them, but dry. From this simple sign, all of the granaries dug into the ground by the people from the village neighboring the fortress of Turquant could be found. They uncovered grain, beans, and peas, which arrived just in time for those aboard the galleys who satisfied themselves with these things so that it seemed like manna from heaven had fallen upon them."[35]

Shortly after daybreak, Cardinal Condolmieri and Regnault de Comfide finally arrived on the scene, while Vlad, who had accompanied them along the shore with the bulk of the Wallachian army, made camp on the left bank. Once again, problems that typically plagued crusading efforts became all too apparent. When the Papal Legate saw that Wavrin had conquered Tutrakan in his absence, he became furious. He refused to return the Burgundian commander's salute as he passed by his galley and laid anchor some distance up river from his. Baffled at this attitude, Wavrin boarded a small boat and went to the Cardinal's galley to find out why he had reacted in this way. When the two came face to face, a heated dispute broke out. The Burgundian Captain recalled that Condolmieri "reproached him for having committed a great act of treason against him, of which he will inform Our Holy Father, the Pope, and all Christian Princes..." Wavrin asked him how this was so and "the Cardinal replied to him that his treason lay in the fact that he came to conquer the fortress of Turquant without his knowledge or approval." He defended himself, saying that he had intended to await Condolmieri's arrival, but that in the meantime the Wallachians had taken the initiative and they needed his assistance. Wavrin then challenged anyone that dared to accuse him of treason to a duel, something which the Cardinal, as a man of the cloth, could not accept. He then told the Papal Legate that if he still wanted "to bring this to the attention of the Pope and the Christian Princes, he was certain that he would be more honored for his actions than blamed." The Burgundian commander then tempered his words in an effort to defuse the conflict, telling Condolmieri,

---

[35]Iorga, "Cronica lui Wavrin," pp. 121-122.

"What I have done, if you think about it carefully, is more for the glory of Your Holiness, as you are my commander, than for my own."[36] After this exchange, the Cardinal regained his composure, but Wavrin, still deeply offended by the accusations made against him, took his leave and returned to his galley.

Back aboard his own vessel, the Burgundian captain, still angry, called Regnault de Comfide before him and demanded to know, "What prevented the Cardinal and the rest of you from following shortly after me as we agreed when I left?..." His lieutenant then explained how "the Cardinal's galley had run aground on a sandbank and because of this, not only did it have to be completely unloaded, but also towed by all the other galleys to free it. All during this time, the Turks remained before them on the opposite bank in battle formation.... Lord Wavrin then observed that it was truly a blessing from God that the galley got stuck on that sandbank, 'Because if you would have left at the appointed time and come after me, the Turks would have arrived at the fortress of Turquant ahead of us and would have defended it so well that we would not have dared set foot on the other shore.'"[37]

After the Burgundians left Condolmieri's galley, Bartholomew of Yano, Guardian of the Franciscan Order at Constantinople, rebuked the Cardinal for his attitude toward Wavrin's actions. Pope Eugenius IV had sent Bartholomew, who Wavrin describes as "a distinguished man, doctor in theology, and a man of good standing,"[38] to the Byzantine capital in 1436 to prepare the groundwork for the negotiations that resulted in the Union of Florence. A long-time proponent of a crusade against the Ottomans, Bartholomew had jumped at the chance to join the expedition on the Danube along with several of his Franciscan brothers, and he did not hesitate to censure

---

[36]Iorga, "Cronica lui Wavrin," p. 122-123.

[37]Iorga, "Cronica lui Wavrin," p. 123.

[38]Iorga, "Cronica lui Wavrin," p. 124. Wavrin does not refer to him by name, but only as the Guardian of the Friars Minor of Constantinople. There is no doubt, however, that this is Bartholomew whose letters from Constantinople provide useful information about Vlad's life and times. Both Nicolae Iorga and Francisc Pall reached this same conclusion, see Nicolae Iorga, "Les aventures 'Sarrazines' des Français de Bourgogne au XVe siècle," in *Mélanges d'histoire générale*, ed. Constantin Marinescu, Cluj, 1927, p. 13; and Pall, "Știri noi despre expedițiile turcești din Transilvania în 1438," p. 14.

Condolmieri for the harsh words he addressed to the Burgundian Captain, telling him that for a commanding officer to behave in such a manner was not only bad for morale, but would inhibit his men from taking initiatives in the future. Realizing that he had erred, the Cardinal dispatched Bartholomew to Wavrin to express his regrets and sent along provisions of bread and biscuits, which were lacking aboard his galley, as a peace offering.

Soon after, Vlad sent one of his nobles to Wavrin "to inform him that, at a distance of a day's voyage from that place, supposing that they will be aided by favorable winds, there is a fortress four times larger than the fortress of Turquant, located on an island called Georgia [Giurgiu], and they could go there to besiege it or to attack it without being threatened by any danger from the Turks."[39] But after what had just transpired, Wavrin refused to take a decision on his own and referred the Wallachian messenger to the Cardinal. When he heard Vlad's proposal, Condolmieri was pleased, but the Cardinal, a man with limited military experience, did not want to commit to anything without Wavrin's approval, so once again he sent Bartholomew to the Burgundian commander to try to convince him to come to the Legate's galley to discuss the Wallachian plan. Wavrin, still resentful of the way that the Cardinal had treated him earlier, told Bartholomew: "I don't see any need for me to go back there again. The Cardinal has only to decide what he thinks is best, to organize a seige or to lead an assault, for I shall always go along with him. From now on I am firmly decided to defer to him and his men, be it to set out first in battle or to lead an assault, so that the honor shall always be theirs, so that I shall never again be subjected to the humiliation I experienced here."[40] But the Franciscan Guardian, a skilled diplomat, never lost sight of the larger objective. In a subtle and tactful manner, he told Wavrin that it was neither the time, nor the place for such an attitude, and reminded him of their common goal — to defeat the Ottomans. In so doing, he succeeded in convincing the Burgundian Captain to accept Condolmieri's invitation to discuss Vlad's proposal.

Meanwhile, as they could not hope to hold a fortress on the right bank of the Danube, Mircea had put his men to dismantle the walls of Tutrakan so that

[39]Iorga, "Cronica lui Wavrin," p. 124.

[40]Iorga, "Cronica lui Wavrin," p. 125.

the Ottomans would have to consume time and resources to rebuild it. As the walls of Tutrakan came tumbling down, Wavrin, Comfide, Bartholomew, and a group of Wallachian nobles, who probably included Spătar Dumitru, met with the Papal Legate aboard his flagship to discuss Vlad's plan for an attack on Giurgiu. The Burgundian commander asked the Wallachians, "who know from their own experience the state of things," for their opinion. They replied that, "for the good of Christianity, it would be fitting for the Cardinal and the Captain of the Duke of Burgundy to honor the request of the Prince of the Wallachians to go to besiege and to conquer the fortress on the island of Georgia. Furthermore, they added that the Prince of the Wallachians has already ordered two large bombards to be brought there for this purpose." Then Condolmieri, who, despite his earlier outburst, deferred to Wavrin's military experience, asked the Burgundian commander what he would do if he were in his place. This gesture soothed Wavrin's wounded pride, and he told the Cardinal that he would go to Giurgiu and do everything that he can to take it, "especially as these Wallachian nobles have affirmed that it is a fortress that has caused great harm to the Christians. We have the means to do this when we consider the strength of the Wallachians, who are six thousand men, and that they have two large bombards, while I also have a very good one, which is very important. At the same time, it is said that there are only about three hundred Turks inside that fortress. Thus, I would very much like for us to take it."[41] The Cardinal concurred with Wavrin's assessment and issued the order for the galleys to prepare to set out for the island of Giurgiu.

Enjoying favorable winds, the fleet arrived there the following day. Vlad and his army on the shore managed to keep pace with the galleys, covering the distance of approximately fifty kilometers by means of a forced march. Giurgiu was a large, spacious square fortress, surrounded by a moat, with high walls and imposing towers, built of massive stone masonry and over twenty-four feet high, on each of its corners, the smallest of which was much bigger than the large tower at Tutrakan, each with battlements and wooden balconies and galleries for defense. On one side, two smaller walls extended down from the citadel to the edge of the river, at the end of which were two smaller towers. Giurgiu had been one of the most important crossing points on the Danube

---

[41]Iorga, "Cronica lui Wavrin," pp. 125-126.

since ancient times, thanks to three islands linking it to Ruse on the right bank. The Romans had built a small fort on the island of St. George, the one located closest to the river's left bank. Later, Vlad's great-uncle, Vladislav I, raised a wooden fortress here[42] during his conflicts with the Bulgarian Tsar Šišman. Near the end of the fourteenth century, his father Mircea had constructed this large stone fortress on the island which fell to the Turks during Mehmed I's attack on Wallachia in 1416; apart from its brief recovery by Dan II, with the help of Sigismund of Luxemburg, in 1427, the citadel had remained in Ottoman hands ever since.

The assault on Giurgiu began on August 31 when the crusaders from the galleys and the Wallachians from the shore descended on the island. The Ottomans came out of the fortress in good order, determined to repel the invaders, concentrating their attack on the Wallachians and wounding several of them, but Vlad's men rallied and drove them back inside the citadel. They then took up positions on one side of the fortress. Meanwhile, across the island, Wavrin spotted several small, four-wheeled carts scattered about and ordered his men to collect them and to fill them with wood. Then they tied them together and used them to cover their advance until they reached the edge of the moat where they formed a barricade protecting the crusaders against Ottoman projectiles. Next, Wavrin ordered his men to dig trenches behind the carts. By sunset, the Christians had the fortress of Giurgiu under seige from opposite sides.

During the night, Wavrin had his cannons and the large bombard brought from the galleys. To bring it into position, the crusaders had to roll the heavy bombard on logs. Then they camouflaged it using wood and branches. At daybreak, the Burgundian commander ordered his artillerymen to train their guns on the area where the wall met the tower and to open fire. The bombard hurled large cannonballs made of Brabant stone, a relatively light and soft type of rock. Its first shot hit right on target and produced a thick cloud of dust. When it cleared, the crusaders thought they saw a slight break in the wall where it joined the tower. Encouraged by this, they prepared to fire again. The second

---

[42]N.A. Constantinescu, "Cetatea Giurgiu: originile şi trecutul ei," in *AARMSI*, series II, vol. XXXVIII (1915-1916), pp. 498-499; and Giacomo di Pietre Luccari, *Copioso ristretto degli annali di Ragusa*, Venice, 1605, p. 49.

shot produced the same results, and when the dust finally settled, Wavrin and his men were convinced that the gap between the wall and the tower had widened even further and they let out loud cheers.

On the other side of the fortress, Vlad heard the shouts coming from Wavrin's men and inquired what all the commotion was about. He was told that the Burgundian bombard had proved highly effective, and that with two or three more shots it would destroy one of the towers. Hearing this news, the Wallachian Prince mounted his horse and rode around to the other side of the citadel to see for himself what damage the bombard had caused. When he arrived, Wavrin recalls that Vlad, "as one to whom the castle rightfully belonged (as his father was the one who had built it and he had been inside of it on different occasions and had not observed the crack), inspected it and at first shared the opinion that the hits from the bombard had produced it. For this reason, he asked the gunners to reload and to fire in his presence. But, as it was already lunch hour and Lord Wavrin had not eaten all day, he said to the Prince of Wallachia: 'I leave the bombard and the gunners at your disposal. You have the latitude to order them to fire as you please; as for myself, I am going to lunch aboard my galley.' Then he left, taking along with him Sir Regnault de Comfide, to dine."[43]

What Wavrin did not realize when he left Vlad in charge of his bombard was that the Wallachian Prince lacked the practical knowledge required to command an artillery unit. Vlad had always excelled more as a statesman than as a warrior, and his inexperience with heavy guns now made itself apparent. After the Burgundian commander left, he ordered the bombard to fire. When the dust cleared, it appeared to him that the gap had widened further and that the tower had begun to incline slightly. He then had the bombard reloaded and fired a second shot which, he thought, produced further results. But, in his enthusiasm, he did not take into account that the artillery of this epoch could not be fired in such rapid succession because, if not allowed sufficient time for the barrel to cool down, it would explode. A series of iron strips formed the barrel, bound together by several metal rings. From the galley where they served lunch, Wavrin and Comfide heard the discharges of the bombard and became concerned. Comfide told his commander: "This Wallachian will fire

---

[43]Iorga, "Cronica lui Wavrin," p. 128.

so much with our bombard that it will break. We should send someone to tell him to let it cool off and not to fire anymore cannonballs with it until we return."[44] But before the messenger from the ship arrived, Vlad fired yet again. Just as Comfide had feared, two of the rings snapped and the flying pieces of metal killed two of the gunners.

Wavrin and Comfide were furious when they heard this news. The bombard, however, did not suffer irreparable damage; the galley's chief blacksmith told his commander that if only two of the rings had broken, and not any of the iron strips, he could repair it quickly. The blacksmith used a long cable to replace the busted rings, and soon the bombard was ready to resume firing. The heavy gun discharged two more rounds, but the frequent firing had taken its toll and, on the second shot, two more rings snapped and one of the iron strips broke, killing another of the gunners and putting the bombard out of commission. Wavrin then ordered it removed to his galley.

Vlad, meanwhile, had returned to the other side of the fortress and put the two bombards he had brought to Giurgiu to work. But, according to Wavrin, "The bombards in question could not be utilized effectively because their barrels were only three-quarters of the normal length without the firing chamber..." thereby reducing their accuracy. In addition, the Wallachians, who had little experience with using artillery in seige warfare, lacked trained gunners. Heavy guns had only recently been added to their arsenal, and the Burgundian captain observed that "they did not know how to aim accurately at the castle, but continually fired their stones over it."[45] The ineffectiveness of the Wallachian artillerymen allowed the Turks to risk venturing outside the walls of the fortress and to launch an assault against their guns. They killed three Wallachian gunners in the attack and disabled their best bombard, but Vlad's men regrouped and drove them back inside the citadel. The damaged gun required delicate repairs and the Wallachians had no one with the necessary experience to effect them, so one of Bartholomew's men, a Franciscan friar named Helye, who had previously served in Jerusalem where

---

[44]Iorga, "Cronica lui Wavrin," p. 128.

[45]Iorga, "Cronica lui Wavrin," p. 129.

he acquired a sophisticated knowledge of ordinance, came and fixed the bombard, but broke his arm in the process.

But the ineffectiveness of the heavy guns against the walls and towers of the fortress soon became apparent to Wavrin. It must be remembered that artillery was still in its infancy at this time. Within a century it would force radical changes in the design of fixed fortifications, but, as Christopher Duffy observed, "in Europe up to the late 1480s we see no convincing evidence that military architects appreciated that artillery had the power to transform the active defense of fortress, from the principle of merely dropping things on people, to the one of hitting them hard and low with missles impelled by gun powder."[46] Despite their previous enthusiasm, the Burgundians had determined that the gap between the wall and the tower which they had observed earlier was not the result of their bombardment, but rather a defect in the construction of the fort.

Having reached this conclusion, Wavrin went to Vlad and told him, "It appears that we will not be able to conquer this castle with our bombards, and that it will be impossible for us to take it unless we employ the same methods we used to win the castle at Turquant. As for myself, I think that everyone should start carrying wood and bringing as many dry materials as he can find so that we can pile them up in a heap as high as possible under the walls and towers on the side facing into the wind and then set fire to it."[47] Vlad agreed, and both the Wallachians and the crusaders from the galleys began the laborious task of gathering the wood and the kindling needed for the bonfire.

As he had done at Tutrakan, Wavrin, despite the fact that he had only one good arm, began to carry wood to set an example for his men. But, at Giurgiu, his rugged determination finally caught up with him. Having refused treatment for his earlier wound, it became infected and the Burgundian commander came down with a high fever. Unable to continue, Regnault de Comfide brought Wavrin back to his galley and called for the doctors and surgeons. When the Cardinal learned of his condition, he also sent his own doctors and surgeons to examine the Burgundian Captain. The medical men decide not to attempt any

---

[46]Christopher Duffy, *Siege Warfare*, New York, 1996, pp. 3-4.

[47]Iorga, "Cronica lui Wavrin," p. 129.

treatment until the next day to see if his fever would break during the night. As he could not move from his cabin, Wavrin turned over command of his troops on the island to Regnault de Comfide.

The Christians filled the four foot deep moat in front of the parapet with wood and kindling and then piled it up at the base of the wall and towers. Seeing this, the Ottomans inside the fortress began to panic. They could do nothing to stop the crusaders whose arbalesters, culvriniers, and cannoneers provided a steady barrage of cover fire. In a desperate attempt to foil Christian plans, the Turks tried to ignite the wood themselves before their enemies could gather a sufficient quantity to threaten the citadel. But, by the time they managed to do this, it was already too late. A fierce bonfire broke out. Flames quickly engulfed the tower supports, balconies, galleries, and roof, and spread to the interior of the fortress. The Ottomans hurried to bring water from the well supplying the citadel to douse the flames, but Christian arrows and gunfire impeded their efforts. Realizing that all was now lost, the Ottoman garrison commander opened negotiations with the Wallachian Prince. The two men knew each other well since the Subashi was the same man who had convinced Vlad to come to Adrianople in the spring of 1442 when Murad had him arrested and imprisoned in the tower at Gallipoli. The Subashi prepared to surrender the fortress if he and his men could leave with their personal belongings and be assured of safe passage across the Danube. Vlad, anxious to get his hands on this strategically important citadel, hurried to consult with his allies before the fire did too much damage to the structure.

Vlad went directly to Comfide with the Subashi's proposal and told him, "For God's sake, let them put out the fire, so as not to burn any more of the fortress, for it is the strongest of all those located along the Danube. It can do great harm to the Christians on this side of the river when it is in the hands of the Turks, because when the Turks make raids in search of plunder in Wallachia or in Transylvania, they first cross over with their horses to this island, then they use the castle's bridge to cross the branch of the river linking it to Wallachia. Then they overrun the entire country and bring back here all the plunder they gather. When the Wallachians set out after them to recover the stolen goods, they can do nothing to them because of this castle. But, when the Turks are forced to cross back directly over the river, the Wallachians can always punish them by striking at the rear of their column, killing and taking many of them prisoner."[48] Comfide, however, lacked the authority to make a decision in this regard, and told the Prince to consult with Condolmieri and Wavrin aboard the galleys.

With no time to waste, as the fortress was still aflame, Vlad mounted his horse and galloped over to the Cardinal's galley. He repeated to the Papal Legate what he had told Comfide. Then, overcome with enthusiasm at the opportunity to regain this vital stronghold, he added: "If I can take this place, which my father built, whole and undamaged, the women of Wallachia alone, with their spinning forks, will be more than sufficient to reconquer Greece." The Cardinal and the others present realized that he exaggerated in his ardor to take possession of the citadel. Wavrin writes that Vlad, "affirmed, among other things, that no stone had been laid in that castle that had not cost his father a block of salt, which in the land of Wallachia they cut from rocks, while in other places it is mined from quarries." Although pleased to hear that the Ottomans would surrender the fortress, the delicate nature of their relations since their dispute at Tutrakan required that Condolmieri consult Wavrin before making a final decision. As the Burgundian commander could not rise from his sickbed, the Cardinal sent Vlad to see him. Even though he was gravely ill, Wavrin "was very pleased to hear him speak of the surrender of the place, saying that the pleasure of the Cardinal was also his. After this, the Cardinal ordered that the fire be extinguished and that the fortress be restored to the Prince of Wallachia, who was overcome with joy."[49]

After receiving a letter of safe-conduct, allowing them to cross the Danube into Bulgaria with their horses and personal belongings, the Ottomans evacuated the fortress. After the surrender, Mircea went to see the stricken Burgundian commander and, speaking to him through a translator, he first swore him to secrecy and then told him of his plan to take action against the Turks. Mircea confided to Wavrin: "My father called me to him and told me that if I do not want to take revenge upon the Subashi of the castle of Georgye, he will disown me and he will no longer recognize me as his son. For this is the one who had betrayed him earlier and who, on the basis of a guarantee of safe-conduct from the Turk [Murad], brought him before the said Turk, after

---

[48]Iorga, "Cronica lui Wavrin," p. 132.

[49]Iorga, "Cronica lui Wavrin," p. 132.

which he was placed as a prisoner in the castle of Gallipoli, where he was held for a long time with both legs in irons. Today, this man, together with his Saracens, surrendered to my father on the condition that he spare them their lives and goods and that they be allowed to cross in safety to the Bulgarian land. And now I will cross the river about two miles from here with two thousand Wallachians and follow them along their way, and, when they turn in the direction of Nicopolis, I will ambush them and kill them all."[50]

Mircea then put his plan into action. The Turks loaded their saddles and personal belongings into small boats and then tied their horses together. After this, they embarked in canoes and began the crossing with their horses swimming behind them; all this time they remained with their arms ready, fearful of a Christian attack. When they reached the opposite shore, they dried off and saddled their horses and continued on their way. Thinking they had escaped unscathed, Mircea's ambush took them completely by surprise. The Wallachians killed all of the Turks except for the Subashi. Then, in an act reminiscent of the terror tactics for which his younger brother would later become infamous, Mircea had his men strip the bodies and line the corpses up along the shore, something which Wavrin admits later "frightened all of those aboard the galleys as they passed by the dead bodies exposed on the banks." Mircea then brought the Ottoman garrison commander back to Giurgiu and turned him over to his father: "The Prince of Wallachia then took him aside and recounted to him his treason; then he cut off his head with his own hand."[51] Thus Vlad exacted revenge for the humiliations and disgrace the Turks had previously inflicted on him.

Having recovered Giurgiu, Vlad took immediate action to repair the damages and to secure the fortress. He dispatched his scribe, Dragomir, to the burghers of Braşov with a letter telling them the news and requesting assistance: "God has granted good fortune to the Christians and given us this fortress which was in the hands of the pagans; all of its buttresses were completely burned and we are now rebuilding it. For this reason, I ask you to help us with bows and arrows and with firearms, and to give us saltpeter so that we can make gunpowder, so we can place them in the fortress, for it is a

---

[50]Iorga, "Cronica lui Wavrin," p. 133.

[51]Iorga, "Cronica lui Wavrin," p. 134.

stronghold for you, and for us, and for all Christians. And furthermore, what My Majesty's servant Dragomir will tell you, believe him, for they are the words of My Majesty."[52]

The victory at Giurgiu did nothing to improve the state of Wavrin's health. The Burgundian commander spent a difficult night aboard his galley; when his doctors came to examine him in the morning they found that the infection had not subsided and that he still ran a high fever. As a result, they decided to perform a phlebotomy, the standard treatment at that time for patients with such symptoms. They made incisions into his skin using razors, and then applied leeches to his wounded shoulder and to his spine to draw out the blood; then they weighed it on a scale to determine how many ounces they had extracted. Jehan de Wavrin, the Burgundian commander's uncle who later committed his reminiscences to paper, reproached his nephew for refusing treatment when he was first wounded: "Here we must observe that when it happens that a captain or a warrior chief feels wounded or burdened by pain, he must not ignore this, but must immediately take proper care of himself so as not to cause graver problems that could affect the fate of an entire people, of an army, or a country."[53]

While Wavrin received treatment, Vlad went before Cardinal Condolmieri with yet another proposal for joint military action. He told the Papal Legate that, "further up river, in the direction of Nicopolis, another Turkish castle is found, built on the Bulgarian shore, called Roussico [Ruse], which in many ways resembles the Turquant castle. Because the river is narrow in front of this castle, the Turks frequently cross there to come to Wallachia to pillage, where they cause great damage. And if they will be left in peace, from now on they will do even greater damage so as to exact revenge.... He humbly requested, in

---

[52]Doc. 277 in *DRH, D*, p. 387. The editors date this document October-December 1445 after Ioan Bogdan (Doc. LV in Bogdan, *Relațiile privitoare*, p. 80), but, as we know that the Ottomans surrendered the fortress to Vlad on September 1, it was most likely written in the immediate aftermath, probably on September 2 before the crusaders continued their journey to Nicopolis. Vlad's emissary Dragomir is presumably the same scribe who penned the diploma issued by the Prince from Târgoviște on August 7, 1445, see Doc. 99 in *DRH, B*, vol. I, pp. 173-175.

[53]Iorga, "Cronica lui Wavrin," p. 130.

the name of God, that they go forward and attack this hornets' nest, for if they did this they could easily take it."[54] Vlad also informed the Cardinal that he had received reliable intelligence that the Hungarians were en route to Nicopolis with a large force. Condolmieri sent word of all this to Wavrin, asking for his advice. From his sickbed, the Burgundian commander replied that, if the fortress in question was no larger than the one at Tutrakan, they should proceed with the attack, but he added that care must be taken to ensure that they reach Nicopolis on time to join with the Hungarians. The Papal Legate then gave the order for the galleys to raise anchor and the Christian forces set out in the direction of Ruse.

It took less than two hours for the crusaders to arrive at the nearby citadel. But, by this time, news of their feats had spread throughout the region. Wavrin relates that "the Turks, who saw the galleys coming and who knew, from news they had received, how the castles at Turquant and Georgia had been captured and how all of the Saracens defending them had been killed, were filled with fear of the Christians. For this reason, observing the approach of the galleys, as we have said, such terror overcame them that they themselves set fire to the castle and to the neighboring village and they fled." Having achieved their objective without firing a single shot, the Christians laid anchor before the fortress, "so that for the rest of that day and during the night that immediately followed, the flames from the castle and the village that were burning provided them with light."[55]

News of the crusaders's successes also reached the Christian population living under Ottoman rule south of the Danube. Wavrin recalls how, "the Christians who lived in Bulgaria began to awaken and, deliberating together, they reached the decision that they would no longer remain under the yoke of the Turks. And once they made this decision, they loaded their women and children and all of their belongings into wagons and carts, bringing along after them all of their domestic animals, and they came to place their fate in the hands of the Prince of Wallachia and those from the galleys, as men who they believed strong enough to resist the pressure of the Turks who remained in those parts.... The Turks, however, who learned in advance of this rebellion of

---

[54]Iorga, "Cronica lui Wavrin," pp. 134-135.

[55]Iorga, "Cronica lui Wavrin," p. 135.

the Bulgarian Christians, went after them with eight hundred to one thousand men, and, when they were within a league of Roussico, they surrounded them on a hilltop. When the Prince of Wallachia found out about this, he had his horses and cavalrymen swim across the river, about four thousand men in all, to hurry to assist those under seige. It is easily understood that the Turks did not wait to confront them, especially when they received news of their strength, but fled as quickly as they could. After that, the said Bulgarians placed their fate in the hands of the Prince of Wallachia, humbly asking him to deign to help them cross the Danube and to grant or to make for them a place in his country where they could live. Then, the Prince of Wallachia, who had a large and spacious country, little populated at some of its margins, satisfied their request and gladly took them under his protection, receiving them with generosity as his own people."[56]

Having agreed to grant asylum to the Bulgarian refugees, Vlad escorted them the remaining three miles to Ruse. He then went to see Condolmieri and Wavrin to explain the situation to them and to ask for their assistance to bring these people across the Danube with their possessions, which they readily agreed to do. Wavrin notes that "they had to work three days and nights to bring them all across. In all, there were over twelve thousand people: men, women, and children, not including their baggage and cattle. Those who saw them said that in their appearance these people looked like Egyptians." Some have suggested that this last observation indicates that the people in question were, in fact, Gypsies migrating to Wallachia,[57] but this is an erroneous conclusion. Gypsies were slaves at this time and, therefore, regarded as property; Vlad could not have welcomed them as settlers. Instead, this remark reveals the strong Cuman influence in the region. It must be remembered that the Slavicized Cumans helped to found the Second Bulgarian Empire and that two of its dynasties, the Asens and the Terters, were of Cuman origin, as was the ruling family of Wallachia from which Vlad himself descended. These kinship ties and the fact that Middle Bulgarian was the language of the Wallachian ruling class during this epoch made it natural for Vlad to welcome these refugees with open arms. "When all of them had finally crossed the

---

[56]Iorga, "Cronica lui Wavrin," pp. 135-136.

[57]Viorel Achim, *Ţiganii în istoria României*, p. 25.

river," Wavrin continues, "the Prince of Wallachia expressed his joy that he had obtained such a large number of people, saying that the Bulgarian nation was comprised of very brave men. After that, he expressed his gratitude to the Cardinal and to Lord Wavrin for all of the good they had done up to that time, saying that even if the army of Our Holy Father and that of the Duke of Burgundy had done nothing else during this entire voyage than to save eleven or twelve thousand Christians from the danger of being enslaved by the Saracens, it seemed to him that this in itself was a great deed."[58]

Bringing the Bulgarians safely across the river had put the crusaders behind schedule. They had agreed to join the Hungarians before Nicopolis on the feast of the birth of the Virgin Mary, September 8, but they did not arrive until September 12. But the delay did not affect their plans for joint operations because when they arrived at the appointed place the Hungarians were still two days away. When the Christian galleys approached Nicopolis they encountered strong opposition. The Ottomans, under the competent leadership of Mehmed Bey, who had boldly attacked the crusading army the year before after forcing them to abandon their seige of the citadel, knew that the Christians were on their way to Nicopolis and prepared to meet them. Mehmed Bey had lined up his bombards and cannon along the river bank in front of the fortress. Seeing this, the crusaders readied their guns aboard the galleys and, as they moved within range, both sides opened fire. In the ensuing artillery barrage, Ottoman cannonballs struck three of the galleys, but caused only minimal damage as they hit them above the water line. The fleet moved safely out of range of Turkish guns and laid anchor up river from Nicopolis, near Turnu on the Wallachian side of the river.

Nicopolis offered the Christian force no opportunity to repeat their successes at Tutrakan and Giurgiu; the powerful citadel had withstood sieges by crusading armies in 1396 and 1444. Wavrin describes the Ottoman stronghold as he found it in September 1445: "The city of Nicopolis is long and narrow, situated on a hill and defended by a powerful castle. On both sides of the city two rows of walls are seen that stretch down to the banks of the river. These walls are strengthened by several large round towers. On the bank of the river, wooden palisades are found which stretch from one side of the

---

[58]Iorga, "Cronica lui Wavrin," p. 136.

wall to the other. In that sheltered place, about six galleys or galliotes were found which the Turks pushed into the water that ran next to the palisades in such a manner that only their sterns could be seen outside."[59]

The day after the crusaders reached Nicopolis, Pietre Vast arrived from Hungary. Concerned to find his commander gravely ill, he reported to Wavrin that the Hungarians were on their way and would arrive in no more than two days. Soon after, Vlad also came to see Wavrin. He too was worried about the condition of the Burgundian Captain which, despite the phlebotomy, had shown little improvement since they had left Giurgiu. As Nicopolis was unassailable, Vlad proposed that they direct their resources against Turnu. He pointed out the window of Wavrin's cabin and said to him, "Do you see that large tower over there, raised opposite Nicopolis, now occupied by the Turks? Because that tower stands in my country, they inflict great damages upon me. Therefore, I ask you to help me once again, either to capture the tower in question or to destroy it."[60] The Burgundian commander agreed to Vlad's proposal and sent his lieutenants Pietre Vast and Regnault de Comfide with him to seek the approval of the Papal Legate. Condolmieri did not hesitate to offer his support and they all agreed to assault Turnu the following morning.

The Ottomans at Nicopolis, however, got wind of Christian plans and saw that they were preparing to lay seige to Turnu. Mehmed Bey ordered his men to load a galliote with food and artillery, and during the night he sent it to relieve the Ottoman garrison defending the tower on the left bank of the Danube. As the galliote eased its way across the river powered by its oars, under the cover of darkness and a heavy fog that had set in, the sentries aboard one of the Christian galleys realized what was happening and sounded the alarm. The galley went in pursuit, but was unable to overtake the lighter, more maneuverable Ottoman vessel before it closed in on Turnu where cover fire from the Ottoman garrison within the stronghold protected it. The failure of the crusaders to prevent the Ottomans from bringing over supplies from Nicopolis would prove decisive in the outcome of the ensuing battle.

---

[59]Iorga, "Cronica lui Wavrin," p. 137.

[60]Iorga, "Cronica lui Wavrin," p. 138.

The fortress at Turnu, called Little Nicopolis, was situated on a plain at the junction of the Olt and Danube rivers, approximately five hundred yards from each waterway. In contrast to the fortresses at Tutrakan, Giurgiu, and Ruse, Turnu, which simply means tower, was just that, a large round tower surrounded by walls. The stronghold had originally been raised during the reign of Roman Emperor Constantine the Great to protect commerce on the Danube and to defend the borders of the Empire from Barbarian invasions. Destroyed during the time of Emperor Justinian in the sixth century, it reappeared in medieval times as a Byzantine fort called Pirgos. Vlad's great uncle Vladislav I rebuilt the citadel during his conflicts with the Bulgarian Tsar Shishman, when, for a brief time, he took Nicopolis, but it fell to the Turks during the reign of his father Mircea and it remained an Ottoman enclave on Wallachian soil for the next five hundred years until the Treaty of Adrianople forced them to dismantle it in 1829.[61]

The Wallachians had surrounded the walls of the fortress and at daybreak Vlad ordered the bombards he had brought along from Giurgiu to begin firing. The artillery barrage continued throughout the day. The Wallachian guns managed to destroy the tower's wooden roof, but the stone cannonballs merely deflected off the cylindrical limestone structure without causing any serious damage.

As the Wallachian artillerymen continued to discharge their volleys, an aged Wallachian boyar, the tutor of Vlad's son Mircea, paid a courtesy visit to the ailing Burgundian commander in his cabin. The old man, who was nearly eighty, had participated in the Nicopolis Crusade when the Burgundians had last ventured to the lower Danube to fight the Turks, where he fell prisoner to the Ottomans who, in turn, sold him as a slave to the Genoese during which time he learned foreign languages before returning to his native land. To help

---

[61]Grigore Florescu, "Cetatea Turnu (Turnu-Măgurele)," in *RIR*, XV (1945), pp. 432-433. Florescu argues that it was Mircea who built Turnu upon the ruins of the ancient Roman fort (p. 439), but it clearly predates the reign of Vlad's father, when it was a focal point of conflict between the Ottomans and the Wallachians in 1394-1395. If Mircea had raised the tower, Vlad would certainly have mentioned this to Wavrin, just as he did at Giurgiu. Vladislav I, who is known to have strengthened Danubian fortifications during his wars with the Bulgarians, is most likely the one who reconstructed Turnu around the time he conquered Nicopolis.

Wavrin take his mind off his illness, the elderly boyar had come to share with him his reminiscences of those times: "Almost fifty years have passed since the King of Hungary and Duke John of Burgundy began their seige before this city of Nicopolis which you see there, and less than three leagues from here is the site where the battle took place. If you could raise your head a little I could show you the place and the way in which the seige was conducted." Wavrin's curiosity peaked and his condition had slightly improved so that, with assistance, he could make his way over to the window of his cabin. The old man then continued, pointing off in the distance: "Do you see that place? There stayed the King of Hungary, together with the Hungarians. Over there, the Constable of France [Boucicaut], and over there Duke John, who was near a large round tower that he tried to mine; when word arrived that the battle was about to begin, everything was ready to set fire to it." The boyar's recollections fascinated Wavrin who later recounted that, "Apart from this, he said that he was then in the service of Lord de Coucy, who made it a habit to keep Wallachian noblemen, who knew the ways of the lands occupied by the Turks, near him as armed companions. One could see that the governor held Lord de Coucy in high esteem. According to him, on the day before the battle, he [Coucy] drove off around six thousand Turks who had come with the intention of surprising the Christians while they were foraging."[62] Wavrin, who had a keen interest in history, thoroughly enjoyed listening to Mircea's tutor recount the Crusade of Nicopolis to him, but their conversation was suddenly interrupted by news of the arrival of John Hunyadi and the Hungarian army.

Ever the knight in shining armor, Hunyadi, as soon as he arrived, dismounted from his horse and, escorted by Pietre Vast, he boarded a bark and went to see Wavrin aboard his galley. But the man his contemporaries dubbed the White Knight could not get though the door of the ailing Burgundian commander's cabin because of the bulk of his heavy armor, so he left to meet with the Papal Legate, promising to return to visit Wavrin later, after he removed his armor. When he returned, Wavrin recalls that Hunyadi expressed his concern over his illness, "speaking to him through his translator, who spoke very good French."[63] The Transylvanian Voivode encouraged him, saying that

---

[62]Iorga, "Cronica lui Wavrin," p. 139.

[63]Iorga, "Cronica lui Wavrin," p. 140.

he had seen people with similar illnesses make a full recovery. Meanwhile, Pietre Vast brought green ginger, sugar almond, and other drugs from the ships well-stocked apothecary for his bedridden Captain. Hunyadi then returned to the shore to consult with Vlad about his plans to conquer the tower.

Given their history, Vlad and Hunyadi did not trust one another, but the arrival of the Christian fleet on the Danube had forced them to collaborate. The artillery bombardment having failed, the Wallachian Prince and the Transylvanian Voivode decided to employ the same tactics against the Turks at Turnu that had proved successful at Tutrakan and Giurgiu. The Wallachian and Hungarian soldiers then gathered wood and kindling, piling it up at the base of the tower. The Ottomans within could do nothing to stop them as the Christian culvriniers and arbalesters provided a steady stream of cover fire, forcing them to remain inside the stronghold. When the pile of flammable materials was high enough, they set the bonfire, but this time the flames did not produce the desired effect. Wavrin explains that "when the fire was lit all around, because the tower itself was round, the fire oscillated in one direction, then the other, instead of concentrating on a single spot to produce the desired effect. Therefore, those inside were not even slightly bothered by the flames for they did not reach above them."[64]

Failing to take Turnu in this way, the crusaders decided to tighten their seige and to mine the wall encircling the tower and to tear it down. They hoped that this would frighten the Ottoman garrison into surrendering. But the Turks remained obstinate, confident that they could hold out, having receiving significant quantities of food and munitions from Mehmed Bey just before the seige began. After ten days of vain efforts to take the citadel,[65] the Christians decided to raise the seige and to move on.

Hunyadi intended to effect a crossing further up river where the Jiu emptied into the Danube across from Rahova. He had given orders in advance for barks

---

[64]Iorga, "Cronica lui Wavrin," p. 141.

[65]Iorga, "Cronica lui Wavrin," p. 141, indicates that the seige of Turnu lasted fifteen days, but this is mistaken because we know for certain that it began on September 13 and that the crusaders arrived at the junction with the Jiu River on the evening of the feast of St. Michael, September 29, after a six day journey. Thus, they had to have abandoned the seige around September 23, after approximately ten days.

to be constructed there to transport men and materials across the river. The morning after they decided to abandon their efforts to conquer Turnu, the crusaders set out. The galleys could not use their sails to take advantage of the winds because they needed to keep pace with the large land army moving along the shore. Hunyadi's force of nine to ten thousand men included infantry and numerous carts and wagons filled with provisions and war materiels; as a result, it took them six days to cover a distance of approximately eighty kilometers.

But this time the Christians had company as they advanced up river. While the crusaders had busied themselves before Turnu, Mehmed Bey had gathered a sizeable force to follow the Christians along the right bank of the Danube to defend against further attacks on Ottoman territory. On the first night of the journey, the Wallachians and Hungarians encamped in a field along the left bank of the river, while the Turks did the same on the right bank; the Christian galleys lay at anchor between them. Around midnight, some of the Wallachians and Hungarians assigned to tend the horses let out a loud cry. The sentries aboard the galleys heard this and thought that the Turks were attacking, so they began shouting for their men to take up arms. When they saw those from the galleys hurrying to board their small boats to come ashore, a group of Wallachian and Hungarian nobles went to them to tell them to stand down. They explained that they used these shrieks "to calm the horses grazing nearby and to stop them from running away. Likewise, this measure is also directed at the Turks who, at that hour, are tempted to attack the Christians when they are able to get close enough to them. For this reason they adopted the practice that, whenever the Christians are encamped under arms in the presence of the enemy, they let out three cries like the one heard earlier, both after nightfall and before daybreak. After he heard these explanations, Lord Wavrin asked them, 'But if the Turks had actually come to attack at that hour, how could we tell the difference between a cry of alarm and that intended to calm the horses?' To which they replied 'If we will be attacked, you will hear the sound of the trumpets and the drums, and the cries will be much louder than the one you just heard.'"[66]

---

[66]Iorga, "Cronica lui Wavrin," p. 142.

A few nights later, Regnault de Comfide came to his Captain with an idea: "'You know that we wouldn't be proper gentlemen if we didn't wake the Turks from their sleep one of these nights.' 'How can we do this?', Lord Wavrin asked him."[67] Comfide proposed that they take the small boats from the Burgundian galleys, as well as those from the Cardinal's ships, and place oarsmen, trumpeters, and culvriniers in each and then have them move up river, under the cover of darkness, close to the Ottoman camp, but out of range of their archers; then, when they were all in position, to begin firing their guns and sounding their trumpets to make the Turks think that the Christians had come ashore and were attacking. After both Wavrin and Condolmieri approved his plan, Comfide prepared to put it into effect, first informing the Wallachians and Hungarians of what they were about to do so as not to create confusion within their own ranks.

Comfide's scheme came off without a hitch. The results were even better than the crusaders had anticipated. Wavrin tells us that "the tumultuous panic lasted for over a quarter of an hour. Soon after, the Turkish fires could be seen going out, until finally all of them were extinguished. From this, it could be deduced that all of the Turks had fled. As this was going on, many Wallachians and Hungarians who were slaves of the Saracens and who knew how to swim, tried their luck and jumped into the water and swam across the river. Arriving at the Christian army, they told how the Turks had fled as quickly as they could, leaving behind all of their baggage, and they said that if two or three hundred men would have landed on the opposite shore at that moment they would have gained substantial booty."[68]

When the Christian fleet set out the next morning, the Turks were nowhere to be seen. They encountered them again around four o'clock that afternoon; the Ottomans had regrouped and taken up positions at a point where the river narrowed. They had readied their artillery and began firing as soon as the Christian galleys approached, but, as they lacked any heavy guns, they did not present a serious threat to the fleet. Instead of returning their fire, Wavrin relates how "all of the Christians, both those on water and those on land, taunted them [the Turks] as much as they could, making fun of them in a

[67]Iorga, "Cronica lui Wavrin," p. 142.

[68]Iorga, "Cronica lui Wavrin," pp. 143-144.

defiant tone for fleeing like cowards the night before."[69] That evening, on the feast of St. Michael, September 29, the crusaders reached the junction with the Jiu River where the barks Hunyadi had ordered for the crossing awaited them.

The Christians now prepared to cross the Danube to Rahova, which Wavrin describes as "a small town, deserted and ruined since the time when Emperor Sigismund of Germany and Duke John of Burgundy battled with the Turks before Nicopolis." The Christian commanders consulted and "decided to disembark the archers, arbalesters, cannoneers, and culvriniers from the galleys in this ruined fortress, together with their munitions. Then, as the walls there were still standing, those who landed would take cover there and arrange to fire in battery upon the Turks to cover the crossing of the Wallachians and the Hungarians, who, as they came over would fortify that place..."[70] The crossing, which went on unopposed, took two days and two nights. On the morning of October 2, the Christian force was ready for battle.

That morning, Hunyadi set out with twelve hundred cavalry to confront the Turkish army less than two miles away. When they saw him coming, the Ottomans began an orderly retreat. When they realized that the Christians intended to pursue them, they began to set fire to their provisions and to the neighboring villages. When Hunyadi observed this, he returned to the Christian camp and ordered his men to cross back over the Danube, telling them that there was nothing more they could do there. The Transylvanian Voivode then informed Condolmieri and Wavrin: "I consider that I have completely fulfilled the promise made under my seal and I declare that the Captain General of Burgundy has also fulfilled the agreement that he made with us. As you have seen, I crossed the Danube River and offered battle to the Turks, but they retreat and burn all of the provisions in our path, thinking that we will follow them. But it is not possible for us to do this as we do not have enough food with us for more than two days. And, as I know the Turks very well, I realize that if I follow them they will just keep retreating before me, trying to draw me deeper into their country so that they can attack me when it will be to their advantage and so that I cannot withdraw, except threatened with great danger and heavy losses. I remember how last year, at the battle of Varna,

---

[69]Iorga, "Cronica lui Wavrin," p. 144.

[70]Iorga, "Cronica lui Wavrin," p. 144.

we lost the King and a large number of the nobles and people of Hungary. This Kingdom, its nobility, and its people are now in my care, and I cannot venture to put them at risk. For if I would be killed, the Kingdom would be lost."[71]

Wavrin and Condolmieri were taken aback at Hunyadi's abrupt reversal. They believed that when the Christian force crossed the Danube to Rahova it had marked the beginning of a new crusade. They even asked Hunyadi if there was a well-fortified port up river where the galleys could spend the winter so that they could resume campaigning in the spring, but the Transylvanian Voivode informed them that there was no suitable place for them to winter and, as it was already late in the season and the Danube would soon freeze over, he urged them to leave for home as quickly as possible. Baffled at Hunyadi's sudden lack of interest in fighting the Turks, the Burgundian commander and the Papal Legate prepared their galleys for the voyage home.

In reality, Hunyadi never intended to undertake a serious campaign against the Ottomans in 1445. His political rivals in Buda had compelled him to accept the Burgundian proposal, hoping to keep him occupied elsewhere while the succession crisis played itself out. But Hunyadi knew that he could not afford to venture away from Hungary for long at this critical time. He worked to undermine the operation before it got off the ground by conditioning Hungarian participation. But Pietre Vast had surprised the Transylvanian Voivode by securing Vlad's assistance and bringing back Daud Celebi from Constantinople. He then had no choice but to gather his army and to set out for the Danube, to the delight of his political opponents in Buda. Already on July 29, the Transylvanian Voivode was in Grosseheuern (Sura Mare),[72] near Sibiu, but he delayed crossing the mountains far as long as he could so that his late arrival would provide a plausible motive to call off the campaign and allow him to return to Hungary as quickly as possible. Even though he told Wavrin and Condolmieri that the Kingdom was in his charge, his position was not yet secure; only in the summer of 1446 did the Diet settle the succession crisis and appoint Hunyadi as Governor of Hungary to rule in the name of the boy King Ladislas Posthumous.

---

[71]Iorga, "Cronica lui Wavrin," p. 145.

[72]Doc. 2519 in *Urkundenbuch*, V, p. 158.

The abrupt end to the campaign of 1445 suited Vlad as well, but for entirely different reasons. From the time he had received news of their arrival in Brăila, the Wallachian Prince had sought to direct the efforts of the crusaders against Ottoman military objectives along the Danube that posed a threat to the security of his border. His success in doing so made him the main beneficiary of the campaign, highlighted by his taking control of the strategically important fortress at Giurgiu. But Vlad had no interest in continuing the campaign south of the Danube or in engaging in an all-out war with the Ottomans. His uneasy relations with Hunyadi also made cooperation with the Transylvanian Voivode difficult. So, when the campaign came to its abrupt end, Vlad had no regrets and felt satisfied that he had achieved some important objectives.

Wavrin and Condolmieri took their leave of Vlad and Hunyadi, expressing their regret that they could do no more against the Turks, and proceeded back down the Danube and out to the Black Sea. They reached Constantinople on November 4. By the time they laid anchor at the Byzantine capital, Wavrin had fully recovered from his illness. John VIII received the returning crusaders with honors. The gifts Wavrin received from the Emperor included "a piece of the precious and holy robe of Our Lord Jesus Christ, worked and sewn by the very hands of his mother, the Holy Virgin.... encased in a gold cross, adorned with large pearls and other precious stones."[73]

After repairing and provisioning his galleys, Wavrin set out for the Republic of St. Mark where Doge Francesco Foscari and the people of Venice gave him and his men a hero's welcome. From there, the Burgundians made their way on horseback to Rome where a grand reception from Pope Eugenius and his Cardinals awaited them. In his audience with the Pope, Wavrin recounted the expedition to him, adding that "if the Hungarians and the Greeks would have organized things better, so that his services could have been fully used in the defense of Christianity, he would have continued in his efforts."[74] The Burgundian commander then asked Eugenius to keep in mind the services that his sovereign, Duke Philip of Burgundy, had provided to the Christian cause. The Pope and the Cardinals thanked Wavrin and his men for their

---

[73]Iorga, "Cronica lui Wavrin," pp. 146, 148.

[74]Iorga, "Cronica lui Wavrin," p. 147.

gallantry. Eugenius then gave Wavrin a series of indulgences to take back with him to Burgundy and told him to express his gratitude to Duke Philip for organizing and financing this expedition. Walerand de Wavrin then made his way back home to Burgundy where he found the Duke in Lille and gave him a full report on his efforts against the Turks and the futile search for the lost King.

Although the campaign of 1445 had strengthened his defenses against Ottoman attacks, Vlad still had to find a way to deal with the Turkish threat after the departure of the Burgundian and Papal forces. But he also faced dangers from other directions. Well-aware that Hunyadi would prefer someone else on the throne of the Transalpine land, Vlad had cause to be wary of his relationship with Hungary where the Transylvanian Voivode's power was on the rise. In addition, his old nemesis Stephen II of Moldavia, who had defeated and blinded his half-brother Iliaş, also began to pose a serious threat as he was determined to recover Kilia which Vlad had seized from him in 1439. Thus, Vlad Dracul entered the new year facing dangers all around him.

Chapter XI

The Raven's Clutches

"Just such a comedy," said Don Quixote, "is acted on the great stage
of the world, where some play the emperors, others the prelates, and,
in short, all the parts can be brought into a dramatic piece; till death,
which is the catastrophe, and the end of the action, strips the actors of
all their marks of distinction, and levels their quality in the grave."

—Miguel de Cervantes Saavedra, *Don Quixote*[1]

E ven after he drove his older brother Iliaş out of Moldavia and
subsequently blinded him, Stephen II still did not rule the Principality
alone. Forced to share power with his younger brother, Peter II, the
sibling rivalry that had plagued the country since the death of Alexander the
Good persisted. This prevented Stephen from attempting to seize Kilia from
Vlad who had taken the strategic fortress near the mouth of the Danube from
him in 1439. But when war broke out between the two brothers ruling
Moldavia in the spring of 1445, Stephen defeated Peter, who took refuge in
Poland, and once again became sole ruler of the country. No longer faced with

---

[1]Miguel de Cervantes Saavedra, *Don Quixote*, Wordsworth Classics, 1993, p. 435.

internal strife, he now had the opportunity to strike back at the Wallachian Prince.

But with Wavrin's galleys anchored at Brăila from May to August of that year and the subsequent campaign of the Burgundian and Papal fleet along the Danube, which extended into October, Stephen had to bide his time. He could not risk taking any provocative action while the crusaders remained in the region for fear that Vlad's new allies would help him in case of an attack. On September 23, 1445, the Moldavian Prince granted the Monastery of Humor, in the northern part of the country, an exemption from all royal duties to transport two cartloads of fish each year from Galați or anywhere else in the country.[2] This is the earliest extant mention in documents of the Moldavian port city on the Danube, located some thirty kilometers down river from the Wallachian port of Brăila. As the Danube was the hub of the fishing industry in both Moldavia and Wallachia, the fact that Stephen specifies Galați in this decree proves that Kilia, a significantly more important port and commercial center at this time, had not yet entered into his possession.

At some point during the winter of 1445-1446, after the departure of the Christian fleet from the Danube and with Vlad busy strengthening the citadel at Giurgiu and preparing for an inevitable Ottoman counterattack in the spring, Stephen II made his move. The Moldavian Prince took back the stronghold at the mouth of the Danube. Although we lack details as to how this came about, by February 1446, Vlad's nemesis once again ruled Kilia. This is confirmed by a diploma issued at Suceava on February 19, 1446, in which Stephen granted to the Monastery of Neamț, "in each year, two maji of fish from Kilia and, from our Princess, three cântare of black caviar. For this, whoever among our boyars shall be Pârcalab of Kilia, together with their officials, they shall give all that is written above to this Monastery of Neamț when the representatives of that monastery will come for them."[3] The loss of the outlet to the sea dealt a serious blow to Wallachian strategic and commercial

---

[2] Doc. 64 in Costăchescu, *Documentele moldovenești*, vol. II, p. 235.

[3] Doc. 68 in Costăchescu, *Documentele moldovenești*, vol. II, pp. 244-246. A *maja* (pl. *maji*) represented approximately 200 kilograms during this period and a *cântar* (pl. *cântare*) approximately 55 kilograms, see Săchelarie and Stoicescu, eds., *Instituții feudale din țările române*, pp. 104, 281-282.

interests, but Vlad could not react. The threat posed by the Turks, who sought revenge for their humiliation at the hands of the Wallachian Prince in the fall of 1445, loomed large and, under these circumstances, Vlad could not risk going to war against Moldavia.

Throughout the winter, Vlad reinforced his newly-won stronghold at Giurgiu and maintained his military forces in a state of alert, waiting for the Turks to launch their counterattack. In the spring of 1446, an Ottoman army led by Davud Bey invaded Wallachia. Although we lack any precise details of this campaign, it was almost certainly directed against Giurgiu, in an attempt to recover the strategically important citadel protecting one of the key crossing points along the lower Danube. The Turks could not allow the Wallachian Prince to go unpunished for his actions of the previous fall. But Vlad inflicted a resounding defeat on the invaders whose shockwaves rocked the Porte.[4]

The situation in the Ottoman capital was tense and the news from Wallachia only made matters worse. Murad's second abdication following his victory at Varna only served to amplify the conflict between the traditional Turkish aristocracy and the new slave elite that had begun to dominate the Ottoman administrative and military apparatus. The young Sultan, Mehmed II, still lacked the political savvy needed to maintain an equilibrium between the rival groups within his Empire. Economic troubles complicated things even further. The wars in Europe and Asia in recent years had drained the Ottoman treasury and the Janissaries had not been paid for the past six months. To deal with the financial crisis, Mehmed II devalued the Ottoman currency, the akçe or asper, by reducing its silver content from 5 3/4 carats to 5 1/4 carats, and then paid off the outstanding debts using the new coinage.[5] But these measures only served to heighten tensions.

When word of Vlad's startling victory over Davud Bey arrived in Adrianople, the conflicts brewing at the Porte reached their breaking point.

---

[4]Gemil, *Românii şi otomanii*, p. 122. An Ottoman calendar from 1452 (Hegira 856) invokes the defeat of Davud Bey in Wallachia in the spring of 1446 as the main reason that Murad resumed the throne.

[5]Gemil, *Românii şi otomanii*, pp. 122, nt. 303, and 213-214; and Decei, *Istoria imperiului otoman*, p. 94. The total weight of the *akçe* at this time was 1.14 grams with a silver content of around 90%.

Mehmed quickly tried to organize a new expedition against the Wallachian Prince under the leadership of Shehabeddin Pasha, the Beylerbey of Rumelia, who had recently regained his former post after his disgrace following his disastrous campaign in Wallachia in September 1442. The Janissaries, however, refused to take part in any military action led by Shehabeddin Pasha, calling into question his abilities as an army commander. They were also unhappy about the recent currency devaluation that had effectively reduced their pay and demanded an increase of one-half an akçe in their daily stipend to compensate for this. The Sultan's elite troops gathered on a small hill outside the Ottoman capital, demanding that Mehmed redress their grievances, threatening to support Orhan Celebi, a pretender to the throne who claimed to be a son of Bayezid I, if he did not. This marked the first time since its inception that the Janissary corps rose up against their Sultan; it became known as the Buçuk Tepe revolt, so-called for the small hill outside Adrianople where they staged their protest. Mehmed quickly agreed to meet their pay demands, but by now the situation at the Porte had spiralled out of control. Once again, Grand Vizir Halil Pasha Cenderli, the leading representative of the traditional Turkish aristocracy, prevailed upon Murad to come out of retirement to restore order in the troubled Empire.

Even though his victory over Davud Bay and the internal strife prevailing in the Ottoman Empire reduced the danger of Turkish attack, Vlad could not let down his guard. The Ottomans could still strike at any time. Despite his strained relations with Hunyadi, the Wallachian Prince maintained cordial relations with Hungary throughout the spring and summer of 1446, allowing him to focus his resources on the Ottoman threat. Peace with the Transalpine land during this period also served the interests of the Transylvanian Voivode. It permitted him to direct his attention to the ongoing succession struggle in the Kingdom and to deal with social unrest that once again beset Hungary and threatened to reach the proportions it had a decade earlier.[6] To ameliorate the trade disputes that had strained relations between the two countries, Hunyadi and Nicholas Ujlaki, together with the Counts of the Szecklers, issued a written

---

[6]Docs. 2547, 2569, and 2570 in *Urkundenbuch*, V, pp. 173-174, 190; see also Radu Constantinescu, "Quelques observations sur l'epoque de Vlad Tepes," in *RRH*, XVII:1 (1978), p. 36.

order to the castellans at Bran on March 15, 1446, not to impede traders from Braşov and the Bârsa land, as well as "all other travellers and merchants of any status" crossing the border with Wallachia, and, "at the customs points at Bran and its appendages, to tax goods according to the ancient customs and the registers established regarding this."[7]

Relations between Hungary and Wallachia, however, began to sour after the Diet, assembled at Pest, appointed Hunyadi as Governor of Hungary on June 5, 1446, effectively making him regent for the boy King Ladislas who remained in the custody of Holy Roman Emperor Frederick III. As ruler of Hungary, Hunyadi now sought to isolate Vlad as he prepared to renew the struggle against the Ottomans, intending to replace him as Prince of Wallachia with a candidate of his own choosing, just as he had done in 1442 when he drove out Mircea after Vlad's imprisonment by the Sultan. As a first step in this direction, on October 25, the newly-elected Governor of Hungary wrote to officials of Braşov and the Bârsa land, informing them of a new monetary issue and forbidding the circulation of Turkish akçe or coins emitted by the Transalpine Voivode in Transylvania.[8] But Hunyadi could not yet take direct action against Vlad. First he had to prepare a successor and, more importantly, to consolidate his own position as war broke out with Austria in the fall of 1446. The Hungarian army invaded southern Austria in November of that year and won a series of victories, but Ottoman attacks along the Kingdom's southern border[9] forced the Governor to pull back his troops and to open negotiations with Frederick III. Vlad also faced renewed Turkish raids into Wallachia.

When Murad finally resumed the Imperial throne, Vlad opened a dialogue with the Ottomans. He needed to secure his southern frontier so that he could direct his resources toward Moldavia to retaliate against Stephen II for his seizure of Kilia, as well as to protect himself in the face of a potential threat

---

[7]Quo. Pall, "Iancu de Hunedoara şi confirmarea privilegiului pentru negoţul Braşovenilor şi al Bîrsenilor cu Ţara Românescă," p. 76.

[8]Doc. 2555 in *Urkundenbuch*, vol. V, pp. 178-179.

[9]Iorga, *Acte şi documente*, vol. III, p. 22. A letter from Frederick III to Duke Albert at Bavaria, dated November 21, 1446, mentions Ottoman attacks on Fürchtenstein and Hornstein and areas around Wallachia.

from Hungary. Peace with Wallachia also suited the Sultan. Murad needed a respite to address the troubles afflicting his Empire and to deal with more pressing matters such as Scanderbeg's revolt in Albania and that of Despot Constantine in the Morea. These same considerations had led him to come to terms a few months earlier with Venice. By the beginning of the summer of 1447, Vlad had once again concluded a peace treaty with the Ottomans.

The new accord restored the previous agreement between Vlad and Murad that had allowed him to return to Wallachia in the spring of 1444. It restored his sons Vlad and Radu to him and also permitted him to retain possession of the fortress of Giurgiu. While the treaty obligated the Wallachian Prince to return 4,000 of the 12,000 Bulgarians who had taken refuge in his land in the fall of 1445, it allowed the remaining 8,000 to stay. One of Hunyadi's confidants, John of Zredna, Bishop of Nagyvarad (Oradea in Romanian; Grosswardein in German), later pointed to this provision to justify the Hungarian Governor's intervention south of the Carpathians; in a letter dated January 15, 1448, he wrote, "the Prince, or as they usually say, the Voivode of the Transalpine land, joined forces with the Turks this past summer and returned to slavery many Christian souls, about 4,000, who he had freed during an earlier war."[10] But despite this propagandistic criticism, Vlad had won another diplomatic victory, obtaining highly favorable terms from Murad. Most importantly, it allowed him to turn his attention to Moldavia.

After Stephen blinded his brother Ilias, thereby making him ineligible to rule, it fell to Ilias's son Roman to avenge his father and to press his own claim to the throne. As early as 1439, Ilias had designated Roman as his heir, when, for the first time, he referred to his twelve year old son in his diplomas with the title of Voivode.[11] When Stephen II, taking advantage of the fact that Vlad

---

[10]Quo. Minea, "Vlad Dracul şi vremea sa," p. 269. This document is mistakenly dated 1447, but the contents of the letter leave no doubt that it is from 1448 as Francisc Pall has conclusively demonstrated, see, Francisc Pall, "Intervenţia lui Iancu de Hunedoara în Ţara Românescă şi Moldova în anii 1447-1448," in *Studii*, XVI:5 (1963), pp. 1050-1051.

[11]Doc. 11 in Costăchescu, *Documentele moldoveneşti*, vol. II, pp. 31-35. This diploma for the Monastery of Moldoviţa, dated March 12, 1439, from Suceava, is the earliest mention of Roman with the title of Voivode.

languished in an Ottoman prison, vanquished Iliaş, Roman fled to Poland with his father and mother. The political crisis in Poland following the death of Vladislav III at Varna made it difficult for the young Moldavian prince to gather the support he needed to mount a challenge to his uncle, but, with help from his cousin Casimir, the newly-crowned King of Poland, and his brother-in-law Vlad, by the summer of 1447 Roman stood ready. But lacking sufficient strength to attack Stephen on his own, he formed an alliance with his uncle, Peter II, who had also sought refuge in Poland after Stephen drove him out of Moldavia in 1445.

Roman and Peter launched a two-pronged attack against Moldavia from the north at the beginning of July 1447. Their invasions took Stephen II by surprise. As Roman's army advanced on Suceava, the Prince abandoned his capital and fled in the direction of the fortress of Neamţ, perhaps in an attempt to reach Transylvania to seek help from Hunyadi. But Roman caught up with his uncle and captured him in the vicinity of the citadel. Then, to avenge the mutilation of his father, he had him beheaded on July 13. The seventeenth century Wallachian chronicler Radu Popescu explains what happened in the neighboring Principality, writing that, "After Voivode Stephen blinded his brother Iliaş in Moldavia, Voivode Roman, the son of Iliaş, could not tolerate this illegal act of his uncle, and he spoke with a large number of the country's boyars and, rising up, they captured his uncle, Voivode Stephen, and cut off his head."[12] Stephen II was then buried at the nearby Monastery of Neamţ. Meanwhile, Peter occupied Suceava. Two Princes once again governed Moldavia, with Peter II ruling in the north and Roman II in the south.

With Stephen out of the way, the fragile alliance between the nephew and his uncle soon unravelled. According to Polish chronicler Jan Długosz, Roman received military assistance from his brother-in-law Vlad and forced Peter to flee the country, thereby becoming the sole Prince of Moldavia. This occurred sometime around the beginning of September 1447. War between the two had not yet broken out on August 22, when Peter issued a diploma from Suceava confirming previous donations received by the Monastery of Neamţ in which

---

[12]Popescu, *Istoriile domnilor Ţării Româneşti*, p. 20. Roman's beheading of Stephen is recorded in some of the earliest Moldavian chronicles, such as those from the Monastery of Putna, see Panaitescu, ed., *Cronicile slavo-române*, pp. 44, 56.

he invokes Roman, whom he calls "My Majesty's brother," as his associate ruler.[13] But Roman's ambition to rule the country alone could already be seen in a letter he addressed to officials and merchants from the Bârsa land on August 4, inviting them "to come to us, to our country, with all of your goods and merchandise, without fear of any losses, because our country is open to you, and you will not suffer any injustices here for we will maintain the same rights and laws for you that you had in the time of our holy departed parent Voivode Alexander,"[14] without making any mention of Peter II. When Roman, aided by Wallachian troops, attacked his uncle, Peter took refuge in Transylvania where he sought help from John Hunyadi to regain the throne.

With his brother-in-law now safely in control of Moldavia, Vlad does not appear to have pressed his claim to Kilia. As long as he had a firm ally on the throne of the neighboring Principality, the fact that the Danubian port remained in Moldavian hands caused little harm to Wallachian interests. But, more importantly, the Polish Crown would have frowned on his retaking Kilia. The Poles wanted the strategic port to remain part of Moldavia because international treaties recognized their suzerainty over that Principality[15] and

---

[13]Doc. 81 in Costăchescu, *Documentele moldovenești*, vol. II, pp. 288-298. The term brother is used for nephew, coveying the sense of equality between the two Princes.

[14]Doc. 283 in *DRH, D*, p. 393. The fact that Roman refers to Alexander as his "parent" has led some to conjecture the existence of an additional Roman, a son of Alexander the Good, see, for example, Stefan Gorovei, *Mușatinii*, Bucharest, 1976, p. 53. There is, however, insufficient evidence to support such a hypothesis, which is contradicted by numerous sources that clearly indicate that Roman, the son of Iliaș, invaded the country at this time and deposed and beheaded his uncle Stephen. It must also be remembered that the Slavic term for parent used in this letter, *roditel*, was frequently employed with a general sense that did not necessarily imply parentage.

[15]This position of the Polish Crown regarding Kilia is clearly seen the following year. In return for Hunyadi's support against Roman, Peter II had turned the fortress over to the Hungarians, but when he reconciled with Poland on August 22, 1448, he promised not to estrange any more of his territories without the approval of "Casimir, the King of Poland, and of his Crown, and those which have been estranged, we want to take back," clearly referring to Kilia, see Doc. 215 in Costăchescu, *Documentele moldovenești*, vol. II, pp. 733-737.

Vlad could not risk alienating this key ally to which both he and Roman now looked for support against Hungary.

Vlad's intervention in Moldavia pushed his already strained relations with John Hunyadi to the breaking point. Having attained supreme power in Hungary, the Governor could now turn his attention to the problems in the two Principalities bordering Transylvania to the south and to the east. Hunyadi began to prepare one of his relatives to replace Vlad on the throne of the Transalpine land. This was Vladislav who, in a diploma dated April 15, 1456, refers to himself as "son of the Great Voivode Dan."[16] While it has generally been assumed that he was a son of Dan II, that Prince only mentions his sons Danciul and Basarab in extant documents, the latest of which recalling his offspring is dated October 7, 1428.[17] If Vladislav was born between that date and 1431, when Dan was killed in battle with Alexander Aldea, he would have been seventeen or eighteen years old when he became a pretender in 1447. In a subsequent diploma, this one confirming the privileges and holdings of the Monastery of Tismana, Dan II only mentions "My Majesty's sons."[18] Perhaps he chose this formula to reflect the birth of yet another son, instead of mentioning each by name. To support the claim that he was a son of Dan II, some equate Vladislav with Danciul,[19] but we know for certain that Danciul is the pretender known as Dan III, who later tried to oust Vlad the Impaler. In a letter to the burghers of Braşov, Dan III calls himself, "the son of the Great

---

[16]Doc. 113 in *DRH, B*, vol. I, pp. 196-197. This is the only extant document from the reign of Vladislav II in which he makes any mention of his parentage.

[17]Doc. 61 in *DRH, B*, vol. I, pp. 117-118.

[18]Doc. 64 in *DRH, B*, vol. I, pp. 124-125. This document is dated either March 20, 1429, or April 9, 1430, as it mentions that it was granted on Palm Sunday which falls on these dates in the respective years. The list of members of the royal council indicates that it dates from the final two years of Dan's reign.

[19]Pavel Chihaia, *De la Negru Vodă la Neagoe Basarab*, Bucharest, 1976, p. 149. Chihaia justifies his assertion by claiming that Vladislav was the name adopted by Danciul when he became Prince, but this is completely false. There was no practice of Princes in Wallachia changing their Christian names upon assuming the throne, instead they added the name John to indicate their status as anointed ruler. In addition, *before* he became Prince, John Hunyadi refers to him as "Vladislav the Wallachian," see Doc. 282 in *DRH, D*, pp. 392-393.

Voivode Dan," and asks them "to remember the services that the Voivode Dan, our parent and our Prince, did for the Christians,"[20] leaving no doubt that he is referring to Dan II who many of the Saxon leaders alive then would still remember. If we admit the possibility that Vladislav II was not the son of Dan II, then whose son was he?

For Vladislav to have been a son of Dan I, he would have been in his early sixties in 1447, which is somewhat unlikely given life expectancy at the time and the fact that he remained in obscurity for so long. Another possibility is that he was a son of Vlad I, who was frequently referred to as Dan after his father. The kinship ties between the Corvinus family and the Wallachian dynasty date to the time of Dan I, and Hunyadi is linked to his descendants and not those of Mircea the Old. One piece of evidence to support this theory comes from Ottoman chroniclers Ruhi Celebi and Sa'adeddin who both say that Hunyadi replaced Vlad with "Ladoglu," meaning "the son of Vlad."[21] If he were a son of Vlad I, who lived in Hungary after Mircea drove him from Wallachia at the end of 1396, Vladislav would have likely been in his forties or fifties when he challenged Vlad in 1447. Ultimately, the only way to shed light on the problem of Vladislav's parentage would be if his body, interred at the Dealu Monastery near Târgoviște, were exhumed and subjected to medical examination to determine his approximate age at the time of his death in 1456.

Vladislav is first mentioned in a letter dated July 13, 1447, in which John Hunyadi informs the officials of Brașov that "this Vladislav the Wallachian, our relative, intends to set out and to come from the Transalpine land with all of his things and his goods to the Kingdom of Hungary. For this reason, we ask that you, as our friends, take notice of this, and that when this Vladislav comes among you with his things, you kindly place at his disposal a house where he can live in your city, and help and assist him..."[22] While some have seen this letter as an indication that Vladislav was returning from a failed

---

[20]Doc. LXXVIII in Bogdan, *Documente privitoare*, pp. 100-101. This letter dates from 1459 when Dan III was in Transylvania trying to gather resources to overthrow Vlad the Impaler.

[21]Aurel Decei, "Oastea lui Iancu de Hunedoara înainte de bătălia de la Kosovo," in *RIR*, XVI (1946), p. 49, nt. 1.

[22]Doc. 282 in *DRH, D*, pp. 392-393.

campaign in Wallachia against Vlad,[23] the phrasing does not support such a conclusion. Vladislav's coming to Braşov clearly was a carefully-planned, calculated move, not a hasty retreat. In addition, the time needed for news of events in Wallachia to reach the Governor at Szecseny in Hungary, from where he wrote to the Saxon leaders, and then for his letter to reach Braşov exclude this hypothesis. It appears more likely that Vladislav had been living in Wallachia up to this time and had somehow managed to stay aloof of the political struggles afflicting the country until now. This would support the conclusion that he was not a son of Dan II, for he could hardly have remained in the Principality had he been the brother of Vlad's rival Basarab II. What is certain is that John Hunyadi, searching for an alternative to Vlad, brought Vladislav to Transylvania to groom him as a pretender to the Wallachian throne.

Now that the Hungarian Governor had a viable and legitimate candidate of royal descent to place on the throne of the Transalpine land, he waited for an opportune moment to act. After Vlad made peace with Murad, effectively renouncing the joint suzerainty of the Ottomans and the Hungarians over Wallachia agreed to in the summer of 1444, and intervened in Moldavia to install his brother-in-law on the throne of the neighboring Principality, Hunyadi decided that he could wait no longer. With the Kingdom bordered by unfriendly states to the south and to the east, the Governor needed to reassert Hungarian authority over Wallachia and Moldavia before he could again turn his attention to the Turks. While he prepared to replace Vlad with Vladislav in Wallachia, Hunyadi forged an alliance with Peter II to drive out Roman from Moldavia. In return for the Governor's support, Peter II promised to turn over Kilia to Hungarian control upon resuming the throne; apart from the military significance of the Danubian citadel, Hunyadi, like Sigismund before him, wanted to secure for Hungary an outlet to participate in the prosperous trade with the Orient.[24] Peter also married one of Hunyadi's sisters or cousins to

---

[23] Andreescu, *Vlad Ţepeş (Dracula)*, pp. 27-28.

[24] Şerban Papacostea, "Kilia et la politique orientale de Sigismund de Luxembourg," in *RRH*, XV:3 (1976), p. 433.

cement their agreement.[25] But the Governor knew that Wallachia was the key to control over the region. If he removed Vlad, Roman would fall. And so, Hunyadi first directed his attention to the Principality south of the Carpathians.

Some have suggested that John Hunyadi attacked Vlad in revenge for his brief imprisonment after his return from Varna in November 1444.[26] Chalkokondyles suggests a connection between these two events, writing, "a short time later [after Vlad arrested Hunyadi], Choniat [Hunyadi] removed him from the throne."[27] But this was not the real motive for his actions. George Branković detained Hunyadi for almost two months after his defeat at Kosovo in 1448, but it did not lead the Hungarian Governor to organize a campaign against the Serbian Despot. Vlad's arrest of Hunyadi three years earlier was just one incident in a long series of disputes between the two men. The Byzantine chronicler concludes that Hunyadi installed Vladislav "in the land of Dacia because of his hatred of Dracula."[28] The Governor's immediate reasons for moving against Vlad were directly tied to the political situation at this time. The Wallachian Prince's renunciation of Hungarian suzerainty in favor of the Turks and his intervention in Moldavia to install his brother-in-law Roman on the throne provoked the wrath of the Hungarian Governor, but, more importantly, Hunyadi planned a new offensive against the Turks and needed military support from Wallachia and Moldavia. In a treaty he signed with King Alphonse V of Naples and Aragon on November 6, 1447, the Hungarian Governor stipulated that he intended to draw 10,000 troops from Wallachia for a new campaign against the Turks.[29] With this in mind, he now prepared to move against Vlad.

---

[25]Minea, *Informaţiile româneşti*, p. 37. Długosz says that Peter married an older sister of Hunyadi, which means she would have been in her forties as the Governor was born around 1407. Peter was twenty-four at the time. It is also possible that Długosz refers to another of Hunyadi's relatives, as kinship terms are often employed with a loose meaning.

[26]See, for example, Florescu and McNally, *Dracula*, p. 38.

[27]Chalcocondil, *Expuneri istorice*, p. 200 (VII, 338).

[28]Chalcocondil, *Expuneri istorice*, p. 210 (VII, 358).

[29]The eminent historians Francisc Pall and Şerban Papacostea support this conclusion concerning the motives for Hunyadi's intervention in Wallachia in November-

John Hunyadi arrived in Transylvania in the fall of 1447 and began to gather an army and to make preparations for a campaign against Vlad.[30] At Schässburg, on November 10, he issued a document mentioning the delay of a trial that had been scheduled to take place the day before, but which he had postponed until January 13, 1448, "because of the setting out of the army raised against the villainous Vlad, the Transalpine Voivode."[31] By November 17, the Hungarian Governor was in Braşov where he joined Vladislav and made final preparations for the campaign; on November 23, he made some last-minute armament procurements before setting out. A few days later, Hunyadi, Vladislav, and the Hungarian army crossed into Wallachia via the Bran pass.

Even though John Hunyadi, also called Corvinus for the raven emblazed on his family crest, had been preparing for several weeks to invade Wallachia, Vlad remained unaware that the bird of ill-omen hovered over him. With winter about to set in, he did not believe that he had done anything provocative enough to incite an immediate attack by the Hungarian Governor, nor did he receive any reliable intelligence from Transylvania to warn him in advance of the imminent danger. According to Długosz, Hunyadi masked his true purpose and entered Wallachia with a large army under the pretext of setting out against the Turks.[32] But as soon as Vlad realized what was happening, together with Mircea, he hastily gathered an army. Chalkokondyles tells us that "this son of Mircea [the Old]; together with his son, prepared for battle. Together, they established their battle lines and stood ready to fight, but the Dacians [Wallachians] abandoned the son of Mircea and crossed over to Dan

---

December 1447, see Pall, "Intervenţia lui Iancu de Hunedoara," pp. 1054-1055; and Şerban Papacostea, "La Moldavie état tributaire de l'Empire Ottoman au XVe siècle," in *RRH*, XIII:3 (1974), pp. 452-453.

[30]Doc. 287 in *DRH, D*, pp. 396-397. This diploma, issued by Hunyadi at Bistriţa on February 1, 1448, confirms the holdings of Ladislas Bathory, rewarding him for his military services to the Crown, including the campaign against "the disloyal, belated Vlad, the Transalpine Voivode."

[31]Doc. 2607 in *Urkundenbuch*, V, pp. 215-216. This motive for the delay of the trial is repeated in a subsequent document referring to the same case dated February 24, 1449, see Doc. 294 in *DRH, D*, p. 404.

[32]Minea, *Informaţiile româneşti*, p. 37.

[Vladislav]."[33] Seeing themselves vastly outnumbered by the superior Hungarian force, it is likely that many of Vlad's troops went over to the enemy. Nevertheless, most of his leading boyars remained loyal to their Prince. One possible exception is his Vornic, Manea Udriște, who had risen to prominence under Vlad and had become the most important official in the country; when Vladislav II assumed the throne, he remained the most powerful boyar on the royal council.[34] His son, Dragomir, would play a leading role in Wallachian politics during the second half of the fifteenth century.

A keen observer of events along the frontier between Christianity and Islam at this time, Enea Silvio Piccolomini notes Vlad's overthrow in his Cosmographia: "the Dans [the family to which Vladislav II belonged] received help from John Hunyadi, who governed Hungary, and he reinstalled them, obtaining for himself glory and wealth, as the one who freed the land of the Dans from Turkish power; he occupied them, keeping them as perpetual possessions for himself and his successors."[35] Długosz also accuses him of intending to seize the throne for himself.[36] Indeed, a conveyance granted by Hunyadi to Peter, the son of Stroya of Ponor, from Târgoviște on December 4, 1447, has led some to conclude that the Hungarian Governor briefly considered taking the Wallachian throne for himself.[37] In the document's salutation, he refers to himself as "Governor of the Kingdom of Hungary and, by the grace of God, Voivode of the Transalpine land."[38] This is the first and

---

[33]Chalcocondil, *Expuneri istorice*, p. 200 (VII, 338-339).

[34]The earliest extant diploma from the reign of Vladislav II listing members of his royal council dates from January 2, 1450. Manea Udriște appears first among all boyars indicating his preeminence at the court of Vlad's successor, a status he probably would not have attained had he not thrown in his lot with Hunyadi and Vladislav in November-December 1447, see Doc. 101 in *DRH, B*, vol. I, pp. 176-177. The shrewd boyar did the same when Vlad the Impaler seized the throne in 1456.

[35]Holban, ed., *Călători străini*, vol. I, p. 472.

[36]Minea, *Informaţiile româneşti*, p. 37.

[37]See, for example, Francisc Pall, "De nouveau sur l'action de Ianco de Hunedoara (Hunyadi) en Valachie pendant l'année 1447," in *RRH*, XV:3 (1976), p. 449.

[38]Doc. 286 in *DRH, D*, pp. 394-396. Hunyadi grants estates to Peter in the region around his native Hunyad in Transylvania in recognition of his services "at different times and places in the interest of the Holy Crown of the Kingdom of Hungary and also

only document we possess in which Hunyadi uses the latter title, but it should not be construed as an attempt to assume power in Wallachia. Although he was related to one branch of the ruling dynasty, he was not a direct descendant of Wallachian Princes and, therefore, the boyars could not accept him as their legitimate ruler. Well aware of this, Hunyadi had taken care to select a legitimate pretender to place on the throne. In addition, had he intended to take the Wallachian Crown for himself, he would have used the proper title employed by rulers of the country, "Voivode and Prince." Instead, he is referring to himself as commander of military forces in Wallachia, in much the same way as Count Stephen Bathory would later call himself "supreme commander of royal troops in the Transalpine land," in a letter dated November 11, 1476, from outside Bucharest,[39] when he helped to install Vlad the Impaler on the Wallachian throne for the third and final time. His use of this title indicates that he had already defeated Vlad, but that Vladislav had not yet been formally invested as Prince. As a result, we can date Vlad's demise sometime between November 27 and December 3, 1447.

Although the evidence as to exactly what happened after Hunyadi entered the country is sketchy, it appears that Vlad, unable to defend his capital, headed east, together with his son Mircea, hoping to organize a force to resist the invaders. But they did not get far before the Hungarians caught up with them. An eighteenth century Wallachian chronicle records that Hunyadi "raised an army and crossed into Wallachia in 1445 [1447] and fought with Voivode Drag [Vlad] at Târgşor in the Prahova district, defeating him..."[40] Mircea was captured during the fighting and taken back to Târgovişte. Vlad, however, escaped the battle and fled south, but the Dragon could not escape the Raven's clutches. Fate caught up with him when he reached the village of Bălteni, near Snagov. A diploma issued by Prince Vlad Vintilă for the Monastery of Snagov

---

of ourself." Undoubtedly, Peter had also distinguished himself in the campaign against Vlad, and the Governor immediately acted to reward him.

[39]Doc. CLXVII in Hurmuzaki, *Documente*, vol. XV, part. 1, p. 95.

[40]Quo. Minea, "Vlad Dracul şi vremea sa," pp. 68-69; see also Nicolaescu, ed., "Letopiseţul Ţării-Rumâneşti," p. 113.

on April 3, 1534, mentions "the Great Voivode Vlad the Old who met his death in the village of Bălteni."[41]

Alternatively, some have argued that Vlad fled south from Târgoviște when Hunyadi invaded the country, following the old salt route leading to Giurgiu in an attempt to cross the Danube to obtain Ottoman assistance. This theory identifies the village of Bălteni, where Vlad was captured and subsequently decapitated, with the locality of the same name located along this route some forty kilometers southeast of Târgoviște.[42] But the document from 1534 clearly refers to the village of Bălteni located in the vicinity of Snagov. Even though he had made peace with the Turks, it is unlikely that Vlad would have turned to them for help. It is more probable that he adhered to the precepts written down by Prince Neagoe Basarab at the beginning of the sixteenth century in his *Teachings*, intended to prepare his son Teodosie to rule: "even if your nobles have abandoned you, God will not abandon you. And those who remain with you, retreat together with them, but do not leave your country, but stay with them, inside its borders, hidden, where you find those favorable to you. The enemies who came against you do not have the power to remain for very long in the country and they will return home, leaving behind a Prince, and he will be opposed by the people. Then, bravely set out against him, in the name of Jesus Christ, because I have faith in God, and if someone praises God, God will help him to bring his enemies under his feet."[43] Such a strategy made perfect sense for a Prince like Vlad who enjoyed a strong base of popular support. In addition, by heading east he could hope to receive military assistance from his brother-in-law Roman in neighboring Moldavia.

---

[41]Doc. 155 in *DIR, XVI*, vol. II, pp. 156-157. There can be no doubt that Vlad the Old is Vlad Dracul because the document recalls his diploma of June 30, 1441, confirming the holdings of the Monastery, including its estates in Dobrușești, the subject of the act of April 3, 1534, see Doc. 95 in *DRH, B*, vol. I, pp. 164-166, mentioning it before a similar deed granted to Snagov by Prince Basarab the Young on March 23, 1482, see Doc. 179 in *DRH, B*, vol. I, pp. 288-292.

[42]Constantin Rezachevici, "Unde a fost mormântul lui Vlad Țepeș?" in *Magazin Istoric*, XXXVI:3 (March, 2002), p. 42; see also Constantinescu, "Quelques observations sur l'epoque de Vlad Țepeș," p. 33.

[43]"Învățăturile lui Neagoe Basarab către fiul său, Teodosie," in Panaitescu, ed., *Cronicile slavo-române*, p. 244.

Soon after his capture at Bălteni, Vlad was decapitated on the orders of John Hunyadi. Beheading was the prescribed form of execution for a man of his rank and status. Some, most notably Nicolae Iorga, have tried to exonerate the Hungarian Governor of responsibility for Vlad's death, placing the blame solely on the shoulders of Vladislav II.[44] But Hunyadi held overall command of all military forces in Wallachia at this time, as demonstrated by his use of the title "Voivode of the Transalpine land" in his diploma of December 4, and it is inconceivable that such an act could have been carried out without his express consent. Informed sources, such as Jan Długosz, Antonius Bonfinius, and John de Thurocz, all concur that Hunyadi ordered Vlad's execution.[45] Ottoman chronicles, such as that of Orudj bin Adil, also relate that Hunyadi "killed Dracula."[46] The Hungarian Governor knew that only by having him killed could he permanently eliminate a popular and capable ruler such as Vlad. Throughout his tenures as Voivode of Transylvania and Governor of Hungary, Hunyadi had consistently tried to place princes subservient to him on the thrones of Wallachia and Moldavia. In a decree of March 21, 1457, King Ladislas of Hungary condemns the former Governor, who had recently died of the plague after defending Belgrade against the Ottomans, for "causing some of our Transalpine and Moldavian Voivodes, faithful to our Kingdom, to be killed and others to be exiled, putting in their place others who he considered to be personally obligated to him."[47]

The location of Vlad's internment is unknown. He may have been buried at Bălteni, the place of his execution, where there is a church dating from this period,[48] but no grave marker remains. Another possible burial site is the nearby Monastery of Snagov. Tradition has linked this monastery with Vlad

---

[44]N. Iorga, *Istoria românilor*, vol. IV, Bucharest, 1937, p. 90; and Constantin A. Stoide, "Contribuţii la studiul istoriei Ţării Româneşti între anii 1447 şi 1450," in *AIIA, Iaşi*, X (1937), p. 163, nt. 2.

[45]Minea, *Informaţiile româneşti*, p. 37; and Minea, *Din trecutul stăpânirei româneşti asupra Ardealului*, p. 27.

[46]*Cronici turceşti*, vol. I, p. 57.

[47]Doc. LXXVI in Hurmuzaki, *Documente*, vol. II, part. 2, pp. 87-88.

[48]Sp. Popescu, "Observaţiuni critice asupra bisericii din Bălteni," in *RIAF*, X (1909), pp. 259-260, and 264.

The execution of Vlad II Dracul at Bălteni

By Octavian Ion Penda

the Impaler, but, as we have already seen, over the centuries the elder Vlad has often been confused with his more famous son. The evidence linking Vlad II to this cloister is stronger than that which connects it with his son. His diploma from 1441, confirming the monastery's holdings and possessions and exempting them from royal taxes and works,[49] is mentioned frequently by later princes; in addition, he donated four mills located at Didrih to Snagov.[50] There is also an erroneous tradition crediting the elder Vlad with founding the monastery there.[51] On the other hand, there is no extant diploma issued by Vlad the Impaler for this cloister or any evidence that one ever existed. Given all of this, and the fact that he was killed in a nearby village, it is more logical to look here for the final resting place of the elder Vlad than for that of his son.

After his capture at Târgșor, Mircea was taken to Târgoviște. Vlad's heir apparent represented an immediate threat to Hunyadi's plans because nobles loyal to his father might coalesce around him in an attempt to oust Vladislav II. To eliminate any danger of this happening, the Hungarian Governor had him blinded;[52] the usual method employed was to place hot irons over the eyes. This was a common practice used to eliminate pretenders, in lieu of execution, as blindness made one ineligible to rule. Iliaș had met this fate in Moldavia, as did the sons of Serbian Despot George Branković when they were hostages at the Ottoman Porte. But some of his enemies did not consider this adequate punishment for the young prince. In a frenzy of violence, possibly to demonstrate their loyalty to the new Prince, a group of boyars seized Mircea and dragged him off to the cemetery in Târgoviște where they buried him alive.

---

[49]Doc. 95 in *DRH, B*, vol. I, pp. 164-166.

[50]Doc. 179 in *DRH, B*, vol. I, pp. 288-292.

[51]Niculae I. Șerbănescu, *Istoria mănăstirii Snagov*, Bucharest, 1944, p. 22. The Monastery of Snagov was founded in the fourteenth century. The earliest extant document mentioning its existence is an undated diploma issued by Mircea the Old, see Doc. 34 in *DRH, B*, vol. I, pp. 74-75.

[52]The chronicles are very confused about what transpired, but several mention that Hunyadi had a pretender or one of Vlad's sons blinded, see Minea, *Informațiile românești*, p. 37; Minea, *Din trecutul stăpânirei românești asupra Ardealului*, p. 27; Nicolaescu, ed., "Letopisețul Țării-Rumânești," p. 113; Gheorghe Brancovici, *Cronica românească*, Bucharest, 1987, p. 64; and Iorga, *Studii și documente*, vol. III, p. XXIX.

The execution of Vlad's brother Mircea by the boyars of Târgoviște
By Octavian Ion Penda

This probably occurred around the time of Vladislav's coronation as Prince on Thursday, December 7.

Soon after he assumed the throne, Vlad the Impaler began to plot his revenge against those responsible for the cruel murder of his older brother. He made his move on Easter Sunday, April 17, 1457. The vengeance he exacted that day left a lasting impression and was set down by many later chroniclers who present it as the most significant and shocking event of his reign. The seventeenth century Cantacuzene Chronicle records that Vlad the Impaler "did a thing to the citizens of Târgoviște, because it was proved that the boyars of Târgoviște buried a brother of his alive. And to find out the truth, he looked for his brother in his grave and he found him face down. And when Easter day arrived, all the citizens gathered for a feast and the young danced. Then, without warning, he captured all of them. All of those who were old he had impaled, encircling the town square with them, while those who were young, together with their wives, sons, and daughters, who were all dressed in their finest clothes for Easter, he took them all to Poenari and forced them to work on the fortress there until all the clothes fell off their backs and they were naked."[53] The Saxon chronicler Johann Filstich adds that he forced them "to work day and night without rest, during which the clothes fell off their backs, so they looked like the Jews oppressed without mercy by the Egyptian Pharoah."[54] Among those who may have fallen victim to Vlad's wrath that day was Manea Udriște, who served as the leading member of his royal council as late as April 16, 1457,[55] the day before the massacre at Târgoviște, and then suddenly vanishes without a trace.

When the Hungarian army advanced on Târgoviște in November 1447, Vlad took the precaution of sending his youngers sons, Vlad and Radu, south of the Danube to keep them out of danger. The fifteenth century Greek chronicler Kritoboulos of Imbros writes that, "This man [Vlad] and his brother [Radu] had fled when John the Getan [Hunyadi], ruler of the Paenonians and Dacians, had come with a considerable force and had murdered their father and given the governorship to another man. The father of the present Sultan had then welcomed these two fugitives who had fled to him."[56] The fact that he did this is another indication that Vlad himself did not intend to desert his country in the face of his enemies. Vlad's young widow entered a monastery, together with her daughter, Alexandra, and infant son, Vlad, where she adopted the monastic name Eupraxia by which she is first referred to in an endowment granted by her son to the Monastery of Filoteiu on Mount Athos, in return for

---

[53]*Istoria Țării Românești, 1290-1690. Letopisețul cantacuzinesc*, ed. C. Grecescu and D. Simonescu, Bucharest, 1960, p. 205; see also Popescu, *Istoriile domnilor Țării Românești*, p. 15; and Nicolaescu, ed., "Letopisețul Țării Românești," p. 111.

[54]Johann Filstich, *Încercare de istorie românească*, Bucharest, 1979, p. 103.

[55]Doc. 115 in *DRH, B*, vol. I, pp. 198-200. This is the first document from Vlad the Impaler's principal reign to indicate the composition of his royal council. Manea Udriște is listed first.

[56]Kritoboulos, *History of Mehmed the Conqueror*, Princeton, 1954, p. 178 (IV, 58): see also Raymond T. McNally, "The Fifteenth Century Manuscript by Kritoboulos of Imbros as an Historical Source for the History of Dracula," in *East European Quarterly*, XXI:1 (1987), p. 7. As Kritoboulos wrote during the time of Mehmed II, "the father of the present Sultan," refers to Murad II.

which he asked the monks, "to write in the prayer book of the holy altar the name of our parents: Voivode John Vlad and my mother, the nun Eupraxia."[57]

After installing Vladislav II as Prince of Wallachia, John Hunyadi returned to Transylvania where he is found at Braşov on December 16.[58] He remained there through Christmas to monitor the situation across the border, perhaps concerned that boyars loyal to Vlad might organize an uprising against his protégé. In his letter of January 15, 1448, John of Zredna wrote to Cardinal Juan de Carvajal, the Papal Legate to Germany, assigned to negotiate a peace between Frederick III of Habsburg and the Hungarian authorities, that Hunyadi could not yet return to Hungary as he was preoccupied with consolidating the results of his campaign in the Transalpine land; the Bishop of Nagyvarad also mentions that the Hungarian Governor had recently concluded a treaty with Moldavia,[59] implicitly with Peter II, with whom he had just formed a marriage alliance.

With the situation in Wallachia seemingly under control, in January the Hungarian Governor turned his attention to Moldavia and to organizing a campaign intended to oust Roman and to place Peter II on the throne. In this scope, Hunyadi visited towns along the eastern Carpathians; documents place him in Sepiszentgyörgy (Sfântu Gheorghe in Romanian; Sankt Georgan in German) from January 5-9, 1448, in Szekelyudvarhely (Odorhei Secuiesc in Romanian; Oderhellen in German) from January 17-23, and in Bistritz (Beszterce in Hungarian; Bistriţa in Romanian) on February 1.[60] In late February, Peter set out against his nephew Roman, probably from Bistritz.

---

[57]Doc. 202 in *DRH, B*, vol. I, pp. 323-326. This is an undated document issued sometime between 1487 and 1492. Vlad the Monk also mentions her in an endowment for the Cutlumuz Monastery on Mount Athos dated August 29, 1492. "They are to pray to God for the souls of my parents, Voivode Vlad and my mother, the nun Eupraxia," see Doc. 231 in *DRH, B*, vol. I, pp. 370-371.

[58]Doc. 2617 in *Urkundenbuch*, V, p. 227.

[59]Pall, "Intervenţia lui Iancu de Hunedoara," pp. 1051, and 1062-1063; and Pall, "De nouveau sur l'action de Ianco de Hunedoara (Hunyadi) en Valachie," p. 448.

[60]Docs. 2622 and 2626 in *Urkundenbuch*, V, pp. 230-231 and 239. On Hunyadi's itinerary during the fall of 1447 and the winter of 1447-1448 see Pall, "Intervenţia lui Iancu de Hunedoara," pp. 1052-1053.

Although Hunyadi did not personally take part in this campaign, Wallachian chronicler Radu Popescu writes that he "gave him [Peter] an army and they drove out his cousin Voivode Roman. Voivode Roman, being a relative of King Casimir on his mother's side, took refuge there [in Poland], where Casimir prepared to give him substantial assistance to retake the throne."[61] But before Roman could strike back, Peter organized a plot against his nephew who, Długosz tells us, died on July 2, 1448, "poisoned by some of his own boyars."[62] Polish chronicler Joachim Bielski adds that just prior to this, Casimir "wanted to make peace between him [Roman] and his cousin or to place him on the throne by force.... The King set out for Lemberg, but, en route, he learned that Roman was no longer alive, having been poisoned by Peter."[63] As soon as he attained the throne, Peter, as he had promised, handed Kilia over to the Hungarians. Thus, by the spring of 1448, John Hunyadi had succeeded in bringing the Principalities to the south and east of the Carpathians under his control in preparation for a new offensive against the Ottomans.

***

"let him who can win fame before death, because that is a dead man's best memorial."

—*Beowulf*[64]

---

[61]Popescu, *Istoriile domnilor Țării Românești*, p. 20. Moldavian chronicler Grigori Urechi provides a similar account, see Kogălniceanu, *Cronicele României*, vol. I, p. 145. The final documents from Roman's brief reign show him in Suceava on February 18, 1448, but five days later, on February 23, he is in Poland at Kolomyja. Peter likely struck when Roman was out of the country on an official visit to pay homage to the Polish King, see Docs. 83 and 84 in Costăchescu, *Documente moldovenești*, vol. II, pp. 299-309.

[62]Quo. St. Nicolaescu, *Documente slavo-române*, Bucharest, 1905, p. 99. Radu Popescu and Grigori Ureche both say that Roman was poisoned at the behest of Peter II, see Popescu, *Istoriile domnilor Țării Românești*, p. 20; and Kogălniceanu, *Cronicele României*, vol. I, p. 145.

[63]G.I. Năstase, "Istoria moldovenească din Kronika polsk al lui Bielski," in *CI*, I (1925), p. 119.

[64]*Beowulf*, New York, 1984, p. 60.

The man called Dracula was a well-travelled and highly educated man who spoke as many as seven languages. The Burgundian crusader Walerand de Wavrin, who met him in the summer of 1445, remarked that Vlad was "renowned for his valor and wisdom."[65] The worthiest of Mircea the Old's successors, he had played a key role in regional politics foe over fifteen years and distinguished himself as a true Prince of the early Renaissance. His practice of *Realpolitik*, to maintain a delicate balance between the neighboring superpowers to ensure the greatest degree of independence for his Principality, had not always been successful, but it was the only course of action available to a strong and resolute leader determined to avoid subservience to either the Ottomans or the Hungarians.

Vlad also enjoyed a solid base of popular support. He carefully protected the interests of his people, such as when he used the presence of Burgundian galleys at Brăila in the summer of 1445 to assure a peaceful harvest. He also promoted harmony among the ruling classes, coopting many of his predecessor's boyars into his administration. He exemplified the maxim later expounded by Machiavelli: "well-ordered states and wise princes have taken every care not to drive the nobles to desperation, and to keep the people satisfied and contended, for this is one of the most important objectives a prince can have."[66] Historian Ilie Minea, author of the first monograph on the life and times of Vlad Dracul, correctly assessed that "he always sought to protect the interests of his country and of his dynasty."[67] Even though Vlad passed from the scene, his legacy lived on. Not only would subsequent Princes follow the political strategy he had developed, but members of his family would dominate Wallachian politics well into the sixteenth century. But when his eldest son Mircea perished along with him at the end of 1447, it left the younger Vlad as his legitimate heir, both to the throne, and to the name of Dracula.

---

[65]Iorga, "Cronica lui Wavrin," p. 61.

[66]Machiavelli, *The Prince*, p. 149.

[67]Minea, "Vlad Dracul şi vremea sa," p. 83.

Chapter XII

Epilogue — 1448

*"it seems to me that the world has always been in the same condition,
and that in it there has been just as much good as there is evil..."*

—Niccolò Machiavelli, *The Discourses*[1]

O nce he had eliminated his long-time adversary Vlad, and placed Princes personally loyal to him on the thrones of Wallachia and Moldavia, John Hunyadi could at last prepare for a new offensive against the Ottomans, one which events following the disaster at Varna had forced him to delay. He had reason to be optimistic about his chances for success. Theoretically, his position was stronger now than at any time before. He ruled Hungary in his own right and he could count on military assistance from the two Principalities bordering Transylvania. In addition, by obtaining Kilia from Peter II he had fulfilled a time-honored objective of Hungarian foreign policy, one that even Emperor Sigismund had failed to realize, securing an outlet to the Black Sea.

But despite these accomplishments, the Hungarian Governor still had reason for concern. Although he appealed to the new Pope, Nicholas II, and

---

[1]Niccolò Machiavelli, *The Discourses*, New York, 1986, p. 266 (II).

other Christian leaders for assistance, he could find little more than moral support in the West for a new campaign against the Ottomans; the crusading spirit had continued to wane since the debacle at Varna four years earlier. With no practical assistance coming from that direction, Hunyadi knew that he needed to rely on his own resources if he wanted to continue the struggle against the Turks. But even this was problematic. The Governor did not hold absolute power and he faced strong opposition in his own country where his aggressive policies stirred controversy; many nobles objected to calls to contribute troops to military actions outside the borders of the Kingdom. But even in the neighboring states, which he had tried to subordinate to his authority in preparation for his new offensive against the Ottomans, he met with difficulties.

Since the Treaty of Lublau in 1412, agreements between Hungary and Poland had recognized the predominant influence of the latter in Moldavia. Even though Peter II had attained the throne by allying himself with Hunyadi, he could not maintain his position for long without coming to terms with Poland, Hungary's traditional rival, which claimed suzerainty over the Principality bordering the eastern Carpathians. The Hungarian Governor had no choice but to recognize the legitimacy of the Polish claim. He negotiated an agreement with Casimir whereby the King accepted Peter as Prince of Moldavia in return for his recognizing Polish suzerainty. As a result of this accord, Peter travelled to Khotin, a fortress on the Dnestr River near the border with Poland, where, on August 22, 1448, both he and the boyars serving on his royal council paid homage to King Casimir, promising to serve him and to assist him, "with all of our power, with our own self, and with our life, against every enemy of our lord, the King, and of the Crown of Poland, without any exceptions....," meaning that any assistance he could provide to Hunyadi in his struggle against the Turks now depended on the state of relations between the two rival Kingdoms. The accord between Hunyadi and Casimir, however, permitted Peter to contribute forces to the Governor's upcoming campaign against the Ottomans; the Polish King also agreed to send a contingent of 1,000 men of his own.

The status of Kilia remained a sticking point. Because he had ceded the Danubian fortress to the Hungarians, an act that met with strong disapproval from the Polish authorities, Peter II had to pledge not to relinquish any other territories belonging to Moldavia to anyone, "without the consent and approval of the aforesaid Lord Casimir, King of Poland, and of his Crown, and those which have been estranged, we want to take them back."[2] But despite this declaration, Kilia did not return to Moldavian control until 1465. Although Hunyadi had secured military assistance for his immediate objective, Peter's submission to the Polish King meant that he could no longer expect unconditional support from the Principality east of the Carpathians.

The situation in the Transalpine land, however, was quite different. Hunyadi could exert more influence south of the Carpathians because international agreements recognized Hungarian suzerainty over Wallachia. The Governor looked upon Vladislav as his vassal, in the truest sense of the word, and he had every intention of subordinating the Transalpine land to Hungarian interests. As a first step in this direction, Hunyadi effected a monetary union between the two countries. He wrote to the burghers of Braşov from Temesvar on March 7, 1448, instructing them: "Because we have decided that our coins will circulate in the Transalpine land just as they do here, we command that you, together with the citizens of Sibiu and the leading men of the Transalpine land, oblige yourselves to consult and to reach an agreement with regard to this..."[3] The fact that the Hungarian Governor unilaterally made a decision of this nature, which blatantly violated Wallachian sovereignty, and does not even refer to Vladislav in his letter, but merely to "the leading men of the Transalpine land," proves that he now regarded the Principality south of the Carpathians as completely subordinate to his authority. But even though he had killed Vlad and succeeded in placing his protégé on the throne, strong opposition to engaging in an offensive against the Ottomans persisted and Hunyadi's actions amplified anti-Hungarian sentiment among the boyars who resented his interference in their domestic affairs. As a result, Vladislav's position was far from secure.

As a prelude to his forthcoming campaign against the Ottomans, the Hungarian Governor decided to attack Turkish positions along the Danube in

---

[2]Doc. 215 in Costăchescu, *Documentele moldoveneşti*, vol. II, pp. 733-737, emphasis added. Peter II's leading boyars also swore to uphold their Prince's oath to Casimir, see Doc. 216 in *ibid*, pp. 737-740.

[3]Doc. 289 in *DRH, D*, pp 389-399.

the summer of 1448, hoping to prevent the Sultan from concentrating his forces. This plan included launching an assault on Nicopolis, defended by Mehmed Bey, one of Murad's most capable frontier commanders. Hunyadi assigned this task to his protégé Vladislav. The fifteenth century Ottoman chronicler Orudj bin Adil relates that Hunyadi "gave Wallachia to the infidel Dan-oglu [Vladislav] and made Wallachia subordinate to him. For this reason, the Wallachian army crossed at Nicopolis and devastated those districts." But Mehmed Bey received assistance from the Beylerbey of Anatolia, Isa Bey, and the Beylerbey of Rumelia, Karadja Bey, and, with several thousand Akingi, "all of these Beys made an agreement among themselves to confront the Wallachian army. Launching a surprise night attack, they destroyed part of it, while they captured many other infidels dressed in mail and sent them to Sultan Murad. When he learned of this victory over the unbelievers, Sultan Murad expressed his great joy."[4]

Although the Ottomans repelled the invaders, their victory was not as spectacular as Turkish chronicles suggest. Vladislav withdrew with his army largely intact. Having completed his mission south of the Danube, at the beginning of August the Wallachian Prince prepared to march to southern Transylvania where the Hungarian Governor readied his forces to invade the Balkans. In preparation for the arrival of his protégé, Hunyadi, then at Kohalm, issued a circular to the Saxon cities on August 7, informing them: "Whereas the illustrious Prince, Lord Vladislav, the Transalpine Voivode, will come to us, for the good of the country and for the benefit of all of Christianity, we command that, on the strength of your allegiance, that after you learn of this, and when that Voivode will arrive in your midst, that you accord him and his men all the proper honors and courtesies, according to the instructions that Anthony of Arapatak will give you."[5] Shortly after, Vladislav joined his suzerain in Transylvania with 4,000 men. Peter II also sent 3,000 mounted

---

[4]*Cronici turceşti*, vol. I, p. 57. An anonymous Ottoman chronicle provides a similar account (*ibid.*, p. 184), as does Sa'adeddin (*ibid.*, p. 316). See also the seventeenth century chronicle of Müneggimbashi, see *Cronici turceşti*, vol. II, p. 246.

[5]Doc. 291 in *DRH, D*, p. 401.

troops from Moldavia to strengthen Hunyadi's army,[6] but the Polish King did not allow his vassal to take part personally in the campaign.

By late August, Hunyadi's army began to move west from Sibiu, and by early September he established his camp along the Danube in the vicinity of Kuvin, near the border with Serbia. When the Hungarian Governor left Transylvania in August, his brother-in-law, Michael Szilagyi, led another diversionary raid against Ottoman positions along the frontier. He attacked the area around Vidin with 1,000 cavalry and 500 infantry, but the Turks easily repulsed the invaders, forcing them to flee back across the Danube. The Ottomans, however, made the mistake of pursuing them into Wallachia. When they set about plundering, Szilagyi regrouped and launched a counterstrike, slaying the Bey of Vidin and killing or capturing numerous Turks.[7]

In preparing for his new campaign against the Ottomans, Hunyadi had also sought military assistance from George Branković, but the Serbian Despot's position had remained unchanged since the Varna Crusade. He adamantly opposed war with the Turks, which he believed could only spell disaster for Serbia. In addition, Hunyadi's seizure of his vast estates in Hungary following the Varna debacle made him even less inclined to aid the Governor. Fearing to become involved in any way in the forthcoming conflict, Branković even refused to allow the passage of Hungarian troops through Serbian territory. But Hunyadi ignored the Despot's protestations. He needed to pass through Serbia to effect a junction with Scanderberg who intended to march east from Albania to join the Hungarians. Finding himself between a rock and a hard place, the Serbian Despot made a last ditch attempt to bring about peace between Hunyadi and the Sultan. He sent Pasquale de Sorgo, a Ragusan merchant in his service, to Hunyadi's camp in an effort to open negotiations between the two sides, but the Hungarian Governor could not be swayed. On September 28, Hunyadi crossed the Danube with a force of some 20,000 men, including

---

[6]Aurel Decei, "Oastea lui Iancu Huniade înainte de bătălia dela Kosovo," in *RIR*, XVI (1946), p. 41. Pasquale de Sorgo, writing from Hunyadi's camp along the Danube on September 11, provides these figures.

[7]Decei, "Oastea lui Iancu Huniade înainte de bătălia dela Kosovo," pp. 43-47. Pasquale de Sorgo's letter of September 11 tells of 4,000 Turks killed or captured, but this figure is probably exaggerated.

his Wallachian, Moldavian, and Polish allies, as well as the Ottoman pretender Daud Celebi who had gone to Hungary after taking part in the campaign along the Danube in 1445. They marched south through Serbia, treating it like hostile territory, pillaging and plundering along the way, and leaving a path of destruction in their wake. Michael Szilagyi crossed the Danube at Severin with his contingent and joined the bulk of the army before they reached Niš, the site of Hunyadi's triumph over the Turks in 1443. From there, they continued on a journey that would ultimately lead them to their fateful encounter with the Ottomans near Kosovo, on the Field of the Blackbirds.

But the Sultan did not sit idly by waiting for the Hungarians to attack. When he learned that Vladislav had gone to join Hunyadi with the bulk of his army, leaving Wallachia exposed, he seized the opportunity to launch a strike of his own. Murad sent an Ottoman force under the Beylerbey of Rumelia, Karadja Bey, to retake Giurgiu,[8] the fortress Vlad had recovered from the Turks with the help of the Burgundian and Papal fleet in September 1445. They then used Giurgiu as a bridgehead from which to stage an attack on Wallachia. Karadja Bey assigned this task to Turakhan Bey, who had distinguished himself during the Sultan's campaign against Despot Constantine of the Morea in the fall of 1446. He instructed him to invade the Principality and to install Vlad's eldest surviving son and namesake, whom the Turks later dubbed Kazîklu, meaning the Impaler, on the throne of his father. The young Vlad had fled south of the Danube, together with his brother Radu, ten months earlier when the Hungarian Governor invaded Wallachia and executed his father. Now, the seventeen year old boy prepared to return home to claim his inheritance.

Before Karadja Bey had set out on his campaign, Murad had formally invested young Vlad as Prince, just as he had done with his father prior to sending him back to Wallachia in the spring of 1444. An anonymous fifteenth century Ottoman chronicle relates that when the Sultan decided to invade Wallachia, and "to put Kazîklu, the son of Dracula, there as Bey, he gave him a flag and a mantle and he granted him many favors." After this ceremony, "he sent him with the Akingi who went and made him Bey in the place of his

---

[8]*Cronici turceşti*, vol. I, p. 58. Orudj bin Adil writes that "Beylerbey Karadja Bey, setting out with the Rumelian army, *repaired* the fortress of Ierkökü [Giurgiu]." This means that he regained possession of the citadel.

father."[9] According to the memoirs of Serbian janissary Konstantin Mihailović, a contemporary of these events who later served in the army of Mehmed II when he invaded Wallachia in the summer of 1462 to drive out Vlad the Impaler and replace him with his younger brother Radu, "the Turkish Emperor, upon hearing of the death of the Voivode of Wallachia [Vlad Dracul], gave his eldest son money, horses, treasures, and tents, as is fitting for a Prince, and sent him with great honors to Wallachia to rule in place of his father, with the understanding that he would come to him each year to pay homage and to bring tribute, just as his father had done."[10]

The Ottoman attack took the Wallachian officials Vladislav had left in his stead by surprise. The fifteenth century Turkish chronicler Enveri, a contemporary of these events, records that "Turakhan Bey won fame devastating Iflak [Wallachia]" at this time.[11] Chalkokondyles confirms the success of Turakhan's mission, writing that "with the help of the Emperor [Murad II], Vlad, the son of Dracula, struck and took the throne."[12] An anonymous letter from Constantinople, dated December 7, 1448, also reports that the son of a former Prince of Wallachia, who was a refugee with the Turks, seized the throne with help from the Ottomans in the absence of the Prince of that country who had gone with his army to Serbia.[13] After installing Vlad as Prince, Turakhan Bey and Karadja Bey returned to Sofia where they joined Murad's army as it prepared to set out for Serbia to confront the invaders. Thus, by late September 1448 a new Dracula ruled Wallachia.

Continuing his march south from Niš, Hunyadi arrived in Kosovo on Tuesday, October 15. He expected to combine forces with the Albanians at any

---

[9]*Cronici turceşti*, vol. I, p. 185; and Iorga, "Cronici turceşti," p. 13, nt. 1. The anonymous chronicler erroneously places these events in 1449, in the aftermath of the Kosovo campaign. The flag and mantle were symbols of investiture accorded by the Sultan to his vassal.

[10]Holban, ed., *Călători străini*, vol. I, pp. 125-126.

[11]*Cronici turceşti*, vol. I, p. 41.

[12]Chalcocondil, *Expuneri istorice*, p. 283 (X, 500).

[13]Doc. III in Iorga, "Les aventures Sarrazines des Francais de Bourgogne au XV[e] siecle," pp. 42-45. The letter is based on rumors circulating in the Byzantine capital at the time, some of which are erroneous, but it largely confirms this scenario.

moment, but he did not know that George Branković had blocked the mountain passes coming from Albania to prevent Scanderbeg from joining the Hungarians. Hunyadi's intelligence service was woefully inept. Not only did he remain unaware of the delays facing Scanderbeg, far more serious was the fact that the Hungarian Governor had no reliable information about Ottoman movements or troops strength. His alienation of the native population by devastating Serbia as he marched through it did nothing to help him in this regard. The Sultan had been in Sofia since August where he gathered a large army of up to 50,000 men to meet the Hungarian attack. Murad left Sofia in early October; when he reached Niš, he followed the path blazed by the Christian army only days earlier. The Ottomans caught up with the unsuspecting Hungarians near Kosovo on Thursday, October 17.

Rather than retreating to join the Albanians, Hunyadi decided to take advantage of favorable terrain and to give battle, thinking that Scanderbeg would soon arrive with reinforcements. After initial skirmishes on the first day, both sides dug in and prepared for battle the next morning. Two days of fierce combat ensued on a plain consecrated with the blood of Serbian heroes sixty years earlier when they suffered their historic defeat at the hands of the army of Sultan Murad I, who himself had fallen victim to an assassin's blade during the fighting. Now his great-grandson and namesake, Murad II, faced another Christian army on this same battlefield, in the shadow of his great-grandfather's tomb, who had been interred near the site of his final triumph. The second battle of Kosovo was one of the first armed conflicts to witness the extensive use of firearms. Hunyadi also employed Hussite tactics, arranging his wagons to create a defensive barricade. The Hungarians held the high ground, but the numerical superiority of the Ottomans ultimately proved decisive.

After some initial successes on Friday, the Hungarians, at the suggestion of Daud Celebi, tried a surprise night attack on the Ottoman camp, but it failed to catch the Turks off guard. According to Chalkokondyles, the Wallachian Prince commanded the left wing of the Christian army.[14] On the last day of battle, Saturday, October 19, Antonius Bonfinius relates that the Wallachian

---

[14]Chalcocondil, *Expuneri istorice*, p. 210 (VII, 358). Chalkokondyles gives the exaggerated figure of 8,000 Wallachian troops present at Kosovo.

contingent, commanded by Vladislav II, led a last-ditch attack on the Turkish lines.[15] This too failed and the Christians spent the remainder of the day desperately trying to hold their lines against Ottoman assaults. Among the Wallachian soldiers who distinguished himself that day was Dan Oteşanul, whom Vladislav later rewarded with an estate in the village of Băleşti for his services at Kosovo.[16]

With his lines on the verge of collapse, Hunyadi withdrew from the Field of the Blackbirds during the night of October 19. Michael Szilagyi led a diversionary attack to cover the hasty retreat and fell prisoner to the Ottomans in the process, but he was subsequently ransomed. Hunyadi managed to escape, but, as he tried to make his way back to Hungary, George Branković captured him and imprisoned him at his fortress at Smederovo. For a long time the fate of the Hungarian Governor was unknown. On November 25, Enea Silvio Piccolomini wrote to Pope Nicholas II from Neustadt, reporting rumors according to which Branković, "the treacherous Despot," had killed Hunyadi during the retreat.[17] Ultimately, Branković freed the Hungarian Governor who returned to his country in mid-December.[18]

While Christian and Islamic forces clashed on the Field of the Blackbirds, the situation in the Transalpine land provoked concern among Hungarian officials in Transylvania assigned to oversee affairs in that region in the Governor's absence. Hunyadi's trusted lieutenant, Vice-Governor Nicholas of Vizakna, wrote to the young usurper, insisting that he come to Transylvania and await there the Governor's return, at which time his claim to the throne would be adjudicated by the rightful suzerain of that country. But the shrewd young Prince refused to fall into the trap laid for him by the Hungarian authorities. Displaying diplomatic skills learned from his father, young Vlad

---

[15]Minea, *Din trecutul stăpânirei româneşti asupra Ardealului*, p. 30.

[16]Vladislav's grant to Dan Otesanul is mentioned in a diploma issued by Vlad the Monk in Bucharest on May 6, 1492, see Doc. 229 in *DRH, B*, vol. I, pp. 367-368.

[17]Doc. XXI in Iorga, *Notes et extraits*, vol. IV, pp. 41-42.

[18]By December 18, 1448, John Hunyadi was in Seghedin where he issued a conveyance transferring ownership of all of his properties in Serbia to George Marnavici, rewarding him for negotiating with the Serbian Despot for his release, see Doc. DCXXIV in Hurmuzaki, *Documente*, vol. I, part. 2, pp. 756-757.

𝕾 tem des selben ars ist er gesetzt worden : den an zu ein,
em herrn in der walchei zu hand ließ er todten den Laszla weyde der

Vlad III Dracula assumes the throne of Wallachia in 1448

By Octavian Ion Penda

wrote to the burghers of Braşov from his capital at Târgovişte on October 31, 1448, explaining his refusal: "we send you news that the distinguished gentleman, Nicholas of Vizakna, has written to us, asking that we consent to come to him until the illustrious John, Governor of the Kingdom of Hungary, will return from the war. We are unable to do this because, this past Tuesday [October 29], the brother of the Governor of Nicopolis [Mehmed Bey] came to us and told us with the greatest certainty that Murad, the Lord of the Turks, fought a battle that lasted for three days without interruption against Lord John, the Governor, who, on the last day, barricaded himself among the wagons of his camp. Then the Emperor himself [Murad] came down on foot among the janissaries, and they attacked them [the Christians] and they killed all those who were outside and inside the wagons of the camp. If we go to him [Nicholas] now, the Turks could come and destroy both us and you. Therefore, we ask you to remain calm and to have patience until we find out what has become of Lord John. There exist doubts as to whether he is still alive. If, however, he returns safely from the war, we will meet with him and make a just peace with him, but if you will be hostile toward us now, and if something happens, it will be to the detriment of your souls, and you will answer before God in peril."[19]

Vladislav learned of what had transpired in Wallachia in his absence en route to Kosovo, so when the battle ended and the retreat began he hurried back to Transylvania where he regrouped his battered army and gathered support from the Hungarian authorities there. In the latter part of November, he crossed the Carpathians and forced the young Vlad to flee south of the Danube. By early December, news had reached Constantinople that Vladislav II once again ruled Wallachia.[20] Despite this inauspicious beginning, the

---

[19]Doc. 293 in *DRH, D*, pp. 402-403. The editors mistakenly attribute this letter to Vladislav II. Nicholas of Vizakna (Ocna Sibiului in Romanian; Salzburg in German), formerly Vice-Voivode of Transylvania, held the title of Vice-Governor at this time, see Doc. 2641 in *Urkundenbuch*, vol. V, pp. 247-250.

[20]Doc. III in Iorga, "Les aventures 'Sarrazines' de Francais de Bourgogne," pp. 42-45. This anonymous letter, dated December 7, 1448, from Constantinople, reports that the Ottomans installed "the son of a Prince of Wallachia" on the throne, but when the Prince of that country returned from Serbia he chased out the usurper. It erroneously adds that the pretender was then captured and killed.

efforts of the young Vlad to follow in the footsteps of his distinguished father had only just begun. He would go on to bring lasting renown to the name he had inherited. But here begins another saga in the Dracula story.

Although Vlad the Impaler's brief tenure on the throne in the fall of 1448 signalled the beginning of his career, the second battle of Kosovo, which had presented him with this opportunity, marked the end of an epoch. Never again could John Hunyadi, who had won fame and glory and accumulated a vast fortune through his military efforts against the Turks, muster the resources to launch an offensive against the Ottomans. He died on August 11, 1456, at his camp in Zemun, near Belgrade, a victim, like so many others of that period, both great and small, of the Black Death. Byzantine Emperor John VIII, who had long militated for a crusade against the Turks as the only means to save the last vestiges of his crumbling Empire, risking the unification of Orthodoxy with the Church of Rome to bring it about, died on October 31, less than two weeks after the battle. Murad II did not live long enough to enjoy the peaceful retirement he so earnestly desired. The Sultan, who had never pursued an overtly aggressive policy, working instead to consolidate his Empire, died at the beginning of 1451. When he heard of Murad's passing, George Sphrantzes prophetically told John VIII's successor, Emperor Constantine XI: "'Your Majesty, my Lord, this is not a cause for joy, but of great sorrow.' But he said, 'How so, man?' I answered him, 'Because he was old and his attempts against Constantinople had failed and he no longer wanted to involve himself in such an undertaking, but he desired only friendship and peace; but the one who has now become ruler is young and since his childhood is an enemy of the Christians."[21] Two years later, Constantinople, the last remnant of Imperial Rome, fell to the Ottomans.

---

[21]Sphrantzes, *Memorii*, p. 76 (XXX, 5).

Great Seal of Vlad II Dracul (1437)

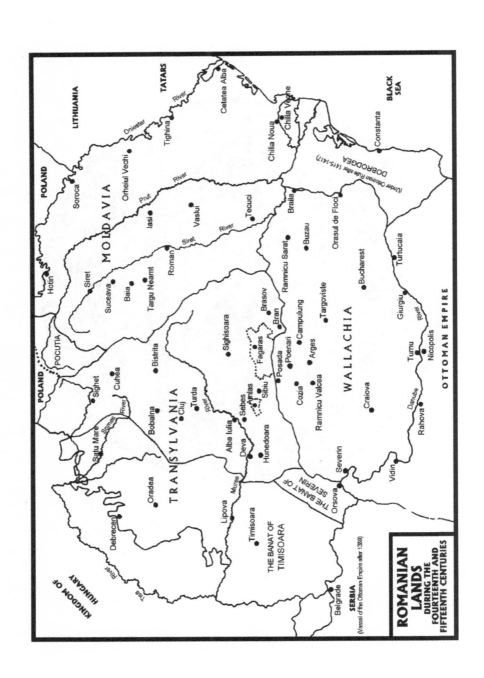

ROMANIAN
LANDS
DURING THE
FOURTEENTH AND
FIFTEENTH CENTURIES

Abbreviations

Found in the Notes

AARMSI = Analele Academiei Române. Memoriile Secţiunii Istorice

AII = Anuarul Institutului de Istorie

AIIA = Anuarul Insitutului de Istorie şi Arheologie

AIIN = Anuarul Insitutului de Istorie Naţională

ARMSI = Academia Română. Memoriile Secţiunii Istorice

ARMSL = Academia Română. Memoriile Secţiunii Literare

BCIR = Buletinul Comisiei istorice a României

BCMI = Buletinul Comisiunii Monumentelor Istorice

CI = Cercetări Istorice

DIR = Documente privind istoria Rominiei

DRH = Documenta Romaniae Historica

MI - Magazin istoric

RA = Revista Arhivelor

RdI = Revista de Istorie

RESEE = Revue des études sud-est éuropéennes

RHSEE = Revue historique du sud-est européen

RI = Revista istorică

RIAF = Revista pentru istorie, archeologie și filologie

RIR = Revista istorică română

RRH = Revue Roumaine d'Histoire

SMIM = Studii și materiale de istorie medie

Selected Bibliography

Andreescu, Ştefan. "Une ville disputée: Kilia pendant la première moitié du XVe siècle," in *Revue Roumaine d'Histoire*, XXIV:3 (1985), pp. 217-230.

Andreescu, Ştefan. *Vlad Ţepeş (Dracula): între legendă şi adevăr istoric*. Second Edition. Bucharest: Editura Enciclopedică, 1998.

Auner, C. "Moldova la soborul din Florenţa," in *Revista catolică*, IV (1915), pp. 272-285, 379- 408, and 552-565.

Bogdan, Ioan. *Documente privitoare la relaţiile Ţării Româneşti cu Braşovul şi cu Ţara Ungurească în sec. XV şi XVI*. Bucharest, 1905.

Bogdan, Nicolae. *Românii în secolul al XV-lea*. Bucharest: Colectia Justiniana, 1941.

Brackob, A.K. *Scanderbeg: A History of George Castriota and the Albanian Resistance to Islamic Expansion in Fifteenth Century Europe*. Las Vegas: Vita Histria, 2018.

Bulat, T.G. "Un document al mănăstirii Cîrtişoara referitor la noi [1440]," in *Revista istorică*, XI:10-12 (1925), pp. 287-288.

Chalcocondil, Laonic. *Expuneri istorice*. Trans. Vasile Grecu. Bucharest: Editura Academiei, 1958.

Chihaia, Pavel. *Din cetăţile de scaun ale Ţării Româneşti*, Bucharest: Editura Meridiane, 1974.

Chihaia, Pavel. *Dela Negru Vodă la Neagoe Basarab.* Bucharest: Editura Academiei, 1976.

Ciocîltan, Virgil. "Între Sultan şi Împărat: Vlad Dracul în 1438," in *Revista de istorie*, 29:11 (1976), pp. 1767-1790.

Ciocîltan, Virgil. "La campagne ottomane de Transylvanie (1438) dans le context politique international," in *Revue Roumaine d'Histoire*, XV:3 (1976), pp. 437-445.

Constantinescu, N. and Cristian Moisescu. *Curtea domnească din Tîrgovişte*, second edition. Bucharest: Editura Meridiane, 1969.

Constantinescu, N.A. "Cetatea Giurgiu: originile şi trecutul ei," in *Analele Academiei Române. Memoriile Secţiunii Istorice*, series II, vol. XXXVIII (1915-1916), pp. 485-522.

Cronici turceşti privind ţările romane. Extrase. Vol. I. Eds. Mihail Guboglu and Mustafa Mehmet. Bucharest: Editura Academiei, 1966; *Vol. II.* Ed. Mihail Guboglu. Bucharest: Editura Academiei, 1974.

Decei, Aurel. "Informaţiile istorice ale lui 'Captivus Septemcastrensis,'" in *Anuarul Insitutului de istorie naţională*, VII (1936-1938), pp. 685-693.

Decei, Aurel. "Deux documents turcs concernant les expeditions des Sultans Bayazid Ier et Murad II dans les pays roumains," in *Revue Roumaine d'Histoire*, XIII:3 (1974), pp. 395-413.

Decei, Aurel. *Istoria imperiului otoman pînă la 1656.* Bucharest: Editura Stiintifică şi Enciclopedică, 1978.

Denize, Eugen. *Ţările române şi Veneţia. Relaţii politice, 1441-1541.* Bucharest: Editura Albatros, 1995.

Documente privind istoria Romîniei. Introducere, vols. I-II, Bucharest: Editura Academiei, 1956.

Documenta Romaniae Historica, B. Ţara Românească, volumul I (1247-1500). Eds. P.P. Panaitescu and Damaschin Mioc. Bucharest: Editura Academiei, 1966.

Documenta Romaniae Historica, D. Relații între țările române, volumul I (1222-1456). Eds. Stefan Pascu et al. Bucharest: Editura Academiei, 1977.

Ducas, *Istoria turco-bizantină (1341-1462)*. Trans. Vasile Grecu. Bucharest: Editura Academiei, 1958.

Fine, John V.A. Jr. *The Late Medieval Balkans*. Ann Arbor: University of Michigan Press, 1994.

Florescu, Radu R. and Raymond T. McNally. *Dracula: A Biography of Vlad Impaler, 1431-1476*. New York: Hawthorn Books, 1973.

Gemil, Tahsin. *Românii și otomanii în secolele XIV-XVI*. Bucharest: Editura Academiei, 1991.

Giurescu, Constantin C. *Istoria românilor, II. Partea întâi. Dela Mircea cel Bătrân și Alexandru cel Bun până la Mihai Viteazul*. Bucharest: Fundatia pentru literatură și artă 'Regele Carol II,' 1937.

Giurescu, Constantin C. "În legătură cu Mircea cel Bătrân," in *Revista Istorică Română*, XV (1945), pp. 413-431.

Giurescu, Dinu C. *Țara Românească în secolele XIV și XV*, Bucharest: Editura Științifică, 1973.

Guboglu, Mihail P. "Românii în bătălia de la Varna (10 nov. 1444) după izvoare turco-islamice și europene," in *Revista Arhivelor*, XLVII:3 (1985), pp. 265-278.

Hajdeu, B. Petriceicu. *Archiva istorică a României*, vol. I, part 2. Bucharest: Imprimeria statului, 1865.

Hale, John. *The Civilization of Europe in the Renaissance*, New York: Atheneum, 1994.

Holban, Maria, ed. *Călători străini despre țările române*, vol. I. Bucharest: Editura Științifică, 1968.

Hurmuzaki, Eudoxia, ed. *Documente privitoare la istoria românilor*, vol. I, part 2. Bucharest, 1890.

Hurmuzaki, Eudoxia and Nicolae Iorga, eds. *Documente privitoare la istoria românilor*, vol. XV, part 1. Bucharest, 1911.

Iancu, Anca. "Știri despre români în izvoare istoriografice sîrbești (secolele XV-XVIII)" in *Studii istorice sud-est europene,* ed. Eugen Stănescu. Bucharest: Editura Academiei, 1974, pp. 7- 41.

Iliescu, Octavian. "Emisiuni monetare ale Țării Românești din secolele XIV-lea și al XV-lea," in *Studii și cercetări de numismatică,* vol. II, Bucharest: Editura Academiei, 1958, pp. 303-344.

Iorga, N. *Acte și fragmente cu privire la istoria românilor,* vol. III. Bucharest: Imprimeria statului, 1897.

Iorga, N. *Studii și documente cu privire la istoria românilor,* vol. III. Bucharest: Editura Ministerului de Instrucție, 1901.

Iorga, Nicolae. "Les aventures 'Sarrazines' des Français de Bourgogne au XVᵉ siècle," in *Mélanges d'histoire générale,* ed. Constantin Marinescu. Cluj: Cartea Românească, 1927.

Iorga, N. "Cronica lui Wavrin și românii," in *Buletinul Comisiei istorice a României,* vol. VI. Bucharest: Datina Românească, 1927, pp. 57-148.

Iorga, N. *Scrisori de boieri, scrisori de Domni.* Third Edition. Vălenii de-Munte: Datina Românească, 1932.

Iorga, N. *Istoria românilor, vol. IV: Cavalerii.* Bucharest, 1937.

Istoria românilor, vol. IV: De la universalitatea creștină către Europa 'patriilor,' Academia Română, eds., Ștefan Ștefănescu and Camil Mureșanu. Bucharest: Editura Enciclopedică, 2001.

Istoria Țării Romînești, 1290-1690. Letopisețul cantacuzinesc, eds. C. Grecescu and D. Simionescu, Bucharest: Editura Academiei, 1960.

Karadja, Constantin I. "Poema lui Michel Beheim despre cruciadele împotriva turcilor din anii 1443 și 1444," in *Buletinul Comisiei istorice a României,* vol. XV. Bucharest, 1936, pp. 5-58.

Kogălniceanu, Const. M. "Cercetări critice cu privire la istoria Românilor: Alexandru II zis Aldea, Domnul Țării Românești (1431; 1432-1435)" in *Revista pentru istorie, archeologie și filologie,* XII:1 (1911), pp. 44-51.

Machiavelli, Nicolo. *The Prince.* Hartsfordshire: Wordsworth Reference, 1993.

Minea, Ilie. *Din trecutul stăpânirei românești asupra Ardealului: Pierderea Amlașului și Făgărașului.* Bucharest: Poporul, 1914.

Minea, Ilie. *Urmașii lui Vladislav I și politica orientală a Ungariei.* Bucharest: Institutul de Arte Grafice 'Speranţa,' 1916.

Minea, Ilie. *Principatele române și politica orientală a împăratului Sigismund.* Bucharest: Convorbiri literare, 1919.

Minea, Ilie. *Informaţiile românești ale cronicii lui Ian Długosz.* Iași: Viaţa românească, 1926.

Minea, Ilie."Vlad Dracul și vremea sa," in *Cercetări istorice,* IV:1 (1928), pp. 65-276.

Mureșanu, Camil. *John Hunyadi: Defender of Christendom,* Palm Beach: Center for Romanian Studies, 2019.

Nicolaescu, Stoica. "Domnia lui Alexandru Vodă Aldea, fiul lui Mircea cel Bătrân, 1431-1435," in *Revista pentru istorie, archeologie și filologie,* XVI (1915-1922), pp. 225-241.

Nicolaescu, Stoica. "Hrisoave și cărţi domnești dela Alexandru Vodă Aldea, fiul lui Mircea Vodă cel Bătrân," in *Revista pentru istorie, archeologie și filologie,* XVI (1915-1922), pp. 243- 270.

Norwich, John Julius. *Byzantium: The Decline and Fall.* New York: Alfred A. Knopf, 1996.

Onciul, Dimitrie. *Originiile principatelor române.* Bucharest: Elzevir, 1899.

Pall, Francisc. "Ciriaco d'Ancona e la Cruciata contra i Turchi," in *Bulletin de la Section Historique,* vol. XX. Bucharest: Academie Roumaine, 1938, pp. 9-68.

Pall, Francisc. "Autour de la croisade de Varna: La question de la paix de Szeged et de sa rupture (1444)," in *Bulletin de la Section Historique,* vol. XXII. Bucharest: Academie Roumaine, 1941, pp. 144-158.

Pall, Francisc. "Un moment décisif de l'histoire du Sud-Est européen: La Croisade de Varna (1444)" in *Balcania,* VII (1944), pp. 102-120.

Pall, Francisc. "Ştiri noi despre expediţiile turcești din Transilvania în 1438," in *Anuarul Institutului de Istorie din Cluj,* vol. I-II (1958-1959), pp. 9-28.

Pall, Francisc. "Intervenția lui Iancu de Hunedoara în Țara Românească și Moldova în anii 1447-1448," in *Studii,* XVI:5 (1963), pp. 1049-1072.

Pall, Francisc. "Le condizioni e gli echi internazionali della lotta antiottomana del 1442-1443, condotta da Giovanni di Hunedoara," in *Revue des études sud-est européennes,* III:2 (1965), pp. 433-463.

Pall, Francisc. "Stăpînirea lui Iancu de Hunedoara asupra Chiliei și problema ajutorării Bizantului," in *Studii,* XVIII:3 (1965), pp. 619-638.

Pall, Francisc. "Iancu de Hunedoara și confirmarea privilegiului pentru negoțul Brașovenilor și al Bîrsenilor cu Țara Românească, în 1443," in *Anuarul Institutului de Istorie din Cluj,* vol. LX (1966), pp. 63-84.

Pall, Francisc. "Identificarea lui Captivus Septemcastrensis," in *Revista de istorie,* 27:1 (1974), pp. 97-105.

Pall, Francisc. "De nouveau sur l'action de Ianco de Hunedoara (Hunyadi) en Valachie pendant l'année 1447" in *Revue Roumaine d'Histoire,* XV:3 (1976), pp. 447-463.

Panaitescu, P.P. *Mircea cel Bătrân.* Bucharest: Casa Scoalelor, 1944.

Panaitescu, P.P. *Interpretări românești: studii de istorie economică și socială.* Bucharest: Editura Universul, 1947.

Panaitescu, P.P., ed. *Cronicele slavo-romîne din sec. XV-XVI publicate de Ion Bogdan.* Bucharest: Editura Academiei, 1959.

Panaitescu, P.P. and N. Stoicescu, "La participation des Roumains à la bataille de Varna (1444)," in *Revue Roumaine d'Histoire,* IV:2 (1965), pp. 221-231.

Papacostea, Șerban. "Kilia et la politique orientale de Sigismund de Luxembourg," in *Revue Roumaine d'Histoire,* XV:3 (1976), pp. 421-436.

Papacostea Șerban. "Populație și fiscalitate în Țara Românească în secolul al XV-lea: un nou izvor," in *Revista de istorie,* 33:9 (1980), pp. 1779-1786.

Papacostea, Șerban. "Din nou cu privire la demografia Țării Românești în secolul XV," in *Revista de Istorie,* 37:6 (1984), pp. 578-581.

Pascu, Ștefan. *Bobîlna.* Bucharest: Editura Tineretului, 1957.

Petrescu-Sava, G.M. *Târguri şi oraşe între Buzău, Târgovişte şi Bucureşti.* Third Edition. Bucharest: Institutul de Arte Grafice "Lupta," 1937.

Popa, Marcel D. "Aspecte ale politicii internaţionale a Ţării Româneşti şi Moldovei în timpul lui Mircea cel Bătrîn şi Alexandru cel Bun," in *Revista de Istorie,* 31:1 (1978), pp. 253-271.

Popescu, Radu. *Istoriile Domnilor Ţării Romîneşti,* ed. Constantin Grecescu. Bucharest: Editura Academiei, 1963.

Popescu, Sp. "Observaţiuni critice asupra bisericii din Bălteni," in *Revista pentru istorie, archeologie şi filologie,* X (1909), pp. 258-264.

Predescu, Lucian. *Enciclopedia cugetară.* Bucharest: Cugetarea — Georgescu Delafras, 1941.

Rosetti, Generalul R. "Care au fost adevăratele efective ale unor armate din trecut," in *Analele Academiei Române. Memoriile Secţiunii Istorice,* series III, vol. XXV (1942-1943), pp. 727-746.

Rosetti, General R. *Istoria artei militare a românilor până la mijlocul veacului al XVII-lea.* Bucharest: Monitorul Oficial, 1947.

Şerbănescu, Niculae I. *Istoria Mănăstirii Snagov.* Bucharest: Institutul de Istorie Naţională, 1944.

Sphrantzes, Georgios. *Memorii, 1401-1477,* ed. Vasile Grecu. Bucharest: Editura Academiei, 1966.

Stefulescu, Alexandru. *Mînăstirea Tismana.* Second edition. Bucharest: I.V. Socecu, 1903.

Stoicescu, Nicolae. *Sfatul domnesc şi marii dregători din Ţara Românească şi Moldova (sec. XIV- XVII).* Bucharest: Editura Academiei, 1968.

Stoide, Const. A. "Basarab al II-lea," in *Anuarul Institutului de Istorie şi Arheologie "A.D. Xenopol,"* vol. XVII (1980), pp. 279-302.

Stoker, Bram. *Dracula.* Wordsworth Classics, 1993.

Sturdza, Dimitrie A. "Dare de semă despre colecţiunea de documente istorice române aflate la Wiesbaden," in *Analele Academiei Române. Sectiunea II. Discursuri, memorii şi notiţe,* series II, vol. VIII (1885-1886), pp. 239-259.

Sugar, Peter F., ed. *A History of Hungary,* Bloomington and Indianapolis: Indiana University Press, 1994.

Tocilescu, Gr.G., ed. *534 documente istorice slavo-române din Țara Românească și Moldova privitoare la legăturile cu Ardealul, 1346-1603.* Bucharest: Cartea Românească, 1931.

Treptow, Kurt W. *Dracula: Essays on the Life and Times of Vlad Tepes.* New York: East European Monographs, Columbia University Press, 1991. Second edition: Palm Beach: Center for Romanian Studies, 2018.

Treptow, Kurt W., ed. *A History of Romania.* Iasi: Center for Romanian Studies, 1997.

Treptow, Kurt W. *Vlad III Dracula: The Life and Times of the Historical Dracula.* Iasi, Oxford, Portland: Center for Romanian Studies, 2000. Second edition: Palm Beach: Center for Romanian Studies, 2020.

Urkundenbuch zur Geschichte der Deutschen in Siebenbürgen. Vierter Band: 1416-1437, ed. Gustav Gündish. Hermannstadt, 1937.

Urkundenbuch zur Geschichte der Deutschen in Siebenbürgen. Fünfter Band: 1438-1457, ed. Gustav Gündish. Bucharest: Editura Academiei, 1975.

Vasilescu, Alexandru A. *Urmașii lui Mircea cel Bătrân până la Vlad Țepeș (1418-1456), I: De la moartea lui Mircea cel Bătrân până la Vlad Dracul (1418-1437).* Bucharest: Institutul de Arte Grafice "Carol Gölb," 1915.

Vasilescu, Alexandru A. "Diplomele lui Sigismund I, regele Ungariei, și Ioan Huniade, voevodul Transilvaniei, dela Mănăstirea Tismana, sunt false," in *Revista Istorică Română,* XIII:4 (1943), pp. 1-115.

Vasilescu, Alexandru A. "Privilegiul comercial latinesc al lui Mircea I cel Bătrân din 25 august 1413, acordat Brașovenilor, este fals," in *Revista Istorică Română,* XIII:1 (1943), pp. 78-96.

Vîrtosu, Emil. *Titulatura domnilor și asocierea la domnie în Țara Romînească și Moldova pînă în secolul al XVI-lea.* Bucharest: Editura Academiei, 1960.

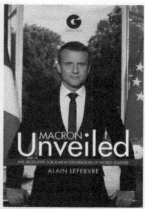